I0080047

10,000 Days In Alaska

Book Two
1990-1997

Norman Wilkins

Copies of this book (volume two of three) can be ordered from any major bookstore or from the publisher. For additional information about the author, go to www.10000daysinalaska.com.

Books by Norman Wilkins:

Volume 1: 10,000 Days In Alaska Book One
Volume 2: 10,000 Days In Alaska Book Two
Volume 3: 10,000 Days In Alaska Book Three

ISBN 10: 1-886352-22-4
ISBN EAN 13: 978-1-886352-22-3

Published by
Cloud 9 Publishing
14051 Oakview Lane North
Dayton, MN 55327
www.cloud9publ.wordpress.com

Volume one transcribed by Nadia Giordana, Cloud 9 Publishing
Volumes two and three transcribed by Linda Law
Technical advisor, Laura T. Behrendt

Front cover photo: Norman Wilkins sitting by a campfire taken by Darrell Breider. Other photos are from the Wilkins' personal archives and include photos taken by family members and friends who have shared their prints.

All names of persons and places mentioned in this book are real; they have not been changed.

Copyright © 2010 Cloud 9 Publishing. No portion of this book may be reproduced, stored in a retrieval system or transmitted in any form—electronic, mechanical or other means without written consent of the publisher except in the case of brief quotations embodied in critical articles and reviews. All rights reserved. Primary and subsidiary rights include but are not limited to, electronic rights, motion picture and television rights, audio book rights, audiovisual rights, merchandizing rights and dramatic or performance rights and the creation of derivative works based on the copyrighted material.

From a 1997 letter written by Norman Wilkins
Nelchina, Alaska

...More has happened since I started the letter, this will fill you in to date.

About a week after the bear hunt, I took the Suzuki to the Ballanger Pass Trail-head for a sight-seeing get-in-the-mountains trip.

Within two miles on the trail, I was seeing lots of caribou. Some of the mountain slopes had groups of several hundred animals, with many groups like that in sight. (Later I heard that a local old-timer bush pilot estimated 10,000 caribou.) I took a picture of a small bunch close to me and slowly drove down the trail, giving them all the time they needed to cross in front of me. At the top of the pass on the other side—the same view, 'boo' everywhere.

I shut off the machine, sat on it, took more pictures, and simply absorbed the sights and sounds. Large bulls, small bulls, yearlings, cows, calves (many at 30-100 yards), were eating, lying down, chewing their cuds, resting. The animal smell, their scent, urine and belching was strong in the air.

Aware that I was there, they largely ignored me, or so it seemed. Few made eye contact. Some cows were making a rapid, grunt-like sound. With luck, I caught a cow doing this; directly, a calf came running to her and began to nurse, butting very hard with its head in the process.

The day was beautiful, warm, sunny, some breeze. Experiencing all of this within yards of me was very moving. I felt lucky and fortunate to have been a witness.

Later, a friend said, "I wish you would have had my camcorder with you."
Yes, it would have made an outstanding film.

Will write again,

Norman

swamp buggy

Norman

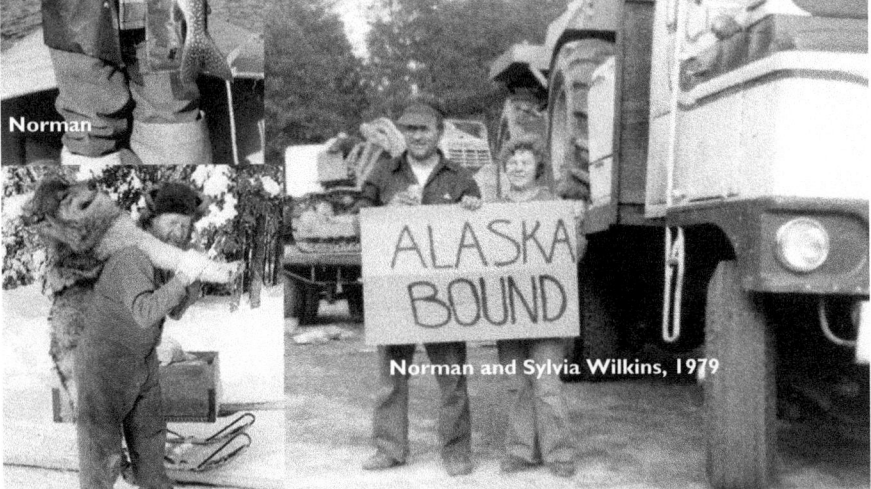

ALASKA BOUND

Norman and Sylvia Wilkins, 1979

Sylvia

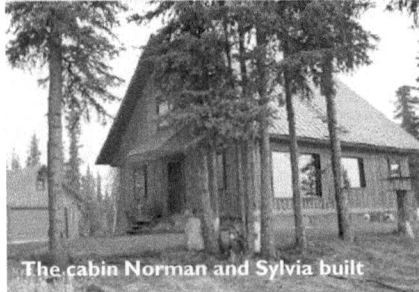

The cabin Norman and Sylvia built

View from the log cabin

Special thanks and recognition go to the incomparable Linda Law of Stillwater, Minnesota who read book one, became immersed in the lives of Norman and Sylvia Wilkins and offered to help bring this documentary series to completion.

Nadia Giordana, Cloud 9 Publishing

FOREWORD

10,000 Days In Alaska is a three-volume, documentary journal written by Norman Wilkins as he and his wife Ladislava (Sylvia) lived it. Norman recorded daily journal entries throughout the entire 25+ years he and Sylvia spent carving out a life on the Alaskan tundra.

The contents of this book have been transcribed from Norman's notebook-style pages as originally written with the exception of occasional edits and insertions for clarity. Every effort has been made to maintain Norman's unique personal style so as not to lose the naturalness of the voice, nor the meaning of his words. His entries are simple, natural, and to the point—bringing to mind another well-known, long time Alaska resident, Dick Proenneke, whose self-documented story, Alone in the Wilderness: An Alaskan Odyssey (written by Sam Keith), has been much celebrated among outdoorsmen and self-sufficiency enthusiasts.

Book one covers the first twelve years of Norman and Sylvia's incredible experience. This is book two, encompassing 1990 through 1997. Book three completes the series, spanning 1998 and ending in 2005 when the Wilkins' left Alaska.

Prior to moving to Alaska in 1979, the couple farmed for more than 25 years in Iowa and Minnesota. At the time of this printing, Norman and Sylvia are in their 80s and living in Little Falls, Minnesota to be near their children.

My friend, Linda Law of Stillwater, Minnesota, upon reading book one, became so interested in the lives of Norman and Sylvia and their friends living around Nelchina along the Glenn Highway, she asked the inevitable question, "What happened next? What's going on with the Smaydas, the Farmers, the Oddens, the Billmans and everyone else?"

In the end, I accepted Linda's enthusiastic offer to transcribe books two and three. Her comments, questions and notes to me in our correspondence throughout this project have helped drive it forward. As a result, we are able to make it available to you the readers, years sooner than would otherwise have been possible.

Nadia Giordana, Cloud 9 Publishing

TABLE OF CONTENTS

Norman Wilkins

1990—crane hunting at Delta, goose at Cordova

Monday, January 1, 1990—light snow, cloudy, ice fog and snow, -22° to -16°. Loafed all day. Sylvia's a little sick. She had Allen, Roxanne and family over for supper. Talked to Dan (who has plow truck).

Tuesday, January 2, 1990—light snow, cloudy, then sunny, and sun dogs. Clear this evening. Took our trash to the dump. We took cupcakes to Charlie Netter and Lloyd Ronning. Then we visited Leona and son Doug Dawson on Lake Louise Road. Looked for ptarmigan and fox, wolf sign—no luck. Doug saw two wolves and drove up to a black wolf that didn't run. Doug left. We had supper at Odden's. John and Coleen were there.

Wednesday, January 3, 1990—cloudy, fog, light snow, -20° to -10°. Sylvia went with the senior citizens. Tom and Lisa Smayda, Tom Huddleston, Mannings, Bonnie Wikle and Allen Farmer all visited. Jim Odden got a grey female wolf today.

Thursday, January 4, 1990—cloudy all day, -10° to -8°. Jim and Mary, John and Coleen Odden were here for breakfast. Tom Huddleston came over interested in the Alpine snowgo (snowgo is a local colloquialism used to denote any snowmobile or snow machine). I ran trapline, no fur. Machine ran well with new plug. Shot a ptarmigan with .223.

Friday, January 5, 1990—cloudy all day, 2° to -3°. Didn't feel well today. Lisa Smayda brought our calendar. Sylvia did some laundry at Nelchina Lodge.

Saturday, January 6, 1990—cloudy all day, -12° to -6°. Parts for snowgo finally got here. Built a fire in the garage and put four new bearings on the snowgo and a new headlight bulb.

Sunday, January 7, 1990—cloudy, clear by evening, -15° to -8°. Worked on snowgo chain case, windshield and tail light. Jim Manning brought over a portable water pump. His trouble was gravel in the pump. Allen Farmer visited about his snowgo in the evening.

Monday, January 8, 1990—light snow all day, -2° to -1°. Finished working on snowgo and small jobs. Visited Smaydas, Sylvia went to Glennallen.

Tuesday, January 9, 1990—sunny, -18° to -30°. Cleaned up a few things in basement. Tried to repair a down parka. Prepared a package for Zappa family in Wisconsin. We had Steve, Karen, Eyan and Caleb Malley for pizza supper. Jim Manning called and wanted to butcher a road kill caribou in our garage.

Wednesday, January 10, 1990—sunny, cloudy in afternoon, -32° to -18°. Tom and Lisa, Tom Huddleston, Allen Farmer, Jim and Elaine Manning all visited today. Phoned our son Paul in Staples, Minnesota. Phoned Lee Siegel.

Thursday, January 11, 1990—cloudy and snow, -10° to 13°. Tom H. borrowed a tool. I ran trapline, got a red fox in first set. Hung five snares and set one Manning (a type of trap). Some moose and caribou tracks. Saw Lisa Smayda skiing on trail. Huge moose feeding across our lake. Six caribou on lake. Odden family was here for supper and bought red fox.

Friday, January 12, 1990—mostly sunny, 3° to -5°. Did a few little jobs. Jim Odden brought his snowgo over to weld and repair it. Smayda family were here for dinner.

Saturday, January 13, 1990—cloudy and sunny, -4° to 5°. Allen and Roxanne had us over to their place for breakfast. Allen, Roxanne, David and I went up Slide Mountain on our snowgos. I made five marten sets. I saw one marten as he was hunting near the trail. Sylvia went to Nelchina Lodge to visit Mae Richardson. When we got back from the mountain, (we had grand views) we went to the lodge for cocoa and coffee.

Sunday, January 14, 1990—mostly sunny, -7° to -2°. Beautiful sunrise today. Watched TV, then took ribcage from the roadkill caribou to the trapline and made some sets. Some hunters killed two caribou at RCA site driveway. I saw three cross near Smaydas.

Monday, January 15, 1990—cloudy, -10° to 0°. Loafed a lot. Sylvia went to Glennallen. I ran traps on Slide Mountain. Nothing. Visited Tom Huddleston.

Tuesday, January 16, 1990—cloudy, breezy, 10° to 24°. Went to Huddleston's for breakfast, back home, then took E.M.T. Oxygen to Secondchief. Came back home and shot a ptarmigan. Read a while and went to gut piles at RCA site. Tried to call a fox with a tape player, no luck. Hoped to get a shot at a fox with the 10-gauge. Set a 1 ½ trap there.

Wednesday, January 17, 1990—cloudy, 10° to 20°. Mike Calahan and Tim Fracina called and asked us to meet them at Nelchina Lodge. Had a nice visit. Visited also with Lee Dudley. I got sick with intestinal flu. Didn't do much today. Checked fox trap and moved it to new trail at the caribou gut piles.

Thursday, January 18, 1990—cloudy, snow in evening, 10° to 19°. Heated the wood shop and put moose turds on Alaska clock and poured envirotex on it, then ran trap line. Reset fox trap and hung fox snare. Another caribou killed nearby. Hauled caribou gut and made a wolf set at Cache Creek with one snare and one Manning. Nothing in traps. Tom Huddleston brought his Jim over to visit.

Friday, January 19, 1990—mostly sunny, 5° to 24°. Distant snow showers. Took snowgo to RCA site, fox trap was sprung. Right snowgo ski broke off at its rear. Went home and put a replacement on and went up Slide Mountain. Got a small female marten in the first set. The rest were empty. Re-made and re-baited all the sets. Tom H. worked on stove parts here. Cut out and sanded a leather, home tanned gun sling. Cleaned house chimney. Oddens had us over for rhubarb pie. They subscribed to a woodworking magazine for me. Jim and Elaine visited and had some of Sylvia's rolls. Checked fox set going and coming from Odden's, no luck. marten is still frozen.

Saturday, January 20, 1990—sunny, 6° to 22°. Checked fox set, nothing. Tom H. made down payment on Alpine snowgo. Skinned and stretched the marten. Oiled gun sling and laced it on gun. Did some small jobs. Jim O. came over to weld on his snowgo. Huddleston family and Odden family were here for supper and we had a fine evening together.

Sunday, January 21, 1990—sunny, cloudy, warmer in evening, 5° to 14°. Tom Smayda. asked me to haul his snow blower down to the lake. They cleaned off a place to ice skate. Some caribou hunters are working the area. The fella with a wall tent on the river, stepped in one of Botley Creek Jim's traps and is upset. Sylvia did laundry at Nelchina.

Monday, January 22, 1990—cloudy and foggy, 18° to 21°. Sylvia went to Glennallen. I stopped at RCA site and loaded the paunch from a caribou kill and ran the trap line. No fur. Made a new gang set, two Helfrich and one snare for wolves. A couple of fox had been on trail. I made a snare set for one fox. Made a trail set with a trap 100 yards west of RCA site for fox. Tom H. visited. Elaine Manning visited.

Tuesday, January 23, 1990—mostly cloudy and foggy, 10° to 11°. Ran line up Slide Mountain. Nothing. Worked on snowgo. Picked up one trap. Visited Lucky Beaudoin. Smayda family had us over for supper.

Wednesday, January 24, 1990—1-½ inches of snow and cloudy, 2° to 9°. Put clock works on moose turd clock. Charged 6V battery. Mannings, Mary Beaudoin and Smaydas visited us. I visited at the lodge and Allen Farmer store.

Thursday, January 25, 1990—mostly sunny, -10° to 1°. Hauled a load of water from Hoffman's. Visited Tom H., also Tom S. (Smaydas will pick up some snowgo parts in Wasilla.) Lisa Smayda and daughters visited after school.

Friday, January 26, 1990—cloudy, ice fog down to 2500' elevation, -26° to -14°. Didn't feel good all night and day. Ran trapline north along Slide Mountain, no fur. Made a fox set south of Cache Creek and north of old trail. Set for a wolf. Missed a fox along highway, one small marten track. Two moose. A lynx came from near Nelchina and north up Slide Mountain.

Saturday, January 27, 1990—cloudy, ice fog, then sunny and -27° to -24°. Beautiful day. Visited T. Huddleston's, Farmer's were there. We all went to Evergreen Lodge on Lake Louise. Kim treated us to a bowl of soup and cheesecake. Saw a few moose, and ptarmigan tracks along the road. Fun day.

Sunday, January 28, 1990—sunny, -30° to -16°. T. Huddleston came over here and watched the Super Bowl game. Sylvia went over there to watch a movie. Smayda family came to borrow some tools and stayed for chili supper and a TV show.

Monday, January 29, 1990—sunny, -34° to -18°. T. Huddleston stopped a minute to bring a curved needle. Didn't do much today, Sylvia went on the senior's van. Tom S. came over to borrow tools. Snowgo dealer didn't send important part. Elaine brought Sylvia a gift sweatshirt.

Tuesday, January 30, 1990—sunny, -42° to -26°. Tom H. visited. I loaned him a saw chain sharpener. Tom S. visited here, and I went over there. Checked Rudbeck's house, flower froze.

Wednesday, January 31, 1990—sunny, -36° to -24°. Fantastic Northern Lights with red in them. Did correspondence, visited Mannings and Tom H. Sylvia did the laundry at Nelchina Lodge. A cow moose is browsing at the back door and a few caribou are traveling across our lake.

Thursday, February 1, 1990—partly cloudy, -35° to -20°. Organized some garden info. Visited at the lodge. Theresa and grandkids called to wish me Happy Birthday. Picked up marten sets on Slide Mountain. No fur.

Friday, February 2, 1990—mostly sunny, -34° to -18°. Sent off income tax to Mrs. Zerbinos. Ran trap line North along Slide. Made one fox set and hung a fox snare. Shoveled out wolf set at trail crossing. No wolves in traps but had 2f red fox in Manning No. 9s at North wolf set. It was caught by lower jaw. Must have bit at trap and hooked teeth and got paw pulled out. Other fox was caught high on front leg. Trail is really rough. Cache Creek is overflowing the trail bad. Moose & boo working along trail. Skinned warm fox. Thawing froze one.

Saturday, February 3, 1990—sunny, -32° to -18°. Fox is still frozen. Cleaning up wolf traps and put them on heater to boil. Organized more hunting info in note book. Wrote daughter Beverly Volk a letter. Mannings brought back bathroom plunger. Henry Johnson brought our water hauling tank back. Allen Farmer brought a socket back and borrowed a pipe wrench.

Sunday, February 4, 1990—sunny., -40° to -15°. Went to Copper Center and bought a wood turning lathe. Visited Lincoln and Ann Smith, Darrel Gerry, Jim & Mary Odden. A young coyote was feeding a few feet from Smith's drive. It was nervous but didn't run from us.

Monday, February 5, 1990—partly cloudy, skiff snow, -16° to -10°. Tom H. helped unload lathe. Allen F. visited. Got some trap gear ready and small jobs. Visited Lisa S. Went over to the lodge. Henry Johnson treated us to pecan pie and ice cream. Sam Weaver was there and we visited.

Tuesday, February 6, 1990—light snow, sunny, -28° to -18°. Waited till early afternoon and ran trap line. Reset the two Mannings I had boiled. Lured with wolf pee soaked, wolf droppings. No fur. Saw moose, boo, fox and marten tracks. A fox had dragged off the piece of boo hide I had cached along the trail.

Wednesday, February 7, 1990—sunny, -42° to -18°. Cleaned guns. Tom H and family visited. I went to lodge to see Lee Dudley. The Odden family visited. We went to Manning's for supper. Darn old cow moose near back door tonight. Beautiful moonlit night.

Thursday February 8, 1990—cloudy, -40° to -24°. Allen F. borrowed some angle iron. Kim Huddleston came to get movies. I sharpened skinning knives and wrote letters and checked Rudbeck's house.

Friday, February 9, 1990—sunny, -36° to -20°. Went with Tom H. to take trash to dump. Split lots of large blocks of wood, hauled and put them in basement. Sylvia did laundry at lodge.

Saturday, February 10, 1990—sunny, -40° to -14°. Ran trap line, had a coyote on trail along highway. This set was a 1-½ Victor & Steel Grapple. The trap pushed under the footprint in the snow. A fox had worked another set and missed pan of trap. Some wolves had crossed the trail east to west, 50 yards south of place I caught young wolf. Gave coyote to Mary Odden. We had supper there.

Sunday, February 11, 1990—sunny, -40° to -18°. Did a few small jobs. Visited at lodge. Lisa S. and girls visited in afternoon. Darrel Gerry visited and had a supper. Jim, Mary and Kari Odden visited. Jim borrowed some snowgo motor repair tools and paid me for the coyote.

Monday, February 12, 1990—mostly sunny, -41° to -20°. Sylvia went to lunch at Glennallen. Tom S. came over. I cleaned rust off some old gun parts. Visited Mannings.

Tuesday, February 13, 1990—cloudy, light snow, -20° to -4°. Read and loafed all day. Lisa S. brought a borrowed book back. Tom H. borrowed ½ extension and 13/16 socket. Tom knows where all my tools are and he's good about bringing them back.

Wednesday, February 14, 1990—sunny, 10° to 14°. Ran trapline. Hung snare for coyote near PCA site. Picked up Helfrich and put down a no 14. at wolverine tree. Nothing in traps. Couple coyotes along highway. Serviced snowgo. Allen plowed our snow.

Thursday, February 15, 1990—partly cloudy, -20° to 4°. Went to dump and made w trap sets. Visited KROA radio station, Charlie Netter was there. Frank Dimick came in. Lloyd Ronning wasn't home. Visited Joe and Morey (Joe's wife) Secondchief. A bearing went out in the motor of our truck on the way home. Called around looking for a pickup.

Friday, February 16, 1990—mostly sunny, -10° to 5°. Went to dump. Nothing in traps. More calling over pickups, no luck. Visited the Farmers. Elaine brought a pattern over for 7 out outs she wants. Cut them this afternoon. Sylvia thawed the ice at septic tank intake.

Saturday, February 17, 1990—snowy all day, 3-4" of snow, 10°. Went to dump. Managed to get Darrel's dog. Tom H. came over and I gave him the Alpine down payment back. Sold Alpine to Mark. Went to Hoffman's for water. Water line was frozen. Came home and unloaded tank. Later Max called and the line was thawed. So we loaded the tank back in Odden's blazer and back to Hoffman's. Got a load of water and plowed some snow there. Came home and unloaded water. Walked over to Henry and Sally's and visited. They paid me for some old dozer work. Jim and Elaine Manning came over to visit after supper. Gave her some wood cut outs for the ladies in her painting class.

Sunday, February 18, 1990—snowy, 6" snowfall, 0° to 10°. Ran trap line. Dug out and remade some of the sets. Overflow at Cache Creek. Snow was tough to travel in. Hung another snare for coyote today. Sylvia did laundry.

Monday, February 19, 1990—snowy, partly cloudy, ice fog, sun dogs, -10° to -4° Still trying to find a pickup to buy. Didn't do much of anything. Jim Odden ran his trap line and plowed snow. Ran out of gas and I took his S10 Chevy and went to meet him.

Tuesday, February 20, 1990—sunny, light ice fog, -32° to -10°. Visited around the neighborhood.

Wednesday, February 21, 1990—mostly sunny, -32° to -10°. Jim came two times to get the blazer to plow snow. Had "Heintz" a German fellow with him. I plowed our lane. Visited Allen.

Thursday, February 22, 1990—mostly sunny, beautiful day, -24° to -2°. Ran Trapline, no fur. Two marten and two fox tracks. Moose along trail and one year bull in Manning trap where I caught first wolf. Some joker slid into Allen's mail box, and mine too—messed them up. Trooper came out. Lucky and Mary here for supper.

Friday, February 23, 1990—mostly sunny, -20° to 3°. Allen and I made temporary repairs to our mail boxes. Jim M. came over to get the parcel we were storing for him. I took Odden's blazer to the dump to look at traps.

Saturday, February 24, 1990—cloudy, 2" of fluffy snow, -4° to 16°. Three cow and two calf boo went east on our lake. A large moose went by west and south side of house, very thin.

Sunday, February 25, 1990—mostly sunny, -10° to 12°. Cow moose lay in snow just off SW corner of house. I took pictures of her from living room window. Cut up and put one quarter cord of wood in basement. Jim and Mary O. came to get blazer to plow dump road. I went along and picked up my traps at dump.

Monday, February 26, 1990—cloudy, sunny, some snow, 10° to 30°. Went Caribou hunting East on our lakes, no luck. Tom H. took the four quarters and back strap off his caribou and left the rest on the lake. A coyote is hanging around and came out on lake this afternoon. I went down to shore to try to call it but the call batteries were down.

Tuesday, February 27, 1990—cloudy, snowed 2", 20° to 30°. No car. Boo (caribou) on lake all day. Allen F. came over to look at mail order catalog. Lucky Beaudoin brought a bunch of tapes (TV). Jackie Beaudoin shampooed our rug, brought Kim and four kids along. Damp in the house this evening. Mail man got a lot of the people's mail mixed up. Elaine Manning visited and also a guy who sells monitor heaters, so I didn't go out hunting boo.

Wednesday, February 28, 1990—sunny, cloudy -15° to 6°. Walked over to lodge. Stopped at Allen's garage. Checked Rudbeck's house. Snow is hip deep, deeper in some places. Ran trap line and picked up fox traps and three snares. One fox track, saw one moose and tracks of another. Got stuck out on first Meat

Pole Hill turn around.

Thursday, March 1, 1990—partly cloudy, -10° to 16°. Went over to Manning to read ad section for a pickup. Walked over to Allen's garage to visit Mary Beaudoin and daughter Donna came to buy children's toys. I've been sick most of day.

Friday, March 2, 1990—sunny, temp got up to 31°. Jim and Elaine M. here for brunch. I cut out and sanded 6 puffin cutouts. Allen F. came for recoil starter rope for Jim of Botley Creek. Moose are hanging around out place for sometime now. Called "Dan" about Dodge truck.

Saturday, March 3, 1990—sunny, 20° to 42°. Took seven puffin cutouts to Elaine. Shoveled snow off woodshed roof. Snow slid off house roof and I shoveled some of it out of the way. Bart Bartley and Henry borrowed water hauling tank and Bart hauled a load for us. Our tank has a dripping leak.

Sunday, March 4, 1990—cloudy, 16° to 24°. Shoveled snow off camper, CAT, woodshop. Bartley was here. Little gas motor wouldn't run. Ok now. Read ads at Smayda's. Mark came to get a different carburetor for Alpine. T. Huddleston came over for info about idle jet on his snowgo. Bart brought water tank back.

Monday, March 5, 1990—2+ inches of snow, cloudy, 16° to 24°. Went to Mannings and to Allen's store. Took more pix of cow moose from out a window. Sylvia went to Glennallen. Elaine drove their pickup off edge of our lane and got stuck against a tree. Didn't feel good all day.

Tuesday, March 6, 1990—1" of snow, cloudy, 15° to 19°. Light snow all day. Ran trapline. Breezy. One fox working wolf sets. Made two trail sets for wolf. Saw one moose and a few new moose track. Meet Lisa S. out skiing on trail.

Wednesday, March 7, 1990—sunny, some breeze, 0° to 14°. Bartley brought over a chainsaw (oiler needed cleaning) and visited quite awhile. Jim and Elaine came over for craft parts. Jim and Mary and Kari O. here for supper and plowed out a place for me to have wood unloaded.

Thursday, March 8, 1990—sunny, -14° to 14°. Our load of firewood got here at noon. Half here and half at Snowshoe. We cut up two sled loads and I sharpened saw. Called to Anchorage about pickups, good one was sold.

Friday, March 9, 1990—mostly sunny, -10° to 20°. More calls for pickups. Put three big sled loads wood in basement. Sharpened saw and swept up saw dust. Went to lodge for pork short rib supper.

Saturday, March 10, 1990—sunny, beaut of a day, -12° to 20°. Put four loads wood in wood shed. Odden's came to get their Blazer plow. Gave them a seat for it. Bart Bartley borrowed the water hauling tank. Tom H. came over to get some acetylene cutting done.

Sunday, March 11, 1990—cloudy, sunny, cloudy, -10° to 20°. Cut up and sledded five loads to wood shed. Harold and Rachel Dimmick came to visit. Gave them a fox skin and two front quarter legs off a boo. Jim & Mary O. brought Blazer for us to use and had coffee. We went to a skating party at Snowshoe Lake.

Monday, March 12, 1990—cloudy, sunny, 7° to 27°. Ran trap line. Red fox had been in wolf trail set. Ran off when I got there. More overflow. Tom H. brought his snowgo over and welded handle bars back on. Cut up and stacked three more loads of wood. Sylvia went to Glennallen. Smayda family visited in evening. Brought over a chickadee nest box.

Tuesday, March 13, 1990—cloudy, sunny, cloudy, snow, -7° to 28°. Cut up and put six loads wood in shed. Some logs rolled down off pile and broke handle of chain saw, had to fix that. Got all the saw dust swept into a pile. Jim and Kari visited while Mary attended a class in painting. Talked to Darrel Gerry about going to look at trucks.

Wednesday, March 14, 1990—cloudy, very light snow, 13° to 27°. Bart B. brought water tank back and welded his snowgo ski. Oddens left Kari with Sylvia while they ran trapline. Sylvia got a little flu today. More calls about trucks.

Thursday, March 15, 1990—up early, 17° to 28°. Darrel got here and we went to Wasilla. He got drywall. I looked around at pickup trucks. No luck. Stopped to see Andy B., a friend Mike Harrison "Ricochet". Lots of very thin moose in Matanuska Valley.

Friday, March 16, 1990—Tom H., his kids, and I went to Anchorage. The kids skated and we looked for a truck for me. We looked at lots of them. Bought one—and then took it back. Stayed overnight with Chad Wilson and family. Went to Eagle River and looked at Dodge 4 x 4 plus plow.

Saturday, March 17, 1990—nice sunny day, 30° here. Looked at vehicles all day. Didn't get anything bought all day—sure tried. Saw a guy drive off into ditch. He appeared drunk. Got home just at dark.

Sunday, March 18, 1990—sunny, light breeze. Got package ready to mail to Nadia. Ran trap line. Cross fox had got in wolf trap. No wolves. Worked a little on snowgo. Helped Tom (he had run out of gas). Rudbecks got back and had supper with us. Oddens visited, also Allen Farmer.

Monday, March 19, 1990—sunny, -9° to 19°. Spent all day on truck transportation problem. Joe Virgin took me to Glennallen to look at trucks.

Tuesday, March 20, 1990—sunny, -8° to 20°. Joe Virgin and I left early and went to Wasilla, Eagle River, and Anchorage looking at trucks. Didn't find one for me but Joe bought a ½ ton Ford 4 x 4. Beautiful Day. The mountains are beautiful. Saw very few moose and they are very thin.

Wednesday, March 21, 1990—sunny, beautiful day, Northern Lights at night, -8° to 26°. A guy brought out a 4 x 4 Chevy with a plow on it. I didn't buy it. Visited Allen and Roxanne in evening. Tom H & I will go look at a pickup and motor tomorrow.

Thursday, March 22, 1990—sunny, beautiful Northern Lights, -7° to 27°. Birds are eating food in front of living room window. Tom H. took me past Copper Center to look at a motor and pickup. They probably are junk, or at least lots of work. Bought lunch at lodge. Looked at another 4 x 4 Ford pickup. Then stopped and looked Chuck Z. 78 4 x 4 Ford. It's pretty nice. Need paint and small repair. Snowshoe rabbit in front of house. Saw a coyote along Simpson Hill.

Friday, March 23, 1990—sunny, Northern Lights, -6° to 30°. Ran trapline. Some marten and lots of fox tracks. Wolves had crossed from west to east. Saw three moose along trail. Snowgo ran. Put pickup in garage and pulled the oil pan off it and couldn't find the bad bearing right away. Went over to lodge and visited with friends.

Saturday, March 24, 1990—mostly sunny, -4° to 30°. Built fires in garage and woodshop. Made wood cut outs for Patty Landers. Joe Virgin came and looked at bad bearing on truck and told me how to fix it. Sylvia went to KROA with Rudbecks to watch ski touring.

Sunday, March 25, 1990—sunny, cloudy, 4° to 30°. Allen Farmer took me to Anchorage and I bought a 1980 Chevy ¾ T 4x4. Looks good, runs good. Went to Odden's for supper.

Monday, March 26, 1990—cloudy, 8° to 26°. Put repairs on drag link on truck. Bartley borrowed water tank. Rudbeck here for tea. Went to Harold and Rachel Dimmick for supper in honor of one of their granddaughters. Clayton and Ruth Midget and Odden family were there too.

Tuesday, March 27, 1990—snow, sunny, cloudy, 20° to 30°. Went to Glennallen and got parts and title for truck. Moose in trouble in ditch. Fish & Game have already been notified. Paid electric bill. Stopped at Rhynell's new store. Worked on truck wiring. Jim O & Kari were here. Jim worked on his Blazer. Sylvia baby sat. Tom S. wants welding done in morning. Jim helped on my wiring. Odden's were here for supper.

Wednesday, March 28, 1990—mostly cloudy, windy most of day, 20° to 32°. Joe Virgin came up and fit the rod bearing on the crank shaft of 77 Chevy. I got the oil pan on starter etc and parked it outside. Put new truck inside. Snow slid off garage roof today. Allen Farmer and Tom Smayda visited—also Karn, then Kim and 3 kids.

Thursday, March 29, 1990—mostly sunny, 20° to 36°. Left for trapline early in order to get back before trails get soft. Saw a moose and fox, moose, boo, tracks. No wolves in traps. Picked all the wolf traps and snares. Hauled a load of water from Hoffman's. Did some door adjusting on truck. Broke one ski of snowgo sled and had to wire, cable and rope a small spruce to sled to get it and load home. Visited Lucky and Mary Beaudoin in evening.

Friday, March 30, 1990—sunny, 20° to 36°. Worked in wood shop most of day. Census taker was here. Edie Griffith and sons stopped by.

Saturday March 31, 1990—sunny, 6° to 36°. Worked in wood shop and delivered the cutouts. Joe Virgin stopped in with a Subaru 4WD. I went to his place in afternoon and bought it. Nice birthday party at lodge for Mae.

Sunday, April 1, 1990—sunny, nice day, 10° to 32°. Went over to dinner at Rudbecks after servicing truck. Went to visit Odden's and Ruth and had supper with them.

Monday, April 2, 1990—sunny, 0° to 22° Saw a cross fox and bald eagle on way to Palmer and Anchorage. Shopped for tools, repairs, groceries. Got home 8:30 PM.

Tuesday, April 3, 1990—sunny, windy, 10° to 30°. Got our state dividend applications mailed. Visited Lloyd Ronning. Karen came to get her groceries. Lisa S. and girls visited. Cut up and stacked the wood Allen F brought. Tried to put sander together, parts missing.

Wednesday, April 4, 1990—sunny, snow skiff in the night. Worked a little on truck. Cut out five dinosaur banks. Sylvia visited Karn. Visited Allen and Roxanne in evening.

Thursday, April 5, 1990—sunny, cloudy, 20° to 32°. Many visitors and phone calls all day. Like Grand Central Station. Did manage to get some work done in wood shop. Sylvia discovered a dead moose on our garden fence. Fred Rungee stopped in also.

Friday, April 6, 1990—sunny, 10° to 36°. Rudbeck brought dividend applications to sign. Worked in woodshop. Sylvia painted. Pat and Patti Landers came to visit and get some wood cut outs. Rudbecks brought Ruth to watch "Dallas."

Saturday, April 7, 1990—sunny, beautiful spring day, 10° to 40°. Brad Chase brought snow plow and we dismounted it from his truck and loaded it in the bed of our old truck. Did some work in the wood shop. Bart and son Bruce borrowed our water tank. I took snow go down hill to garden and broke trail from dead moose calf across lake to a place so the bears won't be at our back door to feed on the moose. My brother Jerry called about the old pictures of mothers.

Sunday, April 8, 1990—sunny, nice day, 17° to 41°. Did some work in wood shop then sent to Snowshoe Lake to watch ski races. Then Pollock eats. Lots of people to visit with. Bob R. and I went back later. I hauled his planks and plywood, sawhorses back to his place. Phoned my brother, Jerry Wilkins about letters. Mannings came over.

Monday, April 9, 1990—sunny, 12° to 44°. Worked in wood shop and soda water on vehicle batteries. Put acid in Suzuki battery. Asked Lisa S. and Allen F. if ok to pull moose calf across lake. Bart Bartley brought load of water. Brad Chase stopped for a couple minutes. Ordered sander from Grizzly.

Tuesday, April 10, 1990—sunny, 12° to 38°. Worked in wood shop a little. We don't feel well. Pulled dead little moose across the lake with the snowgo. Rudbecks brought Sylvia's vacuum cleaner.

Wednesday, April 11, 1990—sunny, 18° to 34°. Left early to go to Palmer, Wasilla. To Doctor, dentist, and to take orders, shop and get repairs. Windy in Palmer.

Thursday, April 12, 1990—sunny, 18° to 40°. Started making twenty-eight sewing blocks and or cabin fever relievers. Changed grease in "80" Truck rear end. Rudbeck borrowed "3/4" brass shutoff.

Friday, April 13, 1990—sunny, 20° to 44°. Eagles and other birds eat on moose calf. Worked in wood shop and did some things on truck. Can't get fuel tanks to switch. Rudbecks were here to watch Dallas.

Saturday, April 14, 1990—sunny, 24° to 45°. Went to Anchorage and bought some cedar lumber and did some other shopping. Found and bought a pickup canopy in Matanuska Valley. Did some shopping for Bob R. Jim Odden borrowed the water tank. Jerry W (my brother) sent a package with old pictures from mother's things.

Sunday, April 15, 1990—sunny, 18° to 46°. My back is "touchy". Read Sunday paper. Unloaded, stripped and stacked cedar lumber. Tom H & Kim drove the Subaru and want to buy it. Sylvia worked all day on supper for Oddens—Ruth, Kari, Mary & Jim.

Monday, April 16, 1990—cloudy, 22° to 42°. Worked in wood shop. Sylvia went to senior's meal. Lisa S and girls came over after school was out to show us their new pickup.

Tuesday, April 17, 1990—cloudy, sunny, cloudy, 30° to 44°. Worked in wood shop most all day. Bart came to borrow water tank.

Wednesday, April 18, 1990—cloudy, 32° to 41°. Harold and Rachel Dimick came to use phone and had breakfast with us. Jim Manning borrowed draw knife, Rudbeck got some plastic tubing. I worked in wood shop. Sylvia made quill bead earrings.

Thursday, April 19, 1990—mostly sunny, 30° to 48°. Finished the mug trees. Went to Glennallen to DMV office. Visited Frank Zimbicki on way home. Did some things at home and went to see John and Coleen at Odden's.

Friday, April 20, 1990—partly cloudy, 28° to 48°. Tom and Jim Huddleston stopped by, and later, Karn Rudbeck. Allen got me to help him set a window in place. I cut out a wood order and found a bad split in the wood and had to re-cut the order. Got it finished. Tom H. came and paid for the Subaru car. We went to the annual Community Co-op Meeting.

Saturday, April 21, 1990—mostly sunny, 20° to 44°. Used snowgo and sled to move rabbit hutches out to where we can load them on truck. Did a few things to truck. Allen was over and I at his store. We went to Lodge to listen to music.

Sunday, April 22, 1990—mostly sunny, 21° to 42°. Did a little work on snowgo. It has bad bearing and seal on crankshaft. Bad headache all day. Had supper at Huddleston's, Oddens were there too.

Monday, April 23, 1990—mostly sunny, 28° to 43°. Sylvia went with seniors to Glennallen. I took motor out of snowgo and took it to Chuck Zimbicki. Heard his bear kill story. Ran out of gas and had to hitch hike back home for gas.

Tuesday, April 24, 1990–cloudy, rain shower, 30° to 34°. Started building planter boxes when Dan Billman drove in the yard. After lunch went to Point of View. He is interest in bidding on the property. Stopped to see Dawsons. Saw a very large moose and a couple caribou. Visited Oddens. Dan treated us to supper.

Wednesday, April 25, 1990–partly cloudy, 32° to 44°. Dan left after breakfast. Loaned Karn a propane bottle. Worked in wood shop all day. More orders from Patty L.

Thursday, April 26, 1990–mostly sunny, 26° to 46°. Worked in wood shop, then we built eight, two foot cedar planter boxes. Supper at Karn's.

Friday, April 27, 1990–sunny, 30° to 50°. Dan Billman was here for breakfast. Then we loaded two loads of rabbit hutches, old stove and garbage cans and hauled to the dump and some to S. Mailly's new house. Looked it over. Took Max Hoffman to the dump and back home. Put more cedar boxes together. Finished assembling the one inch belt sander.

Saturday, April 28, 1990–mostly sunny, 30° to 50°. The swans are really flying west up the valley these days. They are beautiful. It's really nice to see them. Worked at more cedar boxes. Dan B. stopped in. Went to KROA for Sylvia's birthday pizza.

Sunday, April 29, 1990–mostly cloudy, some sun and breezy. 26° to 48°. Worked in wood shop. Harold Dimmick called and invited us to their place for fresh razor clams. We helped clean them while we visited. The clams were very good for supper.

Monday, April 30, 1990–light rain, cloudy. Allen Farmer and Dave, Ellie visited all morning. Worked on truck. Very bad back all day. Straighten up and put sheet metal screws in joints of stove pipe in wood shop. Did this after supper. Allen has tennis elbow from pulling his bow to full draw. He came back in the evening looking for tire tubes for his lawn mower.

Tuesday May 1, 1990–mostly cloudy, rain along Slide Mountain, 27° to 43°. Hauled a load of water. Put eight swan planters together. Visited Allen and Roxanne. Three ladies here to pick up wood to paint and left more orders.

Wednesday, May 2, 1990–mostly cloudy, 26° to 44°. Finished swan hanging baskets. Made two truck wall plaques and 2 heart shaped shaker peg racks. Took truck to Landers and went to visit Lloyd Ronning.

Thursday, May 3, 1990—mostly cloudy, snow, hail, 28° to 42°. Rain in Glennallen. Worked in wood shop all day. Went in to Glennallen and got truck repairs and went to telephone meeting. Visited Farmer and went back to Nelchina.

Friday, May 4, 1990—light snow, mostly cloudy, 26°. Worked in wood shop most of day then took old belts off truck. One of new ones doesn't fit. Tom brought different ones but they sent one wrong size.

Saturday, May 5, 1990—mostly sunny, 30° to 44°. Put a new front seal in rear differential. Suspended the exhaust system. Did some sanding in wood shop. Supper, a very good supper, at the Oddens.

Sunday, May 6, 1990—sunny, 30° to 51°. Put a tarp overhang door on ATV stall in wood shed. Worked in wood shop. Coffee with Mae at Nelchina. Supper at Mannings. Roxanne called Karn who called Mannings, two large grizzly feeding on remains of moose calf I dragged across the lake. I took lots of pictures. Eagle sat in tree over them. Roxanne went to Bartley's and got a bear tag. The bears left before Allen and Roxanne got to them. Probably got Farmers scent as the wind was to the bears. Bartleys came to see bears and visit.

Monday, May 7, 1990—sunny, 33° to 50°. Sighted in the .338 rifle. Worked on truck. More work in wood shop, visited Tom H. Then he came over for a little help. Billman called. They got the Point of View Lodge and will need help for a few days.

Tuesday, May 8, 1990—sunny, 34° to 49°. Worked in wood shop. Went to Sam Weaver's. Took Tom Huddleston to Glennallen and got my radiator fixed and more parts for the steering on truck. Visited Allen Farmers after supper.

Wednesday, May 9, 1990—Tom Huddleston can't trade vehicles now. Then Dan Billman called and wants Sam Weaver and me to go to Point of View Lodge. He has bought it and we are to lookout for his interests. We stayed the night there. Saw twenty plus geese along Lake Louise Road.

Thursday, May 10, 1990—spent all day here. Saw some caribou cross the lake. Did a few other things.

Friday, May 11, 1990—the former caretakers got moved out. Lloyd and Faye Walton (Dan's mother) came to look after the lodge for a few days. Charlie Trowbridge and family are at Nelchina visiting. Ice started out of lake.

Saturday, May 12, 1990—mostly sunny, some showers, 40° to 56°. We picked our mile of road ditches (trash). Cut and started bending willows for medicine hoops. Denise Johnson is visiting with her boyfriend. Had a shake at Nelchina. One fourth of the lake ice is gone.

Sunday, May 13, 1990–sunny, cloudy, 40° to 56°. Worked on truck mirrors. Took Sylvia to Eureka for dinner. Ran out of gas on left tank. Something is wrong there. Lisa S. and Dave visited. Jim and Elaine came over to get a "Puffin Puffin." Not much ice left in lake. Tom H. has his VW Dune Buggy home.

Monday, May 14, 1990–mostly cloudy and rainy, 38° to 48°. Built the boxes for Kim H. Put four cedar wheel barrows together. Started two triple goose head towel hangers. The ice is out on our lake.

Tuesday, May 15, 1990–pretty nice day, 40° to 52°. Got things ready for Sylvia and me to go to Lake Louise. Charlie Trowbridge came over and visited a while. Faye Walton (Dan B's. mom) called and we started for lodge. I forgot fish pole, radio, and flashlight. Didn't go back for them. Saw cow moose with last year's calf., plus boo (caribou). Their horns are started. Loyd briefed me on the latest info about the lodge. Four swans rested the night out on the ice. Water gurgling in the pipes, woke me up so I went out and started the generator.

Wednesday, May 16, 1990–the open water at the edge of the lake had a skim of ice on it. Reached 54° today. Some sprinkles. Spent nearly all day picking up trash. They brought fuel one day early. A light east bound wind moved the ice west and pile up some of the dock units. Popped some lumber and made noise with the 55-gallon drums. Hope the houseboat isn't damaged. Saw five swans flying over the ice.

Thursday, May 17, 1990–partly cloudy and little rain, 44° to 50°. Went to Naomi's gift shop and then to Dinty Bush's to visit. Back to Point of View Lodge and checked oil in generator motor. Henry Johnson, Sally, Bud and Darrel Gerry stopped in. The wind blew one section of dock to shore and I pulled it up and wired it to a willow. Nelchina Mae, Mike Shelton, Sam and Roger brought my hip boots and a heavy rope and visited late. We are all looking out for a man and woman and four kids that the troopers are trying to apprehend. He jumped bail, is a child molester. Someone went down the lake with a small airboat.

Friday, May 18, 1990– mostly sunny, 44° to 62°. Went out to the house boat and dock sections in my hip boots. Got a bunch of them tied up. Later in the afternoon , Loyd & Faye showed up with 160' rope and I encircled the rest of the dock sections with it. We came home and visited with Joe and Morey Secondchief. From them, we got the Athabaskan name for Lake Louise: Shos

Nu Benic. Went on home and unloaded gear, ate, then used the ATV to haul the pump down to the lake and installed it there. Rusty Dimmick came to borrow ½ drill and drill bit. Then went over to Nelchina Lodge for shakes and visiting.

Saturday, May 19, 1990—sunny, good shower with hail in it late afternoon. Thunder also. 36° to 66°. Went to Palmer, Wasilla. Took cedar planter boxes and did some shopping.

Sunday, May 20, 1990—mostly sunny, 40° to 64°. Pulled the pump from lake and welded foot valve housing and reinstalled it. Put dock in lake. Loaded up a load of dirt. Gave Mary B two planters and visited with Lucky. Put three window planters on Kim H. house and filled with dirt. Built flicker house and put in tree. They were looking like crazy for nesting place.

Monday, May 21, 1990—partly cloudy, 30° to 44°. Snow in evening. Loaded up cedar planter boxes and took them to Tazlina at Glennallen. Went on to Kenny Lake and got some spruce lumber and few seed potatoes. Stopped to visit Darrel Gerry for a few moments. Stripped and stacked lumber to dry. Started to cut rawhide strips. Phoned our daughter Beverly Volk and kids in Minneapolis, Minnesota.

Tuesday, May 22, 1990—mostly sunny, 30° to 46°. Worked a little on cedar planters. Did service work on the truck. Quite a few ducks on lake.

Wednesday, May 23, 1990—mostly sunny, 30° to 54°. Sylvia planted the garden. Bud (Michigan) and I took four wheelers and went to Allen F. cabins. Pretty muddy in lots of places. We got splattered. Had quite a time trying to figure out how to get across Cache Creek. Lots of overflow ice still there. Found my 1 ½ Victor (the Manning I couldn't find). Picked up a moose jaw, a boo jaw, skull and horns from up on a high hill. Beaver lodges look good. Two are on one lake. Saw a bear (?) den and some tracks. Some wolf also. Saw an eagle at one beaver dam. We nearly got stuck several times. Broke the stock on the .338 somehow.

Thursday, May 24, 1990—sunny, beautiful day, 31° to 60°. Upgraded plumbing at garden. We built seven smaller cedar planters. Did lots of other small jobs. Visited Allen a few minutes, and Tom H. came over. A real mean cow moose is around here. She stomped Henry and Sally's dog and tried to get "Blue." Ran by our front windows this morning with her ears back and hackles up.

Friday, May 25, 1990—sunny, 38° to 61°. Tom H. was over early and wanted to shorten the wheel base of his VW Dune Buggy. We almost got it finished. We did some other things around here. At Nelchina for supper.

Saturday, May 26, 1990—sunny, hot, 45° to 71°. Took cedar planters to Glennallen. Put one on Rhynell's entry to store and filled it with dirt. Delivered six others to Jo's Flower shop. Sylvia dropped off two tomato plants with Lloyd Ronning. We stopped at Lanegan's and Bonnie's and shopped for dry flies. Went to dump and picked up some steel. Hauled a load of water from Max Hoffman. Lots of traffic on road. Did a few little things around here. Lisa and Dan visited in evening. Sylvia is watering the lawn (it's dry). Bunch of boo bulls with horns in velvet just outside house.

Sunday, May 27, 1990—sunny with a haze, 47° to 65°. Sylvia and I tied thirty willow hoops. She has been watering the lawn. It's quite dry. Made a pattern and cut out 4 moose head clocks. Drilled for clockworks and sanded them.

Monday, May 28, 1990—mostly sunny, shower later evening, 45° to 67°. Worked around here all day. Shot a rabbit out of Sylvia's flowers. Dropped it off at Joe and Morey's on way to Fish and Picnic at Mendeltna Creek. and Oil Well Road. Made six Eskimo wood figurines for Bonnie Wikle. Didn't catch any fish.

Tuesday, May 29, 1990—good rain in night, 43° to 60°. Loaded ATV and went to Palmer and Wasilla to have it tuned. Went to several merchants. Looked at a oil furnace, not what I want. Came home and visited "Bud" at Henry Johnson's.

Wednesday, May 30, 1990—sunny, 45° to 62°. Went to Lake Louise Point of View Lodge to care take it. Washed and waxed truck. Did few small chores. Ice is out. Gulls, ducks, loons and people boating. Mae brought Sylvia and Sam and apples. We fished a little while.

Thursday, May 31, 1990—cloudy, sunny, breezy, rain, 40s to 60. Did a few small jobs. People came and phone calls. Burned trash. Picked aluminum cans. Lots boats fishing. Muskrat feeding. A loon drove two duck from his territory.

Friday, June 1, 1990—cloudy all day and rain late afternoon, 46° to 52°. Fished off the point a couple of times. Forwarded Kay's SBA letter to her. Went to Evergreen Lodge and met "Stormy" the new owner. Some people took their boat out at this landing. Some lady and two boys fished the point. A bear has damaged some of the other cabins.

Saturday, June 2, 1990—mostly sunny, 50° to 64°. Lots people boating and fishing. I didn't catch anything. Some guys from Evergreen Lodge came and started Dan's CAT 12 grader and took it over there for repairs. Sylvia came back from town and the baby rabbits have eaten all her garden. There was a 10 or 12 year old boy with "new" hip boots walking in the lake all afternoon and evening.

Sunday, June 3, 1990—foggy on Lake Louise, 54° to 70°. This morning sun burned it off and it was beautiful all day. Loyd and Faye got here mid afternoon. Saw muskrat swimming under water at dock. I stopped at Ed Farmer's and he looked at my truck.

Monday, June 4, 1990—mostly sunny, shower and breezy, 54° to 70°. Sylvia went to Glennallen. I adapted a auger to my motor for one. Worked on gas tank switches. Lisa S. brought a couple of salmon. We made a cedar planter box for Lisa Smayda. Visited Allen and Roxanne two times today.

Tuesday, June 5, 1990—sunny, showers, raining, 54° to 68°. Set new posts in garden windbreak. Set posts for support wires for raspberries. Cut out a few parts for swan planters.

Wednesday, June 6, 1990—partly cloudy, showers, 44° to 64°. Put new valve cover gaskets and spark plug wires on truck. Salvaged some old telephone wire for raspberries. Three more orders for wood cut outs and worked late at that.

Thursday, June 7, 1990—sunny, cloudy, windy, rain, 46° to 60°. Up extra early and worked on Ruth Midget's wood. Did a little work on truck. Got some used wood off Allen's dump load. Allen's family and Midgets's here for a lunch. They go to Dawson City now. Went over to Lodge. Declined to buy Ed's air compressor. Shot another small rabbit.

Friday, June 8, 1990—sunny, cloudy and rains going by on each side, 44° to 59°. Worked in wood shop all day. Did paint a cooler. Called our son Paul in Minnesota.

Saturday, June 9, 1990—sunny, partly cloudy, 44° to 61°. Worked in wood shop most of day and some other jobs. Cleaned house and made curtains for camper. Ordered gun stock.

Sunday, June 10, 1990—sunny and cool, breezy, dust blowing off the river and a smoky-like haze. 44° to 58°. Went to dump. Visited Odden's and traced a triple heart shelf at Bartley's. Took a quilt rack to Henry's for Doug's wedding gift.

Monday, June 11, 1990—cloudy, sunny, rain and thunder in late afternoon, 44° to 56°. Worked in wood shop all day. Sylvia went to Glennallen.

Tuesday, June 12, 1990—sunny, partly cloudy and light shower, 48° to 70°. Put together seven swan and five wheelbarrow planters. Back is real sore. Lisa S. and Dave's, Peg Virgin stopped for wood. Chad W. and Jane visited.

Wednesday, June 13, 1990—cloudy, some breeze, cool, 46° to 60°. Cow moose and little red calf got real close and startled us both while on my knees counting steel. Worked in wood shop. Dan Billman stopped and visited.

Thursday, June 14, 1990—mostly cloudy, shower in afternoon, 44° to 52°. Propane ran out. Breakfast in Nelchina. Worked in wood shop. Loyd and Faye Walton stopped to give pointers on wood turning. Fixed up some bucket planters for Sylvia's greenhouse. Took Max Hoffman to supper at KROA. Stopped at dump on way home.

Friday, June 15, 1990—mostly sunny, 40° to 60°. Went to Palmer, Wasilla. Got supplies. Wasn't able to get the raspberry seedlings we wanted.

Saturday, June 16, 1990—partly cloudy, breezy and cool, 44° to 58°. Went to Cal G. yard sale and bought some things. Came home and did some thing around here and started to rebuild the table saw Cal gave me. Went to the dump for some iron and shot "Moose Dick" while there. It patterned pretty well and the kick wasn't bad at all for a 10-gauge shotgun.

Sunday, June 17, 1990—partly sunny, a shower, nice day, 39° to 50°. Visited Rudbecks. Worked on restoring the table saw. Sylvia worked around the house. Our daughter Theresa Austin from Minnesota called for Father's Day.

Monday, June 18, 1990—mostly cool and some sun, light shower, 40° to 52°. Worked on the stand for the table saw. Started on a blower circulating filter box for the wood shop. Went to Cal's and got two chain saws some tools and a clothes washer. He gave me a pair winter snow pants and bunch of bolts. He got a load of water. I hauled water from Allen's.

Tuesday, June 19, 1990—mostly sunny, 40° to 60°. Mounted the filter box in wood shop. Then straightened up the brown trailer, the storage shed and a lot of wood shop. Lisa and girls visited. Tom H. needed some help. Painted the out house. Went to the lodge for pie. Rudbecks came over to use the phone. The flickers are back again.

Wednesday, June 20, 1990—mostly sunny, 39° to 52°. Worked on table saw motor mount, sanded top and mounted saw body to stand. Put castors on base of band saw.

Thursday, June 21, 1990—light rain, sunny. Went to Glennallen for truck parts and saw Darrel Gerry. Stopped at Chuck's and picked up snowgo motor and tie rod ends. Decided on a plan for table saw extensions and made a bunch of parts for that. Sorted some bolts. Cleaned up some of the garage.

Friday, June 22, 1990—sunny, some breeze, 42° to 62°. Cleaned up floor and under table in garage. Helped Cal weld up his bumper on '80 Ford Pickup. Tom H. came over to do more torching on VW. Put new tie rod end on my pickup. Fixed a pad short in the wiring.

Saturday, June 23, 1990—mostly cloudy, 43° to 56°. Worked on truck. Welded on snow plow and trap sled. Did a little work on table saw.

Sunday, June 24, 1990—sunny, beaut of a day, 44° to 67°. Worked on saw. Cleaned wood shop. Put a switch on shop air cleaner. Lisa S visited. Bought a pair of mukluks and mittens at garage sale.

Monday, June 25, 1990—sunny, cloudy, sunny, beaut of a day, 48° to 72°. Sylvia went to Glennallen. I worked in wood shop and on cab over camper.

Tuesday, June 26, 1990—sunny, cloudy, shower, 44° to 64°. Went to Palmer, Wasilla. Had truck carburetor and dist. worked on. Did shopping. Sylvia washed canopy top. I dug raspberry and strawberry plants in Palmer.

Wednesday, June 27, 1990—partly cloudy, two light showers, 43° to 70°. Didn't sleep well. Worked on table saw extensions and painted it. Planted the raspberries and Sylvia planted strawberries. Went to Allen's garage sale. Went to dump. Took raspberries to Mannings and Bartleys. Visited Billmans at Point of View. Met Woody and Rub. Don Culp was there.

Thursday, June 28, 1990—partly cloudy, 49° to 72°. Repaired the mountings of brackets for the camper jacks. Painted the saw again. Sorted some junk.

Friday, June 29, 1990—sunny and hot, a few breezes, 54° to 78°. Mosquitoes are pesky some of the time. Sylvia papered the camper inside. I mounted a motor on the saw and wired it through a switch. Painted sides and bottom of table saw extensions. Bob R. went with me to dump to load a cast heating stove for my garage.

Saturday, June 20, 1990—sunny, hot, partly cloudy, light shower and thunder. Put a primer coat on pickup canopy. Then we went to Memorial Service for Leo Zura. Came home and had a nap and rest. Cut out and sanded a double quilt rack for a lady in Copper Center. Cal Gilcrease stopped in to say goodbye. He and his family are moving to Arkansas.

Sunday, July 1, 1990—sunny, and partly cloudy, 54° to 72°. Built a sawdust guard for saw. Attached the saw table extensions. Borrowed a paint sprayer from Lucky B. Lisa Smayda and D's daughters visited. Sylvia worked on camper, lawn, laundry.

Monday, July 2, 1990—partly cloudy, shower and rain, 46° to 66°. Tried to paint pickup canopy. Didn't finish it. Visited Allen F.

Tuesday, July 3, 1990—mostly sunny and hot, 52° to 76°. Finished canopy. Put tie down hooks on pickup. Connected both fuel tanks to one line to carburetor, by passing the tank switch. Did some band saw cutting on some diamond willow for Jim Manning.

Wednesday, July 4, 1990—mostly sunny, some breeze, 50° to 72°. Mounted spare tire and carrier on front of pickup. Cut down large birch tree near woodshed. Trimmed branches off a few spruce near where I drive when storing the cab over camper. Rudbecks visited. Ed F and Kyle came to borrow a movie.

Thursday, July 5, 1990—sunny and hot, 50° to 76°. Lots of bugs. We put cab over camper on pick up and hooked up lights. Made a prototype of a clamp. Sylvia kept Kari Odden all day. Rod and Marty came to pick Kari up in evening.

Friday, July 6, 1990—hot and sunny, 46° to 72°. Painted snow plow. Sylvia put provisions in camper and we started for Fairbanks. Visited Scotty and Ruby Hollenbeck and camped on their farm.

Saturday, July 7, 1990—then on to Fairbanks, Cleary Ski Lodge. Had to drive around a little, after we got close, to find the place. Nice wedding. Met lots of John and Colleen's relatives. Started drive towards home. Didn't get too tired. Got home 1:00 AM.

Sunday, July 8, 1990—partly cloudy, 44° to 58°. Did a few more things to the camper. Sawed out some hickory for wood clamps. Glued some faults in the wood. Had rhubarb pie at Karn's. Allen F. had supper with us. Bob and Karn here for TV in evening.

Monday, July 9, 1990—partly cloudy, 34° to 62°. Frost down on the lake this morning. Went to Point of View Lodge to help Billman's with leveling their lodge. It's a big job.

Tuesday, July 10, 1990—mostly sunny and breezy, 38° to 64°. Real dusty working in the basement at Dan's lodge. Came home early and called sister Virginia (they are coming to visit). Went to visit Oddens. Got truck and camper ready to go to town tomorrow.

Wednesday, July 11, 1990—partly cloudy, 42° to 54°. Went to Palmer, Wasilla on business. Then on to Anchorage and met the flight Don and Virginia Wink (my sister and husband from Iowa) were on. Their luggage was late. Then to eat and shop at Price Savers. Got home and to bed real late.

Thursday, July 12, 1990—rainy and cool, 42°. Decided to go to Denali Park. Shopped a little in Glennallen. Went to Payson and took Denali Highway. Stopped and had lunch. The onto Cantwell and turn right to Denali Park. Made shuttle bus reservations and went north to a state pull off for supper and camp for the night. People in rubber rafts are floating the Nenana River.

Friday, July 13, 1990—up very early. Rained in the night. Went to Visitor Center at Denali National Park. Got on standby list and got on first bus. Saw nice bull moose, then a smaller bull, a red fox, several boo, Dall sheep, 5 grizzly bears, a single at a distance, sow and two cubs, a yearling very near shuttle bus. Some golden eagle. Mt McKinley showed a little sometimes. Went to Wonder Lake. One bull boo lay 30 yards from Eielson Center. Bus driver very good with narration. Got gas at Healy then on to Ester and camped at Cripple Creek campground. Had shower and a good night sleep.

Saturday, July 14, 1990—cool morning and hot, sunny day. Did laundry, grocery shopping and visited Alaska Land Exhibit. Gas for truck and went out Steese Highway 60 miles to another Cripple Creek campground. Dragged in some poor wood for a evening fire. Took some pix at oil pipeline earlier. Nice day and evening.

Sunday, July 15, 1990—warm to hot. Up early and went onto Circle City on the Yukon. Saw lots of mining activity, scenery, etc. Went to Nome Creek on way back at Mile 57 and panned a little for gold. Got back to Fairbanks, gassed up, found a camper park. Showered and to bed.

Monday, July 16, 1990—warm and sunny. Took a slow drive home. A grizzly bear has been nosing around the neighborhood. Got into our garage and my trap bait. Picked up our mail at Rudbeck's.

Tuesday, July 17, 1990—partly cloudy, 50° to 69°. Changed oil in truck. Straightened up the running boards on left side of truck. Put another bolt in rear step on camper. Jim M, Allen F. visited. Rudbeck's brought over some lake trout and we had it and some sweet corn Lefty and Virginia brought all for supper. Don and I canoed and walked over to look down on Nelchina River. Saw bear tracks. Went to visit Billman's at Point of View. They have done a lot of work. Saw cow moose and twin calves just as we were leaving their place.

Wednesday, July 18, 1990—warm to hot. Re-stocked the camper and went to

Valdez. Taking in the sights on the way. Got reservations to do the Colombia Glacier tour tomorrow. Did some salmon fishing for humpies. No luck.

Thursday, July 19, 1990—foggy and hot. Fog lifted by the time we got to the glacier. Saw steller sea lions, harbor seals, flock of kitty wakes, artic terns. Many commercial purse seiners were after pink salmon. The tour boat stopped to watch one of the boats pull up its net of fish. Fished a little after we got back to Valdez. Then on to Glennallen and pizza and on home. Real warm here and much smoke. Tok fire?

Friday, July 20, 1990—mostly sunny, hot and some breeze, 56° to 80°. Unloaded camper and put it on old pickup. Jim Sheldon hauled two loads sand for fill and leveled it. Pushed out some stumps. We had cut the trees and carried the brush off. Visited Manning. Went fishing at Buffalo Lake. Got eight rainbow trout. Don didn't get a fish. Allen had Mike push out the nice spruce tree near mailboxes.

Saturday, July 21, 1990—partly cloudy, hot, some breeze, 52° to 74°. Took canoe back down to lake. Put water tank on truck and went to Max H. and got a load of water. He is depressed. Didn't do much today. Racked some gravel and worked a little on camper window. Lisa S. and girls visited. Lots of little ducks on our lake.

Sunday, July 22, 1990—sunny, haze, and smoke, 51° to 79°. Put a new glass in one of the crank open windows on the cab over camper. Visited Smayda's, Tom's folks. Pie at Nelchina after supper. A Nelchina Glacier lake broke loose. Flooded river and stranded some people on other side of river. Al Lee flew the women out. Men canoed for help.

Monday, July 23, 1990—mostly sunny, 52 to 78. Visited Matanuska Glacier and had lunch at Long Rifle Lodge. Stopped at Musk Ox Farm and on to Hatcher Pass Mine. Got into Anchorage early, ate supper. Went to airport and visited till Virginia and Don boarded their plane for Cedar Rapids, Iowa. We slept in cab of pickup in Sears' mall.

Tuesday, July 24, 1990—partly cloudy, 57° to 70°. Had truck alignment checked. Did some things on list in Anchorage, Eagle River, Wasilla and Palmer. Got home in afternoon. Bob R brought package over. We visited Lloyd and Neva Griffith who are visiting Rudbecks. Lots of little ducks feeding on our lake these days.

Wednesday, July 25, 1990—cloudy, shower last night, 52° to 62°. Tried to repack front wheel bearings on truck. No luck. Right side real bad. Made appointment in Glennallen. Did a few small jobs in wood shop.

Thursday, July 26, 1990—mostly cloudy, 44° to 62°. Sylvia watered lawn and mowed it. Phoned around for airline tickets. Called John O. twice about our claim work. Also Dan B. Fit a new synthetic stock to the .338 rifle. Had to fit a recoil pad also.

Friday, July 27, 1990—cloudy, 40° to 52°. Bought airline tickets. Took truck to Glennallen and had new wheel bearings put in front wheels. Visited with Allen F. Ordered a Toyo oil heater from Paul White.

Saturday, July 28, 1990—rain in night, sunny later, 40° to 64°. We cleaned up, cut up and stacked some down trees around here. Fixed exhaust pipe on truck. Worked on hickory wood clamps. Finished cutting, drilling and got part of the inleting done. Allen and I went to Ed's at Mendeltna for the pipe. Bob R. borrowed a porcelain fixture.

Sunday, July 29, 1990—partly cloudy, 45° to 60°. Started working on snowgo. Then went to Anchorage and bought a fuel tank and stand. Got home late and tired.

Monday, July 30, 1990—mostly sunny, very light showers, 42° to 58° Sylvia went to Glennallen. I unloaded stand and tank, started taking tire chains apart. Lisa S. and girls and Tom's parents came to visit. When Sylvia came home we overhauled L.T. snowgo secondary clutch and installed it and the motor. Replaced the fuel lines.

Tuesday, July 31, 1990—partly cloudy, 42° to 60°. Worked on wolf traps all day. Welded up new swivels, chains and fasteners. Tuned the traps and am boiling them this evening. Bob R. was here for supper.

Wednesday, August 1, 1990—sunny, nice day, 30s to 65°. Tom Smayda's brother John and wife, Sue and Lisa S. and girls came over to visit. Finished boiling the traps. Hauled a load of water from Max H.

Thursday, August 2, 1990—party cloudy, 30s to 64°. Fixed up fuel oil stand and dug out a level place for it. Sanded the 500 gal. tank. Mannings came over and helped put the tank on the stand.

Friday, August 3, 1990—party cloudy, 40s to 70°. Poured epoxy on two clocks. Sylvia went blueberry picking with Mannings. I painted fuel oil tank and stand. We cut down and cut up a couple trees, pulled a half dozen stumps with the pickup. Fun watching the young flickers and young ducks this evening. A shower from NE, sun from SW, double rainbow. Amazing how the lake waters change color.

Saturday, August 4, 1990—mostly cloudy, 48° to 54°. Built a stand for gas storage tank. Sanded the tank. Bob R. lifted tank onto stand with his loader. All welding done. Filter and hose put on. Washed tank out with water.

Sunday, August 5, 1990—partly cloudy, light shower, 37° to 56°. Did a few small jobs. Loaded horns and took them out by the highway, sold one small set. Did more small jobs and loaded pickup with stumps and junk.

Monday, August 6, 1990—most cloudy, 36° to 56°. Worked at cleaning barrel of .338. Rigged up gas station pump to fill over head fuel tank. Elect motor gets "hot." Fit a recoil pad on BPs 10-gauge. Went to Smayda's for supper and homemade ice cream. Lots of neighbors and Tom's brother John and wife Sue. Good music and good time.

Tuesday, August 7, 1990—partly cloudy, light shower, 42° to 55°. Finished pumping gas, some problems with pump. Shot rifle. Started building a fuel transfer pump out of another gas pump. Rudbeck's visited.

Wednesday, August 8, 1990—mostly cloudy, fog early morning, 46° to 56°. Went to Wasilla and picked up our crafts. Bought paint for gas storage tank. Filled Sylvia's prescription. Brought two drums gas home and the transfer pump. Pumped it very well. Dan and Patti Billman visited.

Thursday, August 9, 1990—partly cloudy, 41° to 60°. We laid heating fuel line from tank into basement. Cleaned chimney and painted gas tank and stand. Put a wheel barrow load sand under fuel oil tank. Had a piece of pie at Mae's.

Friday, August 10, 1990—some rain, heavy fog, 44° to 54°. Finished getting ready to leave on trip. Went to Anchorage. Did some shopping. Will park truck at Griffith's while we are gone. They took us to airport. (We're flying to Minneapolis to visit our kids and friends living there.)

Saturday, August 11, 1990—got on plane and went to Salt Lake City and changed planes to go to Minneapolis. Our three daughters and grandkids met us at the air terminal. Went to Beverly's for a few hours, then over to Theresa's.

Sunday, August 12, 1990—rain in night and partly cloudy, 60s to 70s. Slept 12 hours. Loafed and visited around the house all day. Sylvia called her sister Frances Collins in Chicago, Illinois.

Monday, August 13, 1990—mostly sunny, 60s to 70s. Slept and loafed till in afternoon. Went to Fleet Farm store and a couple of malls. Did some shopping and browsing. Earl barbequed our supper. (Holliday Store, Fridley) Super

Canada 12 for $100.00. Huge Magnum 3 for $60.00 Fleet Farm 10 GA steel shot $16.00.

Tuesday, August 14, 1990—partly cloudy, hot and humid, 60s to 80s. Nothing doing until 2:00 PM. Did call Nadia and a couple places for snowplow electric motor. Went to buy one later, stopped at a mall and shopped (Sylvia and I). Took Theresa, kids and Earl out for pizza. Saw 40-50 Canada geese on a green area right in town. One lay dead in the gutter.

Wednesday, August 15, 1990—mostly sunny, a little breeze, 70s to 80s. Loafed all morning and went to Holliday Mall in Fridley. 10 GA steel shot $17.00 per box/1 box weighs 3 ¾ pounds.

Thursday, August 16, 1990—sunny and hot, 70s to high 80s. Laid around here till 2:00 PM, then loaded our gear and Earl drove Theresa and kids and Sylvia and I to Don and Evelyn Caughey (his folks). His brother Butch was there also. Don treated us to great T-bone steaks, barbequed out on the lawn. After a visit Earl and Theresa drove us to Paul and Ruth and Steve's at Staples. Some visiting, then to bed.

Friday, August 17, 1990—foggy morning, high humidity, 60s to 80s. Breakfast, then Harold Hanson came in to town and took us out to their farm. Nice lunch and visit. Dan, Phyllis and Granddad came over. Grandson, Steve Wilkins was with us. Drove around and looked at Harold's corn. Saw a coyote in an alfalfa field. Paul and Ruth picked us up and we stopped at Taymond Hanson's in Motley. He is 92 and looking good. Went back to Paul's and had a good supper.

Saturday, August, 18, 1990—60s to 70s, rain in the night, cloudy all day. Paul and Steve took us to Allen Rollins' to visit. Grand tour of the fields with Allen. Saw a white tail deer. Had nice lunch, Steve got to bottle feed a fawn buck and Lillian took a Polaroid picture of him while Scott's wife Darlene took camcorder pictures. Then on to Jim Rudbeck's. Arlene is in Colorado. Had supper with Jim and heard his side of the story. He brought us to Paul's at Staples in the evening.

Sunday, August, 19, 1990—60s to 70s, some rain, and clouds all day. Visited Eva Adams (an old friend and neighbor who lived near us with her husband Kenneth, son Larry and daughter Rose, when we had the farm in Motley, MN). Spent a lot of time with Steven, and Paul was here all day.

Monday, August 20, 1990—borrowed Paul's car. Steve went with us to Peter and Delaine Achermann's. Great visit with them and John, Mike and Denise and kids. Al Eckes came there to see us. Then on to Harry and Neva McCoy's, then back to Paul's house. Joe Vernarski came there and Scott Rollins called.

Tuesday, August 21, 1990–60° to 80° in Minneapolis, cloudy in Staples, and sunny in Minneapolis. Paul, Steve and I went to a few places trying to get keys made. Looked for good books, no luck. Scott and Darlene Rollins visited. Theresa family and Earl came over at 2:30. Took pix and went to Fridley and Earl and Theresa's. Reorganized and went on to Beverly's, Vanessa and Tyler. Visited awhile and then to sleep.

Wednesday, August 22, 1990–cloudy, and muggy, sweat a lot and allergic to some things here. 60s to 80°. Walked around to a few stores. Visited and watched TV. A nice birthday party for Vanessa in evening. Met Chuck, (Nadia's beau). Theresa's family came. Tyler's other grandmother came. She took Tyler home overnight.

Thursday, August 23, 1990–cloudy and in the 60s. Went for a walk. Then Tyler and I stayed home while the women went shopping. Had a nap. Early evening Kevin took the kids. Bev, Sylvia and I walked to a nearby mall. I bought some metal rings for wooden puzzles. Bev baby sat two little neighbor girls.

Friday, August 24, 1990–cloudy, partly cloudy, hot and humid, 70° to 84°. Went for a walk, loafed around the house. Went for a walk to Woodland Park. Vanessa and Tyler fed bread to the mallard ducks, then home for a good supper. "Rich," Bev's beau, was here this evening.

Saturday, August 25, 1990–shower in the night, hot and muggy, 70° to 80s. Walked. Went to nearby yard sale. Walked over to gun shop. Watched a bunch of movies.

Sunday, August 26, 1990–rain in night, thunder and lightning, 70° to 90°. Took Beverly and kids to breakfast and watched a movie. Then Nadia came to pick up and take us over to her place. Went down to pier and met some of the boat owners there, then back up to apt. for a good supper and some TV.

Monday, August 27, 1990–partly sunny, smog, hot, muggy, 70° to 85°. Nadia drove us around to some craft stores. We walked around some of Stillwater book and craft stores in afternoon. Chuck took us out to dinner in evening.

Tuesday, August 28, 1990–mostly sunny, 70° to 79°. Went to Wisconsin and bought lottery tickets, and on to Fleet Farm for 10-gauge shells. Then to Nadia's. Then to Taylors Falls for lunch and see the park. Not so humid today.

Wednesday, August 29, 1990–mostly sunny, cooler, 61° to 79°. Did a little shopping and left keys to be made. Loafed all day. Nadia had a birthday party for Theresa here, in the party room which looks out on the enclosed swimming pool—kids had a grand time. Then up to the apartment for ice cream and cake.

Thursday, August 30, 1990—mostly sunny, 65° to 84°. Nadia drove us to a mall to do a little shopping. We had a brunch and saw a renovated lodge. We went north a few miles to a park and barbequed some steaks, very good.

Friday, August 31, 1990—cloudy to sunny, breezy, 70° to 85°. Went "malling." Nadia treated us o lunch. We took Chuck and Nadia to dinner in evening. Chuck took us for a boat ride up the river.

Saturday, September 1, 1990—smog, haze, mostly sunny, 70° to 85°. Chuck wanted to go fishing. We went out a mile or so across the St. Croix River. I drove the boat while he trolled, no luck. Did catch sunny and one crappie from under a dock. Ate breakfast and packed our bags. Went to Beverly's then to airport. Theresa and family met us there. Then it was get on the big bird. We went to Salt Lake City. Plane problems and so a 2-½ hour lay over, then on to Seattle. Dennis and Adie G picked us up at airport. Tired when we got here, my hip bothers me.

Sunday, September 2, 1990—partly cloudy, 48° to 58°. Took Griffith family to breakfast. The shopped for groceries and gas. Saw 50 Canadian geese along highway at Merrill Field. Got home early and glad to be here. Allen F. visited.

Monday, September 3, 1990—cloudy, 38° to 48°. Went to Tazlina Gravel Pit to look at junked pickup. Cleaned up moose shoulder blade to help call bull moose. Visited Allen F. Rain in evening.

Tuesday, September 4, 1990—snow on mountain this morning. Most of it melted during the day, 38° to 55°. Opened the safe this morning, went to Glennallen for moose permits for Allen, Roxanne, Mae and myself. Went to haul water from Lucky's. Tried to spot moose from mile 132, no luck.

Wednesday, September 5, 1990—got gear ready and went to Trapper's Den on Glenn Highway and rode 4-wheeler pulling a trailer. Went to 7 mile seismic and went east ½ mi. and put up camp. Ate, and walked east to a tree stand—no moose.

Thursday, September 6, 1990—ice on water bucket. Went west and then north to 9 mile? Trail. Did lots of glassing and walking, no moose. Later Bob and Karn thought I was a black bear in camp and prepared to shoot, then realized I was a person!

Friday, September 7, 1990—Bob shot at a moose yesterday. So we look for it today. A few hair where moose stood. We can't find it. Loaded camp earlier

37

and came out to road and home. Regrouped and went to trail to river near Cal's. Went in two miles and camped, hunted. No moose.

Saturday, September 8, 1990–frosty in night and rainy. Bob and I hunted at old burn, then back to camp. I went out a couple of time hunting. Then Lucky and I went south to swamp. No luck and rain. Nodwell and a plane are hunting. Picked up what traps I could find that Cal left there.

Sunday, September 9, 1990–most of rain has quit. We loaded up camp and Bob borrowed my trailer and we came out and on home. We pulled the pump out of the lake.

Monday, September 10, 1990–foggy and rainy, 40° to 46°. Sylvia went to Glennallen. I paid our bills by mail. Got most of the gear ready for work on the gold claims. John, Coleen and Axle were here for supper.

Tuesday, September 11, 1990–sunny, 38° to 48°. Finished getting gear ready. Mike Meekin called to be three more hours late. John O. came over and we talked about the claims till time to leave. He drove his truck to Eureka airstrip and Mike flew me in to Nelchina Glacier on the first flight. Saw one nice bull moose and he saw another small moose.

We found a campsite that would be somewhat protected from the winds from down the glacier and also sandy for to put tent floors on. John and I put our tents up. Then Dan B and Jed ?, doctor flew in behind us and put their tents up. Then John, Dan and Jed went to the claims for a look see. I stayed in camp and boiled drinking water. Saw two ewe sheep and three lambs on nearby mountain. Saw two hunters come back to their nearby camp, just at dark. Dan fried up some of his fresh moose and we talked till 11:30 PM.

Wednesday, September 12, 1990–cloudy, sunny spells, windy, rain. Saw same five sheep. Also two sheep on another mountain. We got up early, did a breakfast, then went to claims. Dan and I went to No. 1 Claim and tried to get to a gully south of claim. No luck, gusting rain and blowing sand on the way back, we checked claim markers to camp. John O and Jed went up mountain and over to Shoup and back down, taking samples. Dan and I stayed in camp. Saw those five sheep again. Then saw a small black bear near the trail where we expected John and Jed to come down off the mountain. We started over that way glassing as we went. It got too dark to shoot, plus we didn't know where John and Jed were. Then the bear hid in some willows. We started back and spotted J and J down on the river bar, met up with them and came into camp.

Thursday, September 13, 1990–cloudy all day. Slept late, then did a traverse up and back on claims 1-10. Took samples and did evaluations. Saw the same five sheep, then two ewes, plus one med ram and one small ram together on the

South Claim No 1. The glacier calved (large pieces breaking off) lots today, the biggest one while we ate lunch up on mountain.

River is running strong tonight. A whistling marmot kept an eye on me as it rested nearby. Boy am I tired tonight. Legs really hurt. Saw a mature and a immature bald eagles. Windy this evening.

Friday, September 14, 1990—rain off and on in night. It came thru the tent wall and sprayed our faces. Puddles on tent floor in morning. Some fog in mountains and low clouds on east side of river and glacier.

The others got up late and we got to the creek at noon. John and Jed went up shoulder of mountain taking samples west, then up and south across the mountain to the big mineralized outcrop. They did great getting samples. They saw 33 sheep in there. Some were really close and three went up the mountain as far as they could and one slipped but caught itself. Dan and I went to the place minerals percolate out of cracks in the rocks, carried by a small flow of water. I couldn't find the place. I got the quartz sample. We saw eight sheep. A sheep guide and his hunter camp near us. Sure is windy, had to pile more rocks on tent stakes and make tents taunt and well tied down, still my tent shook and "popped."

Saturday, September 15, 1990—partly cloudy, sunny, cloudy, light wind. Late breakfast, broke camp. Packed some gear to air strip. Mike was late coming to fly us out. I flew out first, saw four cows and nice bull moose. Nice party at Nelchina. Café is closing.

Sunday, September 16, 1990—sunny to cloudy. Sylvia dug potatoes and I put the new rear shocks on the truck. Then we put camper on truck and loaded crane and goose hunting gear, food and water and I went to Darrel's. Loaded his gear, stopped at the store for pop and candy, then at gas station. Then had a good visit on way to Delta. Saw two yearling cow moose, eagle spruce hen and ducks on way up. Quite a few hunters along the road. Stopped at farmer and got permission to camp and hunt on his farm. He has buffalo trouble in his wheat field.

Cloudy and windy tonight. Sylvia had sent along a moose roast and veggies for a good supper, then lots hunting talk.

Monday, September 17, 1990—cloudy, sunny, Northern Lights, 30s to 40s. Stalked some geese this morning, no luck. Hunted the crane on Thuringer's and Hollenbeck's and Brehmer's. Didn't get any shots. Only three birds in range. Did shoot a sharp tail with the 10-gauge. Other people hunting nearby. Sharp-tail hunters also drive the fields. A pretty good flight of birds in the afternoon. Some birds caught the thermals and flew south. We went to Al & Wendy Baker's and visited in the evening. Northern Lights.

Tuesday, September 18, 1990—froze last night, warm today, partly cloudy. Cranes left the country. Hundred of flocks, 50,000 total? We had shots at a few crane and I managed to get a young one. 68 bison marched by the goose decoys and grazed on some green wheat, very few geese flying.

Picked up decoys and went to town for gas and a dab of groceries. R. Beaver not home. Darrel went to F. & G. for info. We went to Johnson River, didn't see birds. Talked to Living God Mission on their farm. They use several teams of horses and tractors. Back to look at Delta II. Drove around, no birds low enough to shoot at. Then to J. Thuringer & Hollenbeck farm. Some crane landed out in field and some guy on ATV drove over and jumped them up, wounded one. We didn't get a shot.

Wednesday, September 19, 1900—cool, partly cloudy, 35mph winds in afternoon. Walked and drove all around including Roy Beaver and Scott's land over by the river. Rarely a bird in the sky. Walked up on a single crane and shot him. Then a little later got another one from a small flock. While sitting with my back to the wind and on a tall berm pile, a flock of 20 geese flew over my head. I couldn't move of course until they were past me. Their speed with a tail wind put them out of range before I could get off a shot. Then we went over on Barney's and I went to the big patch of woods and picked up the cow bison head.

After that, we started for the small lake on the other side of Nelson's. I got bad stuck and had to get Scott H. to come and pull me out. It was a long walk to their place. Got to visit with Ruby for a while. Barney is buying 40 elk calves at 3800.00 each next fall. Scott will bring some of his buffalo calves from Kodiak and put them on the farm by the river.

Thursday, September 20, 1990—warm, mostly cloudy, light wind. Crane and geese on the field we hunt. Darrel knocked one crane down and couldn't find it. No more crane or geese to shoot at. We went to the pond north of Nelson's. Jumped a lone Canadian, out of range. Came back to Hollenbeck and jumped some cranes up with the truck. We got water at Hollenbeck's, then over to John T. farm. I got a shot off at a group of four and killed one at 106 Steps. Walked up on another one and killed it at 108 Steps. Broke camp, cleaned the birds.

Got gas and coffee and donuts in Delta Jct. and drove in strong gusty winds and rain almost to Summit Lake. Later the rain quit and I got home after 2:00 AM almost too tired to sleep.

Friday, September 21, 1990—sunny, 30° to 40s. Unloaded camper. Visited Allen F. and Rudbecks. Put tar on a leaky place on roof of camper. Sylvia packaged the cranes. A porcupine wanders around here.

My brother, Jerry Wilkins had a cerebral hemorrhage and is out of intensive care.

Saturday, September 22, 1990—lots of snow till middle afternoon, 30° to 40°. Unpacked new oil burner. Cut out some wood articles for Patti Landers. Went to KROA for pizza. Stopped and visited Landers. Snowing again tonight.

Sunday, September 23, 1990—rain, snow, and fog, 34° to 36°. Drew a couple wood working plans. My back is very sore, rested all day.

Monday, September 24, 1990—light rain, low clouds, 34° to 36°. Sore all day. Hauled water, put away tiller, mower, ATV trailer. Visited folks at Snowshoe Lake. Some swans flying down valley.

Tuesday, September 25, 1990—snow, fog, cloudy, clear, 30° to 36°. Back is real sore. Trimmed five small trees. Cut them and ½ cord wood up and stacked it. Visited Clem in afternoon and Smayda family in evening.

Wednesday, September 26, 1990—sunny, partly cloudy, 18° to 40°. A little ice on lake. Very few ducks, four swans. Back is sore. Visited Jim Manning. Allen came over for 30.06 cartridges. Pulled dock out of lake. Re-plied the two sided logs. John and Logan came to look at the Cat. Jim, Mary and Kari visited in evening.

Thursday, September 27, 1990—cloudy, sunny, 20° to 42°. Back is real sore. Measured up some logs and truck frame and put add on the radio. We worked in wood shop the rest of afternoon. Sylvia made a baby blanket for Mailly's new baby. Karen kids were in Wasilla so we didn't get to see them. The beaver are dragging willow past our dock and to their feed pile in the lake.

Friday, September 28, 1990—cloudy, rain late afternoon, 33° to 36°. Back is very sore. Did some work in wood shop. Test boiled truck thermostat then drained and flushed the truck radiator and installed a 192° thermostat. Lisa S. then Jim M. visited. Swans landed in lake.

Saturday, September 29, 1990—cloudy, foggy, rainy, 30° to 40°. Sore back. Worked in wood shop. Patty Landers was here. Went to Rudbeck's for turkey supper, Oddens were there also. Could hear swans passing overhead.

Sunday, September 30, 1990—cloudy, sunny, 30° to 42°. Went to memorial service for Max Hoffman.

Monday, October 1, 1990—cloudy, snow showers, 30° to 40°. Back still sore. Worked some in wood shop. Made a try for thirteen geese on our lake. They left before I got close. Visited the Smaydas. Allen F. came over for a movie and visited. He thinks a bear might be down around his place.

Tuesday, October 2, 1990—mostly sunny, 20° to 34°. Back is really sore. Worked a little in the wood shop.

Wednesday, October 3, 1990—mostly sunny, 9° to 30°. With hole cutter and chisels I put a four inch hole through a log in south wall of house and setup a Toyo oil burner and finished hooking up the fuel line. Our lake started freezing over.

Thursday, October 4, 1990—mostly sunny, 8° to 28°. Our lake almost froze over. Had coffee with the Rudbecks, supper at Farmer's. Worked in wood shop. Packed gear for Cordova goose hunt. Shot a spruce hen. Back still sore. Six geese on our ice.

Friday, October 5, 1990—mostly sunny, 20° to 30°. Sore back. Did more packing, including crafts. Took some potatoes to Kim H. Our lake isn't completely frozen over yet.

Saturday, October 6, 1990—partly cloudy, 20° to 30°. Finished packing gear in truck camper. Dropped some wood cutouts at Patty Landers. Then on down the hwy. Tried to sell some wood, no luck. Did leave some on consignment at Copper Center. Ferry was late and we had a long wait to get on. Smooth trip to Cordova. Got in after daylight.

Sunday, October 7, 1990—cloudy, windy, rainy in afternoon. We had breakfast at Trowbridge's. Then out to airport. Pilot reports weather not good with high winds. And we must land at low tide on Egg Island. A few hunters are there and Steve didn't see any geese there so we don't fly. We drove out the Cordova Highway looking for ducks. Saw three goldeneye. Found a black bear head, a tanned grizzly cub pelt. Quit hunting early. Beth had a good supper fixed.

Monday, October 8, 1990—warm, cloudy, rainy. Back and leg are very sore. We won't be going out to Egg Is. on that account. Got a late start but drove the road out to the first big culverts past the Million Dollar Bridge. Hunted slowly all the way. Saw a goose and heard others and a few ducks. Silver salmon are spawning. On the way back Charlie spotted Dusky Canada's, just off the road at Mile 33-½. We split up and got on each side and Charlie did a great sneak and got one when they got up. Later we tried for three mallard drakes at a puddle along the ditch and missed them. Then shot two ducks on a gravel pit the beaver had dammed up. The beavers swam right up to us. Heard more geese while plucking the Dusky. Home to supper and heard and saw large flocks whistling swan's flying over in the night.

Tuesday, October 9, 1990—sunny and warm. Got a late start. Went out to highway, saw geese at 6 mile. Couldn't get a shot at them. Charlie shot a green wing teal off a puddle along the road. Went to 17 mile and picked up the two ducks we had shot the evening before. They had drifted to the side and we could pick them up without using the canoe we had loaded and brought along to retrieve them. Then back to town and Charlie worked in the afternoon. We went back out for one hour and he stalked geese at 6 mile. I went east and north 3/8 of a mile. They got up and flew toward me without making a sound till right over me. Came right out of the sun and I missed my shots, poor excuse. Almost immediately four ducks came ripping by and I wasn't even ready enough to shoot at them!!!

Wednesday, October 10, 1990—cloudy, light rain. Back is really sore, laid around the house all day. Patched a hip boot for Charlie. We drove out the road to 41 mi. No geese and few ducks. Good supper. Made ice cream and talked trapping.

Thursday, October 11, 1990—cloudy, up early. Got all packed and to ferry terminal and it was closed as the ferry will be late. Back to Charlie's then another ferry delay till 6:00 AM tomorrow. Sylvia and Beth walked about town. After Charlie got off work we drove out road to 11 mile, saw no geese, back to town and out to Hartney Bay, ducks out a edge of tide coming in and shooting time over before tide gets to shore. Back to house for halibut supper and a BS session. Charlie disassembled his grandfather's Savage 99 to clean it and look at the cracked stock. Found a broken trigger return spring.

Friday, October 12, 1990—cloudy, up early, breakfast and down to ferry. Got on board and got to Valdez mid afternoon. Sold some ski racks at sport shop. Saw some 200 geese on tidal flats very near town. Drove on out to State Gravel Pit east of Robe River. I walked down the river as the road in the trees had been washed away. Prospects looked bleak for shooting so back to camper. Sylvia fixed egg sandwiches and we headed for home. Saw two mallard drakes in puddle but didn't stop to try for them. Rain, snow after Thompson Pass. Gassed up at Glennallen then on home to find 8"-9" snow in our yard. House is 46° and Sylvia's tomatoes are frosted.

Saturday, October 13, 1990—sunny, cloudy, light snow in evening, 4° to 21°. Unloaded gear. Took camper off GMC and put it on old truck. Cleaned garage. Took off bumpers and started to put snow plow on. Allen visited in evening.

Sunday, October 14, 1990—mostly sunny, skiff of snow, 4° to 17°. Slept late. Went over to Manning' and picked up our mail. Started mounting the snow plow on the truck. Lucky came up. I sent a plow motor home with him for parts.

Monday, October 15, 1990–skiff snow, cloudy, 8° to 18°. Back is so sore. Put controls on for snow plow. Lights had water in them. Lisa S. and daughters visited. Patty L. brought a child's rocking chair to be fixed.

Tuesday, October 16, 1990–partly cloudy, -6° to 8°. Mounted plow on truck. Jim O. came along and adjusted lift control cable. Plow works fine and I plowed our snow, moved snow go trailer. Smayda family came over and helped lift canopy onto the pickup.

Wednesday, October 17, 1990–partly sunny, -5° to 10°. Fastened canopy to truck bed. Went to Nelchina School at invitation of students, for grandparents, friends day. Came home and planed some 1" x 12"s. Made a snow deflector and clearance flags for snow plow. Beverly called today. Karn called also.

Thursday, October 18, 1990–cloudy, ice fog, -12° to 8°. Back is still sore. Worked in wood shop. Sylvia paints all day. Made some bearberry jam. Tom Smayda borrowed some tools and brought them back. Sent an order to Bass Pro Shops for fly tying for grandson Steven.

Friday, October 19, 1990–cloudy, 3" snow, clear afternoon, 10° to 20°. Plowed snow for Allen, Lucky, Mannings, and ourselves. Worked in wood shop half the day. Roxanne slid their van off the hill driveway.

Saturday, October 20, 1990–snowed 2-½ inches, cloudy, 14° to 24°. Worked a little in the wood shop. Pat L. and I helped Allen get the van back on the driveway and no damage. He took us all out for a good steak dinner at Tolsona. Saw a fox in the road on way home.

Sunday, October 21, 1990–light snow, sunny, 20° to 28°. Loafed all morning. Cut out a few pieces of wood. Visited Lucky and Mary B. Put a shim under pickup canopy so tailgate would fit better.

Monday, October 22, 1990–cloudy, ice fog just over head, 16° to 24°. Worked in wood shop all day. Wolverine delivered oil. Visited Bartleys. They gave us some buffalo meat. Phoned my brother Jerry.

Tuesday, October 23, 1990–cloudy, sunny, 6° to 24°. Worked in wood shop most of day. Mannings visited. Phoned State appraiser. Went to KROA to MNC meeting in evening. Allen F. called. A coyote to 75 yards and missed it.

Wednesday, October 24, 1990–sunny, beautiful sunrise, 18° to 28°. Put another shutoff valve in stove fuel line. Turned on stove and programmed it. Fired up snow go. Visited Allen at store. Adjusted steering on snowgo. Cut out parts for fly tying desk for grandson Steve.

Thursday, October 25, 1990—16°; up early and went to Anchorage. Shopped for truck, woodshop and spent $750.00 on groceries. Got home late and unloaded everything.

Friday, October 26, 1990—mostly sunny, 12° to 16°. Put away the supplies. Tried to get the heater "programmed". Worked on Steve's fly tying desk. It's all put together ready to put a finish on it. Lots of phoning to get airline tickets for Sylvia to go to Fran's in Chicago. Talked to Darrel and Mike about programming the heater.

Saturday, October 27, 1990—mostly cloudy, snow shower, 14° to 18°. Took pix and varithaned Steve's fly tying desk. Shoveled a little snow. Visited Allen's store.

Sunday, October 28, 1990—cloudy, 15° to 19°. Built a cardboard box to mail the fly tying desk. Varithaned four paper towel racks. Put new halogen bulbs in snowplow lights.

Monday, October 29, 1990—mostly cloudy, 14° to 19°. Tom H. came over for coffee. He is back from North Slope and is on R & R. Worked in wood shop. Tom S. came over to borrow a tool. Sylvia went to Glennallen on senior van. Jim O. borrowed a broom to sweep snow off his plane.

Tuesday, October 30, 1990—skiff of snow and cloudy, 12° to 17°. Worked in woodshop. Dave came over and made some diamond willow lamp uprights. Oddens visited awhile. Mannings brought keys, etc. for when they are gone to N.C. We took pizza down to Farmers for supper. Pat and Patty Landers were there.

Wednesday, October 31, 1990—cloudy, sunny, cloudy, snow flurries, -4° to 16°. Worked in wood shop. Visited Tom H. Worked on snow plow light wiring. Got turn signals hooked up. Kids are Halloween trick or treating this evening.

Thursday, November 1, 1990—cloudy, dry snow flurries all day. 3° to 20°. Did a few odd jobs, called state lands office. Hauled our garbage to dump. Stopped at Bartley's and copied some documents. Went to see Mannings and he showed me how to program his oil heater. Got three packages ready to go to Minnesota with Mannings.

Friday, November 2, 1990—mostly cloudy, some ice fog, 4° to 10°. Worked on snow plow lights. Sanded and inleted heavy wood clamps. Put three coats linseed oil on the clamps. We went to Halloween party at school house. Dave DeJung called and shot a coyote on our lake.

Saturday, November 3, 1990—sunny, and some ice fog, -6° to 6°. Started to put Jorgenson style clamps together. Tom H. came over to visit. Sat on steel swivel chair and folded one leg up on it. He is a big man. We put urethane on 12 moose clocks. Sure had trouble with the paint. Had Huddleston family over for pizza for supper. Mannings stopped to pick up packages to take to our kids in Minnesota.

Sunday, November 4, 1990—mostly cloudy, some ice fog, -3° to 9°. Worked on crafts and some on the clamps. Went to Jim and Mary Odden's for supper.

Monday, November 5, 1990—cloudy, some ice fog, 3° to 12°. Sylvia went in senior's car. I worked in wood shop all day except for adjusting snow plow lights and covering the backside of the plow turn signals. Took some things to Allen Farmer, and Lincoln S. stopped for a few minutes.

Tuesday, November 6, 1990—snow and windy all day, 12° to 14°. Worked in wood shop most day. Went to Glennallen in afternoon and voted. Sylvia got craft paints. Left some wood shavings with Darrel Gerry for dog bedding.

Wednesday, November 7, 1990—mostly cloudy, windy and blowing snow all day, -5° to -2°. Worked in wood shop until evening, then plowed Allen, and Lucky's driveways, and then my own. We had the Smaydas here for pizza.

Thursday, November 8, 1990—sunny and cold, -19° to -15°. John of Kunik Iron Wks made a down payment on CAT. Plowed a little snow, hauled a load of water from Smayda's. Worked in wood shop. Have the periscope finished as far as the wood goes. Worked on Tic-Tac-Toe game. Allen had a hole get burned in the floor of his store.

Friday, November 9, 1990—sunny, cold, -34° to -20°. Worked in wood shop on Tic-Tac-Toe games. Allen F. stopped by to use phone. Gave him stuff to repair his van rear window. Jim Odden borrowed the garage to repair his snow plow. He welded the steel leg on the chair Tom H. broke for me. I changed out batteries in truck and changed to winter oil. Ellie F. spent the afternoon with Sylvia. Northern Lights.

Saturday, November 10, 1990—sunny, sun dogs, -39° to -20°. Worked in wood shop. Got dressed up. Went to Bartley's and got some copies made then on to Billman's at Point of View for a birthday party for Dan. Got to visit with lots of people we know. Tailpipe broke in half on the way.

Sunday, November 11, 1990—sunny, -35° to -16°. Worked in wood shop all day.

Monday, November 12, 1990—sunny, -38° to 5°. Worked in wood shop all day.

Tuesday, November 13, 1990—ice fog, sunny, -28° to -14°. Varithaned two wheelbarrows and 2 towel racks. Put number and clock works on 12 moose clocks. Allen and I visited.

Wednesday, November 14, 1990—somewhat warmer today, ice fog at home. We left early and went to Anchorage to get contract started on the remote parcel. Shopped for truck and snow plow repairs. Got some snowgo oil. Got home about 9:00 PM—long day!! Stopped at King Mt. Café for coffee.

Thursday, November 15, 1990—cloudy, 2" snow, 5° Allen picked up 22 quarts oil and I gave him two cans starting fluid. Cut out and put together five wall hanging moose for Patty Landers.

Friday, November 16, 1990—mostly cloudy, 5° to 15°. Tom S. gave me a saw blade for plywood. We priced and boxed crafts to go to Copper Center Bazaar. Matt from Snowshoe Lake used the garage all day to work on his van. Sylvia and I put another plastic window in pickup canopy.

Saturday, November 17, 1990—cloudy and snow, 5° to 20°. We picked up Rosemary Bartley and then dropped her off at B. Wikles when we went to Copper Center School Bazaar. We hand fun and did well at the bazaar. Had pizza and drove home in a snow storm. Sam Weaver called and let me know about the wolves at Snowshoe Lake and Cache Creek Trail.

Sunday, November 18, 1990—mostly cloudy, 12° to 16°. Repaired the left hand exhaust pipe on the truck. Put snow plow on and plowed Manning's, Smayda, Allen's, Lucky's and our places.

Monday, November 19, 1990—cloudy, snow in afternoon, 4° to 19°. Shoveled snow off some roofs and RV started. Getting trap gear ready. Ran snowgo around. Got 223's out.

Tuesday, November 20, 1990—cloudy, light snow, 12° to 0°. Billmans stopped for a few minutes. Early morning. Worked on snow plow lights. Cut out and sanded 5 Puffin. Broke a trail to Smayda's with snowgo.

Wednesday, November 21, 1990—partly cloudy, -20° to -10°. Went to Glennallen for Seniors' Thanksgiving. Then worked in wood shop. Matt brought truck lights and battery tester. Oddens visited in even. They bought new truck. Dan B. called, gold assays aren't very good.

Thursday, November 22, 1990—mostly cloudy, -15° to -0°. Put new lights on snow plow. We went to Bartley's and enjoyed Thanksgiving. Plowed some snow at there place.

Friday, November 23, 1990—mostly cloudy, 28° to -16°. Wired a large back up light on canopy of pickup. Started installing isolator solenoid so I can install a second battery in pickup to run snowplow. Allen and Roxanne stopped by to borrow movies and ask us to supper. Then we watched some of Allen's 8mm home movies. Luck and Mary got home.

Saturday, November 24, 1990—mostly sunny, -25° to -15°. Worked at wiring solenoid and second battery. Doesn't work, will try another diagram tomorrow. Jim and Mary Odden here for supper.

Sunday, November 25, 1990—partly sunny, -28° to -6°. Coyote chased two boo down our lake. Allen and Sylvia saw them. Worked some more on truck batteries, still doesn't work. Worked in wood shop on baseball racks. Oddens came and got us in their new pickup, went to Snowshoe Lake. Kurt and George NC were there.

Monday, November 26, 1990—mostly cloudy, -25° to 12°. Went to Allen's and Got four mirrors. Worked on candle sconce and baseball mitts. Reattached alternator wires to original schematic. Allen came over and borrowed some Elmer's Glue. Sylvia went to Glennallen.

Tuesday, November 27, 1990—cloudy all day, skiff of snow, -10° to 0°. Worked on both candle sconces and baseball racks. Jim O. brought over a huge pile of tanned furs for safekeeping.

Wednesday, November 28, 1990—sunny, -12° to -6°, dropped to -24°. Checked Manning's house and well—all OK. Allen borrowed some wood filler. Billmans visited a little while over Nelchina claims we plan to drop them. Organized some of wood shop.

Thursday, November 29, 1990—cloudy, then sunny, -30° to -26° to -34°. Put two moose coat racks together, plus five ball, bat, and glove racks. Allen came over for more glue. Ellie F. stayed to visit. I checked Manning's house.

Friday, November 30, 1990—light ice fog, -39° to -34°. Ring around moon (moon dogs). It's bright like daylight tonight. Finished crafts and loaded them in truck. Had a fire in stove in garage today and tonight. Fire also in barrel stove in basement. Allen borrowed some wood.

Saturday, December 1, 1990—cloudy, ice fog, -46° to -36°. Up early and we picked up Rosemary party. Went to Bazaar at Legion in Glennallen. Sold eight things. Considering the cold, people did show up. Got back home and unloaded just at dark. Went over to Allen's soon-to-be store and helped him a couple of hours.

Sunday, December 2, 1990—cloudy and snow, -44° to -26°. Checked Manning house and well. Hauled water from Smayda's. Water pipes had started to freeze. I left hose bib on and when it thawed, ran water all over and made a mess. Steve, Karen Malley and kids were here for pizza supper.

Monday, December 3, 1990—cloudy and snow, -20° to -10°. Went to Glennallen on senior van and got remote parcel contract notarized and mailed to Anchorage. Saw a marten cross the road, sit up in the ditch and watch us go past. Haven't seen or heard of a moose being shot yet in this winter season. Saw two boo on a distant lake.

Tuesday, December 4, 1990—mostly sunny, -28° to -30°. Checked on the Manning place. Allen came and got his trailer, gave me a air cleaner for truck. Cut out three banks.

Wednesday, December 5, 1990—mostly cloudy, light snow, -20° to -16°. Made eight box's for five clocks and three banks. Cleaned chimney. Unhooked isolator as battery was low. Assembled banks and clocks and put in boxes.

Thursday, December 6, 1990—cloudy and flurries, -5° to 5°. Plowed snow here and at Smaydas. Checked Manning stove once, also Smayda's and reset later when electric went off. Hauled ½ load of water from Smayda's. Took clocks and banks to KROA for May. Matt and Bart brought tractor here to service it. We put five sleds of wood in basement.

Friday, December 7, 1990—warmer in Palmer, cloudy all day, -5° to 0°. Sylvia went to doctor, plus we got prescriptions refilled. Brought some groceries and two drums of gas home. Saw two red fox before daylight along the road. Later two moose. Talked to a man with a sawmill about some lumber.

Saturday, December 8, 1990—cloudy and some ice fog, -5° to 5°. Made two clock and bank cardboard boxes. Electrical power went off, reset Mannings and our stoves. Cut out pieces for three fold-up step stools.

Sunday, December 9, 1990—cloudy, ice fog, 5° to 6°. Finished making the wood parts for the stools. Dave DeJung caught small female wolf on Lake Louise Road.

Monday, December 10, 1990—cloudy, -5° to 0°. Worked on the candle sconces' for Mendeltna Chapel. Couldn't find a stain that looked right. So I put sealer on and one coat of varithane. Allen F. visited for awhile. Sylvia went to Glennallen on senior van.

Tuesday, December 11, 1990—mostly cloudy, 0° to 7°. Trying to get a good varithane finish on the candle sconces'. One can had chunks in it. Hope this last coat does it. Went fur hunting with the 10-gauge. and a squealing rabbit tape. Only tried once. This player isn't loud enough. Saw some fox, wolf, moose, boo, ptarmigan, few rabbit tracks and one moose lying down.

Wednesday, December 12, 1990—ice fog and cloudy, -5° to 5°. Checked Manning place. Finished the candle sconces. Put three foot stools together.

Thursday, December 13, 1990—some snow, cloudy, 5° to 14°. Worked in wood shop on folding stools then cut out parts for three more. Took Sylvia and Jane to baby shower for Dee Dee.

Friday, December 14, 1990— -20° to 0°. Allen F. and Ellie visit till mid afternoon so I didn't go on trap line. Mounted the anti kick back mechanism on the table saw.

Saturday, December 15, 1990— -24° to -10°. Made five post, ring, ball and board puzzles. Called Allen Rollins for the solution as I had forgotten that part. Checked Mannings and Smayda's. Tom S. called.

Sunday, December 16, 1990—sunny, cloudy, -11° to -8°. Didn't feel well, so. didn't do anything all day. Tom H. is back from North Slope job and visited us. Allen F. stopped for a while. Steve Mailly visited here while he had the boiler circulating hot water in Tom S. water well.

Monday, December 17, 1990—cloudy, -4° to 0°. Sylvia went to Glennallen. Mike Callahan stopped with Christmas gifts. I gave Mendeltna Chapel a four candle sconces as a gift.

Tuesday, December 18, 1990—mostly cloudy, -27° to -19°. Checked Manning's,, stove was off, started it. Wrote Borstad, (lawyer). Visited Allen. Tom H. called, Jane said Manning stove quit. Went over and restarted it. Temp was 20° in house.

Wednesday, December 19, 1990—cloudy. Helped by cleaning kitchen counter mess and getting it organized. Dave D. came over for a snowshoe binding pattern. Then we went east to past Frank Zimbicki's looking for wolves. Have seen a wolf there at a gut pile and another at another spot along the highway. We stopped near Lake Louise Junction and I cut a hunk off his moose hide at the kill there to send to grandson Steve to tie flies with. Allen F. and sons here for supper.

Thursday, December 20, 1990—cloudy, 0° to 4°. Checked heat at the Manning house every day. Didn't go on trapline. Put new miter gauge together for the table saw. Hauled small load of water from Smayda's. Three lights were on and the door was open. Went to Bartley's. Got some things copied. Tried to stop a seeping leak in some fuel oil line fitting. Phoned Theresa, Darcy (her birthday) and Lee.

Friday, December 21, 1990—cloudy; a red sun peeked under clouds and just on top of some low mountains, 16° to 21°. We went to Glennallen and the senior citizens Christmas dinner. A holiday package came from Nadia today.

Saturday, December 22, 1990—all day, lots ice fog, 16°. Didn't go on trapline. Checked houses. Shoveled snow off wood shed.

Sunday, December 23, 1990—3" of snow last night, sunny, cloudy and ice fog, 12° to 6°. Plowed our snow and over at Smayda's. Steve Mailly visited. We went to Mendeltna Chapel for a supper, program, had a good time.

Monday, December 24, 1990—cloudy all day, 14°. Dave DeJung got snowshoe binding idea here. I helped him lift his snowgo into his truck so he can sell it to Chuck Z. Checked Manning's heat. Shoveled snow off camper, brown trailer, two-sided logs, storage shed and lean to. Raked snow off wood shop and lean-to.

Tuesday, December 25, 1990—cloudy, snow in evening, 16° to 18°. Sylvia fixed sumptuous turkey dinner. Bart and Rosemary, Matt, Anna Marie and two daughters and Darrel Gerry were here to help us eat it. Watched a movie and visited Darrel. Gave a report on North Dakota goose hunting. Brought us carvings and gifts from his folks. We called Beverly, and Theresa called us. Very nice day.

Wednesday, December 26, 1990—Snow all night, wind gusts to 25 mph, 5° to -5°. Checked and reset stoves Smayda and Manning. Pulled snow off fuel tanks and wood shop. Mounted snow plow and plowed Smayda's and our snow. Widened the snow berms back at our place. One drift at Smayda's was four feet deep at its deepest.

Thursday, December 27, 1990—cloudy, -20° to -15°. Went visiting as far as Lake Louise today. Saw a red fox run across road about Mile 6-¾.

Friday, December 28, 1990—a few snowflakes, 4° all day. Allen and Roxanne and kids took us to Eureka in their new car and we had breakfast with them. Sure loafed today. Tom H. brought his "new tech" winter gear over to show me.

Saturday, December 29, 1990—cloudy, more snow, 10° to 15°. Went to Moosey Boo and plowed snow for Jack and Jayne Chamberlain. Farmers and Lee Dudley were there. Did a couple little jobs.

Sunday, December 30, 1990—beautiful sunny day, -9° to -7° to -14° evening. Loafed all day. Nadia phoned. Started snowgo, packed home trails. Shoveled a little snow.

Monday, December 31, 1990—mostly sunny, -12° to -22°. Sylvia went to Glennallen, mailed two packages. Tom H. visited. Checked Manning's house. Plowed snow at Dru Allain's and some at Jim Odden's.

Norman back from a hunt.

1991—caribou hunting, building projects, sheep hunting

Tuesday, January 1, 1991—sunny, -38° to -26°. Checked Smayda and Manning houses and wells. Did a little wood burning. Lots of reading and football watching.

Wednesday, January 2, 1991—partly cloudy, -36° to -18°. Shoveled some snow at Manning's. Wrote Charlie a letter, visited Huddlestons.

Thursday, January 3, 1991—sunny, -26° to -20°. Got some packages ready to mail. Cow and calf moose out by garage. Got a picture of them, I hope. Did a few little jobs outside.

Friday, January 4, 1991—sunny, -24° to -16°. Checked Manning's and shoveled more snow. Cow and calf moose over there. Checked Smayda's. Raked snow off some roofs and shoveled some other snow. Fired up snowgo. Lots phone calls. Supper at Allen F.

Saturday, January 5, 1991—sunny, -26° to -20°. Allen and Roxanne here for breakfast. Then we went with them when they took May's daughter to catch a plane back to NC. We went to the movie "Dances with Wolves." We all liked it. We had a good time. We saw lots of moose and moose tracks. Got back home 1:00 in the morning.

Sunday, January 6, 1991—mostly sunny, -24° to -20°. Checked both houses, took a picture of a spruce hen rest, sleep hole in the snow. Dave DeJung came over twice for information and trap boiling gear. Wolf trapping in Unit 13A is closed.

Monday, January 7, 1991—mostly sunny, -25° to -15°. Put three wolf and three (1 ½ inch) size traps in box on snowgo. I wanted to go east to trap. Got stuck three times first 100 yards going down hill! Got to a snowgo trail on lake and came back home.

Tuesday, January 8, 1991—sunny, -20° to -14°. Dan B. brought the snowplow (Odden's) over and we dismantled my old plow motor and repositioned his brushes and that motor then worked fine. Our sewer froze up. We drained the pipes, ran salt and hot water and thawed the ice.

Wednesday, January 9, 1991—sunny, cloudy, -20° to -6°. Dave D. called about trapping again. I went east past end of a lake a ways. Snow was deep. Stopped and looked in a duck box on way back. It had been used. Stopped at Allen's five minute. Then home and hauled a load of water. Looks like snow tonight.

Thursday, January 10, 1991—fog, partly cloudy, -18° to -10°. Took Sylvia to Mary B. to do some laundry. Dropped some mail off at Bartley's. Looked for caribou to hunt. Went as far as Mendeltna Dump Road. Saw one large moose. Went to Joe Virgin's and looked at a pickup he has.

Friday, January 11, 1991—partly cloudy, -10° to -4°. Checked both houses. Moose were feeding again in Manning's flower garden. Loafed a lot. I helped Kim H. get her car unstuck over at Smayda's place. Shovel, gravel, flashlight, 357 in case of moose.

Saturday, January 12, 1991—partly cloudy, -18° to -10°. Broke out snowgo trail from Nelchina to trap line north along Slide Mountain. Sam Weaver had been snowshoeing a boo hunting trail. I didn't get very far north on trap line trail. I didn't see any caribou.

Sunday, January 13, 1991—mostly sunny, sundog out, -10° to -6°. Checked Mannings. Read the Sunday paper. Loafed all day. Harold and Lorraine H. called. Five Caribou on our lake, three cows, two calves.

Monday, January 14, 1991—mostly sunny, sun dog out, -23° to -10°. Checked both houses. Repaired ATV battery, Five caribou cows on our lake.

Tuesday, January 15, 1991—partly cloudy. -35° in night, -25° to -22° all day. -10° in evening. One fourth frost on ground overnight. Checked both neighbors' houses. Worked a little on ATV battery and started charging it.

Wednesday, January 16, 1991—cloudy, light snow, -8° to -6°. Checked Manning's well. Read a lot today. War started against Iraq today.

Thursday, January 17, 1991—cloudy, 3" snow last night, -10° to 26°. Plowed snow here and at Smayda's and hauled a load water from Smayda's. Our sewer froze again. Sylvia thawed it out. Allen, Roxanne were over to visit.

Friday, January 18, 1991—cloudy, 0° to 6°. Plowed snow for Paul Holland. Cleared snow off camper roof, wood shop roof.

Saturday, January 19, 1991—partly sunny, 20° to 32°. Patti B. called and asked me to build at fire at Odden's house. Went on to Landers and got a pattern Angela H. wants wood cut outs. I cut them out for her. Checked Manning's. Saw a moose in second draw (low area) to the east. Saw a good place to put a snare near the dump today. Rain and windy in evening.

Sunday, January 20, 1991—cloudy, breezy, 26° to 34°. Some snow has slid off roof. Billman was here and we soldered my old snowplow pump motor and put it on Odden's plow. Kim H. and kids visited. Allen and Roxanne took some wood cutouts to Patti Landers for me. Allen visited in evening. Tom H. called to ask me to fix his snowgo brake.

Monday, January 21, 1991—partly cloudy, 15° all day. Plowed the snow at Moosey Boo. Visited Odden's. Good supper at Allen and Roxanne's, Mae was there too.

Tuesday, January 22, 1991—mostly sunny, 17°. Plowed Smayda's snow that slide of the roof. Didn't do much today. Large moose walked from our boat landing south across the lake.

Wednesday, January 23, 1991—most cloudy, 13° to 22°. Charlie T. and Little Charlie and "Dan" here overnight and had breakfast with us. Checked both houses. Checked brake on Huddleston's snowgo.

Thursday, January 24, 1991—mostly sunny, 2° to 10°. Varithaned 4 3/8 buttons for candle sconces. Allen Farmer visited for a while.

Friday, January 25, 1991—sunny, 2° to 6°. Checked both houses, cleaned guns. Went to Odden's for brant duck supper. Went to KROA and took Mae to Odden's.

Saturday, January 26, 1991—sunny, -10° to 16°. I went with Charlie and little Charlie to Tolsona and watched the start of Copper 300 Dog Race. Four well known dog mushers are here this year. Then we went to Brown Bear Roadhouse to see some of them come into the first check point. Odden's brought goulash and cake for supper. Lee Dudley, Charlie and Oddens played music. Allen F. birthday today. Him and Kim H. and both their families here for the evening. We gave Tic-Tac-Toe games that we made as gifts to three families.

Sunday, January 27, 1991—sunny, 0° to 20°. Read paper and visited with Charlie T. Then loaded snowgo and sled and went to Snowshoe Lake. We moved all of Charlie's things from the cabin he used to live in. J and E Manning are back home and were here for supper also.

Monday, January 28, 1991—mostly sunny, -10° to 20°. Freighted Charlie's things with snowgo and sled to his storage shed. He gave me some lumber. I packaged Magnum 10 Barrel to send and get it pro-ported. Managed to pinch my thumb today. Sent 100# gas bottle and gas lamp in van to Lincolns.

Tuesday, January 29, 1991—sunny, some cloudy, 0° to 10°. Hauled a load of water. Then we went with Charlie to Billman's at Point of View Lodge on Lake

Louise. Oddens showed up a little later. There was a cross fox out on the lake. Patti fixed a good lake trout for supper. Charlie, Dan and Oddens played music.

Wednesday, January 30, 1991—sunny, -25° to -13°. Loafed a lot. The Charlie's and I walked over to the "Farmer's Gen Store." Allen brought a van load of stock for store. The Charlie's left for Anchorage and McGrath. Took a little effort to get his car running. He took my gun barrel to post office.

Thursday, January 31, 1991—cloudy, some snow in the evening, -35° to -8°. Checked Smayda's, door open, lights on again. Stopped at Allen's store. Jack Chamberlin showed up. A squirrel is bringing spruce cones out of his cache and eats them on top of the snow. Some caribou are using the lake, but we never see them. Must be crossing at night. Sent letters to all the kids today.

Friday, February 1, 1991—sunny, cloudy, skiffs of snow, -20° to -8°. Wrote garden order and a letter. Oddens came and picked up their furs. We took Bartley's mail to them. Went to Mailly's for supper, very good. Karen baked a birthday cake. We had a good time. Their baby girl Hannah is real sweet.

Saturday, February 2, 1991—mostly sunny, -20° to -10°. Checked Smayda's house. Visited Mannings. Theresa and kids gave me a birthday phone call.

Sunday, February 3, 1991—cloudy 3" of snow, -20° to -2°. Marked sizes on surplus drills Jim O. gave me. Sylvia did laundry at Mary Beaudoin.

Monday, February 4, 1991—cloudy, -10° to 2°. Plowed snow here and Smayda's. Went and got my scoop shovel where I left it on Charlie's Trail. Did a few chores. Elaine brought over some wood cut out work to "bid" on. Sylvia went to Glennallen.

Tuesday, February 5, 1991—mostly cloudy, -4° to 4°. Smayda's got back home. Did a few small jobs. Made small piece of wood for Elaine. Sent the rest of her plans back home with her.

Wednesday, February 6, 1991—mostly cloudy, -6° to 2°. Allen F. and Ellie, Tom and Lisa S. here in morning. Sylvia fixed pancakes. Helped Allen build a produce stand in his store, some in afternoon and some in evening. Repaired ATV battery again.

Thursday, February 7, 1991—sunny, -18° to -9°. Gave Allen a small board and some sealer and helped saw some trim. Smayda family visited in afternoon.

Friday, February 8, 1991—sunny and cloudy, -30° to -10°. Went over and helped

Allen with building a candy rack. Took a 1 x 6 x 12 over. Several people stopped in including Jim from up Botley Creek. Rob is building up there also.

Saturday, February 9, 1991—cloudy, -5° to 6°. Figured a material list to enlarge the wood shop.

Sunday, February 10, 1991—cloudy, 0° to 16°. Read Sunday paper. Sorted my shop tips and idea's in wood and put them in a 3-ring notebook.

Monday, February 11, 1991—mostly sunny, "streamers" of snow blowing off mountain tops to south of us, 4° to 16°. Quiet here. Gave Allen some electrical wiring for his store. Made a false start to go wolf trapping. Aborted plan after talking to Tom S. Then went east on lake and came back. Charlie and Little Charlie are to be here tonight.

Tuesday, February 12, 1991—light snow, cloudy, sunny, cloudy, 9° to 26°. Charlie and Charlie here for breakfast. Charlie Trowbridge gave us a large piece hi dense polyethylene. Smaydas were here for coffee. Gave Sylvia a book and me a couple bungee cords. Didn't do much today.

Wednesday, February 13, 1991—cloudy, 20° all day. Went to Bartley's and got some copies made. Gave Sam Weaver a ride to KROA. Visited there for awhile. Checked heat at Allen's store twice. Organized more wood shop paper work.

Thursday, February 14, 1991—cloudy, 1/2" of snow, 15° to 20°. Made four hi-density poly table saw inserts. Bart borrowed water tank. Mary D. took Sylvia to Glennallen. I'm watching Allen's store. Woke up to cow moose and yearling calf eating flowering cabbages and rubbing up against the house. So glad they didn't break out the dining or living room windows. (This has happened in Glennallen recently.)

Friday, February 15, 1991—cloudy, 10° to 20°. Made three wood and plywood boxes to hold mail order catalogs upright on shelf and separated as to categories. Elaine visited, we visited the Farmers.

Saturday, February 16, 1991—snow, cloudy, 15° to 24°. Worked on Mendeltna candle sconces. Made a center marker for dowels, plus AA depth gauge. Added a tension relieving spring at the motor on the table saw.

Sunday, February 17, 1991—mostly sunny, 16° to 25°. Adjusted table saw. Researched dry sinks. Jim M. came over and took their plants home that Sylvia had been caring for.

Monday, February 18, 1991—cloudy, some snow, 11° to 17°. I built a jig for sawing dado finger box joints. Bart brought our water tank back full of water. Sylvia invited Odden family for crane supper.

Tuesday, February 19, 1991—mostly sunny, snow in the night, 3° to 9°. Plowed snow here and Smayda's. Sylvia did laundry at Smayda's. I finished the jig for dadoing.

Wednesday, February 20, 1991—mostly sunny. Went to Allen's store. Then plowed snow at Moosey Boo. Jack C. and I went to the dump then on to Mendeltna Chapel and put up the candle sconces. I sawed some long fire wood into shorter pieces for wood shop. Started on a jig for cutting panels on the table saw.

Thursday, February 21, 1991—sunny, cloudy, snow, windy, -30° to -5°. Planed installation of washer. Went to store. Dave DeJung brought holster over to make a pattern. Worked on plans for bed. Went to Odden's for supper, homemade ice cream and music and visiting. Borrowed glue from Jim, he returned two books.

Friday, February 22, 1991—sunny, cloudy, light snow, -15° to 5°. Tried to make a shoulder harness. It turned out too small. Kim H. called over and wanted help starting her car. Don't know anything about Mazdas.

Saturday, February 23, 1991—sunny, 15° to 24°. Plowed snow here. Bartley borrowed our water tank. I plowed some for Allen. He gave me some good but going out of condition celery, broccoli and bread. Ground war started in Kuwait.

Sunday, February 24, 1991—sunny, 10° to 25°. This wasn't a happy day. Did some work in shop on a panel cutting jig for table saw. Dave D. visited. Bartley borrowed water hauling tank today.

Monday, February 25, 1991—most cloudy, 10° to 24°. Sylvia went to Glennallen. I worked on panel cutting jig and started the washing machine drain.

Tuesday, February 26, 1991—sunny, warm, 15° to 34°. Most snow slid off north side of house roof. Pushed it off to one side. Built an accessory tray for the table saw. Has expanded metal bottom to let dust fall through. I mounted it on saw stand under saw table. Spare blade for chop saw had fallen behind and under work bench, had a time finding it.

Wednesday, February 27, 1991—sunny, 10° to 36°. Went to see Oddens. He loaned me his dovetail jig and used my tin shears. He and "Ron" were installing a gas furnace. Called Beverly this evening.

Thursday, February 28, 1991—sunny, 10 to 30°. Tom and Lisa S. visited all morning. I mounted the chop "miter" saw on a 3/4" plywood with an extended table to support material being cut off.

Friday, March 1, 1991—sunny, 8°. Up at 6:00 AM and went to Anchorage, warm there. Roads are good. Bought lumber, craft supplies, grocery and went to movie "White Fang." Got medicine for both of us.

Saturday, March 2, 1991—sunny, beaut of a day, 0° to 20°. Worked on two adjustable wood stops for a jig and a cut off box. Denise and her guy, Terry, visited us. I borrowed a 3/8 tap from Allen. Allen phoned that a fox was between us and the lake. I called a red in with a rabbit squeal. Missed him with the 10-gauge as he went away.

Sunday, March 3, 1991—sunny, 4° to 24°. Sweat solder two hose bibs into water lines in basement to hook up clothes washer. Then emptied out room in lumber shed for the lumber we brought home Friday. Got it snickered and piled and all re-piled. Planed a few boards. Planer knives are dull.

Monday, March 4, 1991—sunny, cloudy afternoon, light evening snowfall, 0° to 20°. Finished wood stops. Took tap back to Allen. Planed 19 -1" x 12" x 8" and sacked the shavings for Darrel. Took some ice cream to Farmer and had some Ellie's cake for Roxanne's birthday.

Tuesday, March 5, 1991—1/2" of snow, cloudy, sunny, cloudy, 15° to 25°. Mannings here for coffee. I made some gluing, clamping 90° corners. Put a new sanding disc on sander. Mary & Kari Odden were here for supper.

Wednesday, March 6, 1991—sunny, 5° to 35°. Did a little in the wood shop. Visited Tom and Lisa. Tom came over and we went down on the Nelchina River with our snowgos caribou hunting. We went quite a ways down river towards Tazlina R. Didn't see any caribou. Saw moose cow and calf. Some wolf, fox and marten and boo tracks. Got back just at dark.

Thursday, March 7, 1991—mostly sunny, 10° to 25°. Skiff snow made a couple of push sticks in wood shop. Started on a taper jig.

Friday, March 8, 1991—mostly cloudy, 16° to 26°. Made another push stick. Started repairing the belt sander. Tom H. is home again and visited in afternoon.

Saturday, March 9, 1991—sunny, -5° to 16°. Put belt sander back together. Sharpened two sets planer knives. Tom H. visited. We went to Snowshoe Lake, looks too tough getting down on lake to plow a skating rink. Put 1" x 2" x 8' spruce upstairs in garage.

Sunday, March 10, 1991—sunny, -15° to 11°. Did a few small jobs around the house. Matt borrowed water tank again today. Tom S. called-saw more fresh boo tracks. Harold and Rachel Dimmick were here for supper and a nice visit.

Monday, March 11, 1991—sunny, temp low at Allen's: -40° to -20° to 10°. Went over to Allen's and got him interested in getting wood at Little Nelchina road construction site. We got 2-½ loads of blocks. Ellie's birthday today.

Tuesday, March 12, 1991—cloudy, light snow, -20° ? to 10°. We couldn't get wood today so went to Glennallen and did laundry and lots small errands. Split and piled yesterday's wood.

Wednesday, March 13, 1991—sunny, 1-½" snow in early morning, -10° to 20°. Lisa S. visited for coffee. I finished the taper jig. Made a device to hold circle saw blades while sharpening them. Started a jig to set circles saw teeth. Allen came and took me to a lunch at his store. Quite a few neighbors were there. Got pretty windy at one point today. Blew quite a bit of snow around.

Thursday, March 14, 1991—sunny and some snow, plus breezy, 0° to 25°. Finished the jig to set circle saw teeth. Turned a roller on the lathe and built a frame to hold it.

Friday, March 15, 1991—sunny, windy in early evening, 0° to 25°. Rudbecks were here for breakfast. I hauled a load of water from Smayda's. Went to store. Put roller and frame together so it will mount on a stand. Worked on muffler on truck. Started building a 2' high stool. Built a jig to drill the "rung" holes in the stool legs.

Saturday, March 16, 1991—mostly sunny, -5° to 10°. Visited at store. Worked on stool in wood ship. Rudbeck borrowed some 1" plastic line. Tom Huddleston and family and his sister Kate here for supper.

Sunday, March 17, 1991—sunny, -5° to 25°. Re-squared the table saw cut off box. Worked on the stool then went to Dimmick's and looking for caribou. Visited there. Then stopped at Little Nelchina and checked on wood pile there. Then home and cut fuel wood for wood shop. Tom Smayda got a boo today. Worked a little more on the stool.

Monday, March 18, 1991—mostly sunny, 5° to 24°. Visited T. Huddleston and sister Kate and brother in law, Ron. Fixed trim on pickup. Went east hunting boo (caribou). No luck. Worked some more on the spruce stool.

Tuesday, March 19, 1991—mostly sunny, 10 to 32°. Glued stool together. Bob R. came over later Karn then I went boo hunting. Saw two or three running. Didn't shoot. Saw a couple mink track, marten track and fox of course. I bought 3 Manning traps from Dave DeJung. He wants to go to Colorado, splitting the blanket with Wilma.

Wednesday, March 20, 1991—sunny, 5° to 24°. Went caribou hunting to East, down the drainage to bigger lake and then north to seismic. Saw a boo watching me from behind a spruce. An unknown number ran off. Watched a crossing for quite a while. No luck. Walked back to snowgo and proceeded east. Saw more boo had a clear chance and missed five times. Must sight this rifle in. Checked Toms kill, only the hide left. When I got home I started building some duck nesting boxes. Elaine brought over a couple pieces of cake.

Thursday, March 21, 1991—it was -10° to 22°. Finished three duck boxes. Put them up on the Long Lake a couple miles east. Went looking for boo (caribou). Had a glimpse of one in thick black spruce. No shot. Saw a thick big bodied moose. Came home, finished three duck boxes and one brown thrasher box.

Friday, March 22, 1991—sunny, -10° to 24°. Tom Smayda came over, Lue is here and had boo down near where Tom got one. I went down and got a cow drug home. Hung the four quarters in the garage. Sylvia cut up all the rest of the boo (caribou). I too the head hide feet bones back down for the animals to eat. Put up three more duck boxes. Steve and Ian Mailly were here for a couple of hours. Lue visited a little while. Allen Farmer family and Mae were here for chili supper and movie. They brought apple pies. Rudbecks came over also.

Saturday, March 23, 1991—sunny, cloudy, 0° to 24°. Went to KROA in afternoon to watch ski touring races and kids ski race. Matt borrowed the water tank.

Sunday, March 24, 1991—sunny, cloudy, 10° to 30°. Started getting lumber ready to make some stools. Told Matt and Bart about the caribou. Bart went and shot one. Matt, Anna Marie and Kimberly brought the water tank home.

Monday, March 25, 1991—partly cloudy, sunny, 20° to 40°. Worked on stool legs and planed. Glue up lumber for seats. Allen Baker and Carl ? came from Valdez to hunt a boo for Carl. Lots of good visiting also. Stayed for supper. Snow slid off garage roof, buried his pickup tires—I pulled him out of it. Built flicker box and gave it to Allen.

Tuesday, March 26, 1991—sunny, cloudy, snow in evening, 30° to 36°. The wood for the stools is splitting and cupping as it dries, discouraging. Changed oil and filter on truck, loaded barrels to get gasoline in town. Cleaned up garage. A squirrel chewed up some trap gloves.

Wednesday, March 27, 1991—cloudy, fog, sunny, 20° to 40°. Didn't go to Anchorage. Lisa S. and girls visited. Built a jig to sharpen planer blades, it took all day. Allen stopped in, in evening to borrow a movie.

Thursday, March 28, 1991—cloudy, 10° to 30°. Left early for Palmer, Wasilla, Anchorage. We got all the craft supplies we went to get. Plus 200 gallons of gasoline and a few groceries. Unloaded gas drums.

Friday, March 29, 1991—mostly sunny, 15° to 30°. Built a jig to assist in re-sawing on band saw. Mounted holder on band saw for jig and mitre gauge then removed band saw table and glued wood filler strips to fill out the voids on the table underside and facilitate clamping things to the table. Stacked and striped the 2" x 12" x 8" bought yesterday.

Saturday, March 30, 1991—3" snow, mostly sunny, 18° to 34°. Sharpened three Skill saw blades. Turned a 2" x 14" dowel from a piece of stove wood for Bob R. Helped Allen F make some parts for a simple electric motor for David F. science class. "Carl" Taylor of Valdez and friend Marty shot a caribou east of the gravel pit. Asked me to pull it out to the road for them. Saw Tom S. skiing while on the way to the bull, boo. Snowgo pulled it easy. Put the table back on band saw. Visited Rudbeck a little while.

Sunday, March 31, 1991—sunny, 3° to 30°. We went to Steve and Karen Mailly for Easter dinner. I gave their two small boys a couple of steel tape measures. The sun sets in the west. The low light rays cast pink shadows of yellow gold color to the snow on the mountains to the south. Subtle changes continuous as the sun sets. A very beautiful moon rise later in the evening. The moon stayed yellow a long time and colored the snow and the night. There are quite a few small birds now. Red poll, cross bill, grosbeaks, juncos.

Monday, April 1, 1991—sunny, beaut of a day, -1° to 30°. Lisa S. visited an hour or so. Sharpening three more saw blades. Started repairing Jessica Beaudoin's Dinosaur bank. Visited at store and at Smayda's and filled out dividend applications.

Tuesday, April 2, 1991—sunny, nice, 6° to 30°. Made some trap lure. Repaired Jessica's bank. Went to Little Nelchina construction site for wood. But it is all gone. Turned a few 2" wood balls on the lathe. Visited Sam Weaver, he loaned me a book to read.

Wednesday, April 3, 1991—sunny, cloudy, evening. 7° to 31°. Worked on a toy for kids. Hauled a load of water from Smayda's.

Thursday, April 4, 1991—sunny, worked on Plexiglas side plates for banks. Visited with Mannings.

Friday, April 5, 1991—sunny, 7° to 40°. Went to Art Wikles. He gave us a pot burner oil stove. Then home and onto Palmer. The lumber deal turned out to be a poor deal. So it was a trip for mostly nothing. Saw a couple eagles on Matanuska Drainage side of the pass.

Saturday, April 6, 1991—sunny, beaut day, 10° to 42°. Sanded on 15 rock and roll toys. Cut out 12 penguin and turtle banks. Shoveled some snow. Cleaned and repaired carburetor on the oil heater. Lots red polls, snowbirds, grosbeaks.

Sunday, April 7, 1991—sunny with a few clouds, 10° to 35°. Did a little wood shop. Shoveled a little snow. Lauren and Emily here for supper. Went to Smayda's for ice cream.

Monday, April 8, 1991—cloudy, 8° to 32°. Cut out some wood "deer." Worked on bases for banks. Started "sealer" and stain test pieces.

Tuesday, April 9, 1991—sunny, 10° to 36°. Art and Bonnie Wikle stopped to visit early. Cut out 8 sets of "deer." Put acid in ATV battery, started it and inflated the tires. Put stains on test woods and methods. Allen borrowed some pipe fittings.

Wednesday, April 10, 1991—cloudy, sunny, 16° to 34°. Cut out a wood whale, sanded some banks, did more stain testing. Allen came over to borrow a pipe fitting and I didn't have the right one. Went over to store for coffee and roll. Took the deer models back to Lisa S. this evening.

Thursday, April 11, 1991—cloudy, 8° to 34°. Started for Anchorage, got to Eureka and came back and Ed Farmer listen to truck. He says its fine. Must be my imagination. Gas up, go get lumber, saw blade, etc. Saw one moose on way home.

Friday, April 12, 1991—cloudy, part cloudy evening, 22° to 34°. Stripped and stacked the cedar lumber. Lisa S. visited. Worked in woodshop. Borrowed Allen's meat grinder. Am trying to sharpen the cutter in the grinder.

Saturday, April 13, 1991—cloudy, sunny, cloudy, 22° to 40°. Sanded two sets "deer" or "boo" Put 15 rock roll toys together. Offered Ed Farmer some washer parts. Pat Landers brought a gun stock and sanded the recoil pad down.

Sunday, April 14, 1991—cloudy, sunny, quite windy, 20° to 40°. Went to Dan and Patti's at Point of View Lodge on Lake Louise for a brunch. AK airmen were to meet. Bad weather in Chickaloon Pass kept them away. Only four planes showed up.

Monday, April 15, 1991—cloudy, sunny afternoon, windy evening, 24° to 40°. Ed F. came over to look at pump for washer. Wrong model here. Worked sanding wood all day. Sylvia went to Glennallen.

Tuesday, April 16, 1991—sunny, snow over on Heavenly Ridge, 20° to 42°. Worked in wood shop. Plowed sun softened hard pack snow off to the side. Problems with the palm sander. Returned Allen's meat grinder.

Wednesday, April 17, 1991—cloudy, light snow, more melting, 24° to 38°. Shoveled snow from near a lean to. Sanded dinosaur bank toy.

Thursday, April 18, 1991—cloudy, sunny evening, more melting, 27° to 40°. Finished sanding on dinosaur banks and did "deer" "boo" Also hauled a load of water from Smayda's. Heard swans flying west in evening.

Friday, April 19, 1991—sunny, cloudy, 24° to 40°. Built a jig to hold lake trout plug bodies to rout a dish in front end. Turned two bodies on lathe. Visited Ed and Allen. Sylvia went with Bonnie to Wasilla.

Saturday, April 20, 1991—sunny, 27° to 42°. Went to Glennallen to the health fair. Stopped at Darrel's with some meat and wood shavings. Also at Chuck Zimbicki's. Cut out three quilt racks and turned five fishing lure bodies on the lathe. Allen F. borrowed a paint roller. Rudbecks are back from Anchorage and visited this evening. Man, what a beaut of a view of the mountains.

Sunday, April 21, 1991—sunny, 27° to 40°. Dan Billman called and invited us to their lodge for a couple of days. Lloyd and Faye will be there. We loaded our gear and snowmobiles and sled and went to Point of View on Lake Louise. Nice visit all afternoon and evening.

Monday, April 22, 1991—mostly sunny, 20° to 40°. Dan and I left early in the morning for my trap cabin. Picked up seven traps. Saw two moose and six swans, a couple marsh hawks. Snowgo ½ handlebar broke on my machine when Dan drove it a little ways. He drove a piece of conduit in for a repair. That worked well. Went on to cabin. Stove is rusted out. Threw it outside. Need a roof jack. Covered the hole and closed the cabin again and had a good trip back to lodge. Visited with Dan, Patti and Lloyd and Faye.

Tuesday, April 23, 1991—beaut of a sunrise. Cloudy all morning and hot sunny afternoon. Sun dogs in evening, 20° to 40°. Up early again. Dan and I loaded up some gas, propane and chainsaw on his sled and headed for Crosswind Lakes. Stopped near the lake and cut some firewood. Crossed the lake and unloaded everything at his cabin, then started back. The snow was getting softer by the min. He got stuck bad once and had a hard time staying on the soft trail. The snowgo being large and heavy, we got back to lodge awhile. Ate supper and came on home. Unloaded gear. Allen F. and May J. came over to borrow a Coleman cooler.

Wednesday, April 24, 1991—sunny, 30° to 48°. Welded handle bars on snowgo, adjusted skis. Called our daughter, Nadia in Minnesota.

Thursday, April 25, 1991—cloudy, sunny, 23° to 42°. Tried to get the carburetor on greenhouse oil stove to work—no luck. Worked on quilt racks. Repaired truck taillight. Washed truck and snowgo. Corky Dimmick visited and I took him home. Went to Allen and Roxanne's for a good taco supper and watched a good "Eastman's" hunting movie about North Canol Road and NW Territories and hunting there 1960s era. Saw two moose across lake. Hundreds of small birds. One owl.

Friday, April 26, 1991—sunny, cloudy evening, 30° to 45°. Worked on quilt racks. Kim H. ordered two planter boxes, Sylvia painted dinosaur banks. Put ashes on garden. Two Canada geese flew by lake.

Saturday, April 27, 1991—sunny, cloudy, windy afternoon, 30° to 40°. Worked at lathe on Lake Trout lures. Six swans resting on ice of lake. Two eagles chased a goose west. I asked Mat to come look at oil heater carburetor. Between the two of us, its working!! Went to a picnic at Farmer's Gen Store.

Sunday, April 28, 1991—sunny, some breeze, 20° to 45°. Worked on piggy banks, put ten together. Sam Weaver and friend Roger stopped by. I bought some boards from Roger. Manning here for coffee. Smayda family had us over for turkey supper and homemade ice cream.

Monday, April 29, 1991—cloudy, 25° to 42°. Built 8, two-foot cedar planter boxes. Shot two rabbits and two squirrels. Mae and Karn gave Sylvia birthday gifts.

Tuesday, April 20, 1991—partly cloudy, 20° to 46°. Built more cedar planter boxes. Put up another flicker house and cleaned a squirrel nest out of one of last year's flicker houses. Heard a flicker calling nearby this afternoon. Went over to Tom S. and filled out a forestry paper.

Wednesday, May 1, 1991—sunny, 20° to 46°. Helped Allen work on his store. Tom H. is back from North Slope.

Thursday, May 2, 1991—sunny here, cloudy and windy in Palmer and Wasilla, 30° to 48°. We delivered some cedar planters. Shopped for some craft supplies, groceries and milk for Allen's store. Pretty good trip.

Friday, May 3, 1991—sunny and windy, 33° to 46°. Sylvia went to Glennallen on senior van. I worked on Cedar boxes. Put ¾" clamps together. Started assembly of quilt racks. Visited store. Doug Johnson and wife and another couple visited. Jim Manning came over to get 1" pipe threaded. Rudbecks came over to watch "Dallas" finale.

Saturday, May 4, 1991—sunny and very windy. Lake ice is deteriorating, 34° to 50°. Put snowgo under shed roof. Tried out router bit on fishing plugs. Cut and trimmed a trail to garden and garden road. Cleaned up in wood shop. Re-hung wolf traps. Caribou are coming back. Ordered a hand held marine radio. Put away sleds for winter. Allen F plans to sell his van. Tom H. borrowed brake fluid. Tom and Lisa S. and daughters here for supper and we made ice cream.

Sunday, May 5, 1991—sunny and windy, 36° to 56°. We put eight 2' cedar boxes together. Routed noses on lake trout lures with drill press. We put three double quilt racks together. Improved lure jig. Flickers are active. Shot a squirrel. Mae was here for supper.

Monday, May 6, 1991—cloudy, rained for three to four hors, 35° to 50°. Tom H. visited. Sylvia went to Glennallen. Took pix of bald eagle sitting on tree top 100 feet from house. Worked on lures. Put sides and bases on four banks. Tom H. brought a puzzle order.

Tuesday, May 7, 1991—cloudy, sunny, 34° to 48°. Straightened 4" x 10' piece of steel. Tom H. helped visited store. Testing how to glue hold hooks in lures. Brushed out more of ATV trail to garden. Sylvia transplanted tomatoes etc to greenhouse. My brother Jerry called.

Wednesday, May 8, 1991—sunny, 28° . Five swans and two Canadian geese on lake. Lots of ducks on water around edge of ice. Heat was off last night in greenhouse. No frost in there though. Ordered more supplies. Started putting in clothes dryer. Cut down one set of panty shelves. Bottom part I made into craft table for Sylvia. She transplanted more in greenhouse. Went to see Sam. He wasn't home. Our health fair results came. Asked Jim M. to pick me up some copper line for gas dryer when he goes to Glennallen tomorrow.

Thursday, May 9, 1991—partly cloudy, very windy, 28° to 43°. Hooked pickup by chain to thirteen trees and pulled them over. Got all wood and debris almost cleaned up. Tom H. wife and little Charlie visited. Lisa S. identified the kestrel, (a bird of the falcon family) as the one visiting the nesting box just south of the house. One fourth of ice went out of lake today. River is running strong. Jim M. brought copper tubing etc from town. Allen F. went to doctor today. Sylvia transplanted more plants in greenhouse. Fred Rungee visited.

Friday, May 10, 1991—mostly sunny, very windy, 33° to 41°. Finished cleaning up after trees and cut and stacked the wood. Hooked up the propane dryer. Visited at store and KROA. Took Sylvia out to Tolsona Lake for anniversary dinner.

Saturday, May 11, 1991—mostly sunny, windy, 26° to 40°. Worked on lures. Went to Chamberlains yard sale. Supper at Huddleston's. Called Nadia.

Sunday, May 12, 1991—sunny, 26° to 49°. Worked on lures. Tom S. borrowed metal detector. Family were here for homemade ice cream in evening. Theresa and family phoned. Three boo and one moose on lake shore. Gulls harass an eagle. Ducks and swans feeding together. Tried out L.T. lure and determined where to attach front screw eye.

Monday, May 13, 1991—sunny, windy evening, 30° to 47°. Cut down some small aspen between house and the lake. Switched tires front to rear on pickup. Took the snow plow hitch and power unit off truck and put bumper back on. Shoveled a little dirt. Raked some spruce cones. Six boo bulls (new 16" horns) swam our lake north to south. Other boo went west on our side. Many large scoter ducks here today. A hawk was easting something on lake shore. The wind is breaking up and melting the ice fast. Ice gone at midnight.

Tuesday, May 14, 1991—sunny, windy in evening, 26° to 46°. We took pickup down on Lower Road and cut up one third cord. Down trees and put wood in basement. More caribou going west around lake. Many ducks, one beaver seen, seven swans, the paired kestrels near nest box. Built a frame work to mount on ATV trailer sides to make tent like cover for it. Cut up a tent for cover. Lisa S. will sew it for me. Cut up a ATV trailer load wood after supper.

Wednesday, May 15, 1991—windy in evening, 34° to 53°. Finished getting down wood today. Some caribou going by. Sparrow hawks still mating. See the beaver's everyday. Many ducks. Methane smell from off the lake today. Evidently snow last winter toppled raven next. Mannings came over in evening.

Thursday, May 16, 1991—cool, windy in afternoon, 36° to 50°. Ron Janson, Eagle River, got some steel. Stayed quite awhile. Picked up the lure order Allen got for me. Hauled a load of water from Smayda's. Returned Sam's book. Pumped gas from barrels to tank. We got tiller out, checked oils and started it.

Friday, May 17, 1991—sunny, 40° to 50°. Built a flicker house for Jack Chamberlain. We took a lot of crafts and some cedar planters to Farmer's Gen Store. Lucky wants a flicker house. I've started three more. Lisa S. finished the tarp cover for ATV Trailer. Sylvia planted raspberries and strawberries.

Saturday, May 18, 1991—windy and sunny, 36° to 50°. Saw more caribou. Sylvia saw cow moose and yearling down by the lake. Took more crafts to Allen's store. Hauled dirt for Allen's planter boxes. Built three flicker boxes. Took one of them to Lucky B. Went to dump corp. meeting at KROA.

Sunday, May 19, 1991—sunny, couple of showers, 30° to 48°. Put up a rack to dry fishing lures. Lisa S. and daughter visited. Kyle and David and Ian came over to get a movie. Lucky B. came over wanting to pay for bird house. Coyote came right up to our living room window.

Monday, May 20, 1991—sunny, cloudy, sprinkles, sunny and windy. Worked on lures and lure jig. Sylvia went to Glennallen. I went to Allen's store. Went to Bartley's and got our Tier 2 hunting permits.

Tuesday, May 21, 1991—sunny, beaut of a day, 40° to 54°. Worked on lures. Lots painting problems. Hauled the tiller down to the garden. Checked the culvert, will have to cut it off and move it. Hauled ATV trailer of gravel to pot holes in lane.

Wednesday, May 22, 1991—sunny, really feels hot. Light breeze down on lake, 37° to 57°. Cut 4' diameter culvert off at water level then I built a ramp to roll the 6' long culvert up out of 6' deep hole using a 100' rope doubled and worked good. Sylvia and I then rolled it to new site to try for water. Started getting pump ready to put back in lake. Cut ATV trail to pump site. Sylvia planted potatoes. Went to birthday party for Jack Chamberlain.

Thursday, May 23, 1991—sunny, some breeze, cloudy. Hooked wired pump, put in lake, used water pressure and ½" pipe to locate and thaw a five foot circle thru the frost near the lake. Looks like nice gravel down a ways. Got down about knee deep. Ed and Allen left for the slope to work. Put glow tape on lake trout lures.

Friday, May 24, 1991—mostly sunny, occasional breeze down at the lake, 41° to 62°. Worked all day on getting culvert in. Allen's pump wouldn't work. Got our old pressure pump and are using it. Cow moose and yearling calf feed on lake every day. Saw loons mating. Pair of mallards and other ducks fly by.

Saturday, May 25, 1991—sunny, breezy, 44° to 62°. Worked on getting culvert in and sand and gravel shoveled out of it. Thawed frozen gravel, pumped water out of culvert several times. Lisa S. helped in afternoon. Girls played. Sylvia did laundry also. We are real tired. Put two coats of varithane on seventeen lures.

Sunday, May 26, 1991—mostly sunny, windy and river dust (from dry silt), 41° to 58°. Worked on well and trout lures. Took seven lures to Billmans. Tried radio on way, had contact at 9 Mile. Got to meet Dan's Dad, Vern and Shirley his stepmother. Had supper there and a good visit.

Monday, May 27, 1991—partly cloudy, quite windy, 39° to 51°. Worked on culvert well, cleaned it out, backed filled, put temporary cover and pump in it, changed routing of electric and pipe from garden to lake. Put away most of tools. Tom H. brought his pickup camper over to show us. Sylvia sent some potatoes home with him. Allen F. is back from job on North Slope for a few days. Lisa S. helped again today with well. Ed Farmer saw a cow moose licking her new calf just east of our place.

Tuesday, May 28, 1991—mostly cloudy, some breeze, 41° to 54°. Buried a little water line and filled in some hole in trail. Pulled a few trees over with "come along." Started working them up. Sylvia used the well, pump quite a bit today. Well holds up good. Went to Allen's for supper. Ed Farmer was there also.

Wednesday, May 29, 1991—partly cloudy, windy, 35° to 55°. We went to Anchorage to get materials for well cover, some craft things. Sylvia went to the doctor to have a vein cauterized on her lip. Saw lots of boo, three moose, one yearling on road as we came around a curve. Got stopped in time. Tree blew down on power lines at Don McKee's and started a fire in woods. Lee Dudley on ground and helicopter hauling water in air were working on it. A flicker crashed into house window and died.

Thursday, May 30, 1991—partly cloudy, windy in the afternoon, 37° to 50°. We picked up our mile of road ditch trash. Sam Weaver put his trash in our pickup and after coffee at his cabin we went to the dump. Found a latch and hold open mechanism for rear canopy door. Flattened aluminum cans. Trim limbs off and cut to log length the trees I had down on the hill trail and switch back. Pumped water from well into house. Water looks great. Dan B. phoned. I need to make a change in lake trout lure.

Friday, May 31, 1991—cloudy and rain all day, 37° to 39°. We worked at building the insulated cover for the well at the lake. Got all plywood cut and most put together. Cut the insulation. Fitted some of it. Flickers are nesting in the box directly south of the house.

Saturday, June 1, 1991—rain all night and most of the day, some wind, 34° to 45°. Snow going fast on Ol' Baldy and Heavenly Ridge. Insulated the box and cover for well. Smayda family visited, Tom's birthday. Sylvia gave us strawberry shortcake. Karn came over for a sweat shirt and two kid toys. Painted the well box. Lots of junco's and those beaut finches. Cleaned up construction mess.

Sunday, June 2, 1991—mostly cloudy and lots of rain, a little sun, 40° to 50°. Put lime and fertilizer on grass. Sylvia transplanted broccoli and cauliflower to garden. Visited Smaydas, Tom gone to work. Put second coat of paint on lid of well. Drilled pipe and elect wire holes in insulation box for well. Harold and Rachel Dimick here for lunch.

Monday, June 3, 1991—mostly sunny, 38° to 52°. Sylvia went to Glennallen. Put hinges on well cover. Built a cardboard tray for lures. We loaded well cover on ATV trailer and hauled it down and put it over well. Rerouted water pipe and electric wire. Replaced the tundra around the well. Smoothed and seeded grass there also. Went to Farmers for Lucky and David's birthday party.

Tuesday, June 4, 1991—cloudy, sunny, windy, 38° to 51°. Made 2, six foot, 3 five foot, and 3, three foot cedar planters. Started digging and leveling the ATV trail and switch back up our hill. Cut and sharpened stakes.

Wednesday, June 5, 1991—cloudy, sunny, cloudy, 38° to 52°. Built more cedar planters and boxes. Finished Anna Marie's order. Karn got Sylvia some material in Wasilla. Smayda girls painted two pix and brought them over to us and stayed to watch cartoons. Cow moose and baby walked thru yard and later mid day they swam across the lake. Calf kept up with mother. After supper I worked on the switch back on our hill.

Thursday, June 6, 1991—cloudy, rain, sunny, cloudy, 42° to 54°. We took the planters to Anna Marie at Snow Shoe Lake. Sylvia gave Mary B. a perm. Smayda family asked us to go to Valdez and take a trip to Shoup Glacier with them tomorrow. We gathered up the gear we will need this evening.

Friday, June 7, 1991—cloudy, sunny, partly cloudy, 40° to 56°. Smayda's picked us up at 8:00 AM and we all went to Valdez. Put Zodiac in water at small boat harbor. Went out Valdez arm. Saw sea otters then a whale feeding turned up Shoup Bay, River. Saw many, many sea otter. One with a pup on its chest. Up river the short distance to Gull Island. Many thousands of gulls nesting. Crows rob the nests. Two to four eggs, quite large olive green and brown spots. Only one four egg nest. Gull sometimes try to shit on you. The ladies beach-combed at a place we stopped on way back to Valdez harbor. Tom and I fished for halibut, no luck. Back at harbor, loaded Zodiac, came home. Fine day was had.

Saturday, June 8, 1991–cloudy, rain in afternoon and evening, 38° to 44° Got four pieces and painted them for a drip overhang for the well cover. Went over to Smayda's and helped load a few things for them. Tom gave me a 12V Datsun blower motor. I've started mounting it on ATV to help keep the motor cooler on warm days when ATV is working hard. Called son Paul in evening. 4:40 AM The coyote is back checking out things around the buildings.

Sunday, June 9, 1991–rain, cloudy, 36° to 44°. Finished putting the blower on the ATV.

Monday, June 10, 1991–sunny, cloudy, 33° to 54°. Did odd chores around the place. Sylvia went to Glennallen. Put the drip rim on well lid. Finished the switch back on hill trail for this year.

Tuesday, June 11, 1991–partly cloudy, showers, 36° to 60°. Put grommets in tarp cover for ATV trailer. Refastened trim for truck floor mat. Worked on lake trout lures. Didn't feel well all day. Rudbeck moved Manning cache.

Wednesday, June 12, 1991–partly cloudy, rain, hail, 40° to 54°. Worked on lures. Hooked up propane stove and move p. tank for Mae. Her son Rob is here from North Carolina and helped cut up some wood. Cut roots off the stumps we pulled out so I can haul them away to be burned at 9:00 PM. I saw cow moose across the lake take her calf out into the lake in an effort to defend it from a silvery grizzly. There was another dark bear I didn't get a good look at. I fired 20 rounds or so to scare grizzly away. They left but who knows for how long. Exciting for a while though.

Thursday, June 13, 1991–partly cloudy, rain on each side of us, 42° to 56°. We got 9 lures ready and sent them with Rob to Point of View Lodge. Sylvia worked on sweat shirts today. I raked some yard. Cut up, hauled and stacked some wood. Cleaned and oiled distributor and adjusted drag link on truck. Put two wheel trailer in garage. Flipped the axel over, lowering the bed of trailer 6". Reattached the fenders.

Friday, June 14, 1991–partly cloudy, cloudy and showers, 44° to 64°. Chad, son Frank, and Corky visited. Gave Chad a lure. We went fishing at Mirror Lake and Mendeltna Creek. No luck. Had supper and boys fished in our lake. Chad and I visited. Went to Bartley's and got some copies made. Chad and the boys left. I made plans and looked iron pile over to make ramp for trailer.

Saturday, June 15, 1991–partly cloudy, very light showers, 48° to 64°. Cut and weld up a driving cap so Bart can drive grader blades to anchor his dock at Snowshoe Lake. Cut and shaped two pieces shaker screen 12" x 36" for loading

71

ramps to drive ATV onto two wheel trailer. Put hooks on nine more lures. Checked well while Sylvia was pumping. It seems maintain about 28" of water when pumping it hard.

Sunday, June 16, 1991–sunny, cloudy, 38° to 56°. We walked down to garden. Found a tree swallow egg on ground on way back. Went to chapel picnic at Lake Louise Campground. Then visited Billmans at Point of View. Dan and I went out and dragged lures for awhile till it got windy. The varithane came off the lure so it's back to drawing board again. Theresa phoned Fathers Day wishes.

Monday, June 17, 1991–sunny, cloudy, 42° to 54°. Sylvia went to Glennallen. Worked on truck. Cleaned and painted the lure that shed the varithane. Covered two wheel trailer. Experimented with glues for canopy door. Took down the three small trees at sharp switch back. Nadia called. Great to talk.

Tuesday, June 18, 1991–cloudy, windy, partly cloudy, 40° to 54°. Tried to re-glue plywood end gate where plies had separated. Started building a portable shooters bench. It's all cut out and assembly started. Darrel G. back home, collapsed vein. Sylvia saw another moose swim our lake. I took a dresser over to Mae.

Wednesday, June 19, 1991–sunny, 48° to 71°. Finished assembling shooting bench. Painted end gate for two wheel trailer. Dan B. stopped by. Worked on canopy door. Sylvia baked bread, pies etc.

Thursday, June 20, 1991–sunny, 51° to 80°. Went to Anchorage. Got everything I went for, and got Allen's toilet stool.

Friday, June 21, 1991–sunny, hot, 56° to 82°. Went to senior citizen tour of Pump Station 12. Had nice tour and good meal. Met "goat man" and "Bee." Mae R. rode to Glennallen with us. Went to fuel company for fuel tank charts. Visited Darrel Gerry. So very hot. Jack Chamberlin gave me some Formica. Washed bug guts off front of truck. Some rain, thunder in evening.

Saturday, June 22, 1991–hot, partly cloudy, then cooler. Low 60s to 70s. Built a 4' cedar planter. Build a new rear door for pickup canopy installed nice window in it, latch etc. Nearly finished it.

Sunday, June 23, 1991–hot, breezy, wind switching both from east and west., 44° to 74°. Forest fire on west side Tazlina Lake. Smoke here sometimes. Put canopy door on. Checked on well. Material list for Roxanne. Swans and ducks swimming a lot today.

Monday, June 24, 1991—partly cloudy, 46° to 70°. Tazlina Lake fire flared up again today. Finished canopy door. Built a switch, control box for well. Put new battery in ATV. Sylvia went to Glennallen.

Tuesday, June 25, 1991—mostly sunny, lots of smoke from Tazlina fire. 50° to 74°. Breeze switching east to west and west to east. Smoke drifting north this evening. Repainted acid damage below battery case on ATV. Cutout two moose clocks and four cat napkin holders Sylvia replanted some of garden and tilled it.

Wednesday, June 26, 1991—partly cloudy, smoky some of the time, 48° to 68°. Helicopter and plane fly the fire quite a bit. Took radiator off the truck and soldered some leaks. Dug and buried fuel line to greenhouse. Lisa Smayda and girls here for supper. Rain tonight.

Thursday, June 27, 1991—partly cloudy, smoky some of the time, 52° to 75°. Lisa and daughters here for breakfast. Put in a toilet for Allen Farmer. Finally got Sylvia to help and got it in. Put fertilizer and lime on lawn. Mowed some lawn, also weeds, willows etc down at boat landing. Baby kestrels are being fed now. More rain in evening.

Friday, June 28, 1991—cloudy, partly cloudy, 54° to 64°. Another good shower in evening. Cut some weeds, brush and chopped a couple stumps. Put more tacks in weather strip on canopy door. Flickers and sparrow hawks flying hard to feed their babies. A strange wolf like dog was hanging around Nelchina this morning. Wind carried smoke from fire away from us today.

Saturday, June 29, 1991—mostly sunny, 55° to 74°. Fire is burning over a wider front—over 3000 acres now. Cut out and sanded five puppy napkin holders. Mosquitoes have been bad for two weeks.

Sunday, June 30, 1991—partly cloudy, fire puts out lots of smoke, 56° to 74°. Luckily it's missing us again today. Cut out blanks for AK clocks. Had to jury rig a bearing on lawn mower.

Monday, July 1, 1991—partly cloudy, smoky to the south of us, 50° to 60°. Cut out four Alaska clocks. Sylvia went to Glennallen. Jim McLellan, son of James McLellan of Maine and Forida visited for a while this afternoon. Kestrel's dive attacked ravens. Flew near their nest. An eagle is hunting on lake this evening.

Tuesday, July 2, 1991—cloudy, partly cloudy, rain during night, 48° to 64°. Finished cutting out Alaska clocks. Shot two squirrels. Put them in tree for the kestrels. Put wood filler in voids in clock plywood.

Wednesday, July 3, 1991—mostly cloudy, lots of rain, 48° to 54°. Put movements and faces on two moose clocks. Rigged box's to put clocks in. Took squirrels out of kestrel tree, they weren't touched. (Maybe they only eat their own kills.) Looked in nest box, four babies. Slept lots today. Washed windows, wood shop.

Thursday, July 4, 1991—cloudy, several good rains, 52° to 58°. Arthritis sure is bad these days. Did a little work on Alaska clocks.

Friday, July 5, 1991—mostly sunny, 48° to 60°. Sanded Alaska clocks then burned them. Put sealer on and it darkened them even more. Sylvia mowed lawn and weeded half garden. Went to dump. Got two tires for trailer. Loaded crafts this eve for craft fair, Glennallen tomorrow. Shot another nuisance squirrel today.

Saturday, July 6, 1991—mostly sunny. Went to craft fair in Glennallen at Ahtna parking lot. Sold some things. Visited at Darrel's, Wikles and Snowshoe Lake on way home.

Sunday, July 7, 1991—mostly sunny in Glennallen, 45° to 72°. Quite hot! A shower at home. We went to craft fair and did a little better today. Left some sweat shirts with Cindy Rhodes (Brown Bear Rhodehouse). Glad to be home this evening. Met a nice guy today. Gave me a copy of one of his poems and recited it. Elwood Purcell.

Monday, July 8, 1991—cloudy, windy, rain in afternoon, 46° to 48°. Worked around wood shop today. Sylvia went to Glennallen. Annette got a dinosaur bank.

Tuesday, July 9, 1991—cloudy, light rain, smoky, 42° to 54°. Smayda family visited. Sylvia baked bread, painted on AK banks. I worked on dry flower plaques. Planed lumber to 1/2" thickness.

Wednesday, July 10, 1991—cloudy, rain, some smoke, 44° to 48°. Finished sanding forty (?) flower panels and dipped them in sealer. Gathered up four steel posts, pipe for a more visible marker at property survey posts.

Thursday, July 11, 1991—mostly cloudy, 40° to 57°. Straightened up reloading bench. Loaded 10/338. Had to study up on powders. Cleaned and oiled the press and oil pad. Built a bracket container to catch used primers.

Friday, July 12, 1991—partly cloudy, 42° to 60°. The kestrels came out of nest box last night. Today they sure are messy and bedraggled looking. They stayed nearby on the ground all day. The parents have a keekeekeekee call when "danger" gets near the fledglings. I took pictures. Made five box joint boxes to mount fishing lures in. Drove a steel post at one of the survey marker near lake. Talked to Allen F. on phone from Prudhoe Bay. 9:00 PM is a good time to see ducks feeding. The ravens have been hanging around and calling a lot lately.

Saturday, July 13, 1991—mostly sunny, 44° to 60°. Raked the yard. Hauled more gravel to level up lane. Put primer on five boxes. Found a survey marker and put a tall post there. Sylvia baked a turkey for a picnic at Farmers store. Made a collet to help pull bullets from .338 cartridges. Dan, Denny, Jason Billman dropped off a new air compressor for me.

Sunday, July 14, 1991—mostly sunny, 46° to 65°. Put finish coats on lure box frames and mounted lures in frame. Put air compressor wheels and hose on. Pumped up truck tires. Pulled bullets from .338 cartridges. Went to Lake Louise. Left sweatshirts at Lake Louise Lodge and Dinty Bush's. Swapped out lures at Point of View and left four lures, frame wall hangers. Visited with Denny B and lots other people.

Monday, July 15, 1991—sunny, cloudy, sunny, 45° to 64°. Tried a new way to prepare moose turds for clocks. It didn't work! Cleaned dust from garage and poured epoxy on nine Alaska clocks. Weeded and hilled potatoes. The last baby flicker left the nest.

Tuesday, July 16, 1991—sunny, partly cloudy, 44° to 63°. Went to Anchorage, steel, materials. Picked up some things at Palmer. Smaydas weren't home.

Wednesday, July 17, 1991—sunny, cloudy, rain in evening, 38° to 53°. Worked on clocks. Put air in old pickup tires. Cleaned up and burned some old trash. Made two large rifle reloading trays, resized and primed more .338 cases. Bev called. Sylvia mowed lawn. Pulled weeds in strawberries.

Thursday, July 18, 1991—mostly sunny, breezy, 40° to 58°. Rewired well pump, 220 switch and ran 110V leg to a light receptacle (mounted on underside of lid for heat in the well this winter). Refilled gravel and fill around well and seeded some grass there. The beaver have raised the lake level 8" this summer. Lucky checked out my wiring for me. Put more insulation around the well. Gave Lucky some .300 Winchester shells (for digger).

Friday, July 19, 1991—partly cloudy, 44° to 56°. Boxed clocks. Put bases on two for Farmer's banks. Bob and Jerry R. were over for rhubarb cake. Lots of ducks on lake now.

Saturday, July 20, 1991—partly cloudy, 46° to 61°. Visited at store. Mounted Weaver scope on mod 70. Went to gravel pit and shot rifles. Got mod 70 sighted in. Sight shot loose on other rifle. Sure enjoyed shooting today.

Sunday, July 21, 1991—mostly sunny, 47° to 64°. Went to gravel pit to shoot target. Came home and reloaded more shells. Patched a tarp. Rudbeck brought 100# propane tank back.

Monday, July 22, 1991—sunny, breezy afternoon, 48° to 60°. Sylvia went to Glennallen. I built a tumbler mechanism. Will polish shells when I get a drum. Planned out a stand for the canopy.

Tuesday, July 23, 1991—mostly cloudy, shower in evening, 48° to 54°. Built the stand for the canopy. Made three 10-gauge shot shell loading blocks. Also three 12-gauge. Put tung oil finish on them and seven other loading blocks. Went out after supper. Put tung oil on a wood stool.

Wednesday, July 24, 1991—mostly sunny, 38° to 62° Water proofed goose decoys and both sets steps for house. Sighted in rifle. Started cutting some picture frames. Sylvia mowed lawn again.

Thursday, July 25, 1991—mostly sunny, 39° to 66°. Made three weathered wood picture frames. Mounted two painting, "loon" and "geese" that Beverly had sent us. Also one of mother Canadian honker and her goslings. Started sorting brass. Jerry and Bob R. came over for silicone and gun. Smayda family is up here at their place overnight and visited this evening.

Friday, July 26, 1991—mostly sunny., 40° to 60s. Repaired cigar boxes for reloading. Bartley from Snowshoe Lake wanted a hitch for his plane (Beaver) to pull it out of the water. We got it built by supper time. Sorted more brass in evening. Sylvia went to Anchorage.

Saturday, July 27, 1991—mostly sunny, one good shower, 48° to 68°. Went to Bartley's. We pulled the "Beaver" out of the lake on the wheels. Jim Sparks did the 100-hour inspection and service. Bart and I helped. Then we put the plane back in the water. Tired and back hurts tonight.

Sunday, July 28, 1991—rain, mostly sunny, 42° to 65°. Sorted out more shells. Built a lid for "Peters" box. Cleaned bullet casting blocks. Sylvia got back early evening. Went to Harold Dimmick's for a birthday supper for him. Good time.

Monday, July 29, 1991—rain, cloudy, 44° to 50°. Aching and feel bad all day. Need proper tap and die for one casting block. Made a rack for gun cleaning rods and screwdriver rack.

Tuesday, July 30, 1991—sunny, windy afternoon, 44° to 60°. Fixed casting block and cleaning rod. Made four horseshoe puzzles. Bart brought his tap die set for me to use. Darrel and Ron stop for few min. Gave Ron quills and lure.

Wednesday, July 31, 1991—cloudy, 42° to 50°. Allen F. is back from North Slope. Cleaned gun cleaning brushes. Extended rear seat in canoe 20" forward, hopefully will help when paddling alone.

Thursday, August 1, 1991—sunny, windy in the afternoon, 40° to 55°. Moved a storage (little ex-rabbit food) shed down to dock, wired it to tree to store paddles and gear in. Leveled an area with the shovel. Put small load of gravel on trailer and hauled and put on the lane. Started cutting out a bed frame.

Friday, August 2, 1991—sunny, windy all night, 34° to 54°. Worked on bed frame all day. Did pretty good.

Saturday, August 3, 1991—rain all day, 38° to 40°. Put headboard together for bed we are building. Snow on mountain to the south.

Sunday, August 4, 1991—some rain, some sunny, 42° to 48°. Worked a little on the bed frame. Went to Allen F. with a turkey for a pot luck supper.

Monday, August 5, 1991—some rain, cloudy, and sunny. Mixed some primer and put it on bed frame and some small jobs.

Tuesday, August 6, 1991—partly cloudy, showers, 42° to 54°. Went to Anchorage. Saw young coyote a mile this side of Nelchina. Got most everything we needed from town. Cow moose and calf crossed road mile 14. Unloaded and stacked lumber.

Wednesday, August 7, 1991—partly cloudy, 44° to 62°. Worked all day putting new water line in. Need two fittings and bury the line where it crosses the lower road.

Thursday, August 8, 1991—mostly sunny, 47° to 67°. Re-hooked old water line to well. Buried new water line where it crosses lower road. Put frame of bed together. Had to make some more pieces to shim out for drawer slides. Installed slides on frame. Put one coat varithane on bed.

Friday, August 9, 1991—44° to 60s. Got sheep hunting gear ready. Allen came over for some shim stock for a rifle sight. Went to Allen's. He was sighting a rifle. Then back home for an axe, can opener and jug of water. Ate at Eureka, then on to Old Rd. house area near Gunsight Mountain to unload ATV. Jump started Allen's Ranger. Saw a moose cow on way to camp area. Lots of hunters.

Saw Lucky and Digger in their camp on Squaw Creek 3 mile. We set up our camp at about 8 mile and slept good.

Saturday, August 10, 1991—warm all day, some breeze in afternoon. Up early, ate a little and started up the creek drainage to base of mountain. Saw many moose cows and bulls. Ate a lunch and split up. I went east and up the mountain. Allen and David went south and up the mountain. He saw one full curl ram, tried to get 50' closer and it ran off. He found a dead ewe and got the horns. I saw nine ewes and lambs, five winter kills, two ¾ curl and one ½ curl rams. I had to climb up a Talus Slope to get into position to see the horns on the one ram. My legs did real well. Three caribou bulls were running back and forth trying to get away from flies. One ran by me three times. Once at 15', shook his head and grunted and he went by. Then back to camp by way of creek. Ate supper and Allen and David went exploring on a creek to the west. Sat around camp fire just before bed.

Sunday, August 11, 1991—nice day, some breeze, windy at home. Up late. 8:00 AM Talked Allen into going on down Squaw Creek to Caribou Creek. Glassed rams from camp and again partway and at Caribou Creek. Finally determined the best ram was still not legal. Scouted out best way to get across river and to ridge that looks the best to follow to Fortress Ridge Mountain (for later hunt). Back to camp. Dismantle it, load up and head out. Saw one boo in far distance. Digger got a boo. Allen's Ranger is a slow way to travel, but can haul a moose. Helped a guy load a broken down ATV. Then on home and unload gear. Tom S. phoned. They rented their house out.

Monday, August 12, 1991—mostly sunny, 44° to 60°. Rigged blocks for hauling ATV. Unloaded it. Made clamp brackets to fasten gun case to ATV. Cut plywood sheets for bed frame. Sylvia went to Glennallen.

Tuesday, August 13, 1991—cloudy, partly cloudy, windy, 44° to 64°. Took bed apart. Brought it in and put it back together in the bedroom. Looks good. Ron and Elli Sopko, his and her kids and his folks stopped in for awhile. Welded up two horseshoe puzzles.

Wednesday, August 14, 1991—partly cloudy, 45° to 60°. Went to Wasilla, Palmer for med and truck repairs. Feel sick this evening. Put different temperature gauge on truck.

Thursday, August 15, 1991—light rain, partly cloudy, some breeze, 46° to 66°. Tazlina fire is starting up again. Started on drawers for bed. Finished hooking up one inch water line at well. Rolled up the ¾ inch line. Lucky, Allen and I went fishing in evening.

Friday, August 16, 1991—partly cloudy, smoke to the south. Worked on drawer for bed. Cleaned up garage.

Saturday, August 17, 1991—light rain in the morning, partly cloudy, sunny, windy. Visited store, Allen and Tom. Figured out the dovetail jig. Cleaned wood shop. Chopped roots all around the big birch stump and pulled it out and cleaned dirt off it. Mary and Kari Odden were here for supper.

Sunday, August 18, 1991—partly cloudy, 31° to 54°. Pulled over and cut up three trees near buildings. Trimmed some near green house. Went to Lake Louise. Visited Leona at D.B. and Billmans at Point of View. Met Tom, owner of PA 12 on floats.

Monday, August 19, 1991—28° to 50°. Tom Huddleston, Allen and I went to Copper Center. Tom got salmon from his grandma's and dad's fish wheels. I hauled three small loads of gravel from over lower road and filled a low place out near camper parking place. Went to Mirror Lake after supper and caught a 12" and 16" rainbows. Enough for breakfast and quit and came home. Allen and kids came over with ice cream in evening.

Tuesday, August 20, 1991—partly cloud, light shower in evening, 30° to 62°. Did a few small jobs. Went to Copper Center and got five red salmon from a fish wheel. Mary O. came in evening to use phone.

Wednesday, August 21, 1991—partly cloudy, hard rain with hail in afternoon. Hauled a load of fill for low place near wood shop. Wired a light into each closet upstairs. Rudbecks are back, came over for mail. Lots of ducks on lake, three swans also.

Thursday, August 22, 1991—partly cloudy, 42° to 56°. Worked on bed drawers. Also extended hitch for camper pickup, ATV trailer. Supper at Rudbeck's and worked on floats on Beaver at Bartley's.

Friday, August 23, 1991—cloudy, partly cloudy, 44° to 54°. Finished the extended hitch for use with the camper. Built some parts for the Beaver dolly hitch. Darrel G. here for supper. Jerry and Betty Rudbeck visited. Allen F. over to borrow salt and canning lids.

Saturday, August 24, 1991—Cloudy, some breeze, 44° to 52°. Put truck in garage. Darrel and I worked on front universals. Allen borrowed water tank and trailer. Helped him install new battery on his Ranger. Brought over smoked salmon.

Sunday, August 25, 1991—cloudy, rain most of the day, 38° to 50°. Finished up the front universal joints on the truck. Gave Darrel shavings. Canned meat. Took him home after supper.

Monday, August 26, 1991—rain and wet snow most of day, stopped in evening, 36° to 37°. Lots of duck activity. Loafed at store in the morning. Built loading dock for pickup using old grader blades. Hauled a jag of gravel. Bring dock to level.

Tuesday, August 27, 1991—snow melted up to 4500 ft elevation, 30° to 39°. Did lots small jobs.

Wednesday, August 28, 1991—froze crust on ground, thawed a lot of snow off the mountains. Loaded ATV and went hunting along Squaw Creek. Saw tracks of three moose, four boo, pack wolves and four bears. Saw nine sheep on Sheep Mountain and sheep on Fortress Mountain. Quite muddy. Washed ATV when I got home. Allen gave me three tires.

Thursday, August 29, 1991—froze, then up to 50°. Started old truck and switched the camper over on GMC. Worked all day on it. Went fishing in eve and forgot the worms.

Friday, August 30, 1991—mostly sunny and 38°. Got gear and grub in camper, loaded Suzuki. Allen Farmer and I picked Darrel up to go boo hunting Hogan's Hill area on Richardson Highway. Darrel has five dogs full of porcupine quills. We got to hunt area. Rudbeck's here. Didn't see any boo. Cleaned Darrel's rifle. Camped overnight.

Saturday, August 31, 1991—sunny and 38°. I missed a shot at a boo. Went south to mile 153? Allen saw boo off in trees. Stopped and we shot three boo. Butchered them and packed with ARV to truck. Stopped in Glennallen for ice cream cones on home. Unload and hang meat and load gear for goose hunting. Shower and eat supper.

Sunday, September 1, 1991—froze, some ice, 20s. Finished loading grub and gear, picked up Darrel and drove to Delta. Bought some groceries. Went out to Roy Beaver farm, it's leased out for hunting $45.00 per day per man. John Thuringer gave us permission after giving the buffalo hell. Talked to Ruby Hollenbeck gave her a gift. Scott let us hunt back side their farm. Lots of hunters everywhere. I shot two crane. Marked each one well and found one and where other one landed in 60" oats. It was wounded. Another hunter offered his dog to run the crane down. Dog did fine job. I gave crane to dog owner. Beautiful sunset. Sure like the way this Browning Bps 10-gauge shoots. With the magnaporting, less muzzle jump and no felt recoil. We are shooting steel shot this year.

Monday, September 2, 1991—sunny, nice day, around 40°. Cranes flew well till noon. I missed some easy shots. Did get one crane. Went to Scott's buildings and got our crane decoys. Ground is dry and hard, lots of pounding to get stakes in. Very few crane flew in afternoon. Very few speckle belly geese since the shooting started. Took pix of decoys. Hurt the sides of trailer yesterday. Cleaned the screws etc from them this afternoon.

Tuesday, September 3, 1991—frost, nice day, up at 5:20 AM. Quite a few geese (speckled bellies) and crane flying till 2:00 PM. I got two more crane, one very large one. Did lots of missing recoil of 10-gauge is mild. Decided about 7:00 PM to head for home. Darrel pulled and packed decoys. I jury rigged fastening the ATV down on trailer bed. We ate then loaded trailer sides in camper. Left decoys at Scotts. Went to Delta, gassed up and got home before 4:00 AM.

Wednesday, September 4, 1991—light rain, 40°. Cleaned out camper. Rigged a better way to fasten ATV Down. Gave some plain wood blocks to Dee Dee Johanson for her baby. Worked hard at getting gear ready to go moose hunting tomorrow. Tired tonight.

Thursday, September 5, 1991—44°, finished getting gear ready to go hunting. Lucky is going also. Put handle in Hudson Bay axe. We took three outfits to the trailhead near Trapper Den Lake. Had a fairly uneventful trip in to camp site near 7 mile Seismic Trail. Set up camp and hunted in evening. Started raining in night.

Friday, September 6, 1991—seems warm. Quite a lot of rain. Allen saw and heard some bulls south and east of camp. I walked and drove the trails with no luck. Lots of rain in night.

Saturday, September 7, 1991—rain in the morning. Quit around 10:00 AM. Lucky is wet and went home. Allen can hear bulls in SE. We try to hunt them. In afternoon we go east into swamp area and a bull gets up in front of Allen and he hit once and missed three times. Later he is standing on a knob and shot a 48" bull. We walk out to trail, ride ATV back to camp. Break camp and take Ranger and ATV back to near swamp. Take Ranger to kill sight and butcher, put meat sacks on and load on Ranger. Get back to trail just at dark. Drove out to trailhead in dark, loaded up and came home. Sylvia gave us a bowl of bean soup at 1:00 AM.

Sunday, September 8, 1991—windy afternoon, 47°. Allen came over and we cut back strap, tenderloin, heart, liver and ground neck meat and trim into hamburger. Lots of work and we sure are tired tonight.

Monday, September 9, 1991—light frost, partly sunny. Fooled around here till afternoon. Finally got going. Went to Trapper Den Trailhead and went to hunt area. Hunted trail and picked out camp spot. Allen and Roxanne and two boys and Lucky got there about 7:00 PM. Roxanne missed two boo. Put up our tents and went hunting. No luck.

Tuesday, September 10, 1991—hunted hard. Heard moose, didn't see any. Quite a few boo around. Fun to watch their movements and antics. Bear tracks in trail. Allen hunted with his family in afternoon. They found some horns. Lucky and I didn't find any moose. Lucky and I four wheeled loop hunting. Found small set of horns.

Wednesday, September 11, 1991—thin ice, mostly sunny, rainy night. Allen and I hunted the morning. He saw a big bull and some cows. No shots. We broke camp at noon. Allen told me to pick up moose horns, skull he had found. Uneventful trip out. Loaded up and went home, unloaded and put gear away and washed Suzuki. Went road hunting after supper. Saw a cow and calf moose and a border line moose bull. Herb S. and friend were making a try for it, watch them shoot. Then they left the scene.

Thursday, September 12, 1991—frost, rain, partly cloudy. Allen and I went to Mile 133 to see if pig farmer had killed moose. Worked at putting sides back on trailer. John Kunik and three or four guys tried to get CAT started, no luck. Sylvia and I went Caribou Road hunting, no luck.

Friday, September 13, 1991—mostly sunny, breezy evening, around 20°. Drove Lake Louise Road most of day hunting caribou. Saw several killed. People including video tapers crowded in and chased caribou out of range. So I didn't shoot. A couple hunters were polite. Stopped at Billman's for a minute.

Saturday, September 14, 1991— mostly sunny and breezy, 40° to 46°. Up real early to Lake Louise Road at first light. Got a nice meat bull (boo) down in back of Dinty Bush's. Doug and Steve hauled it to their place and we butchered it there and we gave some meat to them. Then home and hung and meat and cleaned and put gear away. Tenderloin for supper.

Sunday, September 15, 1991—mostly sunny, 34° to 53°. Worked on the camper. Sylvia harvested cabbage and started kraut. Allen came to cut meat.

Monday, September 16, 1991—40s to 53°. Went to Palmer, Wasilla. Forgot list, didn't get everything, got most of important things incl. truck parts. No 10-gauge steel "T" shot shells. Allen and Lucky came over in evening and we cut four quarters of moose, wrapped it and ground some. Finished 2:30 AM.

Tuesday, September 17, 1991—sunny, some breeze, 40s to 52°. Put new ball joints on left side of pickup, screw in mirror, bolts in trailer. Sylvia harvested everything in garden except potatoes. Broke a vice—had it for a long time.

Wednesday, September 18, 1991—partly cloudy and 25°. Get gear ready and went to Squaw Creek. Saw some sheep, none legal. Lots of hunters on ATVs. Went back to camper then went up Ballanger Pass and on up mountains. So I could look for sheep in Horn Mts. No luck. Came back home.

Thursday, September 19, 1991—partly cloudy, 34° to 54°. Redid trailer wiring hook up. We dug, washed and put away the potatoes -fourteen 5-gallon buckets from 4 rows. Rudbecks were here for supper. Washed the 4 wheeler and trailer.

Friday, September 20, 1991—partly cloudy, 30s to 50°. Worked on truck lights. Stocked camper for goose hunting. Mike Zuber brought out a light switch and Darrel to pick up moose bones.

Saturday, September 21, 1991—frost in morning, up to 40s. Up early. Matt stopped by and found thermostat stuck on camper furnace. Loaded ATV, went to pickup Darrel. He was across the road visiting. Went on to Glennallen looking for him. Then back out to Huddleston's to get him. Loaded his gear. Got propane and gassed up in Glennallen. Shopped a little in Delta Jct. Got to Hollenbeck's late. Loaded decoys and got them all set out. Met Brian. He is hunting on same field. Fixed supper and to bed.

Sunday, September 22, 1991—sunny to cloudy and very windy. Got a few shots and one crane. Lots of birds. Quite a few came near our decoys but seem to shy away. Darrel took 4 wheeler for a spin and nearly got lost. Saw moose cow and calf. Thousands of crane left this afternoon. Wind is rocking camper tonight.

Monday, September 23, 1991—warm, high clouds, windy. Went over to John Thuringer Farm and did real good on cranes. Came back to camper and got Darrel and went back. Then cranes quit flying there. Came back to Hollenbeck's and shot more crane and a goose. Darrel got a young crane. Very few birds. Went exploring. Picked up buffalo tooth. Spectacular sunset with dust in air.

Tuesday, September 24, 1991—partly cloudy, warm. Hardly any birds flying. Battery on truck went dead. Took it out and over to Scott H. and charges it up. Put it back in truck. Right foot is still painful to walk on uneven ground. Went to see Al, Wendy, Ross and Jason Baker. Had nice visit and got some water.

Wednesday, September 25, 1991—cold in morning, warmed later, 15°. Missed a crane. More geese flying. None in range for us. Late in afternoon packed up decoys and unloaded them at Hollenbeck's. Shopped and gas in Delta Junction. Unloaded some of Darrel's gear Glennallen and then brought him out to Huddleston's. Then on home.

Thursday, September 26, 1991–two inches of snow, 30°. Staked water line to "grade." Unloaded gear. Removed trailer hitch. Rested. Practiced goose call. Went to supper at school house.

Friday, September 27, 1991–partly cloudy, 34°. Went to Anchorage and got supplies. Got most of what we needed. Center of a sparkplug blew out on East Long Lake Highway. Put in new plugs before dark.

Saturday, September 28, 1991–sunny, 30°. Got truck ready and camper restocked. Sylvia and I came to The Farms at Delta Jct. to hunt geese. Made a unsuccessful stalk on two cranes and stalked somebody's goose decoys–damn. ¾ mile too.

Sunday, September 29, 1991–cloudy, sunny, partly cloudy, windy afternoon, 30°s to 40°s. No geese in the morning. Stalked two crane. No luck. Very cagey. Visited Hollenbeck, gave them two sweatshirts. Visited Bakers. Drove to Delta II farm project, no birds. Back to Hollenbeck's fields, too many hunters. Then over to John T. farm. Saw geese and crane's flying over Carlson's. Appear to land on docs. Walked over a mile over there, birds gone. Came back to Barley field and burrowed into wind row hoping for fly by birds. No luck. Back to camper and coffee. Hunt hours over. Then a hundred plus cranes and eleven geese flew fairly near by. Such is hunting.

Monday, September 30, 1991–partly cloudy, sunny, partly cloudy, 30s to 60s. Saw more geese today. Just didn't happen to be in range of them. Put out decoys this afternoon for morning. Tried to stalk some geese, no luck. Some crane flying, I only got one. They were out of range. Many multi thousands flew out this noontime. Some came back in late afternoon and evening. Large flock of geese left Barley Field after 8:00 PM. One small flock are and left field in about 30 minutes. Saw some large finches, marsh hawk, buffalo track here today. No hunters around.

Tuesday, October 1, 1991–cloudy, partly cloudy, 30s to 50s. Up early and out to goose decoys. One flock of geese and they are decoy smart and won't come in. Saw a few crane far away. Breakfast then drive around to "Rutt" farm, then back over to Reindeer farm. Shot a crane "100 yards" just after the flock crossed the road. Sylvia had just wished to see a buffalo. A herd of about a hundred were on the Reindeer farm. We got a bunch of pix. Then back to rear corner of John T. farm.

"Discovered a fire over on "Doc's" farm. Went to Hollenbeck's to report it. Barney tells me Fish & Game are doing a controlled burn, so we drive some more. Motor home sets at area we want to hunt. Tried again to see Roy Beaver. No Luck. We did meet Vern Weaver who is a mining buddy of Roy's. Then gas up in Delta and head for home. Northern Lights are out. Found a strap ratchet along road. Head wind all the way to Glennallen. Got home after 10:00 PM.

Wednesday, October 2, 1991—mostly sunny, 22° to 44°. Went down to our lake with 12-gauge and put canoe in and paddled around and two shoot two lesser scaup ducks and one spruce hen. Visited at store. Unloaded gear from truck. Put lime on garden and tilled it in. Hauled tiller up and put it in shed. Sylvia fixed a crane and Mae here for supper.

Thursday, October 3, 1991—windy, cloudy, light rain, sunny afternoon, 24° to 44°. Walked around and put things away for winter. Mounted new vise on stand, Sylvia put fertilizer on lawn.

Friday, October 4, 1991—cloudy, sunny, cloudy, 28° to 42°. Made seven sets of "hearts" candleholders. Sylvia put lime on lawn. I put moose wire protection over lilac bush.

Saturday, October 5, 1991—partly cloudy, 22° to 38°. Did small chores. Blew waterline out with air pressure. Helped Ed and Allen a bit. Helped move Mae to house across highway.

Sunday, October 6, 1991—mostly cloudy, 26° to 40°. Tried for ducks on lake, no luck. Packaged sweatshirts to send to Bev and Paul's family. Visited Mae Henry and Sally. Went fishing, caught three rainbows. First one was a really big one. Had him in the bucket, line basket and he jumped back in lake with my Mepps lure and was gone.

Monday, October 7, 1991—partly cloudy, skiffs of snow, 20° to 34°. Did a few things around here. Put new line on fish pole reel. Large flock of cranes went down valley. Jim O. and Kari back home.

Tuesday, October 8, 1991—snow light, cloudy, 17° to 33°. Two family swan groups. Each group had parents and four young. Another group had three adults and one juvenile on our lake today. A few ducks. Lake starting to freeze over. John Kunak didn't show up. I made gun boot holders for mounting on Suzuki four wheeler. Sylvia is sick with the flu. Canvas backs on our lake tonight.

Wednesday, October 9, 1991—more snow, cloudy, 22° to 29°. Large scoters and more swans on lake. Lloyd Ronning brought over some drapes for Sylvia to remodel. John Kunak and some men came and loaded the CAT. Glad he has gotten it out of here. Gave Ed F. some tar and heated it with weed burner and helped him put electric wire across road so he can have lights on the store sign.

Thursday, October 10, 1991—cloudy, 22° to 30°. A little more lake frozen. Patched on old hunting coat. Rested a lot. Sylvia is better. Called Scott H. Tom H. back.

Friday, October 11, 1991—cloudy. 24° to 28°. Visited at store. Loafed mostly. Sylvia remodeled Lloyd Ronning's drapes. One flock of 35 swans and few other groups rested awhile on our lake. Two flocks of buffleheads. Grandson Steven phoned his thanks.

Saturday, October 12, 1991—cloudy, 7° to 20°. Our lake finished freezing over last night. We took the camper off pickup and put it on old pickup for the winter. Tires are worn out on GMC so switched tires and wheels with old pickup. Smayda's were here visiting twice this afternoon. We took Mae to Huddleston's for supper tonight.

Sunday, October 13, 1991—snow most of day, got five inches, 24° to 26°. We put canopy on truck. Mounted the snow plow frame on truck and hooked lights and controls up. Burned three brush piles and one large stump pile. Big day today. Sore and tired. Jim and Kari O. used phone and visited.

Monday, October 14, 1991—another inch of snow, 20° to 32°. Put plow on truck and plowed at home, highway to store and at Moosey Boo. Made three more 12-gauge shot shell holders for reloading. Will give to Jim Odden.

Tuesday, October 15, 1991—2" more snow, sunny, 9° to 22°. Took a tire to Dawson's to get it fixed. Saw bear tracks near road. Visited Leona. Got snowgo out and running. Tom H. visited. Visited at store.

Wednesday, October 16, 1991—cloudy, 0° to 18°. Visited at store. Warmed up wood shop after calling Mary Wilkins. Then carved a diamond willow cane for my brother Jerry. Got one coat of varithane on it. Went to visit the Huddlestons after supper. They were gone.

Thursday, October 17, 1991—cloudy, fog at 3000 feet, 8° to 18°. Put more varithane on Jerry's cane. Mounted gun case on snowgo. Pulled canoe up in tree, near lake. Nadia called, very happy to be out of debt.

Friday, October 18, 1991—cloudy, skiff of snow, 9° to 24°. Sylvia ground meat and made mild sausage. Back is better today. Rested it a lot today. Raked snow off some roofs.

Saturday, October 19, 1991—cloudy, 8° to 29°. Broke trail 12 miles from house on trap line. Saw fox, marten, wolf and bear tracks. 4-wheel ATV had been operating back there.

Sunday, October 20, 1991—1" snow in the night, 20° to 28°. Windy part of day. Sylvia works on sweat shirts. I started making wall hanging wood scissor holders.

Monday, October 21, 1991—cloudy, 0° to 18°. Finished sanding scissor holder. Allen F. visited. Reloaded 300 grain .338. Took trash to dump. Gave clock to the Huddlestons (house gift).

Tuesday, October 22, 1991—cloudy, 8° to 24°. Worked on a "lazy Susan" style pole rack to display Sylvia's sweatshirts.

Wednesday, October 23, 1991—mostly sunny, 20°. Went to Anchorage. Got tire fixed and supplies. Visited Smaydas and looked at the motor at Ron Sopko's. Wrong kind of motor for me. Saw coyote outskirts Anchorage. Full moon and sun rising in mountains was very striking this morning. Foggy in night.

Thursday, October 24, 1991—partly cloudy, 8° to 20°. Put varithane on display rack. Finished unloading truck. Coyote carried rabbit down our lake. Pumped gas into storage tank.

Friday, October 25, 1991—fog, cloudy, snow in the afternoon, 6° to 18°. Put plow on and plowed snow at dump. Checked Jim O. house. Brought Sylvia's sweatshirt tree in house. Cut up stove wood for wood shop. Changed oil in truck and some other small jobs.

Saturday, October 26, 1991—mostly sunny, 8° to 26°. Plowed snow at Huddleston's. Visited with Bart B. Checked Odden's mail and house. Did a little maintenance on truck.

Sunday, October 27, 1991—ice fog, cloudy, 10° to 16°. Read Sunday paper and started making toy pop up toasters.

Monday, October 28, 1991—ice fog, 4° to 14°. Went to Glennallen in senior van and got flu shot and couple pair of socks at Rhynell's. Sanded on toy wood toaster and put a coat of tung oil on them. Returned Allen's meat grinder.

Tuesday, October 29, 1991—cloudy, some fog, 12° to 20°. Visited store. Pumped water, 1/4" ice in well, turned light bulb on in well for heat. Finished the toy toasters. Dump meeting at KROA.

Wednesday, October 30, 1991—mostly sunny, 10° to 26°. Tested TV antenna and then took it over to Mae's. Allen had a pipe for a mast and the coaxial cable. We got her TV hooked up. Sylvia and I went to Dinty Bush's. Visited with Leona and Doug. Doug and I found the leak in the trailer tire (rim leak). Sanded and cleaned it up. Doug sent another rim home with me. Nut on valve stem of truck tire was loose. He tightened that.

Thursday, October 31, 1991—fog, cloudy, highway very slippery, 16° to 28°. Turned the "ends" for the brass polisher drum on lathe. Trimmed up drum. Drilled screw holes and assembled the drum. Put a homemade eye on end of a broken fish rod and rigged it for jigging through the ice. We took a pot of ham hocks and beans and cornbread over to the store for supper. Mae provided Dutch Chocolate Cake.

Friday, November 1, 1991—cloudy, some fog, and flakes of snow, 12° to 17°. Put together a survival bag for me on snowgo. Made a nylon strap sling for 10-gauge. Went to Mailly's for supper. Got a copy made at Bartley's.

Saturday, November 2, 1991—sunny, 10° to 22°. Visited Jim O. and Kari went ice fishing. No luck. Tried to call a fox, no luck. Caller too weak.

Sunday, November 3, 1991—snow, cloudy, 16° to 18°. Mae had us and some other people over for very good dinner.

Monday, November 4, 1991—light snow, cloudy, 16° to 20°. Senior Van driver drove off edge of our drive. Had to come along and jack it back. Plowed snow. Visited at store. Made trap sled hitch.

Tuesday, November 5, 1991—mostly sunny, 19° to 25°. Put tail gate on pickup. Put three small loads wood in basement. Mannings visited at noon. Jim and Kari visited in evening.

Wednesday, November 6, 1991—sunny, cloudy, 7° to 19°. Went fishing at Partners Lake. Got one rainbow. Jim and Kari O were there. Made a improvement on jigging pole. Visited store and the Lodge.

Thursday, November 7, 1991—partly cloudy, skiff snow, cloudy afternoon, 11° to 20°. Started getting crafts ready. Went fishing and got four rainbows. Tried predator call at dump. Call broke. Cashed ck at KROA and visited awhile.

Friday, November 8, 1991—cloudy, 10° to 12°. Boxed crafts. Pumped water. Line doesn't freeze when we blow the line empty with air. Light bulb keeps ice thawed off top of water. Went to Ducks Unlimited dinner at Tolsona Lake

Lodge. Picked up snowgo belt and throttle body from Chuck Z. at Tolsona.

Saturday, November 9, 1991—cloudy, light snow, 2° to 12°. Up early and at Copper Center School to unload crafts and set up table. Didn't sell much. Back home about supper time. Jim, Mary and Kari O. visited in evening.

Sunday, November 10, 1991—cloudy, 12° to 4°. Put new snowgo throttle body on handle bar, also new belt. Got traps loaded on sled. Gave Nordic Ski Doo to Chuck Farmer.

Monday, November 11, 1991—mostly sunny, 0° to 12°. Bart B. came to borrow a pipe wrench. Allen and I went to Little Nelchina River to look at bear tracks. They were Boo tracks. Pack of wolves had been there. Allen and Ed went back and called a fox and missed it.

Tuesday, November 12, 1991—cloudy, ice fog, sunny, ice fog, -10° to 4°. Sewed and made a sheep skin cushion for my marine radio. Lloyd Ronning gave us a birch clock with a wolverine painted on it. Bonnie took her "charge" and Sylvia to Eureka. Mary B. brought a check over for Sylvia.

Wednesday, November 13, 1991—partly cloudy, -18° to -2°. Visited at store. Went on trap line. Made wolf, fox and one marten set. Hundreds of boo between highway and Castle Creek. Saw 38" and bull moose, wolf and fox track. Went as far as second Meat Pole Hill. Jim and Kari O. visited in evening.

Thursday, November 14, 1991—cloudy and snow, -4° to 0°. Cloudy and snow. Went to Highway Camp and Lucky sharpened steel bit. Hung two snare in wolf trail at Little Nell Hill. Tried to call fox, no luck. Went to Jim O. and picked up my two spark plugs.

Friday, November 15, 1991—cloudy, light snow, -1° to 6°. Two coyotes on lake all day, near Allen's. Bart brought tools back. Put new spark plug in snowgo. Shoveled snow off camper and woodshed roof. Allen F. visited in evening.

Saturday, November 16, 1991—sunny, -10° to 0°. Ran trap line, one wolf trap and one number two sprung. Four to five wolves ran part trail. Had a yearling boo in trap, got out when I got there. Remade. Set with clean trap. Some problems with snowgo. Saw boo and three moose bulls.

Sunday, November 17, 1991—ice fog, -9° to 3°. Changed needle. Adjusted snowgo carburetor, cleaned spark plug and tried snowgo on lake. Cleaned Manning trap and put it to boil on heater. Sylvia canned the sauer kraut. Visited Allen but they were going to Eureka to eat.

Monday, November 18, 1991—ice fog, light snow, -5° to 5°. Built a pair of chains for Dan Billman's van. Boiled wolf trap. Jim Odden borrowed snowgo catalog.

Tuesday, November 19, 1991—partly cloudy, 10° to 13°. Bonnie Wikle visited Sylvia. I did some trapping things. Dan Billman brought Bill? (potential Lodge buyer) with him when he stopped in to look at chains. I went to look at wolf snares, tried predator call, no luck.

Wednesday, November 20, 1991—cloudy, light snow, 4° to 0°. Ran trap line. Made two more wolf sets, had fox in one wolf set. Pulled it. Made a fox set along hwy. Went to Dan Billman's, pulled him out of ditch, plowed around the Lodge. Gave him a pair of chains, squared up for flying.

Thursday, November 21, 1991—cloudy, light snow, 8° to -1°. Jim and Kari O. came over and welded his snowgo. I made trap covers and sled hitch adapter. Tried to pump water. Line is frozen. Tried butane torch and hot water to thaw it, no go. Will try something else. Jim and Kari here for supper.

Friday, November 22, 1991—cloudy, light snow, -6° to 3°. Had to cut two long pieces out of water line, bring it into basement and thaw the ice out and replace it, then pump water. Bart and Rosemary had us over for supper.

Saturday, November 23, 1991—3" snow, cloudy, 6° to 8°. Ran trap line. No catch. Made one wolf, one fox, five marten sets. Broke trail to Allen's cabin. Couple moose tracks plus six boo, marten and fox.

Sunday, November 24, 1991—light snow, cloudy, 0° to 6°. Worked a little in wood shop. Plowed our snow.

Monday, November 25, 1991—mostly clear, -10° to 4°. Made some small scissor holders and wood match boxes.

Tuesday, November 26, 1991—ice fog, it raised, then down again, -20° to -10°. Ran trap line. Made wood pee post and one animal trail set. No fur, only bait robber ermine.

Wednesday, November 27, 1991—windy and warmer, 15° to 17°. Went to Palmer in afternoon. Stayed overnight with Tom and Lisa Smayda. She has torn ligaments of her knee.

Thursday, November 28, 1991—breezy, 30° to 33°. Enjoyed a fine Thanksgiving dinner. George, Ted and Sharie and the Oddens came over after dinner and we had pie and coffee together. Home in evening.

Friday, November 29, 1991—mostly cloudy, 10° to 13°. Ran trap line. Didn't catch anything. Pulled a couple sets and made two other sets. Fresh wolf tracks on so go. Tracks - 1 hr? Supper at Odden's.

Saturday, November 30, 1991—snow all day (seven inches), 12° to 18°. Cleaned battery terminals on truck. Visited at store. Jim, Mary, Kari O. here for supper. We got 12" snow total.

Sunday, December 1, 1991—sunny, 24° to 4°. Plowed snow all day. Got stuck a few times, broke a cross bar on chain.

Monday, December 2, 1991—cloudy, light snow, 4° to 10°. Plowed some snow and put different mirrors on truck. Tom H. visited in evening.

Tuesday, December 3, 1991—cloudy, 5° all day. Ran trap line. Pushed snow ahead of snowgo all the way. Unhooked sled near highway. Got stuck a few times. "Broomed" off some sets. Pulled one marten set, got one pale marten, one wolf track, after big storm. One fox track and a couple marten sets. Made a marten set near RCA site. Picked up Dimmick's mail and plowed snow there and at Evelyn's. Checked two wolf snares near Little Nelchina River and got stuck. Tore up truck chain and had a helluva time getting back to highway.

Wednesday, December 4, 1991—sunny all day, -6°. Plowed some snow. Skinned marten. Steve, Karen Mailly and family here for a supper.

Thursday, December 5, 1991—cloudy, light snow, 5° to 6°. Repaired tire chains. Went to Dimmick's twice, feed dogs and start furnace. Made two fox sets near hwy. Manning were here for a few minutes. Ed Farmer found some of our mail, we gave him some moose.

Friday, December 6, 1991—cloudy, light snow, 4° to 6°. Ran trap line. Pulled some and moved them. Some moose and caribou tracks. Jim and Kari Odden visited in evening.

Saturday, December 7, 1991—cloudy, 1° to 8°. Got gloves and some bait ready. Checked fox sets near Little Nelchina. Harold and Rachel Dimmick visited. Kari O. here all day while Jim started setting his trap line. Jim Odden and Kari and Bart and Rosemary Bartley here for supper. Gave Sylvia a poinsettia. Allen and Ed F. got wolf at the state camp gravel pit and want to skin it in my garage.

Sunday, December 8, 1991—light snow, cloudy, 11° to 15°. Ran trap line. Wolves crossed trail east to west. Fresh marten track out where I turned around. No fur. Saw big moose and five boo. Put Helfrich wolf trap and five snares in snowgo and Allen and I went to gravel pit and I put in sets for boo kill wolves Botley Creek. Jim had a very bad day. Lots of troubles.

Monday, December 9, 1991—cloudy, 2" snow, then sunny, 6° to 4°. Nothing in snares. Made a Helfrich set ¼ mi north of Hwy. Saw marten tracks at overflow near highway. Looked for marten and spotted it. It ran up tree and I shot it in eye. Skinned it when I got back home. Got some bait ready. Shoveled snow off wood shed roof.

Tuesday, December 10, 1991—cloudy, -10° to 0°. Went to Hwy Camp and glassed area for wolf tracks. Went on to Little Nelchina area fox set. Had him (red fox) in trap. Skinned it when I got home. Then built a "hobby moose" for Kari O. who Sylvia baby sat again while Jim got more of his trap line out today. Jim had supper with us.

Wednesday, December 11, 1991—mostly cloudy, -14° to -10°. Snowgo gave me trouble starting. Went on trap line. Two fresh marten tracks, no fur. Made fox and marten set. Went to gravel pit, wolves had been there, came back home and got two Helfrich traps and grader blade for drags and set in trails for them. Fox had killed a spruce hen. I gathered up feathers and made a set for her along trail.

Thursday, December 12, 1991—cloudy, foggy, -20° to -14°. Checked wolf sets. Nothing. Shoveled snow off roofs. Allen, Roxanne Farmer and family were here for supper.

Friday, December 13, 1991—cloudy, fog, -27° to -16°. Checked wolf sets. Fox set sprung. Went to dump. Kari here today.

Saturday, December 14, 1991—cloudy, 23° to 20°. Checked sets at State Camp gravel pit, nothing. Ran trap line, nothing. Some marten track. Made Marten set at Cache Creek. Roxanne F. had bad chimney fire, caught house on fire. Lucky got it out. I took water hose down, helped a little.

Sunday, December 15, 1991—cloudy, 4° to 7°, 20° evening. Checked sets at gravel pit, nothing. Tried to call fox at gravel pit in late afternoon. No luck.

Monday, December 16, 1991—cloudy, breezy, light snow, 20° to 10°. Pulled all sets at gravel pit. Serviced snowgo. Plowed our snow.

Tuesday, December 17, 1991—partly sunny, -5° to -10°. Ran trap line. Coyote track, lots caribou—some moose on south end line. Missed marten at Cache Creek set, remade set. Had a porcupine just before Dry Creek. Had to turn loose a young cow boo from wolf set at Allen's tree north of Dry Creek. Kari was here while Jim O. ran his line.

Wednesday, December 18, 1991—evening clouds, -10° to 4°. Sent out lots of Xmas cards. Manning borrowed flour sifter. Tom S. visited.

Thursday, December 19, 1991—cloudy, -15° to -8°. Tom H. and I visited store. He borrowed my weed burner. Drawing for quilt, rifle and party at school house.

Friday, December 20, 1991—mostly cloudy, -10° to 6°. Kari is here. Ran trap line. No fur. Some boo. Remade lots of sets and hung a snare for fox. Saw two ptarmigan. Beautiful full moon.

Saturday, December 21, 1991—partly cloudy, cloudy evening, -20° to -14° to -22° -16° Sun Dogs. Looked for lost camera at gravel pit. Wolfe had been back. Didn't find camera. We pumped water for house. Bart visited and stayed for supper.

Sunday, December 22, 1991—cloudy, light snow, sunny, -6° to 2°. Called all the kids, didn't get to talk to Beverly. Went to gravel pit. Wolf had been back. Made a trail set off in trees.

Monday, December 23, 1991—cloudy, fog, -10° to 8°. Went to gravel pit and made snowgo trail set for old female wolf. Grader blade drag and boo back bone step guide. Ran line north. Trigger creep had sprung trap that I had reset last trip. Wolves on trail there and looked it all over. Wolves on trail near Dry Creek. One marten crossed line. No fur today. Tom H. filled propane bottle and brought it back—nice!!

Tuesday, December 24, 1991—foggy, light snow. Checked sets at gravel pit. Nothing. Visited at store. Sylvia baked pies. A package came from Nadia.

Wednesday, December 25, 1991—cloudy, 4° to -4°. Slept late went to gravel pit with truck. Wolf had stepped in trap. I started walking out the trail, she? Left. Two wolves had walked to the set. This was a trail set, the trap pan was ½ wolf stride at center of a section of boo backbone I used for a step guide. The wolf packed a 40 circle down, 20' chain radius, then took off. I followed 1-½ miles. It had been hung up lots of times but would get untangled and go on. I should have had a regular ½ rebar drag chained to the grader blade. I got tired and came back. We went to Jim and Mary Oddens for Christmas dinner. John colleen and Axel Odden, Smayda family was there also. Jim and John will go with me in the morning on snowgo and have a try that way.

Thursday, December 26, 1991—foggy, cloudy, sunny, -4° to 4°. Jim and John O drove snowgos here and we started tracking that wolf. Lots of hard work breaking trail and walking through the thick stuff. They did all the rough work. She finally went across the river. To dangerous for Jim to cross. She has broken swivel or fastener and lost the grader blade. We gave up and came home just at dark.

Friday, December 27, 1991—cloudy, freezing ice, fog, 24° all day. Went to Little Nelchina are a looking for track of wolf, then on snowgo to Nelchina River south of here, no sign. Then drilled holes for tie wire on trap chain fasteners. Will drill them as I get them home to drill press. Went on trap line, no fur or tracks. Saw one moose and lots boo and moose tracks. Re-made nearly all sets. Raised up lots wolf sets on packed snow. Two were sprung two in packed snow. Sure got tired today. Sylvia baked sour dough bread. She has intestinal flu.

Saturday, December 28, 1991—mostly sunny, -4° to 4°. Got teacher's stove adjusted. Went to Little Nelchina, no wolf tracks. Stopped and picked up a boo stomach from road kill. Took a scoop shovel to area. I caught wolf and found grader blade drag. The "S" link failed and wolf got free. Spent rest of day trying to get snowgo running, no luck.

Sunday, December 29, 1991—snow all day, -5° to 4°. Loaded snowgo on trailer. Visited Rachel & Harold Dimmick, had supper.

Monday, December 30, 1991—snow, cloudy, -7° to 10°. Plowed snow today. Visited Tom Huddleston and Odden's.

Tuesday, December 31, 1991—fog, cloudy, fog, -5° to 10°. Checked trap at gravel pit, nothing. Lots caribou there. Looked for wolf track Little Nelchina area. Tried to run trap line with the 250 colt. Flywheel and motor shroud too bad a shape so came back. Visited at store. Chopped up Boo stomach, put in paper sacks, then sacks in boxes for bait on line. Sylvia and I have colds.

I think a man has missed a very deep feeling of satisfaction if he has never created,
or at least completed something with his own two hands.
—Richard Proenneke

1992—a volcano eruption affects daily life

Wednesday, January 1, 1992—fog, white out, 10° to 15°. Drove to Tolsona Lake and to Chuck Zimbicki's with snowgo on trailer. Timing isn't so bad but what motor should run. Found very low compression, Pulled head and jug. Found lots carbon, rings tight to piston, slight score near exhaust side. Left snowgo and trailer, Chuck will fix it. Dropped off snowgo coil for Tom H. Visited Lloyd Ronning and took Charley Knetter's mail to him at KROA.

Thursday, January 2, 1992—fog, partly cloudy, fog, 5°. Asked Allen to go to his cabin. Rode one of his machines. Checked traps on way. A marten is near Cache Creek. Lots of boo and some moose. Lots of wolf tracks on some of line. They went past six of my sets, didn't use a single pee post. Boo had sprung two of my traps. We saw a few ptarmigan. One fox track up in the high country. We broke trail west and south keeping to high elevation. Saw boo up there. Came past Carrot Lake and hit trail for the pass down south side, Slide Mountain. Then came out at highway camp and on home. Sylvia had a good supper ready for us. Sure grateful for use of one of Allen's snowgo. Tom H. brought me some parts from Zimbicki's to fix the 250 Colt.

Friday, January 3, 1992—foggy, light snow, 4° to 9°. Tried to put parts on 250 Colt, no go as lower case is broke also. Went to gravel pit. Checked trap in wolf trail, walked out Allen's wood trail loop and picked up 750 W Helfrich I had cached there. Tom H. visited. I took Missy's trapping report over to her at store. Pulled Chuckie's pickup out of snow berm.

Saturday, January 4, 1992—partly cloudy, -4° to -1° to -12°. Days are a little longer. Did a few small jobs around here. Tom, Kim H. and family here for supper. Allen came over for some pipe fittings but I didn't have the size needed.

Sunday, January 5, 1992—foggy, cloudy, -19° to -8°. Read and loafed all day. Cole's came over and picked up their key. Allen and Roxanne were here for supper. Jackie and daughters were there also. Sick in night.

Monday, January 6, 1992—cloudy, partly cloudy, -6° to 3°. Loafed most of day. Sylvia went to Glennallen. I plowed snow.

Tuesday, January 7, 1992—cloudy, -4° to 10°. Went to Odden's, needed to talk to John, also Jim. Jim and Mary's friends from Palmer were there. Jim and friend came down after supper and welded snowgo and sled parts. I Checked gravel pit, someone had killed a boo there. Nothing in trap. We pumped water today. I walked to well at lake to turn on pump. Watched boo on lake while pump filled tank in house. Steve Mailly stopped in to borrow a flashlight and knife~ vehicle trouble.

Wednesday, January 8, 1992—cloudy, light snow, 6° to 8°. Tom H. visited. Jim O. came back to re-weld snowgo tie rod. Visited at store. Art Wikle and family here for supper.

Thursday, January 9, 1992—cloudy, 8° to 12°. Tom H. brought me a white Tyvec Coverall. I took the 250 Colt Polaris on the trap line. No fur, one boo in trap (had to take trap off it), one sprung trap. Saw bunch ravens, looked around awhile and found a dead cow boo. Sylvia doesn't feel well today.

Friday, January 10, 1992—cloudy, 0° to 10°. Went to gravel pit. Wolves haven't been back. Ravens nearly cleaned up boo guts. No fox tracks. Repositioned coil on Colt 250 and repaired broken wire. Package came from Beverly. Thumper dropped snowgo oil at Farmer's store. I left a case of oil at store to be sold. Tom and Charley H. visited in evening.

Saturday, January 11, 1992—cloudy, 16° all day. Went to dog race, trade fair in Glennallen old school gym. Didn't sell very much. Visited with friends. Stopped at donut shop.

Sunday, January 12, 1992—2" fluffy snow, 8° all day. Made a five inch box and mounted it on 250 Polaris raising the seat. Nice storage and more comfortable to ride. Mae R. came over and visited. Tom H. got two boo with my 30.06 rifle.

Monday, January 13, 1992—light snow, cloudy, fog, 1° to -1°. A little work on 250 Colt snowgo. Ran trap line. Got a nice female grey wolf. She was in my last wolf set. Put her in sacks and tied her on top of the seat of snowgo and came for home. Skinned it in 2 ½ hrs. Tom H. came to see it. Darrel Gerry and Mike Lanegan called.

Tuesday, January 14, 1992—partly cloudy, 6° all day. Slept late. Real sore and stiff. Visited at store. Sylvia went to late Christmas party in Glennallen. Sewed up cuts in wolf pelt. Got some trap gear ready. Went to gravel pit and Checked that set. Moose calf acting strange down on lake. Some boo going east.

Wednesday, January 15, 1992—sunny, cloudy, snow, -2° to 10°. Went to Chuck's and brought snowgo home. Tried to call lynx, fox at 3 places on way home. No luck. Chuck saw a lynx in ditch while driving down the road. Did some work on snowgo and got it outfitted for trap line. Checked Odden's house.

Thursday, January 16, 1992—cloudy, some sun, cloudy, 20° to 24°. Hauled snowgo to Little Nelchina River. Went down river as far as Nelchina River looking for the trap trail of wolf. Too many boo trails to find it. Some hunters had killed a boo. Snowgo ran great. Back home and did a few things. Am trying out the brass polisher.

Friday, January 17, 1992—partly sunny, breezy, 2" of snow, 24° to 30°. Saw a moose just as I started out on trap line. Re-made most of sets. Put out lots of boo guts for bait. Made two wolf sets out a "Y" on trail. Saw a flying squirrel. No fur and no tracks. Real tired when I got home. Sylvia had Mae and Elaine here for supper. Someone has shot a caribou and left it lay. Then today someone shot and killed a big moose and drove away.

Saturday, January 18, 1992—partly cloudy, 8° to 12°. Put snow plow on truck and plowed for over three hours. Patti Landers came to get some solder for their heating system.

Sunday, January 19, 1992—snow all day (4+ inches), 16° to 18°. Chuck F. asked me to haul his snowgo home from just on this side of Cache Creek. Cole's were here for 5 minutes or so. Patti B called—worried about the gate being unlocked. Reformed the jaws on a Manning No. 9 and boiled it.

Monday, January 20, 1992—cloudy, 5° to 10°. Plowed snow. Pumped water. Checked Odden's place. Patti locked the padlock and I don't have a key for it.

Tuesday, January 21, 1992—sunny, -2° all day. -12° in evening. Ran trap line, moose tracks and one young moose. Wolf tracks at 4 Corners. Bart B. and son Bruce had been boo hunting on trail. Caught a marten. Made two new marten sets and pulled one set. Made a double wolf set. Snowgo maybe to rich, adjusted choke. Sylvia cut Ed F. hair. Jim O and Les, his Dad and Kari visited in evening.

Wednesday, January 22, 1992—partly cloudy, -20° to -5°. Skinned marten. Sylvia went to Glennallen. Discovered she has taped over my Alaska trapping tape. Went to gravel pit and picked up wolf trap and dragged a boo hide out to road. Trail was hard to walk. Snow is hip deep off the trail. Went to dump and tried to call Canines at dump. No luck. Lots of tracks. Stopped to see Oddens. No one answered the door.

Thursday, January 23, 1992—mostly cloudy, -14° to 0°. Turned marten skin on stretcher. Built fire in garage so Jim O. could work on his snowgo and sled. Shoveled snow off camper. Got some fox traps ready. Lester Odden came along to visit.

Friday, January 24, 1992—mostly cloudy, very light snow, -17° to -4°. Maintained heat in garage. Removed starter from truck. Cleaned and dismantled it. Needs brushes and bushing. Sandy F. will bring them from Glennallen this evening.

Visited at store. Quite a few Caribou going east today. Roxanne brought me nine gunny sacks.

Saturday, January 25, 1992—partly cloudy, -15° to -10°. Tried to go on trap line, snowgo wouldn't run. Worked on it all day, no go. Worked on starter on truck in evening and got that fixed. Chuck Z. has been good with advice for snowgo.

Sunday, January 26, 1992—1 1/2" snow, cloudy, -17° to -1°. Sylvia has flu pretty bad for a couple of days. I did more tests on snowgo. It looks like CDI is questionable. Mixed some snowgo gas. A few caribou on lake.

Monday, January 27, 1992—mostly sunny, -17° to -2° Re-torqued head on snowgo. It still doesn't run. Dug the old Colt 250 out of the snow and checked trap line. Wolves have been on south end near top of hill and have been at boo carcass in drainage. One fox track north of Allen's old cabin. Had a boo in Manning trap at "Y." No rope along!! Used starting rope to tie yearling boo, then take trap off. Sally and Kenny out snowmobiling. No fox at dump. Checked Odden house and plugged in his heat tape. Chuck sent a CDI box.

Tuesday, January 28, 1992—partly cloudy, -12° to 12°. Did more checking out of snowgo problem. Talked to Allen F. about it. Finally loaded it up on trailer and took it to Tolsona Lake and Chuck Z. He installed another customer's stator plate so we could tell if my exciter coil was bad, which must be the case as it runs now.

Wednesday, January 29, 1992—partly cloudy, -9° to 10°. Worked at trap gear. Shoveled snow off some roofs. Visited at store. Allen visited here. Jim O. & parents Lester and Lois visited in evening. Kari here also.

Thursday, January 30, 1992—partly cloudy, 4° to 8°. Tied a boo hide behind the sled and started for trap line. Stopped along the way and picked up the head, briskets and some small pieces of hide from the cow moose that someone shot from the hwy. Sam Weaver saw it happen. Lost the boo hide a mile later. Set three Helfrich wolf traps at boo kill in drainage. Went on to Four Corners, dragged the moose parts 40 yards to the southeast. Snow hip deep. Made two trails and set five snares. Bent a small spruce over and wired a cotton wad near the top and soaked it with Canadian Wolf Lure. No fur on line today. Went to end and turned around. Didn't see the glasses I lost, the last trip. Lost both and found one of my Helfrich "setters" today. Eleven boo were on the trail and crossed the highway at Sam W. Oh yes, saw some dry spruce poles appropriate for beaver trapping. Cut six and cached them at the trail that goes to those lakes.

Friday, January 31, 1992—mostly sunny, -5° to 2°. Loaded wolf carcass in sled and started on trap line. Tied on boo hide at place I lost it yesterday. Put wolf carcass at Four Corners. Bait pile. Lost and found two burlap sacks. Found my sunglasses, the sled had run over them and broke a bow. Wired boo hide to a tree near the sets I have at the place I caught the first wolf. I couldn't find the Helfrich trap setting lever. Set another snare at Four Corners bait pile. Picked up marten sets and one fox set. Some moose tracks and signs of feeding. Some boo traveling around. Occasionally squirrel. Lots of ravens flying around. No fur and no tracks. Mike and Steve from Fish & Game stopped by looking for a coyote carcass.

Saturday, February 1, 1992—sunny, -12° to -2°. Visited at store. Checked with Lucky to see if he needed help with well. Ran snowgo hard, it does need ignition advanced a couple degrees. Worked a little with trap gear. Put oil in chain case of snowgo. Nadia phoned birthday greetings, Fran also. Sylvia made pecan pie. Mae Richardson was here for supper.

Sunday, February 2, 1992—partly cloudy, periods of ice fog, -11° to 2°. Read paper. Sorted and organized catalogs. Listened to goose calling tapes. Got some phone calls and made some ourselves.

Monday, February 3, 1992—mostly sunny, cloudy late afternoon, -12° to 0°. Ran trap line. Single wolf track in first drainage along hwy. Left trail soon. Saw a big moose at Four Corners. Lots moose track everywhere. Some boo track. One fox crossed trail. Cut some leaning brush.

Tuesday, February 4, 1992—partly cloudy, -21° to -7°. Sylvia went with Mae R. to Palmer. Built a fire in garage, then Chuck phoned he wouldn't be coming. Cleaned ashes out of stove, went to dump and made two fox sets.

Wednesday, February 5, 1992—cloudy, light snow, -11° to 7°. Checked sets at dump, nothing. Checked fuel oil and gasoline tanks for fuel levels. Worked on snowgo, mixed gas put it in garage. Chuck Z. came in afternoon and timed the motor. I built a box for 110 Coni Bear, to use for wolverine box set. Chuck didn't charge anything to time motor.

Thursday, February 6, 1992—partly cloudy, sunny, partly cloudy, -11° to 5°. Ice fog to east of us. Forgot 330 coni box when I was getting things ready to run trap line. Went to dump and had a male fox there. Back home for breakfast and ran trap line. Moose, boo, fox, marten and ptarmigan tracks. Pumped water when I got home. Lucky borrowed our water hauling tank. Skinned and boarded the fox.

Friday, February 7, 1992—mostly sunny, ice fog nearby, -14° to -2°. Went to dump. Checked trap. Found two wolf trails crossing the highway. They are east of Army Trail Dump. Turned fox on board. Cleaned pitch from four marten and brushed out another fox. Cut up fox carcass for bait in wolverine box. While out in yard I heard wolves howling to east. Took rifle and drove east stopping and listening, no luck. Could hear a plane over at Tazlina Lake. Checked Odden's house.

Saturday, February 8, 1992—mostly sunny, -12° to 4°. Checked trap at dump. Set a snare along hwy near dump entrance. Put in a light switch for Sylvia in kitchen and an outlet out on the "island." Went to Art and Bonnie's for supper.

Sunday, February 9, 1992—sunny, some fog, -10° to 2°. Checked Odden's place. Got a nice cross fox at dump. Drove up Lake Louise Road. Visited Dawson's. Doug mounted a tire for me. Went to Point of View Lodge, visited the new leasers. Bill & Kathy, his daughter Jane, and their two young boys.

Monday, February 10, 1992—snow all day, -4° to 8°. Ran trapline. Made a 330 Coni box set. Re-did some sets. Put out two fox carcass's at snares. No fur. Saw cow and calf moose. Made two fox sets at dump. Saw six boo on our lake. Tom H. stopped by to visit.

Tuesday, February 11, 1992—sunny, -8° to 9°. Plowed snow. Checked dump, nothing no tracks. Visited Jim O., Dan Billman. Last years moose calf is eating old flowering kale plants from alongside the house. We are somewhat concerned it may accidentally break out a window. The moose just keeps coming back. Billman and J. Odden and Kari here this evening.

Wednesday, February 12, 1992—sunny, -17° to -2°. Checked dump traps, nothing. Visited with Lee Dudley at store. Plowed some snow for Roxanne. Tried to fix a leaky faucet. Sylvia went to birthday party for Sandy F.

Thursday, February 13, 1992—snow all day, -4° to 12°. Ran trap line. One wolf, one fox, one coyote track. Remade quite a few sets. Saw a moose cow and yearling calf. Sylvia babysat Kari & Jim and I went to Glennallen to a wolf management meeting.

Friday, February 14, 1992—cloudy, sunny, then light snow, -3° to 10°. Checked dump traps. Plowed snow. Studied Medicare.

Saturday, February 15, 1992—light snow all night and day, -4° to 8°. Sanded points on fur push pins. Ground a notch in utility knife blade for use in skinning. Mannings borrowed a water pump manual and brought a banana bread loaf, so did Roxanne and Ellie. I went down and we took their water line apart and put two lengths of it in house to thaw out.

Sunday, February 16, 1992—sunny, -15° to 0°. Watched Olympics. Helped Roxanne get waterline back out of house and hooked up. Pumped water and filled her storage tank. She gave me a Leatherman Tool!! Took Sylvia to KROA for pizza.

Monday, February 17, 1992—sunny, sun dogs, cold, -30° to -10°. Loafed all day. Jim phoned, he will be hone so I don't have to go to his place.

Tuesday, February 18, 1992—sunny, ice fog to south, full moon, -30° to -5°. Lots of boo going west on lake, as many as 48 in sight at one time. Jim and Kari O. came down. Stayed awhile and we were to go to Mannings for supper. Didn't get to run trap line. Good supper at Mannings.

Wednesday, February 19, 1992—sunny and sun dogs, some distant ice fog, -29° to -6°. Jim Odden came in afternoon and I went to his place and he started his airplane "Rags" and flew it to Gulkana Airport to have it "annualed." Kari and I followed in his pickup. Got back home at 3:00 PM. I got dressed for the trail and ran trap line. No fur. Spruce hen, ptarmigan, fox, coyote, marten, moose and boo tracks. Put two boo hides near sets. Picked up a gut pile from boo some hunter shot near the road. The moon light nights are beautiful.

Thursday, February 20, 1992—mostly sunny, breezy, cloudy, light snow, -32° to -10°. Allen F visited in morning. Sylvia babysat Kari today. Started filling out longevity bonus application for Sylvia today.

Friday, February 21, 1992—mostly sunny, some breeze, -34° to -6°. Did lots reading. We went with Allen, Roxanne and family to Victory School for potluck and prize drawing. I won a drain pan and five quarts of motor oil. Lots boo on road on way there. Beaut evening and night.

Saturday, February 22, 1992—sunny, cloudy, light snow afternoon and evening, -28° to -8°. Drove to dump. Looked at wolf trails and tracks on way. Had another cross fox at dump. Thaw and drying the fox this afternoon and evening.

Sunday, February 23, 1992—light snow all night and day, -18° to 10°. Skinned, fleshed, stretched cross fox. Ran trap line. Saw several moose. Lots boo tracks. Two sprung wolf traps. Couldn't get one reset, brought it home. Hauled another boo hide and guts out to line for bait. No fur in traps. Fox had been working bait on first meat pole hill. Made two sets there. Ate early supper. Art and Bonnie came while we were eating.

Monday, February 24, 1992—partly cloudy, sunny, some breeze, -2° to 15°. Went to Glennallen on senior van and got Sylvia's application for AK Senior

Bonus notarized and mailed off. Saw some ptarmigan along road. Plowed our snow. Visited Allen. Bought some things Wilma is selling off.

Tuesday, February 25, 1992—mostly sunny, 4" of snow last night, 17° to 24°. Plowed snow today. Got stuck once. Only some moose and a few boo tracks along road. Pumped water for house. Snowgo came up the hill, snow had accumulated to about a foot deep. Had to go to Bartley's and pull out the school bus. Pumped gas up into overhead rank and loaded barrels into truck. Thawed wolf hide out and getting ice out of fur so it can be fleshed. Jim and Kari O. visited in evening.

Wednesday, February 26, 1992—1" of snow, cloudy, 12° to 24°. Went to Wasilla. Got some things for house. Dropped off wolf hide to get it tanned. The fur buyer said I was too late in season to sell my furs to him. Got gasoline and dab of groceries and came home. Legs hurt.

Thursday, February 27, 1992—cloudy, snow in afternoon, 28° to 36°. Ran trap line. Saw boo, moose, five marten tracks. Cross fox had got in Manning wolf trap and pulled out. Had a wolf in west trail at "Y" at the turnaround probably by a toe or two for it pulled out, probably when it heard me coming on the snowgo. Unhook sled and went west. Snow very deep. Wolves went north or south. Turned snowgo around in trail by hand (tough going). Reworked that Manning at home. Allen F. family and Mae here for supper. Bartley called, went there and pulled four stuck vehicles out to highway and plowed his driveway.

Friday, February 28, 1992—sunny, 15° to 20°. One control cable broke, ordered one over the phone. Thawed ice off truck chains. Shoveled, chipped ice off garage floor. Gave some No. 2 Diesel to Chuck F. Allen had started Ed's CAT and pushed snow back. Here at our place also. Mountains sure are beautiful.

Saturday, February 28, 1992—sunny, snow late evening, 5° to 11°. Started out on trap line. I have a moose calf in Manning ½ mile south of Cache Creek. Mother cow is with it. Unhooked sled, turned machine around in trail and came back home. Phoned F & G protection. Mike Roscovious and Bob Toby may come out to help get calf out of trap. Toby is flying looking for wolves. Shoveled a little snow. Filed some on the "dog" on one of the Helfrich traps. Hurt my back carrying a trap upstairs pressed against my chest. Lots of boo on lake today. We went to Tom and Kim Huddleston's for supper.

Sunday, March 1, 1992—sunny, light snow, some breeze, 3" snow last night, 4° to 10°. Jury rigged snow plow control cable and plowed snow this morning. Mike R. called that he and the biologist would come out mid afternoon and we went to moose calf in trap. Tranquillized the cow, turned calf loose, gave the cow a revival shot and we came back out to road. They loaded their machines to go back to town and I drove my snowgo home. We went to a ice cream and cake birthday for Robbie F.

Monday, March 2, 1992—mostly sunny, -16° to -2°. Plowed snow. Boiled wolf trap. Sylvia went to town in senior van.

Tuesday, March 3, 1992—mostly sunny, -34° to -10°. Read till 1:30 PM then went on snowgo on trap line. No fur. Lots moose tracks, one moose, cow and calf were gone from wolf set. Lots boo tracks. Three fox and one marten track. Some ermine and squirrel, few rabbit. Picked up four, No. 3 traps. Lost sled and had to turn snowgo around in trail and go back to get it.

Wednesday, March 4, 1992—sunny, ice in air, -38° to 0°. Visited at store and at Mae's. Shoveled snow off camper. Bartley brought air chuck back. Read some. Jim O. watched flight service weather in evening.

Thursday, March 5, 1992—sunny, ice in air, -32° to -8°. Shoveled snow off storage trailer and wood shed. Visited at store. Read. Jim O. came over to watch weather forecast.

Friday, March 6, 1992—sunny, ice in air, cloudy in evening, -26° to 2°. Went to Odden's and helped Jim load his plane, also Tigre, his Labrador. I watched for traffic from east and he took off to west on Highway. Circled and went to McGrath and work. Plowed a little snow for Jack C. Picked up a snare down by dump area. Looked for wolf tracks crossing hwy, none. Sylvia and Mae went to Glennallen. When she got home she helped put the new control cable on snowplow. Days are much longer now.

Saturday, March 7, 1992—cloudy, skiff of snow all day, -15° to 10°. Ran trap line. Four marten, 3 fox track. Lots moose and boo track. Rebuilt quite a few wolf sets. Picked up some wolf and one coni box that I had out there. Ravens are working on bait piles for wolves.

Sunday, March 8, 1992—2" of snow, cloudy, 10° to 16°. Jim M. came over to borrow a TV tape. Neighbor, Cole stopped for a couple min. Sylvia visited Mae. Overflow showing up on our lake again. Reading lots of old trapper magazines these days.

Monday, March 9, 1992—light snow, some sun, cloudy, breezy, 26° to 32°. Plowed some snow. Made a snow rake to pull snow off the roofs. Sylvia went to Glennallen. Tried to plow at Holland's, had to give it up.

Tuesday, March 10, 1992—cloudy, 15° to 20°. Shoveled some roofs off. Used the snow rake also. Tom Dobler stopped to offer to pickup power steering pump for me, but Tom H. was already getting one for me. Snowing hard. 2" this evening. Tom H. dropped off the pump.

Wednesday, March 11, 1992—partly cloudy, 20° to 37°. Ran trap line. Pulled one wolf trap. Remade more sets and snares. A marten lives at one wolf bait. Saw one moose and fourteen marten, and 3 fox track. Fox at Meat Pole Hill was back at bait, seems to be getting around ok since he got out of wolf trap. Started to put new power steering pump on. I don't have proper puller to switch the pulley. Cleaned up the old pump and will take it to Glennallen tomorrow.

Thursday, March 12, 1992—cloudy, 24° to 32°. Tom H. was here before we got out of bed. He took me to Glennallen and the mechanic at the "hub" had a puller that took the pulley off the old power steering pump. Bought a couple new belts. Tom stopped at Chuck Z. I put the pump on when I got home, pushed a little snow. Glad it's fixed. Tom Smayda came up to pull the pump in his well. Lauren and Emily stayed with us. They all had supper with us.

Friday, March 13, 1992—sunny, 20° to 32°. Rest of snow slid off house roof. Re-broke trail to lake and pumped water for house. Lots overflow on lake. Went looking for wolf track on Lake Louise Road. No luck. Saw 2-3 fox track.

Saturday, March 14, 1992—sunny, 0° to 22°. Tom H. came over. We made a couple spacers and found a bolt to repair his snowgo. Went to Odden's. Brought Mary's flowers there. Someone got two caribou east of here.

Sunday, March 15, 1992—sunny, 0° to 26°. Sylvia went to Anchorage with Bonnie W. Bonnie had a moose fall down in front of her car. She thought it was hurt, for me to call F & G. I looked but couldn't find the moose. Art W. wanted me to come push snow for him. Tough going, but got it done.

Monday, March 16, 1992—partly cloudy, 10° to 32°. Ran trap line. Lots marten and some fox tracks. Lots marten hanging around bait station near east west seismic. Wolf tracks in trail just north of there. Went past or around all my sets, left trail at first meat pole hill. Three legged fox has been working bait station there. Went on out to turn around at West "Y." He fooled around there and went on north 100 yards to a Manning set for wolf and put a rear foot in it. He was dead but not frozen hard. A wolf had walked up within a few feet and looked at fox and then cut across the west trail. A wolf had walked on that trail east towards the jct. to very close to where I had a wolf in a trap for a while (that one pulled out) then he turned around and left. Saw a moose run away from the trail and other moose and boo tracks. Skinned and boarded the fox. Put the wolf trap on to boil tonight in logwood dye and spruce bow tips. Turned fox pelt before bedtime.

Tuesday, March 17, 1992—mostly sunny, 5° to 30°. Set one Manning at Allen's tree where wolf dug down to blood from the wolf I killed in trap 1/13/92. Waded snow waist deep. Had to break my way with hard upward and short steps to push my way to set trap. Set three more wolf traps at "Y." Wolf had been walking all around the area. Some more moose, boo, fox, and marten sets. A few ptarmigan also. Cut some beaver trapping poles and brought them home to use for road trapping. Ed Farmer is back from job on slope. Sylvia baked rolls and bread (sourdough).

Wednesday, March 18, 1992—sunny, cloudy, windy evening, 4° to 28°. Visited at store. Read some. Welded a loop on some grader blade for a trap drag. Witched for steel at Art Wikles. He's putting up a large building.

Thursday, March 19, 1992—very windy most of the night. Snow moving in from south, 26° to 34°. Ran trap line dragging fox carcass (till rope broke). Made Manning set in wolf trail on first meat pole hill. Seeing fox and marten track today. Marten have a snow cave dug at the moose head bait pile. Had a red fox in wolf set at Allen's tree. Went on out to "Y" turn around. Fox had been there. Snowing and snowed harder before I got home. Remade Helfrich wolf set across from tree caught big wolf at. Mixed gas and filled snowgo when I got home. Skinned fox and put it on stretcher.

Friday, March 20, 1992—sunny, cloudy evening, 6° to 32°. Read a lot. Lou and his wife are up for ski touring at KROA and boo hunting this weekend. They visited awhile. Tom H. brought a movie out from Glennallen for us to watch.

Saturday, March 21, 1992—sunny, -3° to 29°. Boo on our lake. Read and brushed a fox pelt. Visited at KROA. They had a ski touring meet there. Art W. was flying this area of Nelchina River with his plane.

Sunday, March 22, 1992—mostly cloudy, 7° to 30°. Lou and Sandy were here. Ran trap line. Wolves were on it a little ways near highway. Lou and Sandy came back later and I went with him east of here. We found some boo and shot one and dragged it up here and loaded it to go home to Eagle River. A mink and lots fox and coyote tracks around all the boo gut piles east of here. We went over to Nelchina for a hamburger this evening. Sam Kenny Phil and Arlene (?) were there.

Monday, March 23, 1992—partly cloudy, 24° to 34°. Built a fire in garage and thawed snow loose from the roof. Put plow on and piled it up to the north. Tom H. visited. Brushed some fur out. The ice softened up from truck parking place in garage and I carried it outside. Shoveled snow away from all the mail box's and shoveled through the two snow berms along the road to make a snowgo crossing. Wind is strong. Gusts this evening.

Tuesday, March 24, 1992—sunny, 10° to 34°. Visited at store. Lunch at Mannings. Snow slid off roof at Cole's, blocked driveway. Tried to push it away and got stuck Left truck as we had to go to Huddleston's for dinner. Melanie Cole drove us over there. Chuck Zimbicki was there for dinner also. Tom H. brought us home.

Wednesday, March 25, 1992—partly cloudy, 18° to 38°. Ed brought his D6 CAT through our place. I put in some No 2. diesel. We went over to Cole's and he pulled my truck out of snow bank. Brakes were frozen up. I went home and he cleaned us their driveway. I ran trap line and made one wolf set very close to hwy. Saw a lynx track near top of hill. Some moose and boo track. No wolves in any of sets. Stopped on some high spots and glassed the country in view. Didn't do much at home. Sylvia went to Palmer with Bonnie W.

Thursday, March 26, 1992—partly cloudy, 8° to 31°. Did some reading. Worked a little on snowgo. Replaced a bad bearing. Discovered another bad bearing.

Friday, March 27, 1992—mostly sunny, 10° to 24°. Went to Chuck's and got bearing for snowgo and put it on.

Saturday, March 28, 1992—mostly sunny, -2° to 24°. Ran trap line. Saw spruce hens, ptarmigan and rabbit tracks. Moose along trail. One really huge one. Five fox and one marten track. A wolf walked around four snares (snow crust will hold them up now) and pushed past one other snare. Nothing in any of wolf sets. Picked up one trap and cut some beaver trapping poles. Limiter strap on snowgo broke and gave me some trouble.

Sunday, March 29, 1992—partly cloudy, light snow all around here, -4° to 20°. Read all morning. Took broken parts off snowgo. Called chuck. He has replacement parts.

Monday, March 30, 1992—mostly cloudy and light snow all day, 12° to 26°. Went to Chuck's and got snowgo parts. On to Glennallen. Visited at Lanegan's Glennallen Sporting Goods. Then to F & G. They were closed. (Seward's Day) Had a bite to eat at Caribou Café. Very poor food. The Brown Bear Road House didn't open while we were in town. When we got home Sylvia helped me put the new limiter strap and front spring for slide suspension. Put on a loaf spring slide cushion also.

Tuesday, March 31, 1992—1" of snow in the night, 16° to 27°. Pulled all wolf traps and snares today. Saw one marten, one fox and tracks two coyote. Coyote tracks were on trail between here and school house. Saw a couple moose. Cut and hauled home some dry spruce poles to use in beaver trapping.

Wednesday, April 1, 1992—sunny, 16° to 36°. Stripped trapping box, rifle case, snowshoes off snowgo and went to near Cache Creek to break a trail to a lake 1/3 mile south. Got stuck in just a few feet. Shoveling machine out, turned it by lifting and came back home. Talked with Sally Johnson, Chris Horvath and a small boy along the trail. Unloaded wolf traps into trap shed. Alaska Dividend Application came and we filled it out. Ed and Sandy walked over. I took two fox pelts out of freezer today on stretcher.

Thursday, April 2, 1992—cloudy, 14° to 36°. We took our Dividend Applications over to Mae's and she witnessed them. We gave her an application and we signed for her. Visited at store. Turned the two fox pelts on the stretchers. Bonnie and Emily took Sylvia to Glennallen. Rudbecks phoned.

Friday, April 3, 1992—sunny, 0° to 25°. Visited with Eddie a little while. Sorted some beaver trapping gear. Started getting ready to do some tanning of fur. Tom and Pete Huddleston stopped for coffee. Reloaded forty 30-06 cartridges for Tom H. Got a case stuck in the resizing die, had a heck of a time getting it out. Made a bolt-nut puller. Drilled out the case head and tapped it for the bolt. Use some heat and WD40.

Saturday, April 4, 1992—sunny, -7° to 24°. Made some brackets to mount traps to poles to trap beaver. Tom, Kim H. and family here for supper.

Sunday, April 5, 1992—sunny, -6° to 27°. Put two fox on stretchers. These have been in the freezer too long. Did more readying. Sylvia visited Mae. Tom H. stopped to pick up the cap and glasses he left here last night. I gave him a couple boxes of shells.

Monday, April 6, 1992—sunny, -3° to 31°. Sylvia went to Glennallen. I brought snow in to melt for tanning water. Tom Dobler visited. I started making some highway duty wolf swivels. Took one fox off the board, turned the other one. Brought a fox and coyote into thaw. Went over to Mannings and reset control on stove.

Tuesday, April 7, 1992—sunny, -4° to 35°. Turned the coyote and fox on boards. Started tanning today. Soaked and relaxed the dry furs and mixed tanning solution and put 23 rats, two beaver tails, one mink, six ermine. Started on some swivels for wolf traps. Tried to fix a trap, no luck welding a broken jaw.

Wednesday, April 8, 1992—sunny, 9° to 32°. Removed two fox from boards and brushed out five fox. Mixed up another batch of tanning solution (need to increase because I had too many pelts in first batch). Went to Mendeltna Chapel (Mae's birthday party). Allen F. is back home from North Slope job.

Thursday, April 9, 1992—sunny, 12° to 38°. Made a jig to bend swivel eyes for wolf swivels. Bent 16 pieces. Went to dump. Saw wolf Joe Virgin picked up off the hwy and put in dump. Wish I could have had a chance to salvage it. Visited Allen for awhile. Went to Tom Dobler's after supper and planned our snowgo trip tomorrow. He caught eight rainbows today.

Friday, April 10, 1992—light snow, cloudy, 24° to 32°. Up early. Met Tom Dobler near Cache Creek. He broke trail and we went north and east to a lake with the beaver lodge on it. Saw wolf tracks on the way. Didn't see any open vent hole on the beaver house. Tom told me of how deep the ice is this year. Maybe ice got so deep the beaver froze out? Tom got stuck turning around, so I turned my machine in place. He broke out nice trail on way back. His machine goes good in deep snow. I got stuck once and ran out of power some times. Ravens feed on gut piles along hwy. We each went our separate ways home. I located the "pelt breaker frame" in the garage. Took the coyote pelt off the board. There is a lot of pitch in the fur. So I'm softening it with "GoJo" and combing the fur. Tom stopped in with some maps to look at. He stayed for supper.

Saturday, April 11, 1992—snow all day (6 inches), 12° to 22°. Tried to work with ermine pelts. Hair slips on three of them. Sylvia pumped water for the house today. Allen, Roxanne and family here for chili. Jim O. phoned from McGrath.

Sunday, April 12, 1992—sunny here, snow in mountains to south of us, -5° to 12°. Plowed snow. Visited at store. Visited Mae and had a nice buffet at her place. Shoveled a little snow. Some breeze today. Can hear plane flying. Hunting wolves? Allen Farmer phoned to tell us of three swans flying about our lake. They landed straight out from our house and in middle of lake. Two resting with heads under their wings, third one keeping watch.

Monday, April 13, 1992—mostly sunny, -15° to 12°. Started "breaking" some of the pelts, one mink, and seven rats. Went to Moosey Boo and tried to widen their driveway-got stuck. Sylvia went to Glennallen. Saw another swan resting on our lake.

Tuesday, April 14, 1992—mostly cloudy, 0° to 30°. Worked at tanning and breaking rat pelts. Sylvia replanted her bedding plants. Visited at store awhile.

Wednesday, April 15, 1992—partly cloudy, 10° to 40°. Worked with the pelts again today. Allen came over to visit and later with a nail-string button hole puzzle. Sylvia started tanning a pair of caribou hocks for hopefully mukluks.

Thursday, April 16, 1992—partly cloudy, 25° to 44°. Turned rat pelts. Allen borrowed nail bar. Made six nail puzzles. Repaired snowplow, for Sandy Dino bank. Cake, strawberries and ice cream at Allen's. Lander's there also. Beautiful full moon came up from behind the mountains.

Friday, April 17, 1992—mostly sunny, 20° to 44°. Did gun cleaning today. Saw a marsh hawk today.

Saturday, April 18, 1992—mostly sunny, 15° to 40°. Dust blowing west off the river most of the day. Spent hours scrubbing the bore of the .22. 338 cleaned up easily. Used 3/8" nut and welded them on the swivel eyes for wolf swivels.

Sunday, April 19, 1992—sunny, 20° to 42°. Went to Wikles and helped with building a small section of his shop wall. Checked Odden's house on way home. Changed oil and air filters on truck. Cloudy this evening.

Monday, April 20, 1992—sunny, snow shrinking noticeably, 20° to 44°. Sylvia went to Glennallen. I visited Allen and Roxanne. Did a lot of small jobs. Started 3 hoops for beaver pelt hangings.

Tuesday, April 21, 1992—partly cloudy, cloudy, light snow, 22° to 42°. Made three willow hoops for beaver pelts. Worked some pitch out of two fox pelts, put a marten pelt to soak in salt brine. Allen visit twice and borrowed some visqueen later. Plowed some softened hard pack snow, sure is a headache.

Wednesday, April 22, 1992—sunny, 24° to 45°. Pushed some hard pack snow off to side. Visited Allen. Pushed more hard pack off. Rinsed salt out of marten pelt. Sewed up a rip in it then put it in tanning solution.

Thursday, April 23, 1992—sunny, 22° to 44°. Didn't do much all day. Shoveled a little snow away from a lean to and hurt my back. Sandy F. plans to close the store. Phoned Nadia to wish her happy birthday, also called Bakers at Delta Jct. Phone got repaired by George today.

Friday, April 24, 1992—sunny, breezy evening, 18° to 40°. Bunch of caribou went west on our lake, short while later 20 of them came back to lake. Lay down and stayed for several hours. Two swans flew in and rested among the boo. Went to store to assess Kim H. problem with her car. Later Sylvia and I brought our crafts home from the store. Then Roxanne called me down to their place. She had driven over two milk crates and had them lodged under her car. Jacked the car up and dug out the remaining crate.

Saturday, April 25, 1992—sunny, 24° to 42°. Removed marten from tanning solution, neutralized it, boarded it, turned it, oiled it and boarded it fur side out. The holes where the ski saddles bolt to the steering spindles on the snowgo were worn out, so I rebuilt them with the acetylene torch and electric welder. Beverly called.

Sunday, April 26, 1992—sunny, 14° to 44°. Quite a few caribou spent time on our lake. Roxanne phoned when she saw a coyote testing the caribou. Unknown if it got one in the trees. Sylvia did laundry. I broke three muskrat pelts and turned the two fox pelts in the salt-relaxing solution. Sylvia goes for walks these days. Put two cross fox pelts in tanning solution.

Monday, April 27, 1992—sunny, cloudy and some breeze, 20° to 42°. Loaded snowgo, sled, gear, stove, stove pipe on trailer. Want to leave from Mill Lake Louise Road and go to trap cabin. Sylvia went to Glennallen.

Tuesday, April 28, 1992—light snow, cloudy, sunny afternoon, 28° to 44°. Started on the work of hooping beaver hides. Cleaned up the wood shop. Ed Farmer kids are on their motorcycle. They have closed the store and took the sign down.

Wednesday, April 29, 1992—snow in night, cloudy, sunny, cloudy evening, 26° to 42°. Some gravel got pushed aside last winter. I shoveled some of it back where it belonged. Drew patterns for new fur stretchers. Stirred furs in tanning solution. Sylvia's birthday today.

Thursday, April 30, 1992—snowed all night (6 inches), 24° to 40°. Plowed our lane. Jack called and wanted his place plowed. They had 12" there. Started getting ready to boil wolf and fox skulls. Shoveled a little snow. Fooled around with the .223 Lyman hand loader. Ted and lady friend visited in evening.

Friday, May 1, 1992—sunny, some snow squalls, 16° to 40°. We left early for Palmer. Went o bank, library and machine shop and left oxygen bottle to be filled. Then onto Anchorage, returned power steering core pump and bought gasket and filter for transmission. Then ate and shopped for groceries, stopped at Pay & Save in Wasilla. Didn't do well there shopping. Went to Palmer. Sylvia got medicine. Nice drive home. Unloaded the truck.

Saturday, May 2, 1992—partly cloudy, 26° to 40°. Worked with fox hides and caribou hocks today. Finished with tanning now. Wrote Nadia. Mary and Kari O. and Carol are here from Fairbanks. We were invited to supper there.

Sunday, May 3, 1992—cloudy all day, 25° to 38°. Turned the two tanned fox pelts on the stretchers. Rigged up a rifle bore sighting box. Fred Rungee visited in afternoon. Mary and Kari O., Carol & Paul Wisdom from Copper Center visited and brought homemade ice cream in evening.

Monday, May 4, 1992—cloudy, 24° to 34°. Made some nail puzzles. Started reshaping ermine and marten - mink stretchers. Sylvia went to Glennallen. Ed borrowed a trowel.

Tuesday, May 5, 1992—cloudy, sunny evening, 26° to 36°. Raked gravel on lane. Worked on new fur stretchers. Jack and Jane Chamberlain were here and had tea and sourdough buns this afternoon.

Wednesday, May 6, 1992—partly cloudy, cloudy and windy, 23° to 34°. Up early, drove to Mile 11, Lake Louise Road. Went west with snowgo and sled and loaded with stove and pipe for trap cabin. Saw fox, boo, wolf tracks. Snow and lakes were frozen hard. Trail was rough sometimes, not bad sometimes. Two swans flew over the trail. An owl was hunting one section along trail. After I left the lake, swamp at end of seismic, I didn't get ½ mile. The snow amongst the trees where I had cut a narrow trail was deep, 2 feet and thawed to the tundra in other places. Skis on sled would run under crust after hitting the walls of the holes in the snow. Came to a place to turn around and I went back out to Lake Louise Road and went home. Sylvia put a perm in Mae's hair. We had brunch with Allen and Roxanne. Put gear away and covered snowgo. Looks rainy or snow this evening.

Thursday, May 7, 1992—cloudy, 24° to 44°. Sylvia didn't feel well all day. Slept a lot also. I got a kink in my back. I read a lot. Shoveled and raked a little gravel, leveling and smoothing around the yard. Kim H. came to get a movie Sylvia taped for her.

Friday, May 8, 1992—sunny, light snow in the night, light snow in evening, 27° to 46°. Did some cutting, gluing and sanding on new fur stretchers. Went to visit Jean and Clem Campbell. They now live in the old Max Hoffman house. Jean is dying of cancer.

Saturday, May 9, 1992—sunny, 22° to 38°. Worked on fur stretchers. Started Suzuki. Went to Allen's—nobody home. Took Sylvia to Tolsona Lake Lodge for rib eye steak. Saw a Taverner's Canada goose along the highway, between Mendeltna Chapel and Wood's Creek.

Sunday, May 10, 1992—partly cloudy, 24° to 34°. Loafed and read most of day. Theresa and kids phoned. (It's our anniversary.)

Monday, May 11, 1992—partly cloudy, cloudy, 16° to 42°. Tested the truck rear end for free play. Visited Allen and Ed F. Allen stopped and had coffee. Worked on marten stretchers today. Sylvia went to Glennallen.

Tuesday, May 12, 1992—cloudy, snow in mountains south of us, 32° to 42°. Went to Allen's to thread a brass rod, his tap and die set is missing. Shaped and sanded on marten stretchers. The beaver on our lake is now coming out on top of the ice. Lots of little birds feeding in our area. Some are entering the bird house in our yard. I heard a brown thrasher today. Ed Farmer came over to get some nails and a caulking gun.

Wednesday, May 13, 1992—sunny, cloudy, snow, 34° to 44°. Worked on a platform to access books on the shelves in the stairwell going upstairs. Built a wooden card index file of thin wood. Put two coats oil finish on it. Cut out the card dividers. Saw mature eagle fly by house. Also eagle sitting on ice near south shore of our lake. Beaver is out on ice sometimes. Brown thrashers are singing.

Thursday, May 14, 1992—sunny, partly cloudy, 34° to 46°. Went out to woodshop to put hinges on wood file box I made yesterday when into the yard drove Franz Ackermann. He's now of Bellingham, Washington (formerly from Leader, MN). We spent the day visiting. Drove up the Lake Louise Road and visited Dawsons. Didn't get to show Franz any caribou. He will stay the night.

Friday, May 15, 1992—windy, worked on stretchers.

Saturday, May 16, 1992—cloudy, short blizzard, sunny, 26° to 32°. Did a little bit in wood shop. Ed Farmer borrowed a tool for a little while.

Sunday, May 17, 1992—mostly sunny, 12° to 41°. Worked on the fur stretchers.

Monday, May 18, 1992—sunny, 20° to 48°. Put two coats of tung oil on stretchers and sanded them. Had lunch with Allen and Roxanne. Allen borrowed a brazing rod and flux. Sylvia came home from Glennallen and we cleaned the house chimney.

Tuesday, May 19, 1992—sunny, 34° to 49°. Two swans and some ducks in and near water at edge of ice on lake. Saw a coyote come from trees onto lake. Birds left the area. Coyote trotted across lake to our side. Boiled wolf and fox skulls today. Worked on fur stretchers again. Repaired a cupboard door. Visited at Bartley's in evening.

Wednesday, May 20, 1992—sunny, partly cloudy, evening, 34° to 50°. Worked on fur stretchers. Put a "T" in waterline so Sylvia can water green house and strawberries. Checked our well, some work to do there. Put the boiled skulls on top of storage trailer. Poured the "juice" in a 5-gallon can for Allen's bait. Sylvia did laundry.

Thursday, May 21, 1992—sunny, cloudy evening, 34° to 54°. Did a little more on fur stretchers, stair well, shooting accessories. Cleaned distributor on truck. Phillip Johnson and Eunice, wife, from California visited. Allen F. went with us to KROA to N.M. Corp meeting. We went to dump on way home.

Friday, May 22, 1992—partly cloudy, 36° to 58°. We went to Glennallen and got Sylvia's Medicare (aid) application in. Had a trap movie copied. Went to F & G and got subsistence application to hunt caribou. Paid electric bill. Visited Darrel G. Saw grayling in one small creek.

Saturday, May 23, 1992—mostly sunny, 40° to 64°. Visited Allen. Sandy went with me to school house to get some papers copied. The copier at Snowshoe Lake is broken. Did some jobs, mounted gun case on ATV. Went to Henry and Sally's for music, strawberries and angel food cake.

Sunday, May 24, 1992—mostly sunny, 37° to 62°. Put saw dust in some nesting boxes. Worked on shooting table. Philip and Eunice for coffee. The Smayda family visited for a while. A cow moose walked west along south shore of our lake. She still had a big belly.

Monday, May 25, 1992—light showers, partly cloudy, 40° to 58°. Little jobs with wood shop, stretchers, target shooting. Visited Billmans. Flicker flew into our window, it survived. Lots of ducks on open water. Ice is almost out. Allen picked up a nail in rear tire on his ATV. He brought it over and I helped put a plug in it.

Tuesday, May 26, 1992—shower in the night, 48° to 56°. We went to Palmer and Wasilla. Some grocery, shopping, talked to a couple gun smiths about a problem 22 barrel. Saw several moose, one with a baby moose. Saw Shari Kurt's cousin. Got a load of gas and oxygen. Ice is out on the lake.

Wednesday, May 27, 1992—partly cloudy, 36° to 56°. Visited Allen, Roxanne, Mae & Lucky & Mary there. Serviced ATV, unloaded gas. Made two tire repair plug inserters. Sylvia worked in greenhouse.

Thursday, May 28, 1992—mostly sunny, 38° to 55°. Went up on Slide Mountain to second seismic. Looked for trap, no luck. Flickers are courting. Also ducks and loons. .22 barrel is no good. Will try to order a new one. Did more research in evening. Called Darrel Gerry.

Friday, May 29, 1992—mostly sunny, 36° to 58°. Sylvia planted potatoes. I installed a valve to access water to garden. Hauled tiller to garden. Took snow plow frame off truck. Sure stiff and sore today.

Saturday, May 30, 1992—hard rain, partly cloudy, showers, 39° to 54°. Shoveled some dirt. Started the foot platform in stairwell. Cut out, sanded and sealed it. Neighborhood kids are driving motorcycles and 4-wheelers through yard.

Sunday, May 31, 1992—cool, sunny, rain in evening, 40° to 52°. Put varithane on stairwell and platform. Sylvia got a box of potatoes ready for Darrel. Brother Jerry phoned.

Monday, June 1, 1992—light rain, mostly cloudy, 40° to 51°. Sylvia went to Glennallen, gave Darrel some stuff. I finished stair well. Laced 3 beaver hides onto willow hoops. Sylvia planted more garden. Mae visited. I visited Allen a little while. Shot .223's. Hunted for padlock, keys.

Tuesday, June 2, 1992—partly cloudy, rain, cloudy, 44° to 50°. Removed TV antenna from roof and put it in attic and hooked new coaxial cable to it. TV comes in excellent. Made up some hose connections. Started enlarging the cooking ring on single burner on camp stove. Drove ATV to Cache Creek—too much water to safely cross so came back home. Got home just as it rained. Got stuck several times. Found one nice moose horn from maybe 50" bull. Tried to find the mating horn. Sylvia went to a ladies luncheon and baby shower for Kim H. baby.

Wednesday, June 3, 1992—light rain in night, partly cloudy all day, 42° to 58°. Sylvia sewed Swede sand bags for me. Then we picked the trash from our mile of highway. Finished the wire cooking ring on small Coleman stove. Started on some 4 legged stools. Kim stopped to pay me.

Thursday, June 4, 1992—cloudy, 40° to 52°. Worked on stools all day. Back and hips sore today.

Friday, June 5, 1992—cloudy, partly cloudy, 39° to 51°. Allen, Roxanne, Ellie here for breakfast. Stripped a washing machine. Sylvia helped glue the three stools together. Smashed all the aluminum cans we picked up along our mile of hwy. Lake is beautiful this evening. Small scoters courting now. Two cow moose walked thru yard lately.

Saturday, June 6, 1992—partly cloudy, some showers went by on each side, 38° to 63°. Cut some brush near garden and turn around near well. Put screws in stool legs. Sewed a rip in a tarp. Phoned Paul for his birthday (June 9). Went to Odden's for a barbeque and homemade ice cream.

Sunday, June 7, 1992—mostly sunny, warm, 39° to 63°. Fixed several broken and problem things. Sylvia mowed lawn and watered it. Planted more garden.

Patti Landers came and "looked at" a couple stools I had built. We took canopy
off truck bed. Hauled garbage to dump. Found some "goodies" to haul home.
Beaver and ducks and swan activity on lake. Allen, Roxanne, Pat and Pattie saw
a sow grizzly and cub on a hill on north side of Slide Mt. I phoned Jim O. out at
McGrath.

Monday, June 8, 1992—mostly sunny, 34° to 66°. Did some small jobs. Fixed
leak at fitting at garden. Gathered some gear to hunt black bear. Took gun
order forms to Mary O.

Tuesday, June 9, 1992—mostly sunny, 39° to 66°. Allen and I left very early to
RCA site area to hunt black bear, no luck. Saw quite a few caribou, four moose
cows and calves. One ptarmigan came back home. Started to change oil and
filter on the truck, wrong parts. Pat Landers is to bring parts out tonight. Allen
came over and I went to Jerky Lake and we fished for rainbow trout. I caught
three and he caught eight or ten. Saw caribou there, had a good time. Dave
Johnson was fishing there also.

Wednesday, June 10, 1992—sunny, 46° to 70°. Went to Allen and Roxanne's
for sourdough pancakes. Picked up filter for automatic transmission at his
place. Came home and installed it. Serviced the truck, even washed the
windows. Cow moose and calf escaped the bear. Allen and Ed scared it off with
a few shots last night. Paddled the canoe to that area but didn't see anything. I
unloaded ATV and modified the blocking for it in pickup bed. Swept garage
floor. Emptied sawdust from bag on saw table. Filled with sand and sewed
opening shut on the leather sand bags for shooting that Sylvia had sewed for me.
Modified the bench rest so I could Velcro the sand bag to it. We got screen
door down and put it on Artic entry door.

Thursday, June 11, 1992—sunny, some breeze, hot, 50° to 74°. Took log tongs
back, visited Allen. He was here 2-3 times. Got some salmon eggs. Fixed well
cover. Fertilized rhubarb and lilac bush. Cleaned up some trash. Paper started
coming again. Made a .22 cartridge board. Sorted and boxed old cartridges.
Sylvia washed windows, floor and did laundry. Moose cow and calf spend time
on south side of our lake.

Friday, June 12, 1992—thin clouds, windy in afternoon, evening was mostly
sunny (never really gets dark this time of year), 48° to 74°. Did some fixing on
snowgo trailer. Fooled around with .22 rifles-both are junk. Tom H and T.J.
visited in afternoon. Can't find my valve grinding compound. Cow moose still
on south side of lake. Saw a goose take off this morning.

Saturday, June 13, 1992—mostly sunny, 52° to 70. Polished Remington .22
barrel, its shot and no good. Cleaned up garage. Fertilized strawberries. Sorted

American Rifleman magazines.

Sunday, June 14, 1992—partly cloudy, rain in evening, 54° to 66°. Fooled around with reloading. Did more research. Visited Lucky and Mary B. Cow moose and calf walked up our lane to house yard. Our flickers are gone!! Kestrels didn't come back.

Monday, June 15, 1992—cloudy, rained a few times, 46° to 56°. Sylvia went to Glennallen. I felt sick all day. Repaired a small clamp I found in dump. More reloading research. Got a referral reply on .22 barrel. Jason B brought us lake trout from Crosswind Lake.

Tuesday, June 16, 1992—cloud and light rains all day, 43° to 50°. Made a .224 pilot for cartridge trimmer. Allen came over and we loaded a bunch of .338 for him. I cleaned and reworked the drop primer area on the reloader. A flicker landed on box out front.

Wednesday, June 17, 1992—partly cloud, windy afternoon, 40° to 56°. Didn't do much today. Put varithane on small box. Visited Allen a few minutes. Harvested rhubarb. Young ravens around. Mature eagle hunting along our hillside. Saw moose cow and her calf on south side of our lake.

Thursday, June 18, 1992— partly cloudy, shower, very windy, 38° to 60°. Visited Allen. Sylvia mowed lawn. Did small jobs. Some reloading. Tom H. came over. Helped him with wire for his truck. Eagle hunts our hill every day.

Friday, June 19, 1992—partly cloudy, 40° to 60°. Visited Allen and Roxanne. Four of Mae's grandchildren are here from North Carolina Sylvia watered the lawn. Did some small jobs, loafed a lot. Went to Kim and Tom's for supper, his brothers Mark and Peter were also there.

Saturday, June 20, 1992—partly cloudy, 38° to 68°. Worked some on drawers for bed. Tumbled more cases. Tumbler makes them clean, shiny, look good. Sore, headaches today. More research on loading.

Sunday, June 21, 1992—started raining in the night and rained all day, quit about supper time, 42° to 52°. Worked on 4 cartridge case loading blocks and one block to hold cases for four 5 shoot groups of 3 different loads in each group. Ran a batch of brass through the tumbler also. Nadia phoned, sure great to talk to her. Sylvia picked the first tomato of this season. Robbie stopped by for a couple min on his way to Ms. Cole's.

Monday, June 22, 1992—partly cloudy, light shower, 40° to 54°. Sylvia went to Glennallen. I worked on loading blocks. Had a couple failures-finally made them (two) out of fir. Wrecked one other one. Visited Allen. Chuck borrowed the dump gate key. The young squirrels are invading us. Tom Smayda came up to unplug sewer line at the house he is renting out. Lauren and Emily were here for a couple hours.

Tuesday, June 23, 1992—cloudy, rain most of day, 40° to 44°. Put another coat of varithane on loading blocks. Sylvia and I weeded the garden just before rain. Saw a moose cow swim 2/3 length of lake. Deprimed 300 mil brass in an hour with Lyman Tong Tool.

Wednesday, June 24, 1992—cloudy, showers, 40° to 50°. Tom Dobler here 6:30 AM. We ate breakfast and went to Anchorage. He wanted to pickup a truck of his and take it home. I did some shopping around town and some in Eagle River. Trip wasn't too bad, some rain and construction areas. Some item I couldn't find or were too expensive.

Thursday, June 25, 1992—partly cloudy, some showers, 40° to 54°. Small clusters of ducks on lake. Flickers were here today. Did some small jobs plus made a foot rest to fit the truck for Sylvia's feet. Finished some shelving at reloading bench. Returned some borrowed eggs to Allen and Roxanne.

Friday, June 26, 1992—mostly sunny, 40° to 56°. Sylvia harvested rhubarb today, fertilized green house plants, mowed the lawn. I did jobs around the place. Allen is building a neat trailer for his 4 wheeler. A caribou crossed our lane last night.

Saturday, June 27, 1992—partly cloudy most of day, 42° to 56°. Fertilized the raspberries. Started fitting drawers to bed frame. Finished shelves at loading bench. Made beaver stretching hoop. Made a tool to remove lids from 5-gallon plastic buckets. Tom Dobler brought up a red salmon and had supper (bean soup). Borrowed a ½ drill bit to ventilate a refrigerator he is converting to a smoker.

Sunday, June 28, 1992—partly cloudy, 38° to 73°. Some breeze, lots of mosquitoes. Adj. brakes on ATV. Loafed a lot. Tom D. stopped in. Also Jim Lewis from Chugiak. The little tree swallow babes seem to have flown the bird house. Young robins flying. A flicker spent time at flicker box last evening.

Monday, June 29, 1992—partly cloudy, sunny, cloudy, breezy all afternoon, 52° to 75°. Cut out the parts and put two coats of finish on for a gun cradle to be used when cleaning the bores, installing scopes, sights, bore sighting etc. Repaired the broken handle on grey box and put longer screws to hold handles. Mae was here for coffee. Allen had some pancakes and coffee. Sylvia and Mae went to Glennallen. Bonnie and Emily stopped by. Sylvia and I weeded the garden. The river sure is roaring this evening. Lots of ducks on lake. Swans cruise around sometimes. Painted oil on air tight stove to arrest rust.

Tuesday, June 30, 1992—partly cloudy, 50° to 68°. Finished gun cradle. Don Culp visited, game him four slabs of tanned beaver tail hide. T. Dobler stopped by with a new ½ drill bit. He timed my truck also. We went to KROA. Visited with Al Smith. Strong breeze from the west this evening.

Wednesday, July 1, 1992—mostly sunny, some breeze, 48° to 64°. Lots of mosquitoes, dragonflies. Small whirlwind tired to get started on lake in some lily pads while Allen and David were here. Sure chased the ducks out of there. Voles (probably) took most of Sylvia's transplants out of garden. She replanted with cups around them and watered garden and lawn. I did some small repairs and started more gun cradles.

Thursday, July 2, 1992—sunny, thin cloudy, some breeze, 52° to 80°. Lots of bugs. Finished sanding the four gun cradles and put two coats of tung oil on them. Some tung oil went bad (jelled). Cleaned and prepared some .243 brass for resizing to .22-250. Shoveled some gravel. Sylvia did laundry and washed my wool winter clothes.

Friday, July 3, 1992—partly cloudy, some breeze, 50° to 80°. Watered the trees around the house. Glued sheared sheepskin to forks of gun cradles. Moved water hauling tank. Went to dump and got materials for lead melting pot frame. Stopped at Billman's on way home and borrowed a tap and die set. Cut and welded up the lead melting frame. Now I need to hook up the propane to it. It looks good.

Saturday, July 4, 1992—partly cloudy and cloudy, some rain ant thunder nearby, 52° to 70°. Sylvia watered lawn. I worked on lead melting pot and shot gun cleaning cable. Bugs still bad. Visited Lucky to borrow a pipe tape, he didn't have one. Smaydas up from Palmer and got 20 salmon from fish wheel and visited us for awhile. Allen F. had supper with us. Talked about putting out bear bait on trail above and east of Little Nelchina and on shoulder of Slide Mountain.

Sunday, July 5, 1992—mostly cloudy, shower in evening, 53° to 60°. Sylvia watered lawn again today. I put gun cradles together. Went to dump. Finished two of shot gun plastic coated cable bore cleaners. Ducks take off from lake and swing along side of our hill-here in front of our house-and drop back to lake and land. They have the after burners turned on when they go by.

Monday, July 6, 1992—mostly cloudy, 47° to 60°. Finished the plastic coated cable rifle and shot gun pull thru cleaners. Put knob on brass slotted shotgun cleaning rod. Replaced handle on garbage can. Allen F. visited. I hoed ½ garden. Hilled the potatoes and transplanted a few fill in raspberries.

Tuesday, July 7, 1992—cloudy, some sun, showers, 44° to 55°. We went to Palmer, Wasilla. Shopped for supplies and medicine, got most of what we needed. Saw Mae at Pinnacle Mountain. Saw one moose in highway. Got back after 8:00 PM. Unloaded things. UPS had tried to deliver package. Jim O. called if package had come.

Wednesday, July 8, 1992—mostly sunny, 45° to 60°. Did small jobs. Fixed Case trimmer. 110F Savage .22-250 came today. Clem brought one rear scope base from Glennallen for me. Allen F. visited. KROA unloaded a pickup at my loading ramp. Chuck F. paid for gas and sanding belts. A black bear pursued a woman to roof of her cabin located 15 mile east of here. On roof bear killed and consumed the woman. When husband and help with guns got back to cabin, they killed the bear.

Thursday, July 9, 1992—mostly sunny, some breeze, 43° to 58°. Story about woman and bear in newspaper today. Allen and Roxanne here for coffee. I put a scope on the .22-250 and shot it 25 times. Sure is a joy to shoot. Was fire forming brass for .22-250 cartridges. Went to Allen and Roxanne's for supper and fresh peach pie. Cool this evening.

Friday, July 10, 1992—partly cloudy, 45° to 60°. Allen and I loaded our 4-wheelers and went to gun sight. Went to Sailor Creek, then Southlake then down pass creek and Alfred Creek to Clay Hill which has slid and blocked the trail. Back to another Creek. We went east and north to a pass then thru the mountains. Very beautiful. Allen found a moose horn along the creek. There lots of small waterfalls. Then we started for Ballanger Pass. There Allen spotted a grizzly ahead of us. We went to "Top of the World" and saw it running in the valley floor, a huge Toklat griz. Then on out to hwy, load up and go home. A very fine day. Rudbecks got back today.

Saturday, July 11, 1992—mostly cloudy and showers, 49° to 55°. Rudbecks here for breakfast. Cleaned guns. Lapped muzzle of .338. Bonnie Wikle had us and Rudbecks there for supper.

Sunday, July 12, 1992—cloudy and showers, 46° to 56°. Visited Lucky. Gave him some cartridges. Cleaned guns. Put paste wax on outside. Removed from stocks to do this. Back started giving me trouble.

Monday, July 13, 1992—partly sunny, showers from the northwest, 48° to 64°. Allen came over and loaded 65 30-06 cartridges. David Eastman came over later. Sylvia and Mae went to Glennallen. Dan and Jason B. came to borrow movies. I serviced the Suzuki 4 x 4 and washed the last trips mud off.

Tuesday, July 14, 1992—mostly cloudy, shower late evening, 46° to 59°. Bob and Karen visited in morning. Fred and Ann Marolf from Motley, Minnesota are visiting. We talked most of day and into late evening. Showed them around the place and he took pix.

Wednesday, July 15, 1992—rain all night, showers, lots of rain in afternoon, 46° to 58°. Fred and Ann left in mid afternoon. My back is really bad.

Thursday, July 16, 1992—rain all night and showers all day, about 3/4" rain. Back is real sore. Fooled around with reloading stuff. Tried out the swager for small rifle military primer pockets. It works well. Heated some .22-250 cases in oven to dry them out, must have left them in too long and too hot for they turned dark. Bob and Karn visited in afternoon. Lloyd R. called to offer us some salmon.

Friday, July 17, 1992—rain in night, cloudy, partly cloudy in evening, 45° to 62°. Three black bears seen last evening and this morning. One killed. Two griz all between here and Glennallen. Sylvia and Rudbecks saw the one black. I loaded and shot 15 light loads. They didn't group to well. Sylvia visited all around the neighborhood. Some of the kids came over. Darrel phoned—needed to talk, then called to offer some bear meat.

Saturday, July 18, 1992—mostly sunny, 45° to 62°. Sylvia mowed lawn and replanted some garden and hilled potatoes. I did some things around here. Back is some better. A man lost a bolt out of his boat trailer hitch and got one from me. Allen called to say he was bringing desert over.

Sunday, July 19, 1992—partly cloudy, shower in evening, 48° to 60°. Bob and Karen brought Dennis, Addie, Peter and Gary over for a visit. They didn't do very good at Chitna dipping for salmon. Allen came over to plan a order to Gander Mountain. I rebuilt and renewed the primer arms on the press. Planned and put together a "stuck case in die remover."

Monday, July 20, 1992—partly cloudy, one hard rain, 48° to 60°. Built four fore end stands for shooting benches. Straightened the expander, decapper rods in two rifle dies. Loaded 12 rounds and fired them here at home, they shot well. A grizzly was seen crossing the road 3/8 mile west of here.

Tuesday, July 21, 1992—partly cloudy, light shower, 45° to 58°. Visited Rudbecks. Allen and Roxanne visited here. Plan to go to Homer. Did a few things here. Sylvia did laundry. We went for a drive up Lake Louise Road. Visited Leona D. Cleaned rifle. Reformed .243 brass to .22-250, didn't quite finish. Measured off 25 yards, 50 yards, and 100 yards at gravel pit.

Wednesday, July 22, 1992—mostly cloudy all day. Finished preparing and then loaded 20 cartridge cases. Loaded shooting gear in truck and went to gravel pit. Set up target and bench. Shot 25 times and came back home. Sylvia gave Sandy F. some garden produce.

Thursday, July 23, 1992—mostly cloudy, some sun, 42° to 60°. Started putting the drawers for the bed together. Got seven put together. Robbie Farmer visited in evening.

Friday, July 24, 1992—partly cloudy, 44° to 62°. We finished putting drawers for the bed together. I put one coat of varithane on inside of drawers and two coats on fronts of the 12 of them. Smayda's were up to clean up yard and heat their well. They visited here. Gave Lisa a quilt rack. Allen stopped for a minute on their way to Wasilla. Robby F. was over a half dozen times. Sylvia and I went over to watch him shoot his bow and visit his folks a few min. Annealed 20 -.22-250 brass.

Saturday, July 25, 1992—rain started in the night and quit about 2:00 PM, 48° to 60°. Robbie visited. Put another coat of varithane on drawer fronts. Rest of afternoon and evening is just beautiful.

Sunday, July 26, 1992—mostly sunny, 50° to 62°. Built small night shelves for each side of bed, put one coat of varithane on them. Loaded two transfer cases and took them to Billmans. Visited there. Went to dump. Picked some pipe fittings and oil heater carburetor for repairs.

Monday, July 27, 1992—sunny, 48° to 60°. Sylvia went to Glennallen. I did a few small jobs. Allen visited. Went to Snowshoe Lake and had some copies made. Not good luck at that. Beaut of an evening.

Tuesday, July 28, 1992—cloudy, partly cloudy, windy in afternoon, 46° to 60°. Hoed the garden. Welded fitting on lead pot LP burner. Put drawers in bed. Mounted shelves on wall. Cut some weeds. Picked up all pieces of someone's vent cover from camper. Chamberlains gave us two 5-gallon buckets of salmon. We filleted, packaged and put them in freezer. Supper at Bob and Karn's. Loaded 28 development loads for .22-250. Military planes low overhead one chasing the other. Military convoy also.

Wednesday, July 29, 1992—mostly sunny, breezy morning, 40° to 64°. Went to gravel pit in the morning and shot rifle. Came home and built holder-dispenser for large rolls of freezer wrap paper and plastic.

Thursday, July 30, 1992—cloudy, shower in evening, 43° to 54°. Spent all morning calling F.B Insurance in Des Moines, Iowa and Medicaid in Anchorage. Decided to cash out insurance policy. Made two kinetic bullet pullers. Cleaned rifle. Re-bolted license plate on pickup. Put tung oil on roll dispenser for freezer paper.

Friday, July 31, 1992—rain, cloudy, partly cloudy, nice evening, 42° to 54°. Company all morning. Visited Allen. Used heat to loosen screws holding scope on rifle. Switched scopes on rifles. Loaded some more .22-250. Rudbecks here again tonight to watch the Olympics. Phoned order to Gander Mountain.

Saturday, August 1, 1992—cloudy, rain, cloudy, 40° to 57°. Sylvia went with Rudbecks to fish wheel. Will smoke these fish. I repaired a corner on a cooler. Put a replacement handle in the hand cultivator I found at dump. Haven't felt well all day.

Sunday, August 2, 1992—sunny, beaut of a day, some breeze in afternoon, 42° to 62°. Went to gravel pit and shot .338 + 22-250. Found some shaggy mane and chicken of the woods mushrooms. Did a lot of resizing and neck reaming of the .243 cases to make 22-250. Still having pressure problems. Hope this alleviates the problem. Went to ballgame and picnic at highway camp gravel pit.

Monday, August 3, 1992—cloudy, partly cloudy, 40° to 54°. Sylvia canned smoked salmon (32 pints). I built and put on different hold downs for cab over camper. Most of neighbors are stiff and sore from yesterday's ball game.

Tuesday, August 4, 1992—mostly sunny, cloudy evening, some breeze, 42° to 62°. A two or three year old black bear was in our front yard, a few feet from picture window as I walked out of bedroom when I got up this morning. I phoned Allen and Sylvia phoned Rudbecks. It went west to Allen's sawmill. Roxanne saw it there. I tracked it that far and gave up. Had breakfast with Allen and Roxanne. Did some small jobs. Shot a nuisance squirrel. Picked some mushrooms. Allen came over in eve and we refilled some small propane tanks. Checked Charlie's storage shed. Visited with Ed F. a couple minutes.

Wednesday, August 5, 1992—cloudy and light showers, 50° to 55°. Allen F. stopped by to ask Sylvia to look at some green peas. Robbie visited a little while. Karn and friend Lisa visited and picked corn, mushrooms. Loaded a few cartridges. Read some. Got truck ready to go to town.

Thursday, August 6, 1992—cloudy, fog, rain, sunny, 46° to 60°. Went to Palmer-Wasilla. Visited Lisa S. and girls. Got some of our shopping done in Wasilla then back to Palmer for groceries and stopped at Pinnacle Mountain for gas and visit Mae.

Friday, August 7, 1992—light rain, sun, cloudy, 48° to 60°. Visited Lucky, Allen. Made a lead filled hammer. Went to Bartley's, got some copies and harvest ticket, a duck stamp.

Saturday, August 8, 1992—cloudy, partly cloudy, 50° to 61°. Visited Billman. Went to dump. Shot .338 at gravel pit. Shot some excellent groups. Haven't felt well all day. Resized, primed and trimmed 40 .338 cases.

Sunday, August 9, 1992—mostly cloudy, 51° to 61°. Finished loading .338 cartridges. Got gear ready to go sheep hunting, but I don't feel well. Lucky and Digger ready to hunt. Allen and Ed going hunting. Mae was here for supper.

Monday, August 10, 1992—mostly sunny, 50° to 60°. Finished packing gear, bought plane tickets by phone. Went to Squaw Creek looking for sheep. No luck. Lots of hunters. Digger's friend shot a boo. Saw another hunter with a boo. Allen's group saw grizzly bears on way in. Greg got a horse stuck in a mud hole. I came home, washed mud off truck and ATV.

Tuesday, August 11, 1992—partly cloudy, rain in evening, 43° to 55°. Repaired some gear. Beverly phoned, nice to talk to her. Repaired rear window in truck. Made a gunsmith hammer with 1/2" copper tube and T fitting cap and fill with lead-nice. Allen visited with sheep hunting story - gave us some delicious sheep brisket. Re-worked burner for lead pot. Shot a squirrel last night and this morning.

Wednesday, August 12, 1992—partly cloudy, breeze from east, 44° to 55°. Lots ducks feeding in lake. Sylvia saw a swan this morning. Tried to lap a rifle bore and no luck. Started a goose flag decoy. Fred and Ann Marolf visited this afternoon and evening. Rudbecks dropped in a few minutes.

Thursday, August 13, 1992—partly cloudy, very nice warm day. Marolf's left in the middle of the morning. Nice to have them visit. Shot another squirrel. Put tarp covered "porch" roof on snowgo part of wood shed. Visited Allen, gave him and Ed each "hunters mirrors" Sylvia had a spell of not feeling good. Slept lots today. Doing laundry this evening.

Friday, August 14, 1992—partly cloudy, sunny, beaut of a day, 41° to 62°. Started on "flying" goose decoys. Then hung the door to the wood shop so it opens from outside and to the left. Lots and lots of company. Tom Dobler is back. Denny Eastman brought Lloyd Griffith and three other up the Alcan Highway. Karn and Bob were over. Allen F. brought a jar of currant jelly. Visited with Ed a couple of minutes. Sylvia, Karn and I went to dump area and each picked 2/3 to ¾ of plastic buckets of currants.

Saturday, August 15, 1992—partly cloudy, beaut of a day, 38° to 58°. Worked on woodshop windows. Cut out all goose decoys. Visited Allen. Rudbecks here. Bob took small propane stove home to try out. Allen, Kyle, Ellie here for supper. Went with Allen to see about using a trail to Fortress Mountains. No Luck. Glassed for moose.

Sunday, August 16, 1992—partly cloudy, sunny, cloudy, showers, 41° to 54°. Worked on goose decoys. Sylvia went to a baby shower for Karen Mailly. Mary O, Kari, and Ruth are at Snowshoe now. Went to supper there.

Monday, August 17, 1992—partly cloudy, 39° to 54°. Sylvia and Mae went to Glennallen. I worked on goose decoys. Weeded some in garden. Shot two squirrels. Tom H. borrowed some T50 staples.

Tuesday, August 18, 1992—partly cloudy to cloudy, some breeze, 40° to 55°. Painted the dowels for goose decoy wings and painted the supports flat black color. Went to Tom Huddleston's and helped him and Allen build a water storage room. We got the second floor and four walls up and rafters and sheeting on. Sure tired tonight. Can smell Mount Spur volcano eruption tonight.

Wednesday, August 19, 1992—partly cloudy, smoky tonight, 41° to 56°. Shot a porcupine and gave it to Morey Secondchief. Shot a squirrel. George ? visited. Some people looking for a home to buy stopped by. Ed F. borrowed a propane regulator. Went to Tom H. and helped him finish his water storage shed. T.J., his son, helped a lot. Sylvia is sick with flu today.

Thursday, August 20, 1992—partly cloudy, volcanic haze, 43° to 54°. Did a few small things, cleaned woodshop. Started a decoupage. Hunted two squirrels and got one. Hoed some of garden. Visited Ed a few moments. Smayda family visited and will stay the night. New school teacher will rent their house. Lisa picked orange delight mushrooms, some corrals. Tom ran boiler in his well. Supper with us. Girls are having fun.

Friday, August 21, 1992—cloudy, light rain in afternoon and evening, 44° to 48°. Smayda's had some visiting and things to do. Then girls visited Afton H. Lisa, Tom, Sylvia and I went to Mile 132 and picked blueberries. A few piles bear pooh. Berries weren't real plentiful. We got maybe three gallons altogether. Show two more squirrels. Allen F. brought over Dall sheep steak from ram Roxanne got. Mary O. and entourage are to visit this evening. I put two coats varithane on the decoupage for Darrel.

Saturday, August 22, 1992—fog, light rain to mostly cloudy, 43° to 47°. Pretty sick with the flu. Rested some. Loaded 40 .223's. Karn and Lisa came over to pickup their mail. They had caught some halibut at Homer. The beaver are starting to build their winter feed pile. Some duck broods are flightless yet.

Sunday, August 23, 1992—cloudy all day, windy in afternoon and evening, 41° to 49°. Took front seat out of truck and put seat cover on it. Put gun rack behind seat of truck. Sylvia started sewing cloth for "flying" goose decoys. Made a wrench for CBS die adjustment lock rings. Cleaned up garage. Karn, Allen and boys, Robbie visited.

Monday, August 24, 1992—cloudy, partly cloudy, light showers, 43° to 61°. Sylvia went to Glennallen. She sewed on cloth for goose decoys. I installed a battery isolator on truck. Borrowed some paint thinner from Allen, he got some "locktite" from me. Denny Eastman bought Wilma's place.

Tuesday, August 25, 1992—partly cloudy, 38° to 49°. Went to Eagle River, Wasilla, and Palmer shopping. Saw one moose calf. Quite a few boo racks going towards Palmer, Anchorage. Visited Mae. Saw movie "Unforgiven."

Wednesday, August 26, 1992—partly cloudy, 34° to 54°. Put two loads wood in basement. Visited with Ed a few minutes. Stacked some wood.

Thursday, August 27, 1992—partly cloudy, 32° to 50°. Called Allen and got him to go Caribou hunting on Lake Louise Road. Ed came over to get a plat of Nelchina. Allen and I went hunting. I shot a boo bull (young) at about mile 14. Butchered it out. Left tires and wheels at Dinty Bush's to be changed over. Went on to Point of View for a few min. Talked to Lucky along the road.

Hung the meat in the garage when we got back home. Sylvia fixed hot dogs for lunch then we loaded the ATV's and went to Mile 133 and went to Old Man Creek and partway to Little Nelchina. Explored an old burned cabin. Saw something running in brush. Could have been moose calf or a bear. Bear pooh in road. Got home after 10:00 PM.

Friday, August 28, 1992—cloudy all day, 38° to 48°. Sylvia cut up boo ribs. I cut the butterfly chops. Karn visited a little while. Ed had surveyor out and got Sam's property lines settled. I hunted up Dan B and went to dump. Have flu again today.

Saturday, August 29, 1992—partly cloudy, 40° to 54°. Went to Dinty Bush's and picked up my tires and rims. Left sweatshirts. Visited at Billmans. Sure have the flu. Took picture of Sylvia and decoys. Put different tires on truck. Changed oil in motor. Sylvia is working on sweatshirts for daughters and granddaughters.

Sunday, August 30, 1992—cloudy, few drops rain, 32° to 46°. Sylvia finished cutting the boo meat. I've been sick all day. Teacher's kids came over and borrowed movies.

Monday, August 31, 1992—cloudy, rain in afternoon and evening, 34° to 47°. Watered the trees around the house. Adjusted the kitchen door for new threshold seal. Started getting some gear ready for goose, crane hunting. Did some of the small chores around here. Robbie stopped by after school termination. Dust "snow" on the tops of mountains south of us.

Tuesday, September 1, 1992—rain in the night and all morning, 40° to 44°. Did go moose hunting. Started getting truck and trailer ready to go to Delta. Visited Ed F. Allen came over just in time for fresh buns from the oven.

Wednesday, September 2, 1992—partly cloudy, 34° to 43°. Sylvia went to Alaska State Fair on senior citizen van. I put camper on truck, stocked it with groceries and gear and water. Loaded ATV on trailer. Heard a squirrel near strawberries and shot it with .223. Dug some potatoes and pulled onion to take hunting. Took a shower, went to Glennallen, picked up Darrel. Did some shopping and drove to Delta Junction. Saw people hunting boo near Hogan's Hill. Moose hunter's near Delta Junction. Got some gas. Darrel got some sandwiches. We saw Rhynell's store from highway. Drove to farms, saw two moose cows and two calves on way. No geese or cranes flying. Asked at John Thuringer's to hunt. Other hunters are all ready here. Then saw three flocks of speckle bellies fly over. We are camped at far corner of his place.

Thursday, September 3, 1992—cool morning and hot afternoon, partly cloudy to sunny, very little breeze. Speckle bellies flew all morning. I shot two, did too much missing (wrong choke tube in barrel). Went to Hollenbeck's in afternoon and gave Buckley a hunting coat and a gift for Ruby. Gave Darrel the GI Field Jacket. Sure surprised Darrel when I pulled out the new flying goose decoys I had made. Sylvia sewed the cloth. We set them up on John's off the end of a strip of volunteer grain on Doc's farm. Hauled them down there on ATV. Fox tail (weed) is sure taking over this land. Laid around in sun several hours. Toward end of shooting hours the crane started flying. One large flock flew towards the decoys but shied away. A few minutes later another flock flew right in and over us. I shot two and Darrel wounded one. This choke tube in my gun throws "blown" patters with steel shot. Sure wish I had proper choke tube with me. Four crane's flew a ¼ mile and landed in Doc's field. Later three crane landed with them. Then a small plane flew over and flushed 6 birds up. I just knew there was an injured crane there. Three cranes came back and landed at that spot. Darrel and I made a sneak on them. Three cranes flew away. I flushed the "runner" out of the tall grass. Killed it with second shot. (blown pattern again.) Took pix and cleaned the birds just as it was getting dark.

Finished at 9:30 PM. Great day of hunting. Northern Lights are out tonight.

Friday, September 4, 1992—must have gotten down to the low 20s last night. Good temp to help keep birds refrigerated. We got cooler down off the camper, put birds in it and set coolers in shade of some trees. Spent all morning hunting, no luck, no birds flying. Back to camper AND ate. Flock flew over while I was cooking. Darrel tipped one. He marked it down and we went to look for it but couldn't find it. Probably landed running. Darrel wants to check on his "David." Hunting looks bleak right now so we go to pick up decoys and go home. Sure enough cranes start flying and one flock of speckle bellies fly by. I got one tank of gas at Glennallen on the way home. Dropped Darrel off. Got home 11:30 PM.

Saturday, September 5, 1992—30s to 46°. Cleaned, packaged and froze birds. Sylvia went to Eagle River with three other ladies to watch David Adkins play football, got home around 11:30 PM. I worked on camper. Fixed furnace and adjusted door and drawer latches. Visited at Allen's. Digger and Lucky were there also.

Sunday, September 6, 1992—cloudy, some light rain, 36° to 44°. Dimmick returned some honey. Visited and has some smoked fish with us. Kyle and Evan came to borrow movies. Allen and Robbie came over to get their meat cooling in our garage. Rudbeck and Dennis G came over, Dennis borrowed a pair of hip boots. I stopped at gravel pit on way to Bartley's and found some fired brass. Got my moose harvest tag from Rosemary. Worked on camper light for awhile. Visited Allen about hunting regulations. Considered opening choke on 870 Remington shot gun barrel. Light rain this evening.

Monday, September 7, 1992—mostly sunny, 34° to 44°. Sylvia started laundry but then helped me with the wiring for the camper on pickup. Got some of it fixed and figured out. Some more to do. Smayda's brought a prospective buyer for their property. Robbie puts thru our place on his scooter to see the four girls. Sylvia went out in the evening and picked a gallon of cranberries, then she went back out to pick rose hips.

Tuesday, September 8, 1992—30° to 52°. Sylvia picked over a gallon of cranberries and a gallon of rose hips, then helped me with wiring of truck and camper in late afternoon. I pulled over a few trees with a come along and log chains along the switch back trail. Neighbors are moose hunting. Glued up one of the broken camper tail light covers. Robbie came over to get notches glued on to two of his arrows.

Wednesday, September 9, 1992—shower in the night, cloudy, partly cloudy, and snow. Large flakes at supper time, 34° to 44°. We dug the potatoes and brought the Roto-tiller up the hill and put it and the lawnmower away for the winter. Got the wiring corrected on the trailer. Went down to lake in evening. Ducks are wary. I didn't take canoe out to try for them. Filled out life insurance form to submit policy for cancellation.

Thursday, September 10, 1992—mostly clear, breezy to windy, low 20s to 30s. Gathered gear to go to Delta. Pulled onions. Went to lake to hunt ducks, no luck. Shot a squirrel. Allen and David came over and had some rhubarb cake. Allen, David, Kyle and I went to Cal's old place and drove our ATV's west to a slough and then walked a mile on a low ridge moose hunting. No luck. Some tracks. Bear pooh. Bear muddy tracks out on the hwy. Got home just before 9:00 PM. Darrel called, he can't hunt tomorrow.

Friday, September 11, 1992—shot two squirrels. Pulled onions from garden. Took off screen door and stored it. Put more gear in camper. Allen wanted me to go north of Tolsona Ridge hunting moose. Already committed to Delta and crane and geese. Saw grizzly on way to Glennallen. Picked up Darrel 7:30 PM. Ran into snow at Black Rapids and out of it at Isabell Farm and park in our usual spot at the far corner of his farm. 12:30 AM. Furnace quit at 5:00 AM.

Saturday, September 12, 1992—pretty cold last night. Froze some. Mostly clear. Got up drank coffee. The birds started flying. The cranes came through in waves until around 3:00 PM. We stalked and chased them and had lots of fun. Birds got confused and excited at one point. Darrel got one and I got three. I sure shot a lot of shells to get them. Did lots of missing. Saw a few buffalo at west end of John's farm. Fried boo steak and new potatoes and onions for supper.

Sunday, September 13, 1992—4" of snow on ground and steady snow all day. No flights of cranes. Went looking for cranes riding the 4-wheeler. Jumped 12, then spotted 7, tried to stalk them. They got up wild. One got up with difficulty and one didn't seem right. Had lunch and got warmed up. Went back out. Saw a marsh hawk harassing a single crane on ground. Went and got Darrel to do a pincher stalk but crane was gone. I decided snow would be too deep to get off the field by morning. So we pulled decoys, loaded ATV and went to Al and Wendy Baker's and visited the evening. The kids sure have grown. They had been hunting moose.

Monday, September 14, 1992—close to freezing and snowed all night and still snowing pretty hard. We drove in to Delta Jct. Got gas and started for Glennallen. Some vehicles were in or had been in the ditch, lots of slush in road. Drove slow and easy out of snow and slush before Summit Lake. Road was dry by the time we got to Glennallen. Got fill of gas. Went to Darrel's. He unloaded his gear and a couple of birds and I came on home. Unloaded gear and put wet things to dry. Washed ATV. Visited Allen. He had shot a nice moose. Went with him and Ed to look for moose in evening. Loaned Ed my moose call—he called several moose in at one time and shot a nice one. Allen and I drove the road and didn't see any.

Tuesday, September 15, 1992—2" of snow in the night, very windy in night and all day long, 18° to 30°. Did some things around here. Visited Rudbecks. Allen and Kyle had a bowl of soup with us at supper time. Borrowed my duck decoys and 12-gauge shot gun. The boys want to hunt ducks—great! Allen will help them. Rudbecks came over to borrow a movie in evening. Shot gun 10-gauge sure got rusty from crane hunting trip, cleaned it. Greased two pair of boots.

Wednesday, September 16, 1992—partly cloudy, 9° to 34°. Quite a bit of lake is frozen over. Ducks swim in what is left open. Lots of lake opened up over the day. Late afternoon, 70 sandhill cranes flew over at 200 yards alt. Put away lots hunting gear. Took camper off and put it on old truck for storage. Put snow plow frame and lift on truck. Pumped two barrels gas into over head tank. Loaded five barrels and grey box in truck for trip to Palmer. Have been boiling batches of wolf traps all day. A batch of small traps is boiling now.

MOUNT SPUR ERUPTION

Thursday, September 17, 1992—about ½" volcanic ash fell during the night and this morning from the Mt. Spur eruption, 29° to 24°. I cleaned our truck, camper and canopy plus other things. Parked truck in garage. Started snowing mid afternoon 2" - 3" so far. Jim Manning visited loaned him a TV. Looked like the beaver has started a feed pile midway on the lake.

Friday, September 18, 1992—partly cloudy, 24° to 39°. Blowing ash from the west. Must be wind blowing ash from trees in Chickaloon Pass. Walked down to lake. Got ash all over 20-gauge and started cleaning it when I got back. Ducks stayed out of range. Walked down lake to new beaver lodge and feed pile. Visited Allen and Roxanne for cake and coffee in morning. Sylvia starched the tablecloth for Theresa. Lots of the snow melted, the ash sure is messy now.

Saturday, September 19, 1992—cloudy, snow in afternoon and evening, 1" snow in night, 28° to 30°. Cleaned on shotgun barrel. Sylvia wanted to take flowers (plants) to Point of View Lodge. Highway was wet. Lake Louis Road snowy ruts, snow on divide. Visited with Dan, Patti, and Jason in town. Met Ivory, Joe and another guy. Said Hi at Dinty Bush's. Came right back home. Got our ladder and water hoses, washed roof of house, arctic entry, garage and gas storage tank and truck. Hosed off some log walls and foundations. Scaup are still on our lake.

Sunday, September 20, 1992—cloudy, some light snow, 20° to 30°. Broke the layer of frozen ash mud along each side of the garage over hang. Shoveled some in wheel barrow and dumped it to north, the west side. I threw under the trees. Went down to lake and dragged canoe up here with the ATV. Went to lake on a false goose alert. Did hear sandhill cranes flying over. Spent some time cleaning shot gun.

Monday, September 21, 1992—light snow most of day, 20° to 24°. Sylvia went to Glennallen. Dan B. called several times for a weather report on the valley and Tazlina Lake. Fewer ducks on lake now. Cleaned gun. Enzy delivered heating oil. Did some repair and service work on truck. Loaded gas barrels and grey box for trip to Palmer and Wasilla tomorrow.

Tuesday, September 22, 1992—cloudy, light snow, 22° to 24°. Ash, stirred by vehicles on highway, blows through our house yard. We went to sunny and breezy, Palmer and Wasilla. Shopped for truck repairs and groceries and a load of gasoline. Most of our lake is frozen over. Ducks still sit and feed in the unfrozen leads in ice on lake. Saw two coyotes standing in ditch ¾ mile west of Nelchina, north side of hwy, just after we left home this morning. Looked mature or well grown. Quite pale in color. Fur starting to get longer and thicker.

Wednesday, September 23, 1992—partly cloudy, winds blowing ash around the valley, 0° to 23°. Put front brake pads on truck, unloaded gas. Washed PVC valve, serviced air cleaner. Allen invited us to lunch for roasted duck. Shot two squirrels, loaded more cartridges. Went to Cal's and helped Allen pull a 12 x 50 trailer out of its parking place. He aired tires and pulled it to Nelchina. Rudbeck took floats off his plane, put on tires and taxied back on Lucky's and Allen's property. Got in, in air, ("85 steps") before he got to lake and the ice. Only two small open places and three dozen ducks are using them.

Thursday, September 24, 1992—mostly sunny, lots of ash dust in the air, 0° to 24°. Many "dust devils". Getting ready to go to Minnesota. George visited and went on to Sam Weaver's. Ducks are keeping a hole open in ice on lake. Juvenile eagle keep watch around the lake. Marsh hawk does same.

Friday, September 25, 1992—partly cloudy, 3° to 24°. Repaired truck chains, mounted canopy on truck bed. Straightened out the storage shed. Covered a trailer. Went to dump, KROA, Snowshoe Lake. Coyote circled hole on ice ducks are staying in.

Saturday, September 26, 1992—cloudy, 3° to 26°. Stacked wood in shed. Cut up some to short lengths for woodshop stove. Ravens were trying to kill a duck

Allen had broken a wing on. I killed a squirrel. Coyotes yipping north of hwy.
Welded up three wolf drags. Allen didn't show up to move mobile home.
Lloyd and Dan stopped in for a few minutes.

Sunday, September 27, 1992—cloudy, wind came up in afternoon and blew ash
east, 20° to 28°. The open holes in our lake got larger today. The ravens got the
duck with the broken wing. Cut points on wolf drags, put chains on three stove
wood drags. Steve, Karen Mailly and kids here for supper. Steve came late from
getting wood along Army trail.

Monday, September 28, 1992—cloudy, light snow after supper, 18° to 28° Sylvia
went to Glennallen. Shoveled a little ash and other small jobs.

Tuesday, September 29, 1992—cloudy, skiff snow. Allen and Roxanne were here
for breakfast. Got some trap gear ready. Couldn't get snowgo to run. Lake
thawed some more.

Wednesday, September 30, 1992—mostly cloudy, blowing ash in afternoon, 10°
to 28°. Got snowgo running, excess oil in piston. Changed oil and filter on
truck. Rudbeck brought over 15-gallons of house finish to store here this
winter. Tom S. came up to take care of his rental house. Had supper with us.
Will mail a package for me to Lisa's father in Louisiana.

Thursday, October 1, 1992—partly sunny, some wind and blowing ash in
afternoon, 20° to 40°. Breakfast with Allen and Roxanne. Rode ATV there to
store it while we are gone. Swept garage, tried to figure out wiring in series
electric lights. Shot two squirrels. Lake ice is dark with ash and thawing. Two
swans swimming with ducks. Desert with Rudbecks. Jim Odden is back home.

Friday, October 2, 1992—partly sunny, some blowing ash, 20° to 30°. Got more
things ready before leaving on trip outside. Allen visited. He is storing four
guns for me. Jim O. visited and is storing three guns for me. I took my snowgo
down to Allen's while we are gone. Tom H. took Allen, Roxanne, Sylvia, me,
and his wife Kim to Ranch House Lodge for a very nice dinner and coffee and
cheese cake at their home afterward.

Saturday, October 3, 1992—mostly cloudy, 20° to 30°. Lake thawed out some
more. Put another hasp on a storage shed. Checked out low temp stove
operation. Low temp light control of Lucky's didn't work. Coffee with Allen.
Rudbecks had lots of trouble trying to tow their pickup. Burned tranny and
wrecked the tow hitch. Gave up at the "hub" and came back to Nelchina. We
got some more things ready to take on trip. Pumped water again.

Sunday, October 4, 1992—partly cloudy, 24° to 34°. Rudbecks were here for breakfast. Rush to get ready and go to Anchorage. (We're on our way to Minnesota for a visit.) Left some gifts for Mike Callahan with his wife Shirley. Went to Dennis and Addie Griffith and stayed at their place overnight.

Monday, October 5, 1992—30s here in Anchorage, it frosted. Up early, Addie drove us to airport. Flew to Salt Lake City, changed planes and went to Minneapolis-St. Paul. Three daughters and family met us. Mary Lou drove Bev to airport and back to Bev's house for a welcoming party. We had a nice time.

Tuesday, October 6, 1992—light rain, 60s to 70s. Walked to book store, bought book "50 Yrs Below Zero." Later Bev, Sylvia went to a mall. Made eye appointment for tomorrow. Shopped for some groceries. Bev fixed a very good steak supper. Bev's boyfriend, Asif (Persian) came over again this evening.

Wednesday, October 7, 1992—light rain all day, 40s. Loafed most of day. Visited with Bev. She baby sets a nice baby named Johnny. We went to have our eye's tested. Mine are the same. Sylvia needs a little stronger lens and a new pair will be ready three days. Watched a couple movies.

Thursday, October 8, 1992—rainy, 40s. Went shopping. Got Tyler a birthday present. His birthday is Sunday. Bev had the party today. Nadia, Theresa and family, Tyler's dad and lots of his relatives were here.

Friday, October 9, 1992—cloudy, very little rain, 47°. I walked to a gun shop in the new shoes I bought yesterday. Loafed around house all day. Asif Kahn, (Bev's boyfriend) invited us to his apartment for dinner. He is Persian and prepared his native dishes. Spiced so we could eat it. We found it to be very good. We had a good time this evening.

Saturday, October 10, 1992—mostly sunny, 47° to 60s. Exchanged these new shoes for a better fitting pair. Went to fire hall where Tyler went thru a smoke drill. Phoned Virginia. Phoned Farmers and talked to Roxanne. Allen's friend has killed a grizzly 8' in Allen's yard. In late afternoon we all went to bowling place. Mother and I just watched. Back home, then I went with Asif to his gym and watched him work out. Met Ahmed Abdulcarim (nice man, 57 yrs old), wants to visit Alaska. Ate late in evening, Bev fixed roast chicken.

Sunday, October 11, 1992—frost early, warm and sunny later. Did more visiting and shopping. Asif took me to a pawn shop. We stopped at a garage sale. Theresa and Earl came over late afternoon and we went to their place. Visit with Darcy and Lee and watch "Thelma and Louise."

Monday, October 12, 1992—sunny and nice, 40s. Earl dropped Theresa and Sylvia at grocery store and we went to Northern Hydraulics for snow plow parts.

Had to go to another store so we took women and groceries back to house. Then Earl had company. Later we dropped women and Darcy at a mall craft shop and we went and got plow parts. Back to house for supper and TV. Lee likes his sample of volcanic ash.

Tuesday, October 13, 1992—partly cloudy, 40s. Didn't do anything until afternoon then got ready and went to movie "Last of the Mohicans" and taco's after.

Wednesday, October 14, 1992—partly cloudy, 40s. Went for a walk early. afternoon Nadia came over for two hours to visit. We went shopping when kids got home from school. Supper and watch TV.

Thursday, October 15, 1992—sunny to cloudy and light rain, 40s. Sat with Darcy while she worked on a school assignment. The kids have Thursday and Friday off. Lee and I walked to Holliday Store. I bought some rope and strapping tape to package the snow plow parts. Helped Lee paint his homemade model canoe. Lee and Darcy helped me package and tie with rope the plow parts. I had brought along a drilled out wood handle to make carrying the heavy parts package easier. Sylvia made pizza for supper. Spent evening sitting around doing various things and getting reacquainted.

Friday, October 16, 1992—some snow in night, gone mid morning. Laid around all morning. Went to store for pop and ice cream. Earl up by 2:30 PM. Darcy baked apple pie. Lee went to store with me. Got a buffet supper at Ponderosa for all of us. Then Theresa took us to Omni Theatre to see "Rain Forest." We walked thru some of museum exhibit. Beverly and Asif are coming over tonight.

Saturday, October 17, 1992—mostly sunny. We all got ready, put our bags in Earls car and we went to Don and Evelyn Caughey's. Petted Butch's pet skunk. Had lunch, went to Paul and Ruth's. We all visited till 11:30 PM and to bed.

Sunday, October 18, 1992—sunny. 26°. Gave everyone gifts, ate breakfast, and watched TV. Ate a good dinner. Went for a walk, watched Tom Selkirk in "Quigley Down Under." Taped movie about wolves called Cry of Wild.

Monday, October 19, 1992—cloudy, 20s. Paul is sick. Steven stayed home from school and went with us to visit at Harold and Loraine Hanson's. We had a good visit, chicken dinner. It snowed pretty hard but didn't freeze to windshield. Supper at Paul's and watched TV in evening. Sent order to Bass Pro, Allen's gun boot.

Tuesday, October 20, 1992—cloudy. Went to visit Jim Rudbeck and Arlene. Went with Jim to feed his cows. Arlene fixed a great dinner. We had a good visit. Steve skipped school and went with us. A good supper was waiting for us when we got back to town Allen and Scott Rollins farm and visited them.

Wednesday, October 21, 1992—mostly sunny, 30s. Tried to call various people. Went shopping up town. Took Paul and family out to dinner. Went to "Jigs Place" and picked up my moose horns.

Thursday, October 22, 1992—sunny, Sylvia, Steve and I went to Fred and Ann Marolf's farm. Looked at Fred's projects and visited and had a good meal. Back to Paul's visit and pizza.

Friday, October 23, 1992—windy, sunny, 60s. Watched TV all morning. Talked Paul into taking Steve fishing in afternoon. Both of them caught a perch. Quite a few suckers lying in the holes under the bridge. Five or six northerns, two were big. Steve sure likes to fish. Stopped at the shooting range. Steve picked up quite a bit of brass. Sylvia went with the rest of them to a dance.

Saturday, October 24, 1992—sunny and breezy, 60s. Loafed most of morning. Went to couple garage sales. Taped a movie. Didn't do much all day.

Sunday, October 25, 1992—sunny, 60s. Went to Nadia and Chuck's home at Stillwater. They had fixed a turkey and fixings and ice cream and pecan filling. Others brought pot luck. Kids swam in pool adjacent to party room. Slept on futon bed which is closer to our own bed.

Monday, October 26, 1992—sunny, 60s Went to several places and shopping for some things on our list. Found some books at Goodwill store.

Tuesday, October 27, 1992—sunny, fog, and frost on river, 50s. Saw a few ducks and geese as we drove around today. We shopped for a camera. No luck. Nadia made a casserole and we went to granddaughter Laura's apartment. This is first time got to see great granddaughter Brittany. She is a very nice little girl. Back home in early evening.

Wednesday, October 28, 1992—mostly cloudy, 40s. Went with Nadia and looked up some tax delinquent parcels. None were suitable to build on. Phoned a realtor about one parcel, price too high. Hunted thru bookstore, picked up pix. Venison stew for supper. Watched "Thunderhearts" movie.

Thursday, October 29, 1992—beaut of day, around 26° and up. Left early and went to Cumberland, Wisconsin. Visited Lester and Odden, had lunch then went to Dan Della and Monica Zappa. Got the grand tour of their place. Nice to see them again. Very interesting to see their operation and life style. Back to Odden's. Three of their daughters showed up with husbands and kids. Ate supper and came back to Stillwater. An enjoyable day and fine drive back here.

Friday, October 30, 1992—sunny, 20s to 40°. Beaut of a day. We went to a ammo reloader. I got some bullets. Then to Goodwill store to look for books. Poor luck there. We took Nadia and Chuck out to dinner. Picked up a chocolate pie on way home.

Saturday, October 31, 1992—cloudy, windy, 20s to 30s. Sylvia and Nadia went shopping. Chuck bought cloths and shopped for spaghetti supper. They fixed mussels to go with the spaghetti.

Sunday, November 1, 1992—light rain changing to wet snow, 38° to 30°. We went over to Beverly's. Went to church as Vanessa had a part in the services. Had a time finding the church. They bought movie tickets to "A River Runs Through It." Then to a McDonald's, back to Bev's, then to movie house. Everyone enjoyed the show. Back to Bev's for a minute then stopped at a grocery store, got steaks to fix for supper. Nadia and Chuck are good cooks.

Monday, November 2, 1992—34° All day, 6" of snow in night. More snow during the day, much of it melting. Few ducks flying. Stayed in house all day.

Tuesday, November 3, 1992—cloudy all day, 33°. Went to Beverly's. Nadia went to the Mall of America. We visited with Beverly and Vanessa and Tyler. Asif came over. Had supper at Beverly's, watched a movie, shopped for books.

Wednesday, November 4, 1992—cloudy, 20s to 35°. Went shopping for groceries. Walked down to boat ramp and took pix of some Canadian honkers resting there. Nadia fixed a lasagna supper. Theresa, Darcy and Lee and Earl came over and ate with us and visited the evening. Phoned Bev and Paul. Bev wasn't home.

Thursday, November 5, 1992—partly cloudy, 34°. Left at dawn. Nadia drove us to air terminal. We check in for our flight then a bite to eat. Breakfast in flight. A short layover in Salt Lake City then on to Anchorage. Not too much in view from plane. Fog and rain at Anchorage. Taxi out to Griffiths. Cleaned snow off truck. Spent evening and night with them.

Friday, November 6, 1992—went to Palmer in morning. We both went to see the doctor then to bank, then shopping. Got to visit with Mae. Saw coyote ¼ mile ahead cross in front of a pickup. Everything good here, glad to be home.

Saturday, November 7, 1992—cloudy, some snow, 24°. Had breakfast with Allen and Roxanne. Brought mail home and things we didn't want stolen. Visited Lucky and Mary. His eye operation seems to be healing. Mary tried to tape some movies on our VCR while we were gone. Plowed snow today. Grizzly tore apart my bait freezer and ate all my trap bait.

Sunday, November 8, 1992—light snow, fog, cloudy, 10° to 17°. Installed Hi-Lo thermometer. Unlock all padlocks. Smayda's, Robbie, Lee Dudley, Jim and Kari visited. Sylvia baked buns.

Monday, November 9, 1992—snow in night and all day, 12" to 14". 28° to 24°. Allen stopped for coffee and brought some donuts. Went to Glennallen. Paid light and phone bills. Got flu and pneumonia shots. Rode the senior van. Plowed snow in late afternoon. Robbie stopped by with zipper for Sylvia to put in a coat for his dad.

Tuesday, November 10, 1992—cloudy, sunny, cloudy, 16° to 17°. Visited Ed and Sandra. Plowed snow. Visited Allen and Roxanne. Ed gave me some bait. Ed, Sandy, Robbie visited in evening. F & G appeared to be counting moose this morning.

Wednesday, November 11, 1992—sunny, -13° to 3°. Several phone calls. Jim Odden and Kari borrowed bearing Puller. I went down to Allen's but couldn't start either Suzuki or snowgo. Still can't get Nadia on phone.

Thursday, November 12, 1992—sunny, -15° to 6°. Fred Rungee visited and brought small gift. We gave him rose hip jam, rhubarb jelly and two packages of cranberries. Went to Bartley's and copied bank statement. He will fax a bill for me to Mayflower. Went to Allen's and got my snowgo and ATV. Allen had to put heat on them to get them started. Tried to pump water but we must have ice in the line. Will try to fix that tomorrow. Visited Ed and Sandy a few min. He was watching boo on Slide Mountain. Two boo on our lake this morning.

Friday, November 13, 1992—sunny, -17° to -5°. Allen and Roxanne here for breakfast. Jim Manning came over wanting me to look after his place while they are gone. Went to Bartley's to send a fax. He doesn't know how to use it. Back home and cut up water line and brought it into basement to thaw out. Got snowgo running again. Went to Allen's and got five gal of water. Also ordered a J.S. game caller. Allen called a great horned owl in to 100 yards this evening. Jim O. brought my bearing puller back. I made coffee and popped corn. Kool-Aid for Kari.

Saturday, November 14, 1992—mostly cloudy, 5° to 9°. Went to Allen's and got plastic pipe connectors. Went to KROA and picked up my bottle of acetylene. Pipe is thawed took it down hill and reconnected all three pieces. Heating each as I re-coupled them. Thawed ice out of short pipe at well cover. While pumping water to fill tanks in basement, I shoveled snow to support and cover the pipe to grade as well as I could.

Sunday, November 15, 1992—partly cloudy, -6° to 10°. Allen & I went up trail in back of state DOT camp and around in back of Slide Mountain. David F. got cold and went back home. Saw fox track, moose track, where boo had fed. Animals have to paw through ash to eat. So much country to look at from up there. Snowgo cross shaft bearing failed today. Ed saw a bull moose on side of Slide Mountain thru spotting scope.

Monday, November 16, 1992—cloudy, foggy, cloudy, -6° to 10°. Went to Thanksgiving potluck at school house at noon. Kids put on a program for us visitors. Wildlife caller came in mail today. Shoveled snow off camper, storage and wood shop roofs.

Tuesday, November 17, 1992—cloudy, fog, light snow, -13° to 20°. Put shotgun and predator caller in truck and went to KROA and picked up bearing. Went to Charlie K. gave him some leads for a motor for his tractor. Visited with Lloyd R. for awhile. Some novice is trapping on Tazlina Hill. Started to put bearing on snowgo and found the driven clutch is in bad shape.

Wednesday, November 18, 1992—fog, cloudy, 18° to 12°. Mounted a scope on .223 and tried to sight it in. Fingers got cold, so quit. Tried to put bearing on snowgo. Couldn't get one bolt loose. Ordered a new driven clutch for snowgo.

Thursday, November 19, 1992—fog, cloudy, fog froze on windshield on way to Anchorage, 8° to 4°. Paid off contract to State of Alaska and remote parcel. Shopped for pelts. Some other needed things, plus groceries. Visited a little with Mae when we got gas at Pinnacle Mountain. Jim and Kari visited in evening.

Friday, November 20, 1992—cloudy, clearing, 2° to -4°. Allen and Roxanne brought up their meat grinder for us to use and had breakfast with us. I worked on truck. Bart brought Russ over and he got some of Sylvia's sweatshirts.

Saturday, November 21, 1992—some fog, cloudy, -11° to -6°. Kept a fire in garage all day. Took four hours to put the bearing on snowgo. Allen and David stopped by in time to help me put last two cap screws in the suspension. Tom Huddleston is on leave from his job for two weeks. He visited with Jim O. Welded the frame of his blazer. Sylvia ground 65 pounds of hamburger and sausage and babysat Kari while Jim welded. Lots people for lunch and supper.

Sunday, November 22, 1992—some fog, cloudy, breezy, 10° to 27°. Checked Mannings. Rested a lot. Put snow plow in garage, started to put attachments on. Loaded a few target cartridges.

Monday, November 23, 1992—cloudy, snow, rain, 30° to 34°. All snow slid off house and garage. Finished mounting "wings" on snowplow. Jim O. came over and welded the frame on his snow plow. We all went to Allen and Roxanne's for supper and helped Allen get the new storage tank in the house.

Tuesday, November 24, 1992—cloudy and warm, 34° to 37°. Pumped water. Tightened bearing on snowgo. Pushed some snow for Sandy F. Helped Allen install his new water pump and hook up to new water storage tank.

Wednesday, November 25, 1992—cloudy, fog evening, 30° to 27°. Shot rifle in morning. Helped Allen install some plumbing in afternoon.

Thursday, November 26, 1992—partly sunny, 10° to 12°. Checked Manning's. Bulb at well was burned out. Went to Tom and Kim H. for Thanksgiving dinner. His brother Peter was there.

Friday, November 27, 1992—cloudy, 2° to 12°. Went to Billman's at Lake Louise. Denny was there and got in a good visit with him. Leona Dawson's mother died. Jason B is to be operated on Dec. 1. Saw very little fur sign along the road. Allen and Kyle came over to invite us to dinner tomorrow night.

Saturday, November 28, 1992—cloudy, some fog, few flakes snow, 22° to 24°. Loaded a few cartridges. Helped Allen with his water plumbing. Visited with Lucky. Allen and Roxanne took us out to dinner at Tolsona Lodge.

Sunday, November 29, 1992—cloudy, some fog around, 16° to 8°. Slept late. Read paper. Reset Manning's stove. Steve and Karen Mailly had us over for supper.

Monday, November 30, 1992—cloudy, some fog, -5° in night, 6° to 12° day time. Sylvia went to Glennallen. Mailed tape to Steven. I put cardboard in front of radiator on truck. Shoveled snow at mailboxes. Went to dump and tried to call varmints with no luck. Saw wolf track. Allen came over and got a small piece of 4"stove pipe.

Tuesday, December 1, 1992—cloudy, -6° to 1°. Huddleston's were here for breakfast. Sylvia went with them for the day. I studied Medicare supplement. Reset Mannings stove as the electricity was off. Third reset. Moose cow and calf hanging around Mannings.

Wednesday, December 2, 1992—3 1/2" snow, cloudy, very windy during the night, 30° to 19°. 4th Reset Mannings. Allen was here for breakfast. Studied Medicare insurance. Again. Plowed snow part of afternoon. Visited Allen.

Thursday, December 3, 1992—snow all day, 20° to 13°. Tried to plow out Charlie and Lloyd. Plow battery won't stay up with lights on. Plowed teacher's driveway and part of ours. Went to Allen's for beans and ice cream. David dropped the ice cream mix and spilled it. Allen mixed up more and we all enjoyed peaches and ice cream. Jim O. made it back from Fairbanks. Hell of an adventure though. Plowed Allen's and Lucky's hill so teacher could drive up it and get home.

Friday, December 4, 1992—cloudy, -2° to 2°. Plowed snow. 5th reset Mannings. Snow is deep. Drifts too deep at Dobler and Huddleston's, for me to plow. Snowgo clutch came today. Helped Henry plow his place.

Saturday, December 5, 1992—cloudy, -7° to 2°. Installed driven clutch on snowgo and did service work on it and truck. Pumped water, broke trail to lake. Snowgo clutch's now work very well. Had coffee and donuts at Allen and Roxanne's. Shoveled some snow and rested. Got a bunch of Christmas cards and letters off.

Sunday, December 6, 1992—cloudy, fog all around, -6° most of day. Ms. Banning and daughters came over for some dowels. I made four marten sets along hwy to trap line trailhead. Breaking new trail went good, returning on that trail was a nightmare. Saw a sick young boo bull along snowgo trail.

Monday, December 7, 1992—fog and light snow all day, -9° to 0°. Several phone calls to make this morning. Elect out several times. Reset Mannings twice. 7th reset. Sylvia went to Glennallen. I visited Allen and Roxanne. Went to Odden's. Saw a moose laying in edge of brush. Couldn't see for sure if two marten sets had connected or not.

Tuesday, December 8, 1992—cloudy, -7° to 1°. Went to Tom D. and plowed his snow. He gave me some fish and meat. Checked marten set, nothing. Saw a moose calf. Didn't do much else. Jim O. and Kari, Steve and Karen M. here for supper.

Wednesday, December 9, 1992—cloudy all day, -10° to -3°. Plowed snow from Kim's North driveway. Allen was there to look at her car, it doesn't run. Ran traps and made a fox set, no fur. Talked to Denny B. at Point of View.

Thursday, December 10, 1992—partly cloudy, -19° to -4°. We went to Palmer/Wasilla. Did some shopping. Couldn't get some things. Owners of Reiss Fur weren't there. Saw Tom S. in front of bank.

Friday, December 11, 1992—mostly cloudy, -16° to -6°. Shoveled snow off camper, roofs, log pile, trailer, etc. Allen and David here for bean supper.

Saturday, December 12, 1992—cloudy, fog to south and north, -5° all day. Ran those few traps, nothing. Saw a fox track. Cow moose and calf along our lake. Visited Allen and Roxanne. She had brought a vent value for sewer system for us. I put it on vent pipe. Adjusted snowgo choke by raising stem one thread. Sylvia put perm in Missy's hair. Robbie brought her home on his snowgo.

Sunday, December 13, 1992—cloudy, most of day, 2" snow, -0°. Loafed. Refit the rubber parts on the snowplow wings. Plowed our snow and Banning's. Allen and David visited. Checked well and house at Mannings, pager was squealing.

Monday, December 14, 1992—cloudy, 2" snow, 5° to 7°. Sylvia went to Glennallen. Allen and I went to Point of View. Saw quite a few moose. Some bulls had dropped their horns. Saw one 35" bull. Lynx track near First Hill going north on Lake Louise Road. Saw one fox track, visited with Billmans.

Tuesday, December 15, 1992—cloudy, 1-1/2" snow, 2° to 10°. Got predator calling gear ready and went to Mile 1 on Lake Louise Road. Got a couple hundred yards up trail and along comes Cecil Henshaw. He is trapping there. Checked the dump out, a fox is working that. Stopped at Jim Odden's. He ordered a rifle scope for me. Came home, unloaded some 1" conduit pipe I found along the hwy. Fired up the snowgo and went to check those few traps. A moose calf was getting water at a overflow place. Nothing in traps, a fox was hunting in a westerly direction towards my only fox set.

Wednesday, December 16, 1992—clear and cold, -34° to -30°. Our propane regulator had frost in it. I brought it into house and thawed and dried it. Now it works. Brought some tools etc. in house to so some projects. Pretty boring not having a long trapline to run.

Thursday, December 17, 1992—cloudy, very light snow, -13° to 9°. Checked Manning well and house. Coyote explored our yard. Allen and Roxanne were here for coffee. We are giving crafts suitable for kids to parents around here for Christmas presents for their children. Went to the Christmas program at school house. The teacher asked Jane Chamberlain and I to tell a little Christmas story of when we were young children. Sylvia was too bashful to relate her stories. It was difficult enough for me.

Friday, December 18, 1992—cloudy, ice fog, -12° to -5°. Went to Glennallen on senior van to a Thanksgiving dinner at Kluti Kaah, a group of home study children provided entertainment with songs, recitations and music. Then to Ahtna Inc. to an open house there. We saw quite a few moose along the hwy both coming and going from town. They are out mostly morning and evening. Coyote jumped up on 2-wheel trailer ate the bird's corn bread. It left a calling card in the yard again.

Saturday, December 19, 1992—cloudy, sunny, -11° to -18°. Sylvia went with Sandy to Palmer, Wasilla shopping. Brought tanned wolf hide home. Henry came and stayed quite awhile this afternoon. Nice visit. Allen brought his two snowgos over and put one in my garage so it will start when Suzuki dealer picks them up tomorrow. He'll leave a Suzuki 4 x 4 ATV for Allen. Allen is going to work on North Slope. Bartley called to ask if he son could use my garage if need be, of course he could. Sylvia and Sandy got home around 8:00 PM.

Sunday, December 20, 1992—sunny, -30° to -25°. Checked Manning house, well. No one came this morning to make the snowgo trade. Sandy stopped by for gifts.

Monday, December 21, 1992—sunny, -40° to -28°. Checked Manning house, well. Stratified ice fog in sight at different times. Refracted light distorted Mountains down the valley to the east. School teacher called about her pump house freezing. Jack Chamberlain called for temp here. Mary B. wants Sylvia to put perm in her hair. Sylvia went to Glennallen on senior van. Suzuki dealer dropped off Allen's Suzuki and picked up the two snowmobiles he traded in.

Tuesday, December 22, 1992—sunny, cloudy, -40° to -29°. Took Sylvia to Mary B. to put perm in her hair. Took a movie back to Farmers then plowed Sam's driveway, parking spot. Checked three traps. Visited at J. Odden's a little while. Checked Manning place. Left toy banks and movie at Banning's (teacher). Came home, took off plow and put truck back in garage. Everything is sure cold and stiff today.

Wednesday, December 23, 1992—mostly cloud, sunny, -18° to -10°. Checked Mannings. Loafed. Started snowgo and we pumped water and filled storage tanks. Missy and friend got a pr of earrings. Steve M. and Daughter Hannah stopped by for some presents for their family (kids). Sylvia went to Christmas program at Mendeltna Chapel.

Thursday, December 24, 1992—partly cloudy, sunny, cloudy, skiff of snow, -15° to -4°. Checked Manning's. Started Allen's new ATV and took it to his place and put it in the shed and visited with Roxanne for awhile. Nadia called early in morning. Robbie visited. We went to Odden's for supper and visited. Brought my scope while we were there.

Friday, December 25, 1992—mostly cloudy, some snow, -2° to 2°. Checked Manning's. Went to Jim and Mary Odden's for Christmas day and dinner. The

Smayda family was there also. Charlie Trowbridge phoned while we were there and I visited with him.

Saturday, December 26, 1992—partly sunny, some snow, -20° to -10°. Checked Mannings. Slept late. Tom S. and Jim O. were here several times. Tom is thawing out water system at the house the teacher lives in and needed different things to get the job done. I mounted a scope on the .22-250.

Sunday, December 27, 1992—sunny, -30° to -20°. Checked Manning's place. Cow and calf moose near by and ran off. Lowered light in Manning's well. House ok. Went down to Rudbeck's well, a little ice but ok. Coyote had been all around. Robbie F. visited in afternoon. Borrowed dump key and played cards with Sylvia. Dave DeJung phoned for B. Rudbeck's phone number.

Monday, December 28, 1992—sunny, partly cloudy, -35° to -25°. Coyotes are here most every night. Moose cow and calf wander around browsing for food. Took a 100 watt bulb over to Mannings well in hopes it will thaw the ice. Karen M. came to pick up earrings for Kim H. birthday. Roxanne was with her.

Tuesday, December 29, 1992—mostly sunny, -29° to -15°. Cow moose and calf sure hang around the neighborhood. Have to carry a weapon. Coyotes stole ice cream bars off Sandy F. porch. Stopped there to get my dump key. Then on down to Roxanne's. She had cashed a check for me. Had coffee and a pastry.

Wednesday, December 30, 1992—mostly sunny, -19° to 2°. Ran trap line. Pulled set near school and moved it west to a 6" spruce that is on north side of trail and 20 feet from a phone line steel post marker. Yellow flag tied in small brush nearby. Also a rag poked into small hole in steel post. Sighted new scope on rifle and tested loads and reloaded more and cleaned rifle. Missy and friend borrowed movies.

Thursday, December 31, 1992—mostly cloudy, gusty wind, 20° to 15°. Snow slid off ¾ house roof. Shot rifle testing loads. Loaded more rounds. Sylvia did laundry. Pumped water into storage tanks. Shoveled some snow that slid off roof out into area we walk. Went to Huddleston's for New Years evening. Had nice time watching TV show and visiting. Kids shot off some fireworks. Mailly's, D. Johnson's, teacher and daughters were there.

Sylvia Wilkins at Crosswinds Lake.

Norman with lake trout at Crosswinds Lake.

1993—running trapline, casting bullets

Friday, January 1, 1993—1" of snow, 7° all day. Manning well thawed out. Cleaned rifle again. Didn't do anything all day. Darrel Gerry phoned.

Saturday, January 2, 1993—5° all day, windy 9:00 AM to 3:00 PM, Blew snow and ash out of trees. Quite a mess. Ran traps. Picked up one trail set. Renewed bait at marten sets. Plowed snow. A bolt was lost from plow hitch. Managed to get a 1/2" bolt in. Will fix it right later. Kim brought Charlie, Kendra, and a movie down. Checked Manning's, reset stove.

Sunday, January 3, 1993—sunny, -16° to -10°. Went over to Manning's. Their well is okay. Read and loafed all day. Robbie stopped by for a minute.

Monday, January 4, 1993—mostly cloudy, -16° to -3°. We went to Glennallen on senior van. Sylvia got an Alaska ID card. A little bit of shopping and check cashing. Saw a moose on way home. Very little fur sign.

Tuesday, January 5, 1993—mostly cloudy, 18° to 4°. Had to adjust ski spindle on snowgo, mixed gas for it, oiled clutches. Sylvia went to Moosey Boo for a party for Morey Secondchief. I ran trap line, no fur. Went north on east side of Slide Mt. a mile or so. Turned around and came back. Odden's picked us up and we all went to Billman's Point of View Lodge. Jim, Mary, Dan and Lee D. played music after a very good rib and chicken dinner. Jim & Mary had brought ice cream mix and we made homemade ice cream (Alaska Blueberry) and apple pie. Bob (a trapper), was there. Visited a while with him. Checked Manning's well.

Wednesday, January 6, 1993—partly cloudy, -2° to 22°. A snow shower almost reached us then turned south. Two more boo were in our lane. Roxanne called us when a cow went down our lake. Tom Smayda came up to run hot water in his well, did other things around his property, borrowed a ladder etc. Nice to be able to help him. Mary Odden went back to Fairbanks. Mannings are back.

Thursday, January 7, 1993—partly cloudy, some fog in afternoon, -4° to 6°. Didn't do much all day. Mannings brought a package of raisins and a package of orange slices for a thank you for watching and taking care of their place while they were gone. Chuck F. brought my weed burner back.

Friday, January 8, 1993—sunny, all day, fog most of the night, -6° to 3°. Ed F. visited in morning. Sylvia got things ready for dinner tonight. I checked out places to "call" fur animals. Took garbage to dump. Tom, Kim Huddleston and family, Jim O. & Kari were here for dinner and watch movie. Clouds partially covered the moon, so I didn't try to call any predators.

Saturday, January 9, 1993—mostly sunny, -5° to 14°. Watched football. Allen F. visited. At 11:15 PM, put "Moose Dick" (10-gauge) and caller in truck and went to Tazlina Hill in hopes I could call in a lynx, no luck. Tried to call a fox from on dump road. No luck, got back at 2:00 AM.

Sunday, January 10, 1993—sunny, -10° to 0°. Read until 11:00 AM. Took a Manning trap and set it in a medium size canine trail at gravel pit across from state camp. Got ready to go to Allen and Roxanne's for dinner. Shot a squirrel with 22-250. Tom and Kim and family were at Allen's for dinner, good food and fine time.

Monday, January 11, 1993—sunny, cloudy, some fog, -15° to -10°. Checked canine trap. Went to Glennallen on senior van and recorded a deed and ordered plat maps. Checked trap again when I got back home, and crossed Little Nelchina River looking for tracks. Allen cut off the stock of a rifle to fit Roxanne. Brought it over and visited a while. David came along.

Tuesday, January 12, 1993—partly cloudy, -18° to -8°. Up early, Allen and I went predator calling using his car. Tried for a lynx first, no luck. Then onto Lake Louise Road, tried for fox a couple time and no luck. Drove to end of road, saw where otter and caribou had crossed the road. Some people have been getting caribou. Back home and Sylvia fixed late breakfast. I checked trap to west then checked traps to east with snowgo. A sprung trap at Slide Mountain Trailhead— marten. Re-baited and reset conibear in box nailed on tree. Went north along Slide. Got stuck when slipping off moose tracks just as I was going over a four foot high hump in Cache Creek. Got Lucky and drove snowgo up steep bank and on down trail. Turned around a ½ mile, north of Four Corners. Saw a couple fox and four marten tracks, two of them were fresh. Continued trying to get Remington 22 barrel clean.

Wednesday, January 13, 1993—cloudy, 1" of snow, -18° to 8°. Pulled the trap at State Gravel Pit. Borrowed a sheet metal vise grips from Allen F. Visited there for awhile. Ed F. came in also. Jim and Kari Odden picked up some furs here to take to Fairbanks. Visited awhile. I built a bracket out of Plexiglas and pop riveted it inside a white 5-gallon plastic bucket in such a manner as to hold the speaker off the top of the predator caller when the caller is being carried around.

Thursday, January 14, 1993—mostly sunny, 20° to 22°. Cleaned on .22 rifle some more. Visited Allen. Made lots of phone calls, doctors, insurance, etc.

Friday, January 15, 1993—partly cloudy, -4° to 8° to 2°. Took snowgo to trailhead. Someone had killed a caribou in drainage near our place. Coyote hanging around there. Then saw lynx tracks. Went on to trailhead. No marten in traps. Fuel line came off carburetor, put it back on. When I got back to drainage with boo kill I went north to power line, then east checking out lynx track, it went up Slide Mt. Came home and drove snowgo past green house for Sylvia. Then on down hill and made a trail across lake, came back past boat dock and saw a lynx trail going east. Coyote sure hanging around here. Sign in snow looks like a pair getting ready for breeding season. Looked at old photos all afternoon. Allen brought over a piece of lemon meringue pie. Ed brought catalog back.

Saturday, January 16, 1993—cloudy all day, -4° to 4° Loafed and read most of day. Allen brought his van over and did some mechanic tune up work on it. Sylvia had invited their whole family for supper. Had a nice visit this evening.

Sunday, January 17, 1993—snow, windy morning, mostly cloudy afternoon, 24° to 21°. Truck battery was flat. Put charger on it and visited Ed and Sandy. Got truck started and mounted plow. I had to put two new and different irons on the wings. Shoveled some snow. Plowed our place, teachers, Dobler's.

Monday, January 18, 1993—18° to 0° and around 8° most of day. Re-made one rear shooting sandbag. Tom D. and Tom Huddleston visited. Plowed snow. Played an old violin tape we have.

Tuesday, January 19, 1993—cloudy, light snow, -4° to 2°. From the west on south side of river, snow coming into valley over the Nelchina and Tazlina Glaciers. Slept late. Ordered Gander Mountain boots. Checked Jim's plane, no snow on wings. Went to Crater Lake pullout looking for predator tracks. Saw lynx tracks at Tazlina. Fox at dump. Fox at gravel pit north of Lake Louise Jct. Tried to call this one, no luck. Shot a squirrel at home. Ran trap line. Saw 4-5 new marten tracks. Made a new set for marten. Put flag in a tree 12' from set. Went south of hwy into gravel pit and looked for tracks. Nothing there. Someone had plastic sledded a load out of area south of pit.

Wednesday, January 20, 1993—cloudy, light snow all day, -14° to -7°. Steve M. came to get a 1 ½ pipe coupling. We pumped water. I packed the snowgo trail to the well. Coyote all around here last night. Sylvia and I put a 4" galvanized pipe flu from basement to attic to carry fumes from gas water heater away. Need one more elbow to finish the job.

Thursday, January 21, 1993—partly cloudy, -25° to -13°. Did a few little things in house. Visited at Ed Farmers. Went down to Allen and Roxanne's for moose stew and rhubarb crunch that "Faith" had made. She showed a video movie of her and husband Al hunting cougar in southeastern Cascades of Oregon. Johnny Stewart sent extension wire for the varmint caller.

Friday, January 22, 1993—it was -32° this morning. Plugged in truck for an hour. It didn't start without quite a bit of trouble. Then we went to Palmer, Wasilla. Did shopping then to the Smayda family home. Nice supper and visit.

Saturday, January 23, 1993—stayed over at Smayda's for breakfast. Tom went with me to a gun show in Wasilla. Then Sylvia and I did grocery shopping and drove for home. It was -25° there at Tom and Lisa's and -40° here at home. Picked up some our mail at Allen Farmer's.

Sunday, January 24, 1993—sunny, -43° to -30°. Drew up chart for recording rifle cartridge load testing. Went to school teachers and worked on stove, water heater and propane regulator. Jim and Kari O. here for supper. Sorted a bunch of shot shells, gave 2/3 of them to Jim.

Monday, January 25, 1993—sunny, -47° to -30°. Ed F. sent Robbie over to borrow my weed burner to help get his car started. His antifreeze was frozen also. Allen Farmer visited. Chuck got called back to work. Tom Smayda came up from Palmer to work on the heating stove and install a new water heater in the house is renting to school teacher. I made a threads on black iron pipe for him. He brought treats. Missy F. brought and borrowed movies back. Some of our mail was left in Allen's box and they brought it later.

Tuesday, January 26, 1993—partly cloudy, -35° to -20°. Mailed off application (AARP) for Medicare supplement. We finished the flue hookup to the water heater. We went to Allen and Roxanne for supper. Lucky and Mary were there. We took ice cream and strawberry rhubarb pie for Allen's birthday.

Wednesday, January 27, 1993—mostly sunny, -35° to -8°. Moved some electric wires from near flue. Ran trap line. No fur. One marten track. Coyote track under highline. Repacked trail across our lake, preparing to measure distance across our lake.

Thursday, January 28, 1993—light snow, cloudy, -12° to 8°. Jim and I went to Gulkana Airport. He warmed up his airplane and flew it to his home. I drove his pickup back to his place. Sylvia babysat Kari this afternoon. Kari and Jim had supper with us. I loaned Ed F. some tools to put his roof steel on his house. Charlie Trowbridge phoned. He'll stop by Saturday night late.

Friday, January 29, 1993—cloudy, some snow in the night, 5° to 8°. Squirrel and magpie in confrontation over food Sylvia had put out for small birds. Allen stopped by for coffee. Before he left, Jack and Janet Chamberlin brought some hard board that I am to cut scallop design for them. I've misplaced the charger for cordless driver. Ordered a new gas cook stove for Sylvia.

Saturday, January 30, 1993—sunny, light breeze from west down on lake, -12° to

4°. Wrote lots of letters and put 16 in mailbox. Filled out my longevity bonus application. Drove snowgo down to lake, measured width of our lake south of our well (400 yards). Visited Allen and Roxanne. Broke and packed trail to Charlie's storage shed. Installed choke on snowgo. Darned a pair of wool socks.

Sunday, January 31, 1993—cloudy, light snow, -30° to -4°. Up early and Sylvia fixed breakfast for Charlie, Jim, Kari and I. Plugged in Charlie's car. After a nice visit and Charlie went to his storage shed. He left for Anchorage. Jim and Kari stayed the rest of the day. Frances Collins (Sylvia's sister) called us today. My birthday being tomorrow, Karen and Steve Mailly had us to their place for supper. Karen had made a carrot cake for my birthday. The Farmer family stopped in and had cake also. A cow moose is hanging around our place.

Monday, February 1, 1993—mostly sunny with sun dogs, -18° to -16°. We went on senior van to Glennallen. I got my application for longevity bonus notarized and mail off. Saw one lynx track on Tazlina Hill. Several moose in sight of road. Cow and calf in our yard at home. I picked up marten boxes. Allen and Roxanne had us come to their place to supper. Dave and Dee Johnson from Mendeltna were there also. -38° at Allen's and -28° here, as I write this.

Tuesday, February 2, 1993—mostly sunny, -43° to -30°. Allen and Roxanne came up and had breakfast and we all had a long visit. Ed and Sandy were headed to mailbox at same time. I was there and we visited out there at -30°. Robbie came over on snowgo and borrowed horseshoe puzzle. Theresa and kids phoned in evening. Filled out Sylvia's AARP Medicare insurance application.

Wednesday, February 3, 1993—sunny, some breeze from west, -47° to -20°. Ed saw strange warm air movement on side of Slide Mountain this morning. This is a beaut of a day. Took letter to mailbox and visited Ed & Sandy. Allen stopped there and later came over here and borrowed a 1/2" brad point drill bit. I've been burning wood to supplement the oil this cold spell.

Thursday, February 4, 1993—light snow all day, -28° to -19°. Visited Allen and Roxanne. Visited Ed & Sandy. Wolverine delivered fuel oil today. Darrel is back and called. Coyote got the squirrel and the piece of fat I put out.

Friday, February 5, 1993—mostly sunny, some very light snow, -9° to -6°. Pumped water for house. Can't make the new snowgo choke work. Shoveled a little snow. Plowed snow today. Did some reading. Ed, Sandy, Robbie, Missy and her chum were here for supper.

Saturday, February 6, 1993—mostly sunny, some breeze, fog, -6° to 10°. Wrote some letters. Cut some "scallops" on two - 8 foot pieces of hard board for Jack Chamberlin. Lee Dudley and Sam Weaver stopped by looking for Charlie T.

Henry and Sally called and ask us over to listen to the music. Clem, Henry, and Lee played banjo and two guitars. As we were walking home Charlie T. got here to Nelchina. Unloaded his freezables at our place and went to Henry's to visit.

Sunday, February 7, 1993—mostly sunny, -12° to -2°. Charlie T. got here 10:30 last night and played music at Henry's till 2:00 AM. Charlie made a trip to his storage shed. Lee Dudley visited all afternoon. Charlie went to visit Sam. Back here and we had supper. We had gone over to Henry and Sally's mid afternoon. Coyote walked south across our lake on my snowgo track.

Monday, February 8, 1993—mostly cloudy, -10° to 0°. Sylvia went to Glennallen. I cleaned snow from some roofs. Corky D. asked me to try to plow driveway. Snow too deep and froze hard. Tom H. and friend Mark from W.V. here to pick up his snowgo. Package from South Dakota came today.

Tuesday, February 9, 1993—it was -6° to 6°. We left for Palmer, Wasilla, and Anchorage before daylight and had shopping done by 1:00 PM and headed home. Bought a TV. Saw lots of moose, some very thin, and one coyote.

Wednesday, February 10, 1993—partly cloudy, -4° to 10°. Allen here for coffee. Jack C. here to pickup the boards. I cut scallops on for him. Shoveled snow off roofs. Put choke cable on snowgo. Yearling cow moose hung around here all day browsing on brush. She has a badly injured left rear hock. Lower leg and foot may be frozen. Roxanne's book came today. Tried out snowgo, went to Allen's for coffee. UPS delivered airplane fuel tank for Jim Odden to our place.

Thursday, February 11, 1993—partly cloudy, -4° to 4°. Planned to go to Point of View Lodge and see Denny B. plus hunt, call predators. Hopefully wolves. Had promised some wolf lure to Bob. The lid had rusted on plastic jar. In cutting a hole to drain B.F.F. lure into another jar, I severed a tendon on the top side of my left thumb with a dirty old skinning knife. Very clumsy, dumb of me. Allen drove me to Palmer to emergency room. Thing went slow there (three hours). Doctor doesn't want to sew tendon together till Monday. None of us like this. I think it should have been done today.

Friday, February 12, 1993—mostly cloudy, -4° to 16°. Loafed all morning. Steve M. visited. Ed and Sandy drove us to Valentine children's program. Nice time had by all. Allen borrowed my snowgo and broke a trail to river bluff.

Saturday, February 13, 1993—partly cloudy, 16° to 22°. Allen visited. We took the caller over to river bluff and tried to call wolves, no luck. Got out the old 250 Colt for Allen to use. Stopped at Ed's and looked at his new roof. Allen, his kids and Jim O. and Kari were here for supper. Sylvia fixed sandhill crane.

Sunday, February 14, 1993—mostly cloudy, fog, westerly wind, 18° to 24°. Snow slid off east side garage roof. Put on plow and pushed it into pile. Bonnie W. and Sylvia went to Eureka for pie and brought me back a piece. Allen, Kyle and Ian came over for some hay (lawn clippings).

Monday, February 15, 1993—partly cloudy, 22° to 40°. Allen took me to Palmer in his van. Some snow and rain on the way. I had to wait to see the surgeon. The Doctor opened the cut on my thumb and sewed together the tendon that lifts the end of my thumb. We went to Suzuki dealer (Allen's business). Allen shopped at Carr's. We stopped at Pinnacle Mt. and saw Mae. Saw lots of moose along hwy. We got home about 7:00 PM. Filled Allen's van with gas. Jim O. came over to get some needed fittings to hook up the fuel crossover line on his PA 12 airplane.

Tuesday, February 16, 1993—partly cloudy and sunny, 15° to 32°. Left thumb, hand sore today. Allen was here for breakfast. I went to Oddens. Jim filled his new fuel tank on airplane with gas and fastened cover and fairing down. I forgot the one paper I wanted to copy so I didn't stop at Bartley's. Phoned our daughter Beverly.

Wednesday, February 17, 1993—mostly sunny, very nice day. Thumb feels better. Allen brought over VCR head cleaner tape and had breakfast with us. Didn't do much today. Went to Bartley's, visited and made some copies.

Thursday, February 18, 1993—some fog, cloudy, and sunny, 1° to 10°. Allen was here for breakfast. We went with him to Glennallen. He looked for a job. He got us a lunch. After we got home we visited Jim and Elaine Manning. Elaine just got home from a hysterectomy. Jim and Kari visited in evening. I shot a squirrel this morning.

Friday, February 19, 1993—most sunny, fog early, 4° to 19°. Shot the rifle a few times, trying to lower pressures. Allen borrowed a couple catalogs. Bev phoned, Ivan Bolton passed away.

Saturday, February 20, 1993—foggy till afternoon, then mostly sunny, -3° to 14°. Visited Allen then Lucky's then Sandy and Missy. Sylvia there and we walked home. Read some. Allen brought a sympathy card up. We need one to send to Mary Lou Volk, Ivan passed away. Allen had some pizza with us.

Sunday, February 21, 1993—light snow, cloudy, 8° to 21°. Ash has blown out of trees onto snow. Pumped water today. I shoveled snow off brown storage trailer and two wheel trailer. Picked up some coyote scat and put into a Ziploc bag. Jim Sparks crashed his plane while taking off from the highway near his place. Bart Bartley was with him. Nobody hurt.

Monday, February 22, 1993—cloudy, 10° to 20°. Sylvia went on senior van to Glennallen. Hauled trash to dump for Sandy. Robbie went with me. Allen visited. Later David came over selling cards to Sylvia. Order came from JSC. Most important things didn't come. Will take Allen to Anchorage in morning.

Tuesday, February 23, 1993—cloudy, 13° to 23°. Up at 4:00 AM, dressed and picked up Allen and drove him to airport in Anchorage. He will be working on North Slope. We had breakfast while waiting for stores to open. Did some shopping and picked up Sylvia's new gas stove. I had a rifle head space checked and it was excessive. Doctor looked at my cut thumb and assistant changed the cast. Cast is more comfortable this time. Visited with Mae a few minutes.

Wednesday, February 24, 1993—cloudy, light snow, 10° to 21°. Walked to Roxanne Farmers and got my drill bit. Jim came to watch the TV weather. Stayed for supper and helped install Sylvia's gas cook stove. Big help as I only have one good hand.

Thursday, February 25, 1993—cloudy, 16° to 24°. Did some walking. Moved old stove out to garage. Cleaned up packing and tools. Gathered up some wood cut outs to give to Anna Marie, sort of a thank you for Matt's help. Jim here for weather. We visited and looked at loading tables.

Friday, February 26, 1993—one inch of snow, partly cloudy, 16° to 24°. Did little jobs, put up pegs (child height) for their coats. Went to Bartley's to make some copies. Gave them some wood cutouts to take to Anna Marie. Jim O. here for supper. Jim brought ice cream.

Saturday, February 27, 1993—skiff of snow, mostly sunny, 20° to 32°. Fixed handle on coffee pot. Got truck ready to go to Anchorage to pick up Allen and Ed. Got there a little early. We had supper, left Anchorage, got gas and dab of groceries in Palmer and came on home. Left Allen off at his house and left front hub won't engage. Put chains on to get back up hill and to highway. Left Ed off at his home and went home myself.

Sunday, February 28, 1993—mostly sunny, 20° to 35°. Went to Jim O. and flagged traffic for his takeoff, for Fairbanks. Took a look at front left hub on truck. Something wrong, alright, didn't get it all apart. Lee D. visited and asked about crossing Nelchina River. Mannings had us over for elk hamburger this evening.

Monday, March 1, 1993—partly cloudy, some fog around, 6° to 24°. Cleaned gun. Started fire in garage stove. Worked on truck lock out hub, no luck. Ed Farmer got it dismantled. Allen F. came over and we looked at parts in old truck hub. They are different. Looks like I'll have to get a new hub.

Tuesday, March 2, 1993—mostly sunny, -1° to 24°. Cleaned truck hub parts. Allen and I went to Glennallen in his car and got new guts for the lockout hub. Came home and put it all together. Jacked other wheel and adjusted the wheel bearing.

Wednesday, March 3, 1993—sunny, -16° to 23°. Roxanne's birthday. She went to work. Allen came over to breakfast. I cleaned up tools in garage. Wrote bunch of letters.

Thursday, March 4, 1993—sunny, -13° to 20°. Ed came over and borrowed spinner wrench. Tom H. and son Charlie visited. Covered pr of Sorrel liner soles. Planned and wrote an outline of both rifle and pistol ammo reloading in proper sequence. Tom H. invited us to their place to a stew supper.

Friday, March 5, 1993—sunny, cloudy evening, -4° to 25°. Visited Allen, Roxanne and walked up and down over hill. Visited Ed Farmer. Did some reading. Rosemary and Bart were here to supper.

Saturday, March 6, 1993—mostly sunny, -3° to 20°. We pumped water in top tank today. Water top tank, 2 cups Hilex bleach. Visited Allen. Watched Iditarod start. Walked up and down our hill for the second time today. Red's Gun Repair called to say they were sending my rifle to factory. Rifle to factory, back in four weeks.

Sunday, March 7, 1993—mostly sunny, -4° to 23°. Walked up and down our hill (to lake) two times. Put Tung oil on a folding foot stool for Ellie. Read a lot. Chuck Z. phoned and I got snowgo parts and a ck ready for him.

Monday, March 8, 1993—mostly sunny, several light snows, -6° to 21°. Walked down to Allen's this morning. Sylvia went to Glennallen. Roxanne gave Sylvia a cookie receipt. We ate supper with them. I gave Ellie a folding foot stool.

Tuesday, March 9, 1993—mostly sunny, 3° to 24°. Walked down and up the hill. Ed borrowed snow go and hauled engine stand and crane out to where he could use them. Had to reassemble right lockout hub. Took garbage to dump. Found two woofer and picture frames. Saw fox cat track and two moose at Cache Creek. Mary and Kari Odden visited later in evening.

Wednesday, March 10, 1993—light snow most of day, -5° to 16°. Walked up our hill. Stopped for a minute at Ed's. Rob Yeager is putting a roof on the cabin near Botley Creek.

Thursday, March 11, 1993—cloudy, -4° to 25°. Allen borrowed snowgo oil. Ed needed some steel. Missy borrowed a can of soup. Mary and Kari O. took Sylvia to Point of View Lodge and stayed for supper. Walked the hill again today. Made doctor's appointment for Sylvia.

Friday, March 12, 1993—sunny, -4° to 28°. We went to Palmer, Wasilla. Sylvia met Dr. Cotton and got started on her examinations. We did some grocery shopping. Roads were almost dry.

Saturday, March 13, 1993—sunny, -3° to 28°. Snow slid off north side of greenhouse. Sandy brought over a package that came for me yesterday. I walked the hill twice. Shoveled snow off snowgo trail by greenhouse and off Rudbeck's well. The bulb in their well is still burning and very little ice there. A spruce hen had been eating gravel along the lower road. Tom and Kim Huddleston and family came to supper this evening.

Sunday, March 14, 1993—sunny, 2° to 19°. Took some pix of spruce hen feeding in a spruce tree. Saw her when I was walking on our hill. Phoned Theresa's. Made up package for Lee's birthday. Did some reading. Allen, Roxanne and David and Ellie had supper with us.

Monday, March 15, 1993—sunny, -12° to 20°. Sylvia went to Glennallen on senior van. She mailed package to grandson Lee. I walked our hill twice and did some reading.

Tuesday, March 16, 1993—sunny, -15° to 20°. Sylvia doesn't feel well. She made bread, then rested. I walked the hill twice, to Allen's sawmill and three times to mail box. Copied some recipes onto 3" x 5" cards.

Wednesday, March 17, 1993—sunny, 0° to 25°. Walked our hill twice. Went to Odden's and ran hot water down their drain. Sylvia potted tomatoes and peppers. I did a few non-descript jobs.

Thursday, March 18, 1993—sunny, cloudy evening, -8° to 20°. Still walking the hill. Turned the pump on and off to pump water up to house. Small birds look for food in trees. Saw a squirrel today. Made a chart for Sylvia's blood pressure records. Allen stopped to visit in evening.

Friday, March 19, 1993—sunny, -8° to 26°. Walked hill three times. J & E Manning came over for coffee. Still haven't been able to reach Nadia.

Saturday, March 20, 1993—mostly sunny, -8° to 22°. More walking. Ed borrowed some solder. I had a touch of intestinal flu this afternoon. Nadia phoned. Ed and Sandy asked Sylvia and I to have supper with them.

Sunday, March 21, 1993—cloudy all day, 0° to 28°. Walked hill. Also we went to KROA and watched of ski touring races. Ran water down Odden's drain. Phones about goat and fox skins. Checked Jim's house.

Monday, March 22, 1993—cloudy, 7° to 29°. Visited a few minutes with Allen. Also over at Mannings. Gassed the truck. Loafed a lot. Read. Sylvia worked with her bedding plants. The tomatoes and peppers are looking good.

Tuesday, March 23, 1993—cloudy, got one inch of snow, 7° to 33°. We went to Wasilla. Sylvia had a mammogram and chest X-rays. Doctor then tried to get a biopsy and failed. She (the doctor) gave Sylvia medicine for her cough and lung trouble. Doctor took my cast off. We did a little shopping and got home before dark. We saw three moose calves on way to Palmer. One moose and one spruce hen on way home.

Wednesday, March 24, 1993—cloudy and breezy, ash in the air. Did some correspondence and phoned AARP insurance. Walked hill. Smashed some pop cans. Robbie came over to visit. Tell us his dad broke a rib.

Thursday, March 25, 1993—partly cloudy, breezy, -8° to 24°. Shot a squirrel, walked the hill. Sandy gave us some laundry detergent they are allergic to. We had supper with Allen's. Sam Weaver was there also.

Friday, March 26, 1993—mostly cloudy, -8° to 25°. Walked hill. Sent order to Gander Mt. Talked to Ed. Allen stopped by for coffee and brought chocolate cake and I dished up ice cream to go with it. Rounded up more 3-pound coffee cans for Sylvia to transplant tomatoes.

Saturday, March 27, 1993—sunny, 6° to 28°. Went to dump picked up some .45 cases. Someone had been shooting at a sign and padlock. Tom Dobler is back from his job, visited him. Checked Odden's and ran water down drain. Walked hill. Manning here for coffee. Wants me to do some sawing for him.

Sunday, March 28, 1993—mostly sunny, breezy in afternoon, 4° to 38°. Dust from river very nearly obscured the south shore. Walked the hill, made small stakes for Sylvia's plants. Soaked my hand in Epsom salts. Darrel G. phoned. Did some more research on reloading.

Monday, March 29, 1993—mostly sunny, some breeze and dusty over near the river, 6° to 39°. Visited Allen. Pumped water. Washed ice and some dirt off the truck. Saw the spruce hen. Ed and Sandy went to town. Robbie stopped by after school for awhile.

Tuesday, March 30, 1993—sunny, 5° to 39°. Did hill walk. Lots of squirrels. Shot another one. Put up two small fluorescent lamps for Sylvia's plants. She went to Mary B. house and gave her a perm.

Wednesday, March 31, 1993—mostly sunny, 12° to 41°. Visited Allen. Ed was there. Walked hill. Karn came over and borrowed some canned goods. I fastened some trim on the truck. Shoveled some loose ice off the garage floor. Walked over to teachers place and sure enough the snow had slid off the roof of apt. garage roof. Back home and put snow plow on truck and cleared the teacher's driveway. Slept a little. Tonight was potluck and drawing for Ruger .338 Mark II stainless rifle. It was won by Buck Brown from Gulkana.

Thursday, April 1, 1993—sunny, 10° to 41°. Trail on our hill was too soft to walk by the time I got to it. Allen stopped by for apple pie and ice cream. Ed came over to borrow a long drill bit but I don't have one. Fooled around drilling and prying some Berdan primers - wasn't too successful as there is a anvil still in the way. Crossbills and evening grosbeak were in our trees this evening.

Friday, April 2, 1993—sunny, 11° to 41°. The kids are trying to thaw a sunken boat out of the ice by spreading sand over it. Letter from Nadia (she is now engaged). Allen brought old Colt 250 snowgo back. We had a cup of hot Tang at Rudbeck's. Boy are they busy. Word is that Elaine has MS. Soaked my hand in hot water a lot today. Shoveled some snow off old garage door. A spruce hen slept several hours beside the garage. I had garage door open all day, that helps dry ice and water off the floor.

Saturday, April 3, 1993—mostly sunny, 13° to 35°. Very sick all night and all day. Countless trips to bathroom. Phoned Nadia and congratulated her on the engagement to Chuck.

Sunday, April 4, 1993—mostly sunny, 10° to 35°. Slept late and woke up feeling lots better. Shot another pesky squirrel this morning. Rested today and went to a fine dinner at Bartley's. Rudbecks brought a movie about fishing.

Monday, April 5, 1993—sunny, 11° to 37°. Woke up sick with the trots. Sylvia went to Glennallen. Sylvia gave Karn several dozen hot house plants.

Tuesday, April 6, 1993—sunny, 12° to 38°. Almost well today. Sylvia worked with her plants all day. I made a holder, stand for some dummy cartridges to aid in setting a bullet seater die. Built a simple box to put VCR in and set TV on top. Rudbeck came over and borrowed a screwdriver.

Wednesday, April 7, 1993—sunny, 12° to 36°. Sent longevity form in. Very nice weather, snow is going fast. I moved snowgo to different parking spot so I could get Suzuki out, ran it a little bit. Visited Ed. Built a device to keep outdoor light off TV glass. Sylvia doesn't like it. Opened lid on well. Bulb is burned out and no ice on well. We pumped water today. Letter from Savage rifle repaired.

Thursday, April 8, 1993—sunny, 11° to 41°. Visited Ed and down to Allen's. I had put a boo jawbone in a bucket of dirt last winter. Took it out and scrubbed it off. The soil bacteria had cleaned the tissues off the bone.

Friday, April 9, 1993— cloudy, sun, cloudy, 11° to 36°. Checked Jim's house. Jim's letters were in his box. Tried to forward them. Went to dump. Cleaned ashes from house stove. Reloaded some cartridges. Shot two squirrels. Manning here to supper. Rudbecks came over and watched TV and visited.

Saturday, April 10, 1993—sunny, 21° to 42°. Weaver scope came. Visited Allen. Cleaned spark plugs on ATV. Read some. Rudbeck's here to supper.

Sunday, April 11, 1993—sunny, 25° to 35°. Made some plant stakes for Sylvia. Read some. More water coming up on our lake ice. Took off the rubber bands and wood block from a caribou jaw bone I glued together.

Monday, April 12, 1993—cloudy, partly sunny, 15° to 43°. Made and put up four small shelves in closet on my side upstairs. Painted a tin can. Sylvia went to Glennallen. Allen and Roxanne took me to KROA for a cheeseburger. Rifle came back today. I got started mounting a scope on it. Allen came over for trap bait to put out across the lake. Robbie came over and borrowed power tin snips for his dad.

Tuesday, April 13, 1993—mostly sunny, 13° to 41°. Breezy in evening. Gets pretty near dark at 10:00 PM. Shot rifle sighting in scope. Loaded a few also. Spent time cleaning the bore.

Wednesday, April 14, 1993—16° to 42°. Shot rifle, loaded a few and shot them. I'm disappointed in the chamber of this rifle. Sunny most of day. Cloudy evening. Lots of snow melted. Visited Allen and Ed. Allen came over and borrowed three eggs to make pumpkin pie. Mae is visiting. Last weekend was her 70th birthday. Roxanne fixed a turkey dinner for Lucky and Mary, Allen's, Mae, Sylvia and I and Huddlestons.

Thursday, April 15, 1993—mostly cloudy, 26° to 42°. Didn't do much. Elaine brought Caleb Mailly over to de-sprout some potatoes.

Friday, April 16, 1993—mostly sunny, 30° to 46°. Shot rifle 8 times. Visited Lucky, Allen. Went to supper at Manning's.

Saturday, April 17, 1993—mostly cloudy. Jim, Kari and Ruth visited. Borrowed a coupling. For load development made cartridge board. Sanded slivers off storage shed door. Henry and Sally came over visited and brought some cedar planters. We went to KROA in evening. A band there in new dining room. Got to visit with lots of people.

Sunday, April 18, 1993—mostly sunny, 27° to 47°. Drove ATV down to dirt stock pile and brought two bucket up for Sylvia. She worked with some plants. Tom Dobler visited in afternoon. Gave us some smoked fish and magazines. We gave him some potatoes. Bald eagle hunts along our hillside.

Monday, April 19, 1993—cloudy, sunny, partly cloudy, windy all day, lots of ash and dust, 29° to 47°. Had lunch with Allen and Roxanne. They sent a rhubarb pie home with us. Fred Rungee stopped by with ice cream and visited. He enjoyed two pieces pie and ice cream. Worked at tuning ATV. Shot rifle. Got two good groups.

Tuesday, April 20, 1993—mostly sunny, 24° to 44°. Shot rifle and cleaned it. Allen came over while I was working on ATV carburetor. He stored some rhubarb pie in our freezer and had a piece of pie with me. Sylvia did laundry and some planting.

Wednesday, April 21, 1993—sunny, 20° to 45°. We went to doctor in Palmer and Wasilla for my thumb and meds for Sylvia. Did grocery shopping. Saw eight cow boo 3 miles west of here. Saw one cow moose and a eagle. Some sheep on Sheep Mt. What a beautiful day.

Thursday, April 22, 1993—sunny, 21° to 48°. Visited Ed, then Allen. Allen and boys got the sunken boat up on the ice from in front of our dock and they dragged it home behind their ATV. Lots of swans flying west. Some hung around here today. We think the young ravens are flying around now. Once in a while an eagle is seen. I built two flicker boxes for Henry and took them over there. Shot rifle.

Friday, April 23, 1993—sunny, very nice day, 26° to 51°. A little light breeze. Karn visited. I loaded some shells. Shot some. Cleaned trap, snowgo storage. Moved it all in wood shed. Plan to put a floor in trap, snowgo part. Borrowed a section of Hoffman's harrow from Rudbecks and dragged our lane in an effort to work the volcanic ash down into the gravel. I sure don't like the chamber on this rifle. Sylvia worked with greenhouse today. She has a couple tomatoes started, the pepper is as big as a golf ball.

Saturday, April 24, 1993—sunny, a beaut of a day, 24° to 51°. Went walking around looking for moose horns. Saw tracks of 2-3 wolves. No horns. Nadia called. Loaded and shot a few shells. Denny Eastman and friend Ken got here with Denny's boat. We went to Point of View Lodge and had a nice dinner with Billmans. They also had Jack Hanson and a lady friend as guests.

Sunday, April 25, 1993—partly cloudy, 34° to 51°. Dragged a harrow section around the yard with the ATV in an effort to mix the ash into the gravel. Visited Denny E. and his friend Ken. Worked on trap, snowgo storage. Swept ash off some roofs. Eastman and Ken were here to supper. We talked guns, trapping and I showed them my AK Fish & Game Wolf Canine trapping movie.

Monday, April 26, 1993— sunny and beautiful, 32° to 51°. Lots of swans flying and saw one flock of Canadians. Sylvia went to Glennallen and saw two swans with a duck flying between them. I got a piece of steel and a bolt from Allen. Al & Faith Pakowski from Hatcher's Pass are visiting Farmers. We went down after supper and had homemade ice cream and apple cake with them. Watched a couple movies after ice cream. I've started a mounting bracket and will move the winch on ATV to the front end. Don't like it on the rear. Shot a squirrel this morning. Sent fired cartridges cases to Savage. Otter went east on south side of our lake shortly before dark.

Tuesday, April 27, 1993—sunny with sun dogs!! 30° to 52°. This evening worked on winch mounting for ATV. Pump in well quit. Checked several things and found wire burned in to inline from house to pump. Allen and Karn visited. Sylvia and I went to CVEA Mtg. in Glennallen. Went to dinner for her birthday. I found and picked up a tire and wheel that fit our pickup. It had been there since before the ash fall!

Wednesday, April 28, 1993—cloudy, 34° to 51°. Repaired elect wire to well. Put 2 "tee's" in water line, one at garden and one at edge of lawn. Finished mounting winch on ATV. Cleaned front wheel brake and started on rear brake. Ed borrowed some screws. I borrowed ATV manual from Allen. Sylvia worked in greenhouse. Karn was here to supper. Frances C. called Sylvia this evening.

Thursday, April 29, 1993—mostly sunny, 30° to 50°. Karn and Bonnie took Sylvia to Long Rifle for lunch. I finished the brakes on ATV, started cleaning and painting the rear mtg. Bracket. worked on trap storage. Took Allen's manual back. Allen, David and I went up Slide to a drift near the top that stopped us. Nice view from up there. Didn't see any bears from up there.

Friday, April 30, 1993—sunny, 26° to 50°. ATV has bad tire and oil leak. Put floor in trap-snowgo shed and one shelf. Burned some trash. Shot a squirrel. Sure sore and stiff all day. Shot some mild loads. Roxanne and Allen brought a fried chicken, potato salad, cream cheese custard pie for a birthday lunch for

Sylvia. Very nice. Ed came over in evening and returned some screws he had borrowed.

Saturday, May 1, 1993—partly cloudy, 32° to 52°. Took apart a carburetor I had salvaged last summer and put a spring from it into the carburetor on the oil heater in the greenhouse. Seems to work fine. Visited Allen. Finished sorting, hanging and boxing traps. Burned some trash.

Sunday, May 2, 1993—cloudy, very light rain and clear in evening, 30° to 46°. Pulled recoil starter on ATV and removed oil seal there. We carried the tomato plants out to greenhouse and Sylvia set them into the beds. She went to Karn's to do her hair. I visited Allen. Lucky was there. Two swans on our lake. Heard coyotes to west. Marsh hawk and eagle on lake.

Monday, May 3, 1993—partly cloudy, foggy early morning, 25° to 52°. Ed called and asked me to come watch Mother Griz and two yearling cubs. They were above tree line on Slide Mountain. I pulled the wheels and bearings on ATV trailer. 2 bearings are rough and may run this season—two seals will need replacing also. Took a flat tire off snowgo trailer and put spare on. Shot a squirrel. Pulled canoe out to where it is handy.

Tuesday, May 4, 1993—mostly cloudy, 25° to 43°. Sylvia, Karn and Bonnie went to Anchorage. I went to dump, looked for bear tracks. Went towards Lake Louise Road, picked a truck tire out of ditch, before Woods Creek. Went up Lake L. Road, picked up some brass at mill. Saw boo tracks. Back at home, change oil and oil filter on truck. Allen called and wanted help with getting ready with stakes so Lucky could level the stakes with his transit. The forms are for a garage addition. Started polishing the brass. Arctic terns are over out lake ice.

Wednesday, May 5, 1993—cloudy, sunny, windy, dusty, cloudy again, 33° to 45°. Helped Allen with his forms for cement. Cleaned woodshop, repaired marten box. Cleaned two gal roofing nails. Cleaned and polished some brass. Sylvia and ladies got back from Anchorage in early evening. Brought repairs and repair book for Suzuki ATV.

Thursday, May 6, 1993—mostly sunny, some wind and dust off the river, 32° to 51°. Put new seal and gasket on ATV. Tried again to fix the leak in a rear tire. No luck. Sorted some nails. Went to Allen's to get some tire repair. Went back in evening to give Roxanne a flower. Allen had just come home. Rest of family was at church.

Friday, May 7, 1993—mostly cloudy, some sleet, 32° to 48°. Went to Allen's and we ran cement. Ed, Karn and Roxanne helped. Sylvia did 10 sweatshirts. We went to a little entertainment program the kids at Nelchina school put on. Went to Smayda's place and picked up an old propane water heater. Visited Ed in the evening.

Saturday, May 8, 1993—several snow showers moved through, 31° to 45°. Ask Allen to go with me to Chuck Z. and get ATV tire repaired. Then went up Lake Louise Road looking for a bear. Saw where young griz fed on boo scraps. Picked up some small article that had been lost along the road. Stopped at dump. Found two life jackets, a basketball hoop in dump for Allen's kids. Loaded some cartridges. Mounted ATV wheel. Lots of ducks in all puddles. Ice melting all around our lake.

Sunday, May 9, 1993—mostly sunny, 31° to 42°. Took Sylvia to breakfast at KROA. She left sweatshirts, clocks, 3 hooped beaver pelts for Carol to sell in gift shop. Walked around our place looking for some steel to make a circle to break the bead on rear ATV tire. Sylvia gave some flowers to Sandy. Mannings left for Denali Park for summer. Started widening the switch back trail on our hill. More ice out today. Breezes blowing ice back and forth on lake.

Monday, May 10, 1993—mostly sunny, 31° to 48°. Snow on ground when we got up. Melted off during the day. We went to Glennallen on senior van. Visited Allen. Later Tom S. phoned. I went over to Vernetta's and checked stove out. Then Allen and I went up Slide Mountain and looked for bears with binoculars and spotting scope. Impressive view though. Sure is great to go out and do things. Most of lake ice is out today.

Tuesday, May 11, 1993—mostly sunny, windy in evening, 30° to 46°. Walked around the lake. Looked at beaver house and abandoned houses. Variety of ducks, shore birds, gulls, and a wood cock, loon etc. A moose had died on south east corner very near the lake. The little boy's "fort" is dilapidated!! Saw their canoe paddle floating but out of reach for me. Took snow plow lift off truck and covered it with a tarp. Widened more of switch back trail. Visited Allen a couple of minutes. He and his boys are going fishing. Brought my shovel and wheel barrow home.

Wednesday, May 12, 1993—mostly sunny, 30° to 56°. Very nice day. Some breeze. Last of the ice went out. Cut willows on south side of wind break on south side of garden. Trimmed them, formed them into circles in a 5-gallon bucket and a barrel. Cleaned air filter on ATV. Visited Ed. Chopped a little on switch back trail.

Thursday, May 13, 1993—sunny, beaut of a day, 37° to 56°. Visited Allen. Flickers at nest box. Did a few small jobs. Ed came over and borrowed a nut driver. We went to telephone co-op mtg. Stopped by Darrel's and gave him clothes and some bedding for dogs.

Friday, May 14, 1993—sunny, windy and dusty in evening, 39° to 66°. Built a bore guide for .22 cal. cleaning rod. Sylvia went to Anchorage with Karn. Allen brought garden hose back. Hundreds of lesser scaup on our lake. Widened out more of switch back trail. Bears haven't shown up on Slide Mt. again. Gave Ed a bunch of magazines to read. Two bull boo, two cow boo at the lake shore near our well.

Saturday, May 15, 1993—sunny, some breeze, quite dry and dusty, 38° to 67°. Ash puffs up from my feet when I walk. Visited Ed. Gave Sandy some rhubarb. Got some camp gear together. Cleaned up and burned a lot of junk. Worked some more on switch back trail. Visited Allen and ask if he wanted to go back to his cabin. Cut up a 15-gallon and a 30-gallon drum to make a lead melting unit. Found the misplaced charger for the cordless screw driver.

Sunday, May 16, 1993—sunny, some breeze and dusty, 36° to 75°. Watered some of both greenhouses. Opened vents and doors to cool them down. Karn's temp got to 110°. Went to dump. Checked out gravel pit. Cleaned up more junk around here. Burned some of it. Mary O. visited in the evening after Sylvia and Karn got back from town. Flickers had sex. Tree swallows looking at small bird house.

Monday, May 17, 1993—sunny, windy and very dusty, ash from the west, 37° to 76°. Started on lead melter. Put screen door on. Got boards down for flower box for a picture window. Pressure blew water line apart at a splice. Harold and Rachel Dimmick were here to get water. I went down there with some fiber glass repair for one of his boats. So dusty we stayed in the house most of afternoon and evening. Loaded some shells. Sandy brought Sylvia a nice afghan and two banana nut breads.

Tuesday, May 18, 1993—partly cloudy, a little breeze, 45° to 64°. Worked on lead melter. It's all done except for a shelf to hold the ingot molds. Got started on the molds. Sylvia washed the lawn with the hose and hi pressure nozzle. Phoned around looking for some chairs. Went to Tom Huddleston's for Kendra's birthday. Peter and Patrick H., Dave Johnson and Allen Farmer's— Karen, Malley's were there. Fish have frozen out of Mirror Lake.

Wednesday, May 19, 1993—sunny, some gentle breezes, 38° to 75°. Very dry and dusty from ash. We tilled the garden and planted three rows of potatoes and put in come cabbage plants. The lead melter is finished except for one brace. I finished the two ingot molds. I put handles in three heavy hammers. Allen came over this evening and told me about his latest ATV trip and griz sow, two cubs and one boar and boar tracks north of Cal's, Old Man Creek and

Little Nelchina River.

Thursday, May 20, 1993—sunny, cloudy, 37° to 75°. Sylvia finished planting the garden and watered it and the greenhouse. I finished the lead melter. Put another hammer handle in and an double bit axe handle in. Took all horns out of brown trailer looking for ladle for lead. Cleaned out and burned and threw away some junk. Visited Ed and Sandy. Shot a squirrel that was trying to get in a bird house. Loaded up some more brass for "plinking." Adjusted trigger on rifle. Checked under hood of truck.

Friday, May 21, 1993—mostly cloudy, rain in Anchorage, 37° to 56°. We got some shopping done. No chairs and few primers. No lead sinker mold. Waited 3 ½ hrs and the man's wife didn't come home to sell it to us. Windy evening, huge dust cloud blowing off the Nelchina River bars and flood plain. Disappointed in our shopping luck today.

Saturday, May 22, 1993—partly cloudy, 37° to 59°. Repositioned two shelves upstairs and put up a cupboard like shelf. Cleaned the conduit. Cleaned up garage work bench top. Put up pegboard strip above bench and below window. Sylvia watered lawn, garden etc, gave Karn a perm this evening.

Sunday, May 23, 1993—mostly sunny, some breeze, 37° to 60°. Did some rifle shooting this morning. May have found a good bullet powder primer combination. Sylvia put lime on garden and lawn. Put fertilizer on lawn and did other plant work in greenhouse. She gave Karn cabbage plants.

Allen called and wanted to go to Nelchina River and Sam's cabin and look for bear. We parked at Moosey Boo and drove his King Quad on Lee's trail till Sam's trail forked off. Then we walked on to Sam's old cabin. It is sinking into the tundra. We walked along the bluff to another cabin Allen and Ed had built many years ago. It is in pretty good shape yet, or at least with some work it could be used. Maybe there is 100 traps hanging, rusted on cabin walls. A bear (black) had been digging for roots near by. We spent some time glassing for bears and only saw lots of tracks. There were old powder and cartridge cases lying on the dirt floor of the cabin. The chimney for the kerosene lamp wasn't broke!! Strange with everything else in disarray.

Monday, May 24, 1993—mostly sunny, some dark clouds to the north, 36° to 60°. Did small jobs all day. Tested a method of melting the lead and it worked. Sent order to Lock, Stock and Barrel. Sylvia went to Glennallen on senior van. Allen & I were going fishing and black bear hunting but got to watching a movie Sylvia put on VCR and we didn't go.

Tuesday, May 25, 1993—mostly cloudy, 32° to 57°. Got things ready to melt lead. Sylvia and I chopped several hundred feet of lead covered wire into 12

inch pieces. Piled it all on back of pickup. I melted about ½ of it and had lots
of trouble with frost on outside of my propane bottle. The torch would almost
refuse to burn. I rigged the "grizzly" over a slanting piece of steel and by heating
the propane cylinder with the torch I managed to get the rest of the lead melted
off the wire. Boy and I tired and sore tonight.

Wednesday, May 26, 1993—mostly sunny, 32° to 61°. Sylvia and Karn took
Sandy to lunch and picked up two small bottles of propane for me. I worked at
melting lead and poured it into a variety of ingots. 350# of them and that is
about ½ of the lead I melted down. Visited Allen and Roxanne. Allen and I
went to the dump. I had three garbage cans. I salvaged a 2" x 4" x 6' and a 1
7/8 ball for trailer hitch. Allen got a spare tire and jack, muffler and other
goodies. We weren't able to get my truck back to his logs. Chuck Farmer is
back from his trip. Saw bear tracks in dump.

Thursday, May 27, 1993—good rain during the night, 32° to 61°. It snowed for
awhile around 8:00 AM. Lots of snow down to about 3300' elevation. Repaired
old door on lean-to. Straightened up some things. Hauled two loads dirt for
Sylvia. Allen came over and put air in a trailer tire. Roxanne and Al had coffee
with us. I built a target pistol rest from a picture I saw. Weather looks like frost
tonight so we protected Sylvia's plants the best we can. Started the heater in the
greenhouse. Cleaned a rifle. My back hurts a lot all day, every day. We have
eaten the first bell pepper, very large and tasty.

Friday, May 28, 1993—beautiful day, some breeze and dust devils south of
Nelchina River and over at "Y" on Botley Creek, 20° to 65°. Gathered up
antlers to sell this week end. We went to picnic "last day of school" and ran
some cement at the basketball hoop. Mike Roscovious loaned me a .224 bullet
casting mold. Sat. is his last day as he retires. Built a box and incorporated an
old sweatshirt for a cast bullet cushion and catch container. Darrel G. stopped
to visit. Gave him two tires and a washing machine. A little after 11:00 PM, a
moose walked west on south side of our lake feeding and drinking out of the
lake. There is much swan and duck activity on lake. Flickers are still making
love several times a day.

Saturday, May 29, 1993—sunny, some breeze. Beaut of a day, 32° to 70°. We
loaded horns on snowgo trailer and pulled them out by the hwy. with the ATV.
Only sold one boo jawbone and 2 doz. fish worms. Discouraging. Ed visited,
then Robbie. I quit and brought everything home at 5:00 PM.

Sunday, May 30, 1993—sunny, some breezes and dust devils, 32° to 71°. Sold
some moose and boo horns. Sally and Chris and his bride to be went out on
ATV and terrorized the country. Bob Rudbeck got back from Minnesota. Allen
and Roxanne invited us down for T-bone steak supper—it was good!

Monday, May 31, 1993—sunny, light breeze, beaut of a day, 36° to 70°. Shot a few loads, all flyers. Serviced truck. Sylvia cooked chicken. We went to a picnic at Point of View Lodge. Just a few friends. Dan, Jason, Ian and I went to Evergreen Lodge. There Jack let Dan have a boat for the summer. We had to thicken the transom and rebuild the boat drain plug and put steering handle back on motor. Jason ran boat to Lodge (bow very high). We brought Caleb Malley to his home. Ate a bite and loaded some more cartridges. Trying to develop a plinking load.

Tuesday, June 1, 1993—sunny, some breeze, then none, 39° to 71°. And the mosquitoes are bothersome especially down near the lake as we found out as the waterline parted twice. So I put double clamps on the connection this time. Cut a drum into 1/3 - 2/3rds. Used the 2/3rds end to bury a buffalo skull in so the bacteria clean it up. Some hide and hair on it yet. I cut the chin whiskers off and tied them in little bundles to tie on Indian dance sticks and medicine wheels. Checked out old water heater and salvaged the burner off it. Looked over my small lead melter—but will wait for new electric before I do any casting. Hauled a load of dirt and one of gravel in ATV trailer. Visited Allen. Weather proofed both steps of house. Rudbecks had fried clams with us at supper time.

Wednesday, June 2, 1993—some rain in the night, 33° to 71°. Some light rain occasionally on way to Anchorage. We got up at 5:00 AM. Got caught in construction slow down and got to furniture sale on Elmendorf AFB a few minutes late. Luckily Bonnie Wikle was there and had grabbed up all the tags off the kinds of chairs we wanted. She let us have six of them. Sylvia saw a TV cabinet she liked and bought it. We loaded chests and chairs of Bonnie's on our load and hauled them out of there to her place. I got a sinker mold while in town. Wasn't able to get some things. Some guy got over the center line and broke the mirror on my truck. Lucky I had sun glasses on as glass flew in cab of truck. Only one small cut on my cheek.

Thursday, June 3, 1993—sunny and nice breezes to blow away the bugs, 42° to 71°. A really nice day. Repaired the truck mirror. Took back rest and cushions off the six chairs. Sylvia cleaned (washed) the wood and I sanded the places that needed it. She stained (touch up) and put a coat of tung oil on them. They will be very nice after another couple coats of tung oil. I visited Ed a couple minutes and then Allen in afternoon. We had watermelon at Allen's. Went down to dock on lake and just sat and watched the water and the ducks. Gave Roxanne some fence for her flowers.

Friday, June 4, 1993—sunny and breezy, 42° to 73°. Water line pipe blew off at the elbow in the well. Too much pressure when we only run one hose. Did lots of target practice. 60 gr. Bullets didn't shoot well. Visited Ed. Saw Allen at

Ed's. We went to dump meeting at KROA. Not enough officers present to have meeting, so it has been delayed three weeks. Found a boat fender along highway on the way home.

Saturday, June 5, 1993—sunny, partly cloudy, breezy, 38° to 74°. Dust blowing off river. Very little reached us. ½ day of cleaning rifle. Washed pickup windows. Got ready a wiener roast grill. We had Allen, Roxanne and kids here to supper. Bob and Karn came over and had apple pie.

Sunday, June 6, 1993—sunny and windy, small white caps on our lake, 42° to 60°. I went to Chuck Z. at Tolsona Lake and he mounted two new steel belted tires on the ATV wheels. We had a good visit. Checked out the dump. Mounted wheels on ATV. Pumped gas from drums into overhead rank. Shoveled ash contaminated gravel from parking area at Artic entry. Put on east side and so enlarged the area. Raked some of the other area a dozen times. The wind would carry the ash off. Allen came over and I helped him cut some classifying screen for a sluice box he is building. Sylvia did lots laundry and fixed up two pair Carhartts for me.

Monday, June 7, 1993—partly cloudy, breezy all day, shower in evening, 33° to 60°. Shoveled more ash and top gravel today. Cast some .225 bullets. Cleaned up some trash and hauled it to dump. Sylvia went on senior van to Glennallen. Tried a new way to lube bullets.

Tuesday, June 8, 1993—mostly sunny, light breeze, 42° to 60°. Visited Allen and ask him to help me with the truck. We put new seals, bearings, cleaned the rear brake shoes. Put new gear lube in both differentials and the transfer case. Paid Allen and gave him a chainsaw. He got a job today with Summit Paving. We had supper at their house. Pat Landers brought parts out to us.

Wednesday, June 9, 1993—part cloudy, rain and hail mid afternoon, 43° to 59°. We worked in garden first thing this morning. Sylvia mowed lawn. I cast some bullets. Not having much luck getting good, well filled out, bullets. Called Paul as it's his birthday. Talked to Steve. Shot some cast bullet loads.

Thursday, June 10, 1993—partly cloudy to cloudy in evening, 43° to 63°. Cast more bullets and started on canon ball sinkers. A little trouble there. Lead cools too fast. Shot some of cast bullets. Results about like yesterday. Ed, Sandy, Robbie, Vernetta and Emmi and Sevda, her daughter were here for supper.

Friday, June 11, 1993—partly cloudy, 42° to 64°. We took Mike to Point of View Lodge to get his equipment. We went on to Glennallen and paid for truck parts. Back home and shot some and loaded more so I can shoot tomorrow.

Sylvia and Karn went to Bartley's in evening.

Saturday, June 12, 1993—mostly sunny, 40° to 68°. Did some test shooting. Loaded a few rounds to "wipe" any lead out of the bore that cast loads might have left there. Built a penetration (bullet) box for light plinker loads. Shot the squirrel that tries to get into the bird nesting boxes. Cleaned up more ash. Sharpened Stihl chain saw. Visited Ed. Rosemary, Anna Marie and her two daughters and a lady from Texas visit here this afternoon. I gave Anna Marie some wood craft pieces. My wrists are sure sore the last couple of days.

Sunday, June 13, 1993—mostly sunny, light breeze, 41° to 71°. Sylvia cut aspen on the hill side and vacuumed the truck. I cut down a bunch of spruce so the north sun can reach the greenhouse. I nailed some plywood and dunage blocks together and filled it with gravel for a bullet stop. Shot some targets and got one extra good group. The "flyers" give me the trouble. Trimmed up the trees. Robbie visited. Sevda rode her bike through our yard and said hi. Four girls came over in morning.

Monday, June 14, 1993—mostly sunny, windy in evening, 43° to 74°. Sylvia went to Glennallen on the senior van. Darrel gave her some wheel weights. I jacked up, leveled artic entry. Got ready to pour ingots and casting. Made a repair on Sylvia's entertainment center. Our VCR is out of order. Hoed potatoes in garden. Sylvia did dishes and cut more aspen down.

Tuesday, June 15, 1993—rain last evening, partly cloudy today, shower again this evening, 49° to 69°. Sylvia went to Anchorage with Rudbecks. I cast more bullets and tried them in rifle, trying to get a mix of alloy's that shoots well. Cleaned rifle and weighed each individual bullet and picked out the rejects.

Wednesday, June 16, 1993—rain in night and quite a bit of rain till mid afternoon, then partly cloudy and breezy, 53° to 59°. Cast some different wt. bullets. Tested lead alloy for hardness. Cleaned and tuned molds. Mold handles came loose so I took them off, cleaned and reinstalled them with epoxy. UPS ask directions to neighbors. Mae called, wanted her heating stove started up. Sylvia got back from Anchorage about 5:00 PM.

Thursday, June 17, 1993—mostly sunny, cloudy evening, 37° to 58°. Melted down some more lead. Hauled garbage to dump. Cast some more bullets. Put gas checks on some and lubed and sized them. Robbie came over to borrow a nut driver for his dad. He came back to watch me cast some bullets. Sylvia cut more aspen, some laundry and cut out a stump. She visited neighbors. My back is very bad.

Friday, June 18, 1993—some showers, sun, cloudy, 45° to 62°. Cast some lead.

Melted down more wheel weights. Visited Rudbecks. Load more test loads in an effort to find most accurate load. Those I shot today were not exceptional. The two with magnum primers were best.

Saturday, June 19, 1993—lots of rain, some hard showers, a little sunshine in between, 45° to 58°. Sylvia shortened a pair of down filled North Slope Alleska pants and reinstalled zippers up the outside of legs. Shelly Johnson (not sure of last name) and daughter Tabatha visited in afternoon. Nadia phone to wish me Happy Father's Day. So nice of her to call. I worked on a mold. It had gotten rusty many years ago. It may never be right. I did get it to cast some bullets.

Sunday, June 20, 1993—sun, cloudy, showers, little of bit hail, 47° to 61°. Cast a few bullets. Shot some at a target. Checked cook stove (smelled gas), no leaks. Checked VCR, it's ok. Sylvia cut some aspen. Cleaned rifle. Karn ask us over for walleye supper - very good. Watched two movies.

Monday, June 21, 1993—mostly cloudy, rain in afternoon and evening, 43° to 59°. Sylvia went to Glennallen. I did a variety of small jobs. Goldeneyes are doing their courting flights. A coyote walked up to the SE corner of greenhouse. I called Sylvia's attention to it and it left as she raised her arm.

Tuesday, June 22, 1993—sunny, showers, cloudy, 42° to 59°. Sylvia did laundry. I went to Bartley's and made some copies. Shot rifle and cleaned it. Put up three small shelves. Rudbecks came over in afternoon to tell us they had sold their house and would build another below the hill. A cat tried to get into a flicker box. David F. drove his dad's ATV through our yard—drove into a tree! He didn't get hurt, and will learn how to dodge the trees when they leap out in front of him.

Wednesday, June 23, 1993—fog on our lake, 40° to 64°. Fog and some rain on way to Anchorage. Did some shopping there. Then back to Wasilla to Sylvia's doctor's appointment. Exam and consultation are set up. Home and unload groceries and on to KROA to Nelchina-Mendeltna Corp. Voted in election of officers. Then home. The flickers hatched out yesterday.

Thursday, June 24, 1993—partly cloudy, 45° to 67°. Few light distant showers. Loaded some cartridges and shot them. Got some good groups. Repaired top of bench.

Friday, June 25, 1993—mostly cloudy, some rain, fog on the way to Palmer, 46° to 63°. Up early and in to hospital in Palmer for 9:00 AM appointment for Sylvia's sonogram and chest X-ray. Ate breakfast, checked out Bishops attic, bought gas and on our way home. Sylvia tired and went to sleep. I built a stand to melt lead on. Loaded up 20 cases and shot them after supper. John Odden called about a gold concentrator. We had a good visit about prospecting.

Saturday, June 26, 1993—rain in the night, cloudy morning, sunny afternoon and evening, 45° to 64° Ducks gathering on lake. Sylvia helped and we built two shelves for the entertainment center, they will have full extension slides and will carry the TV and VCR. She mowed the lawn, visited Mae. I put hibachi together as Roxanne wanted to borrow it, then changed her mind.

Sunday, June 27, 1993—mostly sunny, very nice day, 44° to 65°. Serviced the truck. Shot targets and loaded some more for test. Had two very good groups. Lubed more cast bullets. Karn brought some guests over to visit. Sylvia baked bread. Visited Mae and Karn. I shot a squirrel that was trying to get at baby flickers. We went for a walk down to our dock. Saw a muskrat swim by, nice large one. Looked at garden and cultivated one row. Weeds are sure growing. One certain weed is persistently coming every year.

Monday, June 28, 1993—sunny, beaut of a day, 46° to 68°. Sylvia went to Glennallen on senior van. I did a few things here. Bart asked us to go to Crosswind Lake for a few hours fishing. Bartley's friends from Texas (Steve and Barbara) went also. Bart had to make two flights to get us over there. Barbara hooked a nice lake trout but it got off right at boat. We had supper at Bartley's and very good it was and a nice visit afterwards. A very good day.

Tuesday, June 29, 1993—sunny, some breeze, swell day, 46° to 68°. Sylvia went to Anchorage with Bonnie and Rudbecks. I made 15 - .22 cal. Bullets box's. Went to dump and brought home some galvanized tin to make a stove pipe collar for Bartley. Visited Ed F. Talked to Chuck Z about a reverse screw gold concentrator. The flickers are working hard to feed their growing family.

Wednesday, June 30, 1993—mostly cloudy, 45° to 60°. Made the stove pipe collar. Leveled the bottom of an aluminum pot for a lead pot. Got some things ready to go fishing. Started cleaning up the rifle barrel I found yesterday. Sylvia brought three oak cabinets home.

Thursday, July 1, 1993—mostly cloudy, 44° to 64°. Loaded up some fishing gear and a little food. Went to Snowshoe Lake (Bartley's) and Bart flew us out to a cabin he leases on Crosswind Lake. Bart flew us by eagle nest near Snowshoe Lake. We saw at least one baby in nest. I put a piece of tin I had made for a stove to go through the ceiling in this cabin. I put a padlock hasp on an out building. As we would be there overnight. I got up some wood for heat. The wind came up and we didn't go fishing. Wind blew all night and even harder.

Friday, July 2, 1993—partly cloudy and windy most of time, 40° to 54°. I tried a little casting into the wind but it wasn't practicable. We read and slept a lot.

Sylvia did dishes and I got more wood up. Bart brought in three men and gear and brought us out. Saw very few swans. Saw old Boot Lake again. Rosemary gave us ice tea, ice cream and brownies. Then on home. David brought me a check his dad owed me. Robbie came over and got a quart of oil for his sister.

Saturday, July 3, 1993—mostly sunny, windy afternoon and evening, 39° to 63°. Allen F. and Roxanne and David here for breakfast. Went to Allen's and we each sent an order for hunting boots. I got a piece of tin from Allen and made a base for the lead melting pot I've been fabricating. Sylvia mowed lawn and tilled garden.

Sunday, July 4, 1993—mostly sunny, breezy, cloudy evening and windy, 43° to 63°. 20 scoters are rafted out in our lake. We visited Griffiths at Rudbeck's in morning. Wikles came there also. We came home and set up lead melting and casting for ingots and halibut sinkers. We cast about 150 sinkers. Cleaned rifle and phoned my brother Jerry.

Monday, July 5, 1993—mostly cloudy. Rain in night and a couple of showers today, 39° to 54°. Rudbecks brought some smoked fish over. I visited Allen. Sylvia and I worked on her chests for bedroom—almost finished them. Young flickers are flying this evening.

Tuesday, July 6, 1993—hard rain in the night, partly cloudy, 41° to 61°. Visited Rudbecks. Bud and Jerry Smeltzer visited, Sally Johnson's mother and step dad from Michigan. Bartley brought a client down to get some worms to fish with and later dropped off a nice rainbow trout. Sylvia and I stained and varithaned "Elvira" the entertainment center. I did some more plinking –target shooting in evening.

Wednesday, July 7, 1993—partly cloudy, 38° to 63°. We slept late. Rudbecks came over just in time for breakfast. Bob helped carry "Elvira" into the house. Sylvia cleaned up the TV tapes and put them away in "Elvira." I need to assemble 2-6' to 7' coax to complete this project. Did a couple other small jobs.

Thursday, July 8, 1993—sunny, cloudy, 42° to 66°. Worked on some of the furniture. Cut out and prepared for painting the wood for 10 flying goose decoys. Bob brought over a newspaper. We visited Lucky and Mary. Sylvia walked over to Mae's and Rudbeck's.

Friday, July 9, 1993—partly cloudy, 48° to 65°. Started charging "cat" battery. Started cutting the conduit for decoys. Cut out two more wood pieces and sanded all 12. Remodeled a small area of storage shed. Put a "silver bullet" in a .357 cases for Robbie so he can shoot a "werewolf." Smayda's phoned and plan to stay the night with us.

Saturday, July 10, 1993—partly cloudy, sunny, couple of showers, 45° to 70°.
Smayda's here overnight, nice visit. They worked on their property next door.
The girls ran around the neighborhood having fun. Mike Griffith from
Minnesota stopped by. Dale (don't know last name) and two sons from
Chickaloon stopped here. They were looking for Henry Johnson. Dale knows
Andy Boyle. Jerry, Betty and Dana Rudbeck from Minnesota are at Rudbeck's.
Ladies visited here. I worked on goose decoys and cleaned a little storage shed.
We went over to Rudbecks and watched a movie in evening.

Sunday, July 11, 1993—mostly sunny, 47° to 72°. Cleaned sinkers. Welded
steps on flying goose conduit stakes. Smaydas here about lunchtime. Gave us a
salmon fillet (its all we wanted). Allen Farmer family here for shortcake in
evening.

Monday, July 12, 1993—sunny, some breezes, 47° to 77°. Sylvia went to
Glennallen on senior van. I painted primer coat on decoy supports. Cut a 12'
section out of the tree that was leaning so low over our lower trail. Opened up
the choke on the 12-gauge so I can shoot steel shot in it. Chuck Z. sent a 15
minute movie out for me to watch about a reverse gold screw machine.

Tuesday, July 13, 1993—sunny, breezy in evening, 53° to 80°. We went to
Palmer very early. Sylvia to a consultation with Dr. He examined her and
recommended trying to alleviate her incontinence with medicine. The on to
Wasilla and shopping. Got home mid afternoon. Put two new coax cables on
TV, VCR and moved it into corner of room. Allen phoned about an order for
boots for each of us that should have been here 10 days ago.

Wednesday, July 14, 1993—sunny, light breeze, 54° to 80°. Jerry and Bob were
here a few minutes. Brought back my mineral spirits. I painted goose decoys.
Sylvia watered lawn garden and mowed lawn. We went to Tom and Kim
Huddleston's for picnic supper. UPS finally brought Allen and I our shoes.

Thursday, July 15, 1993—sunny, some breeze and smoke from fire across Copper
River, 53° to 84°. Did some service work on truck. Cleaned rifle. Shot squirrel.
Vernetta and daughters brought a BB gun and .22 rifle over and did target
shooting.

Friday, July 16, 1993—sunny, partly cloudy, some breeze, smoke around the
country side, 52° to 83°. Nailed two squirrels. Tightened screws in roof of house
and arctic entry. Went to dump. Stopped at Bartley's and gave them some
elastic, Velcro ankle fasteners. Bart and Steve were taking the tail feathers off
his 180 Cessna in order to find a loose fastening. We went to Vernetta Banning
and daughters to a very good supper. Ed and Sandy Farmer were there also.

Saturday, July 17, 1993—partly cloudy, night shower in night and another in afternoon, 53° to 83°. Allen visited in morning. Sharpened lawn mower blade. Put new fittings on air tools, coupler had been leaking.

Sunday, July 18, 1993—partly cloudy, some breeze, 50° to 77°. Didn't do much today. Soldered a spout on oil can. Visited Allen. We went to local ball game and picnic. Ed and Sandy came over to see "gold screw" machine movie.

Monday, July 19, 1993—partly cloudy, 52° to 77°. Nice breeze, helps hold bugs down. Sylvia went to Glennallen on senior van. I tightened roof screws on garage. Made some cardboard map cases. Made a camber-bullet OAL gauge. Haven't tried it yet. Karn and Company came over and got some fishing worms.

Tuesday, July 20, 1993—partly cloudy, lots of smoke in the air, 54° to 74°. We started cutting a clump of trees to open up the circle drive. This will make plowing snow easier. Blocked part of biggest tree and wheeled it to woodshed. Visited Rudbecks. Installed a light fixture over Sylvia's sink. Made a drawing of camper kitchen, back wall at cook stove. We want to make it brighter and lighter there. Sylvia watered lawn and trees and pulled garden weed and visited Rudbecks. Bob and his brother Jerry came over looking for Dodge pickup wheel bolts, I don't have any. I loaded and shot some ultra light rifle loads.

Wednesday, July 21, 1993—mostly cloudy, light rain, 53° to 69°. We cut and pulled down the rest of the trees we are going take out now. A few stumps to pull yet. Shot a squirrel and it was pulling insulation out from between logs of garage. Visited Rudbecks.

Thursday, July 22, 1993—cloudy, quite a bit of rain, very little sun, 52° to 60°. Rob, Mae's son came over for fish worms. I loaded more cartridges. Made a little tool holder for reloading bench. Finished pulling out the stumps and cleaned dirt off some of them. Sylvia started sewing cloth for goose decoys.

Friday, July 23, 1993—cloudy, sunny, 42° to 68°. Some pretty hard showers in afternoon. Loaded the spruce stumps and hauled them to dump. Put them off to side so as not to fill up dump pit. Salvaged some steel and pipe from a daveno-bed. Salvaged track and bogies from a snowgo. Brought a wheel tire home to fit on snowgo trailer. Sized and trimmed some brass. Got another pesky squirrel. Picked up and took a construction worker to his broken down truck.

Saturday, July 24, 1993—cloudy, sunny, nice day, 48° to 68°. Cut our five more goose decoy bodies. Resized more brass. Chris Rhodes and Suzy Tollman got married this afternoon. We went to that.

Sunday, July 25, 1993—mostly sunny, 41° to 67°. Painted five goose decoy bodies. Cast some 22 bullets. Put fertilizer on lawn. Shot two squirrels. Pulled weeds out of strawberry patch. Tried a new .22 load. Seems very good. Sylvia sewed more goose cloth "wings." The medicine she's taking now leaves her sleepy.

Monday, July 26, 1993—mostly cloudy and showers, 50° to 61°. Karn visited. Bob and Jerry came over to look at my goose decoys. I cast some more bullets to shoot squirrels. Tried different powder weights and found a good 25 yard load and 1 good 50 yard load with bulls-eye and 210 Fed Primer. Sylvia went to Glennallen on senior van. Vernetta and daughter came over in eve and borrowed a drill and drill bit.

Tuesday, July 27, 1993—partly cloudy, lots of smoke, 50° to 72°. Did a few small jobs. Sylvia went to Anchorage with Bonnie. Bob R. came over and got the paint he had stored here.

Monday, July 28, 1993—mostly sunny, strong southeast breeze, 42° to 73°. Did some target practice. Cleaned guns. Sylvia got back this evening. Bonnie had a load of furniture. I visited Ed.

Tuesday, July 29, 1993—sunny, wonderful day, 50° to 76°. So very nice. We built a platform at arctic entry and modified and remodeled the steps. Turned out nice. Took all day.

Wednesday, July 30, 1993—sunny, cloudy, then sprinkles in the evening, 50° to 76°. Re-laid native flat stone walk at arctic entry, steps and stoop. Bud and Shirley (Sally Johnson's mother) visited and borrowed our two pressure canners. Harold and Rachel Dimmick were here to supper. We are planning a trip to Nome to prospect gold. Took a walk down to lake in evening. Saw one squirrel and heard two others. Saw four gadwall hens. Two with three ducklings, one with four ducklings, one with 30 ducklings! She may have taken babies from other hens. Saw a beaver in the lily bed just west of our dock. It would bring up bulbs and eat while resting on the surface. When I rose and started to leave, it slapped its tail as it observed me pass openings in the trees, it would slap its tail again. It's been a beautiful day. Cloudy, this evening, but very warm and nice.

Thursday, July 31, 1993—mostly sunny, cloudy evening, 55° to 75°, some smoke in view. Polished the inside of a .38/.357 sizing die. Did some other small jobs. Visited over at Henry J. Cut up some down trees and stacked the wood in shed. Too windy this eve to try to get a picture of beaver feeding.

Sunday, August 1, 1993—sunny, then cloudy and windy, 52° to 74°. We cut up all down trees and I loaded and hauled them and stacked them in woodshed. Sylvia mowed lawn. Harold D. asked us to a barbecue. Sylvia took a beet salad from our garden. I took Sunday paper over to Ed's.

Monday, August 2, 1993—mostly cloudy and some breeze, 50° to 63°. Sylvia took a wolf pelt to town to sell when she went on senior van. I tried to bring new life to an old .22 barrel - no luck. Tried shooting with L.B.T. lubricating formula on bullets and clean up barrel so it doesn't foul so badly. It's been a bugger to clean. Bud and Shirley visited for an hour or so in late afternoon. Just before they leave Nelchina to go home to Michigan.

Tuesday, August 3, 1993— very nice day, breezy in evening, 48° to 72°. Went to gravel pit and shot rifle and hand gun. Saw bear pooh and large moose track there. Emi Banning visited Sylvia. Jerry and Betty Rudbeck visited in afternoon. We went to Rudbecks for a while in evening. Allen F. stopped by with ice cream.

Wednesday, August 4, 1993—partly cloudy, little light showers, 42° to 64°. I went to Anchorage and got maps of Nome, Koyuk and Noatak areas. Went to state mining office to find out ownership status of these areas. Did some shopping and checked on tent for Allen. Back to Palmer and Dr. looked at my thumb, he seems satisfied. It is doing OK. Came on home. Smayda's are here working on their place. They had supper with us.

Thursday, August 5, 1993—partly cloudy, nice day, 48° to 64°. Sylvia, Karn and Betty went to dump area to pick currants. I went as picker and shot gunner bear protection. Currants were spotty but very excellent in places. I got two rifles ready to sell.

Friday, August 6, 1993—rained all day, 50° to 64°. Wrote some letters. Visited Rudbecks (Bob and Karn). Got gear ready to take to gun show in Wasilla. Jerry R. visited in afternoon. Gun case didn't come so repaired old one. Hope patch's work. Back is very bad.

Saturday, August 7, 1993—partly cloudy and some fog and showers on way to Palmer and Wasilla, 48° to 62°. Gave us a wrong table and we had to move. Sold some things in morning, not a lot. Then very little in afternoon. Ate supper and went to Smaydas took ice cream. Visited, had some ice cream and went to bed. Tom Smayda and girls were on Big Lake paddling a kayak.

Sunday, August 8, 1993—up early (heavy dew here in Palmer). Ate breakfast with Smaydas. Went back to Wasilla and our table at gun show. I didn't sell hardly anything but had some fun trading with other people and visiting. Did some shopping and came on home. This was a pretty day. Sure glad to get home. We unloaded everything except the heating stove Tom sent with me to install in the house he is renting to the teacher.

Monday, August 9, 1993—mostly sunny, 46° to 72°. Sylvia went to Glennallen on senior van. She deposited money for our plane tickets to Minnesota for our trip this fall. I installed heater in teacher's house for Smaydas. Got a very little gear ready for hunting. Repaired exhaust system on the one side of truck. Birthday party at Sandy and Ed's for teacher. Denny Griffith and family drove in this evening. They were 14 days coming from Minnesota. That is a nice way to see the country.

Tuesday, August 10, 1993—mostly sunny, rain in afternoon on Alfred Creek, 44° to 68°. Went to trailhead near Mil 123 and drove in to near old roadhouse, unloaded 4 wheeler and went up trail over Ballanger Pass, down Pass Creek to Alfred Creek. Down Alfred Creek to Clay Hill which was rumored to be passable. Got there and found it impassable to get ATV up the hill. Walked up and glassed the country I could see. No sheep or game in sight. Ate lunch, rain started, so I drove out to truck. Did talk to a few hunters. Two boo kills in Pass Creek. One moose kill near houses. Bob brought some scrap wood over and I gave him some used oil.

Wednesday, August 11, 1993—lots of showers, some sunshine, 49° to 60°. Stiff and sore today. Made some craft things for school kids (teacher). Worked some more on truck tail pipe. Sylvia went to town with Bonnie W. Darrel called and we met at Paul Whites and he gave me some conduit to make flying goose decoy supports. Repaired a few weak leaky places in a pair of hip boots.

Thursday, August 12, 1993—some sun in-between showers, three of them quite hard, 50° to 65°. It hailed 1/2" size pretty hard for a little while. Lots lightning and thunder nearby. Welded 5-10' poles for flying goose decoys. Sylvia and Karn picked some blueberries. Visited Griffiths at Rudbecks. Re-mounting loading press, it much more stable now. A young eagle hangs around the neighborhood. Roxanne stopped by with a pineapple upside down cake and shared with us. Loaded a few cartridges.

Friday, August 13, 1993—partly cloudy, 45° to 65°. We went to Palmer and to one of Sylvia's doctors. Didn't get to go on to next treatment. Stopped by Smayda's. Did some shopping and came back home.

Saturday, August 14, 1993—partly cloudy, 48° to 61°. Put guy wires on goose decoy poles. Tried to wire bulbs in series at well so I'll know when light inside burns out. Can't get both bulbs to light at same time. Lucky and Mary ask us to have supper with them. Visited Jerry and Betty Rudbeck. Bob R. is cutting trees for a road down to his lower property.

Sunday, August 15, 1993—mostly sunny, windy, weather may be changing, 44° to 58°. Target shooting. Worked on elect at well. Visited Rudbecks. Took garbage to dump. Stopped in at Bartley's and visited and got some copies made.

Monday, August 16, 1993—mostly sunny, some windy, 39° to 61°. Shooting using same powder, different weights and different primers. A couple groups show promise. Visited Ed and late he came over here. Robbie stopped by when he heard me shooting. Squirrel was after insulation, so I shot him. Sylvia went to Glennallen. I phoned Fairbanks Fish & Game about sheep hunting. Phoned AK Ferry System and made reservations to go to Cordova October 1st. Packed more gear on ATV.

Tuesday, August 17, 1993—mostly cloud, little sprinkles, 34 to 57°. Did lower frame of stand for pickup canopy down to ground level. Skinned a knuckle doing it. Shot some more test loads. Cast some bullets. Sylvia cleaned house.

Wednesday, August 18, 1993—sunny, then windy, later clouds. Tired to sell antlers, only sold one moose horn. Got one squirrel. Shot some targets. Sylvia went to Glennallen. Lucky visited about moose hunting.

Thursday, August 19, 1993—partly cloudy, windy most of day, 47° to 61°. Put a log chain from up on one tree and anchored on another tree to keep it from possibly falling into the house. Got ATV trailer loaded to go moose hunting. Visited Allen and Roxanne's. Stopped at Denny and Jo's on way home.

Friday, August 20, 1993—mostly cloudy, warm. Finished getting gear ready and loaded. Lucky and I drove to trailhead on east side Slide Mt. Unloaded our ATVs and trailers. We found the trail to be pretty good. We did get stuck a few times and helped pull and winch and push each other out. We saw a caribou on way in. Got to Allen's cabin. Boy have the squirrels made a mess of it. Lots of piss and pellets all over. Two foam and two cotton mattresses, pillows, all ruined. We shoveled out the worse of it, built a fire and burned it. We went out in evening looking for moose. Saw none, no tracks. Saw tracks of a large bear and also of a sow and cub. We slept in the stinky cabin. Rain in evening.

Saturday, August 21, 1993—partly cloudy. We rode our ATV's trying to find a trail Lucky had used years past. After the second try we gave up and went out to North Meat Pole Hill and went east and north on my trap line. I picked up four conibears and boxes and Lucky found he was low on gas, so we went back. Some parts of trail were rough. Some was beautiful. Few game tracks. I was disappointed to not get to end of this trail—better luck next time. Back to cabin. Lucky went back out to look for his lost trail. I walked back down the trail to a small dry Stony Creek. Watched a large area for moose and caribou. No luck. I did see an old beaver lodge on a small lake. At least I didn't see a feed pile started. The lakes are quite low. Saw two loons on one lake and one loon on the other lake. Saw two small boo. Looked for a lost trap. I think hunters picked it up. I ate lots of blueberries. A very good crop of them out here. Back to cabin and roasting wieners at a camp fire. Sylvia had sent a large cake and I fixed large pieces with fruit cocktail on them. Then to bed. 2:00 AM I thought I heard a bear moaning outside. Of course we didn't see anything. We left a Coleman lantern burning and went back to sleep.

Sunday, August 22, 1993—light rain. We packed up our gear on ATV's and trailers. Blocked up and nailed boards over the squirrel holes and the window and started for hwy. At Pimple Hill the hunters had a large moose bull hung up. We again got stuck a few times, but never bad. Loaded up on pickups and trailers and came on home. Then it's unload and unpack to dry out gear. Much appreciation for a hose and running water to clean mud off ATV and trailer. Bartley called and wants to use my welder.

Monday, August 23, 1993—partly cloudy, 35° to 54°. Did some target shooting. Jerry R visited. Visited Ed about my brakes. Rigged a battery in old pickup and moved camper out where I mounted it on the truck. Bad cramps tonight.

Tuesday, August 24, 1993—mostly sunny, 40° to 60°. Bartley brought some steel to cut, grind and weld into a "A" frame gin pole for the back of a truck. He plans to lift his float plane out of his lake and set it on shore. I got a little gear ready for goose and sandhill crane hunting. I took a buffalo skull out of ½ barrel of dirt. The soil bacteria had eaten most all hide and flesh from it. Finished cleaning and washing the skull and put in a cardboard box. Walked down to lake to get pix of beaver and sure enough it came and fed on lilies and saplings and brush it had already pulled into the water. It came to 6' from me. At any movement it slapped the water with its tail and dived for a short time. My, but it is a noisy eater. The jaws move very fast and the teeth strike together probably helping to keep the teeth worn down. Shot two squirrels this morning. Charlie Trowbridge phoned and will stop by Thursday. He wanted info on furniture sales at Elmendorf Air Force Base.

Wednesday, August 25, 1993—sunny, beaut of a day, 32° to 61°. Worked on camper stove and drawers on camper. Bart and Steve were here working on the "A" frame and mounting it back. Again this evening neighbor kids are chasing the ducks with boat and motor.

Thursday, August 26, 1993—sunny, very nice, 32° to 62°. Bart and Steve got a little more done on their job. I put five buckets of dirt in basement for Sylvia. Heard a squirrel but couldn't find it. Put more goose hunting gear in camper. Ed had a little half moon cut in a board to do and used my sabre saw. Jerry R.

visited. I went over to Ed's a few min. in evening. This was after Trowbridge's were here. They had supper with us.

Friday, August 27, 1993—another very beautiful day, 45° to 66°. Darrel called to say he was able to get our Federal Duck Stamps. Jerry R. visited. Sylvia packed trail cookies. Got a little more gear ready for goose hunting. Built a fastener to hold the ATV loading ramps on ATV trailer when traveling. Fixed one tail light on camper. Shot another squirrel today. Checked Manning's heater.

Saturday, August 28, 1993—cloudy, early morning, sunny later, 43° to 63°. Shot at one target. Watched lake and lazed on grass in sun for awhile. Got a few more things ready for hunting geese, cranes. Roger and Jo Ford stopped by. Borrowed 20 HP motor fell off the boy's boat, they found and buoy marked the spot.

Sunday, August 29, 1993—cloudy, some rain, some sun, 40° to 62°. Got more done on truck and camper for hunting trip. Bart and Steve came over, worked a while and took everything home. (Ran out of oxygen).

Monday, August 30, 1993—sprinkles and rain all day, 40° to ? Finished loading gear, of course I forgot a couple things. Went to Glennallen. Stopped at Lanagen's and got my Alaska duck stamp. Put some air in rear tires of pickup. Stopped at coffee shop just as Sylvia and girls were leaving. Ate lunch there. Darrel stopped by and gave me my Federal Water Fowl Stamp and I paid him for it. Pretty good drive all the way to Delta Jct. Some hunters out and about. Got gas and some wheel weights. Then an alarm clock and a little bit of groceries. Oh yes, I stopped at Fish and Game in Glennallen and got regulations and migratory bird shooting times.

Saw 20 geese before I got to Scott Hollenbeck. We visited a little. I gave him a sandhill crane call. Gave his son Buckley a crane call and about 4 box's 20-gauge shotgun shells. Parked camper on Scotts 10 acres. Got furnace and light going. Saw a few geese flying and could hear others. Tired tonight.

Sunday, August 31, 1993—warm, some breeze, few very light sprinkles. Up early-went out to fields to see where geese where flying. They are almost all white fronts (2000). Hardly any Lesser Canada's. Very few sandhill cranes till evening, then several hundred of them.

I did lots visiting with Jim and his father-in-law Charley. Gave Mike and his son Jesse a shooting hours schedule. Finally picked out a place to put decoys. Not a good place. Scott visited this evening and says he has 8 parties out there. Lots of hunters to compete with. I put out all my decoys and while putting up the flying one's two speckle bellies circled me twice. They sure wanted to land.

Put silicone on a leak on the camper roof. Saw ruff grouse and spruce hens in the lane to the camping spot. We dug a knee deep trench in a small berm that was covered with tall grass, to make a blind. I was short 5 cross pieces for decoys so I cut some willow wands for substitutes.

Wednesday, September 1, 1993—mostly cloudy, some rain and windy some times. Got to decoys in pretty good time. Darrel has to pump his ATV tires every few hours. We only had two geese fly over our decoys and we were out working on decoys. We had to set flying decoys on ground a couple times on account of wind. Later in afternoon a few crane flew near us but marginal for height. I didn't try for them. Very few birds and lots and lots of hunters. Saw some ruff grouse at our campsite. They left while I was loading the 12-gauge. Some motor home campers played games with the kids and dog. Poor hunting conditions. We didn't go to end of road to see if Roy Beaver was home.

Thursday, September 2, 1993—partly cloudy, 40s to 50s. Up early and to decoy-blind. Put up the flying decoys and straightened up a few of the others. Very few geese and no crane and none near us. Then back and fix breakfast. Decided to end hunt, packed and loaded up and went to decoys and picked and loaded them.

Mike and son Jesse from Chugiak stopped by just as were about loaded. We started for Bakers where I would have phoned home. I stopped to look at a goose and forgot the trailer and jackknifed it when I backed up and wrecked the hitch. Went on to a gravel pit and hooked a chain to it, straightened it some what. Then decided no to risk bad hitch so won't go to Fairbanks for sure. Gassed up in Delta. Hardy gusty winds the next 150 miles. Sure tense, hard work driving. Saw a place with a wrecked oil tanker. We didn't stop. Got to Glennallen and Darrel showed me his property and we walked it over. Then on home and shower and to bed.

Friday, September 3, 1993—mostly sunny, beaut of a day. Unpacked camper. Repaired trailer and put new loop on ATV winch cable. Shoveled a few rock from fill Mike put in. Boy is there a lot of orange and grape fruit size rock in fill. Shot one squirrel. Serviced the truck. Visited Ed a couple minutes. Made arrangements to go to Nome.

Saturday, September 4, 1993—partly cloudy here, rain west of pass and to Anchorage, 40° to 55°. I parked at airport and tried to check in and the piece of paper I had wasn't a ticket. The counter girl didn't give me a senior discount so I turned around and came home. I didn't get to go to Nome this day. There are some moose, Four bulls and one cow on south side of Slide Mountain. Sandy sent a couple over to look at moose horns, they didn't buy. Harold D. phoned in evening about senior discount—I'm again making plans to go to Nome. Frances (Sylvia's sister) phoned later in the evening to visit.

Sunday, September 5, 1993—up early, repacked clothes, sluice box and grub to go to Nome. Picked up Dimmick's mail and shopped a little in Anchorage, drove to Griffiths, parked the pickup and had coffee and Addie and Gary drove me to the airport. It was still light of course when I got to Nome. Corky, Harold and Rachel met me at the Nome airport. We had supper at "Fat Freddie's" Restaurant. Then drove out the Beach Road to "Irene's" summer camp. They have been cleaning and fixing it up for her. They have borrowed a wall tent from Dan Karmun and Corky and I sleep in it. Home made stoves in both places.

Monday, September 6, 1993—good night's sleep. Low clouds and wind and spitting rain. After breakfast, we looked beach over and dug more sand out of a hole Harold had started. We got a few colors in each pan. After lunch we went to dump on beach where the 1934 Fire Debris remains. We were there three hours. I picked up a few things then found a tooth gold filling and cap. Great find. Then on into town and they did some shopping, then back out to camp and gathered up a little wood and Rachel fixed supper. After supper we drove out past Safety 20 miles or so and got a bucket of water. Someone out there Harold knew wasn't home. Saw some ducks on a bay of a river.

Tuesday, September 7, 1993—wind blows hard and rains sometimes. Wind maybe 50 mph? Tent was really popping. Harold and I built a pole and small log wing break for the tent. High waves and rollers and heavy surf pounding the beach. A barge waiting to unload here at Nome moved farther off shore. Ate breakfast and went to Nome. Rachel and Corky stayed in town and at Dan Karmun and wife Edith. Met there son Bert, and Dan, Gloria, Harold and I went to a small lake and creek to pan. No luck. Then back to Dan, Ethel's. Then went up beach from town with the pickup-parked and walked looking at what few beach operators still working. One of the friendly operations pointed out a patch of red sand and told me to get a shovel of sand from there and pan it out. It was ½ black sand and I couldn't pan that very well. Finally got down to where we could see the gold. More gold in that pan then any I've ever panned. He had a pan of material he did. (We didn't see where he got it). Lots and lots of gold in it. He says much fine gold you can't see with naked eye. Takes a 30 power glass to see it.

Then back to Dan and Ethel's for very good supper other "fixings". After supper Harold wanted to go to Woolly Lagoon to see John Titchuck? Corky drove us, 40 mi on Teller Road then maybe 8 miles on a narrow road to Woolly Lagoon. We saw a couple hundred sandhill crane. Some small family groups plus 20-30 reindeer. Some people were picking berries near Nome. We had Salmon berries. Then to some other relatives for dried fish – then on to the camp. Some more griz sow and cub tracks.

Wednesday, September 8, 1993—very windy, some rain. Harold and I walked up beach to Hastings Creek and panned there, not much color. Saw old abandoned sluice box there. Back to camp and we decided to pack our gear. Me to go home Thursday and Harold's to camp at Dan's summer camp, Mile 58 or Taylor Hwy. Harold and I went up the beach a little ways and Harold found a aluminum sluice (Basic-home bent) then back to Dan and Ethel's for reindeer head soup, willow leaves preserved in seal oil. Very good. Then up the Taylor Hwy 58 miles to Dan K summer camp. They are building a new house there. Saw reindeer on way home and more people out picking berries. Harold, Rachel and Corky stayed over at camp and I went with the Karmuns and stayed the night there.

Thursday, September 9, 1993—wind and seas are down. Dan drove me to airport and I checked in with Mark Air and flew to Anchorage. A phone call and Dennis Griffith came and picked me up at the airport. Then we visited a couple hours at his place. Traffic is heavy in town here. I got gas in Mt. View and went to AK Mining and Diving for books and info on mining at Nome. Got home here a little before 6:00 PM. Had supper over at Rudbeck's.

Friday, September 10, 1993—beaut of a day. Partly cloudy, light shower, some breeze. Put some gear away. Built a new long hitch to pull a trailer while the camper is on pickup. Then went to Glennallen, saw Gene Speerstra, Darrel and Paul White and Rhynell at the new restaurant. Looked for moose all way to town. Talked to the new taxidermist on way home. Pat Landers stopped there also. Then I went to Point of View Lodge, saw Dan and Patti Billman. No moose on way home. Bon voyage. Brought our plane tickets to Minnesota for our trip in October.

Saturday, September 11, 1993—partly cloudy, beaut of a day, 30° to 51°. Paid Ed $12.00 for tire and rim for trailer. Visited for awhile. Showed the gold cap tooth I found to Rudbeck's clan. Went to dump and picked up some bicycle wheels. Hunted. Saw fresh boo tracks at gravel pit just east of us. Worked on camper till supper time. After supper tied canoe on top of ATV trailer. Took shotgun (12-gauge) and shells down to lake and went duck hunting. Managed to get 10 with 14 shots. The beaver are cutting and dragging cottonwood and willow past our dock to winter feed bed. Sun on cloudy sky. Pretty tonight.

Sunday, September 12, 1993—cloudy, light shower, 36° to 48°. Went up on Slide Mt. with ATV to near top. Walked on up, also west and north. Very little boo or moose sign. Very dry up there. Found two boo shed horns. Found a no. 4 Victor trap Allen has lost track of and I brought it down to him. Tom and Lisa Smayda visited. We had fried duck breasts for supper. Went to lake with nine duck decoys and put them out. Beavers sure have been cutting feed for winter. No ducks flying this evening, but I could hear three faraway shots (rifle).

181

Monday, September 13, 1993—foggy, cloudy, sunny, beaut of an evening, 35° to 52°. Drove highway to Mendeltna. Saw a moose yearling get up out of its bed but it got into the brush before I could tell if it was legal. Made some phone calls about mining on Nome Beach. Sylvia went to Glennallen. I made a device to pick black sand off gold with a magnet. Thinned a belt by sanding it. Packed gear to go moose hunting. Allen stopped by to talk going hunting. Brought ice cream. I went down to lake, no ducks on this side. Beaver was upset as I was in his way to haul winter feed to lake. A muskrat swam by 10' away. Dan clued me in as to location of moose.

Tuesday, September 14, 1993—warmer and partly cloudy, 30°. Got more things ready to hunt. Waited awhile for Allen to get family and gear ready. We parked at trailhead near Joe Virgins to go to John Lake. Allen spent some time glassing for moose on way in. After such a late start, we didn't make it to John Lake and parked and camped along the trail. A moose head, hide and feet only a few feet from us. The bears have so many gut piles they can't eat them all. I slept in my ATV trailer. We watched a small herd of moose near John Lake.

Wednesday, September 15, 1993—partly cloudy. Up early and walked a couple miles looking and glassing for moose. Then broke camp and moved to end of trail and parked at some nice trees. Put a nice camp. Allen, Roxanne, David and Kyle and I took off looking for moose. We walked over a couple small hills and looked down on John Lake saw a small group of moose, probably four bulls, one possibly legal. Continued on looking country over and found likely looking "moosey" area. We then determined we could get our outfit moved there, closer to moose. So we did that. Allen and entourage slept in a cabin and I slept in ATV trailer. Wind came up in night and I had to hang on to tarp. Anyway in evening we split up. I went to an area we saw two cows walk to and tried to moose call for a bull. No luck. Allen and family got back just at dark and heard "horn clanging."

Thursday, September 16, 1993—light frost and some rain and wind through out the day. Up early. We went to John Lake and to far side and hunted. The moose had moved. Roxanne and kids were tired of rain and went back to cabin. I convinced Allen we should get farther from lake. We walked away from lake and found another moosey-looking area. I spotted two cows and Allen saw a bull. We couldn't see how many brow tines. Then more small bulls and cows then I saw a bigger bull that Allen didn't. After awhile they all decided to move off. We made a small circle and tried to get up to them again. They stayed farther a way then for some reason some started to cross an open place in front of us. We watched them cross then here came a bull possibly legal. I got ready to shoot (200 yards) by kneeling down and using my knee to help steady the rifle. Allen kept saying "he only has two brow tines." Then we talked that maybe his spread would be 50 inches or more. Bless Allen's young eyes looking through binoculars. He finally said "shoot him." The bull had stood there several minutes. At my shot the bull was knocked off his feet and feet in the air by a .388 -210 grain nosler partition bullet. I walked as fast as I could over the tundra to the bull and finished him with a shot to neck in back of the head. Breaking up those bones kills immediately and helps in cutting off the head later.

Allen could have shot a smaller three tine bull put didn't want to butcher out two bulls at once. We went back to camp. At breakfast loaded up our outfit and went to John Lake. Left one trailer and a pile of gear and drove to kill site. Butchered the bull, sacked the meat. Back to lake, reload our gear and went back to cabin and trail we came in on. Allen picked up a set of boo horns he had found in the brush, then on out the trail towards trailhead. Near junction of trails a guy ran up behind me to ask if I had seen a Bombardier machine. No I hadn't and this time it was pouring down rain with snow mixed in it. On we go and see two guys on ATV that hadn't had any luck hunting, then down the trail at a hunting shack we ran into "Jim," a really full of B.S. kind of guy, but he did congratulate me on my moose. I got stuck a couple times on the way out when the machine would get high centered. Allen would walk back and give me a tug and get me out without having to winch.

Rain, snow, and windy much of this time. Roxanne and David went on to trailhead. When we reached the highway, we loaded up machines and gear and came home. This in the dark, about 10:00 PM. Allen lost a pillow out on Ranger on his trailer. I stopped and picked it up. At home here we hung the meat in the garage and Sylvia fixed hamburger gravy and biscuits. Long day.

Friday, September 17, 1993—cloudy, partly cloudy, 28° and snowing, to 32°. Started drying gear. Sylvia started working on meat. Visited Ed F. and Denny E. Allen and I , Al and Faith P. went down towards the river on the trail to and past the "burn." Walked all over past the end of trail. No sign of game. Only sow and cub bears, probably griz. I went to the burn and glassed it just at dark. Saw a spooky moose cow. Then heard three shots so went the 2 ½ miles back over a rough trail to help if needed. Turned out Allen was guiding Al and Faith to trail by shots in dark. I got home 10:30 PM—tired.

Saturday, September 18, 1993—Sylvia worked all morning with the moose meat. I did the lifting and then started getting gear ready to go hunting in the Tolsona area. Al and Faith, Allen and all his family, Luck B and I all went in together. It's not a long trip 3.8 miles. Some mud and bog though and two steep hills. We got camp set up and hunted a little. Al and Faith left just before dark. I heard two moose fighting. Allen found some "scrapes." We could all hear moose calling in the night. Lazy evening camp.

Sunday, September 19, 1993—light freeze. Up early, went to area Allen wanted to hunt. Tramped a lot of tall brush and only saw three spruce hens and 1 squirrel. A plane (Bart, I wonder) made turn right over my head and ¼ mi back the way he came. He waggled his wings. I caught up with Lucky but he was getting too tired to check it out. Back at camp, Allen wasn't too interested. Later we all made circles out in a swamp. Nothing. Lucky packed up and went out after eating. Later Allen made up his mind to go out also. It was dark when we got out there. I got loaded up and helped him load. Having better lights on my camper I followed him home to Nelchina.

Monday, September 20, 1993—partly cloudy, windy afternoon, 30°. Cleaned up, serviced and put away machine and gear. Got things loaded to go to Delta sandhill crane hunting. Sylvia came home from Glennallen and we put the air compressor in the basement and soon I left for Delta. Did some shopping, cashed a small check and got gasoline in Glennallen. Very windy driving. After Glennallen it was mostly a tail wind. Lots of caribou hunters near Sourdough. Saw lots hunting rigs going home. Quite a few boo had been killed. Rain near South Isabella Pass. Got more gasoline in Delta and drove out to Hollenbeck farm. Saw a cow moose and calf in field. Saw a sharp tail fly out of an oat field. Too windy to hear geese and crane—none seem to be flying. Found a place to park the truck. Furnace didn't work. Fuse holder had come apart and lost fuse. I substituted a piece of copper wiring. Fixed a bite to eat. Checked shooting time and set alarm clock.

Tuesday, September 21, 1993—partly cloudy, cloudy and spitting a little rain turning to snow sleet towards dark, quite windy. Nothing in range so went to camper and fixed breakfast. Sure enough four crane landed within gun shot of my blind. Tried to sneak on them but these were spooky and wild. Nothing came in range so went to truck and fixed a light lunch. Then picked up decoys and went to John Thuringer farm. With his permission I drove out two miles to NE corner of his farm. The "doctors" have three large decoy spreads maybe couple thousand dollars worth of decoys. They have a larger trailer with 4' sides to transport decoys. I only put out one "flyer" decoy this afternoon. The one flock (7 crane) came in range when I had my back turned and was taking a leak. Not good! Saw two flocks of about 60 each of Canadas, one flock of 100 swans and 500 sandhill cranes. As I was walking back to camper tonight I jumped a flock of sharp tails in grain stubble. Knocked feathers out of one with 10-gauge and "T" steel shot—didn't get him. Saw another one near camper and went looking with the 12-gauge but couldn't find it. Red sunset tonight and still windy.

Wednesday, September 22, 1993—cloudy and frost to partly cloudy. Light, occasional breeze till noon. Up early, fix breakfast and leave camper. Had I been one minute sooner I could have intercepted a flock of 20 speckle bellies. Then 120 yards farther on a flock of 60 speckle bellies whizzed by. I tried a shot at bird closest to me and didn't lead enough and missed. Four crane landed in the doctor group's decoys. A flock of 50 crane landed on west in harvested grain field. I walked ½ way there then stalked a ¼ mi. and got as close as I could. Then hunkered down and picked fox tail barbs out of my gloves while waiting and hoping that when the cranes got up I would get a shot at them. After a two hour wait they suddenly got up and came near my hide. They came in three bunches with time in between to reload my shot gun. I missed nine times!!! I grumbled at my bad shooting all way back to camper. I must be stopping my swing? Or just pointing and shooting?

Back at camper I removed the modified choke tube for steel and replaced it with the tube for full choke. Sun is shining and it's beautiful on the new snow on the mountains. Bare ground down here in the valley. Camper furnace has quit and I'll have to check the wiring. Problem doesn't seem to be in wiring or thermostat. Did a little work on camper, then walked way down the field to the place cranes landed this morning. Rested and slept in sun, watched 19 crane catch a thermal and leave.

The doctor group moved two men to their northeast crane decoy set up. So I wouldn't hunt near there? This happened this morning. Now this afternoon they moved two vehicles and decoys to that part of the field I was hunting (within 50 yards). I got up and walked back to camper, disappointed.

A small red squirrel lives in an old berm pile out here in the middle of farm land. Went for a walk this evening and hoped to intercept the speckle bellies. Legal shooting ended before they flew to feed. Speckle bellies, they must rest on Tanana River Flats or North Healy Lake according to their line of flight. Another beautiful sunset. One flock of cranes flying this evening.

Thursday, September 23, 1993—feels cold, mostly clear skies, 10° early morning. The doctor group drove out to field, may have disturbed the speckle bellies usual flight time. No cranes in air early. Drove to Allen and Wendy Baker's home. He had just left for wood lot. Visited with Wendy and called Sylvia. Went hunting for sharp tails and got one bird. Back to Baker's. Allen is there with a load of wood. We visited all afternoon and early evening. Jason and Ross were there after school. Bob (last name?) visited in evening. A while after supper I left for home and got there at midnight.

Friday, September 24, 1993—partly cloudy, 19° to 37°. Ground freezes at night. Visited around neighborhood. Borrowed meat grinder from Allen. Paid Denny for a thermo cube. Got grinder at Ed farmers. Sylvia cut up the front quarter of moose and ground some hamburger. I worked on the camper, cleaning and unloading. Stopped one air leak under fridge. Enlarged "window" between kitchen and dining in camper, so gas light shines into dining better. Removed the trailer hitch from the pickup. Sylvia fixed the sharp tail grouse for supper. We went to school house for Nelchina, Mendeltna dump meeting.

Saturday, September 25, 1993—snow all day, five inches or so, 22° to 30°.

Wired a thermo cube and signal bulb into the light bulb circuit that keeps the well from freezing. Took shot gun to lake and shot two ducks. Saw two wood cock, shot at one and missed. Removed one water hose manifold from the water line. Painted the weld on camper table leg. Re-piled moose and caribou horns in wood shed. Parked ATV trailer and ATV in a stall in woodshed. Rudbecks here for supper.

Sunday, September 26, 1993—snow and cloudy almost all day, 27° to 40°. Went to lake and shot one duck. Removed the hose bibs and replaced them with a coupling at the garden. The water line was frozen. I lifted it out of the snow in hopes the air temp would thaw it out. I had to run hot water and use air pressure but it thawed out in place. Lots of walking up and down the hill again today. Sylvia finished cutting our part of the moose. I sealed a few air leaks on camper.

Monday, September 27, 1993—foggy, cloudy, a little sun, 21° to 37°. Visited Ed. Got a little gear ready for Cordova. Went down to lake and got the gunny sack of duck decoys and brought it up to storage shed. Did a few other things. Sylvia went to Glennallen and then ground some meat when she got home.

Tuesday, September 28, 1993—snow, cloudy, rain, wind from east all day and switched to west and rain, 30° to 38°. Visited Allen. Sylvia packaged ground meat. I got some crafts ready to take to Cordova, read and rested.

Wednesday, September 29, 1993—some rain this morning, later snow that melted, 30° to 42°. Put away a few things for winter. Took meat grinder to Ed's. Offered to help Allen with his garage. He is not ready yet, so I came home.

Thursday, September 30, 1993—cloudy, sunny, 31° to 46°, snow melting. Mentioned moose meat to Allen. Stocked camper. Oiled guns. Put some gear in camper. Waited at home as long as I thought prudent. I wanted to get to Valdez before dark. Had strong head winds all the way, also gusty. So I drove slower and it was deep dusk when I got to Valdez.

It's been raining and the mountain streams are cascading down in a free fall of white water. I got gas and some groceries here in town. Ate a sandwich. Got the camper furnace to run – hurrah!! Now when I got damp putting silicone on camper roof, (yes, the roof leaked again) I can dry off in front of furnace. I must take off the screen that is supposed to keep rocks form breaking the glass in the over cab part of the camper. It jiggles and creates leaks in roof area where it fastens.

Friday, October 1, 1993—seems warm here, must be in the 40s. Rain quit in night. Got up early and signed in to get on ferry for Cordova. The "Bartlett" is making the run. Seas were a little rough just outside the Valdez Narrows. The trip was uneventful. Did see two loner Canadian geese near Orca Bay just outside Cordova. Charlie Trowbridge met the ferry and we went right to his house. Had coffee and went out the road to about mile 35 and didn't see much.

Did a little walking at Salmon Creek. Stopped and talked to Steve (Raimey?) about geese and where located. Then back to town and supper and visit with Cora. The Charlie & I went to his storage area and rigged a carrier for his flat bottom skiff. Repaired a paddle. Checked out his outboard motor. Loaded it and skiff on his pickup and back to his place. I fixed sandwiches and apples for tomorrow. After 12:00 AM now.

Saturday, October 2, 1993—warm, a few showers in the night. Ate breakfast with Charlie. When we went to leave the last headlight went out. We went in and drank coffee till light enough to drive. Went out to Elsinore River, talked to people Charlie knew who recommended against taking a boat down it. We went to Alaganik Slough and put in at boat launch. Drove boat and floated and listened for geese. We saw some geese and ducks fly several different times. Walked up several grassy sloughs and no luck. Then on way back up the Alaganik we saw geese ahead, split up to stalk them. Charlie shot at a duck and missed. In a few minutes a lone goose flew over. Charlie shot at it. As it came past me, I shot and dropped it then on up the slough and stalked more places. No luck.

Ate lunch about 2:00 PM. Some guy came along with an air boat and went where we intended to hunt. We tried to go up river from the boat launch but Charlie gave it up in a little while. Tom and Martha, Roger and ?, ask us to a grilled hamburger which we ate and left me really full. Stopped at airport but didn't get to talk to Steve. Back in town, Charlie got gas and boat gas and some shopping and helped finish picking the goose. Cora got into the act too. Dressed it in Charlie's kitchen. Then ate supper. I have a flat tire. We each took trucks over to the school and Tom the mechanic's teacher jacked my truck and we put the spare tire on it. Then they put a new light bulb in Charlie's truck. His problem is a sticking dimmer switch. Put oil on it and adjusted his driving lights for height. Very tired tonight.

Sunday, October 3, 1993—cloudy and turned to rain about noon. Charlie wanted to get a little later start. We had a good breakfast. I packed a good lunch and we drove without stopping to look or listen for geese. At Alaganik boat launch, unloaded boat, mounted motor, loaded gear. While Charlie packed truck, two ducks flew over me. I should have been ready to shoot. Down the river on a fairly low tide. We don't shoot at a few other small flocks. Charlie wants to get to Tiedeman USFS cabin. We landed on North River bank to look for geese, walked a short way and right to the cabin (surprise). Then back to boat and try to get boat to cabin. Couldn't find deep enough water.

While paddling ourselves to find a channel, two young fellows in a wide long stable John boat with a jet unit on motor came over and ask if we needed help. Very nice of them to stop. Eventually we got to the cabin. Then he wanted to cross slough channel to other side. We had a time getting boat to a place to tie up, then up on bank where we see some ducks and stalk them. Got a shot and missed. Then on to another large pond, made a stalk and missed 3-4 times then hit a teal with one pellet to head. But couldn't get to it wading, so went around pond. About the time I got there Charlie did also. He waded out to the duck and it swam a way a couple times. Eventually he shot two times and hit it in head. He did get a little water in his boots while splashing around. I picked the duck while walking back to boat. Charlie wanted to eat lunch in the cabin so back across channel tie up, got to cabin and eat. Then back to boat. We watch a few flocks of geese fly east near the point on south side of Aleganik but he wanted to go up a side slough and we do and there find a Pete Dahl cabin on Pete Dahl Cutoff Corner. On up water a ways and no bird.

I got very tired this morning and get tired quick now. Back in boat and head for boat launch. Charlie is disgusted and wants to go home. An airboat follows us in at landing and we hurry and load up and get going to town. Charlie stops at airport and gets a can of pop. Back here at camper I get furnace going and start drying wet gear and drink coffee. Beth came home from church with info geese have been flying on Egg Island. Charlie made arrangements with Steve Ranney (air taxi) to fly us out there. Then a mad rush packing gear. Finished getting ready at 12:30 AM.

Monday, October 4, 1993—rain has almost quit. Up early, loaded Charlie's gear into my pickup camper and went to air taxi. Loaded gear into 185 Cessna and Steve flew us out to Egg Island. He flew over thousands of geese. After landing, unloading we packed our gear ¼ mile in to a camping site we selected. We put up the tent and stowed our gear. Loaded our shotguns and headed for the geese. We couldn't stalk the flocks of thousands of geese. Few came even to long range. They did lots of flying "leap frog," moving ever east along the tide line. We did some walking, exploring. Finally shooting time ended and it's back to camp. Charlie came in later. We fixed supper. The sky is clearing and there is a pretty big moon—not a good sign.

Tuesday, October 5, 1993—frost on tent. Up, and had breakfast before shooting time. When we get to the flats, there are a few small flocks, less than 100 geese. I tried two shots. Either missed or they were too far away. More walking and exploring. Found Hermon's camp site. Back to camp and eat lunch. No geese around so we walk to beach. I shot at and missed some ducks that Charlie scared up. We walked quite a bit of beach. I got tired and went back to tent. Take it down and finish packing to beach. Steve picked us up and back to Cordova airstrip, then we went on to Charlie's house. Put gear away. He and I ate downtown. Got ice cream and pie filling cherries for desert at home.

Wednesday, October 6, 1993—warm mostly, sunny day. Got tire repaired. Now

I have a spare. Put exhaust pipe back into muffler. Removed screen and supports from front window of camper and found places to stow it away. Put silicone in screw holes and possible roof leaks. Took a nap. Tried to peddle halibut sinkers, no luck. Put a notice sinkers for sale on Post Office bulletin board. Drove out Harney Bay Road. Ducks were on other side of bay. We didn't go hunting this evening. We went to a "chili benefit" at school at Beth's urging. Looked at catalogs in Charlie's office for plastic ducking that I might use for fine gold recovery. Then Charlie went to play music with friend Tom.

Thursday, October 7, 1993—raining. Charlie and I went to Fish and Game Warehouse and I checked the grease level in the truck rear differential. Then took him to his work. Stopped at a store in town and sold a few craft items. Met Jim? Lab breeder and trainer from Wasilla. Then killed time till loading on ferry. Got in to Valdez about 6:00 PM. Gave a guy a ride downtown. Got gas, shopped at the "prospector." Drove to Glennallen, got gasoline there and then on home. Got here at 10:00 PM.

Friday, October 8, 1993—warm, mostly sunny, 36° to 48°. Up early. Unloaded camper. Jim O. and Kari came over just as we finished putting blocks under the unloaded camper. Then Jim helped put the pick up canopy on and helped mount the snow plow mounts to the frame. Then soup and a visit all afternoon. Bonnie stopped in. Later Jim and I went down to the lake and he shot two great scaup from the canoe. He and Kari had supper with us.

Saturday, October 9, 1993—worked at getting things ready for our trip outside. Finished packing my clothes as Sylvia had already packed most of it. We drove in to Anchorage and to Griffiths and a nice visit that evening.

Sunday, October 10, 1993—up early, light rain. Had a pancake with Griffiths then they drove us to airport. Then to Salt Lake City, short layover between the plane to Minneapolis. Bev, Nadia, Theresa plus lots of grand kids and a couple boy friends met us. We all went to Beverly's. Asif picked up Darcy when she got off work and brought her to Bev's apartment. Got to bed late.

Monday, October 11, 1993—sunny, warm but breeze makes it feel cool. Got up just after Darcy and Vanessa went to school. Tyler went at 8:30. Visited with Bev, then Scott Larson came to work on some of the buildings plumbing. He had a good idea for making a reverse gold screw and had some parts for it. Beverly fixed a very good supper. We had fun visiting with Vanessa and Darcy when they came home from school. Tyler was in and out of the house. We went grocery shopping. Asif rented two movies and we watched "Shadow of the Wolf". Good Eskimo movie. I'm drawing plans for a reverse screw black sand concentrator for gold.

Tuesday, October 12, 1993—nice Indian Summer day, high 63°, some breeze. Took some film to be developed. Did a little shopping mid afternoon. Nadia and Chuck came over and visited. We went for a drive to Minnetonka. Beautiful trees and some mallards and lots of coots on the lake. We picked up the schedule 40 PVC pipe that Scott gave me, while we were in Minnetonka. Then back to Bev's and later we all sat down to a very good taco supper. Then more visiting. My sister Virginia phoned.

Wednesday, October 13, 1993—mostly cloudy, some breeze in morning, 45° to 60°. Went to dentist for X-rays. Phone around trying to find a sheet of PVC compatible with the PVC duct Scott gave me. No luck—disappointed. Bev, Sylvia and I did some shopping this afternoon. Phoned Paul and Steve called back later. Another birthday party for Tyler today. Tyler and I played his arrow game.

Thursday, October 14, 1993—sunny, beaut of a day, 48° to 63°. Ordered some material for gold screw. Dentist cleaned my teeth. Helped Asif cut up some tree limbs. Watched a movie. Lots of visiting. It's good to be with family this way.

Friday, October 15, 1993—cloudy, started raining at noon, 48°. Nadia was at Bev's when I came back from having three teeth filled at dentist. We ate lunch. Then went to pick up the plastic for the gold screw. Then on to Northern Hydraulic and there bought a gas water pump and some parts for gold screw. Then Nadia stopped at her office where she works at Stillwater. Some shopping and a good supper with Chuck and Nadia. Watched a movie. Johnny Kaffel (my nephew) faxed map and directions to Sylvia's sister Francis home in Chicago where we will be going next—and after that, we will swing over to Iowa to see some of the Wilkins relatives.

Saturday, October 16, 1993—cloudy and a few showers, 43°. Up early. Ate breakfast and started for Chicago. Made a couple rest stops and one for gas. Johnnie had faxed a map and directions for Nadia (she's driving). Very good directions. It's about an 8 hour trip and 600 miles. Visited rest of afternoon with Fran and she had a very good dinner for us. Chicago is large and crowded. There were quite a few geese in the air and some sitting in fields along the highway. Sylvia saw a white tail doe deer.

Sunday, October 17, 1993—rain, cloudy, sunny, 63°. Breakfast, then John Kaffel, (Fran's son and our nephew), his wife and daughters Jamie and Nichole came to Fran's house. Fran had fixed a great dinner. We had a nice visit. John drove me around downtown Chicago. He got a Sunday paper. More to eat and more visiting. A nice day. I called Allen, everything good at home.

Monday, October 18, 1993—60°, smog or fog, but sunny from Iowa City to

Marion. John's directions out of Chicago were very good, as were Virginia's directions to their place in Cedar Rapids. Lots of nice corn and some soybeans in Illinois. Crops aren't as nice in Iowa. We passed near the farm in Stockton, Iowa, that we farmed in 1956, 1957 and 1958. Much has changed and some is same. Don and Virginia were just going to a funeral and dropped me off at the Laundromat. My brother, Jerry (up from Kentucky) was drying a sleeping bag there. He had locked himself out of his car. I helped and we got it unlocked with a coat hanger. Virginia fixed a great turkey dinner and afterward I took a picture of three deer just outside their house.

Tuesday, October 19, 1993—sunny, 60°. Jerry got exhaust system fixed on his car. Don and Virginia drove us around Cedar Rapids to some of the sights and places we all had lived. We went to Linwood Cemetery and hunted up dad's grave. It is very close to the southwest corner and near 6th Street. Visited in afternoon. Then went to visit Tim, Ramona and Andy at Columbus Junction. Ate a big Mexican meal near there.

Wednesday, October 20, 1993—43° and rainy (lots of haze and the air had a bad odor at different times all the way to Mpls/St Paul). A light breakfast with Virginia, Don and Jerry. Then after goodbyes we are on our way. Some of the corn and soy beans were harvested, some farmer's were out there combining corn. I got to see a rooster pheasant run across the road. We got to Nadia's at 2:00 PM. It is raining here.

Thursday, October 21, 1993—37° to 31° in Mpls./St Paul area clear skies. Up at 5:30 AM left for Staples, MN at 6:45 AM. Nice drive up. Saw a few ducks and geese. Arrived at Paul's house at 9:30 AM. Loafed around and visited with Steve. He and I went uptown to look for salt peter-no luck. Paul came home from work and after supper we went out and looked in his garage for a speed reducer that I could use on the reverse gold screw. He found one that may work. Phoned a few friends.

Friday, October 22, 1993—sunny, beaut of a day, 18° to 48°. Ruth let us use her car. We went to the box factory where Paul works. Then out to Harold and Lorraine Hanson. Their daughter, Phyllis and daughter-in-law Audrey and Lorraine's brother Al came over. We had dinner there and visited in afternoon. Stopped at Harry McCoy's and Neva, didn't recognize us. We stopped at Bjerga's Feed Store and got a couple of old screens. Supper here at Paul's. Then out to a friend of Paul's. Then over to Allen, Lillian, Scott, Darlene and Andy Rollins visited and coffee and a roll. A beaut of a warm clear evening.

Saturday, October 23, 1993—clear, very nice day, 70°. Up early and went to Bob Rudbeck's place near Pillager. Visited and wrapped the boo mount there. Had lunch and Paul and Ruth came back from Brainerd. Paul found a place in

Brainerd that would cut and roll the grinder screen to make a trommel for my gold screw.

Sunday, October 24, 1993—clear and sunny, some light breeze, 62°. Paul, Steve and I went to shooting range and Steve shot his 30-30. I coached him and he got one shot near the bulls-eye. He then shot the .22 and did well. Paul shot the .22 for awhile also. Then back home at Paul's to a good dinner and a short nap. Steve and I went for a walk and brought back a couple cardboard boxes to box the trommel screens. Then Harold and Loraine came over and visited for awhile.

Monday, October 25, 1993—cloudy, 50s. Jim and Arlene came to Paul's and took us out to their farm. After visiting and a great meal, they took us to John and Rebecca Titerington's, the Chase Place and Bob and Lois Mick home, then back to Paul's home in the evening.

Tuesday, October 26, 1993—cloudy, windy, 36°. Walked uptown a couple of times. Ran into Floyd Griffith. Visited a little. When Ruth got off work and Steve home from school we went to Clarissa and got salt peter for Sylvia (she uses it for making sausage). Went to Hewitt and ordered two shafts for the gold screw jack shaft. Saw 6 white tail deer and a dozen wild turkeys from the highway.

Wednesday, October 27, 1993—some wind in evening, 22° to 40°. Walked around town some. Then at 1:00 PM went to community center and got my "flu" shot. A little later we all went to Wadena-Paul to doctor and have another toenail removed. Ruth drove us to Hewitt and I got my 5/8" shafts for a speed jack for gold screw. Had to chase around to find pulleys and bearing flanges. Lots of geese were getting up from a swamp-resting area in east side of town and presumably out to feed in farm fields. Back to Staples and bought two more pulleys there. Saw a good buy on a scope and gave Steve his Christmas present early as a part payment on scope.

Thursday, October 28, 1993—windy, 30s. Steve said goodbye and went to school. Paul was sick during the night. His toe is sore and hurting today. I packaged the two trommel screens, flat screens, the speed jack and components and about that time Nadia and Chuck reached Staples and Paul's house. We rode back to Minneapolis with them. Stopped along the way for a hamburger. They dropped us off at Beverly's. Visited with Bev, then Vanessa and Darcy came home from school. Later Tyler got home. His dad came and took him somewhere. Bev had a good chili supper cooked. I walked a roll of film over to the mall.

Friday, October 29, 1993—cool and windy this morning, warmer later. Up early and had two teeth filled at local dentist. Did a little shopping later. Asif and I went to some stores that specialize in foods he eats, then back to Bev's and we dress to get pictures taken at photographers. Back to Bev's and she decked Tyler out in his Halloween costume and he went to a Boy Scout meeting. Sylvia, Beverly and Darcy went shopping for supper steaks.

Saturday, October 30, 1993—cloudy, 28° to 33°. Loafed and visited all day. Mid afternoon went to get developed pix and a little shopping. Tyler and I played with a paper airplane out in hallway. After supper, Asif took us all over to Theresa and Lee's.

Sunday, October 31, 1993—about same temp., cloudy, sunny. Watched TV. Went to grocery store, window shopped "Holliday" store.

Monday, November 1, 1993—20s to 40s. Watched TV till Theresa got up at 1:20 PM. Visited till Lee came home from school at 2:25 PM. We all walked east to a mall and a Target store. Did a little shopping and walked back here. Sylvia cooked up a good chicken supper and then more TV.

Tuesday, November 2, 1993—light rain in night, sunny most of day, 28° to 48°. Up early, saw Lee off to school. Sylvia went back to bed for a nap. Nadia came over about 10:30 AM and we all visited for a while and Sylvia fixed sandwiches for lunch. We then did a couple of errands for Theresa and went to Northern Hydraulics store and I looked at engines to power the gold recovery unit. Back at Theresa's I ordered the motor and had it sent parcel post to Alaska. Sylvia fixed spaghetti for supper.

Wednesday, November 3, 1993—sunny, cloudy, 30s to 40s. Watched TV. Made a trip to store when Lee got home from school.

Thursday, November 4, 1993—cloudy, rain in afternoon. Nadia came to Theresa's when she got off work and we stopped by the Fleet Store and did some shopping on the way to her place. Chuck picked up Laura and Brittany when he got off work and brought them here to visit with us. We had a nice dinner.

Friday, November 5, 1993—wind in night and snow, 27° to 24° after dark. Saw ducks flying on St. Croix River. We are enjoying our visit here and getting to know great granddaughter Brittany. Nadia and Chuck worked today. Chuck and Laura fixed supper this evening.

Saturday, November 6, 1993—cloudy, some breeze, 19° to 31°. Chuck played tennis, then cooked dinner. The women went shopping. I got the pump and motor rigged with rope and handle. Same for the box of plastic for the screw.

Sunday, November 7, 1993–cloudy, 24° to 30°. Did more packing. Met Laura's boyfriend "Brad". Went to Bev's with Nadia. Bev sick and in bed. Volk's had Vanessa and Tyler. We visited with Darcy. Shopped in Stillwater. Saw some ducks and geese. Some hunters have their deer. Helped Chuck clean lint out of clothes dryer.

Monday, November 8, 1993–cloudy, 20s to 30s. Saw a few duck and a ½ dozen geese fly by the marina. The marina workers are enveloping the many boats in visqueen, poly tarps. Bev phoned. Nadia went to work for a short time, came back home. We had lunch then mailed the three plastic pipes. Went to Goodwill store, video rental, photo shop and two libraries and gas station then back here at Nadia's. I loaded three heavy packages into Nadia's car, preparing for the trip to airport and home. Nadia and Sylvia fixed a good supper.

Tuesday, November 9, 1993–temperature in the 30s. Up very early and off to airport. Got checked in. At security search some guy tried to go thru same time I did and knocked the thing over. Funny as hell to me. Tiring flight to Anchorage. Got cab and went to Griffith's. Stay the night with them so Sylvia can rest up. Had a nice visit with Griffiths.

Wednesday, November 10, 1993–up early, 20s to 30s. Had coffee and went on our rounds of place to shop in Anchorage, Chugiak and Palmer. Then on home, road in fair shape. Unloaded the truck and went to Allen's and got our mail. Visited a while.

Thursday, November 11, 1993–cloudy, 10° to 20°. Finished unpacking. Put plow on truck and pushed all snow back. Put log chains around the pile of spruce limb trimming and pulled it out into yard so the heat from burning it wouldn't damage nearby trees. Visited with Ed a couple minutes. Sunshine in afternoon. Mary Beaudoin brought us a bunch of video tapes.

Friday, November 12, 1993–cloudy, 15° to 28°. Sylvia did laundry. Kyle Farmer came over to borrow a book for a school project. Spent some time doing a little research for him. Put away a few more things. The three pieces of PVC came in the mail today. When we tried to pump water, I discovered the water line had a ice plug in it. Glad to have the snowgo to run up and down the hill. Brought piece of line in and thawed it out. Tom H. visited.

Saturday, November 13, 1993–mostly cloudy, 26° to 32°. Snow moving in this evening. Visited Allen in the morning. Denny Eastman had Ray McCurdy fly the plane to our lake. Then Ray coached him on landing and take offs. We drank coffee and watched the show from Allen's. At home I unpacked the gold screw parts. Put license plate back on truck, took the snow plow off, put a new weather door sill in the kitchen door. Put away some summer and hunting gear.

Got out some winter gear.

Sunday, November 14, 1993—6" snow and more all day and evening, 23° to 28°. Rested all morning. Packed a CB to send to grandson, Lee Austin. Visited at Ed and Sandy's. Mark Brockman came over to visit in early evening.

Monday, November 15, 1993—cloudy, clearing in evening, 28° to 5°. Plowed snow at home, Chamberlains, Odden's and airstrip. Visited Allen, then Denny Eastman. He gave me a video on dredging for gold. Very good. Visited Mark and his two sons in evening. Reyne was working.

Tuesday, November 16, 1993—cloudy, 1° to 28°. T & K Huddleston took us to Anchorage and to lunch. They did lots of shopping. We did some also. We bought a sandwich at suppertime and shopped at Carr's for groceries. Snowed more than ½ way home and fog on Eureka Summit. Got home at 10:00 PM.

Wednesday, November 17, 1993—partly cloudy, -5° to 23°. 3" snow in night. Snowing again this evening. Sylvia went to Glennallen and mailed book to Lee Austen. I went to Bart's and got my oxygen bottle and some copies made. Picked up some of Jim Odden's mail. Shoveled some snow and plowed the snow that fell last night. Robbie brought the package (B & S Motor) that came in mail yesterday while we were gone. Harold and Rachel visited in evening.

Thursday, November 18, 1993—cloudy, light snow, 0° to 9°. Cut glass for rear view mirror on truck. Wolverine delivered gasoline today. Have had a headache today. Put Jim Odden's mail back in box.

Friday, November 19, 1993—cloudy, sunny, 0° to 14° to -12°. 2 1/2" snow last night. Replaced a burned out bulb in our well. 4" over flow on our lake. Allen's went to "Point of View." Denny E. to Glennallen. Ed is driving truck. I shoveled snow off the camper. Hooked up snowplow turn signal lights. Filled gas tanks on truck. Plowed our snow and snow at Ms. Banning's. We went to a Thanksgiving play at Nelchina School (very good), pot luck supper and a drawing for a win .338 stainless steel. A fellow from Gakona won it. Also loaded a 100 rounds for grandson Steve's .30-.30. Sylvia went over to Elaine Manning to help her. She does get around on her broken ankle and the other is sprained.

Saturday, November 20, 1993—sunny, -30° to -15°. Wrote some letters. Denny and Jo were here for coffee and tea. Wiped the .30-30 cartridges.

Sunday, November 21, 1993—sunny, -31° to 13°. Did some reading and book sorting. Denny G. family visiting Eastman's and riding snowgos here and on lake. Allen and Ellie came up to visit. Later Roxanne and Kyle stopped by and all had soup Sylvia had fixed.

Monday, November 22, 1993—mostly sunny, cloudy late afternoon, -23° to 23°. Gusts of wind here, winds from south over Heavenly Ridge blowing snow 500' higher (to 5400'). Wind and snow like that is impressive. Sylvia went to Glennallen and mailed package to grandson, Steve W. I took Roxanne's mitts down to her. Stopped by to say Hi to Jim and Elaine (broken ankle). Made a couple phone calls to Nome.

Tuesday, November 23, 1993—partly cloudy, 20° to 28° to 14°. 2 1/2" snow last night. Senior van didn't make it out to our place. I plowed our snow and Banning's snow. Made a couple repairs to snow plow. Mixed gas and filled 250 colt and put rest in the long track. Started the colt and drove it over to garage. Shoved the snow off the wood shed. Allen came over and traded movies.

Wednesday, November 24, 1993—mostly cloudy, flurries in evening, 5° to 20°. Went to Glennallen on senior van and did errands. Did a few small jobs outside. Picked up Oddens mail. Nadia and Theresa phoned.

Thursday, November 25, 1993—snow all day, 20°. Shoved snow off two roofs and pulled snow off arctic entry roof. Back was really sore this morning. We got ready to go to Roxanne and Allen's for Thanksgiving dinner. Put plow on and plowed snow and plowed a little for Allen. Plowed the rest of ours when we got back home. We had a good time at Allen's. They had lots of company.

Friday, November 26, 1993—light snow and cloudy, 3° to 18°. Water proofed maps of Nome area. Plowed Vernetta's driveway. Allen, Roxanne, Ed Farmer, Sylvia and I went to Joe Secondchief's funeral at Kluti Kaah in Copper Center. Went there in Allen's van. They did some errands in Glennallen. We had supper with them in evening. We took a pumpkin pie and Pepsi for the supper. Watched a movie, then came home. Steve W. had mailed the old milk strainer to us. I will use it for a material hopper on the fine gold recovery machine.

Saturday, November 27, 1993—mostly sunny, 0° all day and dropping in evening. Plowed snow at Chamberlains, Oddens, and Skoog's. Someone from Mendeltna wanted me to plow but I got out of that one. Grandson Steve phoned, he had gotten the package we sent him. He wants us to send him some traps and trap equipment.

Sunday, November 28, 1993—partly cloudy, lots of fog across the Nelchina River, -6° to +4°. We pumped water. I visited Lucky~Mary had taped more movies for us. I gave him some pictures I had taken when he and I were hunting. Back home I shoveled snow off a roof and pulled snow off two other roofs with the snow rake. Sure tires the arms. Sorted out some traps to send to

Steve. Located a box to send CB Antenna to Lee. Watched eclipse of moon.

Monday, November 29, 1993—cloudy, some fog, -7° to 5°. Allen F. visited. We got ready and went to Dan and Patti Billmans. Had a nice visit and lunch, then watched two tapes: Gold Dredging and Gold Screw. Stopped at Dinty Bush's visited with Leona and Doug. Left a tire to be fixed and gave Doug three old tires. Saw a few boo tracks on Lake Louise Road.

Tuesday, November 30, 1993—cloudy, some frost in the air, -2° to 3°. Checked lights and brakes on colt 250. Adjusted the carburetor float level and long track, folded tent and put it away. Gathered up and packaged lures for Steve. Addressed packages for Lee and Steve. Jim Manning borrowed some chairs. Sylvia and I re-did kitchen sink drain. Mary Beaudoin visited and took some tapes home with her and will return them later. Sylvia sent along piece of lemon pie for Lucky.

Wednesday, December 1, 1993—mostly cloudy, -5° to 3°. Visited Allen, Jack and Denny were there. Talked to Ed a couple minutes on the way home. Sylvia mailed traps to Steve from Glennallen. Phone has been ringing a lot here. Ed borrowed a movie. I didn't do anything except draw some more on the drum-riffles etc for the gold screw.

Thursday, December 2, 1993—sunny, -10° to 4°. Walked down to Allen's. He was hanging garage doors. Ate lunch with them. Walked back past mail box and picked mail up. Did more planning of drum and riffles. We went to Lucky and Mary's for supper. Sylvia put a perm in Mary's hair. Donna was there.

Friday, December 3, 1993—mostly cloudy, some sun in afternoon, -7° to 16°. Walked to Ed's. Denny and Allen went to Glennallen. Saw marten track between our house and lake. Worked on snow plow wings. Sized up supply of steel to make the trommel. Denny Eastman came over to help load snowgo that I have to haul to Tazlina tomorrow. Jim Odden called and gave me forwarding address change.

Saturday, December 4, 1993—sunny, ice fog, -18° to 3°. Took Sylvia's crafts to Glennallen to bazaar. Delivered snowgo. Visited with Mike Lanegan. No one answered door bell at Johnson's so I didn't get copies made.

Sunday, December 5, 1993—snow all day (got four inches), -20° to 1°. Did a few little jobs around the house. Visited with Eastman family.

Monday, December 6, 1993—sunny, 0° to 22°. Sylvia went to Glennallen. I plowed snow. Plowed some at Allen's. Later he stopped by here and cookies and coffee. I gave him three dry wall screw drivers for hex drive. Cut off some steel for gold screw. Carried some frame steel to garage for gold screw. Phoned Sears about stove repair and Sylvia's doctor's appointment.

Tuesday, December 7, 1993—sunny all day, -5° to 16°. Shoveled snow off camper and from brown trailer door. Visited Allen Farmers. Built a fire in wood shop and started getting drum ready to glue.

Wednesday, December 8, 1993—partly cloudy, ice fog, -5° to 4°. Sylvia went to Glennallen. I started the jigs for the drum. Measured the heating oil in tank. Allen brought some tapes back and visited awhile in evening.

Thursday, December 9. 1993—cloudy, ice fog, sunny, cloudy, -17° to -4°. Wrote lots of Christmas cards. Visited Allen. Sears repair service for the cook stove called a few times. Worked some more on the gold drum.

Friday, December 10, 1993—mostly sunny, -16° to 0° to -15°. Glued two parts of gold drum. Denny E. and Allen visited. I took a Christmas card to Mannings. We pumped water this afternoon. A marten is again running around here.

Saturday, December 11, 1993—mostly sunny, -19° to -10°. Tried to make riffles to put in the drum. Material is too stiff, no luck. Jeff and Laurie R. and kids stopped by to look at our house and how it was built. Visited Denny E. in afternoon.

Sunday, December 12, 1993—sunny, -17° to -3°. Brought the Coleman camp oven in and put it on cook stove. Put some riffle material in the oven and heated to "limp" and reformed it. It took the proper "curve", when it cooled down. Later we took a housewarming gift to Eastman's and visited a while. Denny came over and got a couple buckets of water.

Monday, December 13, 1993—sunny, fog later in afternoon, -18° to -2°. Paid some bills. Visited couple min. with Ed. Checked traps on Switch Back Trail. Visited Allen. Sylvia went to Glennallen. Mary Beaudoin taped 6 tapes. Vanessa and Darcy, Tyler and Bev phoned this evening.

Tuesday, December 14, 1993—mostly sunny, -25° to -12°. We went to Dr. Cotton in Wasilla, Dr. Downing in Palmer and Sylvia had blood samples drawn at Palmer Hospital lab. We ate lunch at Palmer Senior Center. Shopped for groceries.

Wednesday, December 15, 1993—mostly cloudy, -19° to -6°. Some phone calls for prescriptions (Sylvia) and about insurance to pay Dr. Denny came over to borrow plunger. Ed is driving truck for Blake. Mary B. stopped by.

Thursday, December 16, 1993—mostly sunny, some ice fog, -15° to -2°. Snow on south side of river. Walked down to Allen's, had coffee and helped him bleed the brakes on his van. Stopped by Denny's a couple min. Ed F. came over to watch the movie about dredging gold. Allen, Roxanne and kids had a chili supper with us. Allen and Roxanne stayed to watch "Geronimo."

Friday, December 17, 1993—partly cloudy, -5° to 16°. We pumped water again today and I packed the trail with snowgo. Lots phone calls today. We went to the Xmas program the kids put on at the Little Nelchina School.

Saturday, December 18, 1993—cloudy and some snow, -5° to 30°. Part of snow on south side of house roof slid off. Took my daily walk, stopped at Allen's and Lucky's. Put antifreeze in leaky radiator. Oil in truck motor. Checked oil in rear differential.

Sunday, December 19, 1993—cloudy, snowed seven inches, 25° to 30°. Plowed snow and got ready to go to Palmer. Someone may be trapping along Slide Mountain Trail (Allen's). Went to Palmer. Went to a hotel for the night.

Monday, December 20, 1993—cloudy, 20° all day. Up early. Went to check into hospital and found the doctor had been hospitalized and operation delayed. Back to hotel until some of the offices and businesses opened up. Dropped cook stove off to be fixed. No luck seeing the "Dixie Doodle Bug Gold" or getting arctic fox hides. Did shopping, got Sylvia's medicine and came home.

Tuesday, December 21, 1993—cloudy, snow across river, 16° to 23°. Some sun, mostly cloudy. Packed trail to well and to Allen's with snowgo. Marten had sprung both conibears. Got a package of cheese from Oddens. We are cooking on a old Coleman propane camp stove. Sears phoned this evening that our kitchen range is repaired. We watched the clouds drop rain that turned to snow about 100'+ above the ground. The interplay with winds, clouds and sun was grand while we ate breakfast.

Wednesday, December 22, 1993—cloudy, then snow most of day, 10° to 18°. Replaced light bulb at well. Built a fire in wood shop and made a jig on table saw to cut riffles for drum. Sanded and cleaned them up. Shoveled snow from well cover and replaced the light bulb. Sylvia helped with the riffles.

Thursday, December 23, 1993—mostly cloudy, 10° to 18°. Up early. Tom H. and I went to Anchorage in his pickup. Our stove was repaired and we picked it up first in Wasilla. Then lots of shopping in Anchorage. Brunch at Gwennie's Restaurant. Some old guy in a pickup pulled out in front of us and Tom managed to miss him. It was close. Tom kept his cool and did a great job.

Friday, December 24, 1993—mostly sunny, 12° to 22°. Plowed the last light snow. Built a fire in the wood shop. Marten has been around again. Eastman drove his Alpine Skidoo out into overflow from Rudbeck's spring. Allen pulled him out. Plowed some snow and watered flowers at Mannings. Hooked up cook stove and it doesn't work. Wasilla Sears didn't check it after working on it.

Saturday, December 25, 1993—ice fog all day, 2° to 8°. Tried to glue the drum PVC sample, no luck. Drilled and screwed it, not good but better. Sylvia wants to buy a manufactured unit. Probably a good idea. She did laundry. We had wild duck I had shot from our lake for dinner tonight.

Sunday, December 26, 1993—mostly sunny, then clouds and ice fog, 1° to 11°. We pumped water and I walked up and down the hill twice. Nadia phoned and we have a nice visit.

Monday, December 27, 1993—mostly clear, cloudy and windy closer to Sutter Palmer area. We got up at 2:30 AM, loaded our things to be gone 4-5 days, also the cook stove. Went to hospital in Palmer. Checked in there and they prepped Sylvia for her operation. Dr. Downing performed and Dr Fawcett assisted. Everything went well. Recovery was slow. I phoned all the kids after 5:00 PM. Sylvia's blood pressure shot up after taking pain killer pills containing codeine. The Doctors and nurses had a difficult time controlling her BP and getting it down. A nurse arranged for me to have a cot in the room with Sylvia.

Tuesday, December 28, 1993—Sylvia's blood pressure is better today. Nurse had Sylvia out of bed and moving around. The machine assisting blood circulation in Sylvia's legs isn't working too well. I stayed at Jean's B & B for the night. Mostly cloudy and warm to about 35°.

Wednesday, December 29, 1993—mostly cloudy, 35°. Had breakfast at B & B then to hospital. Sylvia had been walking and looks much better. After a while I took kitchen range into Sears Repair in Anchorage. Repairman got the range to work by hitting on valve body. They will order out another valve. AK Mining and Diving was closed for inventory. Went back to Palmer and got some sandwich makings and coffee at Carr's. Sylvia has had a shower and is walking in halls. She and I went for another walk. All three daughters phoned Sylvia.

Thursday, December 30, 1993—partly cloudy, sunny, foggy, 20°. Had breakfast and onto hospital. Sylvia already had shower. Nurse took her staples (stitches) out. They moved her to another room. I went to senior center for lunch. Mary B. visited and brought candy. Bev and the kids phoned. Then Laura and Brittany phoned. Theresa called. I went to Wasilla and looked at a "Dixie Doodle" at "Lucas's" (Fine Gold Recovery Unit).

Friday, December 31, 1993—mostly sunny, 10° to 20°. Breakfast at B & B then to hospital. After a certain amount of rigmarole Sylvia got discharged from hospital and we got her prescriptions filled and a few groceries at Carr's, then a good trip home. The roads were fair winter time driving condition. Unloaded all here at home. Brought in propane bottle and camp stove. Got Sylvia settled in, then went to Allen's and picked up our mail.

Sylvia Wilkins

A gold screw similar to the one used by Norman and Sylvia in Nome.

1994—Adventures in Nome

Saturday, January 1, 1994—cloudy, 0° to 10°. Sylvia is doing well and resting a lot. Elaine sent a turkey supper over for us. Sandy phoned and wants to fix us supper tomorrow night. Roxanne phoned. She wanted to fix chicken. Joey E. phoned to say Hi. Robbie came over for a couple minutes. I drove down to Odden's driveway. Gate is locked and no new snow to sweep off the plane. Saw tracks of a fox. Put a note on my trap line sign. A moose has walked by front window. A boo calf walked up to a lean-to door.

Sunday, January 2, 1994—sunny, beaut of a day, -9° to 4°. Went for a walk. Did my exercise routine. Theresa and Bev phoned. Sandy Farmer sent a very good supper over by Ed. I wrote a couple letters and read today. Sylvia got her exercise walking in the house. Lots of overflow on the lake.

Monday, January 3, 1994—partly cloudy, -12° to 2°. Up early and to Palmer. Dr Manelik found a large ulcer in Sylvia's stomach. Her bladder isn't operational yet so she has to have the catheter in another week. She is tired tonight.

Tuesday, January 4, 1994—cloudy, ice fog in afternoon, -9° to -1°. Went to Allen's and he witnessed our dividend check applications and hopefully ordered light bulbs, the long life kind. Took the dishes belonging to Sandy back. Sylvia did dish's and some laundry. I put oil in truck motor and checked the oil in rear differential. Allen brought supper for us. How nice.

Wednesday, January 5, 1994—ice fog all day, -7° to 2° and -2° all day. Oiled a shot gun and a rifle. Made some little sticks for Sylvia's window hangings (frame parts). Jack Chamberlin brought a nice flower arrangement from Mendeltna Chapel. We had a nice visit. Elaine Manning had Missy out hauling her around on a snowgo.

Thursday, January 6, 1994—mostly sunny, -6° to 7°, half inch of fluffy snow. We pumped water today, so I packed the trail to well with snowgo. Returned Roxanne dish. Visited with Ed. Put oil in truck diff. Plowed snow. Shoveled snow off wood shed and pulled snow off arctic entry and woodshop. Made two Plexiglas writing surfaces for Farmer boys. Kim brought a hot dish. Charlie and Kindra were along.

Friday, January 7, 1994—mostly sunny, -23° to -1°. Visited Roxanne and Faith. Then at Lucky and Mary's. Back home I cleaned some more snow off a couple roofs. Jim and Kari Odden were here to supper and picked up their mail. We had a long visit.

Saturday, January 8, 1994—sunny, -30° to -1°. Very bright stars at night and sunlight very bright in day. A breeze from the west. Put order for a book for Mary O. in mail box. Left some tapes with Mary B. and visited with Lucky. Then a couple minutes at A. Farmers. The on up the hill and home. Jim O. came over to watch the Green Bay Packers play football. Sylvia fixed a good corned moose meal.

Sunday, January 9, 1994—sunny, clouds started coming in from south, -36° to -20°. The "high" held them out of the valley. We didn't do much today. Wrote a few letters. Built a fire in wood stove. Put out something for birds to eat.

Monday, January 10, 1994—sunny, sung dogs in afternoon, -37° to -28°. Went to Glennallen and picked up Jerry R's mail. Saw five moose from highway. Allen F. borrowed portable air tank. Chuck Zimbicki phoned about gold screw video tape arrival.

Tuesday, January 11, 1994—cloudy here, warmer in Palmer and Wasilla, -33° to -12°. Got up early and in to Palmer and Sylvia's surgeon. Removed the catheter and checked her for capability to empty her bladder. Everything works. Went to Wasilla for some pills. Back to Palmer, shopping and something to eat. While in Carr's parking lot a raven landed on the truck hood. Walked back and forth and talked with Sylvia. Saw lots of moose along the highway.

Wednesday, January 12, 1994—mostly cloudy, -13° to -5°. Fuel oil delivery. Shoveled some snow. Allen borrowed a tape. Went to Dimmick's and had supper with Harold, Rachel, Rusty, Corky, Sam, Carrie and Charley. Showed gold screw and dredging tapes.

Thursday, January 13, 1994—cloudy, light snow, -8° to 0°. Bart B. came over and we repaired the drive for his snow blower. He visited awhile. Allen and David brought some lasagna for lunch. Then Allen and I went up Slide Mt. Allen broke trail with Denny's Alpine. It doesn't run very well. Allen had to shovel some areas. He got tired and we turned back and came home.

Friday, January 14. 1994—cloudy, -5° to 5°. Bart came over to have me turn his snow blower drive shaft end for end. Then Allen and I and Bart went to his place to look at blower and found more wrong with it. We loaded and hauled it to Allen's and worked on it there. Got it repaired and sent Bart on his way. I met Chuck Z at KROA and he gave me a video tape to view and I bought a needle and seat for snowgo carburetor.

Saturday, January 15, 1994—cloudy. Propane was delivered.

Sunday, January 16, 1994—cloudy, some snow, mostly -2° all day. Visited Ed and Sandy Farmer. Manning brought a loaf of bread. Sylvia gave both families

"Iris" window hangings.

Monday, January 17, 1994–cloudy, light snow, -10° to 5°. Ed F. came over and borrowed a small pulley for electric motor. We pumped water for house supply.

Tuesday, January 18, 1994–cloudy and light snow, -5° to 7°. Up early and drive to Palmer. Roads pretty slippery. Sign in at hospital and Sylvia got her upper GI x-rays then to Sears repair center in Anchorage. Then we picked up the kitchen range. We had already eaten lunch and talked to the manager of Alaska Mining and Diving about sluice's and pumps. Back to Palmer and picked up groceries and on home. Saw seven moose today and one spruce hen. She was in middle of road after sand. Re-installed kitchen range here at home and it seems to work. Sylvia is sore tonight.

Wednesday, January 19, 1994–cloudy, light snow. Loaded snowgo and some food. Denny Eastman and I went to Point of View Lodge. Parked vehicles. Visited Dan and Patti. Drove the trail to Crosswind Lake and across lake from Big Bay to Blackie's Fish Camp now owned by Art and Bonnie Wikle's. We stayed in west cabin. Wikles left soon after our arrival. Later in the evening, Dan B. drove in on his snowgo and stayed overnight.

Thursday, January 20, 1994–pretty nice day. Trapper Bob drove in and had breakfast with us. We all fished all day. Bob got three lake trout. Denny got one. Dan and I didn't get any. Dan and Bob left for Lake Louise at dark.

Friday, January 21, 1994–kind of cold and breezy and pretty foggy. Denny caught two more lake trout. I had three hits, caught none. We packed up our gear. Then while drilling out a hole Bigger lost a fish. Loaded Denny's dark house and went to Point of View. Saw one lynx, seven fox track along trail. Saw a broken down snowgo on Lake Louise. Denny's right "throttle" thumb keeps getting very cold. At Point of View we learn its Dan B's machine broken and Denny pulled it the two miles home for Dan. Trapper Bob brought lake trout fillets to Dan's and they fixed fried trout and French-fries and invited Denny and I to supper. Got home about 8:00 PM.

Saturday, January 22, 1994–mostly sunny, cloudy to south in afternoon. 0° to -8°. Sun dogs. Unloaded snowgo and gear. Gathered some fishing gear for rainbow trout and a couple other small jobs. Visited Allen a few minutes.

Sunday, January 23, 1994–mostly sunny, some overhead fog, -2° to 10°. Tried to fix up a jigging rod for lake trout. Put in screws to hold clothes chests to wall in case of quakes. Eastmans and Griffiths were here for awhile this afternoon. Sylvia baked a goose and invited Jim and Kari to supper.

Monday, January 24, 1994—light snow all day (two inches), 5° to 10°. Visited Ed F. in the morning and Allen F in the afternoon. Steve Malley brought his rangers snow plow blade for Allen to weld. A dog musher from Sheep Mt. area asked about trapping the Slide Mountain Trail.

Tuesday, January 25, 1994—cloudy, sunny, 10° to 20°. Plowed our snow and teachers. Pulled some snow off garage roof. Borrowed a star drill from Allen to drill two holes in cement blocks, hopefully to stabilize the water in the event of an earthquake. Shoveled some snow.

Wednesday, January 26, 1994—cloudy, snow, sunny, 2° to 22°. Sylvia went o Glennallen. I took magazines to Ed. Cleaned snow off greenhouse and several other jobs. Went to Allen's for his birthday and a turkey supper. Kim S, Lucky and Mary were there.

Thursday, January 27, 1994—light snow (three inches), 15° to 18°. Back has been very bad all day. Denny brought some articles (13 +3) over for storage while he goes outside. Visited Lucky at camp.

Friday, January 28, 1994—mostly sunny, 11° to 24°. Plowed snow and shoveled a little. Did couple small jobs. Allen visited for awhile in afternoon. My back is not good these days. Allen came over in eve to borrow a movie.

Saturday, January 29, 1994—partly cloudy, 12° to 20°. I wrote five letters and finished reading "The Eye of the Rainbow" by Ted Mattson. Read a duck hunting magazine. Researched some gun powder reloading information.

Sunday, January 30, 1994—sunny, cloudy at sunset, 11° to 21°. Some breezes blowing snow out of some trees, especially across the river. Did some exercises, loafed mostly.

Monday, January 31, 1994—mostly sunny, beaut of a day, 10° to 23°. Sylvia went to Glennallen on senior van. She did an errand for Sandy Farmer. I fueled the snowgo and drove past the Farmer Bros. at their wood-lot loading area. They hook snowgos tandem to pull a sled load of wood out to a pick-up. I went on to old trap line trail on east end of Slide Mountain Trail has been traveled before and only our last two snows do I have to go through. I saw three sets of marten track (one male and 2 female?). Saw two grown moose and one calf. Two fox traveling together at Cache Creek area. I could smell their pee posts. So breeding season is getting close. Followed trail to the camp on hill between two lakes. Looked at view for a while then back home. Went to Allen's for rolls and coffee and plowed out some snow at his sawmill.

Tuesday, February 1, 1994—mostly sunny, some clouds and a river of fog along

Heavenly Ridge and on east down the valley, 1° to 20°. We pumped water today. Allen invited us down for supper. Sylvia baked bread and a cake for my birthday. We took the cake and ice cream mixer and custard to Allen's at suppertime. Ed, Sandy and their family were there and later Al and Faith Padowski showed up.

Wednesday, February 2, 1994—sunny, cloudy, some fog blowing east on other side of river, 9° to 29°. Theresa and Nadia both called birthday greetings. Quite a bit of snow slid off north side of house roof. Sylvia vacuumed house and I cleaned the vacuum filter. Jim O. brought video of a native man and his woodsmanship. Jim had supper with us. He left a book for me to read.

Thursday, February 3, 1994—mostly sunny after some fog in the morning, 17° to 31°. Some more snow slid off house roof. I shoveled a little more snow and read in book "Shadows on the Koyukuk."

Friday, February 4, 1994—sunny, cloudy, 18° to 24°. Allen heard and saw wolves in bowl of Nelchina River. Came to get me and some traps. He took Al and Faith Padowski along. We drove snowgo to area, saw raven and calf moose kill site. Stopped closer to bluff. Black wolf came out of brush running in deep snow for trees and a ravine. I hit it with .22-250 in liver. Allen hit it high just behind shoulders with a 7mm-08. This is a pup and last one to leave the kill. We made four wolf sets. Anyway I was supposed to be helping Jim O. get his plane to Gulkana to be annualled. So we go back to Allen's and Nelchina.

Allen has given (I think) the wolf to Al and Faith. Al is asking me if I want the wolf. (I previously said we should sell and split it up.) Padowskis want the wolf badly. Jim flew his plane to Gulkana and I drove his truck there. On our way home I asked Jim to stop at Chuck Zimbicki's. There I traded snowgo float needle valves with Chuck. We looked at his new hydromantic gold jig and talked gold then snowgos and other subjects. Back here at home, Sylvia put on supper for Jim and me. Then I called Allen about skinning wolf. He and Al were nearly done. Jim and I turn and walk towards the house. Allen asked us to coffee so we had a cup, visited and Jim brought me home. I checked outside at 1:15 AM and 5:20 AM for howling, and again at 8:15 AM. No howling that I can hear.

Saturday, February 5, 1994—mostly sunny, 5° to 16°. Went down to Allen's and after some jockeying around we went to check wolf kill and trap sets. The wolves had not been back. Allen heard them howl in the night from over at Twin Lakes. My snowgo gave me some carburetor trouble. Lubed the clutches. Shoveled some snow from in front of bullet back stop. Art and Bonnie Wikle ask us to a birthday party for their son-in-law Jeff. He is married to Laurie. This was at KROA.

Sunday, February 6, 1994—cloudy, light snow, 1° to 11°. Read most all day. A spruce hen flew into cable end of house. It hit the house so hard and so loud it really got our attention. The hen didn't survive the crash.

Monday, February 7, 1994—light snow and cloudy, 2° to 11°. Reloaded some FMJ 22-250 for fur. Checked oil in truck. Made a bow saw blade protector. Brought day pack in house for repair. Sylvia went to Glennallen. I visited Ed and talked to Mark near mailbox.

Tuesday, February 8, 1994—partly cloudy. We went to Palmer for Sylvia's check up with her surgeon. Then to senior center in Wasilla for lunch then to Dr. Manelick for Sylvia's ulcer. Then to sport shop and Ace Hardware. Then Smayda's for a short visit. Then shop for groceries, (saw Wikles) and on home. Got tired before I got home.

Wednesday, February 9, 1994—light snow all day, 1° to 16°. Plowed what little snow we had and installed new trip spring on snow plow. Put some air in right front truck tire. Did some reading. Sylvia went to Glennallen and sewed some buttons on my arctic pants. She called Karn about getting stomach pills.

Thursday, February 10, 1994—sunny, -7° to 12°. Sylvia fixed pocket on my parka and installed openings in my arctic pants so I can reach inside pants pockets. I installed a new fluorescent light fixture over her sink. Gathered and sorted game calls. Read a lot. Lanegan called about pelt.

Friday, February 11, 1994—cloudy, light snow, sunny, cloudy and light snow again, -5° to 4°. Smashed aluminum pop cans. Sylvia did laundry. Made a block "holder" to keep Hoppe's No. 9 and bench rest bore cleaner containers upright and in a non-spill position when using them. The order for some different .22 bullets came today. Reloaded some and selected one brand to use. Set up shooting bench and target. Found a compatible powder wt. and got a good group. Fred Rungee stopped for a visit. He left us a sack of pistachio nuts.

Saturday, February 12, 1994—mostly sunny, cloudy evening, -9° to -2°. We pumped water into our storage tanks. I went west on Nelchina River and looked at wolf killed moose and wolf sets. Nothing came near that area except ravens. Did some reading. Cut out and shaped a special cardboard box.

Sunday, February 13, 1994—sunny and beautiful day, sun dogs out, -24° to -9°. Did some reading. Watched the Winter Olympics in Norway. Went to a birthday party for Sandy F. and Patty L. at Sandy's house. Had a great dinner and home made ice cream (we took our freezer over).

Monday, February 14, 1994—sunny, -29° to -2°. Walked to Allen's. They were

going to Glennallen. Sylvia rode the senior van to Glennallen. I pulled some
snow off some roofs with the snow rake. Polished some brass.

Tuesday, February 15, 1994—sunny, -29° to 0°. Read some today. Loafed.

Wednesday, February 16, 1994—sunny, -25° to -2°. Northern lights are bright.
Went with Jim to Gulkana and drove his pickup home for him. He drove his
plane home. He and Kari were here for supper.

Thursday, February 17, 1994—sunny, northern lights at night, -34° to 0°. Jim
wants to go to Old Boot Lake, hauling a cast "prospector" cabin stove. I did
some reading and baked some cookies.

Friday, February 18, 1994—sunny, -28° to 0°. Repaired one of my day packs.
Did more reading.

Saturday, February 19, 1994—sunny, breezy here and more so south in area of
river, -30° to -6°. I got Allen to go with me to wolf sets after he came back from
wood lot. He has quite a few logs out now. A fox had been in area of wolf kill.
No wolves. I visited there awhile at Allen's. Then I packed a trail to shoot at
400 yd targets on the lake.

Sunday, February 20, 1994—sunny, cloudy, some breeze, -29° to -14°. More
snow got blown off the trees and needle and cones. Windy over south in valley.
Watched the Winter Olympics in Norway. Read some. Dave, Dee and son
Colton visited in evening.

Monday, February 21, 1994—sunny, light clouds, some breeze, -24° to -8°. Light
bulb in well burned out. Went to Odden's and watched traffic when he took off
in his PA12 to go to McGrath. Then Joe Virgin asked me in for a cup of coffee.
Visited with him and Peg. Didn't do anything at home today. The northern
lights have been outstanding for quite a while now. I took pictures tonight.
They were yellow-gold and very bright, so much so that the snow looked
yellowish even though the moon was shining brightly. One bright band
stretched northwest to southeast from horizon to horizon plus two other bands
not so bright. They waver and undulate and the intensity changes constantly. It
was fantastic.

Tuesday, February 22, 1994—sunny, -30° to -1°. Didn't feel well today. Sylvia
did some laundry. I shoveled snow off the well. The lid was frozen down. Got
it open and replaced the burned out light bulb. Covered well with snow again.
We pumped water for the house, as I was down at the well anyhow. Went to
east end of lake. Saw a large moose there and come coyote tracks.

Wednesday, February 23, 1994—sunny, -28° to 3°. Sylvia went to Glennallen.

Thursday, February 24, 1994—sunny, -32° to -5°. Allen stopped by for a cup of coffee. Later I took garbage to the dump. Shot the rifle there. It's right on at over 150 yards.

Friday, February 25, 1994—sunny, -30° to 1°. Small birds feeding in the spruce in front of house, disturbing snow on the boughs. Haven't felt well all day. Lots of pain.

Saturday, February 26, 1994—sunny, -34° to -6°. The sun is causing snow to settle a lot. Mary and Lucky brought over three tapes and had coffee with us. Allen and I were to check the wolf sets but he didn't call back.

Sunday, February 27, 1994—thin clouds to cloudy in evening, -33° to -4°. Didn't warm up until early afternoon. Harold and Rachel Dimmick and granddaughter Lilly and Victor and their three kids stopped in on their way home from church today. We had a nice visit and a little lunch. Then I went to Allen's on my snowgo wanting to check to wolf sets. He got ready and we went. He didn't take a rifle along. No wolves have been back. There is a fox in the wolf killed moose area but it doesn't feed on the kill. Two coyotes left tracks in snowgo trail near our lake.

Monday, February 28, 1994—light snow during the night and off and on all day, cloudy, -17° to 5°. Sylvia went to Glennallen. I cleaned up some spilled dirt from the basement floor. Cleaned the ash from the stove in the wood shop. Didn't do much all day.

Tuesday, March 1, 1994— today sunny, thin clouds and cloudy to the south, -11° during night, warming to 21°. I went north on trap line along east side of Slide Mt. Saw tracks of 4-5 fox, one fresh this morning and a big fox. Saw 6 moose, one was a calf. Some boo tracks. I tried to go west from "4 corners" to top of knob. Got up quite a ways and got stuck. Sawn an old wolverine set. Then just before I got near home I took the trail Allen put in going up the face of Slide. It was on this trail that I saw cow moose and calf. More moose were in the area. Saw a couple fox track and one canine trail I should have examined. I took Sylvia's panoramic "throw away" camera up there and took 6 pictures. Back here at home I took the camera down on our lake and took 6 more pictures of the hillside and our homes.

Wednesday, March 2, 1994—some snow showers, also sunny, 0° to 28°. Sylvia went to Glennallen. Jim Manning visited me till noon. I drove snowgo up Slide Mt. and looked at animal trail-turned out to be a boo trail. Repaired my snow gaiters.

Thursday, March 3, 1994—some more snow, sometimes windy, mostly cloudy, some sun, 5° to 18°. Laurie isn't bringing the furniture yet to be repaired. Tom H. visited an hour or so.

Friday, March 4, 1994—5° to 13° and dropping to below zero. Jack Chamberlin returned a book I had asked him to read. Allen stopped in to visit and coffee. I read some. We pumped water. Sylvia did some housework. I took a truck inner tube from near our well on lake to Allen's. The boys had left it there while playing on water last year. I planned and filled out some charts for bullet load development.

Saturday, March 5, 1994—sunny, -15° to 5°. I went down to Allen's and got him to go look at wolf sets. The wolves had not been back and the wind had not blow the sets full of snow. Sylvia roasted a turkey and invited Allen, Roxanne and family, Tom & Kim and family and Lucky and Mary to help us eat it. Still lots left over. Nice visit this evening.

Sunday, March 6, 1994—mostly sunny, cloudy in evening, -20° to 8°. Went to Huddleston's this afternoon to a party for Mary Beaudoin and Roxanne. Someone staying at Odden's. Called Jim and learned it is his niece.

Monday, March 7, 1994—sunny, then cloudy in evening, 0° to 20°. Phoned Dan B. and then drove up there. Saw a fox track and few boo track. Visited and had lunch with them. Stopped at dump. Saw a coyote there.

Tuesday, March 8, 1994—cloudy and snow, sunny, cloudy, 8° to 32°. Cleaned rifle, removed front sight from same. We had Mailly family here to supper. Made homemade ice cream, watched a movie and a cartoon. Enjoyed a nice visit. Their kids are nice and fun to be around.

Wednesday, March 9, 1994—mostly sunny, 12° to 36°. Snow slid off our house and guest house at teacher's. She had me come over and plow the mess out of her driveway. I pulled snow off part of garage roof, woodshop and shoveled snow off storage shed. Wrote two long letters. Visited Mannings. Drove snowgo to river bank and glassed for wolves, no luck. Had coffee with Allen. Sylvia went to Glennallen.

Thursday, March 10, 1994—snowed till noon, not much accumulation, 1° to 30°. Don't feel good. Mid afternoon started preparing some brass for target loads. After supper returned the movie to Vernetta (teacher).

Friday, March 11, 1994—cloudy, sunny, cloudy, -2° to 26°. Mary B brought over a couple movies. Robbie borrowed a movie. Ellie's birthday and party there tonight. Sylvia has some kind of intestinal flu. I took snowgo to Army trail. Unknown trapper was parked there. I unloaded and went to Old Man Lake. He had quite a few marten boxes on trees and two cat sets. I went along shoreline to outlet of Old Man Lake. Saw a otter out on ice. A trapper has some otter sets there. After I got home I looked out the window and saw a Super Cub flying the river. Thinking he might be wolf hunting, I called Allen and I went to look what was going on as we have four wolf sets there. I couldn't find any wolf tracks, nor could I find a place where the plane had landed. Sylvia is pretty sick this evening.

Saturday, March 12, 1994—sunny, a little breeze, 9° to 31°. Visited Ed a few minutes when I took a letter to mailbox. Sylvia is better but still sick. Saw a squirrel in a spruce in front yard.

Sunday, March 13, 1994—sunny, cloudy, 9° to 30°. Saw that same yellow plane. Went out and walked around a little. Sylvia in bed most of day. She's grumpy so I went east on lakes and looked in duck nesting boxes. They are being used. Old coyote track. Some moose track and three recent caribou track, one is a calf. Note: Duck nest box needs a screw in top corner...maybe screw it to a tree (east end of lake).

Monday, March 14, 1994—mostly sunny, 12° to 31°. Thawed the wolf and cleaned a bunch of ice off it. Dried the fur with paper towels the best I could. Took wolf to F. & G. and had it tagged. Got Pepto Bismol for Sylvia, cable for hooking two VCR's together. Cashed check at bank. Stopped at taxidermist Tony. He now says he doesn't have money to pay for wolf. Disappointed.

Tuesday, March 15, 1994—cloudy, sunny, cloudy, 6° to 29°. We pumped water today. I drained down the pressure tank and brought the bladder air pressure up to 20 lbs. Road snowgo to river bluff. Didn't see any wolves. Borrowed a drill bit from Allen and took it back. Put oil in truck. Serviced the snowgo. Visited with Ed. Worked on some of the dies.

Wednesday, March 16, 1994—snow showers, some sun, cloudy and snow, 7° to 26°. Worked some more on dies and finished with them. Laurie and Bonnie came to look at some logs and visit. No money to buy though. We visited Lucky and Mary and brought VCR home.

Thursday, March 17, 1994—cloudy, very few snow flakes, 7° to 18°. We hooked up a second VCR and copied a tape for Chuck and some for me. I made three small rifle brush handles.

Friday, March 18, 1994—mostly sunny, -8° to 8°. Wrote letters to politicians and the White House in favor of conceal and carry law. Visited Ed F. Allen had the kids drag the wolf carcass out on the lake and an eagle is feeding on it.

Saturday, March 19, 1994—mostly snow showers, -12° to 4°. Darcy and Vanessa phoned. Denny and Joey back from vacation, came over and visited and took their weapons home. Allen visited and had supper with us. TJ borrowed a movie.

Sunday, March 20, 1994—some light snow and breezy sometimes, sunny also, -13° to 1°. Phoned Nadia, Theresa, Frances and Jerry. Lou Butera stopped by. He was at KROA for the Ski Touring race and won it.

Monday, March 21, 1994—sunny, -25° to 3°. Sylvia went to Glennallen. I took some magazines to Denny E. and visited a while. Talked to Allen a couple of minutes. He was on the way to wood lot. He has over 600 logs now. David F. and T.J.H. slipped away from Roxanne and stopped to visit and have a cup of coco and cookies. After we had supper Allen, Kyle, David and TJ came over and visited while we munched salsa chips, cookies, cakes and cocoa. Gets dark about 8:00 PM these days.

Tuesday, March 22, 1994—cloudy, sunny, cloudy, -17° to 7°. Something (dog?) has dragged the wolf carcass a hundred yards east on our lake. Denny E. phoned and asked me to ride along with him to Glennallen. Stopped at Lanagan's for some primers and later Denny got a hunting license there. He had some bills to pay and little shopping to do. We went to B.L.M. and I got my federal permits for two caribou. Later Denny, after buying his hunting license went back to Bureau of Land Management and got his permits. I took a rifle along but we didn't see any fur or game. After we got back he came over and borrowed my battery charger.

Wednesday, March 23, 1994—sunny, partly cloudy, -7° to 19°. Sylvia went to Glennallen. I made out an order. Shoveled snow off camper and woodshed. Walked around looking for a squirrel. Loaded some cast bullets.

Thursday, March 24, 1994—sunny, 9° to 40°. Shot a target, loaded a few. Repaired reservoir on powder measurer. Went down on river and checked wolf sets. Nothing but ski and dog tracks, snowmobiles. Caribou are starting to use our snowgo trail. McCurdy went flying with Dennis E.

Friday, March 25, 1994—sunny, windy, cloudy, 8° to 35°. Allen came up for coffee and sticky bun. He's not interested in hunting wolves. He has too many logs in piles at home. Visited Ed a few minutes. Show a few cast bullet loads. Pumped water for house. Drove snowgo down lakes to east. Saw mink, rabbit track. Went over to river bluff. Saw marten and rabbit track. Wind came up and very dusty. Loaded some cast loads to try.

Saturday, March 26, 1994—snowed hard all night (13"), clearing and some breeze later, 27° to 35°. Plowed and shoveled our snow then over to Banning's and did theirs. Then Bart called—went down there and got stuck. That lane is a mess. Cleaned a rifle. Bart called and asked me to go with him to a GOP gun control meeting and supper in Glennallen. Allen stopped in just before I left and had supper with Sylvia.

Sunday, March 27, 1994—mostly sunny, 9° to 31°. A few camp robbers flying around. Read a while. Shot 13 plinking shots and loaded 14 more. Extended the powder cupboard ¾ inch. Made another cleaning equipment block. Bob, Karn, Jerry and Betty were here for a lasagna supper. Denny E. was up flying his airplane. Good for him!

Monday, March 28, 1994—sunny, cloudy at suppertime, -2° to 32°. Shot some more light loads and loaded 15 more. Cleaned rifle. Visited Bob and then Jerry. Sorted through Jerry's dump load and brought home some traps and snares for grandson Steve. Allen and I went to "bowl" and picked up the four wolf traps. Quite a few marten running around now. A fox, a mink and a couple caribou and moose tracks. Allen borrowed a couple movies this evening, and a brake tool.

Tuesday, March 29, 1994—sunny, late afternoon, 12° to 43°. Started getting cloudy with flat light down on the lake. We have at least 6 ice "stars" down on east end of lake. I called Denny E. to inform him about the, so he doesn't fall in one with his plane. Shot some 47 grain bullets and they shot well, so I reloaded the, cases, with the same loading, this is a plinking load. Lubed some bullets. Reworked and refined a tool holder for reloading bench. Ground new ends on a couple allen wrenches. Tried to drill a hole in a couple bullets, no luck.

Wednesday, March 30, 1994—cloudy, sunny, 25° to 45°. Packed trail across lake with snowgo. Got stuck on land near dock. Visited Allen a few minutes. Did a few small jobs. Patched and sewed snowgo cover. Visited the Rubecks. Called around for powder and primers. Tough to find.

Thursday, March 31, 1994—cloudy, sunny in Matanuska Valley, 12° to 43°. We went to Dr. Manelick. Both have appointments. She talked through Sylvia's treatment and did some exams on me. We did grocery shopping. Left wolf hide at Fosters to be tanned. Went to three stores and picked up some powder for reloading. Shopped at the new Wal-Mart in Wasilla. Got a new all fuel camp stove and some soap, shampoo, aspirin etc.

Friday, April 1, 1994—mostly sunny, windy in evening, 27° to 47°. I put up a couple small shelves upstairs. Harold D. called and invited us down for coffee.

We had a very early supper. A friend of his gave him a dredge. He bought a new snowgo and a new Honda 4 x 4. Saw some fox and wolf tracks. I had a rifle along just in case.

Saturday, April 2, 1994—mostly sunny, some breeze from west, 30° to 47°. Shot a rifle at targets. Loaded some more for testing. Laid out and started drilling holes for 100 case loading blocks. Visited with Mark and Ed when I went after the mail. Allen and Kyle were here for a while. Visit, coffee, Pepsi and desert. Snow is shrinking down fast. Forearm sandbag rest needed repairs today. Glued a leather patch on it.

Sunday, April 3, 1994—mostly sunny, a little breeze from west, 27° to 45°. Snow didn't melt as fast today. Denny was out taxiing his plane around on the lake. Shot and cleaned the rifle. Worked a little on two loading blocks.

Monday, April 4, 1994—sunny, 19° to 42°. Sylvia went to Glennallen. I finished the loading blocks and shot more targets and cleaned the rifle. Visited Allen and had lunch with them. Allen brought a borrowed tool back. I got the ATV out of winter storage. Allen found a dead moose over by Rudbeck's storage area. Kim and Charlie H. stopped by on way home from Oregon. Charlie made a gift of a book to me.

Tuesday, April 5, 1994—sunny, more melting, 9° to 41°. We went to Palmer and hospital for my stomach x-ray. Then to Wasilla to Sylvia's two Doctors for prescriptions. Did some shopping then on home. Saw one moose today.

Wednesday, April 6, 1994—mostly sunny, 13° to 41°. Sylvia went to Glennallen. Allen visited in the morning. Denny E. borrowed my foot tire pump. Shot rifle and cleaned it. Checked over rear differential. Chuck Zimbicki called a couple times. I called Mark Air and Kristensen in Nome about freight logistics, prospects etc. The ravens are tearing meat off the dead moose and flying it to their young in the nest. We see them fly by between house and lake.

Thursday, April 7, 1994—mostly sunny, 10° to 45°. We pumped water today. I visited Allen and helped Denny put a ski on the tail wheel of his Super Cub. Phoned out to Nome about an ATV to use when we are out there. Shot rifle and cleaned it.

Friday, April 8, 1994—mostly sunny, 11° to 41°. Shot rifle and cleaned it. Straightened up some in garage. Worked at salvaging some old brass. Put aside two cartridges for future trim length measurement and will use them to set trimmer. Saw an eagle fly by today. Sylvia worked with her plants. Laura phoned twice—once to tell us she shook hands with Pres. Clinton. We got pix in mail from her also.

Saturday, April 9, 1994—cloudy all day, 11° to 35°. Shot two squirrels. Cleaned rifles. Had to pull a stuck case from a die. Phoned another place in Nome about ATV, no luck. The snow is melting off the wolf carcass Allen had pulled out on lake. Ravens are on it this evening. Northern lights most nights now.

Sunday, April 10, 1994—cloudy, sunny, cloudy and snow in Mountains to the south, 19° to 40°. Just after breakfast, a squirrel was fooling around a bird house. They also pull insulation from between the logs. I went outside and shot him. Five ravens are on the carcass on the lake. I am breaking in the barrel of the .243. Cleaned up and rearranged the cleaning area. Sylvia fried some of the fish Charlie T. gave us.

Monday, April 11, 1994—cloudy, sunny, partly cloudy and snow squalls, 22° to 42°. Phoned doctors for appointments. Chuck called about front on gold screw. Shot and cleaned rifle. Denny E. visited. Later he brought Allen and Kyle by and we all went to Mirror Lake to fish for rainbows. No luck. Sylvia saw a wolf at gravel pit on Tazlina Hill (big grey).

Tuesday, April 12, 1994—cloudy, snow squalls, some sun, 19° to 38°. Tried to work on truck but couldn't get the yoke off the pinion. Put truck back together, visited a few minutes with Allen. Beverly phoned in evening. She plans to come and visit us. Yea!

Wednesday, April 13, 1994—sunny, partly cloudy, snow squalls blowing through, 19° to 38°. Hauled garbage and ashes to dump. A bunch of ravens and three eagles are feeding on carcass on lake ice. Went down to Allen's. He and Denny were just going burbot fishing on Snowshoe Lake, so I went along. Made some sets, but no luck.

Thursday, April 14, 1994—partly cloudy, sunny, really cloudy sometimes in mountains, 14° to 33°. Allen and Denny checked the burbot sets. Allen got his sluices bent at Al Lee's. Allen visited quite a while. I cleaned up some ash from brush burning. Tom H. visited then brought Kim and visited .

Friday, April 15, 1994—cloudy, light snow, sunny, windy, with dust blowing from river to us for a short while,16° to 33°. I did some experimental shooting with a weight out near muzzle of rifle. Back and legs are painful. Allen visited in afternoon, let me know no luck fishing. Talked to Wes out at Nome.

Saturday, April 16, 1994—sunny, windy sometimes, snow in mountains, 2° to 18°. Back hurts, stiff and sore. Did some shooting. Blew a primer somehow. Loaded some more. Visited Lucky for awhile in morning. Found a picture and a letter belonging to Sandy and Ed. Had been lost in snow since last October.

Sunday, April 17, 1994—some sun, then cloudy, 0° to 30°. Did more target shooting, loads were better today. Read Sunday paper. Loaded some more to shoot tomorrow, cleaned rifle. Snow turning to ice on lake.

Monday, April 18, 1994—cloudy, sunny, cloudy, 9° to 42°. Ed visited for a while this morning. I cast some bullets. Allen stopped by for a little while. Sylvia went to Glennallen. Bev phoned that she doesn't think she will get to visit us. Broke mold handle and tried to glue it, no luck.

Tuesday, April 19, 1994—partly cloudy, 20° to 42°. We went to Palmer, Wasilla to both doctors, plus some shopping prescriptions etc. Saw a young girly moose on way to town. Saw some nice flocks of geese and a few ducks over Palmer. The swans were flying west up the Nelchina River all day. We learn that Asif has arranged for Beverly to come to Alaska.

Wednesday, April 20, 1994—mostly sunny, 27° to 47°. We pumped water today. I visited Roxanne while the pump did its work. Then home and repair a small break in snowgo windshield so the snowgo cover doesn't get snagged. Made another handle for mould. Started polishing brass. Allen stopped by and had a corned moose sandwich with me. Robbie came over to get Allen home to saw logs. I put gas checks on some bullets. Counted some brass. Started making more loading blocks. A squirrel went in the flicker house so I went out and shot it. I could hear swans flying at several different times today.

Thursday, April 21, 1994—mostly sunny, 30° to 50°. Worked on some loading blocks, drilling holes. Changed the oil in the truck. Showered and drove in to Anchorage. Did a little shopping then on to airport to meet Beverly and Asif at 5:05 PM. Stopped at Royal Fork and had dinner then to Palmer and a little more shopping. Stopped at Long Rifle for coffee. Asif is taking lots of pix. Bev took one of him and a large mounted bear in dining area of Long Rifle lodge. Nice to have Bev here again.

Friday, April 22, 1994—mostly sunny, some afternoon wind, 29° to 49°. We visited Ed Farmers, Lucky and Mary Beaudoin in morning. Denny and Joey E. visited in afternoon. Asif and I cleaned up the new loading blocks and put two coats of tung oil on them. We shoveled snow away from the two lean-to's. Yesterday Allen and Denny dragged the dead winter kill moose (a two-yr-old cow) down the hill and across the lake to far shore. Allen skinned out one rear quarter and the ravens (many) and eagles are swarming all over it. We had 11 ravens flying around and over our house this afternoon. I showed Asif and Beverly my hobby upstairs. Two volumes "Tears of Fire" came in the mail today. Nadia must be behind that. My poem is on page 4.

Saturday, April 23, 1994—mostly sunny, beautiful day, 25° to 50°. We are enjoying Beverly's visit. Asif is a congenial guest. Fooled around outside and in the woodshop. Drove up the Lake Louise Road in the afternoon. Stopped at Dawson's and got some gas and said Hi. Then on to Billman's for a nice visit and a very good supper. We didn't see any animals going or coming today. The eagles feed on the moose carcass from early till late.

Sunday, April 24, 1994—sunny, beaut of a day, 28° to 53°. I left at 2:30 AM with Bev and Asif. Bev and I talked all the way to town. Asif napped. I dropped them at the airport about 5:30 AM. Went to parking log (Eagle) and had a short nap. Then over to Fred Meyer Store and got a case of oil. Then to Wasilla and got a keyless chuck for a cordless screw driver. Suzuki wasn't open. Went to yard sale and got two books. Smayda's were gone (to church maybe). Stopped for gas at Hilltop. Then stopped and watched offhand center fire rifle shoot at King Mountain Fun for an hour or so. Then on home. Sure am tired today. I finished the two GI boxes by gluing the cartridge blocks in them and gluing foam rubber in the lids for a snug, no rattle fit of the cartridges. Sorted some brass. Beverly phoned that she got home OK. Mary Beaudoin phoned to invite us to a supper at Roxanne's for Sylvia's birthday. Fred Rungee stopped by in the evening and brought four quarts of ice cream and strawberries. We had a nice treat and a good visit. We gave him some rhubarb.

Monday, April 25, 1994—sunny, light breeze, beaut of a day, 26° to 55°. Rudbecks came over just after breakfast wanting to look at their mail. Sylvia went to Glennallen. I put snowgo under the roof. Started cleaning up one of the aluminum sheets. Tried casting some bullets, had a problem with "finning." Tom H. and Kim stopped by. Charlie wanted me to cut out an "Awana Race Car" for him. I gave him a basketball I found along the road. I shoveled roof deposited snow off the lawn.

Tuesday, April 26, 1994—mostly sunny, cloudy in evening, 25° to 56°. Sylvia worked in her greenhouse. I worked on a sluice box, cast some bullets, and worked on the "Awana" race car for Charley Trowbridge. Visited Allen for a few minutes while the water was pumping up to house.

Wednesday, April 27, 1994—mostly sunny, 34° to 51°. Some hail about 8:00 PM. Cast a few bullets. B. Rudbeck wanted to anchor a guy wire over our property. I said no. Visited with Ed. Shot a squirrel. Mary Beaudoin fixed a supper for Sylvia's birthday and we ate at Allen and Roxanne's. Denny E. and family and Al and Faith Padowski were there.

Thursday, April 28, 1994—mostly sunny, 26° to 51°. Worked at peeling and sanding two sheets of aluminum. Visited Allen a few minutes. Sylvia made a pot of chili and we took it to Karen Mailly and family. She has recent twin daughters, Elizabeth and Sara.

Friday, April 29, 1994–sunny, around 24°. We got ready to go with the CRNA Senior Tour to Prudhoe Bay. We stopped at Eureka Lodge so some travelers could have lunch. Then on to Anchorage and shopping at the new Wal-Mart on Northern Lights and Benson. Our reservations at the motel were all mixed up, but Sheryl the driver, got that straightened out.

Saturday, April 30, 1994–45° in Anchorage, 15° and wind chill to -10° in Prudhoe Bay. It rained the night. Wake up call at 4:00 AM. We all are breakfast and went to airport and checked in at Alaska Airline for an ARCO flight to Prudhoe Bay Oilfield. The plane was a 737. Saw Yukon River, Brooks Range and Pipeline and Haul Road on the way to Prudhoe Bay airstrip. Once there we went to ARCO operations bldg. for an oil field briefing. We saw the first oil well, main camp and clinic, sea water injection plant, central compressor plant, a tour and lunch at the seawater treatment plant. Then the landfill, gravel pits, flow station #3, Mile "0" of Trans Alaska Pipeline. We rode the tour bus all day. We stopped at the general store in Dead Horse, AK and did some shopping. We boarded flight #272 for Anchorage. On arrival we went to motel then to Royal Fork for supper. To bed early and slept good.

Sunday, May 1, 1994–cloudy, 45°. Wake up call 7:00 AM, breakfast 8:00 AM. Drove to Palmer and shopped for groceries. Visited a lot while riding to Eureka. Had a pit stop there for those in need. Then on home and how sweet it was. Unpacked, read mail, wrote in journal. Partly cloudy and near 50° today.

Monday, May 2, 1994–cloudy, partly cloudy, 34° to 48°. Back hurt a lot today. Sylvia went to Glennallen in the senior van. Saw a squirrel today. Ravens were courting? around here today. Four swans were courting on the ice of the lake this morning. The eagles and ravens fed on the moose carcass all day. I put the wheels on the race car for Charley H.

Tuesday, May 3, 1994–cloudy, sunny, cloudy, 30° to 46°. Shot another squirrel. Did little jobs, wrote four letters, visited Mannings. Kim, Charley, Pook, and Colin brought a birthday cake to Sylvia. We made ice cream. Freezer motor gears quit. Karen Mailly brought our pan back and presents for Sylvia. I did some repair on die locking rings.

Wednesday, May 4, 1994–cloudy, breeze, felt "raw" all day. Sylvia went to Glennallen. Worked on aluminum sheet and cleaned up clutter. Karn visited.

Thursday, May 5, 1994–mostly cloudy, 20° to 46°. Adapted new ice cream maker (motor has quit) to old hand crank drive and painted drive. Cast .22 calibre bullets. Cut a tree that was endangering the house. Trimmed limbs and hauled all away. Managed to fall the tree exactly where I wanted it.

Friday, May 6, 1994—some sun, some snow showers, some clouds, 25° to 45°. Went to school house for a student play, singing and a lunch. Lisa Smayda stopped to visit for an hour. She is a traveling nurse now. Sylvia went to Mary O's with Rudbecks for supper. Mary has a new lady friend with her as well as Jim's niece and her boyfriend.

Saturday, May 7, 1994—mostly sunny, 27° to 50°. Loaded garbage and went to dump. Took two windshield wiper motors off junk cars. Lloyd Ronning stopped to visit while I was doing that. Then Luck and Digger Beaudoin came to the dump to shoot Diggers rifle. After two shots the wind blew sand in Diggers eyes and he had to quit. Digger gave me a framed photo of our lake he had taken. It is excellent photography. I stopped at gravel pit and picked up more brass. Peter Reino is hauling sand in buckets to the land he bought to pour footings for a house. Back at home I soaked the brass in vinegar solution and rinsed it in water and put it to dry. Trimmed and chamfered more brass. Beaut of a day. Some breezy gusts. The ice is turning dark on our lake.

Sunday, May 8, 1994—mostly cloudy, 22° to 42°. Sorted some brass. Went for a walk to lake and over to Charlie T. storage shed. Cut out some ice fishing sticks to wind line on. R. Rudbecks came over to watch the movie "Stand" by Stephen King. Coyote fed on moose carcass.

Monday, May 9, 1994—cloudy, sunny, windy in evening, 22° to 49°. Sylvia went to Glennallen. I repaired the snow plow and took it and the mounting off the truck. Bob R. came over to get some hose. Denny E. asked me to go to Woods Creek grayling fishing with him. No luck. Rudbecks to be back tonight to watch part 2 of 4 of movie.

Tuesday, May 10, 1994—sunny, some breeze, very beautiful today, 28° to 54°. Put bumper back on truck. Tuned distributor etc. Washed the truck. Took Sylvia to dinner in Glennallen. Looked at Darrel's mobile home pad etc. Nice trip for going to Glennallen. Saw an eagle along road. Two swans sitting on ice of our lake this morning.

Wednesday, May 11, 1994—sunny, all day, then windy and dust off the river and clouds moved in late afternoon, 29° to 57°. More birds are using the lake and ice every day. Sylvia went to Glennallen. I made a cover for the snow plow. Dropped the rear drive shaft on the truck. Managed to get the yoke off the pinion this time. Replaced the seal and the lost oil and put all back together again. Chuck Zimbicki phones. The gold screw is in Anchorage.

Thursday, May 12, 1994—cloudy, windy, sunny, 34° to 56°. Checked gas in overhead "84 gal" tank. Sylvia helped and we made a 7" rise for head of mattress on our bed. Did more small fixes and maintenance on truck. Warm strong wind is melting the ice on our lake very fast. Flickers actively courting and using the box outside our window.

Friday, May 13, 1994–rainy, clear and beautiful, 33° to 53°. 2" snow at Eureka Summit and Gunsight. Most of ice is out on lake tonight. We went to Wasilla to Sylvia's doctor. Then to Anchorage and picked up the gold screw at Lynden Freight. Did some shopping, lunch at Royal Fork then to more shopping at Wasilla. Stopped at Suzuki. Visited with the Smayda's. Grocery shopped and picked up prescription at Carr's in Palmer. Got gas at Hilltop. Saw a few moose on way home. Checked Suzuki winch frame.

Saturday, May 14, 1994–sunny, 27° to 57°. Most of ice is out of Lake Denny. E. came over to help unload the gold screw and had breakfast with us. We went to Little Nelchina River to look for a sight to test run the gold screw. Back home and I put it together. Finished the 7" rise for the head end of the bed and we carried it into the house and put it on the bed and turned the mattress. After supper phoned Chuck, discussed the gold screw. Then went to Mendeltna-Nelchina corp. meeting. Ice out on the lake.

Sunday, May 15, 1994–32° to 57°. Small flocks of ducks on lake plus one raft of golden eyes and some swans. Chuck Z. called and offered to help try out the "gold screw." When he came we loaded the machine in pickup. Sylvia went along. We parked at Little Nelchina Campground and looked at a couple locations to set up at. Settled on a bar upstream of the campground. Kind of tough carrying everything to the location. Got it set up, some trouble getting the pump primed. We did lots of experimenting with speeds, water flow and slopes etc. An interesting afternoon. Learned a lot. After helping carry all the gear back to truck, Chuck went on to Eureka to get some parts. We had asked him to have supper with us. He stopped in later and ate with us. Then before he left, we settled up with him for the gold screw. Bob and Karn stopped in and wanted some strawberry Jell-O for Charley Knetter. He seems to be failing fast. They wanted pain pills for him also.

Monday, May 16, 1994–sunny and a little breeze, wonderful day, 31° to 60° Sylvia went to Glennallen and did errand and shopping for some of the neighbors. Cleaned the garage and wood shop. Made a platform for the gold screw. Lots of duck activity on lake.

Tuesday, May 17, 1994–sunny, then very windy from noon on, cloudy in evening, 30° to 64°. Slight earthquake at 2:25 PM. Worked on a tent for camping at Nome. Made new supports, etc. Karn and Dana visited Sylvia. Sylvia and I visited at Ed and Sandy's a little while.

Wednesday, May 18, 1994—cloudy, to partly cloudy and strong gusty winds all afternoon, 30° to 54°. Worked all day on two bicycle wheels and a frame to clamp PVC pipe to in order to keep sand out of the suction hose on the gold screw when we mine on the beach at Nome. Sylvia went to Glennallen. The wind is so strong at times it is hard stand up to it. At least 16 swans on lake. Couldn't see all of east end for the trees.

Thursday, May 19, 1994—partly cloudy, windy most of day, 34° to 54°. Repaired a broken anchor. Hung tent in trap storage to air out. We went for a ride. Visited Leona and left a bunch of tires there. Visited Billmans. Stopped by Charley Knetter. He has lost a lot of weight. Lloyd Ronning is feeling really bad. Saw several caribou bulls along the road.

Friday, May 20, 1994—partly cloudy, sometimes windy, 28° to 48°. Sylvia got sick to her stomach during the night and spent all day in bed. I hoed fireweed out of the garden and strawberries. I made some wood tent guy rope tighteners. I didn't feel good today. I went to Bartley's for a Tier II permit for Sylvia this evening. Stopped at gravel pit, picked up more grass. Saw more boo bulls today.

Saturday, May 21, 1994—cloudy, sunny, windy afternoon, breeze in evening, 30° to 54°. Built a box for junk on seat of truck. We planted potatoes and onions. Cultivated ½ garden, raked some lawn. Loaded a few cartridges as I write this. There is a pretty good size, almost blonde, light colored with dark legs grizzly bear, also another that is slightly darker, feeding on winter killed moose. It tears and feed and when it gets a big piece loose it goes into brush and trees to feed in seclusion. Planted potatoes. Saw two grizzly bears feeding on moose at east side of the lake.

Sunday, May 22, 1994—sunny, beaut of a day, windy from noon on, 28° to 58°. Sylvia raked a little yard. I worked on crating the gold screw to frt. it to Nome. Visited Lucky and Mary. Luck brought me some .22-250 brass, looks to be once fired. I sent plans for a shooting bench and accessories home with him. Mark Brockman brought someone he knew here, loaned him a rifle and the guy shot the smaller blonde grizzly bear. I was right it was a boar. He said it was smaller than he thought it was. Mary Odden and Kari are to bring a couple roast ducks for dinner. Bob R. came along with Mary, then Karn came back from Anchorage. I wasn't able to eat with them (not feeling well). Later I ate something Sylvia fixed. Karn got our gift for Jason's graduation. Karn got White Mt. ice cream freezer at a yard sale and gave it to me. Nice of her.

Monday, May 23, 1994—mostly sunny, windy in afternoon, 32° to 57°. Sylvia went to Glennallen and had her hair done. I went to dump and gravel pit at Tazlina Hill. Looked around for a possible wolf kill-no luck. Finished 11 ice fishing rigs. I felt sick all day. We watched a cow moose swim our lake from near our dock to the other side. As she got out of the water with the spotting scope I could see an udder on her. It appears they use water to break their scent trail at calving time. I took some carpet to Harold for his dredge sluice box.

Tuesday, May 24, 1994—mostly sunny, breezy, and windy, 32° to 58°. Ten swans on our lake. We put the crate for the gold screw up on a work table in the garage. Then we put the gold screw in it. We loaded the crate then re-fastened it with lots of screws. In afternoon Sylvia worked on greenhouse and I helped her with the plant and lawn water system which needed repairs. I rearranged the reloading die rack.

Wednesday, May 25, 1994—cloudy and rainy, 28° to 57°. Sylvia went to Glennallen. I got some gear ready for Nome. Washed the truck. There are more than 125 ducks on the lake. Denny E. was here a couple minutes. Left a battery on my charger.

Thursday, May 26, 1994—snowing hard at 6:00 AM (continued until 4:00 PM), 30° to 40°. Must be 200 blue bills etc. Some beautiful finches, canaries right outside the window in nearby trees. Karn brought some rainbow trout for our supper and visited quite awhile. Later Bob sent her over to borrow a 8mm socket. I loaded some .38 target loads. Burned a brush pile while it was snowing. Snowing hard, ducks rafter up close on lake.

Friday, May 27, 1994—low clouds and rain all day, 34° to 39°. Didn't do much all day. Karn visited here. I visited at Denny E. Sylvia went with Rudbecks to graduation exercises at Glennallen. The ducks seem to have two groups and move from group to group. Rafting up out in lake and drifting with the wind (breeze). Interesting to watch. Lots of other bird activity.

Saturday, May 28, 1994—mostly sunny all day, windy in afternoon, 33° to 54°. Gathered up gear for Nome. Cleaned a little of the basement. Pruned the raspberries. Cut some willow witches for dream catcher hoops. Harold Dimmick called. A motor on one of his boats blew up. His sons, Corky and Rusty pulled the boat to Manley. I loaned him $165.00 so his daughter Arlene and husband Phillip could buy gas to drive the motorhome to Manley to pick up Harold and Rachel. I fastened an electric drill to work bench with plumber's strap. Checked a bolt in drill and with a file shaped a .357 cal. Pilot for my case trimmer. Most of the ducks left this morning, but more are here this evening.

Sunday, May 29, 1994—sunny, beaut of a day, 28° to 57°. Mike? From near Mendeltna (working on his mother-in-law's property) came and asked me to fabricate and install a cat loader frame pivot pin. Stopped at Bartley's to leave off a National Geographic magazine they had loaned me. Anna Marie and her two daughters were there. Repaired rain pants and put Thompson's water seal on a pair of rain pants and the "cook tent" roof.

Monday, May 30, 1994—sunny and cloudy and breezy, 30° to 58°. Later got some more gear ready. Hand cultivated the south half of the garden. Mid afternoon we went to Billman's at Lake Louise. Dan's mother Faye and her husband Lloyd, Patty's mother Betty, Dan and Patty of course and also a guest couple and their son. We saw a moose cow and two Canadian geese picking up gravel off the road. Saw two geese at Mile 9 a little west of 9 mile.

Sunday, May 31, 1994—mostly sunny, some breezes, 33° to 63°. Built a porta-potty like using our old toilet seat and lid with plywood and lid from plastic bucket adapted it for use out at Nome. Installed an oak seat and lid on our toilet. Put heel repair inserts in my hip boots. Visited with Mark B a few minutes. Loaded 17 .357 cartridges to take to Nome. Such a beautiful day.

Wednesday, June 1, 1994—partly cloudy, isolated showers going by our little valley. Dark to the north, 36° to 65°. East near Tolsona, hail near marble size, covered the ground. Sylvia rode through it on senior van coming home from Glennallen. I tried to repair a bag for gear-no luck. I guess the barge cement is going bad. Oiled the straps on another. Got some more gear ready. Visited Rudbeck's building site. Hoed the fire weed out of the garden. Visited Ed F.

Thursday, June 2, 1994—partly cloudy, nice day, 35° to 64°. We worked all day packing for Nome. Lisa Billman fixed it so we could get our tickets, senior discount. Lots of worry and work –so tired tonight. Took garbage to dump. Note: I put the belt for .22-250 in box of lot #3-.22 350 cases.

Friday, June 3, 1994—warm up late and went to Anchorage. Did some shopping, then took our freight for Nome to Mark Air Cargo and consigned it. Then more shopping and supper on down to Griffith's. Visited with Denny and Addie.

Saturday, June 4, 1994—Cloudy and up at 4:45 AM. Addie drove us to airport at 5:00 AM. Got our tickets and flew to Kotzebue, we stayed on plane and went on to Nome. More low clouds and snowing pretty hard. Started getting wet. Harold and Rachel rented a Bronco Ford. We went to Irene's camp and got an old gas can and water jug, axe and 3 sections of stove pipe.

  I called Ken Kristenson and told him we would stop by but Harold didn't stop there, so missed him. We did stop at Wes Perkins' and I won't be able to get the ATV until Monday. Damn. (Sure disappointed as he said I could get it when I got here). Went to Mark Air Cargo and our freight won't be in till Sunday afternoon at the soonest. We did get our luggage and put our rain coats on. We dove west on the beach looking for a place for Harold to put up his wall tent. We spent 6 hours doing that and talking to some of the miners who are friendly. Didn't snow this afternoon, was nice but breezy. Cool this evening. Cramped and poor sleeping in Bronco. Tired, so we slept anyhow.

NOME

Sunday, June 5, 1994—partly cloudy, sunny with breeze, 30s to 50s. The huge dredge just north of us rumbles 24 hrs a day. Planes take off quite often from airport. Dimmicks ran to town a few times, then returned the rented pickup. Gene, Irene's son stayed in town overnight and brought out a young man name of William. Came out mid day and went beach scrounging for stumps for chairs. Rachel moved her fire and put a different grill over it. Harold panned a couple shovels at camp, both had gold in them. We gave him a teacup of sand and it had gold in it.

While they were in town, I picked up some poles and put a 10 x 20 plastic tarp on them, making a "A" frame tent. Blueberry John Andrews stopped at our camp. We tied a small tarp to close the west end. Makes a nice cozy tent. If weather turns bad our gear and selves will be sheltered. We are anxious for our freight to get here and we can get our camp set up where we will mine and get started. Talked to more people here on the beach.

Monday, June 6, 1994—mostly sunny, 40s to 50s. Got up, built a fire in outdoor grill. At 8:15 AM started walking to town. Went to West Perkins Suzuki, he didn't really want to take me over to Dan Stang who has the 250 Suzuki. I am to buy. Dan is kind of non-committal about the machine. I paid him for it and a trailer. Found Ken Kristensen and visited a while. Then to grocery store and got some groceries. Gene was there and asked me to take some articles out to Harold's camp. Our freight was in so I picked up tents, grub etc. filled water jug at Mark Air and started for camp. Checked mail—nothing. The chain on machine's sprocket slips teeth!! Hardly pulls a load. Dan and Wes aren't very straight. Finally got to Harold's camp, ate a little then Sylvia and I go west on the beach prospecting and finally settle on a place about 5 miles west. Then back to camp after leveling a place to erect our sleeping tent. Sylvia stayed to level for cooking tent. After more chain slipping I finally got this load to our tenting site. Cleared driftwood and rocks so I could drive up close to tent site to unload. We put up tent and put gear in tent and came back to our tarp tent near Harold's camp. Rachel had baked potatoes, pork chop supper ready for us. Sylvia had put all our bedding out to air out and dry out, so everything is ready for a good night's sleep. Sure tired tonight.

We see shore birds, sea ducks, geese, sea gulls, even a pair of sandhill cranes. The wind seems to follow the sun and by evening blows out of the west. We saw a raven land and "squak" to us, hopefully that is a good omen. We rested and visited around the fire drinking coffee. Ken and Keven Kristensen came to visit, riding ATV's. The huge company dredge runs all night, I wake up when it stops. It stops intermittently and starts up in 10 minutes or so. Met California Bob, "Andy" John, an Eskimo with cabin at Penny River, Richard Whiteman, also another man.

Tuesday, June 7, 1994—sunny, 40s to 50s. Went to Dan Stang's office and talked to him about the ATV and he traded me the other ATV with the repairs that I was supposed to get. I had to buy a 1 7/8 ball for hitch, then pick up the frt. (gold screw) at Mark Air. Then back to town and air up trailer tires, buy gas, in machine and cans. Filled water jug at Mark Air. Stopped at Ken's. He loaned me a gas jug and glue for ATV seat. The tires on this trailer are small and narrow and pull hard in the sand. I got stuck right in front of Dimmick's camp. Windy in afternoon. Grandson Harold D. drove his grandfathers ATV and went with us to our camp. Good thing he did because the heavy load on the narrow tires of trailer kept getting me stuck, so we roped both outfits together and made it here.

Unloaded the crate with gold screw in it and went to work putting up the cook tent and stocking the groceries in it. Then we put up a wind break of driftwood. The main pole broke and a piece of wood ripped a 14" tear in rear side wall. So we redone the wind break, braced and more sturdy main log. Weighted the base of the wind break with driftwood. Shored up the ocean side of cook tent with driftwood logs and weighted the tent pegs with rock—just in case we get a good hard blow, which is likely. Then we went back towards the jetty at Nome to Harold and Rachel's camp and packed our sleeping gear and tarp tent. Had a snack of walrus meat and a couple of cookies and came back to camp.

California Bob (1st miner east of us) came over and had coffee with us. Then showed us how to prospect this beach and find the pay streak. Nice guy. I did some tidying up while Sylvia fixed chili and macaroni. After supper 9:00 PM went out and patched the hole in ATV seat in hopes of keeping it dry when it rains. Then she sewed the rip closed in tent and we put silicone on to weather-proof it. I carried the sleeping gear in and she did dish's. Two kayakers are camping just east of us. Quite a lot of ATV and some 4 x 4 vehicle traffic and it's after 11:00 PM and Bob is out there shoveling gravel!!

Wednesday, June 8, 1994—mostly cloudy, then partly cloudy and windy about the time the tide came in, 40s to 60°. Did some things here at camp then rode ATV to town. Sylvia cashed her check at bank. I checked our mail at PO box, nothing. Sent of a letter to a guy from Alabama who was interested in buying an ATV. Shopped for supplies and groceries. Invited Dimmicks to our camp to wiener roast, baked potatoes, pork and beans and cookies and a nice visit. We, looked all over for some glue and parts. No luck. Found them in a 5-gallon bucket later in day. Anyway much disgusted with myself, I went back to town and bought what I needed and a cap with a bill to protect Sylvia's "tanning face." Two trips in one day is too much especially when one was unnecessary.

After Dimmicks went back to their camp I pulled 10 or so long poles into camp for tarp supports. We bought mosquito coils today, (yea!!) for they are troublesome tonight. Tide about Noon. People riding up and down the beach most all day and night. A bunch of G.P.A.A. people came in a barge today with two Nodwells.

(Editor's note about June 8, 1994: Sylvia's account of the series events this day is humorous and a bit different than Norman's matter-of-fact journal entry. It is Sylvia's story that gets told among family members. Here, in her own words, is the version she shared with me recently: "Well, as I remember, it was such hard work, I was exhausted and wanted to give up and go back home to Nelchina. When Norman asked me to ride into town with him, I was just too tired and too cold to make the trip on a 4-wheeler, so I said to him, 'Enough is enough!' Later, when he came back from town, he brought back a peace offering for me. It was a cap to protect my face from the sun, and on the front of it were the capital letters, E.N.U.F. I still have that cap to this day.")

Thursday, June 9, 1994—sunny, some clouds and some fog out on the ocean, few drops of rain, 40s to 50s. We spent three hours building frame work for the two tarps over the two tents. 30 some feet of tarp to cover them and a walk way. Maybe just in time as the weather may change. The seas are kicking up tonight. Then we started setting up the gold screw and found we needed more parts. So to town and make do with the parts we could find. Got things together and pump primed and fired it up. Started shoveling sand and rock on the beach at Nome. Made a lot of adjustment tryouts. Ran gas tank dry, so quit for supper then went out and ran the concentrates through again and then shoveled some more. Then the waves got so strong we lost prime to pump and we quit.

Cleaned up the concentrates, pulled pump intake out of ocean. Put everything away and a tarp tied over gold screw. California Bob had loaned me a clean up riffle, so I took that back to him. He gave me some ribbed mat to make my own and showed me a nice pocket six inches red sand deep. He is pleased with that.

Friday, June 10, 1994—partly cloudy, really feels hot at mid day, mild breezes, 40s to near 60°. Up about 8:00 AM. Drank coffee and had breakfast. Pushed pump intake strainer on its little bike wheels out into a mild surf. I had re-rigged the anchor ropes. We pile rocks on the shore end of the 20' section of PVC pipe. We put it in at near low tide. So were able to get it out deeper at best advantage. The waves didn't bother it all day, we are leaving it in all night.

I shoveled a place for Sylvia's port-a-potty, between tent and high beach bank. Then we primed the pump on gold screw and started shoveling gravel and moving rocks. Made some water adjustments and tilt of gold wheel. From all appearances it looks like we are getting the gold and concentrates . A guy stopped to give me some hints on operating a gold screw. He has used one on the beach here. Nice of him to be helpful. Most of the things he mentioned I was already doing, but still I learned from his visit. Then California Bob came over to show us his large flakes from his last cleanup. Lots of traffic every day. (G.P.A.A. and others) one Eskimo. Lonnie and son Ryan from Utah, Chuck Titus.

Saturday, June 11, 1994—partly cloudy and light sea breezes, 40s to 60s. We got up early and I went out and started shoveling gravel. Sylvia came soon after. We got equivalent of 3 full catch pails of concentrate. Shoveled a lot of gravel. We had quite a few visitors, and older guy (GPAA), Stan and wife from Tapper Creek, grandson, a Bill with a flat tire (ATV), Harold and Harold Dimmick stopped in. They got their freight but it had lots of damage. Lonnie and son Ryan stopped, plus a few others.

Bob brought his cleanup trough to use for a few hours. We ran some concentrate through it. When I took it back to him, he showed me how to pan the black sand and get the gold out of it. We are tired again tonight. We took baths. Two Eskimos who drink were traveling the beach. One Eskimo comes to the beach on a three wheeler. He has a 15-gallon aluminum army pot with garbage can lid on the back rack. He was hauling snow for fresh drinking water. They are unloading the third barge this week. We notice several new vehicles in town that have come in on barges.

Sunday, June 12, 1994—hot, sun is intense, even with a breeze blowing, 40s to 60s. Breeze is stronger and the sea is breaking and some curling as it comes to beach. I ran machine and got one container of concentrates. By this time Sylvia got up. After breakfast we ran another one and part of one. Then dug some test holes and panned with machine and gold pan both. We went to visit Jack and Joyce about a mile down the beach. He has built a high bank box with some nice features. They are losing a lot of black sand, so are losing gold. Maybe waiting too long to clean up.

Then back to camp to load water containers and laundry in trailer. Tried to find the short in wiring to I can use battery to start the ATV, no luck. Went to town, saw Dimmicks on way in and in town also. We had musk ox burgers at "Fat Freddies." Did a little grocery shopping, laundry was closed, hardware closed, dump closed. We got water at Kristensen's and came home. Pulled suction hose in on account of the strong running seas. Harold, Rachel and little Harold had coffee and cookies with us. They brought some fresh pineapple.

Monday, June 13, 1994—partly cloudy, windy, so we slept late, 40s to 50s. Panned the concentrate from the little sluice at discharge end of gold screw. Looks like a lot of gold when in pan. We battened down the tarps and got a little ready in case this turns into a blow. I started for town with the laundry, got about a half mile, looked at the weather and went back to camp. Fooled with ATV troubles a while and then started out for Nome again. Said Hi to Dimmicks and went to Wes Perkins (Suzuki). He doesn't act like he knows me now! His mechanic fixed the electrical problem, fried wires, cost $80.00.

I did the laundry and went to S.B.S. out at Icy View. Got turkey drumsticks for supper meat. Really windy when driving into the wind. The sand peppers my face pretty hard. Luckily none got in my eyes. Said hi and bye to Dimmicks. They pulled their tarp tent down and are living in the wall tent. Got to camp, everything OK. Sylvia had secured a couple things and I did a couple more. Now it's hope for the best. Found a 1/2" rope, tied off gold screw to rocks with it. Found old shoe, salvaged shoe string to tie tarp. Found evidence of three old CAT trails on tundra just north of camp. Beach combing was good in evening. Rope, string, fishnet, container for used oil, walrus vertebrae, boards. Breaking waves about 3' – 3 1/2'.

BIRD DRAWING: Whimbrei or Bristle thighed curlew
Brown mottled like nest on tundra in back of camp.
Jaguer like? Fork tail + blackish, whitish back breast osprey

Tuesday, June 14, 1994—windy most all day except a few hours in middle of day, foggy a lot till noon, 40s to 50s. Gulls were flying west along beach in the fog. Their wings almost touching the waves. We saw two arctic loons courting nearby. A large gull was eating on a fairly large object a hundred yards from our gold screw. We got up fairly late. We made a sluice of rain gutter and the ribbed mat that Bob gave me. We glued the end cap and the mat in place with some latex caulk. I started running the machine at 1:00 PM. Sylvia did dishes then came out to throw rocks out of the hopper after washing them.

Almost four hours later and Sylvia was napping, the wind and surf came up and caused the pump intake to take air and it lost suction. So I quit and pulled foot valve in on beach. Went up beach and visited Lonnie and his son Ryan. Beach combed and found a walrus vertebrae. Back at camp I dug a test hole and panned it out. Not looking good there. Dimmicks came to visit in evening for quite a while. When they left I covered the machine and Sylvia fixed supper, then write this and off to bed.

Wednesday, June 15, 1994—rain early then nice with breeze, 40s to 50s. Around 5:00 PM winds picked up and gusted strong sometimes. Re-tied and re-fixed tarps etc. Sylvia helped get tarp tied around the gold screw. We slept late, seas slacked off after we ate and we got the pump intake in place in ocean after only two tries. I got a wet crotch and some water down the inside of my hip boots. We tried out the rain gutter sluice for two hrs, then cleaned it. Looks like quite a bit of gold, but I can't get it panned from the black sands without a lot of work and time. We ate a snack then worked a while longer and the surf broke and lost the pump suction so we quit and pulled pump intake out on beach. We saw more of the same kind of gulls flying up beach, also a few geese. I saw an eagle take off from nearby (near squirrel den) with something in its talons. California Bob hasn't worked out on the beach very much today. Ryan stopped on his way by and said hi. Jack and Joyce did the same.

Thursday, June 16, 1994—beautiful day, 40s to 50s. Winds and seas died down and it was great working at the gold screw. Occasionally a flock of cliff? gulls would go by plus a few other kinds of gulls. Several flocks of brant were flying west along the coast, probably to their nesting grounds. They would fly a little higher and farther out over the water as they approached us at work. One flock of eider ducks went by that I seen. I'm sure we don't notice all of them. One large fishing boat went west. There are two fancy sea going boats at anchor here at Nome. Henry, an Eskimo, who lives in a small house up on the tundra and just west of us, stopped to visit today. A very interesting man to talk to.

The seas got heavier and I got tired after 5 ½ small buckets of concentrate, so we quit. I went to Nome for gas, water and groceries. I phoned Bev's home and talked to Darcy and Vanessa. They are all coming up in August. Great!! Got a letter from Paul and short one from Steve. Winds and seas are running stronger this evening.

Friday, June 17, 1994—overcast, light wind and building seas all day. Around 40°. Waves about 4' tallest. The waves are eroding the beach and are into our old tailing pile. We moved the machine out of the position we were working it in the morning. Later in the afternoon we moved it even higher on the beach. A parka squirrel has adopted us and is less afraid every day. Some geese and other migration birds flew all night and some were seen during the day. I took ATV to the Penny River. Along the way I must have lost my glasses. Saw a good camping spot just past the USGS? Tripod, a few other places as well. Saw a young moose carcass and a dead seal, a couple three houses on this side of Penny River. Visited with Lonnie and Ryan a couple minutes. Then to Harold and visit. Bob brought home baked bread and cookies. Had coffee twice. Then we went back to Dimmicks for a good reindeer stew supper. I'm trying to prospect our next spot to run the machine.

Saturday, June 18, 1994—started clearing up 6:00 PM, 40° most of day. Waves were strong all day. Lower now at low tide and light breeze. I went west to look for my glasses. Found them where I thought I might have lost them. Dug quite a few test holes and panned them. All poor showing. Back at camp, Sylvia had a camp fire going and had been out collecting ocean shaped quartz rocks. She fixed breakfast about noon. Then we watched sea ducks "Eiders" fly west up the beach. The loons spent all afternoon 70 yards out in the sea, riding the waves. I saw a dead baby walrus on the beach up toward the Penny River. I dug a bunch of test holes near here and didn't find much. We are discouraged in that respect.

California Bob came over several times. He brought 4 Dolly Varden and some California brown rice, Sylvia cooked it and made gravy and we pigged out. Very good. A fire is good this afternoon and evening. There is a lot of drift wood along the beach. Bob wants me to go with him to look for some buried silver ore some time in the next two weeks.

Sunday, June 19, 1994—cloudy, partly cloudy, seas moderated, 40s. We put foot valve in water at low tide this morning. Then I went to town for a few grocery and put up adds and mailed the letter to Paul. Forgot to try to call Karn Rudbeck. Visited Harold on way home. Also Stan and Bob. We ran concentrate and hydrauliced a small area. Ate breakfast at noon and shoveled the area we had hydrauliced. Didn't look like we got much gold.

Harold, Rachel and little Harold visited. We sampled some more of the ground here. Looks slim. Jack and Joyce have left. Went to Lonnie and Ryan's camp. Got a suction of 1 ½ pipe near there. Back to camp and secured things around here. Sampled the high beach to east of camp. Some gold but not enough to work.

There have been more ducks, eiders? flying up coast. We saw seals and killer whales just off the beach 4-600 yards. Gulls were feeding in that area. Possibly on the leavings of the animal feeders. Salmon may be running out there.

Monday, June 20, 1994—partly cloudy, sunny and windy in evening, 40s to 50s. We watched the "killer" orca whales feeding about ½ mile off shore in Bering Sea, while drinking morning coffee. This is the third day they have been out there. Sylvia got to see one clear the water in a leap. Occasionally we see seals out about ¼ mile. Every day we see arctic loons and gulls of course. We observed more sea ducks and one flock of brant.

We moved the gold screw about 200' farther west. We got up at low tide and put the water intake in, then had some coffee and moved the gold screw. It sits on a plywood square and I pull it with rope and ATV. Got it in position and shoveled the red sand. We were amazed at how well it went through the gold screw. Prospects look much better at this location.

We quit work in evening and went to Rachel and Harold's. His partner is having trouble with the high banker box of his own design. I went into town and got some groceries and mailed a letter for Bob and inquired of a place to sell the Hauser (rope that washed up on shore. The thing is 87 feet long and two inches in diameter.

Tuesday, June 21, 1994—windy from the north all day, 40°to 45°. Felt cold when we were not working cloudy in morning and mostly clear rest of day. We got out to machine and started work at 10:30 after coffee, get loosened up and panning the clean up from the little sluice the tailings go over. I cleaned the barren sand off and shoveled the better material into the machine. The material from this spot goes through the machine really good. We can't tell how well we are doing for we don't know how much gold is in the concentrate. Consequently Sylvia gets depressed because she expected to see more visible gold. Me too. We pulled the intake pipe and moved the machine back after four hours of shoveling.

Sylvia panned the sluice cleanup and did dishes while I went to Nome for mail, look for buyer for Hauser rope, check plane reservations, and cargo restrictions. Visited with Dimmicks on way home. Then our neighbor Bob gave us four dollys (fish). We ate two for supper and I went up the beach and gave two to Jack and his friend. There is a big minus tide this evening. Very few birds today. Saw a dead arctic loon on beach today.

Wednesday, June 22, 1994—warmed up a little in afternoon, cloudy, 40° most of day. We are at Mile 2.7 from Jetty. Geese flying along the coast this evening. The tide was already coming in when I got up. We hurried out there and got the intake pipe in the sea in time. A bite to eat and coffee. Panned a little concentrate. Then reset the gold screw and shoveled for two hours The tide got so high we quit and moved the machine.

Then to camp and a brunch of bacon and pancakes, with maple syrup. Didn't do much for a while, then I decided to go west on beach and look for a trail to an old drill rig. About 3 miles up the beach I could see it from top of beach bank, off in the distance. Started walking over there and came up on a tent in a low spot. Saw it at 50 yards, so I turned and went more direct to a shack which was part of an old camp for drill rig. All dilapidated. Saw an old forge and two molboard walking plows, a few oil drums, steam boilers, a large fuel tank on skids (maybe 2000 gallons). Lots of drill test holes, some old shafts (filled in). Holes and voids as though dredged? Came to a drill and drilling test shack. Wide steel wheels all around. Very old. Neglected to get the name off it. Took lots of pictures. Lonnie loaned me a screen to classify our concentrate.

Thursday, June 23, 1994—when sun came out and we were behind the wind break, 40s to 50s. We built today to protect camp from a S E wind. It looked rainy and spit a few drops this morning, while I went to Nome to phone the man who is buying the ATV. Got a little groceries for the supper Sylvia fixed this evening. Dimmicks and their gold partners Tom and T. O. and California Bob were here to eat.

When I got back to camp in the morning, I screened panned two gallons of concentrate and returned the screen to Lonnie. The wind and seas are too much to put our pump intake in so we didn't work the gold screw today. We gathered wood and built the wind break. I dug some prospect holes and didn't find any encouragement. Watched the loons.

Tried to take a nap and Dimmicks stopped to leave pork chops and chicken. Sylvia fixed meat balls and spaghetti. Lonnie flagged Tom Massey of G.P.A.A. and we talked of my delivering the 4-wheeler and getting paid for it. Blueberry John prospected west on the beach. He had coffee with us on his way back to Nome. Chuck Titus had me give a wake up call at 8:00 PM.

Friday, June 24, 1994—in the 40s all day. Up at 5:-00 AM and pulled gold screw farther from surf. Drizzled till 6:00 PM. We screened cons all day and panned some of them. Took Andy's blue hose back to him. Several stopped to visit. Chuck Titus visited a long time giving us pointer on the gold screw and how to run it and improve it with some modification ideas he has. We got the intake line in and started shoveling at 8:00 PM. Quit sometime after 9:00 PM. Got a little more than a small pail of cons. Pulled the intake out of sea and put a tarp on machine and back to camp.

I had already gathered the wood. Sylvia fried some Dolly Varden trout that little Harold had caught and brought to us for our supper. The parka squirrel got into our grub, i.e. noodles, cookies, bacon and the butter. Sylvia chases it away with threats. Beautiful red sky when Sylvia got up at 2:00 AM.

Saturday, June 25, 1994—sunny, strong breeze from the southeast, 40s to 50s. Surf pretty strong, tide fairly low when we got up, so we put pump intake in right away. Had coffee and then set up machine and started shoveling gravel. Chuck Titus came along and talked about our little operation. We worked till I felt tired then back to camp and Sylvia fixed breakfast or brunch as the case may be. Then back to machine and shovel till I got tired again. My back and left hand sure give me trouble plus I just don't feel well. Chest hurts too. Lay down and rested, talked to a guy driving the beach with a Honda Trail 90. Panned a sample from little drainage just west of us.

The squirrels (parka) are very troublesome since finding our food. They get into the cook tent all the time now. Ryan Fawset visited. California Bob stopped by just after we had eaten and finished the noodles and corned beef right out of the pan. A cup of coffee and some gab and he went on to his camp. Harold, Rachel, and GS Harold visited and brought us some caribou soup meat.

Sunday, June 26, 1994—beaut of a day, 40s to 50s. Two barges pulled by tugs went west this morning. The squirrel continues to make a pest of itself. Sylvia chased it around and around the cook tent hollering and stomping it once. I was taking a nap at the time. I came out of the sleeping tent to help, the .357 in hand. Not wanting to shoot in the tent (hard on the ear drums and puts holes in tent). I got a 5' stick to jab at it behind the grey box. I think I made a hole in tent floor, not touching the squirrel. It finally got out the door with only a headache from Sylvia's stomp on head.

We got seven little pails of concentrate "cons" and worked about seven hours. We took two rests in between. Working this spot I moved a 5' long rock. The west end of the hole dips down. Hopefully a large pocket of gold rich red sand. I shoveled a few from the low part into the machine and could see the gold going down the little flume. I panned a very large tablespoon of the last bucket of "cons" an there was a nice line of gold in the pan. I went over to Bob's and told him of this hole and he had to come and look at it.

Monday, June 27, 1994—partly cloudy, windy all day, high 30s to low 40s. Very low tide in middle of night. We mined for one hour and got I small bucket of "cons." Seemed to be lots of gold doing down the flume. I went to Nome for water, mail, groceries and check on senior citizen showers.

Wanted "Chuck" to appraise the ATV so I can get paid for it. No luck finding him. I gave "Rob" a 14 yr old miner "on the beach with his dad" a ride from Nome out to his dads here on the beach. He is an avid fisherman and has a pet baby parka squirrel. We pulled our equipment away from the beach as it is too windy to work. We loafed and napped and later in afternoon went to Harold and Rachel's to visit. Tom and T.O showed up so we came home. Seems to be lots of gold at Harold's. Came home, checked equip, shot at parka squirrel and missed. Sylvia fixed a good supper. As sun gets lower and a cloud bank gets darker in back of Sledge Island, it gets cooler here after supper. Went for a little walk on tundra. Close by found an old shaft (mine) and ditch to beach. Also a larger workings just west of this one.

Tuesday, June 28, 1994—cold today, lots of wind from south, 30s to 40s. Low clouds and light rain, wind pushes seas higher on beach. Saw 100 Grant fly west along coast. We ate a little breakfast. I went to our diggings and shoveled some over burden off the area I would to put through the machine next. A skim of oil on the water in our hole, so Sylvia went back to camp and returned with the liquid dish soap and I dispersed the oil with that. We tried to get the wheels and the inlet pipe out in the sea but the seas was too rough. We gathered wood and sat around the fire. We each took a nap.

I built a wind break for our open fire area. Every day a little tweety bird sings here at camp. Bob visited and said he would get around to cleaning our "cons" later to day, but with these conditions it didn't happen. We gave up all thought of mining today and moved equipment farther from wave action. I tipped the machine over backwards onto its top. Leaked some gas that I shoveled away. Lonnie and Ryan just happened by and helped right the machine and pull it farther to higher beach. Went to California Bob's and got the latest weather info.

Wednesday, June 29, 1994—some light rain, gusting winds, seas are building and higher tonight and stacking up, 40°. We re-crated the machine and I hauled it to Mark Air Cargo. Bob and Chuck T wanted to clean my black sand "cons." The waves took out the tripod of poles he had in the surf holding the intake end for his pump. He ran down there and salvaged the intake and moved his pump to higher beach. He gave us a smoked salmon (humpy) and I gave him two quarts of oil.

Sylvia and I took down the cook tent and its tarp and packed the grey box and hauled them to Mark Air Cargo. The third trip they were closed. So I went to grocery store and got a couple potatoes and some round steak. I still can't find "Chuck" to look at ATV. Harold got wet today from the spray his sluice box gives off. I got stuck at the edge of the beach surf this morning and Lonnie and Ryan helped me get out.

Thursday, June 30, 1994—windy, cloudy, fairly strong surf. Warmed up, wind and surf died down in evening, 40° to 45°. Took third load of gear and "cons" to Mark Air Cargo. Kooper Piscoya, an employee there showed an interest in buying the ATV. So he and his wife Annette are trying to get a loan. I still can't find GPAA "Chuck." California Bob has asked me to pick up spark plugs for him at the Bonanza Station. I left Sylvia at Dimmicks to visit with Rachel. I stopped there a couple minutes and then on up to our camp and Bob's with his plugs. Then back to Dimmick's. The beach is getting bumpy like a washboard from all the traffic. Lots of GPAA people coming in this evening.

Visited with Harold this afternoon while he panned the cleanup from his little sluice. It looks to me the place he is working is very good. We ate lunch and supper with them and came home in the evening. I took a short walk along the beach. Found a walrus rib, fishing buoy. The waves almost erased signs of our work and changed the beach from sand to cobblestones.

Friday, July 1, 1994—a warm east wind, 40° or more. Got up built a fire to warm the coffee, then filled the coffee pot with water to heat and mix with some water in a 5-gallon pail. Stood on a piece of plywood and took a bath, put on clean clothes. We packed our clothes. Took down the tarp, folded and packed it. Then the tent and grateful we can pack it in a dry condition, as last nights forecast was for rain. California Bob is already moving his sluice here to our diggings. We wished him good luck. We said our goodbyes and discovered the ATV key was misplaced!! I found it in my rain pants pocket.

We took pix all the way to Dimmick's. We left them more gear, etc. plus more food. Rachel fixed breakfast. Little Harold caught 19 pink salmon. Rachel had them cleaned, cut and hung on a line to dry in the sun and wind. She fixed fried salmon to go with the pancakes. We finished the film roll, checked mail in town, looked for "Chuck"—no luck. On to airport.

Got to put tent poles in grey box. Sold ATV to Kooper Piscoya a Mark Air employee. $500 down, $500 2 wks, $500 2 more wks. A man from Georgia introduced himself and told us about his mining experience 10 miles out on the east beach. He did have about two ounces of gold on his person. Eventually our flight time came and we departed Nome. The route goes to Kotzebue then to Anchorage. We got a splendid view of Mt. McKinley and Mt. Foraker bathed in early evening sunshine. Occasionally we got glimpses of mountains, rivers, valleys, and lakes. What a great and expansive country.

Dennis and Addie met us at the airport. We had a visit with them and their son's Peter and Gary. We stayed at their house for the night. Sylvia and I went to a Wendy's fast food about 11:00 PM and then to bed. I got stomach cramps in middle of night.

Saturday, July 2, 1994—rainy in Anchorage and sunny here at home, 50°s to 65°. Had some breakfast with Dennis and Addie. Then to Eagle Store and to Stoddard's for a plane part for Denny E. AK Mining and diving was closed. We ate on Muldoon at Phillips Int. Went to Palmer and grocery shopped. Got home at 4:30 PM. Nice to be home. Unloaded groceries and gear and put truck in garage. Aired the house out. Pumped water. Allen visited. David and cousin came by.

Robbie came over to show off their new Suzuki 4 x 4. I took a shower. Denny, Jo and friend Jim came over to get aircraft part and visited for a while. We see young robins hopping around the yard. I saw one flicker. There is a raft of young ducks on our lake. Must have been a good hatch. Lake looks as though it is higher again this year. A beautiful evening and nice to be home.

Sunday, July 3, 1994—partly cloudy, sunny here and dark clouds other places, 43° to 63°. Must be well over 100 young ducks on our lake. Sylvia did laundry. I hoed garden. Put away more gear. Visited Rudbeck's, building site. Allen and Roxanne, just before they were to go to an outdoor service at Chamberlins. Allen was here a couple times concerning getting parts for his sluice box. Sylvia baked a cake and made a strawberry glaze. Went to dump and shot rifle a little. Found some steel shafts and roofing I can use.

Monday, July 4, 1994—cloudy and a little rain, 45° to 54°. Put away the treasures I brought home from the dump last evening. Then Jerry R. came over and visited till almost time to go to their place for a 4th of July potluck. Phoned Theresa and Paul, got to talk to Steven. Phoned Chuck Zimbicki.

Tuesday, July 5, 1994—partly cloudy, some light showers here, 40° to 60°. Rain from Sutton to Anchorage, off and on. I phoned Mark Air Cargo early this morning and our freight was in. We went to Anchorage to get it. Did some shopping at Eagle Hardware, Fred Meyer, and Alaska Mining and Diving. Left our Nome film to be developed at Carr's in Palmer. Phoned Nadia this evening.

Wednesday, July 6, 1994—partly cloudy and couple showers, 43° to 60°. Unload all the gear and put quite a bit of it away. We unloaded the gold screw. It got even more rusty in the freight box. Set off the grey box. Drove the ATV down to the well. Found the post supporting the switch box needed to be driven in. Then the small post holding the light bulb came loose and I had to come back up to house for a hammer. Visited Lucky and Mary.

Thursday, July 7, 1994—mostly sunny, 42° to 65°. Worked all day with a wire brush cleaning the gold screw of all the salt water corrosion. Now to get it painted. Ed Farmer visited in morning. We visited Harold and Rachel in evening. Jerry Rudbeck is going to build his airplane hanger in a position that we will look out our window to the lake and see it.

Friday, July 8, 1994—mostly sunny, 47° to 71°. Wire brushed and primed the gold screw. We mowed the lawn. I cultivated 1/3 of garden. Jerry R. has Mike Shelton here with two CATs and a dump truck mining gravel out of the hillside and making a 30' wide fill to the lake. Jim Jr. and Bunny McClellan of Florida visited this afternoon. Lisa Smayda and daughters and Afton H. visited also.

Saturday, July 9, 1994—mostly sunny, 40° to 68°. Started getting ready to clean up the "cons." Panned the little sluice and cleanings from the gold screw. Then we started making a micro sluice with a water bar. Somehow a fuse got loose at well pump switch. Then the kitchen sink faucet started leaking. Cleaned two more brackets for the gold screw. While working in the garage Sylvia heard a noise at the chimney. Upon opening the chimney clean out, we saw a mature golden eye duck. We took pix of her and released her. Then turned to the chimney and removed two dead ducks, and the ash and creosote.

Sunday, July 10, 1994—mostly sunny, a very beautiful day, 44° to 70°. Started work on mining equipment and Jerry and Betty Rudbeck visited and had coffee. Back out to work—then lunch—then work—then Allen and Roxanne visited—then work—then supper and out to work and Allen and Ellie came up. Allen got a 2" pipe elbow and borrowed my dredge to copy. Back to work and in drove Harold and Rachel. We had a nice visit, coffee and rhubarb upside down cake. Karn and a visiting boy stopped by—she was looking for her husband Bob. She has been "guiding" their guest to fishing, halibut and salmon.

Monday, July 11, 1994—sunny, nice day, 48° to 75°. Started working early on gold panner frame. Painted the gold screw also. Sylvia went to Glennallen. After supper I went to Chuck Z. to get information on the motor and pulley size for the gold panner. He loaned me a 50 mesh classifier. Got home 12:00 AM.

Tuesday, July 12, 1994—48° to 75° again today. Woke up late, 9:00 AM. Had breakfast and Ed Farmer came and visited a while. Went out and worked on gold wheel. I couldn't get the brazing to hold on the copper, so I shit-canned yesterday's work and started over using a black pipe and the welder. The result is more satisfying. I think this will work. Chuck helped with more advice and detailed description of his unit. Went down to Allen's once and had some steel cut. A new hatch of camp robbers are around here. Learning to fly, drinking water out of the tub used for panning cons. I just saw a small gull like bird grab a fish out of our lake. Sylvia watered the garden and lawn. She replanted some of the bedding plants. Vernetta's cat is prowling our garage. I went to dump. Got some plywood and rebar, Ford Escort wheels. Will go back tomorrow with metric sockets and get a couple hubs.

Wednesday, July 13, 1994—mostly sunny, some light breeze, 48° to 78°. Karn stopped by just in time to have breakfast with us. I went to dump and salvaged the rear hubs from a Ford Maverick. Quite a job, also got hatch openers. Got 3 toggle switches, 4 hose clamps, air hose etc. Back home worked on gold wheel motor bracket, plastic wheel insert. Sylvia put some fertilizer on lawn and watered it again today. Very hot and dry. Allen was helping Mike haul and spread gravel for Kurt at Snowshoe Lake, Allen's son phone and stopped in looking for their dad. Allen was smoking fish today. We went down in evening. Allen gave me two iron wheels and two, 13" alum wheels with tires on them. We had ice cream cake coffee popcorn and Pepsi and watched the John Wayne movie, *True Grit*. Joe and Peg Virgin stopped a few min at Allen's. Ditto for Denny E.

Thursday, July 14, 1994—sunny, very nice, 47° to 79°. Sylvia defoliated the tomatoes. I gave Allen a micro sluice and Teflon tape. I put primer paint on gold wheel stand. Made an adapter so I can mount a pulley on the wiper motor and power the gold wheel. Made a mounting bracket for switches controlling the wiper motor and a 12-volt bilge pump for a water supply to wheel and spray bar. Allen came up in evening check the throttle controls on my pump. His is a governor controlled motor and different than mine. Our beaver may be dead or gone!!! Allen's boys report the sign's don't look good. We like to see beaver on the lake.

Friday, July 15, 1994—mostly sunny, increasing clouds, cloudy and breezy in evening, 48° to 71°. Had coffee with Allen in morning. Painted gold wheel made modifications. Ed sent Robbie over with the motor drive pulley for the gold wheel. I finished up the old army stove repairs. Hoed ½ the garden. Pulled weeds from raspberries.

Saturday, July 16, 1994—cloudy, partly cloudy, breezy in evening, 48° to 70°. Finished wiring the electrical on the gold wheel. Hoed ½ garden. Did some target shooting found a few (12) .223 Remington empty and loaded. Loaded 14 to shot again. Smashed aluminum cans.

Sunday, July 17, 1994—cloudy, some breeze, clear in evening and light breeze, 38° to 65°. Sylvia heard a squirrel this morning and called me and rifle. There were 3 of them and quite close together but in different trees. I got all three, though one hung up on a limb. We folded three tarps and the two tents and put all away. Swept garage floor. Then we classified a lot of the "cons." Cal and Mary and Phillip Gilcrease are here from Arkansas and may stay. Allen and Roxanne had Gilcreases and us to supper this evening.

Monday, July 18, 1994—cloudy, a little sun, cloudy and windy, 45° to 60°. Sylvia went to Glennallen. I mowed weeds, put up shelf in garage. Serviced Suzuki, remounted the gun case on the Suzuki, cleaned the classifying screens. Karn brought our pix of Nome. Her Bob and Gary visited a while.

Tuesday, July 19, 1994—partly cloudy, mostly nice day with showers in sight all afternoon and evening, 46° to 66°. Swept out garage. Carried the dredge to garage. Cleaned gas tank and air cleaner on it. It fired up on first pull. It tested out good pumping water. The tube to float it that I pumped up yesterday still held its air. Great!! We moved the grey box and Hauser out of garage. Sylvia ran the last of the "cons" through the 50 mess screen. She also mowed the lawn. I sharpened the lawn mower and serviced the truck. Allen visited in afternoon and I gave him two lengths of cast iron pipe and hauled it down to his place. A strong wind blowing down the lake.

Wednesday, July 20, 1994—cloudy, to partly cloudy, some breeze, 45° to 67°. I loaded up the Suzuki on pickup and drove to mile 130 and gravel pit trailhead to Crooked Creek. The trail was quite dry. The caribou are moving east and north. I could smell them and the urine where they were moving through. At the junction of the trail and Crooked Creek. I searched for fire rings and dug under the fire bed in hopes of finding the reputed 80 lbs of gold of the two miners killed by a grizzly in 1919? No luck though. Saw 2 groups (5) people on trail. Then finding no trail to Albert Creek. I went back to the Cottonwood Creek Trail and went to Crooked Creek. No trail to Albert Creek from there either. I did see two hunting eagles. Grayling in the creek.
     Saw one nice meat bull caribou and watched it for a while. There were about a 1000 caribou on Monument Mountain. I saw part of them from a distance. On the way out to trailhead I found a 1/2" steel drill bit and one bungee cord. On the way home I stopped at the gravel pit across from the hwy camp. Sure enough the junk cars were still there. I took the windshield washer motor off of Chris Ronning's wrecked pick up. Then home to supper and a short nap. Went out to garage and put a "U" bolt in front of pickup box so I can winch ATV up tight when I'm hauling it. I made a custom chain to fasten the rear of ATV down. Then we went to Allen Farmer and visited while he fixed a flat tire. Repaired a hand tire pump and loaded his dredge. He cut out a cardboard silhouette of a caribou for David to practice shooting at.

Thursday, July 21, 1994—mostly cloudy, 45° to 59°. Worked on dredge and loading of the ATV. They brought us out a new propane tank late this afternoon. Allen visited twice, once to show me the mounting brackets he made for his gun boot (looks real good). We went to Bob and Karn's for supper. Halibut patties cooked by Frank. Karn and Sharon visited in the morning.

Friday, July 22, 1994—mostly cloudy, 42° to 67°. Drove to trailhead at "big house" near Gunsight Mt. Lodge. Unloaded ATV and went over Ballanger Pass. At the top I shot a few ground squirrels. There are hundreds of them (good fox food). Down near Pass Creek there were caribou by the hundreds on both sides of the trail. Shot squirrels once in a while Down Alfred Creek. At the gorge, the hill had slid into the Mountain and made a small lake. The places I wanted to dredge are under too much water. I went back to the junction of Pass Creek and went up Alfred Creek a little ways, looking at the accessibility to the mountains there for sheep hunting. Later I walked up Pass Creek at lower end of Clay Hill. Saw one small possible place to dredge. Saw a helicopter looking over the caribou. Shot the last of my cartridges (14) on the way up Pass Creek Loaded up again at trailhead and came home. Pretty disappointed about the dredging or lake of opportunity to dredge. I did enjoy being out in the mountains. Unloaded everything here at home. Washed the mud off the ATV.

After supper we went to Allen's for a little while. Talked about the trails and trying to get around the gorge. Back here at home I "retired" the cartridges I have been using and loaded up some different brass. Saw two young red fox near houses. Took some pix of boo.

Saturday, July 23, 1994—cloudy, sunny, partly cloudy, 46° to 66°. We raised the height of the ATV loading ramp. Bob R. loaded my pickup with sand for the fill. Allen and entourage went to Alfred Creek. We went to Point of View Lodge and had supper with Billmans and their guests from Minnesota, Dave and Carol.

Sunday, July 24, 1994—cloudy, sprinkles, sunny, light breezes, a beautiful summer day, 46° to 71°. I hoed the garden, cut some weeds. Painted the cover over the propane valve. Rounded up a spool to make a garden hose holder for Sylvia—she painted it. Pulled some bullets. Switched brand and style. I cut out an extension for the prospecting sluice on the table saw using a carbide blade. Laid out the bends and bent it to shape, got it mostly riveted on the sluice. Allen and David and Lucky went to Alfred Creek yesterday. Lucky and David caught grayling. Allen dredged with no luck. He and Kyle visited this evening.

Monday, July 25, 1994—mostly sunny, light shower out of Sutton a little ways, 44° to 70°. We went to Palmer, Wasilla on business shopping and to doctor. Found a bilge pump at Wal-Mart to provide water for "con's" cleanup. Nice to get back home.

Tuesday, July 26, 1994—rain all night and till noon, then cleared up slowly and real nice in evening, 44° to 70°. Started working on wiring the bilge pump with a power wire from ATV. Need more wire and double plug-ins. Allen was here a couple times to look in my Suzuki shop manual. I went to the dump and partly stripped an Arctic Cat snowgo. Loaded the body and stopped at car pile looking for wiring I could use, no luck. Then home to supper. After eating I went out and finished stripping the snowgo body down to it individual pieces.

Wednesday, July 27, 1994—partly cloudy, a beautiful day, 44° to 70°. Sylvia went to Glennallen. I salvaged a pump and two motors off a washer. Sorted out some junk to go to dump. Worked on two buckets to use in gold clean up. Brushed a mobile home roof covering on our camper. Harold and Rachel had supper with us. We told stories for three hours after supper. They have some funny and interesting stories.

Thursday, July 28, 1994—mostly sunny, 49° to 74°. We loaded our Toyo heating stove and a semi truck tire and went to Glennallen. Traded the tire for cleaning on stove. Got some papers notarized at magistrate office. Did some other errands and a little shopping. Stopped at Chuck Z. and returned his 50 mesh classifier. Showed him photos of our mining on beach at Nome. After supper, I rewired the gold wheel, adding in the 12 V. pump and adapting the wiring to the outlet on the ATV. Beaut of a day and evening. Bad pain on inside of my right arm.

Friday, July 29, 1994—partly cloudy, 45° to 74°. Beaut of a day then cloudy in evening. Shot squirrel early. Loaded ATV and with map in hand went to trailhead east of Eureka. Unloaded ATV and went to Cottonwood Creek, Crooked Creek, and over Cameron pass to Flat Creek. On way over just past, first Little Pass I came to a mobile home and Whitey's airstrip at North Creek. A father and two sons are mining there. Their CAT loader is broke down. I saw an eagle hunting. I shot a ground squirrel. Saw a nice caribou bull high on a sharp ridge. He was running from flies. His tongue was hanging out and he looked haggard. Saw a wolf and pup tracks in mud of trail. Trail is mostly dry and very good traveling. At Flat Creek I turned left and upstream.

When I came to Placer Creek, I thought it was too small for Placer Creek, so went on and when I came to Bubb and Shovel Creeks I went up Shovel Creek a short way. Just to get an idea what it was like. Turned around and went back to Placer Creek. I walked up it a mile or so. It has only a small amount of water running in it and even goes under ground sometimes. Saw a small area someone may have worked in past. Took a small shovel of sand out to Flat Creek and panned out 4 mercury coated flakes of gold. Saw a family fishing down stream on Flat Creek. Uneventful trip back to truck and home. I did find a couple ATV parts and an old pair of needle nose pliers.

Saw a flock of ptarmigan, mostly young birds. Their wings were white already. Allen came by in eve to tell me that he and Cal are working for Blake.

Saturday, July 30, 1994—cloudy and a couple light showers, 55° to 69°. Got an early start and finished a couple jobs. Straightened up the garage and wood shop. Repaired an ATV tire. Checked and put a little oil in ATV. Pulled the nails from the wood shop landing and replaced them with screws. Hopefully I won't catch the snow shovel on the screw heads. The nails would work up and dent the edge of the aluminum shovel. Bob R. brought a broom handle over and repaired it. Jerry R. was with him.

Sunday, July 31, 1994—partly cloudy, sunny, beaut of a day, 53° to 76° got the squirrel early. Adapted a pair of tire chains to front wheels of ATV. Sylvia baked cake and cookies and washed six 5gallon plastic buckets. I cleaned the oil out of them. I cut some brush to access the loading ramp better. Allen came up to show me his ATV chains he put his on the rear of machine. Sylvia visited the Rudbeck outfit. We visited Bart and Rosemary. Their friends Steve and Barbara from Texas are back visiting again this year. Bart made some copies for me. He gave us some phony $3.00 Clinton bills. We gave him a poem etc., to copy and pass on. I stopped at gravel pit checking for brass and found some and a few empty shot shells.

Monday, August 1, 1994—mostly sunny, some breeze and hot, 52° to 79°. Smoke in air coming from west. Sylvia went to Glennallen. I put another coat of roof coating on the camper. Worked some more on gold wheel, found a problem with the speed of the R.P.M. Cultivated half the garden, and did a bunch of little jobs.

Tuesday, August 2, 1994—partly cloudy, 53° to 74°. Sylvia packed a lunch and I gassed the ATV and loaded it. Went to trailhead north of gun sight and unloaded ATV and went over Belanger Pass, trail is very dry. I'm hunting ground squirrels today. Didn't keep count, shot maybe 12-14. Missed some easy shots and made some good ones. Some of them make an easy shot and some are evasive. Went down Pass Creek to Alfred Creek and up it a little ways, then back down Alfred to Fossil Creek. Went up it a little ways and ate lunch. Walked up Fossil Creek, lots of tundra rose in bloom and aromatic. Butterflies flying all around. Saw and shot some squirrels here. Saw lots of old wolf and caribou tracks, a moose track. I walked to a fork in creek and glassed 5 Dall ram's from two miles away. Then back out to Alfred Creek and explore a trail off of it in hopes of getting around the Clay Hill—no luck so back down to Alfred Creek and panned a couple places—no luck. Hunted squirrels on way back to trailhead and truck. Met Lyle, Kathy and Kyle Miller on trail, owns gravel pit where I park. Back at home I washed the ATV and Sylvia had supper ready.

Wednesday, August 3, 1994—mostly sunny, 51° to 80°. Went to dump with junk. Did small jobs. Chuck Zimbicki brought two car spindles to have the extra cast metal cut off. The squirrel was near the strawberries. They sure like berries. Probably a pleasant change from spruce seeds. Seems to be another hatch of camp robbers. I was picking small stones and weed out of the garden, when Allen drove up. We went to house for coffee and cookies. He had brought a box of re-loading components. So we prepared a bunch of cases and loaded three to test fire. We got his dies adjusted and set.

Thursday, August 4, 1994—mostly sunny, some breeze but hot, 47° to 81°. Sylvia went to Anchorage with Karn and Carol Adkins. I went to gravel pit and shot rifle. Tom H. visited in afternoon. I cultivated ½ garden and went over to Bob R building sight. He and Robbie stopped by for iced tea. Sure drank a lot of tea today. Allen came over in eve and loaded some rifle shells. I cleaned rifles. V.H. sent for three magazines. Made out order to L.S.&B.

Friday, August 5, 1994—mostly sunny and hot, 52° to 83°. Went to gravel pit and shot rifles for groups at 200 yards. The barrels got hot so easily I came home. Sylvia helped and we took the large window out of front of cab over camper and replaced it with plywood. We painted the plywood before installation and caulked and screwed it to frame. I sure don't feel well. My back is painful, like never before.

Saturday, August 6, 1994—sunny, some smoke from wild fire somewhere, 57° to 79°. Visited Allen and Roxanne and both Rudbecks. Cultivated garden. Filled a low spot in driveway. Hoed some weeds. Heard a squirrel at strawberries but it hid too well. Cleaned rifles and put oil in truck.

Sunday, August 7, 1994—partly cloudy to cloudy, 53° to 74°. We went to gun show in Wasilla. Did some shopping at Wal-Mart. Cooler in Mat-Su Valley. Grocery shopping in Palmer.

Monday, August 8, 1994—cloudy, partly cloudy, 53° to 74°. Washed the outside of camper, preparing for paint. Had everything ready about the time Sylvia got home from Glennallen. Got camper painted a flat "fudge" brown. Had to borrow paint roller from Allen. He borrowed air tank. Heard a squirrel in "the hole" this evening, can't see it.

Tuesday, August 9, 1994—sunny, some breeze, 52° to 80°. Sylvia cleaned camper. I painted some of it. Changed out some bolts. Put a bunch of screws in the sheet metal on it. Switched two tires and wheels on pickup. Sylvia did some laundry and mowed lawn. I took driver side door off pick up and welded cracks at the hinges. Put some paint on the burn places after sanding and wire brushing. I haven't gotten my sheep tag yet—Bartley's don't have them anymore. We went to Huddleston's for dinner tonight. I stopped at gravel pit and picked up 12 30.06 cases.

Wednesday, August 10, 1994—mostly sunny, some breeze, 49° to 80°. Worked some on camper. Trimmed lawn on north side, looks nice. Made some loading blocks for Allen. Cleaned garage and wood shop. Trimmed weeds and grass. Reinstalled heating shop stove.

Thursday, August 11, 1994—partly cloudy, some breeze, 52° to 78°. Rearranged the beds upstairs. Did some cleaning. Put the camper on truck and hooked up the lights. Took some rhubarb and meat to Dimmicks. Borrowed a paint roller from Bob Rudbeck. Sanded and put tung oil on loading block. Bev called twice. Second time to tell us the kids couldn't get on the flight. Disappointment. Loaded a few squirrel rounds. Sure is dry here. The sand, volcanic ash mix between the garage and wood shop is 1" to 2" deep "loose."

Friday, August 12, 1994—mostly cloudy, some rain here in late evening, 54° to 72°. Bev phoned, the kids are on the plane. We got around and went to Palmer post office and the bank. Then on to airport and met Vanessa, Tyler, Darcy and Asif. Collected their luggage and went to eat. Then took Asif back to airport and we went to Palmer. Did grocery shopping. Saw Kim and T J Huddleston. Joe and Peg Virgin at Carr's. Then on home. The kids got to see "awesome" and "cool" scenery and sights. Everyone was ready for bed when we got home.

Saturday, August 13, 1994—we loaded the camper with food and gear. Loaded trailer with ATV dredge and gasoline. We waited till mail came then started for mile 94 Denali Hwy. Stopped at Glennallen for some groceries and gas. Stopped later for lunch. Got gas again at Paxson, got on Denali Hwy there. I love to look at that country. Quite a few hunters and some tourists. Some hunters have been successful. The black top ends at mi 21. There is some calcium chloride on the road. Some road is dry and very dusty. Sylvia saw a moose near McClaren River. We found Harold, Rachel, Corky, Rusty and great-grand daughter Azalia near mile 94 and we camped beside them. Our grandkids play cards and read a lot. Chili-mac for supper and visit with Dimmicks. We are up high and see no game. Rusty and Corky are hunting boo and seeing lots of ground squirrels. We stay up till nearly dark or about 11:00 PM. The scenery is beautiful. We can see Valdez Creek Mine from here.

Sunday, August 14, 1994—sunny. Saw a raven and eagle and three kestrels. After breakfast Tyler and I unloaded the 4 wheeler and went on the trail south across the road. Got into some mud right away and then the trail was mostly very dry. We stopped on several high knobs and glassed all around for boo, but only saw two swans and small birds and lots of ground squirrels. One of those was harvesting herbage and carrying it in its cheeks to a den. Some squirrels came very close and Tyler liked that. He got tired or bored so back to camper and lunch. Then Harold, Corky, Rusty, Tyler and I went to Canyon Creek and panned for gold. Lots and rock and boulders in this creek. I did get one respectable flake shaped like a "V." Back to camper and load everything and go to mile 48. Looks like a muddy place to cross and a poor place to camp. Maybe we should have spent $5.00 and camped at "Ed Moore's Camp" at mile 52. Anyway we went on and camped at Maclaren Summit Trailhead on the Oscar Trail campground. We ate supper and went out on the Summit Trail and didn't see any game. We saw seven huge bull boo hunters had gotten when we stopped

244

at Gracious House to gas up. Those bulls had been killed about 10 miles west of Ed Moore's camp. There were some pretty colors in the clouds at sunset. I'm tired tonight. The road keeps shaking the trailer side boards loose.

Monday, August 15, 1994—sunny and warm. Got up extra early and went west on the 7-Mile Osar Lake Trail. Corky and Rusty were ahead of me a ways. We would stop and glass from the top of the many knobs. There are lots of ground squirrels here also. We did see two cow moose and two swans, some ducks and some live beaver houses at and near the end of the trail. Then on the way back we stopped and ate some blueberries. Shortly after that we came on two moose bulls, one a spike fork and the other was a "paddle" bull. But no boo. A man and a woman had two pointer dogs on trail, training them to hunt ptarmigan.

Saw a man with a muzzle loader and a woman with a 30-30 hunting. Ate breakfast about 1:00 PM, had a short nap. Harold wanted to move to Moore's camp. But before we could leave, Phillip and Arlen drove in with the news that a friend of theirs had died at Kotzebue so they will go home and then to Kotzebue. The rest of us load up and got to Moore camp, park and unload ATVs and drive out the dusty trail. At four miles, we see two bull boo lying on a partly dried up lake bed. We went on about ½ mile but then turned around and went back and made a stalk on the two bulls. Corky and I were shooting low. I saw two of my shot hit water at bulls' feet and one shot kicked up dust behind them. There were much farther away than we thought so we had to aim much higher. Finally both bulls were down. We got them butchered out. Eskimos have a neat way of taking the hid loose and off an animal.

We loaded meat and horns and went back down the dusty trail to camp. Loaded everything up. Sylvia had supper ready. We are at 11:00 PM. We pulled out of camp, Corky and Rusty going to Tangle Lakes and we headed for home. We got gas at Paxson at 1:10 AM. More gas in Glennallen and on home unloaded and hung up meat and got to bed at 4:52 AM. We are two tired old people.

Tuesday, August 16, 1994—sunny and some breezes. Up at 9:00 AM. Had a shower, breakfast and visit with grandkids. My shoe sole has really come loose. Sylvia package the boo ribs, cooked the heart and tongue. Washed the meat with a vinegar solution to retard bacterial action. I worked on trailer, washed ATV, painted roof on camper, watered some trees. Tyler and I did a few things together. I finished the loading blocks. Then he and I went down to Lucky's and visited him. Allen phoned in evening. Darcy cooked supper. Her and Vanessa did dish's. Beverly phoned at supper time. Tyler and Darcy went down to the lake. Tyler got a leach on him while swimming.

Wednesday, August 17, 1994—sunny, smoky, 39° to 78°. I went to Glennallen, business and a little shopping. Stopped by Chuck Z and got ATV handle bar warmers. Changed the oil, and oil filer and cleaned air filter on truck. Cleaned the ATV air cleaner. Visited a lot with the kids. Bev and Asif phoned. Theresa phoned. Allen and Cal stopped to visit and had some watermelon. Sylvia made homemade pizza, strawberries and cake for Vanessa's birthday. I gave the kids rides on ATV. We stopped at Allen's so they could pet the little puppies. Today is Vanessa's birthday.

Thursday, August 18, 1994—sprinkles, cloudy and sunny rest of day, 45° to 73°. Sylvia finished cut and wrapping the caribou. Fixed the left turn signal on camper. Tyler and I went fishing at Mirror Lake. No luck. Home to lunch and fished our lake from canoe. No luck. Farmer kids borrowed some movies. Karn brought movies she had borrowed back and brought along some of hers. She wanted Sylvia to watch their dog but we may not be here. I hauled garbage to dump. I'm really sick with this head cold and trots both. Saw goose hunter Mike Oz, son Jeff, Barbara, wife and small son on Mirror Lake.

Friday, August 19, 1994—partly cloudy, little breeze, 40° to 74°. Bob and Jerry borrowed my shooting pad. I worked on remodeling the two wheel trailer. We all went to a birthday party for Kyle today. Saw a squirrel and missed it.

Saturday, August 20, 1994—cloudy and a little rain, 52° to 64°. Worked on trailer. Welded stakes on frame. Drilled some holes and cut sides to size. Painted stakes. Sylvia baked a turkey. Allen came over to tell me he got a 56 1/2" bull moose. I showed Tyler and Darcy how I reload cartridges.

Sunday, August 21, 1994—rain all day, 48°. Started taping threads in trailer stakes and broke the tap. My back is really bad today. Went down to Allen's to see the horns of the bull moose he got. Cal, Mary and Allen were cutting and wrapping moose ribs. Vanessa, Tyler, and Darcy played card games all day.

Monday, August 22, 1994—rain, partly cloudy, rain, 42° to 55°. Spent time with grand kids. Worked on trailer till they got up in morning. Finished trailer this afternoon. They were stringing beads. I caught the trailer wiring on fire when welding and had to replace 4-3' pieces of wire. Replaced the lost ATV tie down chain.

Tuesday, August 23, 1994—partly cloud, breezy sometimes, 34° to 56°. "Helped" Tyler fly his balsa wood airplane. We did some repairs and modifications. The girls did some more bead necklaces. They had lots of phone calls this afternoon. They went for a ride on the ATV after supper. I rebuilt the way the camper step was attached.

Wednesday, August 24, 1994—we left about 10:30 AM and went to Palmer and then on to Anchorage and the airport to pick up Asif. We went to Royal Fork for dinner then we went to Long Drug and shopped. Back to airport so they could catch the plane to Minneapolis.

Thursday, August 25, 1994—partly cloudy, 42° to 64°. Shot two squirrels right away. We went down and visited Jerry and Betty working on their hanger. I cultivated ½ garden. Sylvia picked some raspberries and mowed lawn. Denny E. came over and wanted to sight his rifles. We went to a gravel pit and had a lot of fun shooting. I picked up a lot of brass. Then Jerry came over and he, Denny and I drove up Lake Louise Road and down Oil Well Road looking for spruce hens (no luck). Got back 9:25 PM to a late supper. The Mountains (Sanford and Wrangle) had beautiful pinkish light on them and framed in clouds.

Friday, August 26, 1994—partly cloudy, 41° to 70°. Went to gravel pit and re-sighted rifle and checked zero of another weight of bullet. Worked on driver side rear view mirror. Installed ham warmers on ATV handlebars. The grips were on helluva job. Allen here for coffee and pie while I was gone. I visited there a little while. Rudbeck is flying moose meat in from their camp.

Saturday, August 27, 1994—partly cloudy and a breeze from west and feels cooler, 40° to 57°. We loaded up the moose and boo horns and tried to sell them out at end of lane. I had poor luck—most people were looker and picture takers. Allen, Roxanne invited us down to a moose meat supper.

Sunday, August 28, 1994—partly cloudy, rain in evening, 32° to 56°. Frosted the potato vines. Sold more horns. Bob Toby F & G biologist made me quit selling because some the horns were still fastened together. Picked some raspberries again today. Sylvia's cold is some better. Cleaned rifles.

Monday, August 29, 1994—partly cloudy, 40° to 58°. Started loading goose hunting gear into camper. The electric wire to pump has failed, spliced a piece into it. But that isn't the problem or at least all of it. Loaded more squirrel cartridges.

Tuesday, August 30, 1994—foggy to sunny, 34°. Didn't feel well. Rudbecks brought the groceries over that they brought from town for us. Sylvia went on senior van to the state fair at Palmer. I finished loading groceries in camper, ATV on trailer and went to Glennallen. Talked to Darrel about where to meet in Delta Farming project to hunt cranes and geese. Got gas there and went to shooting range. Bob Toby!! Was sighting a rifle. The gas at Paxson. He gave me a handful of wheel weights. I sure enjoyed the drive to Delta Jct. The fall colors were very bright. Got more gas in Delta and put a for Sale Notice up for my D4 Belt pulley. Some smoke from the fire (forest) plus some windrowed trees on farms are burning. Visited with Allen Baker for a couple hours; Jason is at college, Ross at home yet. Wendy was friendly and nice as ever. Went to

Hollenbeck's, no one was out and about. One tractor working in field (Scott?) I drove to the 5-acre parcel of theirs to camp for the night. Turned on propane and lit the refrigerator and camper light and cooked supper. Its 9:30 now.

Wednesday, August 31, 1994—foggy most of morning. Frost early, then up to 60°. Some spruce hens out and about. Jim shot two of them. Saw a few flocks of speckle bellies while visiting Jim and his father in law Charley. Then a couple thousand crane flew over, some quite low. About noon, Darrel and I drove to south end of field and parked his Suburban and my camper. I fixed a late breakfast. Then we unloaded the ATVs and went over to the lake just off Nelson's farm. Scott wanted us to camp there. We want to hunt on the field here. There were five ducks on that little pond. Then we came back here, loaded up the decoys and went up the field to a rise we liked and set stakes and put decoys together and covered them with a poncho. Rigged 3-4 blinds and back to camper. Repaired a light bracket on Darrel's ATV and then Scott and a foster boy came by in the Jeep and shot the bull a little while. It's a nice evening. Smokey to south and east from the fire on Military Reservation, plus some farm tree berms are burning. Off to north it looks rainy. Sunny off towards the sunset and Donnelly Dome. A light cool breeze is moving.

Thursday, September 1, 1994—started raining before daylight, 40s all day. Some buffalo were wallowing in the field dirt near the camper. We were up early and out to the decoys and set them up. Two guys came in the dark, drove in between Jim, Charley and our decoys and set up on next strip. No birds flew for about 3 hrs then these new guys knocked two crane down. One of the birds was a runner and got away from them. Later I saw it, stalked it and shot it. It wanted to fight me on the ground and I hit it in the head with gun barrel. Darrel saw a wolf some distance from us. 10 min later it crossed the field 100 yards west of me, a smaller pup? brown animal. We had lunch and went over to Cummins Sawmill on the Delta II Barley Project Road. Darrel had business with him. Then saw one spruce hen and on back here. The fire on Military Reservation is still burning. The rain quit soon after we got back. We hunted till legal quitting time. I knocked a large hen crane down. It played possum till I started walking over to it. Then it got up and ran a ways and turned to fight and I shot it again. 3000 crane flew down the valley today. We saw quite a few geese, most speckle bellies. The sun tried to shine and the rays coming through the holes in the clouds on the mountainsides with the tree and shrub fall colors was simply beautiful. We saw Charley knock two geese down. I count with tens when counting large numbers of birds.

Friday, September 2, 1994—cloudy and breeze from west, showers blowing through, really foggy before daylight. A few flights of geese, no shots at them from me. Darrel tried once, geese too high. We went to camper for a sandwich and a small flock flew right over my "hide" in some large bales. Sunny all afternoon and I dried everything damp or wet. Darrel wanted to delay going home. All the crane were flying very high and leaving. We picked up the decoys, packed out gear and left about 6:00 PM. Got gas and wheel weights. At Chevron station in Delta. Drove through two fairly hard rains near Delta Junction. The even light made for difficult driving. Got gas again in Glennallen, quick stop and got home 12:00 PM.

Saturday, September 3, 1994—beaut of a day, frost and ice, to 54°. Unloaded food and gear. Sylvia packaged cranes. One front tire started failing on trip, but got me home. Allen took it off the rim and mounted another tire for me. I mounted it on hub at home. We visited with Allen and Roxanne. He borrowed my wheelbarrows. Sylvia picked the ripe raspberries. We had them for desert at supper time, very good. I had an urge to look at spark plugs in truck motor, found a loose one. Pulled all of them, cleaned and gapped them and reinstalled them. We walked over to Jerry R's but they weren't home.

Sunday, September 4, 1994—sunny, some breezes, 34° to 59°. Took the furnace out of camper, looked it all over, put it back in, tried it, no work! Found a burned out fuse, works fine now. Went down to Allen's. He was pouring cement with the help of some kids and Cal G. I helped then went back home, had lunch and went down to canoe and hunted ducks. Got eight of them, cleaned them at lake and Sylvia washed them to freeze. Don't feel good these days. Laid down for a while and felt worse. Harold Dimmick phoned to ask us to have supper with them. They had lots of company. Picked up a "green wood" 2" x 12" x 48" planks lying in highway. Stopped at gravel pit and found a grader blade in junk pile that with some cutting, I could make a blade for out snow plow. Such a beautiful day and evening.

Monday, September 5, 1994—cloudy, sunny, cloudy, showers and snow in mountains to south, 41° to 54°. Sawed horns off of skull plates. Didn't feel well all day. Sized some cases. Went to Bob and Karn R. for supper. Jerry, Betty, Van, Tammy there and Denny E. and family came over later.

Tuesday, September 6, 1994—partly cloudy, 38° to 56°. We went to Anchorage and shopped for a new pump for our well. Shopped groceries in Palmer and stopped at Foster's Taxidermy and picked up the tanned black wolf. Checked on a couple hospital bills and cashed our checks at bank. The truck started "blowing out" the water. Put water in a couple times. Then noticed the upper radiator hose leaking from a couple holes. Shortened hose and re-clamped it and went to automotive store and bought both upper and lower hoses. Managed to get home OK and will repair it here at home.

Wednesday, September 7, 1994—frost and mostly sunny, 27° to 57°. Put new spark plugs in truck and broke one doing it. Put on the two new radiator hoses.

Shot a squirrel with one of my hollow points, seems to work good. The new pump has a check valve I can't remove. I finally managed to get it jammed in open position. We wired it and the new control box. Removed the old pump and its control box and installed the new unit in the well. Sylvia didn't want to try it this evening, in case it didn't work and we would work on it half the night. Rudbeck looked at pump too. Jo and Emily came over to get tomatoes. When we were working on well a duck swam up to shore near by and groomed its feathers ignoring us all together.

Thursday, September 8, 1994—rain, partly cloudy, cloudy, 40° to 51°. The new pump doesn't work either must be the wires going to the pump. Sylvia and Karn went to Anchorage to do some yard sales and will pick up new wire to run to well. Saw 2 squirrels but no chance to shoot. Drilled hollow points in some squirrel bullets. Chopped, cut and leveled some 4-wheel trail to well. Visited Lucky in evening. Gave him some brass.

Friday, September 9, 1994—cloudy, partly cloudy, some breezes, 39° to 54°. Loaded up shooting gear and went to gravel pit to shoot rifle. Forgot chair. Went back home and got it. By then Lucky was there to shoot also. I shot slowly so barrel wouldn't heat up. Breeze opened up groups some. Back at home Lucky found another animal bite in the well pump elect line. I fixed that and took the garden and lawn "T's" out of water line and am pumping water in storage tank now.

Saturday, September 10, 1994—partly cloudy, calm, cloudy and rain in evening, 26° to 46°. Loaded shooting gear and went to gravel pit and shot .243. A couple loads were very good. Back home did a few small jobs. Two women lost the tilt latch pin on their trailer bending the rear part. I cut out all the old and put in new angle iron, just like original and they went on with their hunt. Getting late and Sylvia isn't back yet.

Sunday, September 11, 1994—rain all day, 37° to 44°. Cleaned guns and gut more cleaning patches. Granddaughter Laura phoned and we talked ½ hr or so.

Monday, September 12, 1994—rain, showers, mostly cloudy, 39° to 50°. Sylvia went to Glennallen. My back hurts today. Cleaned garage. Dragged 20' of 3" steel pipe down to lower road to bury so as to protect our water and electric lines as they cross the road with trucks. Cleaned up some junk and we hauled it and garbage to dump. Griz tracks there up to almost six inches wide (front). Checked Army trail, gravel pit and found some rifle brass, fits no rifle I own. Will give away. Crated the gold screw in storage for the winter. Six swans on our lake today. Cleaned a rifle and loaded some test loads.

Tuesday, September 13, 1994—sunny, cloudy, sunny, 30° to 50°. Went to gravel pit to shoot some development loads. Spent 4 hrs at it. White sox got to biting pretty bad today. Talked with Lucky about going hunting. He has built a neat grate support for camp fires. I gassed ATV, checked the oil and started gathering gear for the camping-hunting trip with Lucky. Will take the little pack rod just in case I want to fish. Drilled holes in some antler slices for beaded necklace-chokers Sylvia is making. Four swans on lake today. Went down to lake to get beaver pix, no luck.

Wednesday, September 14, 1994—cloudy all day, 30° to 53°. The forecast of wind and rain didn't materialize. I decided to not go with Lucky to hunt behind Tolsona Ridge. He has decided to go with Allen and Cal to Denali Hwy and hunt Caribou. I visited with Allen and Cal while they were eating breakfast. Back at home I got some things ready for winter. Prepared to re-bury the elect and water line where it crosses the lower road. Jerry R. furnished two pieces of plastic pipe to cross the road. The black flies, white sox were very aggressive.

Thursday, September 15, 1994—mostly cloudy, a little windy at supper time, 37° to 56°. Karn phoned Brown electric. I dug the trench for the new electric wire for water pump. Then rearranged the water line down near the well. Sylvia mowed the lawn.

Friday, September 16, 1994—mostly cloudy, 40° to 51°. Buried the pipe to put well electric wire in near the house and re-sodded the little ditch. Cut a tree near the house and trimmed it. Painted the mail box. Lucky, Allen, David each got a boo. We had supper over at Betty and Gerry R. Breezy this evening.

Saturday, September 17, 1994—partly cloudy, cloudy evening, 34° to 52°. Visited Allen at noon. Al and Faith has brought our electric pump wire out from Wasilla. We hooked it up at house and unrolled it to well and hooked it to switch box there and used the old wire for the heat bulb at well. Dug the potatoes this morning, only "3 crates." Denny E. came over after supper and I went road hunting with him. No luck. Bev phoned and talked a long time.

Sunday, September 18, 1994—fairly hard rain till 3-4 PM, 34° to 53°. Cast some bullets and ingots of wheel weight lead. Cleaned up a little in garage. Jackie Beaudoin and her daughters visited and took a tomato plant home. We went down to Allen's after supper. They and Cal's were canning meat. I'd like to go look at the wing (airplane) part that Allen found while hunting last fall. Don Deering pooh-poohed the find so Allen isn't interested. This evening is beautiful. Clouds reflected in lake. Ducks feed continuously. Allen and Cal are going road hunting this evening. Snowed down to 3600' elevation.

Monday, September 19, 1994—cloudy to mostly sunny, lots of frost this morning, it melted off about noon. Temps, 27° to 49°. Sylvia went to

Glennallen. I put a electrical plug on wire at house, for the light in well. Saw a spruce hen fly into a tree when I went after the mail. Took the .22-250 and a pest load back and shot it in head and ate it for supper. We tried then to push the electrical 3-12 W/G through ¾ plastic pipe, no luck. Cast some bullets. Loaded most of camper and ATV in trailer.

Tuesday, September 20, 1994—cloudy, no frost. Finished loading camper and headed for Delta Jct. Truck steamed a couple of time so bought stop leak in Glennallen. Saw a coyote feeding on a boo. Hide, gut pile in road ditch at Frank Zimbicki's. Talked to Lanagen he had forgotten to call Browning. Got gas and then stopped at rifle range. Picked up a couple gallons of brass. Saw lots of hunters in vicinity of Hogan's Hill hunting boo. Saw some swans on Paxson Lake and Summit Lake. Then rain to Donnelly Dome and a few moose hunters there.

    Got gas in Delta. Drove to rifle range and only found a few pieces of brass. Got some rolls and apples at grocery store. Drove down the Alaska highway and saw a cow and calf moose a few miles before my turnoff onto Sawmill Creek Road. Drove slowly but didn't see any birds. No one at the buildings at Hollenbeck's. So I drove out to the field. E.B. was there helping a hired man with a baler. Got permission to hunt. Walked over to gravel pit pot hole with out my shot gun and sure enough 8-9 sandhill crane got up out of the grass and flew off. So much for being ready!!

    Went to far corner of their farm and parked camper and unloaded ATV off the trailer. Decided to go to the lake just off of the Nelson Farm. Stopped back at gravel pit just in case the cranes came back. They weren't there but a mallard hen jumped up and I shot it. Went to lake by Nelson Farm on ATV. Moved a blown over tree from trail. The buffalo have quite a trail in to this lake to drink. Saw two teal. Sat down in an old bale blind someone else had been using. Soon geese start flying from Clear Water Lake direction. Three Canada geese decide to land in this little lake. I hit one as they were leaving and it circled back and skid landed on the water and coasted up on shore. There it laid its head around on its back and succumbed. I went over, picked it up and brought it back to blind and took pictures. More geese flying but not near here. I picked up what shells were lying around and went back to gravel pit. Nothing there. I can hear geese and crane on the Jerry Brehmer farm. On the way to camper I saw some geese feeding in grain stubble. I'll try for them in morning. Cleaned the goose and mallard. Cooked supper, windy here today.

September 21, 1994—no frost this morning and partly cloudy. Some breeze from the east. I woke up one hour late. Didn't hear the alarms. Threw coffee, shells, snacks, burlap in brown bucket and got outside in time to see cranes landing where I wanted to hunt this morning. I took a round about ½ circle and stayed in low ground to reach a hiding place near where I had seen them. They in the meantime had moved on probably in very low flight ½ mi east. I stayed hid in tall grass. Presently a flight of crane came over and I got one crane, then another group and I got another crane. More crane came by in range of lead shot. We have to use steel shot so I didn't shoot as steel doesn't kill nearly as far. Soon I picked up my birds and walked back to the camper.

Fixed some breakfast and here came a flight of crane near and over the top of the camper. I hit one of these twice. It turned and headed back in direction they came from. I watched it closely as it was loosing altitude then 400 yards from camper it fell straight down over on Brehmer's land. I walked over and tried hard to find it with no luck. Back at camper I cleaned the two cranes I had and then decided to try to locate the down crane. I walked out to where I thought it might be and then not finding it I looked a little more to the west and found it. It is a young one and very fat. One cooler is full of birds now. The camera won't rewind the film. This afternoon is clear, warm, light breezy and beautiful. The bugs are bad. I am burning pic mosquito repellent coil in camper.

Checked gravel pit pot hole twice, no birds. Went to the pot hole just off Nelson's Farm and jumped some crane. Knocked one down and couldn't find it, hard as I tried. Did get a young one from a flock of four. Tried to stalk one, no luck. Some geese landed very near the irrigation system. Didn't fly at all near me. Later after shooting time was over, some geese landed in Brehmer's also. Breeze has died down. Smoke in the air from Fort Greely wild fire and from farmers burning dozing wind rows. The air is warm this evening. There was a sun dog this evening. Clouds are building in the east.

September 22, 1994—light frost, very little breeze today. Up early. Set out decoys near the irrigation center pivot. Six crane and 3 crane flew by while I was setting up goose decoys. I shot once but was too late. Didn't get another chance all day. Saw four spruce hens and found one that had flown into Scott's 8' woven wire buffalo fence. I drove the perimeter of his buffalo and European wild hog farm looking for holes in the fence from bears, moose etc. Got a little chance to visit with Scott while he was working. Went over to Roy Beaver across the road and visited with him. He nearly died from diabetes, lots of problems, health and money. There were thousands of geese on G. Brehmer's farm today. I watched flocks of several hundred Canadian honkers land there. Some left but many more came in from the north. There was a small flight of crane this morning and again this evening. I set in a blind this evening and watched them come into and land on another part of Scott's farm. No way to sneak up on these eagle-eyed birds. None flew within gun shot range of me today. Tired just the same tonight. Looks to be colder tonight. The moon shining through thin clouds on heavy white clouds over the Alaska Range—beautiful. Met Gary Allen and Phil (Cole?) from Anchorage Sport Clay Shooters. Met Gene and wife Johnnie.

September 23, 1994—light frost, mostly cloudy. Up early and went to my blind near head of center pivot irrigation. Nothing flew close enough for a shot. Some cranes landed a ¼ mile closer to Hollenbeck's. A few geese ¼ mi closer to the air strip. But over on Brehmer's the huge flocks of lesser Canadas were dropping out of the sky and landing in droves. When they circle they stay well within the perimeter of Brehmer's farm. Gary and Phil managed to get permission from Shultz bros. to walk on to that farm and hunt the geese.

Phil got four Canadas this morning. They invited me to shoot sporting clays at the "Eagle Nest Ranch"? Even offered to supply the shells. I met them at Cherokee II Café. Tried to phone Sylvia, no luck. Then followed Gary and Phil to place we were to shoot. As they claimed, I did have fun and enjoyed it. I shot a score of 24 of a possible 50. In retrospect I should have stayed and shot another round and even shot a pheasant or two. Gary and Phil offered to freeze my birds and stay longer and hunt with them. I should have. I visited the "Big Horn Gun and Ammo" shop in Delta. High winds blowing against me for first 40 mi going home. Road was rough of coarse and I drove slowly. A spark plug wire came loose near south end of Paxson Lake. I got home just after dark a little while.

September 24, 1994—snow most of morning and snow all around us for most of day. 33° to 40°. Sylvia cleaned and packaged the birds. We unloaded the camper and I put the gear away. Did some small jobs. Then cast some wad cutters and melted down the rest of that box of wheel weights. Sylvia is fixing the mallard for supper tonight.

September 25, 1994—some snow and rain, low clouds, 31° to 40°. Cast some bullets. Repaired the mold. Cleaned shot gun. Checked switch box at well, one fuse was loose. The beaver have sure been working hard at getting their winter feed pile. Much, much sign on this lake. Harold Dimmick phoned. Bob, Karn, Betty, and Jerry were here for supper. Allen and Kyle brought us some of their smoked sausage.

September 26, 1994—sunny, very light breeze, 32° to 45°. Loaded up shooting gear and rifles in to the camper and drove to gravel pit for a session of load development for these two rifles. Morning shooting is good in that there usually isn't much wind, but the sun shines at me and not at targets. Made some horn buttons for Sylvia's crafts. Cast some more bullets, rebuilt the hinge bolt arrangement of the mold. Some squirrels around but no chance to shoot one. Sylvia saw the beaver working like a beaver does.

September 27, 1994—cloudy and a few flakes of snow here, then clearing and sunny, then cloudy, 27° to 40°. We took the camper off the truck and onto blocks. Then Sylvia went to Betty's to have a perm put in. I did some small jobs. Loaded the ATV in truck bed and went to Dimmick's. They needed a plug to repair a tire. Had coffee and roll with Harold, then went to the gravel pit just east of Call's/unloaded the ATV and drove 3 ½ miles south on a trail there. Parked ATV and walked west according to Allen's directions, I found one of the lakes he told of and not knowing which to go around the lake I chose left and walked ¾ way around the lake and came upon the other lake Allen described and after a little search found 5 feet of the end of an airplane wing. It had been hack-sawed off, not torn off. Saw what appeared to be small CAT tracks to crash site. Oxidation on aluminum and red and green or cream fabric, plus the small ran down spruce lead me to guess this happened about 20-25 yrs ago. Tried to phone Al Lee, no answer, so I left a message. Found a dime in trail. Saw a very sharp pointed rock. Stopped and knocked it out of the trail, with another rock. Saw old wolf scat in trail and caribou bones. Fox scat in gravel pit. Started preparing more brass.

September 28, 1994—sunny, beaut of day, 20° to 44°. We went to doctor appointments in Wasilla and got groceries and four drums of gas. Uneventful trip till we got back to Tahneta Pass. There were 40-50 swans on Leila Lake. We saw other groups also. The beaver in Weiner Lake have a large feed pile.

September 29, 1994—some clouds, light snow and snow south across the river. Unloaded, pumped off, gasoline drums into overhead tank. Denise Johnson Crisp visited a long time today. Later I installed one new plug in truck, tightened valve covers, cleaned PVC value, checked antifreeze level, added oil, adjusted head light, moved rear view mirrors, stored gas drums. Then raked some leaves and mulched some raspberry plants.

September 30, 1994—fog on lake, 19° to 39°. This morning gravel froze around here. Readied more things for winter. Removed screen door from arctic entry. A small dresser had sticky drawers. I put two coats varithane where it glides in the dresser frame. Built three fires in wood shop to help varithane dry. Sylvia fixed sandhill crane meat loaf for Harold and Rachel to eat with us this evening. We made ice cream (pumpkin pie flavor) for desert. The homemade hollow point .22's really work.

Saturday, October 1, 1994—partly cloudy, cloudy in evening, 12° to 36°. Quite a lot of lake had a skim of ice on it. Big beaver swims the lake. Some ducks are left. A family of swans—two adults and five young made a beautiful landing this evening. I visited Allen this morning. Went to gravel pit and target shot with rifle this afternoon. Allen, Roxanne and family were here for supper this evening.

Sunday, October 2, 1994—cloudy and snow to south, partly cloudy, cloudy in evening, 29° to 43°. Strong breeze west on lake all day. The swan family of seven left in mid morning. Another family of three are here this evening. Bob Rudbeck is working down by the lake so I didn't try for duck. Karn came over this evening for cold meds for Bob and a couple movies to watch. We mounted the frame and pump for the snow plow on the pickup. I've mislaid my ½ breaker bar.

Monday, October 3, 1994—cloudy and fog all around, 31° to 37°. Walked down to lake, no ducks to be shot from shore. Beaver has a feed pile in front of his lodge. Shot another squirrel. Cut some dead spruce near house, blocked it up and put it in basement. Polished some neck expanders. Sylvia went to Glennallen on senior van.

Tuesday, October 4, 1994—rain in night, cloudy, some clearing and a shower in afternoon. 34° to 44°. Beaut of an evening. Decided to put a little gear together and went to Oilwell Road—off Lake Louise Rd. My plan: hunt mallards on Mendeltna Creek. I shot two spruce hens on way in. Started up stream-lots of bear trails. So much so I turned and went down stream as the salmon spawning beds are up stream. I jumped three mallard drakes. Missed first shot and knocked the second drake down with my second shot. Got over there as fast as I could but I couldn't find him, even after looking far down stream. Perhaps I only tipped him over and he recovered and flew on. I don't like steel shot. In driving back up the road I had a another chance at a spruce hen and missed both shots. Checked out two gravel pits on way home for brass. Cleaned the birds and Sylvia fixed one for supper. Very good!! Walked down to lake twice today but no ducks to be shot from shore. Saw a muskrat swimming. Lots of beaver activity. Brought a paring knife to house that I had left on dock.

Wednesday, October 5, 1994—kind of windy all day, sunny sometimes, 26° to 45°. Didn't catch any ducks near enough to shore to shoot. Found my breaker bar. Picked up a couple things for winter. Did a few odd jobs. Sylvia went to Glennallen on senior van.

Thursday, October 6, 1994—nice day, clouding over in evening, 26° to 42°. Rudbecks stopped by on their way out of state for winter. Put the canoe in lake to hunt ducks. Some of them still can't actually fly. I knocked one down but it got away. I pulled the canoe up on the dock, probably for the winter. Later I got Sylvia to help and we put chicken wire around the raspberry plants. I cleaned the chimney, very little creosote in it.

Friday, October 7, 1994—very nice day till late afternoon and a cloud cover, 24° to 44°. Allen and Roxanne were here for breakfast with us. We cut the big dead tree near greenhouse and one other dead one. Then we cut two green trees that the wind tries to blow into the house. We cut and stacked the wood and gave some logs to Allen. We put some dry wood in basement.

Saturday, October 8, 1994—partly cloudy, beautiful, snow in evening, 29° to 43°.

Moved some more trimmings from trees via wheel barrow to a place to burn. Took shotgun for a walk, no ducks, but watched muskrats swimming. Checked Charlie T. storage shed. Did some reading and loafing.

Sunday, October 9, 1994—snow till noon, some sun in afternoon, 30° to 37° to 25°. I burned the tree trimming brush pile. Hooked up control cables on snow plow and the electric wires. Phoned Nadia. Washed the brass that I picked up earlier. De-primed 200 mil brass. Sylvia went to a baby shower for Roxanne. I heard Tundra swans calling as they were leaving Alaska, some flocks I could see. Some are above the clouds or out of my vision. This has been going on for a few days. Denny Eastman's dogs have been barking at something over on river bank for weeks. Maybe keeps some bears at bay.

Monday, October 10, 1994—mostly sunny, 16° to 32°. Denny E. came over and wanted me to ride along to Glennallen, so I did. Took varmint rifle along but saw no fur. Polishing brass in tumbler this afternoon and evening. Sylvia rode senior van.

Tuesday, October 11, 1994—cloudy, light snow, 20° to 29°. Denny and Joey E. were here for breakfast. The women watched movies. Denny and I went to Glennallen as he needed diesel fuel. Then we went to Lake Louise Road to Oil Well Road. We planned to hunt ducks on Mendeltna Creek. There was other hunter there. We hunted a little, no luck and no game. The Alaska Range was lighted with a neat light effect. After supper we saw a beaver crawl out on top of the ice near its lodge. Our lake is nearly frozen over.

Wednesday, October 12, 1994—mostly sunny, nice day, 20° to 38°. Sylvia rode van to Glennallen. I put 10 wheelbarrows of wood in basement and stacked it.

Thursday, October 13, 1994—mostly sunny. I called and ask Denny E to go with me to Klutina Lake. The 23-½ miles of road to the lake along the Klutina River is pretty rough. Denny shot three or four spruce hens. We saw some ducks with maybe two dozen mallards. There were some swans at the outlet of the lake. Some spectacular scenery and an enjoyable day to be remembered. Back at home Cal, Mary and Phillip Gilcrease were here for supper. After supper I froze some ice cream. Then Allen, Roxanne and family came up for a moment and had cake and ice cream with us.

Friday, October 14, 1994—cloudy all day,16° to 32°. Burned papers, repaired the ½ chair, moved the ash pile, started the snowgo, put a 40 watt light bulb in well but didn't turn it on. Got a few small things ready for winter. Gave Lucky some brass. Lee Dudley visited. Phoned Nadia. Muskrat is keeping a hole open on lake.

Saturday, October 15, 1994—cloudy all day, with snow in late afternoon, 24° to 30°. Hauled a load of junk and garbage to dump. Checked out two gravel pits. We put the canopy on truck then I decided to take tires and wheels off old truck, in case I want to mount new tires on the wheels. Dittman polling called to ask questions regarding oil companies.

Sunday, October 16, 1994—snowed, 10 to 12 inches of it—wet too, 26° to 34°. Plowed our snow. Shoveled off the camper and all the snow where I walk to garage. Got stuck a couple times and had to put chains on. I got snowgo fired up and took a broom down to Denny's plane and brushed the snow off it as Denny is in Anchorage. He did call and ask about weather. We see muskrats and beaver coming out on the ice of the lake.

Monday, October 17, 1994—partly cloudy, 18° to 33°. We had two to three more inches of snow last night. I plowed it. Then shoveled the walk and the woodshed roof. Used the uniformer on 75 primer pockets. Put some hunting gear away both away at the outside storage shed but here in the house also.

Tuesday, October 18, 1994—cloudy, partly cloudy, very little snow, 9° to 24°. During the night. I changed the oil and filter on the truck. Shoveled and raked the snow off the rest of the roofs. Sylvia fixed a supper and we took it down to Allen and Roxanne who are back home with a new daughter Samantha.

Wednesday, October 19, 1994—cloudy, very light snow-frost falling, 10° to 17°. Moved the gold concentrate and gold wheel etc into the basement. Shoveled snow, put up protection for log pile. Covered Suzuki. Sylvia went to Glennallen. The neighborhood kids ride their snowgos through our yard. They are having fun. We were invited down to Eastman's for dinner and cake and ice cream to celebrate Denny's birthday.

Thursday, October 20, 1994—cloudy, snow in afternoon and evening, 5° to 21°. Wrote a letter to Steve. Visited Denny. Took the huge "CAT" battery out of old pickup and got it into the basement and put the charger on it. I'll use it to power the water pump (12v.) and motor (12v) that runs the gold wheel. Bev phoned in the evening.

Friday, October 21, 1994—cloudy and four inches of snow, 5° to 21°. Raked the snow off arctic entry and the greenhouse. Took the truck license plate off the camper and put it back on the truck. Cleaned and oiled the shot gun and put a full choke for lead in the 10-gauge. Plowed our snow. Allen stopped for coffee.

Saturday, October 22, 1994—cloudy, flurries, one inch of snow, 4° to 15°. Cut and sanded more horn center pieces for Sylvia's "chokers." Made a tin deflector to aid the gold separation using the gold wheel. Shoveled snow up to and on foundation of the house.

Sunday, October 23, 1994—cloudy, foggy, 10° to 20°. Fog lifted some by evening. Hunted all around the place looking for fire clay. Found it on the second search. Billman wanted it for his fire brick job. He and Patti visited in afternoon and picked up the fire clay. Denny E. drove down to his plane again and checked the ice thickness in a few places.

Monday, October 24, 1994—cloudy, very little snow, 13° to 20°. Sylvia went to Glennallen. I started on basement and Sylvia worked at cleaning and straightening her craft stuff. Denny E. stopped by for a cup of tea. Kyle and David F. stopped by to get movies to watch. My brother, Jerry W. phoned.

Tuesday, October 25, 1994—foggy, till afternoon, then cloudy, 11° to 22°. Much overflow on our lake. I started putting the Nome Beach concentrates through the gold wheel. Doesn't look like the yield will be very good. Sylvia is sewing clothes to take to Minnesota.

Wednesday, October 26, 1994—partly cloudy. More overflow on our lake. Ran one bucket of concentrate through the micro sluice. This material I ran through the gold wheel yesterday. There wasn't much gold from either operation.

Thursday, October 27, 1994—cloudy and snow all afternoon, 13° to 24°. Put concentrate through the gold wheel till 5:00 PM. The 50-mesh concentrate has quite a bit of gold in it.

Friday, October 28, 1994—cloudy, some clouds down to 2800 feet. Worked with the "cons" again today. Cleaned the ashes out of barrel stove.

Saturday, October 29, 1994—clear cloudy, -1° to 20°. Took ashes and garbage to dump. Note: Made new targets to copy.

Sunday, October 30, 1994—clear, beautiful day, 4° to 15°. "Panned" concentrates most of day. Kids are playing and snowmobiling around the lake. Grosbeaks feeding in spruce trees.

Monday, October 31, 1994—ice fog, sunny in Glennallen, -10° to 10°. Went to get flu shots. Went to Halloween party at school house.

Tuesday, November 1, 1994—ice fog that lifted later in afternoon, -10° to 10°. Back hurts a lot today. Lifted the magnetite out of some more "cons." Went to dump and picked up the two pieces of light sheets of steel I had seen there previously. Went on to Johnson's to make some target copies, but the copier was too low on ink to make dark copies. Did some reading. Phoned the NECP help line to get eye care for seniors. Allen phoned to ask about hunting coyotes. Seems he has lost-misplaced his hunting regulations copy.

Wednesday, November 2, 1994–2° to 34°. We left home at 4:00 AM. The road and weather was good to Palmer. On the way home was rain, snow, fog. We had colonoscopy procedure done. I had an upper endoscopy done also. Sylvia picked up medicine from her Dr. Allen and David visited this evening.

Thursday, November 3, 1994–mostly cloudy, some wind, 18° to 32°. Visited Eastman's when I took movies and book back. Asked Allen to pick up our mail. Steve Mailly was there. Ate lunch with Allen and Steve. Sylvia and I went to Glennallen. Paid phone bill. Cashed our checks. Voted by absentee ballot. Started getting stretchers, snares and traps ready for Steve W. Will load some 30-30 for him.

Friday, November 4, 1994–mostly cloudy, some wind and a couple inches of snow in the night. Windy tonight, 15° to 22°. Plowed our snow, shoveled off camper. Packed up stretchers, a few traps, snares etc. to take to grandson Steve. Allen and Roxanne ask us down to supper this evening. The boy's needed a roof jack for a stove pipe from their stove in the "fort." I had one I gave them. Sylvia held baby Samantha a lot this evening.

Saturday, November 5, 1994–it's -10°. Finished getting ready to go to Minnesota. The road was icy in quite a few places on way to Anchorage. Shopped at Long Drug. Went to new sports equipment store down on Diamond and Old Seward. Got some socks there. Went to a restaurant to meet Chad Wilson, but he didn't come. We ate dinner and went to Griffiths. Visited and watched some TV, parked our truck there. Dennis E. and family were staying there also.

Sunday, November 6, 1994–snowing pretty hard with four inches on the ground. Dennis E. took us to airport. Our flight left on time. We had a short layover in Salt Lake City, our plane for MPLS/STP was on time. Bev, Darcy, Nadia and Chuck met us and took us to Bev's. We all visited and looked at pix. Tyler came home after a while. Asif dropped in.

Monday, November 7, 1994–sunny, strong breeze. Went for walk to a gun shop on Lyndale Avenue. Played some pass football after getting the ball off the apt. complex roof.

Tuesday, November 8, 1994–cloudy, went for two walks. Looked at books, crafts and a drugstore. Played soccer with Tyler when he got home from school.

Wednesday, November 9, 1994–warm, sunny day. Got up before daylight (6:00

AM) walked to dentist office for appointment to clean my teeth (7:00 AM) then back home laid around house all day. Read a little. Went with Sylvia and Bev while they did some shopping. Tyler and I played with the glider Sylvia and I got him. Then a little soccer. Watched a movie then a good supper.

Thursday, November 10, 1994—sunny and warm, -50s. Tyler and I walked down Lyndale to the gun, pawn shop—looked at the guns and walked back. Played some soccer. Vanessa and Darcy stayed from home school. The kids played at building and tearing down domino castles. Theresa came and had supper with us. Phoned grandson Steve Wilkins, he got an 8-point white tail deer last Saturday—big day for him. Phoned Billmans, got news from there. His rifle is .300 H & H.

Friday, November 11, 1994—cloudy and windy, 50°. Went to grocery store. Read newspaper. Later went to Kinko's and made some copies of a prairie dog target. Girls came home from school first, then Tyler. Bev, Sylvia and two girls went to grocery store. Tyler and I played with the dominos. Bev fixed supper and we went to Asif's apartment and watched a Clint Eastwood movie. Then visited with Vanessa and read a little.

Saturday, November 12, 1994—cloudy, 50°. Sylvia, Tyler, Darcy, Vanessa went to nearby Hub shopping center in afternoon. Bev slept 'til mid afternoon. Except for taking garbage out, I stayed in all day. Three boys visited the girls late afternoon.

Sunday, November 13, 1994—rain in night, cloudy and some wind today, 50s. Went for four walks. Kids went to church Bev slept. One walk was with Tyler to K-Mart. Some crows around today.

Monday, November 14, 1994—cloudy, then mostly sunny, high 40s. Nadia came over to Bev's and took Sylvia and me over to Laura's. Later, after Nadia left, we went with Laura to her place of employment and then to a bank, then to a bookstore. Back at her place we played with great granddaughter Brittany. Laura served a very good roast beef dinner. We watched a movie afterward.

Tuesday, November 15, 1994—sunny, 50s. Played games with Brittany in the morning. Went to a small nature program with Brittany in afternoon. Laura's boyfriend, Brad and Nadia and Chuck were here for supper. Then we had a nice visit afterward. Called Paul's that we were coming up tomorrow. Will try to call Allen Farmer in Alaska.

Wednesday, November 16, 1994—frost this morning, 40s today. Ate breakfast. Laura drove us to Staples. Brittney got sick on the way. We had lunch in Motley. Visited with Paul for awhile. Britt really liked playing with the turtle.

Then Steve came home from school. I gave him some 30-30 cartridges, fur stretchers, snares and traps. Steve showed us the horns of his deer, also some pix. We had a good supper and watched movies. Ruth's brother Joe spent the evening here.

Thursday, November 17, 1994—cloudy, light rain in afternoon. Watched movies in morning. Steve made an appointment to shoot sporting clays. We drove out there for a 1:00 PM shoot. Steve shot a 20 and I shot 19. They also have pheasant and Chukar. We had a good time even if the shotgun would jam. Finally had to shoot singles only. Then we drove over to a gunsmith and inquired about a scope ring clamp. Then back to Staples to a chicken supper. Steve started cleaning the shot gun right away. Sylvia gave Ruth and Steve some Indian choker necklaces.

Friday, November 18, 1994—freezing, cloudy, strong winds. Light snow blowing around. Trash in air. Paul, Steve and I went to Coast to Coast stores for a scope part for Steve. No luck then to pawn shop to look at rifles. Then to Vern Drake Gunsmith. Still no luck. Back at Paul's. Scott Rollins phoned. Watched some good movies.

Saturday, November 19, 1994—freezing, sunny, cloudy. Watched TV till noon. Then we went to shooting range. Steve shot 20 clay pigeons. His dad ran the trap thrower. Then they shot .22 at target. Remington game load .22's with poor ignition, accuracy was bad. Paul and I picked up some brass. Visited with a shooter from Staples with a son (teacher) in Delta Jct. AK. Read some magazines and watched some movies on TV. Steve worked at trap preparation all evening.

Sunday, November 20, 1994—cloudy and light rain. Did lots of reading and visiting. Phoned Lee at his Dad Larry's. Larry brought Lee over to visit and came and got Lee after supper. Virginia phoned about our plans.

Monday, November 21, 1994—mostly cloudy, freezing and windy. We went to Harold and Loraine Hanson's. Harold's health isn't good. Nice visit and meal Steve was with us. Back to Paul's, Sylvia and I got the pizza and pop for supper. Then we went to Jigg's place to see Steve's fox and mink. Took pix, then back to Paul's and watch movies.

Tuesday, November 22, 1994—frozen again this morning, mostly sunny today, some breezes. Went to Allen, Lillian, Scott, Darlene and Andy Rollins'. Visited and had lunch. Allen went to Dr. Sylvia visited with Lillian and Scott, me and Steve went to gun dealers and a gunsmith looking for a scope ring bolt for Steve and some things I needed. Steve got his bolt. Couldn't find what I wanted. Supper with Rollins' then back to Paul's and phoned a couple of Rudbeck boys.

I stopped at the shooting range at Motley and we picked up some brass.

Wednesday, November 23, 1994—frost, sunny nice day. We went to Jim and Arlene R. and had a good breakfast and visit with them. Then to B & K Rudbeck and picked up caribou mount. Steve with us again today.

Thursday, November 24, 1994—beautiful, sunny day. We got up early. Paul, Ruth, Steve, Sylvia and I went to Minneapolis. Steve saw all the muskrat houses and geese both flying and sitting on lake along side the highway. I saw some crows and two large owls. Sylvia and I treated everyone to Thanksgiving dinner at Old Country Buffet. It was a nice dinner. Then Nadia and Chuck drove us to their place. It is nice and quiet here.

Friday, November 25, 1994—frost, then a little warmer, sunny. Showered. Sylvia did some laundry. Chuck went to Northfield to see a friend. We went with Nadia for a little shopping.

Saturday, November 26, 1994—frost, beautiful day, some breeze. We went to a gun show at Hastings. I couldn't decide on a rifle to buy. After Chuck and I went for a walk.

Sunday, November 27, 1994—snow and windy all day. Shoveled a little snow. Aborted the trip to Hastings, Burger Bros and picking up Theresa. Picked up a Sunday paper. Heard crows and saw one. Sylvia slept a lot today. She phoned Beverly. Had to let Theresa know we wouldn't be picking her up. Laura phoned several times. Chuck cooked a ham, scalloped potatoes, baked bean dinner.

Monday, November 28, 1994—cloudy. Shoveled snow. Nadia and Sylvia went to Theresa's place and brought her over here at Nadia's to visit for a few day's. Met Chuck and Nadia's landlord Joe. The women went grocery shopping. Chuck and I went to Burger Bros. Sporting Goods and looked at rifles and walked around the store looking at all the "goodies."

Tuesday, November 29, 1994—mostly sunny, 17° to 28°. In the afternoon, Nadia, Theresa, Sylvia and I went to Stillwater and searched for books at the antiquarian book store. I saw two books that I was interested in years ago. I didn't get them. Back at Nadia's, Laura and Brittany came to visit and were here for chicken thighs Chuck baked for our supper. Nadia had to work a couple of hours. Chuck took Theresa over to her place and Laura and Brittany went home early - work day tomorrow.

Wednesday, November 30, 1994—mostly sunny, 11° to 30°. Saw a gray squirrel and a few crows flew by. Did a little reading and packaged the .22 cartridges Chuck gave me. Nadia and Sylvia went to a craft shop and left some of Sylvia's necklaces. Chuck had a couple errands. Nadia went to work for a few hours.

Thursday, December 1, 1994—sunny, 47°. Nadia and Sylvia went to Stillwater. Chuck and I shoveled the big snow berm over the edge into the swamp. Later in afternoon Chuck and I went for a hike on a trail. We aborted the hike when his shoe and sock gave problems. Some deer and mink tracks and a few crows.

Friday, December 2, 1994—warm, more snow melted. Darcy was sick yesterday through today, is getting better. Nadia and Chuck went to his brothers and found my slide projector in storage there. Nadia and Sylvia did some shopping and picked up my slides at Theresa's. Chuck and I went to Wipaire. He sold a labeling machine. We got to see some floats that cost $180,000 that fit a Caavan I Cessna. Then we went to see the 3M Jet fleet in an old World War II Hanger. A car hit 10 point buck near Nadia's driveway.

Saturday, December 3, 1994—above freezing and cloudy. About 11:00 AM Nadia took Sylvia and me over to Bev's. Visiting with Vanessa, Darcy, and Tyler. Went with Asif to look at a Bronco 4 x 4 then back to Bev's for a good steak supper. Asif and I went after movies and some shopping for him. I looked for books at book store in afternoon.

Sunday, December 4, 1994—cloudy and melting, 32° Plus. Went to K-Mart and got a Sunday paper. Read for a while. The kids went to church and then to Nancy's. Later they played a game. Bev fixed tacos. Asif and I went to get a movie. I shoveled leaves and trash from around the dumpsters for Beverly.

Monday, December 5, 1994—froze during the night. Bev and family decide we will all go to "Mall of America." Missed the first bus. Cold and windy waiting for next one. Spent an hour at mall then came back home so Vanessa could get ready for work.

Tuesday, December 6, 1994—up early and Nadia took us to airport and flew to Anchorage. Shoveled snow off our truck, started it and went to Costco's and had 4 new tires put on. Got a bite to eat, gas for truck and back to Griffith's and stayed the night.

Wednesday, December 7, 1994—cold, up early and off to Palmer's Hospital for Sylvia's endoscopy exam. Some grocery shopping, got home 3:30 PM. Good trip and unpacked. Everything fine, glad to be home and eating a boo burger.

Thursday, December 8, 1994—sunny, beautiful sunrise, cloudy. -36° to -16°. Got caught up on correspondence. Tom Huddleston visited in afternoon. Phoned Billman, he and Lou Butera went through the ice on Crosswind Lake near Dan's cabin. Dan and a couple friends got the snowgo out a few days later.

Friday, December 9, 1994—mostly sunny, -26° to -11°. Put plow on truck and plowed our snow and pushed it back. Shoveled some snow. Sylvia tried to pump water, no luck. So I started snowgo and tried to get to well. Got stuck. Shoveled machine out and manhandled it back around and got it back up on the road. Walked down to the well. I had forgotten to turn the light on in the well when we went to Minn. So it is frozen over. Turned on the light and hope that will thaw it out in a few days. Got snowgo back up the hill and parked and covered up. We went to Odden's for supper. Jim's folks Les and Lois are there visiting. They are very nice people.

Saturday, December 10, 1994—mostly cloudy, -26° to -10°. School teacher (Bruce?) and Jan phoned up and ask to borrow my water hauling tank. He and his wife came over and visited quite a while. Later Allen and David stopped by. Then we all went out and loaded the water tank in my truck, went down to Allen's and he pumped water in it. The Bruce went to Eastman's where Bruce and Jan are house-sitting to unload the water. We got everything set up then the water pipes blew apart. So we brought the water back to our place and dumped it. Allen asked me to ride along to Eureka. He cut a Christmas tree along the way, then got spark plugs for his snowgos and treated me to coffee and pie.

Sunday, December 11, 1994—mostly cloudy, -19° to -5°. Read a lot. Bruce brought over a movie for us to watch. Got into a discussion of gun control, gold and life in the villages.

Monday, December 12, 1994—foggy, then cloudy, -10° to 23°. Sylvia went to Glennallen on senior van. I scooped the snow off the camper and "raked" the snow off the wood shop roof. New neighbor Jan brought over some Christmas cookies. I went to Johnson's at Mendeltna and did some copying of snowshoe plans, a crow target and assembly of Steve Wilkins' deer rifle.

Tuesday, December 13, 1994—much the same.

Wednesday, December 14, 1994—cloudy, some ice crystals fell. Sylvia went to Glennallen on senior van. I went to Odden's and ordered a rifle etc. After supper we went down to Allen and Roxanne's to visit. I pulled snow off the roof of arctic entry and greenhouse.

Thursday, December 15, 1994—cloudy, some ice fog, 7° to 13°. Wrote some letters. Shoveled snow off more roofs. Sylvia had Oddens and his folks, Les and Lois for a spaghetti supper.

Friday, December 16, 1994—cloudy, light snow, clear and bright moon in evening, -2° to 7°. Sylvia went to a shower for Lauri (W) and baby Swaby. I went to Tom Huddleston's for coffee. Met Tom's new neighbor, Chris, who lives in Rhynell's apartment across the road. I feel sick most of night and today.

Saturday, December 17, 1994—foggy, beaut moonlight, fog sometimes and cloudy, -1° to 9°. Sylvia went to a ladies dress up Xmas party at KROA. I read. Early evening. I hauled a load of water for Bruce White, school teacher. Jim O., Lester, and Kari came over to borrow dovetail machine instructions.

Sunday, December 18, 1994—mostly cloudy, 2° to 10°. We visited Lucky and Mary B. Tom H. brought my Pepto Bismol over. Allen, Roxanne and family visited in evening.

Monday, December 19, 1994—cloudy, 2° all day. Sylvia got ready to got to Glennallen and the senior Christmas party and dinner. Then got suddenly sick to her stomach. I have sinus and very sore throat and feel queasy in my stomach.

Tuesday, December 20, 1994—cloudy, sunny and ice crystals falling, -8° to 2°. Sylvia feels better. Did dish's and baked Christmas cookies. Bruce and Jan came over to borrow a ladder. I'm still sick but some better.

Wednesday, December 21, 1994—cloudy, light snow -7° to 13°. I am sick with this bad crud. Sylvia went to Glennallen on senior van. She did some groceries shopping there. Medicine came today. Saw two moose east of our place ¼ mile browsing.

Thursday, December 22, 1994—cloudy, fog, a little snow, 5° to 19° Felt pretty sick most all day. Bruce and Jan brought the ladder back and had coffee and exchanged baked goodies. Later Allen brought "Rocky" (the other teacher's husband) over. They needed some stuff to repair a snowgo.

Friday, December 23, 1994—fog, cloudy, sun, cloudy, 0° to 18°. A little snow and some wind last night. Didn't do much all day. Tom Huddleston stopped by, Gillcreases also. Sylvia gave them a tray of goodies. Gillcreases left a tray with us. Nadia phoned Christmas greetings. The Farmer family took Sylvia to KROA for a Christmas party.

Saturday, December 24, 1994—clear, below zero all day, -15° to 5°. Bruce was over with a movie and visited a while. Sylvia visited with Sandy with goodies in hand. Bev phoned twice and Darcy's grad picture came. We phoned Theresa— Lee was there.

Sunday, December 25, 1994—cloudy and some fog, -16° to -8°. We went to Billman's at Point of View Lodge in afternoon. Trapper Bob was there. Later we ate Christmas dinner there. Jason and friend, Lisa, Ann? were there. Later the Odden clan, Jim's, John's, Rod's family and Les and Lois came and made ice cream and music.

Monday, December 26, 1994—clear and cold, -32° to -28°. We took trays of goodies to Lucky, Mary and Roxanne and Allen. Mary G and family were at Farmers. I visited Ed Farmer.

Tuesday, December 27, 1994—mostly clear and some fog. Visited the Oddens. They have 16 guests. Jim had my order. Visited Huddelstons also for a while.

Wednesday, December 28, 1994—clear, snowy looking in evening, -18° to -10°. Tried to help Dana with the steamer, no luck. Sylvia went to Glennallen. Jackie B and Dave, Jamie brought Ray, Nancy, & Kim Lawrence, now from Georgia, to visit and reminisce. They've been outside for 11 years.

Thursday, December 29, 1994—cloudy, foggy, light snow, -17° to 12°. Granddaughter, Laura B. phoned us from Minnesota at 6:00 AM our time. Then Allen and Roxanne asked us down to breakfast. Dana asked me to find out if "Rocky" has thawed steam boiler. Then visited Cal, Mary and Phillip Gilcrease.

Friday, December 30, 1994—sunny, some fog to south, 6° to 14°. Sure have lots of aches and pains. Looked at wolf traps today. Read, and loaded five cartridges.

Saturday, December 31, 1994—partly sunny, some low cloudy and ice fog around, 10° to 17°. Bruce W. brought another movie over. We loafed all day. Took showers. Phoned the Smayda family.

View of Scoter Lake, the Nelchina River bluffs, and mountains in the distance, from Norman and Sylvia's oversized picture window.

1995–Hunting at Delta farming project

Sunday, January 1, 1995—mostly a nice day, some ice fog on each side of us, -5° to 2°. The grosbeaks fed in spruce trees. Sandy brought the calendar over. Fresh snowgo tracks on lake.

Monday, January 2, 1995—sunny, cloudy, -8° to 7° Allen was here to breakfast. Sylvia made bread, raisin bread and baked a lemon pie. Cooked a caribou roast and the goodies to go with it and ask Allen Roxanne and family to have supper with us. We watched a movie afterwards. Beverly phoned to talk things over with us.

Tuesday, January 3, 1995—partly cloudy, some fog, 2° to 17°. We left for Wasilla early. Couple things to do in Palmer then to Dr Manelick, then to Dr. Kase. He evaluated my right shoulder. Then to Anchorage and got an eye exam. Ordered glasses at Costco. We grocery shopped at Costco. Ate at Royal Fork and drove home in the dark on icy roads. Beverly, Vanessa, Tyler, and Darcy sent us a Christmas package.

Wednesday, January 4, 1995—mostly sunny, 1° to 9°. Sent off some letters. Went to Jim O's for supper with Mary and Kari also. Jims wants to go caribou hunting tomorrow.

Thursday, January 5, 1995—mostly sunny, -4° to 5°. Went to Jim O's early and we went to Glennallen. Jim had a couple errands and we got our fed hunt permits. Then we went to the West Fork Trailhead. There unloaded his snowgo and sled and went west on trail a few miles looking for caribou. Saw some tracks. This trail is part of the Copper Basin dog race trail. No luck hunting. Later on way home I spotted a beautiful red fox in the ditch. Jim tried for it, but the scope cover got in the way. More errands in Glennallen then on home.

Friday, January 6, 1995—sunny, with fog all morning and again in evening, -12° to 0°. We went to Gilcreases's to return movies. Looked for caribou on the trip. I checked out a place to trap wolves. Decided to not trap there now.

Saturday, January 7, 1995—sunny, -13° to -6°. Phoned Beverly. Talked to Vanessa and then to Tyler. Didn't do anything today. Visited Allen and Roxanne a little bit. Bruce White stopped by. Gave him access to trapping information for school kids.

Sunday, January 8, 1995—sunny, some fog across the river, -18° to -6°. Chickadees and grosbeaks looking for food in the trees and shaking frost off boughs. Darcy phoned in evening.

Monday, January 9, 1995—foggy all day, -22° to -11° We went to Glennallen on senior van. Paid phone bill, cashed checks and did shopping. Anchorage news: Moose stomps man to death.

Tuesday, January 10, 1995—partly cloudy, cloudy, clear, -22° to -13°. More moon every night. Checked fuel oil and ordered same. Put up a bird feeder. Did a gun oil cold test. Dr. Kase phoned. Harold and Rachel ask us to supper. Harold told hunting stories after supper.

Wednesday, January 11,1995—mostly sunny, fog in sight, -25° to -10°. Sylvia went to Glennallen. I brought a dozen large pieces of fire wood in basement. Phoned Dr. and Oxford minerals. Magpies and camp robbers use the feeder.

Thursday, January 12, 1995—mostly sunny, some fog, sun dogs, -22° to -12°. Went to Dinty Bush's (Leona & Doug) gave them some used tires and met Daryl Douthat, trapper from Loon Lake. Then on over to Billman's and visited for a while. Back home just in time for supper. Tom Huddleston and his kids here for supper. Before we were done eating, Denny, Joie, Aaron, Emmy Eastman drove in from their trip to Minnesota. A little later Allen, Roxanne, Ellie and Samantha dropped in. Eastmans will stay overnight. Bruce White stopped to see Eastmans.

Friday, January 13, 1995—partly cloudy, -24° to -10°. Company here till after 12:00 PM. Then we went at mid afternoon with Allen and Roxanne to Glacier View School to watch the Nelchina school kids play a hockey game with the hockey team there. Three wolves killed by a hunter near Porcupine Lake, according to Jim Fimple, and one more killed the next day.

Saturday, January 14, 1995—sunny, -25° to -15°. Visited Allen and got my Locktite back for a job here. We are burning wood to extend fuel oil supplies till next delivery. I mounted the bullet luber on a board and made some bullet boxes. Cal and Phillip stopped by for rabbit cages we gave them. Robbie and Coyote came over to borrow movies.

Sunday, January 15, 1995—cloudy and fog nearby, -26° to -20°. Lubed some cast bullets today.

Monday, January 16, 1995—cloudy and some ice fog all day, -25° to -10°. Went for a walk, did some exercises. Lubed more cast bullets.

Tuesday, January 17, 1995—sunny and cloudy, full moon, -10° to 2°. We left at 10:00 AM. Went to Palmer and had right shoulder examined (X-ray, dye) result, torn rotator cuff. Expect to operate Jan 27th. Saw a few moose on way to town. Bev phoned in evening.

Wednesday, January 18, 1995—warmed up thru the night, 10° to 12° in afternoon, snowed 2". Ordered medication from AARP. Walked down to Allen's - no one home. Then back home, shoveled a little snow. Battery on truck is low. Tom H. plowed our lane. Sylvia baked a new prune-apricot recipe.

Thursday, January 19, 1995—cloudy, foggy, some snow, 4° to 10°. I have the trots today. Wrote lots of letters. Allen visited in afternoon.

Friday, January 20, 1995—cloudy and snowed 5". -5° to 20°. I went for a walk to Eastman's. His new water pump doesn't work. He burned the instructions for it. Daryl Douthat visited a couple hours. He is interested in my trap line. I plowed our snow. We went with Farmers to another hockey game at Glacier View School to KROA at Mendeltna for pizza after the game.

Saturday, January 21, 1995—cloudy and snow in Palmer-Anchorage, 10° to 28°. I plowed our snow then rode with Denny E. to Wasilla. There we attended a gun show. Enjoyed that. I didn't buy anything. Then on to Long Drug Anchorage where I left the camera to be fixed. Denny had to pickup some airline tickets, then back home.

Sunday, January 22, 1995—mostly cloudy and snow this evening, 10° to 28°. Nadia phoned that Ruth is in hospital in St. Cloud. I cleaned snow off roof. Plowed some snow. We saw a hairy woodpecker today. Jim O. borrowed our water tank and we pumped it full for him. Jim and Kari were here for supper.

Monday, January 23, 1995—cloudy, some sun, -15° to 5°. Sylvia put food out for the birds. Red polls, grosbeaks, 2 kinds chickadees, camp robbers, we see a raven or so every day. I cleaned snow off a bunch of roofs. Chuck Zimbicki visited for a while in afternoon. Started new method of reloading record keeping.

Tuesday, January 24, 1995—cloudy, some sunny, -4° to 7°. Cleaned off more roofs. Allen stopped by and we had coffee and cookies. Jim and Kari stopped in and more coffee and cookies. Bev phoned about things, Ruth and all. We phoned Staples and learned Ruth had been operated on (angioplasty), seems to be ok. Moved a book shelf at reloading area. I am still drying concentrates from Nome Beach.

Wednesday, January 25, 1995—cloudy and sunny afternoon, -15° to -8°. I pulverized the Cottonwood Creek sample with a motor and pedestal. Screened it through a 30 mesh. Sylvia went to Glennallen. The birds sure flock in when she puts out food for them. The kids are practicing their hockey game. We watch them from up here, skating on their expanded to full size hockey rink.

Thursday, January 26, 1995—clear with ice fog, -25° to -18° to -28°. Plowed a little snow, took garbage to dump. Stopped at both Tom H. and Jim O. places for coffee. Measured fuel oil again.

Friday, January 27, 1995—it's -35°, Allen drove us to Palmer Hospital. Dr. Kase did a right shoulder rotator cuff repair on me. Good nurse, "Judy".

Saturday, January 28, 1995—I developed diarrhea, chills, fever of 103.8. Hospital trying to find problem. I'm in pain killer fog most of time.

Sunday, January 29, 1995—hospital used temp control machine to get temp down. Nurse Bev "froze," 38° my buns, then heated the pad way too hot.

Monday, January 30, 1995—Dr. Manelick is back and took over my treatment. Medication change, diet change etc.

Tuesday, January 31, 1995—sick, sick, diarrhea.

Wednesday, February 1, 1995—four nurses brought in a small cake and sang "Happy Birthday." So very thoughtful of them. I'm still sick, weak and body is water logged.

Thursday, February 2, 1995—Allen and Roxanne brought Sylvia and I home. How great it is. Still sick.

Friday, February 3, 1995—temp is right at 0° I'm feeling better but still sick. Ed Farmer visited.

Saturday, February 4, 1995—0° Allen visited couple minutes. Still sick. Still on this B.R.A.T. diet. Ugh.

Sunday, February 5, 1995—mostly sunny, -10° to 16°. Better diet. Tore a muscle in my left shoulder getting out of bed. Very painful all night and day. Cal and Mary G, Allen, Kyle and David visited. We watched a wolf trapping movie and talked gold mining.

Monday, February 6, 1995—mostly sunny, some breeze, cloudy evening, 10° to 30°. Sylvia went to Glennallen. Allen visited a couple hours. Kids practiced hockey.

Tuesday, February 7, 1995—sunny, cloudy afternoon, 10° to 30°. Bart Bartley brought some movies over and visited 3-4 hrs. Sure helped pass the day. Still get the scoots every time I eat.

Wednesday, February 8, 1995—mostly sunny, 3" of snow during the night, 20° to 30°. Sylvia went to Glennallen. Allen visited in afternoon. I gave him some brass and bullets. Then Tom H. plowed our snow and had coffee and some of Sylvia's candy. Maillys brought some reading material and a plate of cookies.

Thursday, February 9, 1995—ice fog here all day, 10° to 20°. Allen drove us to Palmer and Wasilla. Cloudy and rain there. Went to two doctor appointments. Did some shopping, had a bite to eat. Saw a few moose along the highway.

Friday, February 10, 1995—snow, foggy, partly cloudy, cloudy, 20° to 30°. Muscle in left shoulder very sore and very little sleep. Read and did my exercises. Sylvia had a long nap. Sylvia went with Odden's to Glacier View School and the hockey game.

Saturday, February 11, 1995—some fog in the distance, mostly sunny, beaut of a day, 2° to 21°. Allen and Kyle borrowed a rope. Odden family was here for supper.

Sunday, February 12, 1995—cloudy and snow late afternoon and evening, 10° to 21°. Watch TV, exercises, and read a little.

Monday, February 13, 1995—snow (4" in the night), cloudy, sunny, partly cloudy, 10° to 20°. Jim O. came over to haul water. Our water line is frozen. He checked the well bulb, has it thawing. Denny E. had tea with us.

Tuesday, February 14, 1995—clear and sunny, some breeze from west, -10° to 15°. Watched movies and read. Allen visited in morning. Odden came over and plowed some snow and welded some cracked places on his plow. Tom H. brought a magazine and a couple tapes and had cake with us. The last snow is causing "stars" to show up in the ice on the lake.

Wednesday, February 15, 1995—sunny, -8° to 9°. Sylvia went to Glennallen. Allen and Denny hauled water and filled our water tanks. Nice of them!! My left shoulder still very sore. Phoned two places that have the rifles I want.

Thursday, February 16, 1995—mostly sunny, cloudy evening, -22° to -1°. Read and did exercises. Smashed some cans. Took letters to mail box, got mail when it came. Watched TV.

Friday, February 17, 1995—some snow early morning, sunny later, -20° to 4°. Read, watched TV. Tom H. needed some rivets. David F and Tahoue borrowed a movie. Jim phoned. He has ordered my rifle.

Saturday, February 18, 1995—sunny, ice fog, breeze from west, -8° to -1°. Exercises, reading and TV again today. Allen F. visited. Tom H. brought a couple movies back. Granddaughter Laura phoned. She cut a finger. Will change jobs soon.

Sunday, February 19, 1995—sunny, snowy, clouds moved in just at dark, -28° to -6°. I've felt sick all day. Huddelstons had a party in afternoon and Tom came and got us so we could be there. Neighborhood friends and relatives. Tom borrowed three movies when he brought us home.

Monday, February 20, 1995—some snow, sunny, cloudy, and snowy, -20° to 3°. A downy woodpecker and a couple hairy woodpeckers were at the bird feeder while Ed Farmer was visiting us. Did some reading and later Chuck Z. and Tom H. with Charlie and Kindra visited for awhile. Called Bev's place and got to talk to Darcy and Vanessa.

Tuesday, February 21, 1995—sunny, -8° to 14°. Allen visited at noon. Sylvia was sick last night, but better today.

Wednesday, February 22, 1995—sunny, -10° to 13°. Lots of over flow showing up on our lake. Sylvia went to Glennallen. Denny E. took us to Odden's, Mary had fixed a good salmon loaf supper. Nice visit afterward. New rifle came today.

Thursday, February 23, 1995—sunny, some breeze, -22° to 2°. Allen stopped to get some antifreeze. Cal and Mary brought a movie back and loaned us one. Tom H. stopped in and left off some movies he had borrowed. Bev phoned.

Friday, February 24, 1995—sunny, -19° to 4°. Denny packed his air strip on our lake with his snowgo. We got another package of videos from Nadia. Sylvia vacuumed the house. I read a lot and did my exercises. I am increasing them in number every day. There were lots of birds at the feeder today. We think the birds go from feeder to feeder along the ridge. Probably making out like bandits. Harold Dimmick called. Their oldest daughter died.

Saturday, February 25, 1995—sunny, -26° to -1°. Slept poorly last night. I overdid the exercises yesterday. Sam Weaver visited this morning and we witnessed his AK Dividend application. Bartley came to get a 1/2" bolt he needed. Allen visited a little while.

Sunday, February 26, 1995—cloudy, sunny, cloudy, -18° to 7°. Didn't sleep good last night. Took a nap today. Read a lot. Smashed some cans. Put two wolf traps back in trap shed. Allen visited—David came to tell him to come back home. Robbie brought a couple movies back.

Monday, February 27, 1995—sunny, light, thin, cloudy later, 0° to 14°. Sylvia went to Glennallen. I visited Ed and picked up the mail on way back home. Read some and did my exercises. Stoned a rough place on bolt of new rifle. Tested the trigger pull on it also. Allen visited for a while in afternoon. David drove his snowgo up and down airstrip (packing it) on the lake. Denny was out flying his plane late in afternoon.

Tuesday, February 28, 1995—sunny, 2° to 17°. Allen came and got us for steak, biscuits and gravy at their place. Denny was out flying his plane. Later he and Ed unloaded 325 gal of water in our tanks.

Wednesday, March 1, 1995—cloudy all day.,2° to 18°. Did my exercises and some reading. Some snow in evening. Sylvia has seeds started.

Thursday, March 2, 1995—sunny, a nice sunrise and a small river of fog glowing east from Nelchina Glacier, 3° to 29°. Sylvia put a perm in her hair. I took a shower and read some. Allen visited for a while in afternoon. Quite a bit of snow slid off the north side of the greenhouse.

Friday, March 3, 1995—sunny, beautiful sun rise and another river of fog, -3° to 28°. Shoveled a little snow. Did exercises. Wrote Shilen (rifle company).

Saturday, March 4, 1995—sunny, some fog off the two glaciers to south, -6° to 25°. Slept a lot today. Did exercises. Allen borrowed air tank. Mary O. came and got us to have supper with her and Kari.

Sunday, March 5, 1995—sunny, cloudy, some snow mostly south of river, -5° to 25°. Pretty bored today. Harold and Rachel were here to supper and we had a nice visit with them. We phoned Lee to wish him happy birthday.

Monday, March 6, 1995—sunny, -5° to 25°. Denny went flying today, right after I visited him this morning. Sylvia went to Glennallen. I did my exercises.

Tuesday, March 7, 1995—sunny, -11° to 24°. Allen's stove smoke drifted east in two layers this morning. A canine left tracks on our lake last night. Allen and Cal had coffee and rhubarb upside down cake with us. Dan B. phone in evening.

Wednesday, March 8, 1995—sunny, -9° to 27°. Lots of birds using the feeder. Sylvia went to Glennallen. I visited Ed and Sandy. Sylvia went over later. Harold and Rachel brought our repaired camera from Long Drug in Anchorage.

Thursday, March 9, 1995—clear, 4° to 20°. We went with Kim H. to Palmer, Wasilla. Roxanne, Samantha, Sylvia and I. Mary C. met her daughter in Palmer. The rest of us did some shopping and I went to doctor and the therapist who will direct the rebuilding of my shoulder. Saw a red fox 1-½ mile west of Eureka.

Friday, March 10, 1995—cloudy, snow in the air and windy sometimes, -18° to 12°. Rigged up the ropes and pulleys to stretch the soft tissue of my shoulder. Rudbecks phoned us in afternoon. Nadia sent three tapes and a nice letter.

Saturday, March 11, 1995—sunny, -22° to 3°. Took a birthday balloon down to Ellie Farmer, visited awhile. The exercises for my shoulder take a lot of time. Denny E. visited and had tea. I rode with Allen, Cal, Phillip and Kyle to Glennallen Church and a wild game feed and three speakers.

Sunday, March 12, 1995—cloudy and snowy late evening, -27° to -5°. Mary O. came and picked us up about 1:00 PM and took us to Billmans at Lake Louise. We stayed till about 5:30 PM.

Monday, March 13, 1995—1-1/2" Snow, snowy then clearing, -14° to -7°. Mary O brought some packages over and Sylvia took them with her when she went to Glennallen today and mailed them for Mary.

Tuesday, March 14, 1995—sunny, some snow later, -34° to -10°. Read some. Allen visited a while in afternoon. Sylvia put out bird food. They sure like it when it's this cold. A sparrow owl flew into some of the trees in front of the house while Allen was here. Lorraine Hanson called, Harold talked a little. He has had more heart trouble.

Wednesday, March 15, 1995—cloudy, then snow in afternoon, -34° to -9°. I went with Allen and Roxanne to KROA for coffee. Visited with Jeff Routt. Put two small loads of wood in basement. Sylvia went to Glennallen. Offered to trade Chuck Z Honda pump for Suzuki repair.

Thursday, March 16, 1995—snow most of night and all day—about 16 inches of it, -3° to 24°. Tom Huddleston plowed our snow. Mary O. and Kari stopped in after school to visit.

Friday, March 17, 1995—sunny, with a few light snow showers, some breeze, 18° to 38°. Allen had breakfast with us. He fired up Ed's D6 and pushed our snow back as well as a lot of snow in the neighborhood. David Farmer came over and shoveled the snow off our camper. I pulled some snow off garage and greenhouse roof.

Saturday, March 18, 1995—sunny, 3° to 27°. Shoulder is sore today. I removed a scope and bases from the savage, replaced bases with weaver bases. In afternoon Tom Huddleston plowed some snow and had cake and ice cream. Then Allen and Denny brought water and unloaded it. Had cake and ice cream and a "bull" session. Got the first mail in three days. I shoveled out Allen's mail box (and ours). Lots of birds at the feeder. A squirrel showed up today.

Sunday, March 19, 1995—sunny, -12° to 23° Sore and aching all over. Read some today. Sylvia phoned Fran. Squirrel is back again today. Allen dragged Denny's airstrip on the lake.

Monday, March 20, 1995—cloudy, windy, and snow in evening, -8° to 18°. Lincoln brought meals. Bruce White (teacher) stopped by. Little birds are on a feeding frenzy. Weather related?

Tuesday, March 21, 1995—mostly sunny, cloudy in evening, -4° to 12°. Read Ted's book again. Ran snowgo, did exercises. Phoned Chad. Granddaughter Laura phoned.

Wednesday, March 22, 1995—sunny, -21° to 2°. Allen visited in morning. He uncovered our water line and the direct sun light thawed it out and Sylvia pumped water. She went to Glennallen also. Allen, Roxanne, Ellie, Sammi and Anne visited in afternoon. We went to a supper at Mary O. Billmans and Kurt were there. Sent order to Sinclair.

Thursday, March 23, 1995—sunny and some breeze in open, -27° to 2°. Did exercises. Walked down to Allen's. Picked up mail on way home. Looked up some lumber for Allen. Cal and Mary G. visited a while. Sylvia watched a movie. I cleaned some brass for Dan B. Allen drove snowgo up for the piece of lumber. Then David drove the van here. Kyle with him and had cocoa with us. Denny E. came over to repair his heater.

Friday, March 24, 1995—sunny, -32° to 4°. Tom H. invited us to lunch at KROA. Allen drove us down. Lots of neighbors there. Many snowbirds at the bird feeder. Very few tracks of animals along the road. I started polishing Dan's brass today. Steve and Nadia both sent letters today.

Saturday, March 25, 1995—sunny, -32° to 12°. We went to Valdez to a craft and gun show with Denny, Joey and Emily E. We ate lunch when we got there, then went to the show. It was rather small. We drove around Valdez a little. Saw a bald eagle and a moose on way home. Some fox tracks, game was scarce. Snow boards and snowmobiles have been out on the snowy slopes of mountains. Some skiers in evidence. Denny's borrowed some tapes.

Sunday, March 26, 1995—sunny, snow to south of us, -10° to 18°. Mike Ackermann and (Dave?) from Motley and Pillager Minnesota are visiting this afternoon and will stay the night.

Monday, March 27, 1995—sunny, -11° to 22°. Mike and Dave had breakfast with us and then left for Valdez and then home to Minnesota. I visited at Allen's. Then later he hauled my ATV to Chuck's to be repaired. He had some peach upside down cake with us and watched part of a movie. I gave him a can of mixed gas that I won't be using.

Tuesday, March 28, 1995—light snow in night, sunny today, 2° to 40°. Visited Allen. Ellie and Emily drove Emily's snowgo into Allen's 2-wheel trailer. Neither was seriously hurt. Very lucky. Sylvia was sick a lot today. Beverly phoned. Janette Wilkins had called her. I scoured the worst of the tarnish off Dan's brass and then tumbled it. Rudbecks came back today and visited for an hour or so. Snowbirds on a feeding frenzy.

Wednesday, March 29, 1995—sunny, 12° to 36°. Had a visitor from Anchorage. Did exercises. Bart gave Robbie some forms for us to sign in support of the Inter Tie Transmission Electric Line (No Way!) Polished more brass today, cleaned both powder measures. The TV signal now comes in very good!!

Thursday, March 30, 1995—6° to 41°. We went to Palmer and Wasilla. Went to doctor. Did some shopping. Saw the 5 "baldy" caribou at Tanita Lake. Also one moose calf near Palmer.

Friday, March 31, 1995—sunny till noon then cloudy, 20° to 43°. Allen had coffee with us. I called Tom and thanked him for plowing the snow that slid off our roof yesterday. Then we went to KROA and treated Allen, Roxanne, Tom and Kim to lunch. Backed home and I worked on brass for both Paul and Dan.

Saturday, April 1, 1995—mostly sunny, 14° to 40°. More snow settling and shrinking. Stopped by Rudbecks shop on way to Allen's. Allen and Cal and Phillip were sawing 2 sided logs. Had coffee then stopped to see Lucky and Mary, had coffee again. Visited a while, gave him some brass for Digger. Sylvia cleaned and arranged the pantry, also did laundry. I did a little with Dan's brass.

Sunday, April 2, 1995—cloudy, light snow, sunny, 22° to 40°. Wrote lots of letter. Sylvia transplanted some plants. Carried garbage cans out of snow and put bags on the garbage before it starts leaking. Shot a squirrel with .22 revolver from out of upstairs window. Mannings stopped in on their way home from church and visited for a while. Sylvia fried some of the venison that Mike A. left with us. Very good. Allen and David visited and had ice cream with us.

Monday, April 3, 1995—sunny, cloudy, wet hard snow, 17° to 40°. Sylvia went to Glennallen. I resized more brass for Dan. A female red fox "stalked" birds at the bird feeder. Sylvia saw her first. I took pictures. She acted real hungry. We really enjoyed watching her and so near to house.

Tuesday, April 4, 1995—cloudy, foggy, cloudy, sunny, two inches of snow last night, 25° to 40°. Visited Allen and Roxanne. Gave him a powder measure. Denny and his pal Scott came to Allen's also. I worked some more on Billman's brass. Shoulder joint is sure sore. We both feel kind of sick. Beverly called then later Laura phoned. Mary B. gave some things to Sylvia.

Wednesday, April 5, 1995—cloudy, sunny, cloudy, 18° to 42°. Did some of exercises. Walked down to Allen's, had coffee the worked on D B's brass. Sylvia went to Glennallen. Tom H. stopped by to visit and coffee.

Thursday, April 6, 1995—sunny, beaut of a day, 13° to 42°. We went to Wasilla to Dr. Kase. I've injured my shoulder and have to rest it a week, thus delaying the physical therapy. Had to have x-rays—the screws were still holding. We did a little shopping. Stopped at Suzuki to ask about motor repair.

Friday, April 7, 1995—sunny, 9° to 40°. Went on a walk. Stopped and visited with Allen and Denny. They have found wolves out at Marie-Nye Lake area. Numerous kills out there plus they are hanging around the Denning area. I did a few little jobs. Rested shoulder mostly.

Saturday, April 8, 1995—sunny, 8° to 43°. Walked down to Allen's and back up the hill. Sylvia ground caribou meat into hamburger and sausage.

Sunday, April 9, 1995—sunny, windy in afternoon, 24° to 42°. Shot a couple squirrels with 22R. Sylvia finished packaging the hamburger and sausage.

Monday, April 10, 1995—mostly cloudy, windy some times, 15° to 42°. Worked on a few pieces of brass. Allen had coffee here. I stopped at Tom H. had coffee and visited about CVEA election. Then went on to dump with garbage.

Tuesday, April 11, 1995—mostly sunny, mountains were very beautiful this evening, 17° to 45°. Shined a lot of brass today. Sylvia pumped water. The fox cleaned up chicken bones, a squirrel and some old bread. We took Allen's grinder back and visited and watched the movie "Point of Honor."

Wednesday, April 12, 1995—sunny, windy in afternoon, 13° to 42°. Sylvia went to Valdez with Karn and Mary O. I worked on brass. Allen and Cal stopped in for pizza and lemon pie lunch. Allen needed some gun grease and motor oil. The fox was back last night. I shot the squirrel from out upstairs window with .22 revolver.

Thursday, April 13, 1995—sunny, 10° to 42°. We went to Wasilla to the physical therapist and received instructions and a demonstration on rebuilding my shoulder muscles. We got a few groceries. Nice driving conditions. Allen stopped in for coffee in evening.

Friday, April 14, 1995—sunny, 12° to 42°. Visited Allen. Sylvia went to a little program at school. Then to a shower for Missy F. at Mendeltna. Mary O. and Kari came down with the makings for ice cream. They leave for McGrath soon.

Saturday, April 15, 1995—cloudy, very windy most of day, 12° to 40°. Jim M. had tea, then Tom H. stopped by to pick up turkeys. He and Allen and Roxanne had ice cream with us. We went to a pot luck and a drawing for a .338 stainless Ruger at the school house.

Sunday, April 16, 1995—mostly sunny, 26° to 44°. At A & R Farmers invitation we went to Easter Sun services at Mendeltna Chapel. Then in afternoon we went to Tom and Kim H for a nice turkey dinner. Lots of our neighbors and their relatives and Chuck Zimbicki were there. The fox is coming by every night now. Polished more brass.

Monday, April 17, 1995—partly cloudy, nice day, 18° to 44°. I did my exercises and worked at polishing and sorting brass. We walked over and visited Mannings. Sylvia went to Glennallen with Kim H. in evening. I visited Sam W., who just returned from North Carolina. Denny Eastman was flying today.

Tuesday, April 18, 1995—mostly cloudy and windy, 15° to 40°. The fox came around again today in daylight. I took lots of pictures. Her belly is bulging more now. She eats everything we give her. Cleaned more brass. Broke my decapper.

Wednesday, April 19, 1995—mostly sunny, 25° to 43°. Sylvia went to Glennallen. Jim and Elaine stopped a couple min. wanting some earrings she has altered. I polished more brass.

Thursday, April 20, 1995—sunny, 15° to 45°. Sylvia worked with her plants and planting seeds. I shoveled some snow and put snowgo in its place in shed. I made a wood box to put load note books in. Karn stopped by for tea. Ed and Sandy visited. Robbie showed us his learner's permit. Allen visited later and we had ice cream and I gave him a reloading handbook. Wrote G.A.R. about tin.

Friday, April 21, 1995—sunny, cloudy afternoon and evening, 25° to 45°. Did some small jobs. Sylvia went to Mendeltna chapel and helped ladies clean the church. After supper we went to the Nelchina, Mendeltna Corp meeting.

Saturday, April 22, 1995—mostly sunny and windy in evening, 31° to 46°. Did exercises and Sylvia got two tomato plants ready and we took them to Dan and Patti Billman at Lake Louise. We had a nice visit and lunch with them. Dan shot his rifles and the loads all look okay. Everyday there is more water on top of the ice on our lake.

Sunday, April 23, 1995—sunny, beautiful, 28° to 49°. Three swans sat on our lake most of the day. An eagle landed in top of a tree in front of our house. I did my exercises and visited with Lucky while on my walk. Loaded brass for D.B. Sylvia did laundry. We called Nadia (her birthday).

Monday, April 24, 1995—cloudy, sunny, 29° to 49°. Sylvia sick all night and a lot of today. My shoulder really sore today. Loaded more brass for D.B. Visited Allen on my walk this morning. The squirrel ran for thick trees at first sign of me. A very nice spring day.

Tuesday, April 25, 1995—cloudy, all day, 25° to 48°. Moved my exercises upstairs. Had coffee at Allen's. Snow is low enough to walk to "out house" by around about. Sylvia saw robins. Loaded water hauling tank from off a snow bank and unloaded it closer to the stand I store it on. Swans are flying west.

Wednesday, April 26, 1995—cloudy, sunny, 32° to 51°. Sylvia went to Glennallen. I did an experiment with adhesives, rubber and wood. Tom H. brought me two cookies and showed me a rifle he bought. Tom and I went to Allen's and had a piece of blueberry pie. I took some homemade ice cream to put on it. Fred Rungee stopped by for almost an hour and had tea and a nice visit. He gave us a gasoline jug. Saw a very large flock of swans.

Thursday, April 27, 1995—sunny, some breeze in evening, 28° to 50°. Did exercises and went for a walk before breakfast. Worked on a new gun cradle today. Cal and Mary G. visited. After supper I walked southwest of our house to find what the eagle, hawk, and ravens were flying around a few days ago—I found the feathers of a spruce hen. I loaded 50 light "fun loads" for the .357 this evening.

Friday, April 28, 1995—light snow in the night, cloudy, windy, then nice and sunny, 30° to 43°. Accomplished some more on the gun cradle. Shoulder, back, hip and right knee hurt tonight. There was over 30 swan's resting on our lake ice when I got up this morning. Other large flocks were battling a west wind. They were headed for Tahneta Pass.

Saturday, April 29, 1995—sunny, very nice day, 21° to 53°. Worked a little on the gun cradle. Got ready and went to Missy Farmer's wedding to Tim D. Rudbecks visited in afternoon. Then we went to Harold and Rachel Dimmicks for supper and watched a video of their 50th wedding anniversary. (They celebrated in Hawaii.) Sylvia noticed an eagle standing on our lake ice at a muskrat push up. I watched as it grabbed the rat with its talons and pull it out onto the ice.

Sunday, April 30, 1995—sunny, beaut of a day, 20° to 55°. Lots of birds singing. Worked on gun cradle and got most of it varithaned. Cleaned, sanded the outhouse Styrofoam. Did a few small jobs. Took my walk. Talked to Lucky a couple minutes. Sized some brass. We went over to Manning's for supper. Jack Chamberlin was there also.

Monday, May 1, 1995—sunny and very nice, 26° to 57°. Sylvia went to Glennallen. I finished varithaning the gun cradle. Sized some brass for Paul. Helped Denny Eastman maneuver his plane off the lake ice on to Jerry Rudbeck's ramp. Had coffee with Allen and we watched an immature eagle try to get rats out of push ups.

Tuesday, May 2, 1995—sunny, cloudy, breezy in evening, 30° to 60°. Did small jobs. Swadged primer pockets. Put gun cradle together. Hauled garbage. Took books back to Mailly's. Had supper with Bob and Karn Rudbeck.

Wednesday, May 3, 1995—partly cloudy, some breezes, 30° to 52°. Sylvia went to Glennallen. I had breakfast with Allen and Roxanne. I chopped some wild rose bushes. Repaired a door latch. Put up a powder storage box in storage shed. Some other small jobs. Lake is turning dark. Phoned our son, Paul.

Thursday, May 4, 1995—mostly sunny, 29° to 57°. Went for walk. Had coffee with Allen. Chopped out more rose bushes and burned them and some trash. Did a little more on Paul's brass. Denny E. brought his new GW Polaris ATV over.

Friday, May 5, 1995—low cloudy, partly cloudy, 33° to 53°. Finished chopping roses. Cleaned up and burned some trash. Started another shooting bench. Cleaned lube from the base of some cast bullets. "Found" our lawn and garden lime. We visited Lucky and Mary.

Saturday, May 6, 1995—windy, sometimes strong, partly cloudy, 31° to 50°. Had coffee and lunch with Allen, Roxanne. Sylvia went to Palmer and Wasilla with the ladies. Finished loading brass for Paul. Sized, lubed, boxed more bullets. Bob R. borrowed the Epsom salts.

Sunday, May 7, 1995—some breeze and cloudy, then partly cloudy, 34° to 52°. Charlie Trowbridge called this afternoon. Nice visit. I finished putting a shooting bench together. Clean lube off some .30 caliber bullets. Made a better board support for the lube/sizer. The swans hang around the thawing edge of the lake. Some ducks flying. Some birds chased the juvenile eagle.

Monday, May 8, 1995—cloudy, partly cloudy and lots of wind today, 38° to 57°. More open water on the lake tonight and more ducks. Sylvia went to Glennallen. I rebedded the receivers in two rifles. Started cleaning the new one. Allen had cake and strawberries with us and we asked him to bring Roxanne and the kids up later. While Roxanne and Allen were here eating strawberries, he saw a light brown grizzly bear going west on the other side of the lake. I got to see it for 50 yards. The bear didn't stop at an old bone pile. Allen wanted to shoot the bear and tried to get someone to go with him. I can't with my shoulder like it is. I put linseed oil on the one gunstock.

Tuesday, May 9, 1995—some breeze, but mostly sunny, 38° to 65°. Put a couple more coats of linseed oil on gunstock. Visited Tom H. to get his ideas on selling our old pickup. Went to Dave and Dee Johnson's and got some copies made. I traded work remodeling two display fixtures for a radiator for our truck. Sylvia worked in green house all day. I completed one display fixture. More ducks and loon on the lake. More ice is out. The kids were canoeing. A large inner tube has drifted east on south side of lake.

Wednesday, May 10, 1995—beautiful day, 34° to 67°. Had coffee at Allen's. Sylvia went to Glennallen. Finished the display cabinets. Allen came over and helped take the canopy off the truck. Repaired a moccasin. Lubed some bullets and real tired tonight. Denny came over to have me drive his ATV.

Thursday, May 11, 1995—beautiful day, windy in evening, 40° to 70°. We are seeing golden eye ducks flying low and fast past the house. Allen helped me put the roof ladder on the garage and I put a cover on the chimney to keep the ducks from trying to nest in the chimney. Sylvia and I took the snowplow off the truck and we put the garden and lawn manifolds in the waterline. Allen, Roxanne, Sammi and Anna visited. We took the chicken wire from around the raspberries. I full length resized Steve's brass. Cleaned and swept the floor of garage. Covered snowgo and snow plow.

   Lonnie Fausett and son Stewart brought (Tom?) and visited most of one hour. We met them on the Nome beach last year. They are all going back again this year. We talked mining and they showed gold they had gotten last year. Lonnie had his well put up and plans to merchandise it to tourists. We surely enjoyed visiting with them. The west wind is breaking up and melting the ice on our lake.

Friday, May 12, 1995—partly cloudy, 38° to 62°. Ice is out of our lake. Serviced the truck and put the new radiator in it. Cleaned the dirt off some beads. Karn was here for coffee. We walked down to their building site and then over to Allen's for a little while. Cleaned some primer pockets for grandson. At 6:45 PM a Coast Guard helicopter passed low (200 ft) over our place while circling Manning's. It moved off towards south end of Tazlina Lake.

Saturday, May 13, 1995—partly cloudy, windy and cloudy, 39° to 54°. We picked the trash out of our mile of highway ditch. Modified the gun cradle I just built. We went to the potluck and ball game at Allen and Roxanne's. Visited with Sam who was walking to work at Henry and Sally's.

Sunday, May 14, 1995—cloudy, light rain, snow to the south and also on top of Slide Mountain, nice day later, 35° to 56°. I washed the truck, fixed table saw switch, cut new threads on a bolt for the snow plow, watered some trees, lubed some bullets. Took Sylvia to Eureka for a Mothers Day prime rib dinner. Dan visited us and I gave him his reloads and a shooting bench.

Monday, May 15, 1995—partly cloudy, cloudy windy afternoon, sunny windy evening, 30° to 55°. Sylvia went to Glennallen. Fixed bathroom faucet and towel, closet knob. Made lots of calls pricing a muffler system for truck. Gave Tom H. 5 - 2 x 12 x 8' planks when he offered to put the exhaust system on the truck. Started mounting a scope on a rifle.

Tuesday, May 16, 1995—partly cloudy, then windy in afternoon and evening, 28° to 53°. Allen, Roxanne, Sammi and Annabelle were here for breakfast. Jim Manning showed up and ate the remaining food. They stayed until 11:00 AM. Jim borrowed our roto-tiller. I put a scope on one rifle and reinstalled the scope on another one. Jack Chamberlin stopped by with some bean seeds for Sylvia. The ravens hunt for voles along our hillside. The flickers are breeding. David and Jahobbi left some .38's they want loaded. Flickers are mating.

Wednesday, May 17, 1995—partly cloudy, 28° to 58°. Sylvia went to Glennallen. I visited Allen. Stopped by Rudbecks—they are busy now. Worked on truck manifold. Measured exhaust system. When Sylvia came home she helped put bumper on truck. Loaded two empty gas barrels, two coolers and grocery box. I saw duck down on two of the duck box's I looked at. Started prepping cases for the Remington 700.

Thursday, May 18, 1995—cloudy, some rain here, sunny, partly cloudy in evening with distant snow and rain, 34° to 53°. We saw a moose and four caribou bulls between Eureka and Gunsight Lodge. Went to pay hospital. Bought weld rod, bank not open, stopped at Nugent's Ranch and bought some seed potatoes. Went to physical therapist and two doctor appointments. No luck buying muffler parts. Got 100 gallons of gas and some groceries (Safeway Wasilla) and then prescriptions at Carr's in Palmer. Got home about 6:15 PM. Allen visited later in evening. Sylvia saw a fox dropping in the yard.

Friday, May 19, 1995—sunny, some wind. Unloaded gas. Looked at truck gas tank. Took bin to Allen and had coffee. He brought tiller home and tilled our garden. He had serviced the tiller. I built a extension on a curtain rod for Sylvia. Water pump wasn't putting out any water. Will check it tomorrow. Allen, Roxanne, Ellie and David and Sammi had supper with us. Called Chuck about my ATV.

Saturday, May 20, 1995—partly cloudy, 37° to 58°. I picked up some tree trimmings, raked some lawn and burned it all. Sylvia planted garden. Tom H. and friend Mike came over and Tom pulled my left fuel tank from the pick up. It has a large rotted place in it. Tom will look in Copper Center tomorrow for a tank. Allen took Ed's D 6 down to Lucky's property and is clearing a large area.

Sunday, May 21, 1995—cloudy and a light shower in afternoon, 35° to 56°. We went over to Sandy F. for a good lunch and homemade ice cream. Back home a little while and in drove Tom and Mike with a gas tank for our truck and we put the gas tank on my truck.

Monday, May 22, 1995—mostly cloudy, 37° to 54°. Started another front rifle rest. Washed the truck tool box I gave Tom H. Cleaned the garage. Sylvia went to Glennallen.

Tuesday, May 23, 1995—cloudy, windy evening, 31° to 53°. Looked at Rudbeck house construction. Got sand and sorted leather for rear rifle bag. Worked on front rifle rest. Prepared aluminum and loaded it in truck. Gasoline filter plugged. Changed filter, raked a little yard. Visited Bartley's and got Tier II hunt applications. Cleaned .338 rifle.

Wednesday, May 24, 1995—partly cloudy, 41° to 59°. Light rain in Anchorage. We got up at 4:00 AM and drove to Anchorage and had an exhaust muffler system installed on truck. Saw some caribou in vicinity of Eureka, one moose later. We did shopping, sold aluminum cans and dropped my .338 rifle off to have a muzzle brake installed. We got back home about 9:30 PM. Tired.

Thursday, May 25, 1995—mostly sunny, windy, 37° to 59°. Worked on "new" leaking gas tank. Took the fuel pump off. Unloaded barrels and gas. Couldn't get the welder started. Wanted to modify the brass polisher and weld the front rifle rest. Harold Dimmick wants to borrow a wood drill bit. Sylvia had a battery put in Karn's watch and Karn picked it up today.

Friday, May 26, 1995—some wind but a sunny day, 34° to 64°. Did some small jobs, then Rudbecks brought out my new fuel pump for our truck and I put it on. Came in house and napped for an hour and Tom H. and Mike drove in our yard with a gas tank off Ed's old parts Chevy and put it on our truck. We filled it with water to test it for leaks. Then they had supper with us. Later I put the brass tumbler together. I had already realigned the rolls. I worked some on the rear sand bag. Sylvia worked in greenhouse and with her flowers and then curtains in house. Allen came over to get a catalog. Sandy and Lois visited Sylvia.

Saturday, May 27, 1995—partly cloudy, windy, 36° to 59°. Worked on rifle rest, glued a rug on top of shooting table. Prepared some plywood for a floor in upstairs closed. Hauled trash to dump. Had supper with Tom H. and family and guest Mike from Louisiana.

Sunday, May 28, 1995—partly cloudy, 37° to 54°. Sylvia watered the lawn. I sewed the rear rifle bag. Then gave the truck a tune up. Then drove to Tolsona. Chuck and I settled on a cash + trade for a pump + repair of my ATV. Painted rifle rest. The loons are mating.

Monday, May 29, 1995—partly cloudy, windy, cool, 37° to 56°. Sorted books to take to Gilcrease's. The truck wouldn't start. Got Allen to help. It was out of gas-sitting still. Loaded some old rabbit food and went to Gilcrease's. Gave them the books and rabbit food. Had coffee. Cal wanted to pay me for the two sacks of cement he had borrowed. Ron was there and offered us some paint that we needed. Nice trade all round if Ron comes through with his end. Back home I finished the front and rear sandbags and refilled the old rear sandbag. Checked the proper air pressure in ATV tires. Denny E. came over to air up a low tire on his ATV. The raven's hunt for voles along our hillside each day. Eight swans on our lake over night. Ellie and Emily have a soft drink stand and sell antlers of their dad's. Evening: cow moose hurried (20' from front window) past here with a red new born calf. Hackles on cow were up and calf with mouth open from hurrying.

Tuesday, May 30, 1995—cloudy, partly cloudy, sunny, windy sometimes, 30° to 58°. We washed the upstairs windows and made and put on the inside trim for them. Allen borrowed oil, visited, then he and David visited late afternoon. Robbie borrowed a movie. I resized some more brass to use in USSF. Got another squirrel with revolver.

Wednesday, May 31, 1995—Mostly sunny and some wind, 30° to 58°. Sylvia went to Glennallen. I shot rifle to start breaking in the barrel. Patti Billman phoned. Then Elaine called, very excited. A griz was in her next door neighbor's yard. She wanted help. I grabbed the 44 magnum and went across the highway with the truck. The bear was eating spilled dog food that had been raked up with some grass. It ran when I got there and I hurried it on with three shots over its head hoping it would be scared enough to stay away.

Got to meet Bob and Noreen (?). Visited Allen and Roxanne. On way home saw the bear, back in same yard. Denny E. had a bear tag and wanted to shoot it, so he drove over close to bear and shot it with his .338. Bear dropped instantly but didn't die quickly. It bothered jack Chamberlain that the bear was thrashing around, so I drove over there and told Denny to kill it. Allen was there and the three of us skinned the bear. I guessed the weight at 220 lbs and 60 inches long, a male. After supper Elaine came over, borrowed a movie.

Thursday, June 1, 1995—some rain in night, partly cloudy and windy in afternoon, 35° to 55°. Sylvia cleaned upstairs. I washed truck and garage windows, burned some trash. Shot rifle to break in barrel. Loaded some more to continue break in.

Friday, June 2, 1995—partly cloudy, some rain going by on each side of us, 37° to 61°. Got some craft ready and took them to Dee (gift shop) at Mendeltna. Then we drove up Lake Louise Road. We ate lunch at gravel pit at 10 mile, nice overlook towards my trap cabin. Then we went on to the Point at Lake Louise. Visited Billmans. Stopped at dump on way home and picked up some lumber scraps and an electric lamp (needed a little repair), a small clevis. Allen stopped by, returning some borrowed oil, at supper time. He helped me carry a chest of drawers out of the basement and over to wood shop. I took the chest of drawers from there (it's much nicer) and put them in the garage and plan to refinish them and put them in bedroom reloading room.

Saturday, June 3, 1995—cloudy, sprinkle of rain, 39° to 59°. Worked on a chest of drawers today. Allen, Roxanne and Sammi visited. We ate supper with them. Sylvia painted the inside trim and window of one upstairs window (soldier blue). Neighborhood kids came to borrow a glue for their raft. I didn't have a suitable glue. Beverly phoned and talked for a long time.

Sunday, June 4, 1995—party cloudy, cloudy and much needed rain in evening, 38° to 55°. Finished remodeling the chest of drawers. Sylvia painted another window and painted the chest of drawers. I cleaned out some of woodshop and burned trash. Visited Lucky. Tom and Mike and Afton stopped by. Phoned Paul to wish him a happy birthday.

Monday, June 5, 1995—rained a lot last night, snow on Slide Mountain down to about 3100 feet elevation, 36° to 58°. Sylvia went to Glennallen. I went to Glacier View School ground breaking with Allen and Roxanne. Cal's was there. Allen left his resume. After lunch we came home. Sylvia was back and getting ready to finish painting the chest of drawers. I cut out the framing for the bottom of the upstairs cold and hot air registers. She has done a lot of cleaning and straightening up, upstairs. Quite a few canvasback ducks pairing up on our lake.

Tuesday, June 6, 1995—partly cloudy, windy afternoon, 34° to 56°. Sylvia worked upstairs. I painted some, visited Allen. Took truck to Glennallen. Kim H. brought me back home.

Wednesday, June 7, 1995—mostly cloudy and then light rain in early evening, 37° to 58°. Did some phoning about our address change July lst. We went on senior van to Glennallen. Ran a few errands. Stopped by Pharmington Services, they couldn't find anything wrong with choke (maybe we need a new carburetor). Picked up some brass at shooting range. Did some electrical wiring on house. We watched a cow moose (faded haircoat) swim parallel to our lakeshore. Saw a bull moose cross they hwy about mile 162.

Thursday, June 8, 1995—sunny, partly cloudy, 38° to 59°. Trimmed and put screen in heat-air return ducts to upstairs. Some other jobs including hoeing in garden. Borrowed a drill bit from Allen after he got home from job. Damn truck quit on Lucky's Hill and he pulled me home.

Friday, June 9, 1995—partly cloudy, 42° to 66°. Got truck running again. Shot rifle 20 times-breaking in the barrel. Tried to make a bullet puller. No luck. Took borrowed gas back to Lucky. He gave me some books. Bev called.

Saturday, June 10, 1995—mostly sunny, very nice day with breezes, 47° to 75°. Sylvia worked in greenhouse, watered lawn, did laundry, vacuumed and baked finest rhubarb pie ever! I worked on the welder, points and plugs. Salvaged alternator of old truck. Put screen door on arctic entry. Denny E. had his airplane E.L.T on in his plane. Don Deering of Search and Rescue, (from air) dropped a message at our place asking him to shut the device off.

Sunday, June 11, 1995—sunny, some haze, a shower far to north, 47° all the way up to 84°!! Cleaned the bench in the garage. Sylvia treated me to a dinner at Eureka Lodge. Back at home, I advanced (adjusted) the spark on the truck in an effort to end its "dieseling."

Monday, June 12, 1995—sunny, breezy, 54° to 83°. Went to gravel pit and shot rifle at targets. Visited Tom H. and Mike worked on truck again. Then Tom and Mike came and we worked some more on it. Sandy F. gave us a mix of ice cream to freeze. Then a little later Robbie dumped ATF in their truck oil. I gave them new oil. Tom, Mike, Allen, Roxanne, Ellie, Sammi, had pie and ice cream with us. Allen left some rug-like material, salvaged from Glacier View School.

Tuesday, June 13, 1995—partly cloudy, 50° to 79°. Smoke in the air from a run away fire at Pinnacle Mountain. We went to Palmer, Wasilla, some shopping and Sylvia seen her Doctor Cotton. The doctor was late so we got to Anchorage too late to get the exhaust system corrected. We didn't find a mattress. I was able to get my rifle as the muzzle brake was installed. Got a lot of groceries. Lots of pretty scenery but we are tired tonight.

Wednesday, June 14, 1995—partly cloudy, some breeze, 44° to 71°. Worked on truck distributor. New one I got is for newer trucks. Tried to test the primer and paint we got yesterday. Test got messed up a couple times, so is meaningless. Karn was here three times. Brought fish the last time. I hoed in garden and cut down some large willows near there. Stopped and said Hi to Lucky. Bob R. came over and got an "O" ring.

Thursday, June 15, 1995—mostly cloudy, bugs are troublesome, 46° to 64°. We slept late, then Karn and her friend visited. Got a late start putting the primer on the room upstairs, plus the door, shelves, craft table and some plywood for a floor in one closet. Took a lot of time preparing to paint. Allen's rifle stock came today. He was home alone so we had him come and share lake trout that Karn gave us. Real tasty. Lucky is moving to Palmer today.

Friday, June 16, 1995—rain most of night, several showers today, mostly cloudy, 40° to 54°. We put a semi-gloss coat of latex on everything. We put primer on yesterday. Worked on Allen's rifle and cleaned the loose powder out of mine. Cleaned the press. Went to KROA and got a moose clock for a wedding present tomorrow. Rudbeck came over and got his paint roller. They fished today but didn't catch anything.

Saturday, June 17, 1995—rain most of night, 3/8" - 1/2", showers till a little after noon, 42° to 62°. Beautiful evening. We cleaned one room and put plywood down in ½ the north closet. Closet looks neat and orderly. We went to Artic Wikle and Michelle's wedding at their friend's house. Back home I wired in a light and fixed up some on bench.

Sunday, June 18, 1995—partly cloudy and breezy, 47° to 71°. Smaller mosquito's here now and bite anywhere out of the breeze. Cleaned and put a coat of Varithane on the bench top. Denise and her husband Terry (?) visited, they moved back here from NC. Allen and Roxanne took us to Eureka for pie. Allen shot my .338 with the new stock on it. Bob Rudbeck is flying his Minnesota friends out to different lakes for their fishing. Karn and Dana stopped by for cash for paint and Sylvia's prescription. Allen came over after supper and we got further inletting of his .338 barreled action into the stock I got for him. The magazine release has a loose fit. Tom H. and Mike visited for a while later in the evening.

Monday, June 19, 1995—sunny and some breeze to blow bugs away, 44° to 77°. The aspen seeds (fuzz) are blowing around now. We prepared the next upstairs room for painting. I spent all afternoon in the garage making an (O.V.L.) overall length gauge and a .22-250 + .243 modified cartridge cases. Took two borrowed movies back to Farmers. Flickers are mating again.

Tuesday, June 20, 1995—partly cloudy, some breeze but lots of bugs, 48° to 77°. New batch of camp robber fledglings. Worked on truck till 1 PM. Reworked the gas line, drained the left gas tank. Visited Ed F and got a couple ideas to try on the carburetor. Came home tried those, "seems" better. Stripped the paint from a spare wheel and primed it. Did other odd jobs. Sylvia mowed the lawn and painted some more upstairs.

Wednesday, June 21, 1995—rain early morning, partly cloudy rest of day, 44° to 67°. We put primer on an upstairs room. Painted spare truck wheel. Worked on truck. Hoed weeds in garden plus other jobs.

Thursday, June 22, 1995—showers, partly cloudy, showers in evening, 46° to 71°. Worked all day on house, painting etc. Finished hoeing the garden. Phoned Bev's and got to talk to Tyler.

Friday, June 23, 1995—rain all night and most of day, light rain, low clouds this evening, snow in mountains to south, 38° to 41°. Cut out of cardboard boxes and glued magazine holders. Carried books and replaced them on shelves. Sylvia went with Karn to Anchorage. Legs tired tonight. Cleaned and oiled three revolvers after supper.

Saturday, June 24, 1995—partly cloudy, with breeze from west, 39° to 56°. Took books wood cut outs and petex cutting board to both Mailly's and Huddelstons. Went on to dump with garbage. Cal drove in after I did. Checked out two gravel pits. Nothing. Right big toe joint very sore. Cleaned rifles and loaded a few rounds.

Sunday, June 25, 1995—mostly cloudy, strong breeze sometimes, 38° to 64°. I started trying to figure out the light fixture at the kitchen sink. No luck. So after some talk we decided to install a splash board around the kitchen sink. We had everything on hand. After emptying it, we took the top cupboards loose. Cut, fit and glued the splash board on and screwed cupboard back on the wall. Went down to Allen's-they must be gone for the weekend.

Monday, June 26, 1995—mostly sunny and some breezes most of day, 42° to 65°. Worked on a wiring problem. Lucky came over in the evening and found a loose wire. Cut some weeds. Cleaned wood shop. Walked down to lake. Saw Jerry R. down at his hanger. Talked a little. Lucky, Roxanne, Kyle, Sammi and Allen here and nice visit.

Tuesday, June 27, 1995—mostly sunny, 42° to 68°. Wired in florescent light over the kitchen sink. Built a rack to display some plates, on top of cupboard over sink. Tried to make a drain board. Weeded the raspberries. Went down to Allen and Roxanne for supper. Lucky and Samantha and Kyle there. The job Allen was on was shut down because of old diesel and paint thinner contamination in soil.

Wednesday, June 28, 1995—partly cloudy, 48° to 72°. Sylvia went to Glennallen. Got some nails for Rudbecks. I replaced a broken glass in greenhouse door. Put a screen over the wood basement chute for air circulation. Revamped the drain board base. Dug some raspberry plants for Elaine. Put a handle in a garden fork. Had lunch at Allen and Roxanne's.

Thursday, June 29, 1995—cloudy, light showers, cloudy to a very nice evening, 51° to 73°. Lloyd and Faye Walton, (Dan's mother and step dad) visited a while this morning. I took a truck tire off a wheel. Cleaned up some trash. Sylvia mowed lawn and painted later in afternoon. I cast some bullets. Lubed them after supper.

Friday, June 30, 1995—fog, cloudy, sunny, cloudy, 44° to 65°. Made a stand-cover for powder scale, cover for trimmer. Sylvia painted. I pulled weeds in strawberries. Dropped the left gas tank on truck-shortened gas line hoses and put it back up. Sylvia handed me tools. She put up curtains in the other bedroom upstairs. I cleaned the carburetor on the welder. It still doesn't start. Will work on points condenser next. Allen stopped by for a while. He went to Palmer again. Greg and Natilee may come out and he is excited about that.

Saturday, July 1, 1995—cloudy, fog, cloudy most of day, 45° to 63°. Painted new mail box numbers. Cut throw rugs from the piece Allen gave us. Tried to fix tail pipe, no luck. Weighed up wheel weights lead and tin for #2 Lyman's alloy. Shot squirrel while Allen, Roxanne and Sammi were here. They brought sticky buns and we had coffee. Later Mannings came over to get more raspberry plants and to tell us they had bought the house next to theirs.

Sunday, July 2, 1995—cloudy most of day, rain in afternoon and evening, 49° to 62°. Cast some bullets. We had supper with Jim and Elaine and watched a movie. Fixed a package for son Paul.

Monday, July 3, 1995—cloudy and rainy, 47° to 57°. Sylvia and I went on senior van to Glennallen. Mailed package to son Paul. Ate at Rendezvous Café. (They now have the contract). Got electrical supplies at Blake and Jackie's. Back at home Allen came over and we decided to replace our mail box supports. We used my telephone cross arms and a 4' piece of 2" x 12" A.W.W. He gave me the mail box Lucky gave him. He ate supper with us and brought watermelon and ice cream. Then he got a call from home he was to go to Kim's for supper!!

Tuesday, July 4, 1995—50° to 70°. painted numbers on mail box and made a base for it. Visited Allen. Picked, washed, and cut up rhubarb. Sylvia put contact paper in cupboards. Baked a rhubarb cake. We went over to Jerry R. for supper. Several couples there. I have felt dizzy all day.

Wednesday, July 5, 1995—partly cloudy, sunny, some breeze, 50° to 77°. I drove the truck to Glennallen to have carburetor worked on. Ate dinner at Rendezvous. Got wire nuts at lumber yard. Sylvia got a perm in town. She mowed lawn and I wired some outlets upstairs. We went to a picnic at Allen and Roxanne's and had a great time.

Thursday, July 6, 1995—partly cloudy, 53° to 76°. Finished wiring upstairs. Sylvia cleaned the mess and did laundry. Painted the top and side of mail box again. Case a few bullets. The voles got in garden. Sylvia put cans on plants again. I tilled the garden and pulled some weeds.

Friday, July 7, 1995—cloudy, partly cloudy, cloudy, 48° to 70°. More cleaning and vacuuming. I cleaned vac filter twice. Took pictures of property line between Jerry R and us. Cast some more bullets. While drinking coffee this morning. I saw golden eye duck fly up to our roof as to land there. Later I checked chimney clean out and sure enough it had fallen to chimney bottom. Took a picture of Sylvia and duck before we turned it loose to fly back to lake.

Saturday, July 8, 1995—rain in night and some showers today, 45° to 62°. Got up a little after 5:00 AM. Dave Johnson came from Mendeltna and took me with him to Glennallen. He dropped me off at Pharmington Services (Pete Butaric). My truck (carburetor and power steering and timing) was repaired and ready to be picked up. I went to shooting range and picked up some brass. Back at home I did a few small jobs. Allen came over and we put up our new mail box posts and attached our boxes. Later in eve, Tom and TJ H. stopped by and tom shot our east property line with his company's survey equip. Denny E. flew some fisherman today. He made an excellent landing on our lake this evening. Golden eyes are trying to nest in the flicker box.

Sunday, July 9, 1995— partly cloudy and a few sprinkles, 48° to 67°. We drove the survey lathes this morning. I worked on truck floor mat and washed and cleaned the motor. Sylvia waxed bathroom floor and washed the outside windows. Tom H. stopped by with his calculations of land parcel area. Four neighborhood girls brought a movie back. Cast some 30 -06 bullets.

Monday, July 10, 1995—partly cloudy, shower in evening. We went to Glennallen on senior van and paid bills, ate at Rendezvous. Put primer on our old mail box and put cross bracing on our box's we put up Sat. Tumbled some brass. Visited Allen and Roxanne a little while. Saw fox dropping in our lane. Got letter from my brother, Marion and his wife, Rae that they plan to visit us.

Tuesday, July 11, 1995—fog, cloudy, partly cloudy and a very nice evening, 46° to 68°. Did a bunch of small jobs. Sylvia waxed the floors. Finished painting mailbox and took it and shells down to Allen in evening.

Wednesday, July 12, 1995—partly cloudy, sunny, 44° to 70°. Hauled garbage to dump and went on to Glennallen and Pete adjusted my truck choke. Ate at Rendezvous. Bob Rudbeck came over and ripped some of his kitchen cabinet parts on my table saw. We walked down and look at the house they are building. Gave some lettuce to Betty R. I pulled the weeds in the garden. We went to Tom and Kim H. to supper.

Thursday, July 13, 1995—cloudy, partly cloudy, breezy all day, 50° to 68°. Shot rifle for load development. Did lots odd jobs and mount camper on truck. Sylvia did lots cleaning. I started on basement. Sylvia saw a squirrel but I kept missing it and it got away.

Friday, July 14, 1995—rain most of day, starting to clear in evening, 48° to 60°. We had to put a new gasket in lavatory water line. More house work. Sylvia saw a squirrel; it would hide in thick branches. I emptied the revolver, scaring it out, in hopes of a clear shot. Emptied the cylinder. Sylvia kept him in tree and I got the .22-250 and 40 GR Nosler B.T. It knocked the squirrel 18' out of the tree. Sylvia laughed so hard at the "overkill" results she peed her pants laughing. Theresa phoned this afternoon.

Saturday, July 15, 1995—partly cloudy, breezy, 41° to 70°. We started for Anchorage, within a mile turned around and came home and adjusted the mirrors for use with the camper. Did some shopping in Wasilla. More shopping in Anchorage. Went to airport, Marion and Rae's flight isn't coming in on time and there is a mix up. We do more shopping, visit Addie G. Go back to airport and lo and behold Marion and Rae are there. They switched to Alaska Airline and got here on time. We start for home and get groceries in Palmer. We got home about 4:00 AM, put groceries away and go to bed.

Sunday, July 16, 1995—partly cloudy and breezy, nice day, 41° to 68°. We slept till 9:00 AM. Visited and ate a lot. Marion and I went for a walk down to lake in afternoon. Both Cal and Allen stopped by to visit in evening.

Monday, July 17, 1995—partly cloudy and breezy, 42° to 71°. We got fishing gear ready after a phone call from Dan Billman. We went to his lodge. He flew Marion and I to Kianna Creek on Tazlina Lake by way of an overhead look at my trap cabin. We saw a cow moose and calf near Mendeltna Springs. We could see king salmon lying in clear stream water that flows out into the grey glacier water of Tazlina Lake. Dan caught first fish and released her. The fish all left that hole and we went back closer to the plane and ate sandwiches. Later as sun got lower Dan caught two and Marion fought one of them. I rested for a while then decided on three casts and hooked one on last cast. It gave a very good fight. Dan netted it for me. Maybe a 30# fish. We got back to Lake Louise about 12:00 AM, had a bite to eat and got home at 2:00 AM.

Tuesday, July 18, 1995—mostly sunny, 43° to 70°. We slept till 8:00 AM, visited and then Marion and I tried to find out what is keeping the gas from leaving the auxiliary tank with no luck. Sylvia fried a big mess of King Salmon for supper. Very good.

Wednesday, July 19, 1995—partly cloudy, 41° to 70°. Loaded up camper with necessities and drove to Valdez. Marion and Rae enjoyed seeing the mountains and views and took lots of pix. We drove around Valdez and Rae did a little shopping. Drove up pipeline terminal road, parked camper and fished for a while with no luck. Kind of nice to watch the seals feed on the salmon. Saw trooper car at Lloyd Ronning's cabin.

Thursday, July 20, 1995—mostly sunny here, cloudy in Valdez, 41° to 69°. People caught salmon on both sides of us. No such luck for us. After breakfast and while getting ready to go home, Wendy Baker, working for Fish & Game, drove up and we got to visit with her for a few min. Had a nice drive home. Truck doesn't run right. Marion and Rae took us out to supper at KROA. After eating Vern told us the gift shop had blown up and the wolves and other fur had been ruined. Dee hasn't called or told us yet. Lloyd Ronning died yesterday.

Friday, July 21, 1995—mostly sunny, cloudy and rain in evening, 50° to 76°. Marion and I brought the canoe up from the lake, got some fishing gear ready and after lunch we went to Buffalo Lake and fished for rainbows. We caught nine on the fly rod. Marion got most of them. Saw an arctic loon and a very large gull there. Cleaned the fish, ate supper, invited Allen and Roxanne over for pie and ice cream. We all had a nice visit. Dee phoned to tell us about the explosion. She had insurance and we will get paid in two weeks.

Saturday, July 22, 1995—some rain, mostly cloudy, 49° to 59°. Marion and I walked down to Jerry R's hanger. Visited with his son Nick. Soon Jerry came along and I suggested he build his own road from his house down to his hanger as we were concerned about the use our property is receiving. Jim Manning came over to get a electrical wire repair done. Marion and Rae wanted to go gift shopping and get us dinner in Glennallen. We stopped at Dave and Dee Johnson's on way home and picked up crafts that had not been damaged in the explosion and fire. Talked to Jerry about road.

Sunday, July 23, 1995—rainy, cloudy, rainy, 48° to 60°. Slept late. Marion and I took the windshield wiper switch off my truck. Cleaned and greased the contact points on it and replaced it in the truck. It works fine now. Sylvia fixed caribou steak for supper, very good. We watched the goose and duck hunting tape after supper. Gave Marion and Rae "Alaska" clocks for them and their son Ken. Packaged these for travel.

Monday, July 24, 1995—rain, 43° to 53°. Talked to Mike about our road. Later Marion and I walked over to Nelchina River. Ducks appear to be rafting up on our lake. Lots of little ducks.

Tuesday, July 25, 1995—rain most of day, 42° to 54°. Marion and I put new plug wires on welder engine, adjusted points. It started very nicely. Towards evening, we loaded their luggage and started for Anchorage. Ate supper at Long Rifle Lodge. Went on to Anchorage and the airport. Visited with Marion and Rae till 12:AM then drove to Wal-Mart parking lot and slept in camper.

Wednesday, July 26, 1995—50s (Anchorage) to 60s. Did a little shopping. Visited Rosemary Bartley in Alaska Regional Hosp. More shopping. Not successful in waiting out the line at Motor Vehicle (state). Got home about 4:00 PM. Visited Allen and Roxanne. Seventy ducks in view on lake.

Thursday, July 27, 1995—cloudy and rainy, 48° to 57°. Slept late. Started preparing some brass. Did a few small jobs, oiling hinges, burn trash, level the gravel Jerry R. hired CAT tore up. Got some lettuce and cauliflower from garden. Tried to find out why windshield washer runs all the time. Put old vacuum cleaner in hip boot to blow warm air and dry it out.

Friday, July 28, 1995—most, partly cloudy, 38° to 64°. Did rifle load development. Shot some excellent targets. Shot the .338. No detrimental effect on my shoulder. Visited Ed Farmer. Replaced the welder starting rope. Camper roof is leaking, painted cracked places with mobile home roof paint.

Saturday, July 29, 1995—partly cloudy, 41° to 60°. Cultivate some garden. Pulled weeds and hilled potatoes. Started fixing camper cupboard over the stove. Tried to repair truck windshield. Visited Gilcreases.

Sunday, July 30, 1995—partly cloudy, rain during night, then rain and hail in evening, 43° to 66°. Worked on windshield. Pulled weeds and cultivated garden. Jacked keel of canoe back where it belonged. Finished camper cupboards. Sylvia painted and papered them. Shot a few cart loads and started preparing more. Ed borrowed spade bit and brought it back.

Monday, July 31, 1995—one inch of rain in the night, partly cloudy today, 45° to 64°. Took the trolling motor apart today. Helped some neighbors take up some tile at Bartley's today. Finished loading some cast bullet rifle loads for load development.

Tuesday, August 1, 1995—partly cloudy, 46° to 64°. Shot the cast bullet loads. Three look promising. Took the heater core out of the truck. Straightened up the stove in the camper. Cleaned and re-lubed the burner valves on it also. Put some fertilizer on lawn. The eagle gets ducks everyday. We visited Allen and Roxanne and borrowed movies. Cal and Mary came there also. Cal is working on Allen's house.

Wednesday, August 2, 1995—mostly cloudy, 43° to 59°. We went to Glennallen on senior van. I got my migratory bird hunting stamp, post card stamps and a new heater core for the truck. Shot three loads of three cast bullets. They didn't shoot well. Installed the heater core.

Thursday, August 3, 1995—rain all night and day, quit in evening, 40° to 53°. Wrote a lot of letters. Loaded more .22-250 for load development. Two beaver planes landed on our lake this afternoon.

Friday, August 4, 1995—mostly cloudy, 44° to 53°. Loaded up shooting gear and drove to gravel pit. Too windy to shoot load development. Repaired bullet backstop here at home. Straightened and stretched truck seat cover. Found a small bird fluttering against window inside garage and released it outside.

Saturday, August 5, 1995—partly cloudy, some breeze, showers, partly cloudy, 43° to 62°. Slept late. Went to gravel pit and shot rifles. Cleaned and started preparing brass to reload. Sylvia is making quilts.

Sunday, August 6, 1995—mostly cloudy, 40° to 66°. Developed loads and assembled. Three young kestrels here today. I found a coral mushroom today.

Monday, August 7, 1995—mostly sunny, 40° to 65°. Went to Glennallen on senior van. NAPA didn't have wiper switch for my truck. Shot a rifle when I got back. Ellie fell and hurt her ankle. We loaned our ice pack outfit for her.

Tuesday, August 8, 1995—mostly sunny, 41° to 67°. Took a card down to Ellie.

Went to gravel pit to sight in .338, after some stock work on it. Took quite a few shots but the last three shot group measured 7/8" at 100 yards. Visited Tom H. Back at home I cleaned the rifle. Sylvia worked on more quilts. Mike Griffith from Staples, Minnesota stopped in.

Wednesday, August 9, 1995—mostly sunny, 40s to 60s. Dan and I decide to go to Meirs Lake, Paxson, Denali Highway and hunt caribou and subsistence moose. I met him and Patti in Glennallen. He got his permits and something to eat. I stopped at rifle range and picked up some brass. We looked for boo and a camping place.

Thursday, August 10, 1995—partly cloudy, little shower, 40° to 60s. Lots of bugs here on Denali Highway. Not many caribou. Not a lot of hunters. Some boo have been shot. We talked to some hunters and pointed out caribou to them. We hunted for moose in another area. We unloaded the Suzuki, fixed a good place for Dan to ride and drove 2 ½ miles to a large open area. The game sign was several days old. Walking slow and quiet, I heard a sound. Got Dan stopped and shortly two wolves broke out into the open. I must have gotten "wolf fever" for I tried to shoot without a cartridge in rifle chamber. The black wolf ran back into the brush. Before I could find the light grey wolf the black one ran out again. I held the crosshairs over its back and missed it. In retrospect I should have held the crosshairs at the bottom of its chest. So goes hunting. Later we went to Tangle Lakes Lodge and visited there. We parked the camper back in the same place tonight.

Friday, August 11, 1995—partly cloudy, 40s to 60s. We drove the road a lot, saw a few caribou, and three cow moose. The only boo we might have shot was too small so we let it go. Not many caribou around. Saw (2nd boy) one of Bakers sons, hunting also. We unloaded the ATV on the Alascom Tower on a high hill. Drove over some hills and couldn't see a boo anywhere with the binoculars. Along in afternoon gassed up once again and hunted on the way home, not a ½ mile south of the hunt area a boo was standing in middle of the road. It ran down the road quite a ways ahead of us before it left the road.

Came to an old man who had dropped his boat trailer tongue on the road. We helped get it hooked up so he could continue on. Some reservations on this as he had been drinking. Windy from Glennallen to home. Drove Dan home up to Lake Louise. Mike from NC was there. Glad to get home and rest.

Saturday, August 12, 1995—30s to 50s. Cleaned out the camper and unloaded the Suzuki. Rested a little then hauled the garbage to the dump. A very large griz has been seen in the dump. It had wrecked some of the dump fences. Stopped by Tom H. but didn't see anyone around. Worked on windshield wiper till Allen F. came over to find out how hunt went. He asked me to go hunting with his crew this evening but I declined.

Sunday, August 13, 1995—foggy, cloudy and a little rain, 43° to 55°. Read some. Loaded .38's and a few 300 H & H then tried to put the windshield wiper from the old truck on this one, but the wiring didn't fit. Put the old one back on. Ate Montana Mule deer steak for supper. Sylvia made a cake and I froze homemade ice cream and we took it down to Allen and family. Allen and Al Padowski and Kyle were hunting on Slide Mountain. They saw a big bull caribou. Al shot at it but missed and ringed his eye with the scope. Al shot five spruce hens with his bow and arrows. I shot a squirrel with a cast bullet. Devastating results for the squirrel.

Monday, August 14, 1995—rain all night and day, 44° to 51°. Sylvia went to Glennallen. I corrected the wiper position on truck. I removed the screen from wood chute into the basement. I reloaded .38 SPL and P Brass and sorted some of it. Dan stopped by and visited.

Tuesday, August 15, 1995—mostly sunny with hard rain between here and Glennallen, 45° to 63°. We went to Glennallen to BLM office, DMV magistrate's office and DOT trying to find ownership of a sliver of land between us and the hwy. Not much luck. Stopped by Pete Butorac and he tried our truck. I sold him our old pickup. We bought a new windshield wiper unit at NAPA store. Pete came and got the pickup tonight. We picked up a few brass at shooting range.

Wednesday, August 16, 1995—partly cloudy, cloudy, sunny and very nice, 44° to 65°. Sylvia went to Glennallen. I put the new wiper, pump on the truck. Then went to gravel pit and shot the .338 at 200 yards. 2 shots into 2" and I came home. After Sylvia got home she handed me tools and I took the gas tank off the truck, found the strainer in the tank was folded over. Put a different fuel pick up unit on tank and replaced it, along with the rubber hose fuel line to the "Y" connection with the other tank.

Thursday, August 17, 1995—sunny day, very nice though lots of bugs, 45° to 67°. I went to gravel pit, hoping for a caribou but shoot at target instead. After lunch we went blueberry picking west side of Little Nelchina River. Roxanne and her "crew" came there to pick a little later. Back at home I did more target shooting. Just as I finished with the 44 magnum, Jeff Routt, Laurie and their kids drove in. He needed 5-2 sided logs. We visited a while mostly talking, hunting and guns. He showed me his latest buy. Raining south across the river right now.

Friday, August 18, 1995—partly cloudy and rain in Tahneta Pass while we coming home, 39° to 65°. We went to Wasilla and Anchorage shopping. Didn't find everything we needed. Saw Lucky in his pickup.

Saturday, August 19, 1995—partly cloudy, 41° to 63°. Did a few small jobs on truck. Shot another two squirrels. Practiced with .44 magnum again today. We went blueberry picking on west side of Little Nelchina River. Bugs were pretty bad. Roxanne and crew were in area picking also.

Sunday, August 20, 1995—partly cloudy and a couple showers, 45° to 63°. Got a squirrel right away. Karn had toast and coffee. Reloaded some more pest loads. Put the electric trolling motor back together but it doesn't run well and then only in 4th speed both rev and forward. Sylvia rested then we went to hill just west of Little Nelchina and picked blue berries.

Monday, August 21, 1995—mostly sunny, 39° to 63°. Sylvia went to Glennallen. I worked on truck and went to gravel pit and shot targets. Three ex-groups, 2 less than 1/2" 1-.32" 5 shots. We picked blueberries for a little while in afternoon.

Tuesday, August 22, 1995—partly cloudy, 34° to 63°. A little frost on a few potato plants. Pulled weeds in ½ the garden. Dug enough potatoes for a couple meals. Went to gravel pit two times, trying new loads. Hunting caribou traveling back and forth. Visited Allen in evening.

Wednesday, August 23, 1995—cloudy, rains going by on each side of us, 44° to 59°. We went to Glennallen on senior van. Paid electric bill and got a tranny filter kit and oil seal for truck. I tried to glue a couple places on my boots. A couple swans are on our lake.

Thursday, August 24, 1995—cloudy and rainy all night and day, 45° to 56°. Cut cleaning patches this morning. Wrote Theresa. Loaded a few varmint cartridges. We drove to dump. Lloyd's old bear skin is in dump. Lots of live bear shit there. Went on to Dan and Patti's and visited a while. Didn't see a caribou coming or going. Allen visited after supper.

Friday, August 25, 1995—cloudy and lots of hard rain all day, 47° to 51°. I prepped some brass today. Sylvia fixed a nice supper and had Ed, Sandy, and Robbie over to eat with us. Harold D. phoned in afternoon. Ed and family saw a nice bull moose run by their house, down to lake, swim across and run off into the woods.

Saturday, August 26, 1995—cloudy, sunny towards evening, 44° to 61°. Shot two squirrels. Loaded 127 rounds for practice. Sick all night and not well all day. Ate supper and don't feel well now. Doing maintenance and modification of reloading press.

Sunday, August 27, 1995—mostly sunny, then cloudy and a shower in evening,

41° to 60°. Visited Allen in morning and he paid me back gas he borrowed. But a new filter and oil in tranny of truck. Sylvia mowed lawn. Harold, Rachel, Rusty Dimmick and Robert were here for supper. They showed us a video tape of mining in Nome and their trip by boat up Yukon River to Nenana. Their friend Tom (?) came here to see the Dimmicks.

Monday, August 28, 1995—sunny and nice all day, 44° to 60°. Went on senior van to AK State fair in Palmer. Ate lunch at senior center and did a little shopping before coming home. Got home 9:00 PM.

Tuesday, August 29, 1995—cloudy and windy, 46° to 56°. Put a new valve on toilet tank. Had a hard time getting old seal out of transfer case on truck. The new seal was the wrong one. Brushed, waterproofing on both porches and steps.

Wednesday, August 30, 1995—cloudy, some rain in night and rain in afternoon and evening, 43° to 53°. We went on senior van. Sylvia got groceries, I got an oil seal for truck. Put the seal in when we got home. Rechecked the oil level in automatic transmission. The ermine sure scarfs up the squirrels I bring to it.

Thursday, August 31, 1995—cloudy, mostly sunny, cloudy in evening, 38° to 56°. Recovered the 2 sided logs. Sylvia picked cranberries. They aren't quite ready yet but very good. I did other small chores. Cleaned 2-5 gal buckets. Removed the garden and lawn water manifolds from the water line. Pulled weeds from garden and also the compost pile.

Friday, September 1, 1995—rain in evening, 35° to 56°. Sylvia went to Anchorage with the Rudbeck women. I cast some bullets. Shortened the stock on the .338 rifle. Shot three squirrels, missed another and saw two others. The ermine is well fed.

Saturday, September 2, 1995—intermittent showers, partly cloudy, 42° to 56°. Rigged the axe and shovel so they won't rattle when ATV is in motion. Cut some more off BPS 10-gauge stock. Went to gravel pit and shot .338 to check the zero after removing and replacing the stock yesterday. Allen & kids ask me to go camping and hunting with him. Cal was going also. I have so many aches and pains I declined his offer. Snow on some Mountain tops south. Saw a spruce hen in lane.

Sunday, September 3, 1995—partly cloudy, some breeze, 38° to 60°. Cleaned a rifle and got ready to go to gravel pit and shoot targets. At the pit, someone is sitting in their vehicle "hunting". I leave and go home, will shoot another day. Roof of camper is still leaking a little so I painted (leaky looking spots) it with aluminum paint. Very thoroughly cleaned two revolvers. The cylinder of one was quite leaded. Shooter's choice black powder gel worked very well. The ermine is getting lighter colored as he changes to winter fur.

Monday, September 4, 1995—mostly sunny, frost early, 31° to 56°. Sylvia picked a nice bucket of cranberries. I put more aluminum paint on camper. Repaired a broken part of camper mirror. Shot .338 and .22-250 at gravel pit. Shot very well. Put camper mattress out to dry a wet spot where the roof leaks. The ermine is now exploring the garage. Hauled garbage to dump. Allen, Roxanne and Ellie were here to have hamburgers with us. Later we had ice cream they had brought. Then Cal, Mary and Phillip G. brought a pumpkin pie and borrowed some video tapes. Then Allen and I went to dump in hopes of seeing a grizzly bear. No luck in that respect but I brought home a patio screen door and garden hose that needed an end.

Tuesday, September 5, 1995—partly cloudy, 40° to 49°. Waited ½ the day for a call from doctor's office. Sylvia picked cranberries. They look beautiful. Welded a hinge for storage trailer, plus a few other small jobs. Mary and Kari O. were here for supper.

Wednesday, September 6, 1995—some showers, mostly cloudy, 40° to 49°. Sylvia went to Glennallen and I went to Palmer, Wasilla to get medicine and a prescription filled. Stopped by Lucky and Mary B. Fixed door latch-knob.

Thursday, September 7, 1995—showers, cloudy, partly cloudy evening, 41° to 47°. Loaded some more target loads. Started loading gear in camper (goose hunting). Had supper at Mary O. Dan, Patti and Kurt were there. Saw cow and calf moose near the school house.

HUNTING AT DELTA FARMING PROJECT

Friday, September 8, 1995—mostly sunny, 40° to 50°. Loaded crane hunting gear and food. Forgot one medicine. Uneventful trip to Delta Jct. Got gas and some wheel weights. Some brass at the shooting range. 14 mi of new tar being laid on AK Hwy east of Delta Jct. Stopped by John Thuringer farm and gave them one of sweatshirts Sylvia made. Visited short while with John. He hasn't seen many geese and crane but I am welcome to camp and hunt. I saw a hundred cranes right away, stalked these, no luck, and 27 more a little later. Drove to other end of farm and cooked supper and saw maybe 1000 crane catch a rising thermal and head east. A few geese and crane flew low after shooting hrs. Saw a wolf track. Visited Scott H and camped on his place.

Saturday, September 9, 1995—partly cloudy, low fog this morning, 40s to 50s. Drove over to John's place while a little foggy. Parked and walked a long way. Couldn't get close to some cranes. Back to camper and fixed breakfast. Missed a sharp-tail. Took goose decoys out into field and set them. Three crane came close before I was hidden. Flared off and I missed the bird I shot at. Two cranes flew low over camper while I was out in field. Fixed lunch, no birds in afternoon. Went in to fix supper and a large flock flew near camper. But no chance shot for me. Went back out to lie under a straw windrow my back resting on pack frame and it leaning on a plastic bucket. No birds, the only action being John combining barley.

Sunday, September 10, 1995—partly cloudy, sunny and windy in afternoon, 40s to 60s. In field early, lots of dew. No birds, back to camper. Fix bite to eat. Back to decoys. Some cranes flew by on east side. Turned a nice flock of Canadians with call but they were alarmed by another blind with flapping burlap. I gave up about 11:30. A large 100+ flock of cranes had landed ½ mile away. No self respecting crane would fly by my goose decoys with the "real" thing so close. I pulled my decoys went to camper, fixed lunch. Put camper in order. John Thuringer came by on a tractor just then and I thanked him and drove over to Scotts. The guys I met last year (from Anchorage) are hunting the far corner at Scotts. I went on to the water hole in gravel pit nothing there.
    Drove over to Scotts other farm with buffalo and wild hogs. Took pix of buffalo—they are thin. Stopped to see Roy Beaver across the road. He looks much better this year. He was just about to haul a 350 JD CAT to Fairbanks and trade for a 1066 International farm tractor. I can hear cranes over on Schultz's farms. Parked on Scotts where Jim usually is parked. Walked to a grassy berm pile. Soon some crane flew by—too faraway. A speckled belly goose went over too high. More cranes flew directly over me. I screwed up, didn't even get one. Heard other hunters shooting. Saw a hunter walking, appeared to have something in his game bag. Lots of shots out along the road (hunting spruce hens?).
    Bartley flipped his plane in Tazlina Lake and got hurt. (It was windy with rough water.)

Monday, September 11, 1995—foggy, 40s to 50s. Up early and out to the blind Jim built. Heard a couple speckle bellies. Saw a nice flock of Canadas. A couple large flocks of sandhill crane, none flew near me. Gave it up about 10:00 AM and left for Delta Jct. Didn't find any wheel weights or rifle brass. It rained in Black Rapids-Summit Lake area. Some people are hunting boo north of Meyers Lake. No brass at Glennallen range. Stopped at Homestead Lumber and priced 3" ABC rigid plastic pipe. Scott Lawrence was there. He is visiting Jacki his sister for a week. Haven't seen him for 12 years.

Tuesday, September 12, 1995—partly cloudy, very nice, 37° to 57°. Sylvia picked cranberries and washed 6 plastic buckets to store berries in. I went up the trail to top of Slide on ATV looking for moose, boo or black bear. Didn't see any game and little sign. Shot .44 at targets. Washed mud off ATV. Reloaded 64 .44 magnum.

Wednesday, September 13, 1995—partly cloudy, 31° to 54°. Went to gun sight, didn't buy the 4" pipe he had. Looked for moose-caribou as I drove. Did some target shooting. Oiled some door hinges. Had to re-tighten the exhaust nuts on truck. Went to gravel pit to look for tracks. A couple boo had crossed the road there. I found (4) -.30 -06 shells where the boo went in the brush.

Thursday, September 14, 1995—sunny, beautiful, 34° to 53°. We took the camper off the truck and it's on blocks. Loaded ATV on truck and we went to Lake Louise Road looking for boo or moose. I was looking for a trail at about Mi 3 and found it. Back home I fixed a fender rattle and put the license plate back on truck. After supper we drove to mile 120 and glassed for moose. Saw a cow and yearling near dark on way home. Saw a cow at edge of ditch.

Friday, September 15, 1995—cloudy, little misty rain, 32° to 49°. Scott Lawrence visited about 7:00 AM. Nice to see him. I went to Mile 4 on Lake Louise Rd. Unloaded ATV and looked for trail west to my old trap line in that area. I got the machine down a steep rough place and had to turn around, cut brush and shovel dirt off level and winch and drive the machine back up to level trail. On way back to pickup I saw a martin in a large spruce tree. Drove around looking for a moose or boo—no luck. But did see two guys butchering an animal a little way east of Al Lee's. Sylvia went to a program put on at school house by the little kids. I readjusted the lights on the truck, oiled the door hinges. We will go to a supper at Allen and Roxanne's, cake and ice cream in honor of Faith Padowski.

Saturday, September 16, 1995—sunny, very nice, 31° to 56°. Went to about mile 12.6, parked the truck on north side in a gravel pit. Unloaded ATV and drove up to a small low hill and glassed for game. Saw first a moose, cow and calf. Then two hunters stopped by. After they left, they went somewhat near where the moose were last seen. The moose moved south towards the hwy with a bull following. I couldn't determine horn size and if the bull was legit.

A plane flew up the valley to the south and circled the reputed big bull over there. I tried to stalk the big bull I saw. I couldn't get through a thick deep swamp. Back at the pickup I loaded ATV and drove east and glassed but they were in brush. Went to Cal's to enlist his interest but he thought it was a bull with 2 brow tines on each side and not legal. I didn't feel well anyway and went home. Then down to Farmer to visit Lucky and Mary B. for a few minutes, back home and supper. Then Mary O. & Kari visited. Then Jeff Routt and Laurie came over to have holes drilled, ends radiused and sanded on steps and spacers for a circular stair.

Sunday, September 17, 1995—cloudy, partly cloudy, nice day, 32° to 54°. On the way to Squaw Creek Trailhead I glassed for the bull moose I saw yesterday-no luck. Unloaded ATV/Luck, Digger, David and a stranger "Carl" were getting ready to hit the trail. The trail was pretty good, though Lucky did get stuck three times. I spotted sheep on Sheep Mountain a protected area. After watching them (14) rams for awhile I saw two ewes on out side of Squaw Creek. Digger thought there might be more sheep out of sight and he went up that mountain. We continued on and saw grizzly bear tracks and a skinned rear ½ of a sheep in trail. It was well ripened. Possibly we had scared the bear off, but why didn't he carry it into the brush? We climbed up on a high bench but couldn't see any game. We explored a couple trails—no luck. Some ground squirrels were out this afternoon. A few moose tracks in mud. Visited another hunter and boy. Saw 5 other hunters. Looked for bull moose on way home. Sylvia dug the potatoes today. They are large and yielded well.

Monday, September 18, 1995—cloudy, partly cloudy and windy, 38° to 57°. We didn't leave the trailhead at RCA Hill till about 10:00 AM. Digger and Lucky were late. I road hunted while waiting on them. Digger saw a man shoot a illegal bull moose. The trail was very good. We were so late starting and left so early in afternoon that virtually no hunting, but a nice ATV ride on a fall day. We were high about the Nelchina River, which was running a lot of water.

Tuesday, September 19, 1995—I tried to drive ATV from home to trailhead at Hwy camp, couldn't do it so came home, loaded on truck and drove there. Met Geo (?), owner of "A" frame. Went up to top of Slide. Didn't see any game. Saw a fox dropping and a small grizzly track in the trail. Took trail to east and saw two bear dens dug into the face of Slide Mountain. Went a little way north along west side of Carrot Lake. A few caribou tracks here. Walked on a ways, then came back and ate lunch, down off the mountain. I looked for another trail, then came home. Went west, road hunting. Late afternoon, stopped at Dimmick's and talked to Rusty—they got a 56" bull moose.

Wednesday, September 20, 1995—cloudy, some showers, 46° to 64°. Up early and drove highway hunting to Mile 120. Didn't see anything. Came home, ate lunch, rested, fixed light switches at reloading bench. Then decided to hunt the trail on east side of Little Nelchina River. Once there, I saw very little moose sign. One pile bear pooh. Gave it up for this season and came home.

Thursday, September 21, 1995—hard rain all night and some this morning, 46° to 53°. Then partly cloudy and cloudy and very windy in evening. Wrote a letter to Jim M. Put screen door upstairs in garage. Cast some bullets with new mold. Anxious to try them on targets. Cal and Phillip were here borrowing TV tapes. He didn't get a moose. Washed the ATV. Cut a tree near the highline. Lubed bullets after supper.

Friday, September 22, 1995—partly cloudy and windy, 46° to 59°. Nelchina

River running strong—I can hear it from house yard. Did a few small jobs including grounding the left gas tank on truck—now the gauges work properly. Delta Application sent.

Saturday, September 23, 1995—cloudy, low fog, 36° to 50°. We mowed lawn. Fertilized, lime and tilled garden. Hauled garbage to dump. Cast some more bullets. Went over to Jerry and Betty Rudbeck's for supper.

Sunday, September 24, 1995—cloudy, foggy, some light rain, 39° to 47°. Weighed up wheel weights. lead and tin in 5 lb packs for casting bullets. Raked leaves. Cut a couple small trees and limbs in regards of future snow plowing. Visited Allen and Roxanne when they ask us to lunch. "Roma" the new teacher was there. Read a lot today.

Monday, September 25, 1995—foggy, cloudy, partly cloudy, 46° to 52°. Worked on Sammi Farmers hi chair tray. It's repaired and I'm staining the repair. Truck power steering hose leaking so I put another clamp on it. Sylvia went to Glennallen. She got Karn started in making corned moose meat.

Tuesday, September 26, 1995—partly cloudy, 32° to 53°. Dan and Patti drove down here and Dan went with us to Palmer to pick up their van that has been repaired. I had a doctor appointment then chased around looking for a threshold seal, no luck. Did a little shopping, plus 4 drums gasoline and came on home. Saw a 35" horned bull moose and a cow at mile 133.

Wednesday, September 27, 1995—mostly sunny, 33° to 53°. Pumped off the four drums of gasoline, took gun, trolling motor and battery down to lake, put canoe in and paddled to west end of lake. Shot a duck there. Paddled along south side and shot two more ducks with 1 shot. Went on to east end and got two more ducks there. Waited a while for some ducks to return, no luck. So used the trolling motor to come back to our dock. Cleaned the ducks. Cut the last of the rhubarb. Cal and Mary came to borrow some movies. We took the repaired high chair tray to Sammi F. in evening. Saw 200 swans very high, 5500 ft. Sun was shining on bottom of their wings.

Thursday, September 28, 1995—mostly cloudy, 27° to 43°. Replaced the security 5 gal bucket. Rearranged some of garage. Realigned the water line down near the lake. Saw two ducks swim past. Filled seven bags of sand for canoe ballast.

Friday, September 29, 1995—partly cloudy, 33° to 50°. Dan B. phoned and suggested we go caribou hunting in the Federal Hunt area. I gathered hunt gear, then trimmed a couple small trees until he got here. His "new to him van" is real nice. We did a little business for him in Glennallen then stopped at shooting range. He shot his rifle twice and mine once and hit a quart can with mine. At mile 10 Denali Highway I shot a small bull boo. Back at Glennallen we attend a meeting by Air Force who want to over fly our area.

Saturday, September 30, 1995—partly cloudy,34° to 49°. Sylvia cut up and packaged the boo. I re-bolted the exhaust pipes to the manifold of the truck. Checked the power steering. Covered a bare place on a electrical truck wire and tied the wire away from the exhaust pipe. Pick up a little more stuff before snow falls. Built a 1/4" gravel sieve. Hauled one small load of gravel with the ATV and trailer. Manning had us over to lunch. Mary O., Kari and Kitten R. visited late afternoon.

Sunday, October 1, 1995—cloudy, snow showers, melted as they hit the ground, then mostly sunny, 36° to 46°. Hauled a little gravel. Cleaned up some spilled oil. Packed two trailers and covered one. Went to gravel pit to target shoot. Polished some brass. Allen, David, Kyle and friend visited and had blueberry pie with us. Went to work scrubbing a pistol bore. Found a blemish there. Damn!

Monday, October 2, 1995—partly cloudy, light breeze on lake, 27° to 47°. Eight swans and three ducks on lake. I spread fertilizer on lawn. Sylvia went to Glennallen on senior van. Jim Manning borrowed my shooting bench and sand bags etc. to sight in his rifle. In afternoon we went to Bart and Rosemary's and visited for awhile. She recovers from a stroke and operation. He recovered from injuries received during an attempt by a helicopter to rescue him after he flipped his 180 Cessna Float plane upside down in Tazlina Lake. He clung to the plane floats, wet and cold in a high wind for seven hours. The chopper attempted the rescue, struck the plane floats and sank. Bart's plane sank later. Bev phoned.

Tuesday, October 3, 1995—partly cloudy, 36° to 46°. Wrote letters. We took ½ caribou meat over to Dan at The Point. Patti was in Anchorage. Had chili with Dan. Then drove down Oil Well Road saw about 60 caribou in all our driving today. Jumped five ducks at Mendeltna Creek. I didn't shoot, couldn't retrieve them. Water too swift and deep. Back home, changed oil and filter on truck.

Wednesday, October 4, 1995—partly cloudy, very nice today, 27° to 44°. Sylvia went to Glennallen. I shortened the stock on 12-gauge shotgun to my length of pull. I cut off and filled with accu gel the stock of .338. Started sanding the recoil pad for that stock. Bob and Karn visited for a while after Sylvia came home today. I could hear swans, or maybe they were geese, in flight today. Six swans, six ducks still on lake. The beavers are working like beavers.

Thursday, October 5, 1995—mostly cloudy, 30° to 40°. Snow on mountains to south. Finished putting recoil pad on rifle. Mounted snow plow frame to truck. Went to gravel pit to practice. Bev called. More ducks on our lake today.

Friday, October 6, 1995—mostly sunny, nice, 22° to 39° Did a few small jobs. Tried to shoot a spruce hen with .44 and bird shot – was too far away. Cut off a rifle stock and re-glued recoil pad back on. Sylvia fixed a turkey dinner and had Bob, Karn, Betty and Jerry Rudbeck over.

Saturday, October 7, 1995—light snow, cloudy, partly cloudy in afternoon, 30° to 43°. Started building two gun cradle vises. Burned the little pile of tree trimmings. Sylvia saw thirty ducks get up and fly off our lake. Saw a spruce hen picking up gravel and feeding on berries

Sunday, October 8, 1995—partly cloudy, 24° to 40°. A few ducks still on lake. I went to look for trees to cut for wood, no luck. Looked for more discarded mail, no luck. Elaine M. here to lunch. Worked on gun cradles. Sam Weaver visited. Then Allen F., Mary Odden, Kari and friend, then Scott and Diane came. Did some load development for Paul.

Monday, October 9, 1995—partly cloudy, 30° to 40°. We went to Glennallen on senior van. Cashed check at bank. Sylvia shopped. I went duck hunting on our lake and got three ducks. Didn't feel well this afternoon.

Tuesday, October 10, 1995—snow and cloudy, 27° to 37°. Cast some bullets. Worked on gun cradles. Bob and Karn visited a while. Two swans and five signets spent time on our lake.

Wednesday, October 11, 1995—Snow in night, cloudy, partly cloudy and windy, 29° to 37°. More ducks today and swans flying around. Sylvia went to Glennallen. My back is better. I worked on gun cradles. Target shot with revolver. Cal, Mary, and Philip visited.

Thursday, October 12, 1995—mostly clear, then cloudy in evening, 15° to 35°. Quite a bit of thin, slushy ice on lake this morning. Another three signet swan family and maybe 30 ducks. I worked on gun cradles. Cal G. came over and visited in afternoon. Sylvia fixed ham, beans, and cornbread and ask Allen and Roxanne to supper, Ellie and Sammi came also.

Friday, October 13, 1995—partly cloudy, 22° to 34°. A west wind broke up a lot of the ice that was on our lake. Sylvia went to a "puppet" show by the kids at school. Tom H. stopped by and we mounted his new scope on his rifle. I started another gun cradle (one will now go to Steve).

Saturday, October 14, 1995—mostly cloudy, a little sunny around noon, 9° to 29°. We got our butchering gear gathered up and went to Tom H. He treated us to pizza first, then we went out and butchered his two hogs they raised this summer. We had a good time doing it. I brought three little Dimmick boys here till their grandparents could come and care for them. Our lake is frozen over except for a small hole with seven ducks.

Sunday, October 15, 1995—mostly sunny. From 2 to 5 goldeneye ducks are using the little open water on our lake. We saw four swans fly down the lake. We went to Tom and Kim's and helped cut up the two hogs. They gave us some pork. Peter H was there when we got there. Back at home, I loaded wood on truck and unloaded it in basement.

Monday, October 16, 1995—cloudy, 12° to 28°. We rode senior van to Glennallen and got our flu shots and a TB test for me. Tried to fix a tarp cover for pickup camper, no luck. Worked on gun cradles. Clouds are down to 3500' elevation. A couple ducks still keep a hole open on lake.

Tuesday, October 17, 1995—low clouds, hiding the top of Slide Mountain, 10° to 29°. I put the three gun cradles together and I put three coats of tung oil on the one for me. We went to a birthday party for Samantha Farmer.

Wednesday, October 18, 1995—mostly cloudy here and looking like snow this evening 9° to 27°. We went on senior van to Glennallen. We tied chicken wire along and over the raspberries. Put canoe on dock and tied it down. Visited Bob and Karn Rudbeck. Jerry came over there then we all went spruce hen hunting. No luck but did see some caribou. The little duck can't fly!! and is still keeping the hole open. It dives and feeds OK.

Thursday, October 19, 1995—mostly cloudy, skiff of snow in the night, 21° to 35°. Did a few little jobs and worked on gun cradles. Sylvia quilts. Little duck persists in keeping hole open in lake ice. Griz, last night, on lower road.

Friday, October 20, 1995—partly cloudy, low clouds just at dark, 21° to 40°. Left front brake was frozen on ATV. Took it apart and put WD 40 on it, after wiping it dry. Finished the gun cradles. Cast 10# of bullets this afternoon. Visited Jerry at his hanger. Our lake thawed a lot this afternoon.

Saturday, October 21, 1995—low clouds, light snow, 26° to 37°. Finished lubing the bullets. Loaded some hunting varmint loads. Drew out a design for a shooting stick. Went down to Allen's but he was gone; he and family visited in evening.

Sunday, October 22, 1995—cloudy, all day, 25° to 33°. The grizzly was into Mannings garbage cans again last night. We hauled our garbage. Went on to Jeff and Lori's, gave him a gun cradle-vise and two sizes of cast bullets to reload. Art and Bonnie were there also. Jeff gave me some bullet lube to try. We looked for a place to cut fire wood while on way home. No luck. Ed Farmer brought over a parka and asked Sylvia to repair it. He needed an oil filter too. He had his son-in-law Tim and Pat Landers with him.

Monday, October 23, 1995—cloudy, all day, some snow around us, 26° to 32°. Sylvia went to Glennallen on senior bus. I didn't need anything. Shortly after Sylvia got home, Lee Dudley visited. We talked guns and reloading. Great! Then just as I got started casting some decoy anchors for grandson Steve, Bob R came over on their mule ATV and gave me a ride on it. It needs a lot of work. Good project for him. Finished the anchors. We just finished supper and Robbie brought back an oil filter replacement.

Tuesday, October 24, 1995—cloudy and hard snow in the pass on the way home from Palmer and Wasilla, 20° to 36°. We went in to get prescriptions filled. Did a little shopping. Stopped at Glacier View School, didn't look up Allen though (he was working). Made an attempt at adjusting the timing on the truck.

Wednesday, October 25, 1995—cloudy, some snow, 27° to 33°. We went on senior van to Glennallen. After lunch, we attended a "hands on" class using a fire extinguisher to put out a fire. I bought a "low temp house minder" at the lumber yard. We brought the air compressor into the basement. I cut and sanded moose horn slices for necklaces Sylvia wants to make those for grandchildren. We visited Jerry and Betty R.

Thursday, October 26, 1995—snow all night and day, 25° to 31°. We put canopy on pick up. I blocked ATV off its tires. Started snowgo and drove it a little. Did a couple little jobs for Sylvia. Put new screws in M 70 action, then cleaned the barrel.

Friday, October 27, 1995—we have 4" snow now, cloudy and some snow most of day, 20° to 31°. Packed snow on driveway with truck. Gathered, packaged and boxed some things I don't use any more and will take them to Steve when we got to Minnesota Nov 8. We made reservations this morning. We think Jim O. flew over in "Rags" his plane while on his way home.

Saturday, October 28, 1995—cloudy, 11° to 21°. Jim O. visited in afternoon. Gave him some cast bullets and a gun cradle vise. We went to a potluck remembrance of Lloyd Ronning.

Sunday, October 29, 1995—mostly sunny, 10° to 25°. Cleaned and oiled two shot guns. Read some, wrote my brother, Marion. Sylvia finished the necklaces and did laundry. More overflow on lake. Canine tracks crossed the lake.

Monday, October 30, 1995—mostly cloudy, 13° to 27°.   Bob and Karn were here for coffee this morning. I did some target practice. We have lost Sheryl's caulking info. Two red polls hit garage window and died. I started some cartridge key rings.

Tuesday, October 31, 1995–cloudy, rain just at dark, 16° to 29°. Finished cartridge key ring. Loaded the cartridges I emptied yesterday. Jerry R. borrowed some electrical and pipe fitting. Read some. We went to the Halloween party at the school house.

Wednesday, November 1, 1995–rain in night, black ice on highway and lots of accidents, 21° to 35°. We went on senior van and had a good meal. Sylvia got a birthday card for Carol Adkins. Back at home I did a couple of small things. Cal G. brought some tapes back and picked up his tapes. We had coffee and visited.

Thursday, November 2, 1995–mostly cloudy, 15° to 27°. I cleaned the well and turned the light bulb on to keep the well from freezing. Sylvia gave Missy a permanent. We went to a birthday party for Carol Akins.

Friday, November 3, 1995–cloudy, light snow, 9° to 22°. Tried to fix an adjustable desk lamp. Rigged up the low temp light to put in bathroom window while we are in Minnesota. Dan B. stopped by for a few minutes. We went to Odden's for supper. Lee Dudley, Bob, and Karn R. were there also. Jim, Mary and Lee played music.

Saturday, November 4, 1995–very windy all night, cloudy all day, 17° to 23°. Breakfast with Allen, Roxanne and family. Jim M. brought back a borrowed catalog and showed pix of him and son Jamie hunting elk on Afognak Is. De Johnson brought us some insurance money she owed us. Karn R. brought a petition for us to sign, an effort to get rid of Officer Stevenson. We moved Odden's rug out of upstairs closet and got closets ready for winter.

Sunday, November 5, 1995–mostly clear, sun dogs out this morning, 3° to 17°. Cal visited and had sausage sandwich and coffee. Rudbecks brought a package for Sylvia to mail then changed their mind and took it with them to Anchorage. We visited Rosemary and Bart in afternoon. Put on snow plow when we got home. Doesn't lift well, will add oil tomorrow.

Monday, November 6, 1995–finished getting ready to go to Minnesota.

Tuesday, November 7, 1995– it's -12°. Bart and Rosemary picked us up at 9:00 AM. We stopped at Eureka and had breakfast. Dr. appointment in Wasilla. Then on to Eagle River and ate lunch. Then Bart and Rosemary got motel room in Anchorage. We went to "Get Shorty" movie. They then dropped us off at airport. Our flight left at 2:00 AM.

Wednesday, November 8, 1995–45°. We arrived at Salt Lake City, two hour lay over and got to Minneapolis about 1:30 PM Minnesota time. Nadia met us at the gate. Gathered our luggage and drove to Nadia and Chuck's. Visited with her till Chuck got home and we visited and ate supper. Lots going on here with the magazine and all. Chuck is good at selling the ads for magazine. Some of kids and grandkids phoned to visit.

Thursday, November 9, 1995–some snow and windy. Warmed up and melted snow off roads after breakfast and Chuck went to work his rounds. Nadia, Sylvia and I went to Staples. Had lunch in Royalton on the way. Filled Nadia's car with gas at Ruth's station, said hi to her and went to see Paul and Stevens. Nadia left soon after we got here. Opened the boxes of trap gear for Steve and reloads both men. Read some and watched TV after supper. Paul and Steve have picked up a lot of brass at the two nearby gun ranges.

Friday, November 10, 1995–fairly cold and some breeze. We went to Harold and Lorraine Hanson's. Visited and had lunch. Saw some successful deer hunters. Back at Paul, Ruth and Steve's for supper and movies. They got gear ready to hunt tomorrow.

Saturday, November 11, 1995–close to zero, and up to 20°. Paul, Ruth and Steve back at mid afternoon. Didn't get a shot at a deer. Visited and watched TV. Called and invited Lee and girlfriend Kelly to a turkey dinner tomorrow.

Sunday, November 12, 1995–skiff of snow, 10° above to 22°. Sylvia fixed turkey. Lee and Kelly showed up and we had a nice dinner. Sylvia gave Lee a quilt. I gave him a pair of choppers, liners and a .357 key ring.

Monday, November 13, 1995–1/2" snow, 10° to 20s. We went to Rollins, had lunch and visited with Allen, Lillian, Scott, Darlene and son Andy. Marty (MN) F & G was there. We looked at some of Allen's projects. Back at town did a little shopping. Steve and his partner Arron started trapping near town.

Tuesday, November 14, 1995–partly cloudy, 10° to 30s. We went to Jim and Arlene R., had lunch with them. They asked John Titterington and wife over for dessert and we got to visit with them. Went to Mike Ackermann's. His dad, Peter, and Clarence Miller was there. Had coffee and donuts and visiting. Saw a cottontail rabbit near Mike's. We got Steve back home too late as his trapping partner had left for trap line. Paul and I drove Steve to his trap line. We saw a couple hundred Canadian geese on the way. After leaving Steve, we saw a woman and two retrievers in ditch watching a small flock of geese in flight. Steve made more sets. He didn't catch anything.

Wednesday, November 15, 1995—cloudy, 15° to 32°. Stayed here with Paul all day. Read some, watched TV, Steve ran his trap line. He and Arron each got a muskrat. Steve had a rat ring off also. Back home in Steve's fur room they skinned and stretched the rats. Arron missed a fox at a set. We all watched the fur put up and took pix.

Thursday, November 16, 1995—partly cloudy, 20° to 40°. We all got around fairly early. Loaded luggage, duffel bag in Paul and Ruth's vehicle. Steve skipped school and went with us. We stopped at El Ray Café and had breakfast. We saw a fork horn white tail south of Motley and geese on Long Prairie River at Motley. Steve notices all the rat and beaver houses in sight of the road. We saw lots of ducks and Canada's geese in fields and on water and ice all the way to Minneapolis. Found our way to Nadia and Chuck's OK. Had lunch and visited a while. Paul and family then went back to Staples. Chuck went to dentist. I walked to a Quick Stop store and got a newspaper.

Friday, November 17, 1995—cloudy, 32° to 40°. We went with Nadia to Stillwater. She did errands. We shopped.

Saturday, November 18, 1995—cloudy, 25° to 30s. Went to Stillwater PO, then to Wal-Mart and Fleet Farm to shop. Back at Nadia's I walked to the Quick Stop and got Sunday paper and ice cream. After supper, Chuck and Nadia went to his nephew's football game.

Sunday, November 19, 1995—cloudy, light shower, 30° to 38°. After lunch Nadia took us over to Ranette and Janette (my brother, Jerry Wilkins' twin daughters). We met Ranette's daughter. Salina and her daughter. Angelique. We didn't get to meet Peter or her (Ranette's) husband the last time I saw her because I was in Alaska hunting in the fall 1972. She lived with Jerry a short while at that time.

Monday, November 20, 1995—cloudy and windy, 33° to 30s. We went with Nadia as she did some errands. We grocery shopped and came back for a late lunch. Nadia and Chuck's landlord came over and wanted to visit with me.

Tuesday, November 21, 1995—windy, 29° to 30s. After lunch, we went with Nadia to PO, errands and did a little shopping. Chuck was out and about today. I tightened a door hinge this afternoon. Laura and Brittany were here to dinner this evening.

Wednesday, November 22, 1995—mostly sunny, 15° to 30s. Chuck and I went to Bayport. He had things to do. We tried to find bungee cord "S" hooks and a electrical breaker. I got a turkey, pies and snacks for tomorrow's dinner. Nadia and Sylvia went shopping. Sylvia got birthday present for Brittany. Laura dropped by at dinner time and ate here. She took the turkey with her. We plan to eat at her place.

Thursday, November 23, 1995—sunny, -3° to 31°. We all went over to granddaughter Laura and daughter Brittany's place. Laura had fixed the turkey and all the fixings. Very good. Visitors, TV and games going on in afternoon. Nadia and Chuck went back to their place about dark.

Friday, November 24, 1995—cloudy, partly cloudy late afternoon, 20s to 30s. Laura went to work. Brittney stayed home from school. Laura came home early afternoon. Her boyfriend Brad came about supper time. We watched movies.

Saturday, November 25, 1995—partly sunny, cloudy late afternoon, 10° to 30°. Stayed here today. Darrel Breider phoned. Brittany's father came and took her for the night. Laura and Brad went out for a few hours.

Sunday, November 26, 1995—one inch of snow in the night, 20s to low 30s. Cloudy and warm enough to thaw most of the snow. Laura fixed a lunch shortly before Nadia came over. We went with Nadia to Theresa's place. Theresa came out and went with us to Nadia and Chuck's place, so she could visit with us for a little while. Darcy couldn't arrange her time to see us. Chuck fixed a good supper.

Monday, November 27, 1995—six inches now, some windy. Snow melted on hwy. Nadia took Sylvia to shop for Sandy's present and drove us to Beverly's. Tyler was home and Vanessa came home from school and showed us her graduation picture and gave us, big, med, small pictures. Good supper and fun with Tyler and movies.

Tuesday, November 28, 1995—mostly cloudy, a little sun in afternoon. 5° to 20s. I walked with Bev to auto teller to get money orders. Check out the book store on way home. Watched a lot of TV. Took out the garbage.

Wednesday, November 29, 1995—cloudy, sunny, 5° to 20s. Mary Lou drove Bev and Sylvia to Sylvia's eye exam and new glasses. Back to Bev's to pick up Bev's laundry and over to Mary Lou's to do laundry and lunch. Tyler went to church after school. Vanessa went to "McDonald's" meeting. I did a little reading and TV watching.

Thursday, November 30, 1995—cloudy, sunny, cloudy, 30s to 40s. I walked south on Lyndale to a gun shop and back. Stopped by the book shop. Mary Lou came over and Bev, Sylvia went to lunch and grocery shopped. Mary Lou spent the afternoon and early evening here looking at pictures.

Friday, December 1, 1995—mostly sunny, snow and ice is shrinking, 20s to 30s. I walked down Lyndale again today. Legs got tired and back is sore. Bev's neighbor Florence visited a little while. Vanessa stayed home from school. Tyler played outside after he got home from school.

Saturday, December 2, 1995—mostly sunny, snow and ice is melting, 30s to 40s. Helped Tyler with his math. He and I tried to rent a movie, no luck. He did get to play with a video game. Then we did a little grocery shopping. Sylvia and Bev cooked a Thanksgiving dinner. Invited Mary Lou. We watched TV later. Tyler went over to his dad's with Mary Lou when she went home.

Sunday, December 3, 1995—sunny, cloudy afternoon, 20s to 30s. The kids went to church. Mary Lou took them to lunch and got here late. Bev fixed shish-kabob. I walked over to the Quick Stop and got a Sunday paper. Tyler and a friend played. We watched TV.

Monday, December 4, 1995—cloudy, snow flurry, windy in evening, 20s to 30s. I walked over to hardware store and then picked up a gallon of milk on way home. Laura called about 6:00 PM and Nadia got on phone. She is hospitalized over night. Dizzy spells and couldn't drive her car. Not sure what the problem is. We hope she is well in morning.

Tuesday, December 5, 1995—mostly sunny and windy 20-30 mph., 10° to 23°. Took a nap in morning. Nadia phoned several times to keep us informed. Her condition is much better. Tests indicate an inner-ear infection.

Wednesday, December 6, 1995—sunny and windy sometimes, 5° to 20s. Bev, Sylvia and I walked over to mall and did a little shopping. Back at home I needed packaging tape, so went back and got some. Theresa called in evening. I phoned Steve and got news of his folks, fishing and trapping.

Thursday, December 7, 1995—sunny and some breeze. 10° to 30°. We all walked over to mall and did a little shopping. Confirmed our flight for tomorrow. Nadia called. Theresa called.

Friday, December 8, 1995—snowing here in Minneapolis, 10°. Nadia and Chuck came over to Bev's to take us to airport at 5:00 AM. Our plane had to be de-iced and we got to Salt Lake City 20 minutes late. We hurried through the terminal to the gate for our flight to Anchorage. Made it with a few minutes to spare. Jim and Mary Odden met us in Anchorage. We shopped in Eagle hardware store for an air purifier and a speaker telephone. Went to Royal Fork for supper. Had prescriptions filled and shopped for groceries in Palmer. Nice visit on way home. Sure great to be home. Hooked up new phone.

Saturday, December 9, 1995—23° most of day. Finished packing and getting things back to normal. Jim M. was out at mail boxes when I went out for our mail. Ralph, teacher's husband, stopped by for a visit. Jim M. came over a little later. Shortly after they left, Allen came with ice cream in hand and stayed for a bite of supper and visited over 3 hours. I sorted an answered some mail.

Sunday, December 10, 1995—mostly sunny, -18° to -6°. Wrote some letters. Drove truck down to Allen's and dropped his ice cream off, drove on lake and over to our well and checked it . The light bulb is keeping ice off the top. Ralph borrowed my CAT Claw. Robbie F. borrowed our dump key. I thanked Sandy for watching our place. She needed my truck dip stick to ck their transmission oil.

Monday, December 11, 1995—mostly cloudy, -13° to -3°. We rode senior van to Glennallen and did errands. Picked up magazines and junk mail at post office. Jim and Mary O. stopped by towards evening and had supper with us. Harold Dimmick ph. from Arizona and wanted me to go check on heat in their house. Sent off papers to Energy A.

Tuesday, December 12, 1995—mostly cloudy, ice fog around us, -11° to -4°. Visited Ralph, Roxanne, talked to Mark and then over to Mannings. Got a couple more Christmas cards out and wrote one letter. Phoned Jim O. His eye may be improving. Cal G. stopped by and had coffee and cookies. After baking cookies, Sylvia worked on quilts.

Wednesday, December 13, 1995—mostly cloudy, -15° to -2°. We went to Glennallen on senior van. Sylvia works on a quilt. I made two marten sets and took plow off truck and gassed it. Allen visited in evening.

Thursday, December 14, 1995— it's -6° to 2° in Anchorage. We left early and returned the new telephone to Eagle Hardware in Anchorage, then got prescription quotes. Ate lunch and shopped Northway Mall. Sylvia got a lot of quilt fabric, then on to Wal-Mart, Wasilla, then Cottonwood Mall, Carr's Palmer and then home early in evening. Plugged phone in. Tired tonight.

Friday, December 15, 1995—mostly cloudy and lowering in evening, -9° to -1°. Big marten is running around our place. It likes duck cleanings. I wrote a lot of Christmas cards today. Tom H. called to invite us over Christmas Day (evening) and to Mendeltna Chapel for a Christmas Party. Roxanne stopped by with a more formal invite to Mendeltna.

Saturday, December 16, 1995—cloudy, -7° to 4°. Caught a marten. Later went to Cal and Mary's with a couple wolf traps and set them along a trail the wolf had used last night. Visited and had coffee and cookies. Came home and went right over to Ed and Sandy's. Sylvia with "brass" gift for Sandy. Visited and came home and shortly Bartley's phoned and came over with a poinsettia for Sylvia. They visited and had coffee pie and ice cream.

Sunday, December 17, 1995–cloudy, -6° to 6°. Visited Allen in afternoon. Lucky and Mary B. were there. Later I rode with Allen to Eureka hunting caribou, no luck. We got ready to go to Mendeltna Chapel Christmas program. Ralph Fuson and Roma Lee returned my Cat Claw bar. The Christmas program was nice, with lots of kids participating. Visited with lots of people.

Monday, December 18, 1995–cloudy, -5° to 0°. Sylvia worked on quilts. I read.

Tuesday, December 19, 1995–cloudy, partly cloudy afternoon, -8° to -1°. We went to Christmas party at Kluti Kaah Hall in Copper Center. A dinner, gift exchange and a cake walk for gifts. Talk is wolves are eating pet dogs in Chistochina, Chitna Copper Center, and Glennallen. Jeff King calls 140 wolves, fox and coyote per year according to friend of Mark Weitslhist.

Wednesday, December 20, 1995–cloudy, -8° to 10°. Set for marten again. Read quite a bit. Made some phone calls. Worked on my chair seat and did my exercises. Patti and Dan Billman stopped by for a few minutes and left some home canned salmon and sauerkraut and pickled string beans. We gave them a small Christmas wrapped cake. Sylvia made sugar cookies and brownies for folks who drop by. Allen brought ice cream and watched TV with us.

Thursday, December 21, 1995–cloudy, fog afternoon, 0° to 15°. Shoveled a little snow on top of the septic tank. Put some repairs on a bullet mold. Cast 160 .45 cal. bullets. Temp in the garage wasn't too bad even with the doors open for ventilation. Read some and took a nap this afternoon. Phoned William Gilliam (American Legion, Glennallen) about getting my P.U.F. life membership transferred.

Friday, December 22, 1995–cloudy, fog, 0° to 8°. Did some reading. Took a nap. Jim and Elaine visited and brought cookies. Phoned Cal and Jim with hunting information I got from Fish & Wildlife Protection-Anchorage.

Saturday, December 23, 1995–cloudy all day, 5° to 17°. We visited Allen and Roxanne in morning. Did some reading and exercises. Sylvia sews quilt covers. Nadia, Chuck, Laura, Brad and Britt phoned Christmas greetings. Charged the wildlife caller.

Sunday, December 24, 1995–cloudy and fog all around, 4° to 16°. Small birds feed on what Sylvia gives them. Put bulb in yard light. Spent some time with wildlife caller. Read a lot.

Monday, December 25, 1995—cloudy, fog all around, 10° to 20°. I have some kind of sinus cold. We went to Odden's for Christmas dinner. John, Coleen and their two sons were there, Jim and Elaine Manning, also Morey Secondchief. Very good and enjoyable. Got back home and Theresa phoned.

Tuesday, December 26, 1995—cloudy, fog around, 6° to 17°. Sick with a cold. Slept late. Allen called and we had him, Roxanne and Sammi here to breakfast. I gave him a couple of bungees. Sylvia went to Glennallen with Roxanne. I worked on a hose on the water works in the basement. A marten was into my bait box last night. I made a set for him.

Wednesday, December 27, 1995—foggy all day, 10° to 21°. Went to Jim's and he ordered some things for me. I made a fox set in gravel pit on way home. Sylvia had pumped water and it was murky!! Drove truck through Allen's and down lake to our well. Bulbs were burned out!! And the well has lots of ice in it. Put a heat bulb in hoping to thaw the well.

Thursday, December 28, 1995—foggy, windy down on lake, cloudy, 5° to 12°. Got a nice male marten. Put another heat bulb in well, covered well with a tarp. Checked trap at gravel pit.

Friday, December 29, 1995—partly cloudy, -2° to 2°. Shoveled some snow over septic tank. Jim and Mary Odden visited in evening.

Saturday, December 30, 1995—mostly sunny, -5° to 10°. Checked well, bulb is thawing ice. Sylvia did a little sewing for me. Our septic system is frozen up. Visited Allen and Roxanne.

Sunday, December 31, 1995—mostly sunny, -10° to 7°. Did lots reading. Still fairly sick. Allen and Kyle had coco with us. Later Allen and Roxanne and family took us with them to Tom Huddleston's home. We ate supper there. Visited and watched some TV and video.

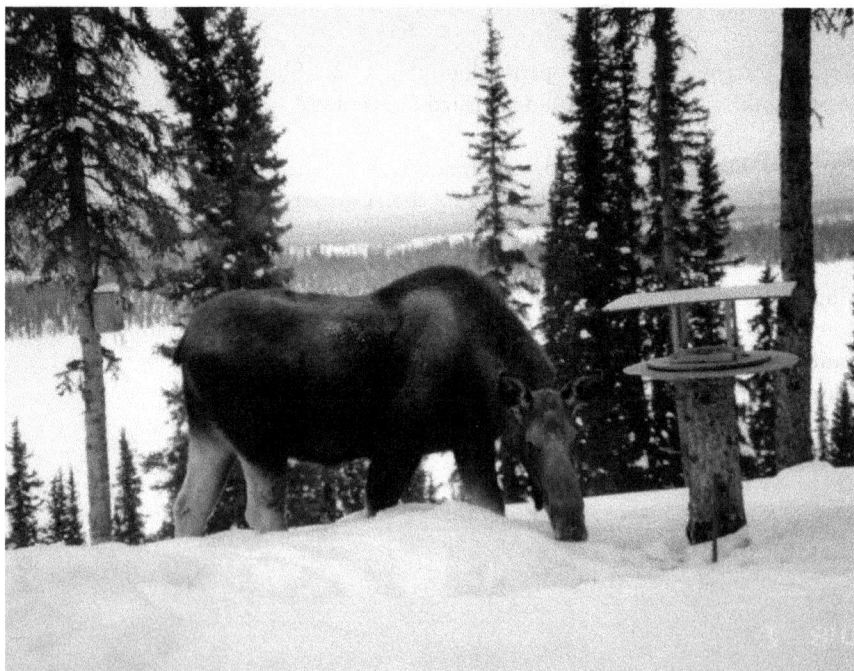

A moose browsing just outside Norman and Sylvia's picture window.

1996—moose hunting, duck hunting

Monday, January 1, 1996—mostly sunny, -2° to 12°. Read some and wrote another page in letter to Beverly. Sylvia baked Kyle's gingersnap dough—good and worked on her quilts.

Tuesday, January 2, 1996—mostly Sunny, -7° to 9° Fog, snow moved in across the river. Sylvia went to Chamberlain's for a party for Morey Secondchief (her 86th birthday). I read. Jim phoned the gun has arrived.

Wednesday, January 3, 1996—partly cloudy, -5° to -2°. Sylvia went to Glennallen on senior van. Jim came over and I filled out the paper work to buy the gun. Polished some brass in afternoon. A very large, strange dog ran through our place last night. Mary and Jim and Kari O. brought corn chowder and flan (a custard) and ate supper with us. We watched a movie of native early schooling then loaded the rug and pads Jim and Mary had stored here. An owl flew into the big window as we ate, but didn't break it.

Thursday, January 4, 1996—light snow all day, -4° to 5°. Checked trap at gravel pit. It was sprung. I brought it home. We took the heat bulb out of the well and put a 100 watt bulb in. Lots of ice has been melted. I shoveled more snow around the well. A part in yard light receptacle is broke. I won't fix it till spring.

Friday, January 5, 1996—snow all night and day (4"), 4° to 8°. Did some reading. Birds are at feeder. I got most of my snow plowed at home before the plow lift quit working. Talked to Ralph Fuson a little while. Jim brought over most of an order that came in for me. Allen visited and had pie with us.

Saturday, January 6, 1996—cloudy, very little snow, -2° to 8°. Jim left snow plow manual. Had trouble getting a set screw loose. Adjustment didn't cause plow to work. Loaded some M5ACP. Feel sick this evening.

Sunday, January 7, 1996—cloudy + 1" snow, -2° to 5°. I had Sylvia move the snow plow control lever while I tried to see why the pump wouldn't activate the cylinders. Possibly the bypass valve or pump itself is bad. Did target practice with the .45 to check its function. Asked Mark B. about pump—no luck.

Monday, January 8, 1996—mostly cloudy, a little snow last night. Sun dogs, -14° to -10°. We went to Glennallen on senior van. D. Johnson paid us some more. Cashed our check and ate lunch. Back home fooled around with snowplow. It worked for 15 min. and quit again. I loaded some .45ACP. Mark B. stopped by to see if our plow was working.

Tuesday, January 9, 1996—mostly sunny with sundogs, -24° to -12°. I put the new battery in the truck on the snowplow side. Hoist works now. Shot a target with 185 GR .45ACP. Trooper Lt. Al Cain phoned to discuss our problem with officer Stevenson. We didn't get very far into our discussion when Allen and David came. I gave Allen his share of the black wolf money. Ralph Fuson visited in afternoon to make plans to call varmints.

Wednesday, January 10, 1996—mostly sunny with sun dogs, -34° to -20°. Lt. Al Cain called again this morning. He has only talked to Herb Simon and me so far. He hasn't done much of an in depth investigation into Officer Stevenson's conduct. Many other people should be heard. We went to Glennallen on the senior van. Sylvia did a couple loads of laundry while we ate lunch. I got copies made of Jim D's Western Snowplow Parts Book and Owner's Manual. I prepared some more .45 ACP cases/ready now for powder and bullets. I didn't see any tracks of fur or varmints in the ditches today. We did see two moose. One near the highway and another some distance out in the edge of a swamp.

Thursday, January 11, 1996—sunny all day, few clouds, a little breeze, -34° to -18°. Did some reading. Polished the .45 ACP sizer die. Cleaned and oiled the decapper bell and the seater dies. Cleaned 10 gallons of ashes out of stove in basement and built a fire there.

Friday, January 12, 1996—sunny, -45° to -28°. Visited Jim and Elaine. Brought mail on way home. Loaded a few cartridges and shot some. Went to Jim and Mary Odden's for supper. Jeff and Laurie Routt were there. We had a nice visit. Paid Jim for rest of supplies.

Saturday, January 13, 1996—sunny, -42° to -30°. Visited Ed and took some magazines to Sandy when I went out to get the mail. We are burning quite a bit of wood these days.

Sunday, January 14, 1996—sunny, -41° to -32°. Read most of the day. The light bulb that heats the well has burned out.

Monday, January 15, 1996—sunny, -42° to -29°. Pulled two plastic sled loads of wood to house and put in basement. Sylvia and I drove to lake and put new bulb in well. Visited Roxanne and kids. Jim Odden came there for Kari. Scott Rollins phoned. Wrote lots of letters. Put bulb in well.

Tuesday, January 16, 1996—sunny, -40° to -30°. Visited Ralph, no school today so Roma was there also. Back home I built a bullet trap by filling a 50-gallon drum with snow to freeze, then hang a target in front of frozen snow to catch the bullets for recasting. Brushed and prepared the two marten for shipping to sale. Mailed holster order to Cabela's.

Wednesday, January 17, 1996—sunny, -40° to -30°. Jim M. visited this morning. After I got the mail, I shot a couple targets. Cal called to report the wolf with a trap on its foot went past his place last night. Tom H. visited and I let him shoot a target with the .45 ACP. My back is very bad. Allen, Roxanne, Ellie, Sammi and Kari visited us. Cabela's cap from order came. Shirts back ordered.

Thursday, January 18, 1996—sunny, -43° to -28°. We did a few little jobs. I took my two marten to Missy Farmer to take to Glennallen for me. Shot another target. Jim and Mary Odden picked up Sylvia's prescription. I took two wolf traps to Cal's and we set those and checked out the north gravel pit. Had coffee, then went to highway camp gravel pit and made a trail set for wolves there.

Friday, January 19, 1996—sunny, -42° to -30°. Some fog on Nelchina River. Probably caused by overflow on top of river ice. Smashed aluminum cans. Tried to fit Packmayr grips on .357, no luck. Reload some .45 ACP. Harold and Rachel Dimmick visited.

Saturday, January 20, 1996—sunny, -44° to -31°. We put wood in basement every day. Sylvia baked bread. She went with Allen and Roxanne to Eureka. Allen had killed two caribou. We ate supper with them.

Sunday, January 21, 1996—partly cloudy, -44° to -27°. Nadia phoned 9:00 AM urging us to plug in our CO alert. The furnace heating their aptartment had just set off her alarm. I plugged ours in, she had given it to us last fall. Odden's got back 2:00 AM this morning and had gotten Sylvia's medicine. Roma Fuson dropped it off at our place. Allen and David brought one side of boo ribs and one side of back strap this evening.

Monday, January 22, 1996—thin clouds, -39° to -25°. Sylvia cut and packaged the meat Allen brought over last night. I checked the wolf sets and had a mature male grey wolf (weight, 102 lbs., length of carcass 66"). Made a snare set on north side of highway ½ mile west of highway camp. Cal came down and helped me skin the wolf and had coffee and soup with us. Allen stopped by with a pistol he is trying out.

Tuesday, January 23, 1996—high layer of clouds, -33° to -17°. Did some chores. Took some money to Odden's. Jim is out on trap line. Went to Cal's to set some snares but prospects didn't look good, so gave it up. Had coffee, saw four moose on way home, some quite a distance out, cow and calf near hwy. Sure stiff and sore today. Jim Manning and Ralph Fuson stopped by while I was gone.

Wednesday, January 24, 1996—sunny, -30° to -15°. Sylvia went to Glennallen on senior van. I got some snare supplies ready and set another snare for wolves.

Visited Jim O. then onto to Tom H. He had just returned from a snowmobile trip to my place. He had frosted his nose. Looked for fur tracks at gravel pit on way home.

Thursday, January 25, 1996—mostly sunny, -35° to -18°. Visited Jim and Elaine Manning. Couldn't fix kitchen door latch so I moved the one from the front door to kitchen. Ralph stopped by while I was at Manning's and returned later in afternoon. He wants to call predators when weather warms.

Friday, January 26, 1996—sunny and a little breeze from east, -40° to -23°. Sharpened some skinning knives. The holster from Cabela's came. Cal G. took us down to Allen's birthday party and brought us home.

Saturday, January 27, 1996—sunny, -37° to -24°. Jim Odden and Ralph F. came to get water tank to haul water for school teacher Amy. Allen's water was frozen over so they all came here. Allen and Jim shot .45 at targets then we tried to pull water here. Water quit at about 100 gallons. Our water line froze up. Jim, Mary, Kari O., Allen and Ellie were here for supper. Wild duck and sauerkraut. Mary brought mincemeat pie. Sylvia is feeling sick tonight.

Sunday, January 28, 1966—sunny here, clouds both north and south, -43° to -18°. We checked the two snare sets. Then went to Tom and Kim to watch the super bowl game. Quite a few people there. I take a rifle everywhere I go, just in case I get a chance at a varmint.

Monday, January 29, 1996—cloudy, warmed up thru the night to -9° morning and -4° afternoon. Did some target shooting, brass cleaning and loaded 35 cases. Jim and Elaine had tea and snacks.

Tuesday, January 30, 1996—sundogs at noon then cloudy, -10° in night to 9°. Jim came over and we uncovered the well. Light bulb was burned out but well wasn't frozen. Our water line was frozen for a long way towards the hill. So we plan to wait for warm sunshine to thaw the line. Sylvia made kolaches and we all had some. Mary Odden brought a package that had my "ProChrono" in it and a box of .338 bullets. After Jim went home I checked my wolf snares, nothing.

Wednesday, January 31, 1996—cloudy, snow in sight and freezing mist in evening, -5° to 14°. Went to Glennallen on senior van and I mailed the wolf pelt to the tannery. Ralph and Jeff Routt went calling predators' (wolves) and got back too late for he and I to go out. We plan to go in morning. Went to Jim Odden and paid him for ProChrono. Talked over my sale of trap line equipment and the wolf kill Ralph and Jeff found. Nasty driving this evening.

Thursday, February 1, 1996—cloudy, light snow, ice fog, 5° to 10°. Ralph came over early and we went to Oil Well Road and tried to call in wolves. The moose kill Ralph and Jeff had found was consumed. The wolves seemed to be gone. We tried three stands. Stopped in at Jim O. on way home. Back at home, I left and checked the two snares I have out. No new sign there. Did target shooting. Cal G and family, Allen F. and family visited. Nadia called to tell me "Happy Birthday".

Friday, February 2, 1996—cloudy, ice fog, and frost and snow in evening, -15° to -5°. Took the bathroom stool off the drain and turned it upside down looking for a reason it doesn't work, no luck with that. Did a couple little jobs and shot a target. Cleaned pistol. We went to the pot luck supper and drawing for a video camera at the school house. Bev and family phoned birthday greetings.

Saturday, February 3, 1996—mostly cloudy, lots of ice fog, -13° to -3°. Sam Weaver stopped by and visited for awhile. We had coffee with Allen and Roxanne and checked the outside bulb at the well. Loaded some .45 ACP cartridges. Jim Odden stopped by to air up his trailer tires. I hooked up the hose to pump water off and into house storage. Jim asked to get the trap line when I'm finished.

Sunday, February 4, 1996—snow all day (2"), -10° to -5°. Slept, read, looked at pictures, then showered and warmed up the truck and went to Jeff and Lauri Rhout's place for turkey supper. Art and Bonnie, Ralph and Roma and Jim and Mary, Kari Odden were guests also.

Monday, February 5, 1996—cloudy, very little snow (3" now), -10° to -3°. We went to Glennallen on senior van. Called our checks and did a little shopping. Plowed our snow, plus in front of Ed F. and the lane down to Allen's. Then I plowed a road to our well.

Tuesday, February 6, 1996—snow all night and morning 3", -10° to -3°. I tried to shovel snow off wood shed roof-too slippery. Cast some bullets. Shoveled snow up to north side of house. Plowed out our snow and Allen's snow. Jim O. came over to weld/repair, his snowgo sled. We drove out the rear sight on a rifle of his and put in a new one I had that fit his rifle. We ate supper with Allen, Roxanne family and Roma drove their pick up over the edge of a steep bank sideways.

Wednesday, February 7, 1996—partly cloudy and snow in evening, -9° to 12°. Shoveled snow of wood shed roof and raked it off greenhouse. Tried to find Jeff for Lauri (baby was sick). Made a spacer for bed mattress. Did .45 ACP target shooting. Getting much better. A squirrel evades me. It is jumpy and has excellent hearing. Door opening, foot steps etc.

Thursday, February 8, 1996—mostly cloudy and 2" snow overnight and snowing again this evening, -3° to 11°. Shoveled and raked more snow off roofs. Plowed our snow. Visited Ralph, his left pickup door and rear cab corner is severely damaged. He gave us some pickled fish. Target practice again today. Jim O. hauled us a load of water and welded the hitch on his snowgo sled. Saw two spruce hens picking up gravel in our yard.

Friday, February 9, 1996—1 1/2" snow in night, cloudy all day and snowing in evening, 4° to 13°. Shoveled and raked more snow off roof. Visited Cal and Mary in afternoon. A little target shooting when we got back home. Tom H. visited for a little while after supper.

Saturday, February 10, 1996—3" snow, 8° in night to 18° this morning and reach 32° this afternoon. Plowed our snow and cleaned around the mail boxes. Tom borrowed our snowgo trailer. Turned too short and broke off his ball hitch bolt. Luckily I had a replacement. I did more target practice. Theresa called early morning and Bev phoned this afternoon. Snowing all afternoon.

Sunday, February 11, 1996—3-1/2 more inches of snow, 31° in night to 10° morning and 19° in afternoon. Plowed our snow and went to Bartley's and plowed theirs and had coffee with Rosemary. Loaded more .45 ACP then started snowgo and broke trail to well. Got stuck twice, pulled a hamstring, walked and packed rest of trail to lake on foot. Allen visited and brought cake, borrowed a rope, asked me to plow snow at his saw mill. David stopped by too.

Monday, February 12, 1996—sunny bright and beautiful, -3° to 17°. Saw a set of canine tracks down on eastern end of our lake. Sylvia went on senior van. I shot a target. Went to Allen's and plowed snow at his saw mill.

Tuesday, February 13, 1996—foggy most of day, -8° to 10°. Sylvia sewed quilt. I packaged a gun to send off for repair. Allen brought a tub of ice cream, Roxanne and girls came by later and had ice cream on a no crust pumpkin pie Sylvia had made.

Wednesday, February 14, 1996—cloudy, snowy in evening, 3° to 16°. Sylvia went on senior van and mailed my 44 magnum to Ruger for repair. I did some target practice. Ralph visited and I gave him some window plastic to rig a temporary window in his truck. Ravens are courting.

Thursday, February 15, 1996—1" snow in night, 12° to 25°. Sunny, cloudy, partly cloudy and low clouds just at dark. Sylvia went to a ladies luncheon. I plowed snow. Made some plow adjustments. Target practice. Tom Huddleston brought snowgo trailer back and visited. Allen came over and borrowed the old blue rope. I advanced the spark on truck.

Friday, February 16, 1996—7" snow, mostly cloudy, 9° to 24°. Plowed our snow and the mailbox's and Bartley's when we went to Oddens for supper. I shoveled snow off the camper. Fired up the snowgo and broke trail down to the well.

Saturday, February 17, 1996—sunny, -10° to 9°. I shoveled off woodshed roof. Target practice. Allen and David visited. David left and later Roxanne came and Allen went home with her. They called at supper time for us to eat with them. Denny E. showed up at Allen's and called his brother Chuck. Chuck then told me how to try to get the gold out of our ruby sand.

Sunday, February 18, 1996—partly cloudy, light snow evening, -8° to 8°. Raked some snow off roofs. Shot target. Went to Cal's and we picked up the wolf sets. Elaine borrowed and returned some movies. Tom H. came over to weld and repair his snowplow.

Monday, February 19, 1996—partly cloudy and gusty winds, -9° to 9°. Cleaned off more roofs. Ralph visited, Sandy F, and Cal G. also all while I'm baking cookies. Shot a target. A cow and calf caribou walked through the yard.

Tuesday, February 20, 1996—sunny, ice fog in air, -30° to -10°. Finished cleaning snow off roofs. Walked over, visited Ralph Fuson this morning.

Wednesday, February 21, 1996—partly cloudy, cloudy and light snow in evening, -39° to-16°. Allen came and got us to have breakfast with him Roxanne and Sammi. More caribou were in our yard. Jim O. came over for some pipe fittings to make a water tank vent. He wants my trap line. -60° at Snowshoe Lake.

Thursday, February 22, 1996—morning, cloudy and light snow in night. Sun dogs at noon. Sunny afternoon cloudy and clearing in evening, -36° to 5°. Visited Ralph in morning. He gave us some caribou jerky. While there Sylvia called that the tannery has our wolf pelt done. Visited Allen and had a bowl of ice cream. Target practice back at home. I saw a fat ermine in the woodshed. It was -60° at Snowshoe Lake.

Friday, February 23, 1996—sunny, -32° to -5°. Coyote tracks on lake. Target shooting. Loaded a few. Allen got stuck in overflow but got out by himself and no frost bite. He had coffee with us. Moose has been feeding on browse in the yard. Sent a letter to Nadia and a letter to tannery.

Saturday, February 24, 1996—partly cloudy, -29° to -7°. Target shooting and gun cleaning. We watched a cow moose and yearling calf walk across our lake.

Sunday, February 25, 1996—mostly cloudy, -17° to 17°. We went to Dimmick's. Met Claude and Dora from Kotzebue. Had supper with Harold, Rachel, Corky and Rusty. Two skidoo's were here while we were gone.

Monday, February 26, 1996—mostly sunny, 2" snow in night, -12° to 26°. We went to Glennallen on senior van. Shot some loads over the ProChrono with the 22-250. It worked fine, my first experience. Plowed our snow. Looked all over for a box of cartridges. Mary and Kari O. came by. I went with them to their place and brought their truck home to take to Jim in Anchorage tomorrow. Cal visited in morning.

Tuesday, February 27, 1996—partly cloudy, foggy through the pass, -7° to 23°. Up early and drove Jim's pick up to Anchorage airport. Met him there. We did errands and shopping for Jim and us. Finished up shopping in Palmer. Got gas and drove on home. Unloaded groceries. Sylvia heated pizza for a snack. Mary Odden phoned. Wanted the warm pickup, take a visitor home. Jim ate banana split with us. I left a wolf skull with a guy in Peter's Creek. He is to buy it.

Wednesday, February 28, 1996—mostly sunny, 3° to 28°. I made three skin sewing ulus. I cut a used blade of Sylvia's fabric cutter into three pieces and glued them into toy wood wheels.

Thursday, February 29, 1996—sunny, 4° to 30°. A little target shooting. Repacked the trail down to the well. With snowgo and went onto east end of lake. Saw fox tracks there. There is a fox den about 3/8 of a mile east of beaver dam. Mike from Louisiana is back at Tom H. He was babysitting Kindra and came over to visit a little while. After he left, I took the snow plow off the truck and went to gravel pit across from hwy camp. Walked and snowshoed to a wolf snare and picked it up. It gets dark about 7:00 PM now.

Friday, March 1, 1996—sunny, 5° to 34°. We took garbage to refuse container, then onto Glennallen. Got some wheel weights and brass. Sylvia did a little shopping. Saw where a pack of wolves crossed Lake Louis Road, just a little east of Mile Post 9. Some rabbit, ptarmigan, moose and caribou track. We visited Dan and Patti. Trapper Bob was there and I gave him and Dan some photos I had taken of them. Visited Leona, Doug and Tom on our way home. Snow had slid off north ½ house roof. Had to shovel some of it out of way. Phoned Nadia this morning.

Saturday, March 2, 1996—sunny, 4° to 31°. Called Jeff and he suggested he, Ralph and I go to the gun show at Palmer Hi. We got there around noon and left around 5:00 PM. Saw several people I new. Had a good time just walking around looking at all the guns and accoutrements. We got home shortly after sundown.

Sunday, March 3, 1996—sunny, -5° to 25°. Cleaned and polished brass. Chronographed some loads—interesting. We had Odden family and the Farmer family here to supper and blueberry pie and ice cream.

Monday, March 4, 1996—sunny, some breeze, -4° to 30°. Sylvia went to Glennallen. I did a few little jobs, then Sylvia took some pictures of me and a trap, later shooting pistol over the ProChrono. Then Ralph drove over to shoot his pistol and let me shoot also. I let him shoot mine. I've lost seven brass. Sure gets dark later now.

Tuesday, March 5, 1996—sunny and windy, 0° to 25°. Got wolf trap, snare and hunting gear ready. Picked up Ralph and we drove up Lake Louise Road. Saw lots more wolf tracks today. They must be hunting along the road. Stopped by Billman's. Dan is fishing at Crosswind Lake with Don Kulp and Trapper Bob. Ralph and I hunted (called) from a couple locations on way home, no luck. I shot a target, then cleaned a pistol and uniformed the primer pockets on some .45 ACP brass. Allen F. stopped by and had ice cream and pie with me.

Wednesday, March 6, 1996—sunny, not windy, -5° to 20°. We went to Glennallen on senior van. I prepared and sorted some brass. Started the snowgo and drove to Farmer and back. We went to a party at Oddens. Jim leaves for work and Smayda's are visiting. Sent check to Ruger.

Thursday, March 7, 1996—sunny, -16° to 16°. Smayda family visited a while in afternoon (enjoyed that). I loaded some more 45 ACP target loads. Cleaned the seater die of some lube.

Friday, March 8, 1996—sunny, -15° to 15°. Walked past Ralph's (he wasn't home) to Allen's. He was at work. David and Kyle are home on spring break. Shot one clip. Cleaned up some water Sylvia spilled in toilet. Loaded up some load development cartridges with a different powder than I have been using in .22-250. I cleaned that rifle.

Saturday, March 9, 1996—cloudy, snow all day, -14° to 14°. Billman called and wanted help with a C of C turkey shoot at the spring celebration at Tolsona Lake. The man who was to do it backed out at last minute. So I said I would help him and got Ralph to go along. Things were not organized. Ralph and I did out best to get things ready. The clay birds were broken!! Luckily there wasn't any one there with a shotgun who wanted to shoot for a turkey. I phoned the tannery and they are sending my wolf pelt. I phoned Tom Lessard and he called back. My wolf skull is worthless due to the broken teeth. Phoned tannery. (It was an old wolf.)

Sunday, March 10, 1996—snow all night and most of day & snowing again this evening, 12° to 22°. 6" to 7" fluffy snow. I loaded two more weights of powder for the development of the .22-250 loads. Then I went out and plowed snow here at home, the mail box's, past Brockman's, Ed Farmers, Ralph Fuson, and Allen's driveway widening it in a few places. I lost a bolt and had to replace it.

Monday, March 11, 1996—4" - 5" fluffy snow during the night and snow all day (2"). I plowed our snow and the mailboxes. Engaged in some target shooting. Only 10 old bullets left. Pounded some dry meat and put it out for birds. Boy did the red poll's flock in for it.

Tuesday, March 12, 1996—3" snow last night and today, 9° to 19°. Tom H. and Mike had cake and coffee with us this morning. I reloaded some .45 ACP brass. Plowed our snow. Manning visited.

Wednesday, March 13, 1996—nice sunny day, 11° to 32°. We went to Glennallen on senior van. Saw fox, lynx, rabbit, and moose tracks. Did a little target shooting and cleaned the bore of the .45 ACP. Visited Allen and Roxanne.

Thursday, March 14, 1996—sunny, breezy sometimes, 4° to 34°. I took Ralph with me up the Lake Louise Road looking for wolves and or signs. No luck. Did see two moose, some fox, caribou and ptarmigan tracks. This afternoon I ran seven 3 shot groups over the ProChrono. Very informative. Pete H. brought our water hauling tank home. A beautiful evening.

Friday, March 15, 1996—sunny, cloudy evening, 0° to 34°. Did some target shooting. Serviced snowgo packed trail to well. We went to students program at the Little Nelchina School. Allen saw a black wolf on south side of Tahneta Lake this morning.

Saturday, March 16, 1996—2" snow, quit about noon, 15° to 32°. I plowed it. Pulled a muscle in calf of my left leg while putting plow on truck. Noticed two loose bolts and tightened those. Packed trail to lake with snowgo. Stopped at Allen's but he was gone.

Sunday, March 17, 1996—sunny, -12° to 26°. Did target shooting and checking out a different primer. Harold, Rachel, Dora, and Claude were here to supper and a good visit after. Mary O. stopped by for some Epsom Salts to soak a cut hand. Ralph phoned wanted to go wolf hunting tomorrow.

Monday, March 18, 1996—sunny, 0° to 32°. Ralph and I drove up the Lake Louise Road, found wolf tracks coming off lake and up to the road. Didn't see where they left the road. Then we drove to Eureka and Ralph got some snowgo oil. West of, at Gunsight someone camping in motor home w/two dog-wolf crosses. I loaded some more .22-250 load development rounds. Ralph borrowed a snowgo gas line filter. We visited Allen and Roxanne in evening.

Tuesday, March 19, 1996—sunny, -12° to 21°. Don't feel good today. Looked for some papers, no luck. Ironed some maps flat. Roxanne, Sammi and Kyle visited. Kyle is writing a paper defending trapping in Alaska. He wanted to run his ideas past me and ask for suggestions. The northern lights were very bright.

Wednesday, March 20, 1996—sunny, -15° to 27°. Allen had -28° at his place. I adjusted the choke on the snowgo again. I drove it down to lake and circled the lake. Saw lots of mink track. They may be attracted to the boo trimmings on south side. Allen stopped by; he had been setting snares for wolves. We may set some of my traps tomorrow. Did some target shooting. Sylvia went to Glennallen.

Thursday, March 21, 1996—sunny, -14° to 21°. Some breeze on Little Nelchina on river. Loaded some wolf traps, went to Allen's. There we loaded his logging sled with alpine and went to Little Nelchina campground. Saw some other snowgos. They were hunting caribou. We went down river. Lots of wolf tracks. Made one set quite near where he had made a snare set. Then we went up river past campground a couple miles but made not sets up there. Back at Allen's he fixed a lunch and we visited awhile.

Friday, March 22, 1996—sunny, -3° to 25°. Went for a short snowgo ride on our lake. Shoveled some snow. Allen brought some caribou sausage, visited about lunch time. Jim Manning brought a bunch of our tapes back. They leave to visit outside. I did some cast bullet load development. Found two promising loads. Ralph visited for awhile this afternoon. Wants to drive Lake Louise Road tomorrow.

Saturday, March 23, 1996—thin clouds, -7° to 30°. Ralph came over about 8:30 AM and we drove the Lake Louise Road. Wolves had crossed near Woods Creek Oil Well Road. Fox at even more places. Moose and boo also but we didn't see any. Ralph pulled a pickup that had slipped off the road. The package with the wolf pelt in it came today. The guard hair is relatively short on this wolf. The tannery did a poor job. The lips are ruined. Ear and feet shrunken and hard. The length is shorter by 10". When the tanner fleshed it, the leather was thinned so much, hair roots were cut off and hair is falling out. I'm very disappointed. Clouding up this evening.

Sunday, March 24, 1996—thin clouds, 10° to 36°. I drove down as far as Cal's driveway looking for a caribou—no luck. A wolf crossed hwy going north at mi 142. I glassed the wolf set on river bank-nothing. Prepared 144 .45 ACP cases for powder and bullet. Allen, Roxanne, Kyle, Ellie and Sammie brought ice cream and a movie of spearing black bears and hunting polar bears.

Monday, March 25, 1996—sunny, 7° to 34°. Drove snowgo to Allen's. They were gone. Ralph walked out to end his driveway as I went up hill on way home. We visited a little. Picked up mail on way home. Melted down wheel weights, fluxed the lead and poured it into ingots. That batch yielded 65 lbs. Ralph stopped by on his way to school house. Darrel Douthat (trapper) visited with the news that Tree Farmer (Wolverine Lodge) has punched a trail through my old trap grounds. Darrel took a good observation-inventory around the cabin for which I am very grateful. Went out at 11:00 PM and got to see the comet Hyakutake thru holes in clouds.

Tuesday, March 26, 1996—sunny, 18° to 37°. We drove to Eureka and back looking for a caribou to shoot. No luck. Talked to a hunter who had found them north and east and in the brush. I cast some bullets. Cal, Mary, and Phillip visited in evening. I took a picture of Hyakutake Comet.

Wednesday, March 27, 1996—sunny, some wind, 21° to 34°. We went to Glennallen on senior van. Paid a couple bills and did laundry. I nearly finished a fleshing tool for Steve. A bald eagle feeds at Allen and Ralph's.

Thursday, March 28, 1996—sunny, -5° to 34°. Missed a squirrel. Rode snowgo to Highway camp. No one had a broke trail up slide from there. Saw wolf tracks. So came home. Allen visited and had a bite of supper with us.

Friday, March 29, 1996—sunny, some haze, -5° to 36°. Went to Odden's. Mary drove Kari, Sylvia and I to Meyer's Lake hunting caribou. No luck. Other's snowgo away from road and get a few animals. We did see a coyote at Woods Creek. Picked up a few brass. Ralph visited awhile.

Saturday, March 30, 1996—sunny, -2° to 28°. Hunted caribou. Stopped and told Allen that wolves had passed by his snares. He is committed to freighting for Al P. to John Lake. I lubed some bullets. Target practice. Made ice cream for a birthday party for Ralph Fuson at Mary Odden's.

Sunday, March 31, 1996—sunny, breezy, -1° to 29°. We road hunted this morning. Loaded .45 in afternoon. Ralph visited. Got a stove ready to take to trap cabin. Allen visited awhile. We road hunted after supper. A bull caribou with no horns and thus illegal ran towards us in middle of the road at mile 133. He was very tired, mouth open, stumbling. We went on to Cal and Mary's and visited awhile. Fixed a package for Steve.

Monday, April 1, 1996—sunny, windy, -5° to 20°. Loaded snowgo and gear on trailer and Ralph and I drove up Lake Louise Road to 11 ml trail. Unloaded machines and headed for trap cabin. I lost the trail, so we back tracked and tried a different trail. A ways down on this one the steering broke on my machine. We turned it around in trail by hand, I cut a suitably sized green spruce, tied it between the skis, with a loop to hook over Ralph's hitch, thus he could keep my skis straight. I used my motor for power. Back at road, loaded up and went home. Disappointed but it sure could have been worse. Feel sick tonight.

Tuesday, April 2, 1996—mostly sunny, -17° to 17°. Tried to vacuum clean the TV. It still doesn't work. Repaired the steering column on snowgo. Packaged some traps and a knife for Steve. Wrote Paul. Started to hook up the 5" TV, but Sylvia doesn't want TV.

Wednesday, April 3, 1996—mostly sunny, started snowing 4:00 PM, -15° to 20°. We went to Glennallen and mailed four packages to Minnesota. Ralph came over and I went with Ralph to look at a wolf snare set along hwy across the road from Slide Mt. trail. Someone had caught one and maybe two wolves. Tom H and TJ brought over a TV for us to use until we get one of our own. 2" snow.

Thursday, April 4, 1996—partly cloudy, 6° to 30°. Allen visited and Ralph borrowed a water tank. Did some target shooting and reloaded a few. Tried to improve timing on truck. Cleaned snowgo plugs and adjusted the choke. Wrote a letter.

Friday, April 5, 1996—cloudy, sunny, windy, 15° to 42°. Allen, Roxanne, Sammi and Nicky had breakfast with us. Ralph and I went to Eureka-he needed spark plugs and car adj. advice.

Saturday, April 6, 1996—partly cloudy, snow, very windy. Target shooting and cleaned gun. Ralph stopped by a couple min, to make plan for Mon. Put handle in salvage alum shovel to carry on snowgo. Snow slid off garage roof, cleared it away from east side of garage with snow plow. Made Jell-O. Mary O. wants to visit.

Sunday, April 7, 1996—mostly sunny, 10° to 34°. Beverly, Vanessa and Tyler phoned. Read a lot. Eagle, ravens and magpie feed on bone pile across lake.

Monday, April 8, 1996—sunny, 10° to 30°. Left home close to 9:00 AM, after loading Ralph's snowgo on my trailer. We unloaded machines at Mill Trailhead Lake Louise Road. Into parking lot drove Douthat and his friend Jack. They are freighting Darrel's cabin building materials to his property on Loon Lake. Tom Murray and other friends are doing the construction. After visiting awhile and looking at his map that he loaned us, we left for another try at getting to trap cabin. Whoever (Darrel Douthat) tried to put in the trail to Blue Lake sure got a lot of loops in it, plus dead ends. When we reached the Little Lake southeast of Blue Lake, I recognized the area. We followed their trail past my old turn off, turned around and came back in hopes of losing the curious. Took off up the trail to my cabin. Snow was deep, but it went well and we arrived in good time. Really great to be here. An emotional time for me. Ralph and I looked things over. We spent quite some time cleaning the mess the porcupines left while living in my cabin. Put new plastic on windows. Burned a lot of things the porcupines had peed on. Had some lunch. Ralph wanted to see Hole Lake, so we drove over there for a look see. Back at the cabin, more cleaning and straightening up. One support log of the cache has broken and dumped the storage drums and snowgo gas buckets on tundra. We picked up the 5-gallon buckets and will bring out all the trash and the old stove. Ralph put the foam mattresses and sleeping bags out on a line to air out on a rope between two trees. I shoveled some snow and we straightened the outhouse up. We are on daylight savings time and it stays light till about 10:00 PM. Ralph snowshoed, went to Hole Lake and tried to call wolves in with a rabbit squeal call. I shoveled snow off cabin roof. Saw four boo on Blue Lake.

Tuesday, April 9, 1996—sunny, thin clouds, 0° to 38°. Ralph fixed breakfast. Then went to Hole Lake and tried to call wolves again. I did the dishes, cleaned cabin again. Ralph loaded trash. I put shutters in the windows and prepared to close the cabin. We saw a spruce hen along the trail at jct. We took the Loon Lake Trail and found Douthat's cabin. His friends were started on a 12 x 24 cabin for him. After visiting a while we drove on. Left Darrel's map at Tom's cabin. Darrel then showed up to fix lunch for his help. We went to parking lot, loaded and went home. I put gear away. Rusty Gaines, an archer, stopped to visit on his way to Dan and Patti's. His wedding reception will be there July 25? Visited Allen in evening.

Wednesday, April 10, 1996—sunny and thin clouds, 0° to 38°. I noticed a couple small planes flying just behind Slide Mountain. I thought wolf hunters. Ralph thought bear hunters. We got Allen to go with us and try to get a grizzly bear. We hauled snowgos to Slide Mountain Trailhead and left from there. We soon saw wolf tracks and scat. A kill must be near by. North of Four Corners and near a place I caught a wolf once we came upon a moose front leg laying in the trail. We took trail west from Meat Pole Hill. I couldn't find the bear den I had in mind. We went west to trail going east. Allen spotted digging well up on a high hill. He led the way on his Alpine and broke trail past that area. We stopped and admired the view then turned down past the two digging areas. These were fox dens or two tries at one den, a neat thing to see. Then down the hill, stopping again at the camp between the two lakes. We continued on and past the Four Corners at Cache Creek. Two snow machine new tracks over ours turned up Cache Creek. We followed ¼ mile and turned back not wanting to

332

interfere if they were hunting bear. The bear may have been spotted from the planes this morning. Then back home. Allen stayed to have coffee and blueberry pie with us. I unhooked the snowgo trailer. Loaded gas drums and coolers in truck in preparation for our trip to Anchorage tomorrow.

Thursday, April 11, 1996—sunny, 3° to 41°. We left early for Anchorage. We shopped there including a new TV. Saw a couple moose and a few eagles today. Hooked up and programmed the TV this evening. Cal and Mary G. visited and borrowed movies.

Friday, April 12, 1996—sunny, 3° to 42°. Unloaded, pumped off the gasoline we hauled home yesterday. Visited Allen, Ralph. Tried programming TV. Lunch and Roxanne and Allen had pie with us. I went with Allen to his property and helped a little with his cabin project. After supper we returned Tom H's TV to him.

Saturday, April 13, 1996—sunny and a little breeze, 9° to 43°. Took garbage to dumpster. Picked up quite a bit of rifle brass there. Cleaned and polished it at home. Shoveled some snow and little jobs. Went with Ralph when he sighted his rifle in.

Sunday, April 14, 1996—high clouds, light breeze, 13° to 40°. Ralph and I went to Slide Mt. east side trailhead. Went north and Ralph saw a sow and calf moose before Cache Creek. There we went west and south following someone else's snowgo tracks. Turn and came back and went north to Meat Pole and west 2-3 mile then back to hunt camp between two lakes, then back out to hwy and home. There I moved drum bullet trap with ATV. Then moved water hauling tank closer to its storage place.

Monday, April 15, 1996—cloudy, sunny, cloudy, 20° to 46°. Target practice and polish brass. Small jobs. Allen and Ralph brought about a cord of wood, very nice of them. They had lunch with us. I did some load development with the .22-250. Checked the F.P.S. of my .338/300 grain bullets. Sylvia sewed a new cover for the snowgo from an old tent.

Tuesday, April 16, 1996—thin clouds, 26° to 46°. Up early, went to Allen's after had breakfast. He, Ralph and I went to Little Nelchina and got two large pickup loads of wood, cut up stove length. We have yesterday's load of wood cut up and all of it stacked in the woodshed. Really nice of Allen and Ralph to do this for us.

Wednesday, April 17, 1996—27° to 50°. Allen and Ralph visited. Ralph adjusted the choke on our pickup. UPS delivered my .44 magnum from Ruger's repair shop. I went to Allen's. He and Ralph were putting a new tranny in Ed's pickup. Sylvia cooked some of the Jambalaya Joe and Shirley sent us. After supper I adjusted the brake pedal travel on our pickup. Dan Billman visited in eve and we showed him the bush pilot movie that Nadia sent us.

Thursday, April 18, 1996—mostly sunny, cloudy evening, 25° to 50°. Visited Allen in morning. Put trap boiler together and boiled the wolf traps I had used this winter. Shot the .44 magnum. Need to adjust sights some more. I missed a squirrel today. Mary O. gave Ralph and I some left over water. Dimmicks phoned and ask me to feed and water their dog. Sylvia and I stopped at Gilcrease's on way home. Mary was in town, visited with Cal and Philip a while. Cal is working on his store.

Friday, April 19, 1996—again today sunny and thin clouds, 25° to 50°. After a couple phone calls, Allen, Ralph and I decided to go bear hunting on back side of Slide Mountain. After reaching the top of Slide Mountain, plus a half mile or so, we came across a bear track. After glassing the country for a while, Allen spotted a bear about one mile away, at a possible den site. After a circuitous route to put us at an advantage regarding the breeze, we drove our machines to the brow of a ridge over looking the bear. Ralph overshot and drove over the edge a little, then ran down the hill 50 feet. Allen and I glassed the area of interest and saw a blonde, a honey brown cubs with a sow blonde with brown legs and lower body—a Toklat color bear. The cubs looked to be three years old. The sow is very large. Mostly they just lay there soaked up the sun's rays. The sow looked our way just as we were leaving, probably not recognizing us for what we were. We left before provoking a confrontation, of course. Shooting a cow and or cub is unethical and illegal. Just seeing them is a fine and rewarding experience. We then back tracked the first bear tracks and they led us to the southeast corner of Slide Mountain and tracks and evidence that another group had hunted these bears. After again admiring the view out over many 100's of thousand acres we went down the mountain and home again. The trail had softened up and was difficult to negotiate. I was getting tired.

Saturday, April 20, 1996—sunny, 22° to 50°. Visited Allen Farmer. Some owl hawks are hanging around Allen's and Ellie imitates their call and they respond. Allen filmed Ellie and the bird on our VCR camera. Shoveled the snow off the water line. Bulb burning in well and it is thawed out. We had supper at Tom and Kim H. The Odden family were there also. Nice time and visit.

Sunday, April 21, 1996—sunny, thin clouds, 20° to 47°. Did lots target shooting. Having trouble with base pin on the .44. Re-trimmed some brass and polished .44 magnum brass. Cleaned guns. Called Nadia and she called back. Harold and Rachel had us to supper. No more than got home and Allen and Roxanne, Ellie and Sammi visited. Allen pulled bones over to river and back to a tree in a natural opening that is across our lake and east a little way. He wants to see what animals come in to it.

Monday, April 22, 1996—partly cloudy, cloudy, 24° to 50°. Did some target practice. Loaded some more. Cut some aluminum circles out on band saw. Used by Ralph building an air cleaner for truck on Allen's sawmill. Allen came up and got some large chain for a sled hitch. Rode with Allen when he picked up the boys from school bus over at Cal's driveway. On way home I suggested stopping by to investigate large bloody place on hwy, ½ mile west of our mail box. Wolf tracks in blood and on hwy. Caribou had been dragged 40 feet off hwy. Wolves, eagles and ravens are feeding on it. Imagine a wolf kill on highway so near habitation. Shoved snow off water line (lawn) and at septic tank site after I got home. Grandson Steve phoned: He's trapped two beaver so far. Nice to have him phone. Saw coyote on west end of our lake, and a wolf kill caribou on highway.

Tuesday, April 23, 1996—cloudy, sunny, 27° to 48°. Reworked the toilet seal. Some other small jobs. Ralph came over after lunch and worked on my truck brakes, much better now. He has shaved his beard. I visited Allen and he borrowed my level. I took pix of blood, tracks on hwy and caribou carcass (Monday's wolf kill).

Wednesday, April 24, 1996—cloudy, thin clouds, 27° to 48°. .44 magnum target shooting, testing another powder. Shoveled more snow off sewer drain field. Worked a little on water line to well. Gave Ralph a piece of angle iron he needed. Jack Chamberlin came and got a flower planter box and we visited a while. Allen came over to look at Suzuki repair manual and stayed for supper. Three swans sitting on ice of lake. Loaded more .44 magnum shells.

Thursday, April 25, 1996—partly cloudy, 29° to 50°. Shoveled some snow off sewer field. Hauled a load of water from Odden's. We got ready and went to Glennallen to do errands, shopping and went to the CVEA annual meeting. Got a few lbs of wheel weights at tire shop and some brass at shooting rifle range.

Friday, April 26, 1996—partly cloudy, 28° to 50°. Sylvia helped me put the snowgo back in its stall for summer. Sharpened chainsaw. Shoveled more snow off sewer field. Did some target shooting. Glassed Slide Mt. for bears-no luck. Reloaded some more brass.

Saturday, April 27, 1996—windy, partly cloudy, 26° to 48°. More target shooting. Gathered some broken tree tops and trimmed them. Allen wanted to borrow some glossy black paint but I didn't have any. My left shoulder is very sore.

Sunday, April 28, 1996—sunny, 21° to 46°. Burned trash and odd jobs. Beaver is dragging wood. Saw spruce hen and marsh hawk.

Monday, April 29, 1996—sunny, 26° to 49°. Breakfast at Allen's, Lucky and Mary there. Digger and Caroline gave a slide show of Diggers photos at school house. We went to Eureka for Sylvia's birthday dinner. Not good food. Visited Cal and Mary on way home.

Tuesday, April 30, 1996—partly cloudy and snow squalls blowing through most of day.,27° to 47°. Worked on .44 magnum load development. Took garbage to dumpster. Found some brass. We went onto visit Billmans at Lake Louise. Lots and lots of caribou crossing from east to west, headed to calving ground. Rusty and Corky Dimmick came over to drill two holes and install a trailer hitch...their dad's van.

Wednesday, May 1, 1996—mostly cloudy, snow showers, a little sun, 30° to 46°. Tried to thaw the water line near the house, little progress. Tested more .44 magnum loads. Allen and family came over to visit. Picked up a few spent bullets from a melting pile of snow I've been using for a bullet backup. A few ducks on the open hole in our lake. A marsh hawk appeared to be eating something on top of a muskrat pushup. ...the muskrat perhaps? Robins are around now.

Thursday, May 2, 1996—sunny, some breeze, 25° to 46°. I loaded the wolf carcass on the ATV and went up Slide as far as I could get and left it there. I walked around on the Slide area looking for fossils and had no luck. Saw the skull of a half grown marten. Old wolf and bear tracks. Snow was deep in protected places. Shot one load, .44 magnum. It shot accuracy very good. Picked up a few spent bullets. Allen used our water tank to haul Amy some water.

Friday, May 3, 1996—sunny and warm, 22° to 51°. Raked some leaves. Kim came by wanting donations for a school yard sale. Cast some bullets. Went to Allen's but he was gone. Started thinning the leather of a home made belt.

Saturday, May 4, 1996—cloudy, cool, 33° to 51°. Cast some more bullets. Raked some more of yard and removed some snow and ice. Fred Rungee visited, left a gift of potatoes. Lubed some bullets.

Sunday, May 5, 1996—sunny, beaut of a day, 33° to 53°. Did some target shooting. Finished thinning the belt and put a buckle on it. Sam Weaver wasn't home. Checked out gravel pit on way home, found some brass. Saw the remains of a snowshoe rabbit and fox at old RCA Site. In walking about the gravel pit across from DOT Nelchina station I found two places the road trapper made sets. I stopped at site of wolf killed caribou. The carcass has been pulled a hundred feet farther into the willows.

Monday, May 6, 1996–sunny, really nice, 28° to 56°. Cast more bullets. Had to work on a sprue plate. We pumped water to the green house from our well. The line into the house is thawed out. Cleaned up some old tree roots. Swan's, gulls, ducks, eagle, hawks on our lake. Allen's invited us to dinner. We made ice cream to take. Chuck Zimbicki stopped by to borrow my Suzuki manual, visit, ask about tires and will do something about smoke from Suzuki exhaust.

Tuesday, May 7, 1996–cloudy, few sprinkles, 39° to 52°. Put snowplow on and parked it for summer. Removed snow plow mounting from truck. Changed the oil and oil filter and air cleaner. Allen, Roxanne, Sammi and friend Nicki brought a nice lunch at noon. I walked around the lake this morning. Didn't see any fresh beaver sign. Not even at the dam on the east end of the lake. Northing has disturbed the hides or the bone piles. Saw several kinds of ducks, 3 swans and some gulls.

Wednesday, May 8, 1996–cloudy morning, sunny afternoon, 36° to 52°. Removed the canopy from truck. Installed front bumper. Parked the trailers out of sight. Cast more bullets. Target practice and chronographed some speeds. Watered the trees around the house. Put a cover on garage chimney to keep ducks out. A pair of swans is doing their courtship dance this evening.

Thursday, May 9, 1996–sunny, 25° to 60°. Started out to walk over to Nelchina River and Allen decided to go along. When we got there we had a great view from a narrow spine like projection out from River Bank, which is 125'-150' high in this area. We saw no game. Had lunch with Allen. Then took donated some things to school yard sale. I bought a vest and cup there. Sylvia and I went to Glennallen. Paid phone bill and cashed some checks. Ate supper and went to telephone coop meeting. Met a nice guy names Bill at Glennallen range. Checked little creek near Frank Zimbicki's for grayling going upstream to spawn. Didn't see any. Stopped by Kim Huddleston's. Sylvia paid her for some sewing stuff. Tom had left me a plastic cap for our well but it is all oily. I didn't bring it home.

Friday, May 10, 1996–sunny and a little breeze, 38° to 60°. Visited Allen. He didn't want any help. Sylvia and I decided to pick up the trash on our mile of hwy. Sure made us tired. Sam Weaver was picking trash also. We took the trash he had picked up with ours to the dumpster. I picked up a lot of brass at the dump, cleaned and polished it at home. I smashed the aluminum cans at home. Got in some target practice. Beverly phoned late at night. Sylvia took plants to green house.

Saturday, May 11, 1996—mostly sunny. Cleaned guns. Dug around on top of septic tank and found opening. Could see ice inside pipe. Loaded some more target loads. Don't feel well. Allen, Roxanne, and family were here to supper.

Sunday, May 12, 1996—sunny, breezy and beautiful day, 36° to 64°. Missed a squirrel. Picked up more bullets out of snow berms. Ralph came over and used my vise to repair the driveline on his truck. The Farmer family brought a corsage for Sylvia and Kyle gave it and a hug to Sylvia. Later Allen and Kyle visited. Allen gave me an engine block heater and I'm trying to thaw the septic tank with it. It may be too low a wattage.

Monday, May 13, 1996—sunny, breeze, 34° to 67°. Cleaned up and burned some trash and moved two sleds out of sight. Picked up bullets, watered trees, went down to well. Our septic tank isn't frozen. Swept the garage, put the screen door on arctic entry. Sylvia went to Glennallen with Roxanne to mail a package and get a graduation card for Vanessa.

Tuesday, May 14, 1996—partly cloudy and windy, 41° to 54°. More open water on the lake today. We watered the rhubarb and strawberry. I cleaned up some more of yard. Cast more bullets. Returned Allen's engine block heater. He visited here in afternoon. Chuck Zimbicki stopped by with his pick and will re-torque the head bolts on the Suzuki at his place. Lubed some bullets.

Wednesday, May 15, 1996—sunny, 25° to 53°. Worked on a pistol holster. Carried Mannings for rent sign up out of ditch and stood it back up. Watered trees again. Both Rudbeck families arrived from Minnesota today. We visited Jerry's Bob and Karn came over to pick up a key to Odden's gate lock. Harold and Rachel visited this evening.

Thursday, May 16, 1996—mostly cloudy, 31° to 57°. Started an ATV ramp. Repaired a yard light socket.

Friday, May 17, 1996—mostly cloudy, one light sprinkle, 34° to 56°. Couldn't find Allen at home. So cut steel with my torch. I got the two ramps assembled and welded today. Real tired tonight. Bob R. came over and brought Odden's key back. Chuck Z. phoned. It will be a while before he gets my ATV problem found and repaired he was in his bear bait stand last night late and killed a 200# black bear. A well furred animal. Took four shots—one of which was a miss. The bear climbed a tree and Chuck killed with the 4th shot using a 30-06.

Saturday, May 18, 1996—partly cloudy and some showers, 35° to 50°. I finished the loading ramps. Swept the garage. Cut some brush. Ran more water on the septic system and it's now thawed out. Sylvia went to Glennallen with Karn. Allen visited in evening.

Sunday, May 19, 1996—partly cloudy, 31° to 52°. 2" snow in night, melted off by noon. Sylvia worked in greenhouse. I cut out some wood figures for Elaine M. Went to gravel pit to target shoot. Lots of ducks on our lake, courting and feeding before nesting. An eagle keeps an eye out for meals.

Monday, May 20, 1996—partly cloudy, 33° to 47°. We drove to Glacier View School this morning. Allen works on the crew tearing down the old hockey rink. We loaded up some used lumber materials and the posts and brought them home. The highway construction crew started laying asphalt down today. Less ice on the lake. Eagle gets the ducks up and flying sometimes.

Tuesday, May 21, 1996—partly cloudy, 31° to 54°. Strong breeze in afternoon. Cut some brush and finished raking the yard. Started rebuilding a set of saw horses. Denny Eastman and Frank M. of Pillager visited. Then Rudbeck's Bob and Karn brought tier II Fish and Fame permit applications. I reloaded some .44 magnum with a different powder. Allen came over after supper and visited then I went with him to Eureka to pick up Kyle. Allen showed me his cabin he is building.

Wednesday, May 22, 1996—mostly sunny, some breeze, 30° to 58°. Held the ladder while Sylvia washed the house windows on the outside. Finished rebuilding the saw horses. Loaded up the shooting bench and all the goes with it and went to gravel pit and fired the .44 magnum loads testing this powder for accuracy and velocity with ProChrono. I shot quite well (accuracy), the velocity was higher than I expected. Visited Bart at Snowshoe Lake and picked up some subsistence hunting applications. Went to Bob and Karn's for supper. Jerry and Betty were there and Mary O. came later. Ellie F. and Kari O. put on a little dance for the grownups.

Thursday, May 23, 1996—partly cloudy, cloudy and windy, 27° to 55°. Filled out Tier II Hunt applications and mailed them. Worked at developing reduced loads for .223 Remington. Imr 800X powder and mini 14 for a rifle. Used the ProChrono for F.P.S. and Ave at 1500 F.P.S. Had a very accurate load with cast bullets. We went to a 75th birthday party for Jack Chamberlin at Mendeltna Chapel with pot luck supper.

Friday, May 24, 1996—partly cloudy and windy, 35° to 56°. My back is pretty bad. Got off to a slow start this morning again. Tried to repair a garden rake. Then loaded and test some more .223 loads. Cleaned the rifles. Loaded 20 of the last load @ 2000 FPS. Allen and Dave hunted a grizzly with no luck. Allen stopped in here and visited on his way home. I told him about a big black bear east of us. We may put out a bait station and try for it.

Saturday, May 25, 1996–cloudy and light showers, 35° to 50°. Sylvia went to Glennallen with Betty and got some flowers. I went down to Allen's thinking we might set up a bait station for black bear. Al Padowski had come out from Palmer and brought some dog food. Allen and Al set up the bait station last night!! I'm disappointed. I tried to add to the lighting in my closet w/no luck. I did add one small shelf that will help a lot.

Sunday, May 26, 1996–mostly cloudy, 36° to 52°. Cut and burned some brush. Ralph came over and borrowed the water tank full of water. Cal visited a little while. The .357 lube die was leaking so bad that I took it out to garbage and put a think wash of solder on top rim. After reinstalling it worked well.

Monday, May 27, 1996–cloudy and light showers, 30° to 56°. Sunny some times. Loaded a 100 pistol cartridges. We took garbage to dumpster. Looked around for some bear tracks with no luck. We went on to Woods Creek and fished with a Mepps spinner with no luck. We stopped by Oddens and gave Kari a birthday card. Back at home I loaded targets etc and went to gravel pit for target practice. Shoveled gravel over a screen to recover all the bullets I could. Will re-melt and cast them to use again. Cleaned pistol and the brass when I got home. Quite a few caribou had been walking around in gravel pit.

Tuesday, May 28, 1996–mostly sunny and light breeze, 36° to 61°. We put a 2" x 10" support across the front of trap, snowgo and gold screw storage area. Rebuilt and repaired two saw horses.

Wednesday, May 29, 1996–sunny, 36° to 68°. Went to Glennallen and paid electric bill. Talked to Darrel about Green Acres Land. Mailed Poetry Magazine to Charlie Trowbridge. Visited Blackie Zimbicki. Watched closely for a black bear. Found a piece of 1/2" plywood with some damage. Went to supper at Dimmicks. Met Rod and a ½ dozen other people. Stopped by Cal and Mary's on way home and visited. The new black top is laid to Eureka now.

Thursday, May 30, 1996–partly cloudy, 40° to 70°. Took the two tarps Beth left here to Charlie's stove and two wheel trailer and covered them securely. Visited with Jer and Betty at their hanger while on my way home. Allen came over and visited three hours. Later I cleaned some steel and plywood from along the side of the garage. Harold and Rachel stopped by with their guests. Sylvia served cake, blueberries, tea and coffee. Allen borrowed our garden tiller. I game him two grease hub caps for his ranger. Mary Odden and Roma Fuson were here to supper. I'm planning a trip to Anchorage.

Friday, May 31, 1996–partly cloudy, shower, 48° to 66°. We went shopping in Anchorage. A tiring trip. Saw a moose two miles west of Eureka and a caribou two miles east of Eureka.

Saturday, June 1, 1996—partly cloudy, a very nice day, 39° to 70°. Today was cleanup day at the dump site. I picked a couple bags of trash but mostly carried the shotgun and looking out for a bear. Lots of women and kids around. I installed the new distributor cap and rotor, put one pint oil in motor, adjusted the mirror mounting bracket on truck. Emmi and Sevda Banning visited a little while. Ralph left a couple guns here. Later he and Roma took picture of Sylvia's greenhouse and us.

Sunday, June 2, 1996—partly cloudy and windy, 46° to 72°. Melted down and cleaned the wheel weights I got in Anchorage Friday. Cast them in 1oz, ½ oz ingots. Went to gravel pit for target practice. Found some .223 Remington brass. Cleaned the pistols. Adjusted the mirror and tailgate on the truck.

Monday, June 3, 1996—mostly sunny, some breeze, 45° to 64°. Finished rebuilding the saw horses. Mounted an extension light in upstairs closet. Tried to determine feasibility of a road down our hill. Will need one other person.

Tuesday, June 4, 1996—partly cloudy and very windy, 36° to 54°. A tree blew down across our lane during the night. I cleaned it up and got the big tree that blew over in the hole, down on the ground. Visited Allen and Roxanne. Built and installed another shelf upstairs.

Wednesday, June 5, 1996—very nice day, 30° to 62°. Took trash to dumpster. Visited Tom H. on way home. Removed ¾ of wood shed roof and started putting used plywood sheathing on the roof. Allen invited me down for soup at suppertime. Sylvia came home in time for pie at Allen's.

Thursday, June 6, 1996—very nice day, some breeze, 34° to 65°. Finished putting the sheathing on wood shed roof. Visited Allen in evening.

Friday, June 7, 1996—nice day and some breeze to help with the mosquitoes, 38° to 72°. We put the brown roll roofing on the woodshed today. Stiff and sore and glad it's done. Supper at Jerry and Betty Rudbecks.

Saturday, June 8, 1996—couple of showers, mostly cloudy, 42° to 59°. Worked in garden. Started working on lawn mower. Needs a bearing. Called Chuck. It will be two weeks to get Suzuki fixed. Looked at Mark Brockman's TV dish. Allen brought over onion sets and eggs that we needed. Jerry R. wanted to borrow a cement drill and I don't have one. Called around about TV dishes.

Sunday, June 9, 1996—partly cloudy, 38° to 64°. Repaired lawnmower. Went to dump and rolled 4 heavy drums up out of a ravine and loaded them on the truck. When we got out to the gate someone had ran off with the padlock for dump gate causing us a lot of confusion. We took the drums to Dan at Point of View. Just as we got to dock area, the left rear axle came out of housing. Dan's helpers helped me get it back together.

Monday, June 10, 1996—but cooler later when it clouded over and got real windy, 35° to 61°. Pulled wheel and axle out of truck. Allen is to get me a new key and oil seal. Helped Sylvia with a cedar border for some flowers. Tried to check out the grade of the proposed road down to lake. Sure seems too steep.

Tuesday, June 11, 1996—partly cloudy, cloudy evening, 31° to 55°. Checked well and two duck box's. Bob Rudbeck wanted me to see part of their file on Brian Stevenson. Started planning wood shed roof overhang. Made a water tank rim support for Jim Manning. Allen and Roxanne stopped by with the oil seal for my truck. They had supper with us. Our lake water level is very low. I tapped three times very gently on one duck box and the hen flew out and landed close to shore and appeared to coax me away from the next box. Put left rear axle back in truck.

Wednesday, June 12, 1996—rain in night and snow on mountain peaks and Heavenly Ridge to the south, 37° to 56°. Mostly cloudy today. Visited Allen a little while. Wrote three letters. Thought some more about the roof overhang. After supper we went to KROA and talked to Fred Cristofferson about a TV receiver dish. Visited with Mike Shelton and Vern Adkins. Harold and Rachel visited in evening and brought us three heads of lettuce. Very cool this evening.

Thursday, June 13, 1996—off and on rain showers all night and day, 39° to 55°. Sylvia went to Glennallen with Karn and Betty. I went to target practice at gravel pit.

Friday, June 14, 1996—mostly sunny, 38° to 58°. Mosquitoes troublesome. Started cutting trees down to make way for a road down the hill to reach the lower road. Cut 16-18 smaller trees, trimmed them and piled the limbs. Went to Allen and Roxanne's for a late baked salmon lunch. Fresh salmon and very, very good. We took a watermelon down to share. Started cutting some more trees when we got back home. The sprocket in the bar broke!! Allen, David and Kyle came up and cut down a lot of trees. David left his saw here for me to use.

Saturday, June 15, 1996—partly cloudy, nice day, 38° to 68°. Cut a few trees. I'm pretty sore from yesterday. Piled more limbs and trash. Re-piled the wood we trimmed yesterday, plus a couple other little jobs.

Sunday, June 16, 1996—sunny and nice breeze, 45° to 72°. Some mosquitoes. I made a tumbler to remove brass from polishing media. New boots hurt my feet. Loaded powder and bullets into 100 brass. Lots of drake goldeneye on our lake.

Monday, June 17, 1996—sunny and nice breeze, 46° to 77°. I went to
Glennallen. Saw a flock of 25-30 Taveners geese near Tolsona Creek. Got
chain saw repairs and came home. Lunch and then cut 6 to 8 spruce at a switch
back on road to lake. Stumbled and fell on broken off stump and broke a rib or
two. Jerry and Bob want to buy lots from us. Allen and I hauled garbage to
dump. Four grizzlies are hanging around the dump.

Tuesday, June 18, 1996—sunny, breeze, and very nice, 48° to 76°. The rib is
better tonight. I tried to shorten the old chain saw chain, no luck. Sorted and
rearranged brass and boxes. Loaded some .357 target loads. Allen visited quite
a while in afternoon.

Wednesday, June 19, 1996—sunny, with a breeze, 44° to 72° Mosquitoes are
persistent. Built a saw horse extension to be used in target shooting the .338
magnum. Sylvia went to lunch at Eureka with neighbor ladies. Wayne
Sorenson (from Staples MN) and wife visited in afternoon as they were on their
way to Valdez. Sylvia got mixed up on the evening. We were to go to Cal and
Mary's. It was to be tomorrow night. Visited Allen and Roxanne in morning.

Thursday, June 20, 1996—sunny and some breeze, 42° to 71°. Tried to plan the
rafters for wood shed overhang. Built a plywood container to bring window
home. Did some repair and adjustments to lawn mower. Piled a little brush.
We went to Cal and Mary's to a Barbeque picnic. Took some cukes and a
freezer of ice cream. Allen stopped by afterward and helped load our TV on
truck.

Friday, June 21, 1996—sunny, 43° to 75°. We left before 6:00 AM for
Anchorage. Got a window for house and cement for dish base. Shopped for
some other necessaries. Saw a very small red moose calf about thirty miles west
of home. Sylvia's doctor's report was very good. We returned one TV and they
gave us another one in replacement.

Saturday, June 22, 1996—sunny, some breeze, 46° to 75°. Thunder shower in
distance. Did some planning to build window sash. Went to gravel pit for
target shooting. Cleaned guns and reloaded 50 rounds. We went to Art and
Bonnie Wikles for supper. Some other people were there. Eagles and raven
hanging around Bob Rudbecks.

Sunday, June 23, 1996—sunny, bugs bad, 49° to 78°. Sylvia went to Mendeltna
Chapel to services and local native singers. Walked down to lake and planned
the road some more. Switched clips on two clipboards. Possibly duckling have
left the nest near the dock. Reloaded some .44 magnum for practice. Our TV
antenna needed alignment. Took a while to determine that. Still not right.

Monday, June 24, 1996—partly cloudy, and light rain, 46° to 66°. Started building the window sash for upstairs. Hoed some grass from parking area. Cal borrowed a little cement. Allen visited and I gave him a canoe paddle I had found. Took a dead goldeneye duck out of house chimney.

Tuesday, June 25, 1996—partly cloudy, breeze, 42° to 67°. Worked on window sash. TV still doesn't come in very well. Shot a porcupine in yard. Allen wanted it.

Wednesday, June 26, 1996—partly cloudy, windy, 41° to 62°. Worked on window sash. Went to Cal's to get some paint for it. Had to fit and cut and plane it five or six times before it fit the opening. It is in there now. Bob R. was over a couple times needing wood plugs for some holes in his retaining wall and to cover bolt holes in his mantel at his pellet burning stove. David wanted to borrow a fishing pole but thought ours was too nice if he lost it. Lucky is up here and they are going to Gulkana River over night and canoe, float and fish for King Salmon. I borrowed Allen's air powered finish nail gun to use on the window. My ribs hurt an awful lot tonight.

Thursday, June 27, 1996—mostly cloudy, windy, 40° to 56°. Wrote letter. Jay and Sherlene Hole visited a couple hours. Harold D. phoned. They got a road kill cow moose and gave us some. Took the paint and movies back to Cal G. Had pie and coffee with them and gave them some meat. I turned a piece of wood for Bob R. on the lathe.

Friday, June 28, 1996—partly cloudy and cool most of the day, 40° to 61°. We went to Glennallen on senior van. Paid electric bill and ate lunch. Home early, rested. Started mower and Sylvia mowed grass. I hoed grass in driveway. Shot three squirrels today. The baby (Tundra sparrows?) have left the nest. The lettuce and cucumbers are sure good.

Saturday, June 29, 1996—mostly cloudy and some rain in late afternoon, 41° to 55°. We went to Cal's and got the meat grinders and Sylvia ground and packaged the moose meat. We ate some for lunch and supper. Fresh moose tastes good. Shot some pistol loads over the ProChrono. Hung tarps in garage to cover benches and tools etc. from public eye when Sylvia has her garage sale. I took Allen's nailer back. He was gone dip netting salmon. Lucky is still at Allen's. Checked the chimney and found a live golden eye duck and released it to nest somewhere else.

Sunday, June 30, 1996—mostly cloudy and several nice showers. Put up a pipe hung from ceiling of garage for Sylvia to hang cloths on during the garage sale. Rudbecks are fishing Kianna Creek. They fly guests over there to fish for King

Salmon. I went to gravel pit to target practice. When I finished I shoveled the gravel into a ¼" classifying screen to reclaim the bullets. Will melt and recast them to use another time.

Monday, July 1, 1996—cloudy, showers in afternoon, sunny evening, 44° to 58°. Painted garage sale sign. Hoed some grass. Opened Gold screw crate to service motor. Put a little wood in basement. I returned Allen's meat grinder. A beautiful rainbow from out of Botley Creek.

Tuesday, July 2, 1996—partly cloudy, 45° to 69°. Worked a lot on the TV antenna. Sorted a couple boxes of books. Hoed the garden. Mike Shelton will be here tomorrow to put in a road down our hill.

Wednesday, July 3, 1996—mostly sunny, a couple showers, 44° to 73°. We went out early and piled wood and slashings out of the way of road building. Mike started on the road about 8:00 AM and 5 hrs later he had it built. He ate lunch with us. Allen and Sammi brought over an apple rhubarb crunch. Sylvia had baked another kind. We worked at getting ready for garage sale. I raked the cat tracks out of lane and the grass from the area that I had hoed. I drove the truck up and down our new road. Mike came by later and ask if I wouldn't drive him to school house. Karen, Ian and twin girls (Mailly) came over for surplus bedding plants. After supper we visited Mike, Shirley Callahan and her mother, at KROA campground. He gave us some halibut and smoked salmon.

Thursday, July 4, 1996—partly cloudy, beautiful day, 42° to 73°. Lots of mosquitoes. We had a garage sale all day. Sold some thing for a few bucks or nickels as the case may be. Lee Dudley visited. Fred Rungee visited and Harold and Rachel D. visited in evening.

Friday, July 5, 1996—mostly sunny, 43° to 72°. Garage sale all day. A few people came by. Nothing to shout about. One guy stayed quite awhile. Did a few odd jobs today.

Saturday, July 6, 1996—sunny, very nice, 45° to 76°. Garage sale all day. Very few came, did sell a little stuff. Cleaned up and landscaped upper part of road. Sylvia went to Glennallen with some women. Cal and Mary visited. Scott Hinson and son Steve stopped by. Denny and Joey E. were here. Allen, Roxanne and kids brought Dr Natalee Manelic and her three kids.

Sunday, July 7, 1996—sunny, 50° to 75°. Very few stopped for garage sale. Mark B. visited a little while. Wheeled a little gravel up hill. Hoed strawberry and cut roses from near rhubarb. Sylvia watered the rhubarb, flowers, garden etc. I reloaded some revolver cartridges.

Monday, July 8, 1996—rain in night and till noon today, sunny this evening, 47° to 66°. We visited Allen and Roxanne. Took the propane tanks to Allen. Straightened up some of mess from garage sale. Filled a few low places in lane. Shot targets at gravel pit. Roxanne brought from Glennallen back a birthday card Sylvia needed. Loaded a few cartridges while it was raining.

Tuesday, July 9, 1996—partly cloudy, 43° to 65°. Some breeze on lake but lots of mosquitoes some of the time. Cast and lubes some bullets. Shoveled gravel. Straightened up garage. Folded and put away the tarps. Sylvia went to a birthday luncheon for Betty R. at Lake Louise Lodge.

Wednesday, July 10, 1996—mostly sunny, 42° to 68°. Pulled dead raspberry bush's and weeds at garden. Planted a few spruce and one willow along new road. Then started putting a roof overhang on front of woodshed. Enzy brought propane. Took garbage to dump. Brought back some nice aluminum roofing.

Thursday, July 11, 1996—mostly cloudy, 43° to 67°. Pulled more dead raspberry and weeds. Looked for my glasses again. I have misplaced my good tri-square. We worked on the overhang on woodshed, getting the rafters all up.

Wednesday, July 12, 1996—sunny, cloudy evening, 48° to 68°. We went on senior van to Glennallen. Cashed checks and paid phone bill. Put purlins on roof overhand rafters and put about 16' of metal roofing on. This is mobile home siding. Cal and Philip brought some movies and borrowed some and visited. We put the aluminum overhang roof on after supper.

Thursday, July 13, 1996—mostly sunny, some dark clouds moving by, 40° to 68°. Put ridge cap on woodshed overhang. Closed the ends. Cleaned up the mess. Put away tools. Cut up and ricked some wood. Put some lumber overhead. Hung up the antlers. Carried the aluminum roofing and put it up under the overhang roof. Visited Allen a little while. Ralph stopped by with two of Jeff and Lorri kids.

Friday, July 14, 1996—cloudy, sunny, cloudy, 39° to 68°. Started raining 11:00 PM last night and rained till 9:00 AM today. Snow in and on top of mountains to the south. Cast over 400 /250 GR SWC. Jim and Elaine Manning visited. Ed Barno (Willow Lake) and son Jason stopped by for some wood cut outs.

Saturday, July 15, 1996—partly cloudy, 41° to 63°. Pulled some more raspberries out of garden. Used the truck to pack the road to lake. Allen visited for a while and just before he left Jim and Bunny McClellan from Florida visited. While they were here Lee Dudley stopped by and gave us another short story by Louis L'amour on a tape. He visited quite a while. I gave him some .44 cal. bullets. I sharpened the chainsaw and cleaned and oiled the .338 magnum. Getting ready to load Barnes bullets.

Sunday, July 16, 1996—beautiful day, 40° to 71°. Packed road to lake. Pulled weed and cultivated garden siliconed the joints in metal on wood shed roof over hang. Did load development with Barnes bullet using the chronograph. Interesting and fun. The rifle shoots lots of bullets very accurately. Rudbecks came after their mail. Allen and Kyle took me fishing at Jct. Lake. No luck. We saw salmon in Mendeltna Creek. Theresa, Ed Barno stopped by.

Monday, July 17, 1996—mostly sunny, beaut of a day, 52° to 75°. Cleaned and rearranged the trap, snowgo, gold screw part of storage shed. Moved junk from in front of two dead and dying trees near gas barrel in preparation to cutting the trees down. Allen visited a while in afternoon. Took a couple of pix of Sylvia and flowers. Bev Tyler and Vanessa phoned. Such a hot beautiful day.

Tuesday, July 18, 1996—mostly sunny, 52° to 77°. Hauled trash to dump. Saw tracks. Grizzly sow with two small cubs. She had tore canvas off dumpster. Mike Shelton is hauling gravel from this pit to the new transfer sight. Sorted more trash. Gathered aluminum copper brass and removed the steel from five radiators. Got pretty tired today.

Wednesday, July 19, 1996—sunny, 52° to 78°. Allen and Roxanne and Sammi visited Sylvia went to Glennallen on senior van. Cal and Mary came over. Mary brought frozen clams. She selected some clothes from yard sale and borrowed some movies. I cast some bullets and quenched them in water for Lee D. Resized and trimmed 115 brass. Pulled weeds in garden.

Thursday, July 20, 1996—partly cloudy, some wind and thunder in afternoon, 51° to 75°. Worked most of day cleaning up junk and preparing scrap to sell. Greased the truck.

Friday, July 21, 1996—cloudy, 52° to 65°. Wrote letters. Went to gravel pit target shooting. An eagle hunted along our lake. We visited Allen's. They have gotten 35 salmon- fishing at Valdez. We loaded the scrap metal to sell in Anchorage.

Saturday, July 22, 1996—lots of nice rain in night, 49° to 66°. Cloudy looked to be breaking up when I got up, so decided to go to Anchorage. Sold a little scrap and did some shopping. Had a lunch. Returned home about suppertime.

Sunday, July 23, 1996—beautiful day, 52° to 72°. Allen brought us two smoked salmon fillets. Very tasty. I welded extensions on the new door lock for kitchen. Put lock back together and installed it on the door. Moved the front door lock back to front door. I refilled, with shovel, a couple low places in new road to lake. Rolled the wire and pulled the posts of the raspberry support. Steve Malley brought a burn permit by. I packed a little of new road. Loaded two heavy schedule 80 pipes down at old road. Picked up raspberry wire, posts and some chicken netting with truck and brought it up the hill for storage here. Lee Dudley stopped by with his new GPS and showed me how it works. Very nice and very interesting. I gave him some water quenched bullets for his .444.

Monday, July 24, 1996—beaut of a day, 42° to 71°. Worked some more on rifle carrier for freighter pack frame. Installed special new spark plugs on truck motor. Runs better now. Visited Allen. We ate supper with Harold and Rachel Dimmick. Stopped by Cal and Mary's got two loaves bread and visited a while.

Tuesday, July 25, 1996—very nice day, 41° to 68. Pulled constant velocity shaft off track to replace the oil seal. Worked on rifle carrier. Plugged a few old nail holes in roof overhang. Mannings brought over a couple movies. Allen and David visited. Sylvia went to Palmer with Roxanne. I visited at Brockman's. Mark gave me some coax for satellite dish. Ed Farmer saw a black bear on Slide Mountain.

Wednesday, July 26, 1996—45° to 69°. We went to Glennallen on senior van. Shopped for truck repairs. Ate lunch. Started putting part on truck, seal in transfer case, cross on constant velocity shaft and new oil in transfer case. After supper I put new spark plug wires on truck. Sure tired and back is very sore.

Thursday, July 27, 1996—cloudy, 48° to 63°. Worked on the steel pipe post for TV dish. Went down to Allen's after 10:00 AM—they were still in bed. Back home and cut and weld till I got the post finished. I put a coat of primer paint on it. Ralph Fuson was here this afternoon. He had picked up some pistol and rifle brass, bullet lube at a yard sale and shared it with me and Jeff. It was like Xmas in July. Sylvia made a huge pot of clam chowder and strawberry shortcake and had Cal and Mary Gilcrease, Allen Roxanne, Elli to supper.

Friday, July 28, 1996—sunny and very nice, 44° to 76°. Did some more work on satellite dish post. Painted it too. Walked down to lake. Our well needs attention. Walked on over to Charlie Trowbridge's property. Everything there is okay. Resized and trimmed 60 brass for Ralph just in case he will need it. Allen brought a spotting scope over and showed use a sow grizzly and 4 cubs up on face of Slide Mt. Sow looks like the sow we saw just north of there last spring.

Saturday, July 29, 1996—very nice day, 49° to 69°. Built and installed a shelf to store bullet lube on. Stripped some old 3-12 wire and soldered 2 pieces together. Will use it for a pull through wire for the satellite dish co ax cable. Went to gravel pit for pistol target practice. Adjusted timing on truck. Moved some wood. Cleaned pistols and resized a bunch of brass. Chuck Z. phoned, he didn't get ATV back together yet.

Sunday, July 30, 1996—nice day, then showers in evening, 45° to 66°. Did some small jobs. Shot rifle at gravel pit. Went to well and made a plan to redo the cover. Rounded up the materials. Plan to start on it tomorrow, weather permitting. Prepared a few .338 brass. Chuck brought my Suzuki repaired home. Mother duck and seven ducklings use this side of lake this evening. We went down to Allen and Roxanne's for German Chocolate Cake.

Monday, July 31, 1996—beaut of day, 44° to 68°. Nice breeze too. Hauled two small loads of small course gravel and placed it around well culver. Put down oak 2" x 6"'s w/fir 4" x 4"'s on top and then lowered the well cover down on the lumber gravel foundation. Softened, shaped and put home made of plastic bottle stiffeners in the ears of wolf pelt. Shaped nose also. Piled more tree trimmings to burn later. Fred Rungee visited and ate with us. He brought ice cream and we sent him on with blueberries. He just came in off a canoe trip on local waters of 39 miles. He will float the Copper River next.

Thursday, August 1, 1996—rain shower in the morning, beautiful evening sunset, 49° to 64°. Extended the floor of trap snowgo area out under roof overhang. Burned four trash and slashing piles. Carried a lot of old slashing and stump etc. from along our driveway and burned it also. Finished loading a 100 .357 target loads. Invited Allen over for cake and coffee.

Friday, August 2, 1996—partly cloudy, some breeze, 46° to 63°. We went to Glennallen on senior van. Paid bills and I got a can of urethane. I tried to fill in the empty spaces in well cover insulation. I got about ½ the spaces done. My left knee is very sore today. We had Dimmicks here to supper. They leave for a stay in Deering soon.

Saturday, August 3, 1996—partly cloudy with occasional showers, 41° to 61°. Burned more junk wood. Cut up some for firewood. Piled some that I might use. Reloaded some target loads.

Sunday, August 4, 1996—mostly sunny, 42° to 63°. Hauled some gravel down to well to fill some low places. Sylvia picked some blueberries down by lake. Cleaned woodshop. We went to the currant picking place near KROA, gravel pit area. We got four gallons. Sylvia picked most of them. She juiced them this evening. I reloaded some target brass. Really nice day today. Lots of travel on highway. Allen went to John Johnson's to get the back hoe he bought from John.

Monday, August 5, 1996—many showers during the night and all day, 43° to 54°. Visited Allen and Roxanne in morning. Cal and Phillip showed up at Allen's. Cast some target bullets.

Tuesday, August 6, 1996—mostly cloudy and some showers, 41° to 57°. Hauled some more gravel and placed it around the well. Started trimming and cutting up the trees we had felled to put in the road. Hauled two loads of ash from the burning of limbs and slash and spread it on the bare gravel exposed when putting in the road cut. After cutting the wood to length I stacked it in the wood shed. The ducks are exercising their wings every day now. Not very many this year, only 20 or so. Maybe the eagles have eaten them.

Wednesday, August 7, 1996—partly cloudy, 42° to 62°. We went to transmitter site at mile 119 and picked blueberries. I didn't think we did very well, but Sylvia was satisfied. Also she picked the most berries. Stopped at Gilcrease's store on way home and got a loaf of bread from Phillip. His dad had gotten a 40" moose and was at Allen's cutting it up. Sylvia baked a blueberry pie and I trimmed and cut into stove length some of the trees along the road we put in. I hauled and stacked the two little jags of wood in the wood shed.

Thursday, August 8, 1996—mostly cloudy, light frost on potatoes, 35° to 67°. I cut and stack two more small jags of wood. Did some reloading and lots of shooting at gravel pit. Bob Rudbeck borrowed two 1" plastic pipe elbows. I had done some lathe work for him also.

Friday, August 9, 1996—mostly cloudy, 44° to 63°. We went to Glennallen on senior van. Did a little shopping. Back at home, we got a call to pick up a road kill boo and I turned it down, as I was in a mad rush getting gear ready to hunt with Allen, David and Kyle. We drove west as far as Allen's property and stopped to evaluate the weather to the west and the area we wanted to hunt. Look so rainy we decided to abort today's hunt and try Monday. Just then Kim H. drove up wanting Allen to look at something. I came home and unloaded ATV from truck, ate supper and cleaned some more on the .338 magnum. Getting the bore really clean is a big job.

Saturday, August 10, 1996—mostly cloudy and cooler, 43° to 56°. Loaded two pickup loads tree slashing and hauled it to gravel "cut" and burned it. Fred stopped by and did our "sat site." We paid him for the satellite dish. Went to gravel pit and shot a .338, 2 shots, group that measured ½" from 200 yards. Very happy with it. Tended the brush pile fire. Visited Bob R. at his hanger. Jerry came over at Bob's and then Allen showed up looking for grader blade bolts, but I don't have any.

Sunday, August 11, 1996—partly cloudy, 40° to 60°. Pulled six stumps to brush burning site, burned two loads of spruce boughs plus a lot of stuff I carried to fire. Sparks and heat started in a few places so I hooked up a hose and soaked the area. Looks better where it's cleaned up. Jerry rides by several times and doesn't stop to visit. They, Jerry & Bob, flew somewhere today. Jerry's plane makes a strange exhaust? Sound. We went to Cal's for a fried chicken supper. Cal gave us some moose meat.

Monday, August 12, 1996—mostly sunny and some breeze, 40° to 69°. Burned brush. Cut a few trees. All rotten except one. Cut it up for wood. All brush is burned for now-area looks good. Left knee hurts like blue blazes. Must be 2 weeks or more it's sore. Sylvia was gone all day gallivanting with Karn. Visited Allen in evening.

Tuesday, August 13, 1996—partly cloudy and numerous light showers moving west to east, 44° to 62°. Allen with backhoe, David, Cal came over and dug hole for the satellite dish and the PVC pipe ditch for the co-ax cable over to house. Bob r. brought his cement mixer. It took two sacks of cement for enough mix to fill four feet of steel drum. I scattered the ashes from brush burning. Loaded the wood blocks I had cut yesterday and put them in the wood shed. Replaced the sod and the dirt back in flower bed.

Wednesday, August 14, 1996—Sunny with occasional showers, 47° to 65°. Cut the dying double tree from near the gas barrel. Burned the limbs and stacked the wood in the shed. Cast some target bullets. Re-hung a door on the brown trailer. Cal visited a while in evening. Finished urethaning the well house.

Thursday, August 15, 1996—partly cloudy, 45° to 66°. Cut a couple dead trees and burned the limbs. Cut and piled all the wood in shed. Opened the boxes of satellite dish components. Read some instructions. Dan B. stopped by with the concealed carry applications, videos and required reading materials for the pistol class.

Friday, August 16, 1996—mostly cloudy, 46° to 61°. Did some small jobs. Cal came over and helped me put up the mast-post for the satellite dish. We visited a while. When he left I cut a tree in the way of the dish. Put fertilizer and lime on lawn. Fred Christofferson drove in and asked if I could get Mark to come over and help put the dish up. Mark came over and was a lot of help. It's all hooked up. Now we have to learn to run it.

Saturday, August 17, 1996—partly cloudy with several good showers in later afternoon and evening, 43° to 65°. Did a little finish work on satellite dish. Allen was here to breakfast. I reloaded some practice rounds. Cal and Mary visited. They liked the dish-TV performance.

Sunday, August 18, 1996—lots of rain in night, 42° to 65°. Nice day today. Did a few little jobs. Then tried to retrieve the 4' x 4' piece of culvert from first well effort. It seems to be frozen at the bottom. A lot of work for nothing. Cut up a little wood and cut off four stumps. The young golden eyes are doing aerobatic flying now. Bob and Jerry R, Karn, Betty and Lisa, Nikiniki were here to supper.

Monday, August 19, 1996—partly cloudy, 42° to 66°. We went to Allen and Roxanne and ask them to sign our absentee ballots. It's the day before moose hunting season and Allen discovered a cracked drive axel on his Ranger. I went target shooting. George came to gravel pit hunting mushrooms.

Tuesday, August 20, 1996—partly cloudy, 37° to 60°. Beth Trowbridge, Little Charlie and Cora stopped in on their way to Anchorage. (Beth is pregnant). Sylvia fixed a breakfast for them. Charlie Sr. is in Homer AK, working for a little while. I built a little storage area on east end of wood shed.

Wednesday, August 21, 1996—partly cloudy and a couple showers, 45° to 54°. Visited Allen about his rifle stock and arranged a new stock to be shipped here. Hauled two small loads of brush. Picked up and arranged tires/wheels etc. Phoned about Allen's gun stock.

Thursday, August 22, 1996—very low clouds in early morning, partly cloudy later, 44° to 61°. Left shoulder very sore today. Did some small jobs. Loaded some .44 magnum to shoot at target to qualify for a concealed carry weapon permit. Classes tomorrow and ½ day Saturday. Two shots over the ProChrono this afternoon. Phoned Nadia.

Friday, August 23, 1996—partly cloudy and some showers, 35° to 63°. Up very early and had to hurry to Lake Louise and "The Point." We were a little late to CCW class held at Andy Runyan's place. Bill Bahleda is our instructor (very good). He instructed on gun care, handling, types, use etc. In afternoon we all qualified on the required pistol shooting at a life size target. Then we did the non-required three yards, three shots, three seconds target exercise. Back at Dan's for dinner with some of their lodge guests. I stayed the night at "The Point."

Saturday, August 24, 1996—partly cloudy and a shower, 34° to 62°. Up early and hurry to get over to Andy's to class. Ed Bryant, Anchorage PD detective instructed us on CCW and the law, use of force, how to conduct ourselves etc. Very interesting. Back to "The Point" for lunch. Then home. Unload gear. Clean guns, sort brass. Allen stopped by and I gave him the replacement stock for his rifle. He went moose hunting at mile 133. I returned Mark B. his co-ax cable.

Sunday, August 25, 1996—mostly cloudy, windy, Mendeltna area, 41° to 60°. Took garbage to dumpster. Windy there. Picked up some aluminum there. Shot some of the .44 magnum I had loaded earlier. Did fair at 25 yards, poor at 50 yards. I just can't see open sights on a pistol very well anymore. Fooled around with the remote control and got the VCR tape off the satellite and play the tape on the TV. Ralph visited and had supper with us. Cleaned the .44 magnum and made some "dummy" .357 cartridges for dry firing and practice loading with the speed loader.

Monday, August 26, 1996—mostly cloudy and some sprinkle of rain, 37° to 54°. I just got started cleaning up and moving some steel and parts etc. Mike Griffith from Minnesota stopped by on his way back to Minnesota. Visited for a couple hours. During the visit he told me had seen a bull moose 5 miles west of here. After he left I went down to Allen's—Cal was there. We ate a bite of lunch and then decided to hunt the moose Mike G. had seen. Allen followed its trail for ½ mile saw the moose watching him. It had three brow tines on one side and four brow tines the other side. Allen shot and nicked a front leg—missed second shot and got in a killing shot through the chest. We butchered it out. Hung the neat at Allen's. I brought brisket, flank steak, heart, and tongue, home. Later Cal came over and borrowed a tube for stuffing sausage. Chuck Z. brought back a rope of mine.

Tuesday, August 27, 1996—mostly cloudy, light showers going past, 39° to 52°. Removed magnetite from some Nome concentrate. Allen and Roxanne brought us a couple quart jars of canned moose. I moved some goodies on out in thicker trees. The area around the gas barrel stand looks better all the time. Moose ribs for supper and very good. Cal and Phillip visited in evening.

Wednesday, August 28, 1996—partly cloudy, 33° to 56°. Sylvia went to Alaska State Fair on senior van. I finished cleaning the area just east of the gas barrel. I moved the stand and the water hauling tank to that area. Hauled junk and garbage to dump. Dan and Patti stopped for a couple minutes. Checked two fans I brought home a few days ago.

Thursday, August 29, 1996—partly cloudy, some rain in night, 39° to 56°. Went to Allen's and cut up meat today. Hauled a load of brush to lower road to burn. Puts silicone in some nail holes in roof of tire storage. Allen, Kyle and I went to John Johnson's in evening. Went up Tolsona Ridge to Antenna—communication site and glassed the surrounding country in hopes of seeing a bull moose. We did see two cows and three calves along the road. No bulls though.

Friday, August 30, 1996—a couple of showers and mostly cloudy, 33° to 52°.

Using a handyman jack I raised the brown trailer to level it. Replaced the blocks. Jacked up the storage, shed in same manner and using 3/4" to 2" shims under the runner, I got it level. Of course I had to then raise the lean-to attached to it in order for the doors to close properly. Using a hacksaw, drill tap and grinder I fashioned a devise to facilitate pulling bullets (.30 cal.) from cartridges. Mary and Kari Odden visited a while after school was dismissed. Phillip G. borrowed some auxiliary audio cables. He is putting music to a home video of Roxanne's This is a nice early fall evening.

Saturday, August 31, 1996—cloudy, couple showers, 33° to 51°. With ATV, trailer and shovel I hauled a couple loads of gravel. Visited Allen, Luck was there and had caught over 200# of halibut and cod. Allen and I checked out the burn for moose. Very little sign. Glassed a couple other areas, nothing. He walked over to the moose gut pile. Bears have cleaned it up except for a few bones. I spotted a nice bolt and piece of Plexiglas along the road.

Sunday, September 1, 1996—mostly cloudy and showers and rain, 38° to 57°. Spent a lot of time reloading cartridges today.

Monday, September 2, 1996—sunny, beautiful day, 32° to 61°. Went down to Allen and Roxanne's to see when we would cut up meat. Allen has things to do today. Dr. Natalie Manelick and her three kids were there. We returned the meat grinder and came home. I spent the day cleaning up and rearranging the area just north of the woodshop.

Tuesday, September 3, 1996—sunny, very nice, 32° to 63°. Cleaned a storage lean-to. Carried lots of junk wood into basement for kindling. Then I took the crate that the D47U belt pulley came in and put the belt pulley in it. Made cover for the crate to protect it from weather. Pulled weed in garden, carried cabbage leaves out of garden. Applied water seal on both steps of house. Cal stopped by to visit. After supper I repaired and put a wood pallet in storage shed. Cleaned a handgun.

Wednesday, September 4, 1996—sunny and beautiful, 33° to 65°. Went to Squaw Creek Trailhead. Drove Suzuki 23 mi round trip. Saw some sheep in the distance on "fortress" and Sheep Mountain. One small bear track, a few small moose tracks. Trail is good. Saw cow moose and calf at 133.5 on hwy. Sylvia was helping Allen and Cal cut meat when I got back, so I helped.

Thursday, September 5, 1996—sunny, beautiful, 29° to 59°. Did a few jobs that make this place nicer. Allen and Roxanne here to breakfast. Joe and Peg Virgin came to look at our satellite dish installation. Our water line blew apart at a connection. I double clamped it in another place. Cal phoned about a spike fork moose near his place. Allen went along with me to Cal's but we couldn't spot it. Then there was a long BS session. Got home late. I found a pair of porcupine teeth.

Friday, September 6, 1996—sunny, very nice, 25° to 59°. Allen phoned with news of Chuck's death. Later he came over and I drilled a couple holes in his new loader teeth. Later I went to Cal's and we took a walk near his place looking for a moose. No luck, but Cal found a misplaced trap and a caribou horn. Allen, Cal and I had lunch at Cal's. Then unloaded some building materials for Allen. Went to Eureka and loaded a Jeep swamp buggy on Allen's trailer. Cal has traded a snowgo for it. It needs a lot of work but shows potential. Allen had bought a snowgo passenger sled at Tom's yard sale and we loaded that in the van. We unloaded the swamp buggy at Cal's and I came home. Then stopping in at Mark Brockman's to ask of circumstances of Chuck's death. Found out Chuck Zimbicki drowned on hunting trip while crossing Maclaren River.

Saturday, September 7, 1996—sunny again today. 28° to 60°. I dropped off a movie at Cal's on the way to Alfred Creek Trailhead. Drove ATV over Ballanger Pass. While descending Pass Creek I found a pair of leather gloves. Before I got to Alfred Creek, I met the owner of the gloves walking back to look for them. He and his son will camp up Alfred Creek for tonight. Miner Jim Luhrs and Ed have punched a CAT trail around the gorge. I met two sheep hunters glassing sheep that were at the end of Wood Creek and Valley. The very valley and creek I wanted to explore. I encouraged them to get a good head start and I would follow behind. They worked their way off to the left and I went straight in line with Creek on high ground. About halfway up the valley as I topped a rise I saw the cabin I was curious about and came to see. Elevation of Alfred Creek, 3000'—at cabin 4300'. I walked slow and favored a bum left knee. On arriving at cabin I found it to be pole frame with ship lap boards 8' x 12' w/pitch roof and dirt floor. Some tar paper has blown off roof leaks and cracks between boards on sides. Door (south end) is on hinges. A small door opens on west side. Has dirt floor. Small work table and iron cot. A small steel stove to burn willow wood (the only wood there). After the first ¼ or 3/8 mile an ATV could make it all the way there. The trip out to trailhead was marked by very fat parka squirrels and one couple out joy riding on an ATV. I washed my machine when I got home. Saw some sheep. My spotting scope couldn't define the horns. Saw an eagle perch on the pinnacle of a peak.

Sunday, September 8, 1996—beautiful, sunny day, 40° to 59°. Rested. Got ready and went to Tolsona. Met Chuck's brother Mike and wife Pat, father Tony and mother Mary. Spent some time with them then went to Chuck's Uncle Bruno "Blackie" and visited with him for a while. Then on to Glennallen and the rifle range. Very little brass. Stopped by the Rendezvous café. Had pie and coffee and visited with Darrel Gerry. Then we went to the visitation for Chuck at the

Catholic Chapel. Maybe a dozen and half people were there. The sun was still up and shining in my eyes while driving home. Got home about 8:00 PM. Chuck Zimbicki brother Mike and wife Pat, Father Tony and Mother Mary.

Monday, September 9, 1996—partly cloudy, 29° to 57°. Attended funeral for Chuck Zimbicki at Glennallen Catholic Church. Quite a few people wee there and refreshments afterward. Tom Huddleston delivered a very nice and appropriate eulogy. We knew lots of people there.

Cashed a check at the bank. Left my CCW application at trooper office. Went to Tazlina Trading Post to get my Alaska Migratory Bird stamp. We saw two vehicles parked along the road-probably had seen moose to hunt. Picked up a 4' x 6' piece of 1/2" plywood from ditch bank. Picked up brass cartridges at gravel pits. Found a spark plug socket in gravel pit driveway. Gave Allen 2 sacks cement. Left CCW application with troopers.

Tuesday, September 10, 1996—partly cloudy, nice, 28° to 54°. Wrote a long letter. Sylvia went along on a trip to Lake Louise. We didn't see a single moose or caribou. Some hunters scattered around. Got some gas at Leona's. Stopped by Andy Runyan's, talked to Ruthie. Saw Dan at Leona's and Patti at The Point. She gave Sylvia a tea and culture called Kombucha, a health tea. Back at home I added water to ATV battery and am charging it now. I added some protection from snow to the pile to two sided logs.

Wednesday, September 11, 1996—rain in night and a shower in afternoon, 39° to 52°. Raked some leaves. Wrote a long letter. Hauled garbage and went to Mendeltna and got copies made of the letter. Put up a sheet of plywood on end of wood shed. Put lawn mower away. Saw a bull caribou near Odden's but it ran off into trees. Cal and Mary G. visited in evening.

Thursday, September 12, 1996—cloudy all day, 34° to 49°. Burned a brush pile. Drove ATV up Slide Mt. Walked around up on top, mostly to north. No sign of caribou. Heard a moose grunt three times. Some shots in distance to east. Bear Pooh in trail. Back at home replied the live coals at fire to finish burning. JR visited a little while. Talked to Bob a little while in morning. After supper road hunted to Cal's and took him along to mile 120 and back to his place. Saw two cow moose, three calves and one other moose. Plan to hunt in morning.

Friday, September 13, 1996—cloudy, light rain near Gunsight, Tahneta Pass, 38° to 51°. Got up early, picked up Cal at his place and we road hunted to Mile 120. Saw a cow with calves. Then a cow running with a small bull following her. We watched them a while then tried to get in position ahead of them, with no luck. Back at Cal's for lunch. We did find an axe for Cal and a light nylon strap binder for me. I put up two tarps to keep weather out of wood shed and trap storage area. I went east road hunting in evening. Talked to two young hunters that had just killed a goat. They were going to have Bart fly them to the Alphabet Hills and hunt moose and caribou. Stopped a gravel pit at Army Trail and picked up some more brass. Stopped at dump site. Allen was working late constructing the shed for the dumpsters. Took a shower. A Greg Anderson of ND called from Eureka and came over and bought a rifle I had for sale. He had a canoe wreck on Birch Creek up in the central area out of Fairbanks. Lost his food, clothes, shoes, rifle, etc. Some hunters befriended him. He wants to hunt moose. I sent him to Bartley's. It looks like he will fly out tomorrow. Allen and David came over. Allen borrowed my set of carving tools.

Saturday, September 14, 1996—cloudy, partly cloudy, then cloudy and rain at suppertime, 34° to 47°. Up early and drove the road. Lots of traffic. Picked up some stuff people had lost. Left a pair of glass that I found at Eureka Lodge. Didn't see any game. Ralph Fuson stopped by but I was hunting. Did some small jobs. Clothes washer pump got plugged. Backed up pulley and it started working. Missed a squirrel. Found quite a few .44 magnum brass. Polished it.

Sunday, September 15, 1996—partly cloudy. Sylvia and I drove to and up the Lake Louise Road hunting. Turned around at Mile 11. About ¾ mile S. saw several hunters with rifles at ready, looking east. Two very nice bull caribou were walking south on the east side of a lake. One nervous trigger finger shot once. The caribou were two rifle shots distant. No one there had Tier II permits. Sylvia and I did but my knee is too sore to try for these bulls. Rested for awhile after returning home. Did a few little jobs around here. Allen borrowed some gun grease. Jim and Mary Odden phoned that they would visit in evening. After supper Allen came over with some fresh cookies and wanted me to hunt with him. But Jim was coming over. When Jim was really late, I went to Little Nelchina and looked for a black bear. Saw some old tracks in mud. Back at home, Jim was there and we visited.

Monday, September 16, 1996—partly cloudy, up early, 28° to 52°. Jim O and I drove to Mile 120 and back looking for a bull moose and no luck. I got a little more ready for winter. Weld repaired two log chains. After supper I went to Cal's and we road hunted. Saw lots of cows, moose and calves. Got gas at Eureka. Odden's drove in to get milkshakes while I was gassing up.

Tuesday, September 17, 1996—snow on nearby mountains, rain with snow fell here, 28° to 55°. Left at daylight. Stopped by Cal's and he went road hunting w/me. Saw cows and calves and a couple bulls but were unable to tell if they were legal. It was rain/snow, pretty hard at the time and difficult to see with binoculars plus the bulls were moving through closely spaced trees. Jim Odden was out also. He drove up just as we were trying to see the bulls. It quit raining and I nailed a tarp in the front of tire storage area. Saw a squirrel, didn't get a shot. Mid afternoon, I called Cal and we went looking for those bulls. A stiff

357

breeze came up out of the East and the sun came out drying the brush. We walked to and past the area where we saw the bulls. They were gone. Visited with Corky Dimmick a couple minutes. After a nap and supper I caught sight of a small flock of Canadian Honkers flying quite fast into a breeze out of the east. Visited Allen, Lucky and Mary and other relatives there.

Wednesday, September 18, 1996—partly cloudy and windy, 41° to 50°. Drove west as far as construction gravel pit Mil. 33. Glassed from there. Saw no game. Don Makee visited when I was at gravel pit. After breakfast, I went to the trailhead on east side of Little Nelchina River. This goes around the west side-shoulder of Slide Mt. This trail is in exceptional condition this dry year. I saw a cow and calf tracks in part of trail. I drove as far north as other people had drove ATV's. I got off and walked around a bit. Found a pile of fresh glistening moose droppings. The foot prints with it were quite large. Glassed and looked for moose all the way back to truck. Loaded up and started home. Stopped on way back and checked out a possible place to set snares for wolves. It is a prominent game trail. Bears use it, for I found five piles of shit in a short distance—this trail has possibilities. 300 yards down it is what is left of a plywood cabin overlooking the Little Nelchina River as it flows east here. Ate a sandwich at home, rested. Later we went to Odden's. Sylvia gave Jim a cabbage. Mary was gone. A cup of coffee and pie crust treats and we came home. Removed the screen door from the arctic entry and stored it over head in garage.

Thursday, September 19, 1996—rain, snow during the night and occasionally during the night, 33° to 45°. Picked up Cal in a snowstorm, road hunted 6-8 miles and saw Jim O. and gave it up and came home. Stopped home for breakfast and when weather started clearing in the north. Sylvia and I drove the Lake Louise Road. Saw a few caribou killed between Mile 10 and Mile 11 on east side of road. Eight men hurried down to small lake area and killed 4 boo, one cow had been killed shortly before. We looked and I walked around a little in areas away from so many people with no luck. Picked up rifle brass at 10 mil gravel pit and some more at Army Trail gravel pit. I had planned to hunt the burn this evening but it's rain/snowing.

Friday, September 20, 1996—some rain with snow, partly cloudy also, 32° to 46°. Went to trailhead for west shoulder of Slide Mt. Drove in 1 ½ mi on ATV parked in Lee of spruce tree to keep some of rain off. Walked north to A Lake, ducks on it. Then west to crest of low ridge. Someone had fresh blazed a trail N. & S. No moose or caribou. Few tracks, fresh blueberry and hair pooh (Black Bear?) in trail. Back home to lunch and rest. Allen came over, he needed treated poles. Ate supper and went to "burn area" to hunt. No luck there. Came home at dark. I tried the moose call. Lost a bungee. Beaut Sunset. The ramps I made to load-unload ATV work well.

Saturday, September 21, 1996—cloudy, 27° to 39°. Started snowing pretty hard about mid afternoon, could feel it in air before it got here. Seven spruce hens in yard this morning. Six eagles hunting and soaring over our lake and south side of Slide Mt. Put some wood in basement, to make room in wood shed for some green wood that is stacked in the winter place I park the snowgo. After supper I loaded the garden tiller in the ATV trailer and hauled it up from garden and stored it in the lean to.

Sunday, September 22, 1996—some snow and cloudy, 23° to 33°. Snow melted a little. A fairly large flock of swans spent most of day here. Were here at dark. We assume they are resting. I re-piled some green spruce into the area where I vacated the dry wood. Had to split some large pieces. Cut up some green spruce poles and dry diamond willow for fire wood. Jim, Mary, Kari, Ellie, Allen and David here for ice cream, cake and watch movie.

Monday, September 23, 1996—snow (2-1/2 inches), clearing in evening, 17° to 30°. Slept late. Got well ready for winter. Removed the two water hose manifolds from water line. Re-piled scrap lumber and plywood. Readied Suzuki for winter. Loaded four barrels, chest and coolers on truck, preparing for trip to Palmer and Wasilla. Allen brought some steel over and used my acetylene torch to cut it. Kyle and Lucky were with him. Cal phoned and talked a long time. 71 swans spent the night and all day on our lake.

Tuesday, September 24, 1996—cloudy, some snow and colder, 8° to 28°. We went to Palmer-Wasilla. Cashed some checks. Bought groceries, gasoline and some drug store items. The swans flew away today. Unloaded the groceries, gas etc. Put away barrels, coolers, box etc. Cal and Mary visited and had a hamburger with us. Ice cream makes me sick to my stomach. Both Jerry and Bob R. were flying today.

Wednesday, September 25, 1996—cloudy, rain, sunny and snow after supper, 27° to 43°. Went up Lake Louise Road and down Oil Well Road to Mendeltna Creek. Saw tracks of sow griz and two, 2 year old cubs in road. They investigated every camping place and fire pit. They turned off the road ½ - ¾ mile before the cr. Saw small bunch of about a dozen caribou close to 4 miles from where grizzly tracks turned off. Boo were moving south and east. Looked around a little at cr. It was raining pretty hard. Saw some teal and got two of them. Back at Lake Louise Rd, I went north. Picked up some caribou hides. Saw a cross fox cross the road at 7 mile. Back home I hung up the boo hides. Washed the truck and put some special glass wax? On windows. Did a few other odd jobs. Cleaned teal and saved skin feathers, guts etc for trap bait. Sylvia cooked the teal for supper. After supper we went to a gathering for Rudbecks as they are leaving for Minnesota.

Thursday, September 26, 1996—partly cloud and breezy, 20° to 36°. Drove to west of Little Nelchina and picked up a caribou hide for wolf bait. Didn't see any spruce hens in gravel pit. Visited Cal a few minutes. Removed spare wheel and bumper from truck and put the mounting for the snow plow on. Advanced the timing of the truck ignition slightly. The air movement and temp has removed some ice off our lake. It's about 2/3 open now. Ducks still feed, preparing for migration.

Friday, September 27, 1996—cloudy, sunny, cloudy, 19° to 38°. Put the canopy on the truck. Allen and Kyle stopped by. Prepared the caribou hides for use as trap bait. Took garbage to dumpster. Checked out two gravel pits, couple pieces brass. Mary Odden had the kids from Nelchina School and was looking for a place to pick berries. I got a spruce hen. Came home and hunted the ducks on our lake. Got seven.

Saturday, September 28, 1996—cloudy, with some snow, 27° to 38°. Put a new headlight in truck. Melted down salvaged lead bullets and poured them into ingots. I got the two-burner Coleman stove out of storage. Cleaned it up. Put some gasoline in it and burned it awhile to be sure it worked OK and Ralph and Jeff intend to use it when hunting brown bear on Montegue Island. The beauty of the sun on the clouds and the reflection to the lake is almost beyond comprehension.

Sunday, September 29, 1996—partly cloudy, very nice, 15° to 37°. Cut up the tree that blew over earlier in summer. It broke over four smaller trees. The wood is wet, green and heavy to carry up out of that deep hole. Stacked some of it in the wood shed. Walked down to lake. No ducks, near shore. Fred Rungee stopped in and stayed to have bean soup and blueberry pie with us. He had a neat story of his and a few friends raft trip down the Copper River from Chitna to Million Dollar Bridge. Lots good conversation and stories. He leaves soon to go to Labrador on a trip. Farmer boys chased the ducks around.

Monday, September 30, 1996—cloudy, 17° to 33°. Lots of swans flying. Some stop to rest at our lake. Quite a few teal? Very small ducks. Our lake is nearly frozen over. Piled some slashings from the tree that blew over in the "hole". Carried the blocks of that tree up to the driveway and split them and moved them with the wheelbarrow to wood shed and stacked it. Got a spruce hen and a young cock today. Cast some bullets. Sewed buttons on shirt. Lake has four small holes that aren't frozen over.

Tuesday, October 1, 1996—cloudy, 24° to 32°. I burned the slashing pile in the "hole" and carried all the wood remaining up to the driveway. Split and wheeled it to wood shed and stacked it. After lunch I cast quite a few bullets. Robbie returned a movie. Later David returned a movie. More swans came in the night. Lake opened up a little bit. Swans came and went during the day. One lone signet left on lake at dark. Quite a few ducks remain.

Wednesday, October 2, 1996—mostly cloudy, sometimes sunny, 18° to 36°. Went to Jim O's. Visited a little while he is starting a water room. Drove through gravel pit. Stopped at the construction of a building at the transfer sight. Quite a thing to see. Split three large blocks of wood. Cast more bullets. Loaded a few cartridges. Our lake is nearly frozen over. Signet walks around, sometime sitting all alone in the wind and blowing snow on the ice.

Thursday, October 3, 1996—snowed all day (about 6 inches), 18° to 29°. Cal phoned to visit. Jim and Elaine came over and had coffee and kolaches. Cast some more bullets. The signet is still hanging around our lake. This snow is pushing the thin ice down and water is coming up into the snow. Did some letter writing. Kim phoned and wants me to plow snow from the school yard. I put plow on truck in the dark.

Friday, October 4, 1996—mostly sunny, snow in the night, 8° to 34°. Got up before dawn. Drove to school and started plowing snow. Before long the plow wouldn't raise up. So I finished the plowing with the plow down all the time. Even drove down the hwy home with plow down. At home I took plow control lever mechanism apart. Tightened one nut and bent tabs in. Seems ok now. Allen visited. Jim came over and we went to estate sale of Chuck Z. things. I didn't buy anything. Mike Z. gave me some pint jars and rings. Sylvia fixed Jim and me a hamburger when we got back. I loaded some .45 ACP target brass. Cal visited and brought three chain saw chains and we had coffee and visited. Lake froze over.

Saturday, October 5, 1996—mostly sunny, -2° to 36°. Prepared some brass, shoveled a little snow. Jim Odden came over and welded some fatigued places on his snow plow. I welded four places on my plow. Mike and Phil brought some of Chuck's food down to us so we are sharing with Cal and Mary and Allen and Roxanne.

Sunday, October 6, 1996—Cal and Mary visited. Cal brought two more saw chains for me to try for fit on my saw. Allen and Kyle visited in afternoon. I shot some loads over the ProChrono. Robbie asked how to prime a water pump.

Sunday, October 6, 1996—sunny, 0° to 36°. Slept late. With Jim and Cal's help I found out that my snowplow solenoid is shot. Patti B brought the health drink mushroom as far as Snowshoe. We drove up and got it.

Monday, October 7, 1996—sunny, 12° to 39°. Melted some snow. Snow slid off house and garage roofs. Jim Odden got me a snowplow solenoid in Glennallen. Plow still doesn't work, so I will have to find out what is wrong. I straightened the support for the left set of plow lights. Did some target practice. Polished some brass. Repaired the screw holes in the lid of my brass tumbler. Put the belt on snowgo, started the motor. Covered the Suzuki.

Tuesday, October 8, 1996– mostly sunny, 14° to 40°. The Zimbickis, Mike, Anthony, Phil left some more food here. They were on their way to Anchorage and on to Michigan. They plan to be back in the spring. Jim O. stopped by and tested all the solenoids. I tried a different electrical wire. Cleaned and polished the contact tabs. New solenoid doesn't work. Old one works now-will it work after warmed up by use? Resized and primed more brass. Read some. Feel tired tonight.

Wednesday, October 9, 1996–sunny, cloudy in evening and snowing nearby, 17° to 37°. Resized more brass. Put a different alternator on truck (85 amps). Hope it helps with plowing snow. Allen visited, then Tom, Kim and Kindra Huddleston visited.

Thursday, October 10, 1996–mostly cloudy, some light fluffy snow, 19° to 29°. We went to Tom and Kim's for breakfast. Stayed quite a while. Back home I walked over and looked at Charlie T. storage shed. Saw an eagle fly by today. Jim Odden came over in evening and we talked about his water room and a few other interesting subjects.

Friday, October 11, 1996–cloudy, some snow going by on each side of valley, 20° to 28°. We went to Glennallen on senior van. Pd. some bills and errands. Worked on some chains for the senior vans. Checked voltage in a couple batteries. Read some. Visited Brockman's to see their new baby. Visited Allen and Roxanne also.

Saturday, October 12, 1996–snow in the night and almost all day (6" plus), 21° to 29°. Plowed most of our snow. Tested the new solenoid, doesn't work. Tested battery, ok. Allen, Roxanne took Sylvia down there for a perm. Cal was here to look at snowgo repair manual.

Sunday, October 13, 1996–mostly cloudy, 24° to 31°. Went to Cal's and plowed his snow. The solenoid quite completely just as I finished. Got it home. Installed a battery Cal gave me. Jim Odden loaned me the solenoid from his snowplow. I plowed the dump and the school yard. Also Kim's driveway. Finished plowing our snow. Ralph Fuson phoned in evening. Plowed school and Secondchief.

Monday, October 14, 1996–snow all day, 7° to 22°. Did a couple little jobs, then had to go down to well and turn on light bulb as there is a little skim 1/4" ice on top. More than a foot of snow out there. Phoned Steven and Paul.

Tuesday, October 15, 1996—cloudy, light snow in afternoon, 13° to 21°. Plowed drive to Allen's campground. Plowed Cal's place. The solenoid he brought is the wrong one. His friend brought out another one to try. Finished plowing our place. Saw 32 swans flying east, apparently following the hwy? Karen Mailly gave us a dozen eggs, some cookies, tea and get-well wishes for Sylvia. She asked me to plow out Morey Secondchief, which I did. Back home I replaced a fuse in the truck. Brought a frozen section of water pipe into the basement to thaw. The deep snow and hill make my legs ache. Started the snowgo and drove it around a little. Gave Allen a piece of ABS pipe for his campground septic system.

Wednesday, October 16, 1996—cloudy, light snow in evening, -02° to 12°. Cal brought over another solenoid-it doesn't work on snow plow. Allen brought over some jerky that Ed had made. I gave him some plumbing parts. Tom H. sent a pair of shoes that are too small. Kim is sending them back. The lake has over flow and I couldn't make a snowgo trail over to dock from well. I walked the water pipe down hill and hooked up line to pump in well. Works good now. Moved distributor a little. Spent a lot of time putting on and testing solenoids. Tonight I phoned Nadia and had her order one from Northern Hydraulics and pay with her credit card so it will get here sooner. Nadia ordered solenoid.

Thursday, October 17, 1996—sunny, thin clouds in evening, -10° to +13°. Read some. Wrote letters. Walked down to well. It's ok. Lots of overflow.

Friday, October 18, 1996—partly cloudy, cloudy evening, -15° to +12°. Went to Glennallen on senior van. Sylvia to a baby (Adam) shower. Welded 4 heavy steel rod wolf trap drags. A blue bill duck flew by mailbox. Ralph Fuson stopped by on his way to Valdez. He borrowed my Coleman camp stove and will go with Jeff to Montegue Island to hunt brown bears and deer. He had a moose hit and break out a side window in his pickup this evening.

Saturday, October 19, 1996—mostly sunny, -12° to +13°. Some fog flew by on south side of river. Found a weak spot in one of my welds and I re-welded it. Sorted winter clothes and a few other little jobs. Watched some TV hunting shows. May get cold tonight. Lorraine Hanson phoned.

Sunday, October 20, 1996—clouds came in overnight, clearing again in daytime, -8° to 9°. Slept late. Went to Jim's and installed his plow solenoid back in his blazer. Fired up the snowgo and packed the trail to the lake. The overflow is now frozen. Tom and T J Huddleston visited in afternoon. A coyote came out on lake. I poked a couple shots at it but missed. We went to Tom and Kim's for supper. Had a good time. Readjusted the left headlight when I got home.

Monday, October 21, 1996—sunny, -19° to +11°. We went to Palmer-Wasilla. Bank, welding shop for rods. Shopping in Wasilla and Dr. appointment for me. Saw 5 moose along road. Saw wolf tracks crossing highway near trail to old cabin. I hope to trap that trail.

Tuesday, October 22, 1996—sunny, -16° to +7°. More overflow on lake. Allen and Roxanne ask us to breakfast. Lee Dudley stopped by for a visit. Jim O. came over also. After Lee left Jim weld repairs on snowgo slide. He dropped off my #9 trap wire. After supper, Allen came up and took me and a flat tire to his shop and repaired the tire. Brought me home afterward.

Wednesday, October 23, 1996—sunny, -14° to +11°. Put the repaired tire and wheel on the truck. Did some reading. Allen, Roxanne and girls, Tom, Kim and family and their neighbor boy were here to supper.

Thursday, October 24, 1996—sunny, foggy early morning, -12° to +10°. Lots of overflow on our lake. I walked down to Allen's. Gave him a handful of steel drill bits. We gave Mark Brockman a recliner chair. He and a friend came over and got it. Tom Huddleston came over for some fittings to get a heating oil drum set up for his Toyo stove. I gave him some drill bits and a box of bolts. The neighborhood kids pull a snowboard behind a snowgo down on the lake. Snow board doesn't get through the overflow very well.

Friday, October, 25, 1996—sunny, -23° to +8°. We went to Glennallen on senior van. We had to go to Gulkana to get our flu shots. Back to Glennallen and are lunch. Paid electric bill. Picked up solenoid package at post office. Back home, changed clothes and installed the solenoid on truck. It raises the lift cylinder ok. I didn't attach the snow plow and try that. Read a while.

Saturday, October 26, 1996—sunny, -19° to +3°. Up early and taped some hunting shows. Sorted the leather working stuff. Phoned Beverly. Lee Dudley copied a few of our tapes and brought us a couple of new ones. He picked out some loads from manuals. Visited quite a while. I did some target shooting. Allen asked me to go up Slide Mountain with him but I am too sick to go on that trip. He stopped in when he got back with a nice report and ate supper with us.

Sunday, October 27, 1996—sunny, a little fog in early morning, -20°to +3°. Laced some on a holster. Sized and primed some brass. Took a nap. Talked to Jeff R. He and Ralph didn't get a brown bear or any deer. Ralph stopped by later and related more about the hunt. He and I split the roll of No. 9 wire.

Monday, October 28, 1996—partly cloudy, cloudy evening, -13° to 10°. Went to Allan and Roxanne's. They signed our absentee ballots. Then I went to Cal's gave them some box's of clothes and returned his saw chains. My snares came today and I put 12 together. Switched spare tires on the truck. Fired up the snowgo and went down to well. It isn't started freezing yet so I didn't put a 100 watt bulb in there. Jim and Elaine were here to supper.

Tuesday, October 29, 1996—cloudy all day, -5° to 15°. George borrowed my compression tester. Harold Dimmick phoned and asked me to check on Rusty and Corky. They were OK. Harold called back later after I got back home. I took the garbage to dumpster. Read and did some reloading research. Allen visited and watched some TV.

Wednesday, October 30, 1996—1/2" snow, cloudy all day, 11° to 23°. Did some letter writing and target shooting. Reloaded more cartridges both target and varmint. George brought compression tester back and visited a while. Brought in the TV Antenna I salvaged from dump.

Thursday, October 31, 1996—cloudy, sunny, 17° to 36°. Visited Allen with snowgo. Target shoot with 22-250, very, very good group. Checked head space on .338—ok. Put together another TV Antenna up in the attic. It works well. Water line from well is frozen again. I have the lower end ice free. Neighborhood kids are trick or treating this evening. Some of the older ones were using snowgo to pull a snowboard, through our yard, down the hill and all around the lake.

Friday, November 1, 1996—mostly sunny, 10° to 30°. Sylvia went on senior van to Glennallen. I got the ice out of water line and our water tanks are full again. Snowgo is running well. Went to a Halloween party at Nelchina School.

Saturday, November 2, 1996—fog and cloudy, 3° to 16°. Went to Jim's and disassembled, cleaned and reassembled rifle bolt. Used rifle barrel arrived today for .22 rim fire. It doesn't fit. Needs modifications in the pin area. Allen visited in afternoon.

Sunday, November 3, 1996—low clouds and fog all day, 10° to 20°. Put out some fat for magpie. Fitted new (used) rifle barrel to receiver. Attached sling to stock. Mixed gas and put some in snowgo. Put hard gun case on snowgo. No one showed up to snowgo up Slide.

Monday, November 4, 1996—low clouds and fog all day, 13° to 21°. Snowing in late afternoon. Allen, Jim and I decided to wait for better weather to snowgo up Slide. I returned the .22 R F barrel-action to its stock. Remounted the scope on it. Fired it at 25 and 50 yards. Rifle is exceptionally accurate and scope is zeroed in now. Allen visited and needed some oil. I didn't have the right wt. oil for him. He also wanted an old file to weld on Bart's snowgo skeg. I didn't have one large enough. I loaded 6 - .38 spl with 6 possibly oil contaminated primers as an experiment. Loaded 6-.357 magnum dummy rounds.

Tuesday, November 5, 1996—cloudy, 3" snow last night. Up early and plowed snow off wood shed, camper and wood shop and its lean-to. Jim O. came over and welded up one of his snow plow shoes. Did some target shooting, getting a rifle ready to take wolf trapping. Jim, Mary and Kari were here to a halibut supper and a nice visit. Plowed snow at school house.

Wednesday, November 6, 1996—fog, cloudy, snow in evening, 9° to 18°. Jim couldn't go up Slide Mt today, so we called the trip off. I added black wire to two dozen of my new wolf snares. Built a fire in wood shop and worked out there. Made two small supports for the blinds at the dinning room window. Packed snow down trail to lake and wood hauling to house.

Thursday, November 7, 1996—fog, cloudy, light snow most of day, 10° to 20°. Added black wire to the rest of the wolf snares. Allen, Roxanne, Sammi and Nicky visited. Harold Dimmick phoned and wanted to relay a message to Corky and Rusty. Plowed our snow.

Friday, November 8, 1996—sunny here, cloudy in Glennallen, -10° to +6°. Went to town on senior van. Cashed our checks, ate lunch and shopped a little. Pd ph. bill.

Saturday, November 9, 1996—fog and cloudy, -12° to -3°. Read and watched TV. Taped some hunting shows. Pumped water and I went down to hand drain the lower water line. David F. came over, borrowed a couple movies. Allen and Sammi came later. Allen tells me he and Jim went up on Mt. and looked at partial bear dens while I was gone to Glennallen.

Sunday, November 10, 1996—fog all day. Read most of day. Reloaded some pistol cartridges. David brought a couple movies back.

Monday, November 11, 1996—cloudy, fog, rain, snow, sleet, -11° during night, +9° most of day. Did some target practice. Cleaned pistol. Cleaned and lubed some brass. Cal visited. I gave him some drill bits.

Tuesday, November 12, 1996—fog and one inch of snow today, 8° to 15°. With snowgo and sled I put quite a few loads of wood in basement and stacked it. Sorted magazines and read some.

Wednesday, November 13, 1996—snowed 3", some fog and misting rain, 14° to 21°. Plowed and shoveled snow. Checked oil levels in truck. Packed trail to lake and rode around the lake a couple times. Stopped by Allen's. He was plowing snow. Later he came over and had coffee. Tried to adjust the choke on the snowgo, not much luck.

Thursday, November 14, 1996—foggy in our neighborhood, -2° to +16°. Cal G. had breakfast with us. I went to his place and plowed snow, shopped his store and got a choke cable for snowgo. No fur, animal tracks along highway. Did some target shooting.

Friday, November 15, 1996—ice fog all day here, -4° to +3°. I went to Anchorage foggy for 40 miles, then ice. Foggy from Cal's to home on way back. Got a new pair shoes and lots of groceries. Saw lots of moose along road. One in road. One eagle at Palmer Hay Flats. Not much for fox tracks, 2 ptarmigan in road.

Saturday, November 16, 1996—foggy, sunny, -19° to -6°. Taped some outdoor movies. We went to "The Point" and Dan's birthday skating party. Saw lots of people we know and good food.

Sunday, November 17, 1996—sunny, -20° to -4°. Taped some more hunting shows and a rodeo for Billman. Read some. Reloaded some pistol cartridges. Rigged some snares with support wires.

Monday, November 18, 1996—sunny, -17° to +1°. Called Jasper at service oil. He explained how to fix odor leak from the Toyo heater. After cleaning it and reassembling, it works fine with no odor. I had planned to set some snares for fox at old dump site, maybe tomorrow. Phoned Paul and Steve in evening.

Tuesday, November 19, 1996—sunny, -16° to +6°. Temps fluxuated sharply in the morning. Read a lot. Went to Jim O's. Got key for old dump. Supposedly there was a black-silver fox there. Didn't see much for tracks. Went to gravel pit on Tazlina Hill. Lots of rabbit tracks. Tired to call fox and or lynx. No luck. Visited back with Jim. Shoveled some snow up to house foundation.

Wednesday, November 20 1996—sunny, -22° to -7°. Slept late. Allen and Roxanne had us to breakfast. Came and got us and brought us home. Cleaned the fur on tanned wolf hide. Did some target shooting. Cleaned and prepared that brass for reloading.

Thursday, November 21, 1996—sunny, cloudy and clear in evening, -26° to -8°. Did some reading. Sewed up holes in tanned wolf skin. Tannery sure did a poor job. Actually ruined this hide. Snowgo wouldn't start. Went to Cal's and got two new spark plugs. Left wolf hide there for him to try to sell. Didn't see any wolf tracks along highway.

Friday, November 22, 1996—sunny, -21° to -12°. We went to Glennallen on senior van. I can't get the choke cable to work as it should on snowgo. Saw an ermine at the wood shed.

Saturday, November 23, 1996—sunny, -27° to -15°. Taped more hunting shows. Made up .357 - .44 magnum and .45 ACP cartridges with rubber in primer pockets. These I'll use to practice dry firing these pistols.

Sunday, November 24, 1996—sunny, -29° to -17°. Read a lot. Trimmed excess rubber from dry practice rounds. Allen and Kyle visited in afternoon. Brought movie back, borrowed movie. Watched a little TV.

Monday, November 25, 1996—sunny, -30° to -18°. We went on senior van to Glennallen and Thanksgiving dinner. Lincoln drove.

Tuesday, November 26, 1996—cloudy, -13° to +1°. Went to pick up moose gut pile for wolf bait, it was gone. Visited Cal. Put choke back on snowgo. Renee Brockman brought her three sons and Mark's mother over to visit.

Wednesday, November 27, 1996—cloudy, -10° in night to +3° afternoon. Took Garbage to dumpster. Tried to call a fox, no luck. Shot a varmint. Did some target shooting.

Thursday, November 28, 1996—cloudy, some frost, -9° to +3°. Read a lot. Went to Jim and Mary's for Thanksgiving dinner. John, Colleen, Alex and Eric, Jim's brother, were there from Fairbanks. Lots of good food and visiting.

Friday, November 29, 1996—cloudy and ice fog, some snow, -2° to +10°. Ralph, Jeff picked me up and we went varmint calling. No luck, but a good time. Saw two moose. First place was breezy and cold. Down on Mendeltna Creek it was warmer. We talked hunting and guns.

Saturday, November 30, 1996—cloudy and 4" of snow in the night, 7° to 15°. Plowed Cal Gilgrease and our snow. Thawed water line and pumped water. Ralph and Roma brought magazines back. His glasses screw came loose, luckily we had a screw driver that fit.

Sunday, December 1, 1996—cloudy, frosty, a little snow, -6° to +7°. Did a few little odds and ends. Taped some hunting shows. Jim and John came over and welded on his snowgo sled. We went to their house for a turkey supper. Allen, Roxanne Farmer and girls came over at desert time. We all had a nice visit.

Monday, December 2, 1996—cloudy, some frost and snow fall, -10° to -2°. Plowed the dump transfer site. Visited Jim and John Odden. Plowed school yard. Removed dash from truck and re-plugged electrical wires to heater switch. Jim and John brought their families over in the evening. Had a nice visit. Colleen bought our tanned muskrat pelts. Plowed dump site transfer. Plowed school house.

Tuesday, December 3, 1996—cloudy and snow in afternoon, -10° to +4°. Plowed out water hauling tank. Oddens can get by till next delivery. Using snowgo and sled, I put a few loads of wood in basement.

Wednesday, December 4, 1996—3" snow, snow all day, 0° to 8°. Plowed our snow and the snow at school teacher residence. Went on in to Glennallen and looked at guns.

Thursday, December 5, 1996—snow all day, 3° to 11°. Shoveled the snow off wood shed roof. Rebuilt snow rake. Plowed our snow and pulled snow off greenhouse roof. Allen, David visited in evening.

Friday, December 6, 1996—cloudy and some snow, -10° to +4°. Got up early and plowed snow at school house. Saw some canine tracks. Went to Glennallen on senior van. Left an article on black powder cannons at Rendezvous Café for Darrel. Paid bills and shopped. Back home I closed the hooks on a set of chains for senior van. Cal stopped by for a cup of coffee. Then I went to dump and plowed it. Someone threw their sacks of garbage on top of the wire lid. John Dimmick called-his truck is in ditch and wants me to pull it out. Plowed school and dump.

Saturday, December 7, 1996—sunny, 1" of snow in the night, -13° to -4°. I went to Dimmicks and took John to their pickup in ditch. He and I shoveled it out. Too much shoveling for my own good. Quite a few people stopped to offer assistance. Nice of them! I declined help as it was already shoveled out. Had to try three times then pulled it up on the road. Saw a nearby fox trail, so when I got back home I grabbed the fox snares and went back and made two sets using duck feathers to attract the fox. Visited Cal. When I got home I fired up the snowgo and packed the trail to the well.

Sunday, December 8, 1996—cloudy, -23° to 0°. Cleaned a gun. Taped some shows. Allen came over and borrowed rubber sanding wheel. Sylvia phoned Bev and we got to visit with Tyler also.

Monday, December 9, 1996—partly cloudy, -6° to +6°. Went to Glennallen. Stopped by Jeff Rout's place and took him along. I had several errands and some shopping. We stopped at two places that sell guns and traps-snares. We didn't see any fur to hunt. Very few tracks. I checked my snare set before I came home. My new .45 ACP dies came today and I put them together.

Tuesday, December 10, 1996—partly cloudy, -17° to -1°. Slept late. Ralph phoned a couple times. Read some. Rode with Odden's to The Point, Lake Louise and had supper with Dan and Patti. Trapper Bob was there also. Back at home, Odden's visited a short while.

Wednesday, December 11, 1996—cloudy, 1/4" snow, -13° to 0°. Cal welded a snowmobile part Mary visited. I read some and reloaded a few rounds with the new dies. I like them! Jim is going outside (lower 48), brought some food they won't use.

Thursday, December 12, 1996—cloudy, skiff of snow, -16° to -2°. Wrote Christmas cards. Pumped water. Water line was frozen again and had to thaw it out. Mary O. brought over some postal envelopes for us to forward their first class mail. I had hoped to set some fox snares but ran out of time.

Friday, December 13, 1996—mostly sunny, -23° to -13°. Some ice fog in sight. Sylvia went to Glennallen on senior van. I went to Cal's. Had planned to set some fox sets. But opportunity just wasn't there. Cal did make a fox set in house yard. The wolves crossed hwy just on this side of Nelchina River. Allen saw me looking at tracks. Don't think he had noticed before. Anyway he wants to trap them later in winter - maybe. They had us to supper. Sammi is cute.

Saturday, December 14, 1996—partly cloudy, -26° to -10°. Taped some hunting – shooting movies. Sylvia went to a luncheon at Mendeltna. I split some wood. Target shot and reloaded those 15. Practiced trigger pull. Bev called at supper time.

Sunday, December 15, 1996—sunny, -26° to -20° all day. Got up early to tape hunting movies - not much luck so I went back to bed. My back is very bad today. Watched the tape Marion sent. Wrote him a letter.

Monday, December 16, 1996—cloudy all day, -24° to 0°. Dan Billman phone, ask me to round up some people interested in improvements to Lake Louise air strip. Art Wikle was only one I could get to go to the meeting. He rode with me. I did some target shooting and reloaded some more with a different powder. Checked Odden's house and mail.

Tuesday, December 17, 1996—cloudy, ice fog, light snow, 0° to 10°. I went west and tried calling in canines with no luck. Checked the fox snare, so had someone else. Made a wolf snare set in some willows near campground. Visited a while with Cal and Mary.

Wednesday, December 18, 1996—cloudy, ice fog, some light snow, 0° to 11°. I went to Jeff's. He had already driven the Lake Louise Road looking for a lone wolf that the school bus driver has been seeing. He did see one fox. I drove and he went with me. We saw some ptarmigan. No canines. Then I went with Jeff, Lauri and their son to Glennallen. Jeff shot a ptarmigan. While we were on way home Sylvia feels sick. Allen visited while I was gone. We will miss the kids program at school house. Cal phoned. He saw fresh tracks of large wolf feet near his place.

Thursday, December 19, 1996—cloudy and snow flurries, 19° to 21°. Plowed our snow. Split and hauled some wood to basement. Allen came over and I went with him. After he started his loader we went to Eureka for a bite to eat. Back to loader. He drove it home and I drove his van home. I checked the fox and wolf sets on the way.

Friday, December 20, 1996—2" of snow in the night, 6° to 10°. Plowed that and went to Christmas party at Klutina Hall in Copper Center. Did some shopping in Glennallen. Cal visited a little while in evening. Mailed Odden letters to Wisconsin.

Saturday, December 21, 1996—mostly sunny, -12° to -2°. On way to Cal's I stopped by the Hwy Camp Gate and got some of moose guts from the moose Jahobie hit with his new snowgo. Mary had a catfish dinner ready when I got there. After we ate, Cal and I went south to jct. with east west trail and I set a Manning trap in wolf trail there. Then we went east and on a small rise put out the moose gut bait and set two Mannings there. We should have made the circuit again and ran over our man tracks. I saw where the wolves had crossed over the hwy fill. Checked my wolf snare set and looked for fox set location. Didn't make a set. Fox has quit using the trail I have snares on. Checked Odden's mail and house. Didn't find a place to set anymore fox snares. I loaded the rest of moose guts and brought them home. I couldn't find the head. Read a lot. Cal and Phillip came over and got a cross tanned fox pelt and three tails to sell in the store. Sylvia went with Renaye B. and her three sons to Glennallen to see Santa Claus.

Sunday, December 22, 1996—sunny, -20° to 0°. Some strong breezes. Read most of day. Taped some outdoor shows.

Monday, December 23, 1996—sunny, -22° to 0°. Some strong breezes. Got out the slides, projector and screen and looked at slides of 1974 Hunting in Alaska. Allen visited in afternoon. Practiced trigger control – dry firing.

Tuesday, December 24, 1996—sunny, -22° to -10°. I checked my snare sets. Also the wolf trail to traps sets. Took garbage to dump. Picked up Jim's mail and checked on house. All is ok. Allen brought over popcorn balls and candy. Borrowed my wide chisel. He invited us to Xmas dinner tomorrow. Jim Odden phoned. Checked Jim's house.

Wednesday, December 25, 1996—sunny, -24° to -10°. Read some. Slept. Allen came over to borrow meat saw. Tom, Kim and Kindra visited and brought gifts. We went down to Allen and Roxanne to supper. Grandson Steve phoned. Talked to his dad also.

Thursday, December 26, 1996—sunny, -23° to -12°. Didn't do anything today but read. Supper at Huddleston's - Allen's came also. Huddlestons showed up later.

Friday, December 27, 1996—sunny, -13° to 10° and -8° most of the day. Went to Glennallen and mailed packages. Ate, paid light bill. Ralph brought out some cotter keys for me. Brought steak and Sylvia fried it for supper.

Saturday, December 28, 1996—sunny, some high clouds moving in, -22° to -11°. Ralph and Jeff came over. Jeff can't hunt caribou till Jan 5th, so we visited awhile then drove Lake Louise Road. Didn't see any predators to hunt. Saw moose, sharp tail grouse and ptarmigan. Saw a family hunting birds. We drove to gravel pit west of Tolsona Creek and tried to call in a fox. No luck. They brought me home. Then I checked Oddens house. I tried to call fox near home – no luck. Picked up a road kill rabbit. Checked Odden's house and mail.

Sunday, December 29, 1996—partly cloudy, -27° to -11°. Taped a program. Wrote letters. Checked snares. Visited Cal - left a plate of cookies. Researched info on rifle.

Monday, December 30, 1996—thin clouds, -23° to -6°. Tried to pump water – no luck line froze. Must be accumulated frost slowing and freezing the water. Tom H. borrowed our water tank to haul a load for their place.

Tuesday, December 31, 1996—sunny, -36° to -30°. Allen visited early in afternoon. Later Tom brought the water hauling tank back. I'm trying to super glue one of the cords in the window at the dining table.

Photo from a hunt at Delta Junction.

Norman with wolf.

1997—a wolf in a trap, caribou by the thousands

Wednesday, January 1, 1997—sunny, -39° to -34°. Sent off order to "Cheaper Than Dirt". Walked down to well and stuffed a sock in water pipe in order to help keep cold out. Walked on over to Allen's. They were just having breakfast. Visited, then walked home. Read this afternoon. Mike Callahan phoned greetings. Allen visited and offered to haul a load of water.

Thursday, January 2, 1997—thin, cloudy, -44° to -30°. Checked Jims place (all okay) and picked up their mail. Checked my fox and wolf snares. Nothing. Someone made a wolf set on south side of hwy at Slide Mt. Trailhead. The wolves haven't cross hwy near Cal's. Visited Cal and Mary. Did some dry firing practice this afternoon. Jeff Rhout brought me 50, .45 ACP loads. He needed some sand paper and I gave him also a cutting board for Lauri. He and his neighbor Doug have both seen a blue coyote at Jackass Curve.

Friday, January 3, 1997—thin clouds, -37° to -28°. We went to Glennallen senior van. After lunch we cashed checks at bank and did a little shopping. The van died at Al Smith's place. Al dropped us off at our place while on his way to Anchorage.

Saturday, January 4, 1997—thin clouds, cloudy evening, -34° to -30°. A little snow last night. Checked Odden's mail and house. Put out bird food there. Checked my snare sets – nothing. Talked to Cal a couple minutes. Allen got our water hauling tank and brought us a tank of water. Ralph called while I was gone. I called places in Anchorage for water pipe.

Sunday, January 5, 1997—1 1/2" snow, cloudy, -20° to -10°. Plowed the snow. Noticed a loose bolt and tightened it. Cal, Mary, and Phillip visited for a while in evening.

Monday, January 6, 1997—skiff of snow, -21° to -12°. Left early, in the dark to go shopping in Anchorage. Got groceries and some small things. Also 500' – 1 1/2" poly pipe. Stopped at Cal's on way home with two gallons of milk for them. Saw quite a few moose on Palmer Hay Flats. Checked Odden's mail and house.

Tuesday, January 7, 1997—it's -44° to -30°. Warmed truck. Checked snares on way to cat fish lunch at Cal and Mary's. Stayed until mid-afternoon. Back home and later Allen and Roxanne came over and borrowed a movie Sylvia had taped that Roxanne wanted to see. We ate supper at Farmers.

Wednesday, January 8, 1997—mostly cloudy, -45° to -30°. Early afternoon after truck warmed I went to Dave and Dee's at Mendeltna and made some copies.

Saw Jeff Routt there, also Mike Roscovious. Checked Odden's house and picked up mail. Looks like Kurt Skoog is home. Note: it was -71° at Kenny Lake. Caught wolf.

Thursday, January 9, 1997—mostly cloudy, some snow, -30° to -11°. On way to wood lot, Cal found a wolf in a trap. Mary called and I went down to take pictures and help skin and get the pelt on drying board. I checked Odden's house. Allen visited in evening. Note: Born: Paul Elias Trowbridge, 8 pounds, 2 ounces.

Friday, January 10, 1997—4" of snow in the night, cloudy all day and areas of fog, -6° to 0°. Took senior van to Glennallen. A little shopping. Sylvia did laundry. Ate lunch. Mailed letter to the Hansons. Plowed our snow.

Saturday, January 11, 1997—foggy sometimes, sunny too, -2° to 12°. Packed snowgo trails. Started getting poly pipe ready to go down hill to well. Allen called then stopped by also in regards to a death of a trooper and search for suspect (lots of rumors). Tom H. visited Charlie Trowbridge. Phoned with news of birth of a son Paul Elias. Lisa Smayda had a gall bladder operation. Phoned Nadia.

Sunday, January 12, 1997—16° to 18°. Jeff Routt visited for an hour or so. Trooper supposedly died of a heart attack.

Monday, January 13, 1997—sunny and thin clouds coming from west, 16° to 19°. I got a hundred feet of water line out but ran into trouble with the 300' roll. Allen came and helped me with it and the next 100'! I finished by tying the water line off in basement. I hung up the two old pieces of water line. Put away all the tools etc. Sylvia went with Gilcrease's but they had went to Anchorage. We went across the road to see Allen working on a cabin there. Roxanne, Sammy and Clinton Johnson were in cabin also. Checked my snares— nothing. Phoned Theresa.

Tuesday, January 14, 1997—some fog, cloudy, -2° to 11°. Wrote letters. Hauled three small sled loads of wood to basement. Did a little target shooting. Sylvia cooked a lasagna dinner. Cal, Mary, Phillip, Allen, Roxanne and their four kids were to enjoy it. Nice time visiting also.

Wednesday, January 15, 1997—sunny, thin clouds, -1° to 10°. Didn't feel good today. Allen came over early in the afternoon. He wanted a heavy piece of pipe that I had. I started cutting out snowshoe binding.

Thursday, January 16, 1997—partly cloudy, -2° to +9°. Worked on snowshoes. Allen came over and got a cable clamp. Gathered up some traps and gear and went to Cal's. Rigged up a milk crate on and old Arctic Cat snowgo. Put in traps, setters etc. Cal broke trail to the "burn" with his alpine. I followed on the Arctic Cat. We made a set at edge of burn. Saw a couple moose. We went south on trail a mile and turned around and made a set at a stump the wolves were using for a pee post. Back at Cal's we had a roll and coffee. The kids all got off the bus there. Soon Allen drove in with his Snotrac. He was pulling the snow trail groomer that he had been working on. It seems to work well. I picked up a wolf snare and two fox snares while on way home. I don't think anything will use those trails again.

Friday, January 17, 1997—partly cloudy, 3° to 12°. Sylvia went to Glennallen on senior van. I didn't feel well today. I did some more work on snowshoe binding fit. Put some epoxy on a few weak spots in the babiche near the front of the snowshoe tip. Allen's dad, Herb has passed away. We didn't have sympathy cards and got a couple from Cal and Mary. Herb Farmer passed away.

Saturday, January 18, 1997—mostly cloudy, 3° to 11°. Had Allen, Roxanne, Elli and Sammi were here to breakfast. Before they left, Jeff and his sons visited. Jeff gave me a .30 cal. 125 grain bullet mould. I gave him some .30 cal. 178 grain bullets. Cal phoned then came over after dropping Phillip at Robbie's. I loaned him 6 traps for marten, then we went to his place. He drove his Alpine and I drove his Panther and finished breaking trail south. I broke through in some overflow-2' deep. Got out without getting my feet wet. We turned around and left by a different place. I think he made four marten sets and I made two wolf sets. I got stuck in snow twice and he was stuck once. He got slapped on nose and cheek by a piece of brush that brought blood. We had coffee and cake at his place and he brought me home. Sylvia and I went to Allen and Roxanne's for supper.

Sunday, January 19, 1997—ice fog, the cloudy, 7° to 16°. Anchored the water line to garden corner post. Removed the rust from the mould Jeff gave me. Polished it and blued it. Switched the choke cables on snowgo. Put oil in truck and a little antifreeze cast about 100 .30 cal. 120 grain bullets for Jeff.

Monday, January 20, 1997—ice fog, cloudy, snow in late afternoon, 1° to 10°. Built a new lever to set Manning traps. Have a catch under my right shoulder blade. Punched more holes in a sling strap for rifle and sling will go over a parka. Waited all day for Jeff and his brother Dale to bring over a rifle for me to look at. I liked it and bought it. We had a good visit. Allen phoned and asked me to plow snow from his driveway while he goes outside to the funeral for his father. We called and talked to Beverly and Tyler. Vanessa wasn't home. Cal, Mary and Phillip brought some movie back and borrowed more. We have a good visit.

10,000 Days In Alaska Book Two 1990-1997

Tuesday, January 21, 1997—mostly sunny, -1° to 10°. We went to lunch in Glennallen then to Copper Center Cash Store and took advantage of their gift certificate Sylvia drew at Christmas time. I found some usable brass at the shooting range. We pumped water. The line tried to freeze. Sylvia had washed and cleaned both tanks. The roads today were slippery. I cleaned the brass at home.

Wednesday, January 22, 1997—sunny, ice in the air, -21° to -8°. Ice fog on river and along Heavenly Ridge. Went to Cal's and we drove snowgos on trap line. Nothing in traps. Track of one marten. Saw 5-6 moose. It's hard to count them in brush at a distance when moving on a snowgo. Coffee there. Tom H. was here when I got home. He visited a while and borrowed a couple movies. I sorted some brass and started polishing it.

Thursday, January 23, 1997—sunny sometimes and ice all around, -26° to -16°. Worked on some brass. Cleaned rifle. Shoveled snow off snowgo trailer. Tom H. brought over a pair of Tom's shoes for me. Kindra came with him.

Friday, January 24, 1997—sunny, almost full moon, -25° to -17°. Worked on brass all day. Jeff and I didn't go hunting. Checked wt. of trigger pull on new (to me) rifle. Did some reading. Moose cow and calf went east, down lake.

Saturday, January 25, 1997—sunny, cloudy and skiff of snow, -33° to -16°. Don't feel well. Did some reading, rifle loads research. Phoned Cal for a few minutes.

Sunday, January 26, 1997—partly cloudy, -32° to -4°. Did some research on the Mini Mark X. Pumped water in the afternoon. Worked okay, but somewhat troublesome. Fired Mini Mark on a target and got the scope sighted in close enough to start load development for this rifle.

Monday, January 27, 1997—cloudy, -21° to -4°. Took my snowgo to Cal's and ran our trap line. Snowgo weekenders had run over two wolf sets. I reset them and Cal made another master set. I made two more snare sets.

Tuesday, January 28, 1997—partly cloudy, -25° to -12°. I may have fixed the "rattle" in the oil heater. Jim Odden came over and welded a break with the "A" frame of his snowplow. Jeff drove in and we all had a nice visit. Paid a visit to Ed Farmer with condolences on the loss of his father.

Wednesday, January 29, 1997—partly cloudy, a nice day, -10° to +2°. Up early, fixed a couple sandwiches, went to Jeff's, and we went up Lake Louise Road hunting. Only saw one ptarmigan and it flew right away. Tried to call in a fox. No luck. Leaving Jeff, I stopped and visited Tom H. on way home.

Thursday, January 30, 1997—mostly sunny, 2° to 18°. I went to Anchorage with Jim Odden. Did a little shopping and had a good visit. Saw quite a few moose both coming and going.

Friday, January 31, 1997—sunny, 2° to 20°. Sylvia went to Glennallen. I went to Cal's and we ran the trap line. No fur. Two sets fox track. Back home, I plowed our snow and Allen's driveway. My back is very sore. Did some target shooting. Brass polishing. Phoned about pistol cast bullet molds.

Saturday, February 1, 1997—mostly sunny, 2° to 16°. Cal phoned birthday greetings. Roxanne brought a cake. Fran called. Jim and Mary O. came over. I put together a few key rings on cartridges.

Sunday, February 2, 1997—mostly sunny, a little breeze in the afternoon, -4° to 18°. Fooled around with method of attaching key rings to cartridges. Tried to pump water – line was frozen. Jim and Elaine visited.

Monday, February 3, 1997—partly cloudy, 11° to 30°. Wind blew most of snow out of trees. Tried to pump water but thin ice in pipe dammed the flow. The light bulb that keeps the well thawed burned out and I replaced it. Highway was frosty when I went to Cal's. We drove snowgos on trap line. No luck. Jeff visited; but I was gone.

Tuesday, February 4, 1997—mostly cloudy, 10° to 32°. Warm till past 10:30 in the evening. Polished some brass for key rings. Did some reading. Wrote to Steve. Tom H. returned water hauling tank and borrowed a movie.

Wednesday, February 5, 1997—cloudy, snow in the evening, 29° to 31°. Water line is plugged with ice. Allen and Sammi visited. Jim O. came over and welded some on his snowgo tub. I worked a little on my snowgo straightening the bumper and revamping fuel line. Drained carburetor and blew out the jet. Visited Allen and Sammi in the afternoon. Jeff came over and we did some target shooting.

Thursday, February 6, 1997—cloudy, 2-1/2 inches of snow, 22° to 31°. Plowed our snow. Shoveled snow off woodshed roof. Put a little wood in basement. Cast a few bullets. Jim and Mary brought a car over and gave it to us. We are overwhelmed. They had lunch and coffee. Cal and Mary returned some movies. Visited for a while. Good thing Sylvia baked a cake this afternoon.

Friday, February 7, 1997—partly cloudy, 15° to 29°. Went to Cal's and we ran the trap line. He got a marten in a trap I loaned him. Back home I made a pipe fitting w/valve stem to put in water line to blow out i.e. empty the line of water.

The water line is still frozen. We made ice cream for the party at school house.

Saturday, February 8, 1997—mostly cloudy, 7° to 21°. Neighbors are snowmobiling today. I loaded the water hauling tank and the pump from my dredge. Went to Little Nelchina River and hauled a load of water. Assembled and packaged some more cartridge key rings.

Sunday, February 9, 1997—cloudy and overhead fog, 13° to 22°. Did some fire lapping of pistol barrel.

Monday, February 10, 1997—foggy, sunny, cloudy, 14° to 21°. Loaded snowgo. Went to Cal's. Ran trap line. There had been two marten but they didn't go in or get caught in trap. Lots of overflow at south end. Ate lunch with Cal. Visited Allen a few minutes in the afternoon. New Hornaday pistol dies came, cleaned and adjusted them.

Tuesday, February 11, 1997—cloudy, 11° to 22°. Stopped by Jeff's and he went to Glennallen with me. I had the title of the car transferred to my name. We found a few brass at shooting range. Ate lunch at Rendezvous Restaurant. Shopped for groceries. Cashed checks at bank. Went to post office. Saw a couple moose today. Didn't see any varmints or fur to shoot. Stopped at lumber yard, gun shop and had car keys made at the other lumberyard. The Huddleston and Routt families had supper with us.

Wednesday, February 12, 1997—fog and cloudy all day, 0° to 15°. We ate breakfast with Allen and Roxanne. Then I went to Odden's and helped Jim with some walls in house.

Thursday, February 13, 1997—low clouds, some fine snow, 10° to 18°. Cleaned snow off lean to roofs. Cast some bullets with new mould and lubed them. Cal brought us some valentine cupcakes Mary had made.

Friday, February 14, 1997—sunny and very nice, 5° to 18°. Cal was sick so I ran trap line alone. Wolves were on line, so I came back to house and got a sled. Had a small female wolf in first set, a trail set. They didn't go in a pee post set ¼ mi south. They then left the burn. Several moose in burn. No marten or wolves on rest of line. These wolves spent some time near place we caught first wolf this winter. They ate carcass of first wolf. Cal helped skin and stretch the wolf. Philip and Robbie rode to Nelchina with me. Wolves have crossed hwy east of Little Nelchina River. I saw where a marten has crossed ? the road just went of highway camp. Really tired. Took a shower and feel better.

Saturday, February 15, 1997—low, cloudy, 5° to 15°. Went to Cal's and turned wolf hide. Philip rode home when I went. I made a marten set on each side of road where marten crossed. I used duck cleanings for bait. Took our garbage to the transfer site. Stopped by Jim Oddens and had coffee and rice pudding. Ralph Fuson phoned. He has met a pilot who has gotten 188 wolverines in last 15 years and more than 100 wolves.

Sunday, February 16, 1997—partly cloudy, 4° to 20°. Checked marten sets. Last some .45 SWC's. Treated and loaded 30 and fire lapped the .45 ACP pistol barrel.

Monday, February 17, 1997—partly cloudy, 7° to 20°. Gathered up more trap gear and went to Cal's. Ran the line, pulling the wolf carcass looking for a good place to leave it. The wolves had been on the trail again. Three marten had crossed it also. Nothing in the traps. Left carcass where Cal had last cut wood. Set two traps and one snare in that area. Made a box set for a marten closer to highway camp. Allen visited and told me of a wolf crossing near mile 132. I did some target shooting with the new bullets. That barrel shoots much better after fire lapping it.

Tuesday, February 18, 1997—sunny, clouded over in mid afternoon, 3° to 23°. Loafed all morning. We went to Cal's. Sylvia visited Mary. I took Cal south and west to a big swamp area and tried to call wolves with my Johnny Stewart caller. Used the Coyote Challenge call and Screaming Rabbit. No luck. We did make another set with a trap at same place we caught the first wolf.

Wednesday, February 19, 1997—foggy and mist all day, 9° to 18°. Did some target shooting and load testing. Checked marten sets. Visited Allen. Put gasoline drums in truck. Added one quart oil to motor and a little oil in power steering reservoir. Auto tranny is ok.

Thursday, February 20, 1997—foggy, clearing, light snow in evening, 10° to 18°. I left early for Wasilla. Did a lot of shopping. Got back home about 4:00 PM. Jim M. came over as I was pumping gasoline from drums into storage tank. Jim, Mary, Kari Odden were here to supper.

Friday, February 21, 1997—sunny, cloudy in the afternoon, snowy windy evening, 8° to 30°. We went to Glennallen for lunch. Went to Cal's and we ran trap line. No fur. I did remake one wolf set. Cal spotted a trap hanging from a tree limb about 50 feet off the present trail he now uses. I've started load development using a new powder.

Saturday, February 22, 1997—cloudy, some snow and fog, 26° to 34°. Trooper Scott Keiffer phoned a couple times in regard to the moose cow that Jim Luce caught in a snare, 2.4 miles down river from Botley Creek. I am to get the moose but Jim didn't call me early enough in the day to go to the moose kill and butcher it before dark. Serviced the snowgo. Cut out and put together some shelf brackets for reloading supplies. Checked the three marten sets – no luck.

Sunday, February 23, 1997—sunny, 25° to 38°. Went to Cal's. Loaded his Alpine and sled on trailer and hauled them and him here. We followed the trail to Nelchina River and down stream past Botley Creek. There I broke through the trail into overflow. Walked down the snow for 50 yards and with much effort got the snowgo to good dry snow. Then dragged the sled one step at a time out of the water also. Got some water in my boot. Sure glad it was a warm day. Then I had to tromp down the snow and make a turn. After I get my machine up the bank and turned and started back up river, Cal drove his Alpine over. I've decided I won't continue to look for the moose in the snare. I have gotten to tired to continue trip. Back home we load his machine and sled. Then eat lunch in the house and I drove him back to his house. The snow slid off the house roof so I put the snow plow on and pushed it out of the way. It was so warm I tried to pump water but the line is frozen near the house. I did get the ice out of a lot of the pipe. We ate dinner with Jim and Elaine Manning. After we came home I shoveled the roof snow that had covered the water line, off to one side, because it would be to frozen to move it tomorrow. I put in a very hard day today. The moon is beautiful tonight.

Monday, February 24, 1997—partly cloudy, 1° to 26°. Worked on shelves in upstairs closet. Went to Cal's and ran that little trap line. No fur. One wolf trap sprung by falling clump of snow. Cal gave me the little wolf to bring home!!

Tuesday, February 25, 1997—mostly sunny, 10° to 31°. Started working on the shelves before breakfast. Finished putting them up before lunch time. Cal and Mary came over about then and Sylvia fixed lunch. After they left I cleaned up the mess from the carpenter work. Then I cleaned and brushed the wolf hide.

Wednesday, February 26, 1997—cloudy, 5° to 21°. I took wolf pelt to town (Glennallen) to have it tagged at Fish & Game. Stopped by lumberyard. Sold some key rings and my buffalo rug. Ate lunch with seniors. Stopped by Jeff's on way home and visited a while. Boxed the wolf pelt for mailing to tannery.

Thursday, February 27, 1997—mostly sunny, 6° to 23°. Put up a little shelf in closed. Tried to sharpen the cutter knife for our hand meat grinder. Did some target shooting. We went to Odden's for supper "Doc" Watson and Allen Farmer Roxanne and Sammi were there.

Friday, February 28, 1997—fluffy snow all day, 8° to 21°. Picked up the marten sets. Checked the wolf traps. Nothing. Cal sold the other wolf and got $250.00 for it. We went to KROA and enjoyed Pop Wagner show. Someone requested "The Strawberry Roan" in my name. We had a good time. Sylvia mailed the wolf to Idaho. (Wolf was back to Glennallen post office 5/6/97).

Saturday, March 1, 1997—cloudy, sunny, 4° to 19°. Some guy came to look at pool table. Cal asked me to come plow his snow. I plowed our snow. Drove to Little Nelchina, using the dredge pump, loaded the water hauling tank. We pump it off with the house water system pump.

Sunday, March 2, 1997—sunny, 0° to 14°. Modified the tray holding the new gunsmith punch's to fit into an old Hoppe's Plastic Gun Cleaning box that I don't use for its original purpose. Sam Weaver brought over a couple curtains he wants Sylvia to alter. Did some target practice. This powder burns clean. Put gas in snowgo. Neighborhood sure is quiet. Elaine Manning phoned at 10:00 PM. Comet Hale-Bopp is in sight due N by NW over Slide Mt. Appears large yellow and a long tail. Junior Bloomberg died.

Monday, March 3, 1997—sunny, -21° to -3°. Boxed some of my buffalo (bison) hooves, skull, wolf skull. John Kunik and wife Jane had vehicle trouble. Used our phone a couple times, tow strap etc. Brought strap back later. We had lunch at Mannings. After supper we went to Roxanne's for ice cream and some of her birthday cake.

Tuesday, March 4, 1997—sunny, -24° to 8°. Helped Mary Odden thaw their frozen sewer. Cal and I checked the wolf sets. No luck. Snowgo odometer quit.

Wednesday, March 5, 1997—sunny, -11° to +9°. Sylvia ground some moose meat and added pork trimmings and sausage seasoning. I pumped Odden's water from outside tank to their upper storage. Some water left over so I brought it home and pumped it into our holding tank. Allen had breakfast with us. Mary G. phone and asked us to a catfish supper. Allen and Roxanne, Ellie, Sammi were there also.

Thursday, March 6, 1997—sunny, light snow in night, -4° to 16°. Went to Glennallen. Sold my buffalo robe. Did a little shopping. Jeff R. went with me. I put a little wood in basement. Phoned my brother Jerry, his birthday today.

Friday, March 7, 1997—sunny, -3° to 21°. Serviced the car. Got ready to go to Cal's. Allen invited me for a bowl of beans at lunch time. I drove to Cal's to run trap line, only to find out he had gone to Glennallen. So back home. Did some target shooting and cleaned the gun.

Saturday, March 8, 1997—partly cloudy, -8° to 22°. Ralph and Jeff phoned, we decided to go to gun show in Palmer tomorrow. Tried fire lapping .357, finished with J-B compound. Reattached unhooked odometer on snowgo. Unloaded snowgo, took a new bulb down to well. Skim of ice in well.

Sunday, March 9, 1997—scattered snow squalls here today, 3° to 23°. Jeff and I went to Palmer Lions Gun Show. Nice day there. Met some new people. Jeff's brother Dale Rhout was there. Ralph and Roma Fuson came later. Saw a few people from Glennallen at show. Mike? an old acquaintance was there. Talked to two carvers of horn. Bought another pistol, a part box of bullets, three plastic boxes for loaded rounds. Had a lot of fun. A very enjoyable day. Picked up some groceries.

Monday, March 10, 1997—sunny, 2° to 18°. Went to Cal's and we ran wolf sets. Nothing. Had coffee when we got back to his house. The pin holding the trailer and its tongue together broke while I was crossing the Little Nelchina Bridge. Trailer whipped all around. I got it under control without any damage. Made a temporary repair and fixed it good when I got home. I tried out the new pistol. It shoots very well. Reloaded some more ammo to practice with. Polished more brass.

Tuesday, March 11, 1997—sunny, windy in places, -12° to 17°. Went to Glennallen. Hunted all the way, plus some of Lake Louise Road. Nadia phoned. Good to talk to her. Found a rubber plug for chain case on snowgo. Put a little more of the junk wood in basement. Sorted some brass and loaded 20 to get that lot of brass evened up. Cal visited and had a piece of the cake Sylvia baked today. I have a bad headache and don't feel good.

Wednesday, March 12, 1997—sunny, -12° to 24°. Wrote some letters. Did some target practice. Jeff came over needing a couple of bolts. He shot that pistol also. I drove west, looking for wolf tracks and or a caribou for meat. Stopped at Allen's cabins as he was working there and encouraged him in his efforts. He showed me wolf tracks through his campground property. Visited with Corky and John Dimmick. They aren't seeing any caribou.

Thursday, March 13, 1997—sunny, -10° to 20°. Visited Mannings. Target practice at home. Cast some bullets. My back hurts really bad between my shoulder blades.

Friday, March 14, 1997—sunny, -8° to 29°. Jeff and Shobie visited for awhile. I had just hooked up to snowgo trailer. Cal stopped by on his way home from Glennallen. Did some target practice and got one ex group. Cal and I ran trap line. No wolves. Saw marten and fox tracks. Sylvia went to Glennallen. Neighborhood kid snowboard on our switch back road to lake. Cleaned pistol.

Saturday, March 15, 1997—intermittent snow, sunny, 7° to 24°. Cast some more practice bullets. Cleaned garage a little. Did some target practice. We went to Jeff and Lauri Routt's for dinner this evening.

Sunday, March 16, 1997—mostly sunny, cloudy evening, 0° to 10°. Wrote and loafed all day. We haven't felt good all day.

Monday, March 17, 1997—light snow all day, -10° to +7°. Wrote a letter. Loaded more pistol practice loads.

Tuesday, March 18, 1997—snow showers and clearing, 0° to 19°. I plowed out snow. Drove to Cal's and ran that wolf line. No wolf. On way home I saw a coyote trotting up the driveway of the gravel pit across from the Nelchina DOT Station. It took me quite a way to get stopped on the snow pack. Grabbed a rifle and walked back to the driveway. Just as I got to it someone stopped and asked me what I was doing! Like a fool I answered "hunting." Then he hollered asking what I was hunting. I ignoring him, and continued on. The damage was done. The coyote had been moving away from our talking and was at the SW edge of the pit. I kneeled down but missed the shot.

I did some target practice at home with pistol. Then I saw Cal driving his old Arctic Cat. It couldn't get up sharp rises in the trail, simply dug down into the hard pack. I helped him lift and pull and push trying to get up the little hill. Finally he gave up and I drove my machine around him. I had a 50' x 1/8" cable for such emergencies and pulled him up the hill.

Wednesday, March 19, 1997—sunny, -5° to 29°. Went to gravel pit where I took a shot at the coyote. I had hit it but it left few drops of blood. I trailed it on my snowshoes. Tough going. It made a loop I gave up for today and went home. The rifle and I got lots of snow on us from trees and brush. I dried, cleaned and oiled the rifle when I got home. Rested a little and went to Oddens. When Bishop delivered their water I hooked the pump up and filled their upstairs storage tank. There was enough water left over to fill our tank. Showered and we went to Mary and Kari (who has chicken pox) for supper. Kurt Skoog came there also. Nice visit.

Thursday, March 20, 1997—sunny, -2° to 33°. Mixed some gas for snowgo. Jeff called and offered to go with me to look again for the coyote. He retraced my trail of yesterday, while I followed its trail east. Jeff caught up to me after I had passed the place the coyote had stopped and rested for some time. There wasn't much of a blood loss, probably from matted fur. It was walking right along and crossed the hwy to the north. We then walked back to Jeff's car, satisfied the wound was superficial. Wiped water out of and off of the rifle Jeff carried. The front swivel stud had to have Locktite applied to it. Finished shooting Lot #5, .45 ACP.

Friday, March 21, 1997—sunny, 6° to 30°. Gathered some predator gear and drove snowgo towards AK Hwy camp. Saw where coyote came onto trail.

Another machine had then run over its tracks. Wolves had also been on trail after the snow last Monday. No luck calling with dying rabbit screams. On way back to Nelchina met Sally Johnson, Chris and Suzie Rhodes. I followed them up Slide Mountain. Chris fresh broke the upper part of the trail. Sally and I didn't try to get to the top. The view from where we were was grand. Back at home I shot some experimental pistol loads. Mannings came over for a donation of a gift for a prize at some games Elaine is getting together. Location: KROA.

Saturday, March 22, 1997—sunny, thin clouds, -2° to 29°. I got confused the date of Gun Show in Glennallen. Drove in and no show. Stopped by lumberyard. I won't be getting a holster from them. Didn't see any fur or game along highway. Saw rescue helicopter at clinic. Found an owl killed squirrel lying on snow with wing marks. This was halfway between house and outhouse. Loaded more pistol target loads. Possibly a bear hunter parked at school house driveway.

Sunday, March 23, 1997—cloudy, snow and windy in evening, 7° to 27°. Put some wood in basement. Did some reading. Reloaded some more pistol rounds.

Monday, March 24, 1997—sunny, windy in open places, 0° to 17°. Ran trap line with Cal. Saw a fresh fox track. Wolf had been along highway last Thursday. Picked up two sets. Saw three moose and a calf. A bunch of school kids rode home from Cal's to Nelchina with me. Sylvia is still sick. Cal and Phillip came over to borrow some movies.

Tuesday, March 25, 1997—clear, -23° to 21°. I went to Copper Center and attended the 55/Alive Mature Driving Class at Kluti-Kaah Hall. At Copper Cash Store I found some cold medicine for Sylvia. She is some better tonight. I saw a moose lying down in some black spruce near Woods Creek, also ice fisherman on lake at Trapper Den.

Wednesday, March 26, 1997—clear. Went to driving class at Copper Center. Finished class and drove straight home. Sylvia is feeling much better. Possible: bear hunters parked at trailhead.

Thursday, March 27, 1997—clear, thin clouds, -11° to 25°. Sick with the flu last night and today. Rested this morning. Jim Odden flew his plane in from McGrath. He phoned. I offered to help plow the snow off his air strip. We had coffee and visited later. He loaned me fur handling video from Alaska Department of Fish & Game.

Friday, March 28, 1997— mostly clear, -2° to 28°. Sick with flu. Pulled a car back on the plowed roadway for an Eagle River couple. Did some taping for Steve.

Saturday, March 29, 1997—snow showers all day, 6° to 30°. We both still have the crud. I only swept snow off the car and covered the snowgo. Packaged a video tape for grandson Steve.

Sunday, March 30, 1997—Clear, -4° to 27°. Rested all day. Went to Odden's for supper.

Monday, March 31, 1997— clear, some breeze in the afternoon, -10° to 30°. Waited at mail box this morning for a COD Package. Cal stopped by on his way home from Glennallen. After lunch I went to his place and we picked up the wolf traps and snares. I forgot to bring the wolf stretcher home. We both still have the flu and my back is really sore.

Tuesday, April 1, 1997—cloudy then sunny most all day, 8° to 26°. Pain in my back is really bad. Read and rested all day.

Wednesday, April 2, 1997—sunny, 21° to 34°. 11" fluffy snow. Settled and melted some today. I plowed our snow and Odden's. Pumped Odden's water and brought what was left home and put in our tanks. My back is worse.

Thursday, April 3, 1997—mostly sunny, -2° to 31°. Didn't do much today. Jim & Elaine walked over late morning and stayed for lunch. Helped make our day.

Friday, April 4, 1997—sunny, cloudy, 0° to 33°. Went to Glennallen on senior van and mailed a trapping video tape to grandson Steve.

Saturday, April 5, 1997—sunny, cloudy, 13° to 42°. I drove Jeff and we went to Gun Show in Glennallen. Got home and snow had slid off east side of garage. So I put plow on and pushed it out of the way. We went to Mary O. for supper. Jeff and his family and mother-in-law and her brother Justin were there also.

Sunday, April 6, 1997—sunny, clouding over late afternoon, 18° to 44°. Snow is shrinking fast. Loafed all day. Allen visited in the afternoon. Super Cub looking at SE Corner of Slide Mountain.

Monday, April 7, 1997—sunny and windy, 22° to 46°. Lots of snow melting. Repaired my buck knife holster and sharpened the knife (the one Nadia gave me). Phoned Marion his birthday greetings.

Tuesday, April 8, 1997—sunny, 19° to 45°. I brought a five gal bucket of dirt into the basement. Covered one wolf skull with dirt in another bucket. The microbes in the soil will eat the meat off the skull. Removed the rest of the ice from the large waterline. Put a couple more bungees on the gun case on snowgo. Shot the .338 to check the scope zero. Did some pistol practice. I may have found a bear trail in snow on Slide Mountain. Sure looks like it through the binoculars. Cal and Mary visited.

Wednesday, April 9, 1997—sunny, 12° to 44°. Sylvia went to Glennallen on senior van. I got another bucket of dirt. Cut most of the meat from a wolf head and covered it with dirt in a 5-gallon bucket. Put some oil in snowgo gear case. Tried to spot a bear on Slide Mountain with no luck. Mary Odden phoned. Went to Allen's and had cake and strawberries. Al Eckes phoned.

Thursday, April 10, 1997—sunny, 12° to 44°. Shot up some .223 at off hand practice. Spent a lot of time and effort cleaning the bore on that rifle and it isn't clean yet! Allen phoned – he saw three snowgos being unloaded at Slide Mountain Trailhead. Bear hunters?

Friday, April 11, 1997—sunny, very nice, 12° to 46°. Sylvia went to Glennallen. Cal came over and got some barrels of water. I filled our water storage tanks from our well. Put some gas in snowgo. Shoveled a little snow. Denny Eastman drove in and visited a while. I glassed for bears on Slide Mt. Didn't see any. The people snowmobiling out North are back again today. I visited Allen about tires for a few minutes.

Saturday, April 12, 1997—sunny, cloudy evening, 16° to 47°. I got my gear ready and loaded, snowgo on trailer. Ralph and Roma showed up mid morning. Got Ralph ready and went to trailhead on east side of Slide Mt. Just as we were unloading a pick up with father + son from Copper Center crowded right in and unloaded their snowgos and sled. The son had shot a 8 1/2' grizzly, black legs, brown body, blonde head collar and hump with a .30 -06 rifle last night. Left it overnight and were going in to skin it this morning. We went north to first meat pole hill. West then looking for a den first – no luck. Then south climbing some hills at 33-3400'. The snow was 33" deep and wouldn't support a snowgo. Got badly stuck Ralph was stuck several times and couldn't get up to me. I got snowgo turned around and we got back to the trail and went on west. Saw another trail south of us. Six snowgos went east on it. We went over to the trail and went east on it. We were looking for another bear den. Just couldn't get our machines to it. We talked to the other riders, then continued on back out to the highway. Loaded my machine and I started for home. Ralph missed the trail home and got stuck in road ditch snow. He did get back to our place. He and Roma brought steaks for our supper. After supper he and Roma went to visit Mannings. Cal and Phillip brought my wolf stretcher back home.

Sunday, April 13, 1997—sunny, 23° to 45°. Ralph came over about 11:00 AM.

We went up the trail on Slide Mt. north of our place. The snow was soft. Ralph led and got stuck often breaking trail. We gave up the effort at the lower of the slides. We walked up on it, rested and looked out over the country. Then back down the mountain and home. He left his machine here. I did a little reloading. The squirrels I got early morning. One hung up in the tree. The snow at this elevation is settling down and melting. A swan flew up the lake today.

Monday, April 14, 1997—partly cloudy, 23° to 43°. I got a mid morning start and went to the east Slide Mountain Trailhead. Drove snowgo a mile and 1/3 north, the 1/3 mile west. Parked and with rifle on one shoulder and the .44 magnum on the other shoulder and snowshoes in one hand I walked the bear hunters snowshoe trail. They made lots of switch back getting 400 ft of elevation on Mt. and close to a mile east. Near the bear carcass an eagle flew away. While glassing the dead bear, a fox trotted off into the trees. When I was sure no other bear had claimed the carcass I crossed a gulley and went over there. The bear (a boar) had run 80-100 yards that I could see after being hit. I measured the bear at 7 ft. long. Hind foot 6" x 11" if claws had been on it. Then shot 5 slugs from the .44 magnum, 3 crossways through the shoulder and 2 length ways. I was disappointed that none of them exited. Possibly because the meat was cool and stiff. Saw a raven fly by just as I left.

Walked back down to snowgo. Trail had warmed up and I stepped down past my knees in the snow quite a few times—still that was easier and safer than going down on snowshoes. Drove snowgo out to hwy, loaded snowgo and came home. Allen and Roxanne had brought some borrowed tools, a fuel drum and a new generator to replace the one he borrowed from me last fall. That one burned out while he was using it. I moved it into storage. Glued the rearview mirror back on the car windshield. Checked the snowgo over and put the cover on it. Called a couple people looking for rims for the car. Joe thought he had a couple but they didn't fit. Visited Allen and filled him in on the bear.

Tuesday, April 15, 1997—partly cloudy, 22° to 41°. Wrote letters all morning. Scraped and sanded the wolf pelt stretcher clean. Shortened it 10". Cut 2" from the inside to let more air in when pelt is on stretcher. Re-attached the adjustment boards at the bottom. Visited Mark and Rynee and family in evening.

Wednesday, April 16, 1997—snowed 1-1/2" all day, 24° to 32°. We went to Glennallen on senior van. I greased my brown boots. Measured bolt pattern. One of Molly's wheels.

Thursday, April 17, 1997—mostly sunny, 2° to 31°. Wrote a letter. Did some reading. Looked up some prices of old gun sights. We visited Cal's in evening.

Friday, April 18, 1997—sunny, a little windy, 2° to 33°. We went to Glennallen on senior van. Paid phone bill. Stopped by Blake's new hardware store, nice. I was looking for bear and or dens of the face of Slide. An area I was interested in a couple weeks ago looks even better today. Ralph plans to come out tomorrow morning and we'll go look that area over. Cal visited in evening then Mary O. came over.

Saturday, April 19, 1997—sunny, some breeze, 3° to 31°. Ralph showed up and brought bacon and eggs for breakfast. Brought us some canned veggies that Carr's had on sale. After we ate, we loaded gear and snowgos on my trailer and went to hwy camp, unloaded snowgos and took that trail up Slide. Saw wolf, fox, marten, rabbit, spruce hen, squirrel, moose tracks. Drove our machines as far as practicable. Then tried to snowshoe to the area we thought might be a bear den. Snow conditions were too bad to snowshoe. Tough to get snowgos back to trail but we managed. Then back at home ate lunch, took a nap and Ralph went to Art's and they flew Slide Mt. and didn't see bears or den. We visited Jeff and Laurie in evening. Ralph, Dale, Heidi, Justy, Art and Bonnie, J & L kids were all there. Had a nice visit.

Sunday, April 20, 1997—sunny, 0° to 35°. Ralph came over in the afternoon and I put a different front and sight on his rifle. I put a tarp over the snowgos. Ralph left his here on the trailer till next weekend. Allen visited in the afternoon and then came over later for a bite of supper and watched a movie.

Monday, April 21, 1997—sunny, 3° to 39°. I lost my snow shoes off the snowgo Saturday up on Slide Mountain. I brought the air compressor up out of the basement and took it out to garage and put air in snowgo trailer tire. Greased the snowgo. Drove to Nelchina DOT and parked along the driveway. Drove up the trail. Saw some moose and marten tracks. I saw where three? machines had been on the trail since I lost my snowshoes. I didn't find them of course. I did drive on up to the top of the left shoulder. I visited Allen in evening. Henry and Sally visited us later.

Tuesday, April 22, 1997—light snow, cloudy, 13°. Lee Dudley visited while he was here. Three moose walked out on the lake. One of them had a broken left rear foot. One of the other two moose would lay its ears back, run and strike at the other moose—perhaps to protect the moose with the injured foot. It would be interesting to know the whole story. I put the ATV in garage. I think the battery is bad. Three robins in yard at supper time.

Wednesday, April 23, 1997—sunny, thin clouds, 27° to 50°. Lots of melting snow. The squirrels are in love. Saw two marsh hawks coming home from Glennallen on senior bus. I tried to glue a crack in snowgo gas cap. ATV battery seems to be taking a charge. Got the truck ready to go to Anchorage. A griz recently broke into freezer at Moosey Boo.

Thursday, April 24, 1997—cloudy, windy on top of Slide Mountain, 27° to 49°. Allen and Kyle wanted me to go with them up on Slide Mt. to look for griz. Allen was late and had to go back for his binoculars and spotting scope. His Alpine snowgo broke trail really well. Both his machines would "vapor lock," but mostly we went right along. Because his machine didn't run well, we kept our distance as we watched the den where we had seen a sow with cubs last year. We also saw ravens flying in and out of Cache Creek, as well as over to the bear-kill site that I had walked to. We got back home in good time. I hauled our garbage to transfer site. Went to De Johnson's also and used the copy machine.

Friday, April 25, 1997—mostly sunny, breezy late afternoon, 32° to 52°. Two swans sitting on lake ice. We went to Glennallen on senior van. Ron gave me four rims for "Molly" but the hole pattern is too large. We went to Allen's for ice cream. Saw an airplane that appeared to be flying hunters and or spotting bears. I am putting Tung oil on the wolf stretcher.

Saturday, April 26, 1997—cloudy, 25° to 48°. Did some target shooting. Reloaded 100 more for target practice. Put some more Tung Oil on wolf stretcher. Pumped water into house storage tank. Two swans still rest on our lake. Jim, Mary and Kari Odden plan to visit this evening. Cal visited a little while this afternoon. Many 100's swans fly west up the valley.

Sunday, April 27, 1997—sunny, 27° to 50°. Got up extra early, are and got ready for Ralph and Jeff to come over. They were on time. Loaded Ralph's machine and we drove to east trailhead Slide Mt. unloaded machines and went north, glassing and we went looking for a bear. I was leading and turned up the trail to the camp between two lakes. We glassed there for awhile, seeing no bears and/or tracks. Then probably upon hearing us talking, a sow was trying to lead two large, two-yr-old, cubs out of a thicket. They had a den there. Ralph had a time deciding if he wanted to shoot one of them. He saw them first. Jeff and I felt the larger two-yr-old cub was a boar and large enough to shoot. We tried to circle ahead of them. The snow was deep and walking in it was slow. The wind was wrong, for they didn't move as fast as we thought and they scented us and crossed the little valley and went west on the snowgo trail to John Lake. Jeff and Ralph followed their trail later and it went north. Then we went north and West and they scented us on the back east trail and went north again. At that time we turned around drove out to the road, with some stops to eat, drink pop. Snow was getting warm and soft. Ralph and both got stuck a lot. Out at road they went home and I did too.

I lubed some more bullets. Elaine came over and picked up their mail and newspapers. Allen and Roxanne, Sammi visited. Allen might want to ride to Anchorage with us.

Monday, April 28, 1997—sunny, 28° to 50°. Allen went to Anchorage with us. He had business and shopping. We had a lot of shopping to do also. We got back in the late afternoon, early evening. It was an enjoyable day. I did get pretty tired.

Tuesday, April 29, 1997—partly cloudy, 25° to 52°. Did some target practice. Allen and Sammi visited. Sylvia worked in the greenhouse. I worked at timing the truck. Drained water from water hauling tank and straightened some dents. I took Allen to dump transfer site and we pulled the dumpster into proper position. Went to Tazlina Hill gravel pit and looked at a winter killed moose. No bear feeding on it. Looked for bear on Slide at old bear kill site, no luck.

Wednesday, April 30, 1997—partly cloudy, 32° to 48°. Snow melting fast. We went to Glennallen on senior van. Reloaded five different pistol powders, 10 of each. Will shoot them over the ProChrono to determine their velocities. Unloaded and parked Ralph's snowgo. Mary O. phoned. She and the girls will come over after supper. They brought ice cream and strawberries to help celebrate Sylvia's birthday.

Thursday, May 1, 1997—sunny, some breeze, 24° to 48°. Loaded the moose stomach on a piece of plywood and slid it into bed of pickup. Allen, Kyle, and Sammi came over and brought lunch. After lunch, Allen, Kyle and I went to Allen's. He hitched his Alpine to a sled and across the lake to make a bear bait station. We looked at the bear tracks left there last evening. Looks like a two year old. We walked over to the river bluff. Very little water running so far. Maybe one set of bear tracks in the distance. Some ducks in a pool on the river. Saw one silt-gravel slide, of 5 to 10 yards of material. It took some time for it to slide the 150' down to the river bed. Allen brought up some ice cream to go with some of Sylvia's cake. I repaired the choke on the snowgo, then rebuilt some of the suspension on snowgo. Called Ralph about material to repair hinge area of my snowgo hood. Told him about the bear that was on our lake.

Friday, May 2, 1997—sunny, 22° to 50°. Went to Glennallen on senior van. Got some wheel weights. Chronographed 5 different loads for .45 ACP. Allen stopped by about 8:00 PM. He had noticed griz tracks crossing the hwy about ½ mi. east of our place. I drove over there and measured front foot 6 1/4" wide, rear 9" long. Jeff dropped off a couple cans of powder Ralph had picked up for me. Gladys Schmidt phoned.

Saturday, May 3, 1997—partly cloudy, 28° to 50°. Spotted a trail down off Heavenly Ridge. Went down to Allen's. It looked like snowshoe tracks to him, then he saw the tracks went to two bear dens. Later I found another den ½ mile west of those two dens. I shoveled a lot of snow off the septic drain field, plus some off the lawn. I took the two wolf skulls out of black dirt. Scrubbed and cleaned them up. Sorted some wheel weights for Allen. We went to Steve and Karen Mailly's to supper. Steve's birthday. Lee Dudley was there as well as Pat and Patty Landers. We had an enjoyable time.

Sunday, May 4, 1997—mostly cloudy, a shower of snow, rain mix, 28° to 50°. Replaced the firing pin spring in the bolt of win mod 70 with a 25# wolffe spring. Fired it a few times for function as well as practicing close range quick shooting. Then shot a box of .22's practicing off hand shooting. Cleaned a pistol. Washed-cleaned and installed outlet plugs on a pool table light and a cold beer sign. Glassed for bears from off dinning room table. A few dozen duck on our lake including mallards.

Monday, May 5, 1997—rainy and cloudy most of day, 34° to 48°. Allen dismounted "Molly's" snow tires and mounted the new non-studded tires. He and Sammi came for pizza lunch and brought ice cream. Lee Dudley visited. Sylvia worked with her plants and the greenhouse.

Tuesday, May 6, 1997—mostly cloudy, a couple light showers, 31° to 52°. Snow and rain in mountains to south. Allen and Sammi came over to tell us of a moose cow over on the other side of our lake. She didn't appear to have a calf or to being chased-followed by a bear. They had breakfast with us and I gave Sammi a little wooden wheelbarrow. Sylvia worked with her plants and the greenhouse. I fire lapped the barrel of the Minnie Mauser. Also loaded and fire some load development rounds through the Mini Mauser. Mailed wolf to be tanned February 28, 1997, returned to Glennallen 5/6/97. Delivered 5/7/97.

Wednesday, May 7, 1997—partly cloudy, some rain in night and snow rain shower passing through, 31° to 52°. We went to Glennallen on senior van. I shot the .338 once at close range target. Picked expended bullets out of pile of snow. Did some more load development work. Tried to repair the garden rake. Cal and Mary were here to supper.

Thursday, May 8, 1997—mostly cloudy, snow-rain in area, 32° to 51°. We drove up the Lake Louise Road hunting bears and or porcupines. Visited Billmans. Sam is working there. Then on to Glennallen and picked up shocks for car. Stopped at John Kunik's machine shop. He bought our old DH CAT and is completely rebuilding it. Actually every part. Then to rifle range and picked up some brass. Then we went to the Copper Valley Telephone Coop Annual meeting. Got home about 10:30 PM. Drove through some hard rain on the way home, but it was dry here.

Friday, May 9, 1997—mostly sunny, 29° to 55°. Boiled wolf traps and snares. Practiced "bear" head shots. Jim and Elaine Manning brought their son James and his wife over to visit in the afternoon. I polished some brass and prepared some to reload. The kestrel drives other birds including ravens from its territory.

Saturday, May 10, 1997—cloudy and windy, 33° to 48°. We went to Glennallen to the Health Fair. Put a quart of oil in car and gassed it up. Nadia and Bev each phoned Sylvia. She wanted me to take her to Tolsona to dinner, we had prime rib.

Sunday, May 11, 1997—sunny, windy, 35° to 57°. Boiled traps. Cleaned and straightened up trap storage. Got ATV trailer out of storage and made snowgo storage area ready for machine as soon as I get the hood fixed. Got a lot of exercise today. Cal and Mary brought Sylvia a flower and a gift and borrowed some movies.

Monday, May 12, 1997—partly cloudy, 30° to 53°. Made two sets of Helfrich 750 wolf trap setters. I even coated the steel handles with plastic dip. Also made a snow paddle. Started soaking the wolf skulls in a solution of baking soda and water to kill the bad odor. The kestrels are mating.

Tuesday, May 13, 1997—snow in the morning, cloudy all day, 32° to 58°. I got one front shock absorber on the car. Then Allen visited for a while. After he left I put the other one on, then greased the front end, changed the oil, put new oil filter and cleaned the air filter. Washed the PVC valve. Quite a bit of ice melted at west end of lake. Goldeneye ducks fly by looking for nesting places.

Wednesday, May 14, 1997—partly cloudy, snow in evening, 31° to 49°. Did some load development with the .223. It isn't shooting well. I'm disappointed. Allen brought some barbeque pork ribs at lunch. We had Sylvia's cheese cake for desert. I made a patch repair to car tailpipe. I went in evening to American Legion Post 27 and met with some people from the VA about available health care. Looks good.

Thursday, May 15, 1997—mostly cloudy with snow, rain showers, 30° to 44°. Didn't feel well today. Visited Allen. Ed gave me a small book as I passed his place. I read it and took it back to him along with one of my books. Built a cartridge measure device. Tried to modify the claw extractor on the Mini Mauser. The nut on trigger over travel needed adjustment and tightening.

Friday, May 16, 1997—mostly sunny, 27° to 53°. Ice is going fast from lake. Lots of snowshoe rabbits every where this spring. I found the tail of one laying in the grass this morning. I washed the windows on the car and truck this morning. Then rotated the tires on the truck and mounted the front bumper on the truck.

Saturday, May 17, 1997—mostly cloudy, some showers in the afternoon and evening, 30° to 55°. The eagle hunts our lake. Went to the yard sale and pot luck lunch at the school house. I got three books and Sylvia got a puzzle. I vacuumed the car. Cleaned the filter on the shop vac. Picked us some bullets from out of a snow pile. Lots of ice went out in our lake. Maybe ¼ is left.

Sunday, May 18, 1997—sunny, beaut of a day, 29° to 54°. Lots more ice is gone from the lake. A few more ducks and eight swans this evening. The snowshoe hare were breeding today. The flickers were mating. I read some today. Went to gravel pit. No new tracks. Put gas barrels in bed of truck. Walked down to lake. Mary Odden and Kari came over.

Monday, May 19, 1997—partly cloudy, very nice, 32° to 62°. The rest of ice went out in the lake. We went to Doctor's appointments in Wasilla. Did some shopping. Brought home 200 gallons of gasoline. Ice is out on the lake.

Tuesday, May 20, 1997—sunny and breezy, 34° to 66°. I re-hooked up the old water line, put the two water manifolds for (garden and greenhouse) hoses. Picked up some expended bullets from a melting snow bank. Will re-melt and cast them into bullets again. Removed the snowgo hood and tried to glue the left side of the hinge area. Hope it works. Visited Allen. Rudbecks are back from Minnesota.

Wednesday, May 21, 1997—sunny and breezy, 40° to 71°. Re-attached the two front arm rests on the car. Put a piece of carpet on the worn out place on the driver's side. Put the snowgo in its storage place for the summer. Visited Allen and gave Sammi, Clinton and Kindra little toy wheelbarrows. Stopped by KROA for garbage sacks put roadside trash in. Left to (two) little toy wheelbarrows at Mailly twin girls. Dumped our garbage in dumpster. Went to Tazlina Hill gravel pit with some caribou hide. Possibly saw a small black bear west of there. Changed oil, filter in truck. Sylvia saw caribou from senior van.

Thursday, May 22, 1997—sunny and breezy, cloudy and windy, 36° to 65°. We planted potatoes, onions, cabbages, and sweet corn. Allen visited. I took the belt shield loose on garden tiller and placed the reverse belt back on pulley. Mary Odden brought a new battery from town for the Suzuki and I installed it.

Friday, May 23, 1997—partly cloudy and breezy, 39° to 60°. We went to Glennallen on senior van. Sylvia got some tomato plants and turnip seeds. I replaced the battery light cover on the ATV. Wrote to Bob D. CBA

Saturday, May 24, 1997—mostly sunny and breezy, 32° to 60°. We helped pick up the trash at old dump site. Raked some of yard and burned trash went to KROA for pizza. Visited Mannings on way home.

Sunday, May 25, 1997—sunny and breezy at times, 30° to 61°. We picked up the trash from our mile of road ditches. Sylvia watered the garden.

Monday, May 26, 1997—sunny and breezy, 33° to 65°. Jerry drove over our waterline so I pulled it up hill, then shoved it through the pipe under the road. Cleaned up a screen door latch and put a primer coat on it. Allen, Roxanne and Sammi here to lunch. We went to Bob and Karn's for supper. Jerry and Betty and Dana were there, Mary and Kari Odden. Jerry asked if he could have fuel delivered over our land and store it in a tank.

Tuesday, May 27, 1997—sunny, breezy, 37° to 67°. Started putting a screen door together for the front door. Cal borrowed my pipe threader. Started loading some .45 ACP.

Wednesday, May 28, 1997—sunny, 33° to 69°. We went to Glennallen on senior van. Sylvia got a sharp pain under her right ribs and we went to the ER at clinic. After x-rays, blood test, diagnosed as arthritis pain. Did some shopping and paid electric. Did some work with the water line. Allen visited.

Thursday, May 29, 1997—partly cloudy, 46° to 68°. Worked some on screen door. Visited Allen. Later Lee came to Chronograph some loads. Then Allen came over to look at snow plow. Ed brought back a book. Karn brought over a clipping from a paper. We went to Dimmick's for Supper. Rachel and Arlene came to get some Epsom salts for Corky's hand. I finished loading the .45 ACP after casting the bullets.

Friday, May 30, 1997—rain all day, 38° to 56°. Sylvia went to Glennallen on senior van and picked up some aluminum pop rivets and 2 3/4" pipe couplings. Painted the screen door hinges and cast some .45 bullets. Swept and vacuumed in the basement.

Saturday, May 31, 1997—new snow on mountains to the south, down to 3300' elevation, 36° to 52°. Very few snow and or rain showers today. I hung the front screen door and put a latch on it. Extended the phone extension wire to the TV Dish control box. Took garbage to dump. Phoned Paul and family.

Sunday, June 1, 1997—intermittent sunny, cloudy, showers, some with snow-like hail, 29° to 55°. Fired some .223 over the Chrony to obtain velocity and at a target to check for accuracy. Cleaned rifle and loaded some more brass with a different powder and will perform that same test on it. Read the Sunday paper. Lee Dudley stopped by and I miked some brass for him. He visited awhile and gave me shark medicine pills for my bad shoulder.

Monday, June 2, 1997—mostly sunny and very nice, 31° to 69°. Melted a batch of wheel weights and poured them into ingot mould. Drove Suzuki up Slide Mountain looking for moose and caribou tracks. Walked west on top rim looking for a black bear. No luck. But did see a blonde-chocolate legged grizzly. It was about 500 yards west and looked to be soaking up the sun and sleeping. Came home and drained the gas out of the Suzuki and cleaned the fuel filters. After supper I drove to Tazlina Gravel Pit. The bear has pulled the moose winter kill carcass farther in the brush. Allen and David were in the pit. I went around on top. No bear has been to the caribou hide. Didn't find any cartridges. Stopped at Army Trail Gravel Pit. Met a truck driver "Peter." He was resting from driving. I found 19 .44 magnum brass. A couple .223 +.30 - 30. No brass in pit across from old RCA site. Visited with Allen for a while.

Tuesday, June 3, 1997—beautiful day, 35° to 74°. Windy on Eureka Summit. I loaded the Suzuki and drove 11 miles to trailhead on Eureka Summit. On the way to Crooked Creek. I drove by 50 bull caribou in groups of 2-10-12. They are shedding; shaggy and ribs show. Horns are well started. The trail was very good. I got to Crooked Creek and found the ice still frozen to creek banks. The stream, it's flowing free. I couldn't get across so ate my lunch and came back. Pretty tired tonight.

Wednesday, June 4, 1997—sunny, some breeze and hot, 39° to 75°. Worked on car. Succeeded, I hope, in getting a piece of carbon out of valve seat. Cast 200 bullets. Changed the upper water manifold and ran 3/4" plastic 50' closer to greenhouse and 50' closer to strawberry bed. Lee Dudley visited and I gave him some wheels for his swamp buggy.

Thursday, June 5, 1997—sunny, windy sometimes rain in evening, 39° to 76°. I drove Suzuki up Slide Mt. on trail out of hwy camp. Stopped on numerous knolls to use the binoculars. Saw one nice bear den and two other older ones. Saw three caribou. Drove on over to the lake and wished I had brought my pack rod to fish for grayling. Some pairs of ducks on lake. The trail was very good. Found some .44 magnum brass. Took Cal's paint back to him. Gave him pictures of him on trap line. Karn visited. I went to gravel pit to shoot but it started raining.

Friday, June 6, 1997—rain, cloudy and windy, 40° to 56°. Went to Glennallen on senior van. Cashed checks. Fish and Wildlife Protection gave seniors some red salmon. We saved one to bake later. Fried a piece for my supper. It was firm and tasty. Sylvia canned the rest, in pint jars.

Saturday, June 7, 1997—rain and fog all night and day, 41° to 51°. Allen came over and copied the tape we made last night. Then I made two more copies. I drove Allen to Mendeltna to pick up his van.

Sunday, June 8, 1997—rain and fog, clouds are thinning some what, 40° to 49°. I spread fertilizer and lime on the lawn. Reloaded some .357 practice loads. Phoned a happy birthday to Paul. Talked to Steve and Ruth. Bob and Karn visited this evening.

Monday, June 9, 1997—partly cloudy, some rain south of river, 39° to 58°. Put some different spark plug wires on car. It still had a miss so I started checking the spark plugs. The right rearmost plug was badly fouled w/carbon and water crud. Went to gravel pit for target practice. Sure wrecked two joints of my right forefinger today. Saw a sparrow fly up out of some blueberry stems. Looking closer I saw the four tiny eggs in the well-hidden nest. Sylvia saw a snowshoe hare out by the garage. Visited Allen in evening.

Tuesday, June 10, 1997—rain in night and partly cloudy, 39° to 62°. Went to Glennallen and helped Darrel put his 3" cannon w it's four iron rimmed wagon wheels together. Went to Glennallen shooting range and picked up some brass I can use. Cleaned and sorted it when I got home.

Wednesday, June 11, 1997—sunny, 39° to 67°. Took Karn's book back. Bob gave me a few blocks of green firewood. Split and piled some of it. Hauled two loads gravel and filled some low places in our lane. Checked plug in car, its OK. Used the tiller. Got lawn mower out. Sylvia mowed lawn. Went target shooting and brought back 12 buckets of crushed gravel for her green house floor.

Thursday, June 12, 1997—partly cloudy, 46° to 63°. Split and piled the last few pieces of green wood. Missed a rabbit near the woodshop. Counted out and put in paper sacks 100 dream catcher hoops. Raked lawn and mulched the raspberries with it. Hoed out the grass that tries to grow in the parking area gravel. Lee Dudley visited in evening. Allen visited late.

Friday, June 13, 1997—partly cloudy, 41° to 63°. We went to Anchorage. Did lots of shopping. Got nearly everything we went to get.

Saturday, June 14, 1997—partly cloudy, 39° to 60°. Made a cleaning rod protector. Put stop leak in car. The store sent me with wrong headlight bulb. Did some target shooting with the .223.

Sunday, June 15, 1997—partly cloudy and breezy keeping, 38° to 64°. Chronographed some rifle and pistol loads. Reloaded some more. Cal came over to get a hole drilled and tapped. Lee Dudley stopped by to get a tire I gave him. Allen, Roxanne and family visited in evening. Allen went down to lake and brought TJ Huddleston up to our house. Sylvia fixed him a couple large hot dogs, milk and cookies. While Allen's were here we saw a spike horn young bull moose swimming down our lake. It got out on south side and walked off into the trees.

Monday, June 16, 1997—partly cloudy, breezy, 37° to 62°. Lots of bugs in protected places. Lee Dudley wanted to bring back the tire I gave him but I urged him to try it for size at least. Went to gravel pit for rifle handgun practice. Tried without success to change the fuel filter on the truck. Nice outside today.

Tuesday, June 17, 1997—sunny, some breeze, 37° to 70°. Lots of mosquitoes. Cleaned carburetor on chainsaw and cut the brush back away from garden. Hoed four garden rows. Lee came for some swamp buggy advice. Nadia called, bless her heart. Loaded up some 250 grain Nosler. Went to gravel pit after supper and chronographed them, some 210 grain and some .223 Remington. That old .338 win shoots so many bullet weights to same or nearly same point of aim. Very accurate rifle.

Wednesday, June 18, 1997—lots of clouds and breezy, 46° to 70°. Visited at Cal and Mary's. I went to Eureka Summit. Took the trail to Crooked Creek. Met and visited with a man out for a ride on the trail. Ate my sandwich at Crooked Creek. Scattered caribou every where moving west. Went partway up Monument Mountain. Walked over to a small hill to look for the 80 pounds of gold. No luck. On way back I went down Cottonwood Cr. Started raining so I turned around and started for trailhead. After 3-4 mi met two men and two boys on ATV's. One man is the one who found the dinosaur bones at Mile 121 gravel pit. I got rained on pretty hard before I got to truck. Unloaded everything at home.

Thursday, June 19, 1997—cloudy and some light rain, 45° to 63° mostly in 50s. Didn't feel good all day. Did a few small jobs. Loaded 100 .223's. Made a nice shot on a varmint.

Friday, June 20, 1997—mostly cloudy, 42° to 61°. Made pistol bore cleaning rod. Repaired chainsaw chain breaker. Shortened chain for chainsaw. Visited Allen.

Saturday, June 21, 1997—sunny and warm, 40° to 76°. Ralph ate breakfast with us. Loaded my gear and we drove to Chitna and got our dip netting permits at F & G. Hundreds of people in the area dip netting fishing the Copper River. We saw maybe 30 fish caught. We watched how this fishing is done. We had a good time. Found some brass. We didn't even try to fish -too slow for us. Back at home, Sylvia fixed a good supper with Ralph's steak and hash browns. I cleaned the brass and put it away. I had misplaced some gear in a cooler and it was lost for a while. Allen brought some crushed rock for the septic system.

Sunday, June 22, 1997—partly cloudy, thunder showers going on both sides – little here. 49° to 73°. Lee Dudley wasn't home. Visited a little with Karen Mailly. Found some brass in gravel pit. Cleaned and sized it. A moose cow stood out in the lily pads of our lake for quite some time then crossed to south side. Dan Billman visited, enjoyed that. Just as he was leaving Ralph and Jeff stopped by Jeff with some salmon. After supper I shot some factory .223 Remington over the chronograph checking F.P.S. out of barrel of a mini 14.

Monday, June 23, 1997—mostly sunny, 43° to 76°. Thunder showers in the distance. I cut some trees from near the septic tank. Blocked them up, loaded in ATV trailer. Hauled to wood shed, split and piled them. Helped Cal pour ¾ yards of cement. Got ready to go to town tomorrow.

Tuesday, June 24, 1997—cloudy, 47° to 65°. I went to Anchorage to pick up my eyeglasses, also some drain field pipe. Visited with Leona Dawson who was waiting in line at construction sight.

Wednesday, June 25, 1997—mostly sunny and some breeze, 49° to 75°. Sylvia went to Glennallen. Cleaned up and piled all the branches from the spruce and a birch I cut down. Blocked the spruce split and pile it. Painted out the bad places in the paint on the car. Replaced the high beam bulb on the car. Practiced off hand .22 rifle shooting. Plus 50 - .45 ACP and 24 - .44 magnum moderate loads. Karn and Sheryl visited Sylvia. Bob and Karn brought some grayling and lake trout. Bookmobile stopped by.

Thursday, June 26, 1997—sunny, breezy, 50° to 75°. Worked in garden. Loaded some target practice .44 magnum. Trimmed some branches out of some trees. Walked over to Charlie's Storage, it's ok. Allen visited in evening.

Friday, June 27, 1997—partly cloudy, 55° to 78°. Sylvia went to Anchorage with Karn. Showers in afternoon and evening. Cut some witch's broom off a few spruce trees and burned it. Dismantled the bumpers and plywood from the pool table. Brought the piece of roofing steel. I plan to paint and use on front porch roof. Did some digging near the septic tank. Allen wasn't able to dig the drain field line today.

Saturday, June 28, 1997—partly cloudy and breezy, 50° to 75°. Put two coats paint on steel for porch roof. Worked on a shooting gear box for rifle range, not finished. Drew up plan for porch rafters. Harold and Rachel visited in evening.

Sunday, June 29, 1997—mostly sunny, 53° to 79°. Mosquitoes not quite so bad. Cleaned and painted the flashing for front porch roof. Glue wouldn't hold it together. Build a small tray for shooting gear box. Went to gravel pit for target practice. Sylvia brought home a lawnmower from Anchorage.

Monday, June 30, 1997—sunny and some breeze, 52° to 80°. Pushed the well cover back down over the culvert. Put in an over ground drain line from the washing machine. Weeded the garden and thinned the turnip and cauliflower. Built another tray for shooting gear box. Allen came over this evening and dug about ½ of sewer drain field. We have to rip out one line and are going much deeper under it. He hit frost at about 50", at a 10" layer of pure black soil. There is sand-gravel under it. That is what we are trying to get to and fill with rock.

Tuesday, July 1, 1997—sunny, some breeze and lots of bugs this evening, 52° to 80°. Cleaned the well. Put some sod back in place. Chopped a bunch of roots. Cut down a bunch of trees near the septic drain field. Allen came over and finished digging the ditch. Roxanne brought over a cake at break time this evening.

Wednesday, July 2, 1997—sunny and a shower after supper, 52° to 79°. Did some digging in ditch and shoveled loose material away from ditch. Cleaned out and washed part of line that will use again. Cleaned the .22. Worked some more on the drain system. Allen hauled gravel.
A black bear stopped in front of the picture window and exchanged looks with Sylvia. As soon as it moved on she called down to Allen's as I had taken him home. He got his rifle and Kyle. I hurried home and got .338 and started tracking the bear. He had gone between the satellite dish and the heating oil tank, down a short bank to our switchback road that goes down to the lake. Lost his tracks at our south garden fence. Allen, Kyle and I dropped down hill to lower road and turned east. Just past Jerry's hanger a little ways the bear walked out on the road. I immediately made the decision it was plenty big enough to shoot. I kneeled down on one knee and quickly shot. Allen said, "He is hit." The bear galloped out of sight in a heartbeat. We moved up the road tracking the bear--seeing no blood. (The bullet had passed through the lower 1/3 of heart). Very shortly it turned off into the brush. We split and Allen spotted him down and expiring. The bear had traveled maybe 40 yards. I gave him another on in back of the neck to be sure of a quick death. Time: 11:50 PM. Then we went to our place, got the Suzuki and trailer and back to kill site. Dragged the bear the short distance to the road and loaded it into the trailer. Back up the hill to the garage. Gathered the butcher gear, skinned the bear, put the meat in the freezer and I took Allen home. Time 2:00 PM. Then I hosed the bear hide on both sides with water and spread it in bed of pickup for the night. I got to bed 2:30 AM.

Thursday, July 3, 1997—partly cloudy and a hard shower in the afternoon, 50° to 75°. Took more pix of bear and put the hide in the freezer and worked on the ditch. Allen visited then hauled gravel, and put it in the ditch. I placed the pipes and tarp and plastic covering and shoveled a lot of material and Allen moved the old ditch material on top of the new. Cal brought over a rug washer for Sylvia to wash our rugs. He wanted to hear the bear story. Mark Brockman and Nickie came over hoping to see the bear. Nickie got to see the meat in the freezer. The kids play a lot on their raft out in the lake. Phoned Steve and told him about the bear adventure.

Friday, July 4, 1997—partly cloudy, some showers all around us, 48° to 72°. I shoveled and carried gravel. Moved some sod. Cut down some more trees near drain field. Visited Cal. Stopped by McKee's moving sale. Sylvia and I returned the rug washer to Mary and Cal.

Saturday, July 5, 1997—partly cloudy, one good rain. 52° to 75°. Shoveled a little gravel. Went over and told Jerry R about the black bear. Dennis and Addie Griffith were there also. Allen visited and I gave him some steel and some money on the work he done. Cut the quarter opening on the range box. Went to Huddleston's barbeque picnic supper and good visiting after.

Sunday, July 6, 1997—partly cloudy, really nice, 45° to 77°. My left shoulder is really sore. Shoveled a little gravel. Did some more on range box. I've put too much strain on left shoulder. We went to a Mendeltna church service and barbeque picnic after at Allen and Roxanne's. Ralph visited a little while in the afternoon. Phoned Nadia.

Monday, July 7, 1997—partly cloudy, breezy sometimes, pretty hard rain mid afternoon, 53° to 77°. I offered Bob R. some smoke house shelves. Finished painting the range box and trap setters. Reloaded 250 45 ACP. Put bear skull out to thaw.

Tuesday, July 8, 1997—partly cloudy to cloudy and breezy, really smoky, 49° to 75°. Took bear hide to Glennallen F & G and they put seals on hide and skull. Picked up some brass. Skinned feet our on bear hide. Preparing it for shipping to tannery.

Wednesday, July 9, 1997—partly cloudy and breezy, 51° to 75°. I went to Lee's place. Had a nice time. The dumpster at the transfer site is full so I didn't put our garbage in. Packaged the bear hide. Boiled the bear skull, cleaned it of meat and scrubbed it. Then put it to soak in Hilex solution. Beautiful evening. Back has hurt a lot all day.

Thursday, July 10, 1997—partly cloudy, loaded gear and Suzuki in truck and drove to trailhead for Ballanger Pass. As soon as I reached the flat going to the pass, I started seeing caribou by the thousands covering many square miles. The

smell of them every where. I stopped and took pictures. At top of Ballanger
Pass I stopped again and watched the interplay of the herd members. They were
closest at 30 yards. Listening to the sounds they made, such as cows calling their
calves to nurse etc. It was a moving experience. After a while I continued to
Pass Creek, then Alfred Creek. The clay slide ("dam") was washed out. I went
around it on the western upper trail. When reaching Alfred Creek I explored
both up and down it. On the way back I shot at some rocks and squirrels
shooting 8. Visited Cal and Mary on way home. At home I found Darrel Geary
had brought his brother and wife of Connecticut to meet us. They stayed for
supper. They got the grand tour.

Friday, July 11, 1997—cloudy, a few sprinkles, 48° to 65°. Shoveled some gravel
in drain field. We got our septic rank pumped today. Unloaded the Suzuki and
hosed it clean. Put my gear away. Worked on range box correcting my mistake.
Allen visited in evening. Bev and Tyler phoned to visit. Cal brought us some
fish. Sylvia canned them. Allen came over and asked me to move his Ranger to
our place. Job went well. Found some buckets Roxanne lost off Allen's truck.

Saturday, July 12, 1997—cloudy to partly cloudy, 47° to 71°. Worked on range
box. Sure am having problems getting it built. Went to gravel pit and shot
three handguns and the .338 magnum.

Sunday, July 13, 1997—cloudy, Partly cloudy, cloudy, 49° to 72°. Less bugs right
now. Worked on range box. It's mostly finished. Sylvia packaged more bear.
She baked a lemon pie and fixed a basket of flowers for Elaine (just out of
hospital back surgery). Met Elaine and Jim's Dave Loretta. Visited them for a
while. Allen came over and we took the blade for his Ranger down to his place
and he did some welding. Then he dressed up our drain field covering material.

Monday, July 14, 1997—partly cloudy and rain in evening, 47° to 69°. Worked
on rafters for front porch. Visited Peter Heino and wife. Saw the home he is
building. Came home, car overheated, finished the rafters. Put away tools.
Started three reloading blocks. James Callahan phoned. He will be here Aug 3rd.

Tuesday, July 15, 1997—mostly sunny, shower in evening, 48° to 66°. Finished
putting the holes in three loading blocks. Put porch rafters, purlins, and steel
on west end of house over the front door. Painted the outside of upstairs
window above the new porch. Put one coat of paint on loading blocks. Pulled
the weeds out of 2/3 of garden. Hauled garbage to dump. Bears are in the
dumpster. Damaging the covering wire and scattering garbage. Hauled Allen's
plastic pipe down to his place—they were gone. Bears have been in dumpster.

Wednesday, July 16, 1997—mostly sunny, rain in night, 48° to 69°. Worked on
front porch all day. The military war games refueling jets fly very low over-

through our little valley.

Thursday, July 17, 1997—mostly sunny, 37° to 70°. Early morning, left for Anchorage. Shopped for building materials—some groceries, lime and lawn fertilizer. Had to run around town too much. Waited on road construction.

Friday, July 18, 1997—rain in morning, partly cloudy, 46° to 69°. We went to Glennallen on senior van. Painted the plywood for the ceiling in front porch inlet the porch light switch box in the log by the door using a drill and a chisel. Drilled through the header log and ran wiring out to porch. Switch light worked the first try. Pretty tired tonight. Allen, Ellie, Jamie, Sammy came over with ice cream. Later I drilled the hole he needed in his receiver hitch he is building on his truck.

Saturday, July 19, 1997—partly cloudy, some breeze, 46° to 69°. Finished the front porch. Fiber glass repaired the snowgo hood. Visited Cal and Mary.

Sunday, July, 1997—partly cloudy, cloudy and a shower in the afternoon, 43° to 63°. Pulled weeds in garden and hilled the potatoes. Pulled the fire weed on west outside. Glued a wolf skull together and glued the teeth back in. Visited Allen and Roxanne after supper and borrowed meat grinder.

Monday, July 21, 1997—rain all night and most of day, 48° to 58°. Put the RCBS primer together, mounted it on a board and adapted the board to reloading bench. Returned the meat grinder to Allen's. Sylvia ground some of bear meat and made 28 large patties.

Tuesday, July 22, 1997—partly cloudy, 47° to 65°. Removed the radiator from the car. Cast some bullets. Went to gravel pit after supper for target practice. Found some brass. Shot a varmint with .44 magnum.

Wednesday, July 23, 1997—partly cloudy, a few showers around, 49° to 68°. Loaded ATV in truck and went to Mile 133 trailhead. Saw a couple moose and caribou tracks on way to Old Man Creek. Drove thru a real deep hole crossing the creek. Stopped at Trailside Lake to watch grayling feeding. Ate lunch on top of a knob. A ways farther on, I was turned back by a deep, fast running stream in a swampy place. Saw a wolf track, a spruce hen and chicks, a ptarmigan hen and family. Took pix of hen. Visited Cal and Mary's. Washed ATV at home. Straightened the ears of the wolf pelt so they will dry straight.

Thursday, July 24, 1997—cloudy, rain, 51° to 60°. Went to road construction office at Mile 115. No culvert to be had. Picked up trash at a spill along highway. Found Styrofoam cooler and piece of plywood along highway. Cast more bullets. Got mattress from Don Makee B & K. Supper at Rudbeck's.

Friday, July 25, 1997—mostly cloudy, lots of rain in night and more today, 49° to 66°. I went to Wasilla for paint, groceries and gasoline.

Saturday, July 26, 1997—cloudy, sunny, smoky, 49° to 72°. Visited Allen and Roxanne. Soldered radiator and installed it in truck. Tough job. Glued on a wolf skull.

Sunday, July 27, 1997—partly cloudy, 46° to 76°. I cut out parts for well cover. Sylvia painted primer coat on them. Did some target practice. My sister Virginia phoned.

Monday, July 28, 1997—partly cloudy, thunder showers near us in evening, 56° to 77°. Cleaned the gravel in parking area. Measured window trim. Reloaded .38 spl. Electricity was off in the evening.

Tuesday, July 29, 1997—partly cloudy, showers in evening, 51° to 67°. Sprayed wolf skulls with acrylic. Visited Cal and Mary. They gave us some paint for well cover. Cast some bullets. Loaded some .338.

Wednesday, July 30, 1997—partly clouds, a little rain, 50° to 64°. We went to Glennallen on senior van. Painted some more on lid for well. A man's truck broke down near here.

Thursday, July 31, 1997—rain in night, partly cloudy, rain in evening, 48° to 64°. Sprayed acrylic on wolf and bear skulls. Started assembling the cover for the well. Cal, Mary and grandchildren Hanna, boy? plus Harold and Rachel Dimmick were here for a bear roast supper.

Friday, August 1, 1997—partly cloudy, some showers, 49° to 67°. We went to a senior picnic at Lake Louise. Visited Andy & Ruth Runyan's trophy room. Visited Patti Billman. Back at home we put Styrofoam insulation in the well cover and nailed the top on. Wonderful evening.

Saturday, August 2, 1997—partly cloudy, 50° to 65°. Worked on cover for the well. Cleaned wood shop. Sylvia painted some and I did some.

Sunday, August 3, 1997—sunny, light breeze, a very beautiful day, 48° to 70°. Painted more of the well cover. Pulled weeds, raked spruce cones. Waited on James to show up. Allen visited and brought over some more fresh corn. We gave him a box mattress springs.

Monday, August 4, 1997—sunny with a breeze, very nice, 50° to 76°. More painting of well cover. Started planning the plumbing change in the well. Still waiting for James.

Tuesday, August 5, 1997—sunny with a breeze, very nice, 54° to 80°. Assembled the plug for well top. Some other little jobs. Sylvia went to a ladies luncheon. Cal came over just as I was going to haul the well top to the well and he helped me with it. I gave him the rest of the paint he gave me. I gave him a propane fitting he needed. Reloaded some target loads and used the last of the World War II surplus Bulls Eye Powder. In evening we hauled the garbage to transfer site. Stopped by gravel pit and found some brass. Some smoke up in the air.

Wednesday, August 6, 1997—cloudy, foggy, lots of rain night and day, 48° to 52°. Went to Glennallen for some parts to change the plumbing and wiring in the well. When I got home, Henry Johnson, James Callahan and Mike Shelton were here and visited quite a while.

Thursday, August 7, 1997—cloudy, partly cloudy, 47° to 65°. Visited Roxanne and Lucky. Looked at Allen's drain back check valve in his well. Visited James at Henry's house. Compacted gravel at home. Cut trim for house windows.

Friday, August 8, 1997—partly cloudy, 49° to 63°. James Callahan was here when I got up this morning. We visited all day, then went to Sam's and visited till supper time. James went over to Henry's to get a beer.

Saturday, August 9, 1997—mostly cloudy, 49° to 58°. James visited a few minutes. Sylvia gave trim 2nd coat. I hauled two loads gravel down to trail to well with the ATV and trailer. Did some target practice and found a lot of brass there. Polished it at home.

Sunday, August 10, 1997—mostly cloudy, 46° to 62°. James stopped by, he is on his way to Anchorage. We put up trim on house windows.

Monday, August 11, 1997—cloudy, windy in the afternoon, 43° to 67°, mostly less than 60°. I worked some more on window trim. After lunch I went to gravel pit and shot a couple rifles from 200 yards. Cleaned guns after I got home. We keep a low fire in garage to help dry paint on window trim. Allen stopped by for coffee and cookies. Sylvia gave him zucchini relish.

Tuesday, August 12, 1997—cloudy, sunny and very nice, 45° to 70°. Worked on well. Raised the box around it by putting 4" x 4"s under it. Put the top on and screws in the hinges. Hauled old top to wood shop. Sylvia helped. She painted window trim while I pulled weeds in garden. Cleaned woodshop.

Wednesday, August 13, 1997—cloudy and rain showers all night and day, 48° to 56°. Shoveled a little gravel in a few small depressions in our lane. I sharpened hunting knives. I gave Bob four cans of oil and he gave me some used plywood. Elaine visited. Karn came over twice.

Thursday, August 14, 1997–sunny, some breeze and beautiful, 46° to 70°. Worked on the well cover, wiring for light bulb to heat the well. Pulled the pump. Assembled and installed some of the well plumbing. Put more trim on house windows. Rudbeck bros. graded our lane. Went to cook-out supper at Gilcrease's. Met Rose and Ron.

Friday, August 15, 1997–partly cloudy, 46° to 67°. We shopped in Anchorage and Wasilla. Groceries and materials for the well. Visited Allen at his campground. Gave him a fuel drum and transfer pump.

Saturday, August 16, 1997–cloudy till 2:00 PM and clear by evening, 48° to 63°. Started working on the well and rained out in morning. Finished wiring the pump. Hooked up the plumbing to water line. Had to lengthen the chain that suspends the pump motor. Tried putting another pair of hinges on well cover lid. No style hinges seem to work, so I painted the screw holes full and will do without hinges on it.

Sunday, August 17, 1997–foggy, cleaning to partly cloudy in evening, 40° to 65°. Very nice day. Went to gravel pit and fired the .338 and used scope cross hairs to measurer target. Horizontally 14" Vertically 22". Will use this hopefully to measure distant moose horns. Almost finished all the work on front window sill. Sylvia worked on floors and mowed lawn. House looks great. Saw a moose at SW corner of our lake.

Monday, August 18, 1997–partly cloudy and very nice, 47° to 63°. Mike Griffith and Bob Nickels visited at lunch time. I was working on window trim for garage. When they left I finish that job. Sylvia painted it. I cleaned up the floors in garage and woodshop. Measured car muffler outlet. Hauled gravel fill for 5 small depressions.

Tuesday, August 19, 1997–sunny, 45° to 64°. Went to Glennallen and mailed a letter to Vanessa in Australia and a parcel with Mike and Bob's caps in it. Pulled a few small trees from along trail to well. Tightened two plastic threaded fittings at well. New plumbing works OK. Sylvia painted garage trim.

Wednesday, August 20, 1997–partly cloudy, 40° to 62°. Moose season opened today. I got up early and hunted ½ mi west of DOT station. No luck. Had coffee with Cal. Had to remake the vertical trim for the garage then prime it. Ate lunch, loaded ATV and drove up the trail in back of DOT station to top of Slide. Didn't see any game, just a few tracks. Saw cow moose north side highway near Little Nelchina River.

Thursday, August 21, 1997—cloudy, rain in late afternoon, 44° to 58°. Painted the last of garage window trim and put it on later in the afternoon. Cleaned garage and wood shop and some junk lying around. Cousin Gladys and Harold Schmidt arrived to visit. They live near Manning Iowa.

Friday, August 22, 1997—cloudy, rain in night and occasional showers today, 43° to 46°. Visited all day with Gladys and Harold.

Saturday, August 23, 1997—partly cloudy, light shower, 45° to 60°. We went with Harold and Gladys to Copper Center. Had a sandwich. Visited Georgia Strunk's home to see her collection of artifacts. While in Copper Center we visited a art gallery and museum. Our guests wanted their picture taken at the oil pipeline. A young GI (Marine) was having brake trouble, I had him follow us home and gave him a bolt to fix it and got it repaired and sent him on his way.

Sunday, August 24, 1997—partly cloudy, 45° to 61°. We took Gladys and Harold to church at Mendeltna Chapel Service. Pot luck after. Then drove up Lake Louise Road to look at what sights there was to see.

Monday, August 25, 1997—partly cloudy, 44° to 62°. Gladys and Harold left after breakfast. I went hunting on trail on east side of Little Nelchina River. Very little sign. Met a man and woman camping. Drove the highway in evening. Saw Allen and Ed glassing a couple cow moose. Saw a moose in ditch on way home.

Tuesday, August 26, 1997—mostly cloudy and a little sprinkle of rain, 42° to 52°. Got up early and drove a little way west and walked out to a slough. Did not see any moose. Pulled some weeds in garden. Tom and T J Huddleston visited. I changed the way I hang tarp in front of trap, snowgo part of the wood shed. Visited Allen after supper. David forgot to return my electrical connectors for me. They seem to be temporarily misplaced.

Wednesday, August 27, 1997—partly cloudy, 33° to 59°. Moved some black dirt with wheel barrow. Cut down two birch, piled slash, started cutting it into stove length and the chain broke. Went to Tazlina to get copies made but they were poor copies. Found a lot of .44 magnum brass at gravel pit. We painted the east upstairs window. Went to Dimmick's for supper. Sylvia showed Rachel how to get batter to stick to halibut and deep fry it. We had a good supper and visit. Didn't see any moose along the road.

Thursday, August 28, 1997—mostly sunny, 35° to 63°. Sylvia went on senior van to Alaska State Fair at Palmer. I repaired chain for chainsaw and finished cutting and stacking the birch wood. Moved distributor on truck. Glassed Slide

Mountain for game. Cleaned dirt off tree stumps and piled them. Moved the dirt over by Sylvia's wild flowers and the cut of the road down to lake. Karn and Bob brought over a couple quarts of really nice large blueberries. Little time to visit.

Friday, August 29, 1997—a beautiful day, 48° to 64°. Trimmed and cut up some small trees from near the septic drain field. Sharpened the saw chain a couple of times. After Sylvia came home from Glennallen we augered holes and reset the posts in the garden fence. The second crop of radishes and lettuce is coming along nicely. Allen stopped by and picked up 13 steel posts. Went target shooting.

Saturday, August 30, 1997—a nice day, 41° to 62°. Trimmed and cut up and stacked more wood. Drove Suzuki up Slide to near top. Walked on up and found two guys camping up there!! Someone has had to tell them where the trail is. A couple old moose tracks were all the sign I saw. Reloaded some .44 magnum. Phillip, Evelyn and her son borrowed some movies.

Sunday, August 31, 1997—cloudy, rain, partly cloudy, 39° to 55°. Tom came and got a load of water. I took the pool table apart and cleaned the wood of staples and hardware. Sylvia fixed a huge meal. Huddleston family, Allen and daughters, Jim, Mary and Kari Odden were here help eat it. We have a nice visit afterwards. I found our well has silted in a lot.

Monday, September 1, 1997—partly cloudy, 34° to 55°. We took the dredge down to the well. Had a lot of trouble with air leaks and getting water to the pump. After getting the pump working, it wouldn't lift the sand from the bottom of the well. We got pretty tired. Brought everything back to the house. Rested a while. Ate supper. Took garbage to transfer site. Very little luck looking for brass at gravel pit. Had fun "plinking" with the .44 magnum.

Tuesday, September 2, 1997—partly cloudy, 32° to 61°. Sylvia went in well with a shovel and put the sand in a bucket and I pulled it up and carried it away and dumped the buckets. Will try to get more tomorrow. Got 2 squirrels today.

Wednesday, September 3, 1997—beautiful sunny day, 33° to 62°. Shot a spruce hen and a squirrel. We got a little more sand out of well. Pumped it lots of times to clear the water up. Then we built a trough to lay the water lines in an effort to keep them draining this winter. The turnips, radishes and lettuce sure are good. We went to a cookout at Manning's. Rudbecks flew in to repair their moose hauling rig.

Thursday, September 4, 1997—cloudy, 35° to 60°. Shot a spruce hen, butchered it. Shot a squirrel. Pretty well finished up the work on the supports for the water line down at well. Dave and D came over to look at some logs we have. Sylvia didn't feel good all day. With rest she's better tonight. A 24-hour flu is going around. Went out after dark and looking up at the sky I notice a "hole" in the clouds shaped with east-west axis with feathery clouds that appeared to be wind driven in center.

Friday, September 5, 1997–cloudy to partly cloudy, 41° to 61°. Loaded the Suzuki and went to Old Man Creek then down the trail from there to the Little Nelchina. Talked to a couple guys eating their lunch. I went up the Little Nelchina River a couple miles and glassed for game, no luck. Did see a porcupine. Back out on trail, back to truck met a man and a boy. Saw a larger moose track. Went to look at Allen's septic tank installation. David brought over the electrical connectors that were lost.

Saturday, September 6, 1997–partly cloudy, 38° to 57°. Finished getting the well ready for winter. Re-attached the tail pipe support on truck. Put a plug in gas line from the left gas tank on the truck as the tank leaks really bad. Helped clean blueberries Sylvia picked. Ralph and Roma Fuson are visiting. They brought steaks and other goodies for supper. Ralph and I went road hunting.

Sunday, September 7, 1997–cloudy, partly cloudy, 38° to 57°. Ralph and I hunted the road early morning. Ate breakfast, did a few little things then we drove up the Lake Louise Road. Talked to a few hunters. Stopped at Dinty Bush's. Visited about "Mean Machine" with Steve, Doug and Leona. Got some gasoline there. Hunted back down the road. Saw a very small cow with a very small calf. Of course, I didn't shoot her, though she was legal. Shot a rabbit later.

Monday, September 8, 1997–partly cloudy, 37° to 56°. Shot six spruce hens. Bob and Karn came over to visit. Had lunch. I tried to put wax on garage and house roofs. Was only partially successful. The applicator I tried didn't work very well. We drove the Lake Louise Road but didn't see any caribou. Saw a mature eagle in a low tree 20' from road way. After supper we drove west on hwy looking for a legal moose bull. Lots of glassing with no luck. Saw Allen looking also. Had coffee with Cal and Mary. They still have lots of company. He saw a moose that might be legal and will go look in morning.

Tuesday, September 9, 1997–cloudy, 37° to 52°. We drove up the Lake Louise Road to Oil Well Road and down it to Mendeltna Creek. Saw two spruce hens. One was real young. Sylvia didn't want me to shoot them. Didn't see any moose or caribou. Went on up the road to 10 ½ mi and saw two caribou on the road. Couldn't shoot them on the road, once they got in the brush I couldn't see them. We went onto Lake Louise Lodge and had a hamburger. On the way home the truck motor started putting out a lot of blue smoke and quit.

Steve Mailly saw it happen. He went home and got his Jeep and pulled our truck home. Sure was a life saver for us. We had a good visit over coffee.

Wednesday, September 10, 1997—a shower, mostly cloudy, 47° to 52°. Joe Virgin dropped off a puller for a balancer crankshaft pulley on truck. Ed F. came over and checked the motor out. He found that something went wrong w/#5 cylinder. Motor will probably have to be replaced. Reloaded some practice ammo.

Thursday, September 11, 1997—mostly sunny, 44° to 60°. Drove east hunted on Lucky's old cabin site. Saw a cow and calf moose. Hunted west 10 miles didn't see anything. Cal was busy so didn't stay. Ed came over to borrow my pickup over cab rack, I gave it to him. Hauled the canoe down to lake. Went up Slide on Suzuki. Walked west and north. Didn't see any game. One fresh moose shit and tracks to go with it. Back home I built a receiver hitch and mounted it on the car. Really tired tonight. Got a spruce hen.

Friday, September 12, 1997—mostly sunny, 34° to 59°. Up very early and went to trailhead at mi 133. Unloaded Suzuki. Drove past the mud holes parked and walked two miles plus loops off trail looking for a legal moose w/no luck. Came back to hwy and glassed the valley off towards the river. No luck. Talked with a guy who had killed a nice bull caribou out of the Mulchatna herd. Stopped by Cal's. Did a few small jobs at home including waxing the roof of both the garage and house again.

Saturday, September 13, 1997—really nice day, 42° to 57°. Ralph and Jeff got here and Sylvia fixed breakfast. Then Ralph drove and we went to Lake Louise Road. We hunted, ate and took naps. Didn't see a caribou. A few caribou were killed by other people. We heard distant shooting. Many, many people were driving the road and hunting. It was a fun day to be out with these two guys.

Sunday, September 14, 1997—another very nice day, 27° to 55°. Jeff came over. He, Ralph and I went up the Lake Louise Road. Less hunters and still no caribou or moose to be seen. Back home, Ralph and Jeff prepared our truck motor for removal. In one hour it was ready to be lifted out. Tried the rest of the day to find Allen in hopes he could lift the motor with his loader—no luck. He did come over and tell us about his moose hunt. He got a 51" 48 brow tine moose bull and brought us a little back strap. Cal changed his mind and decided to keep his motor. Tom H. wants me to wait and give his brother a chance to sell me a motor. Mary Odden is bringing in new cranberry pickers to pick berries on our ridge. Brother Jerry phoned today but I was hunting. Beverly called to tell us that granddaughter Darcy delivered a baby boy last week.

Monday, September 15, 1997—partly cloudy, 24° to 55°. We drove up the Lake Louise Road at the junction, someone was butchering a moose. We parked at 11 mile. I drove about 6 miles on Suzuki to Bob Lake. Didn't see any caribou. Talked to three luckless hunters. We came back home, rested a while, ate supper and I drove to pull off at mile 133 hill. Drove and walked three miles in to hunt moose. Suddenly the sound of many "shots." After 10-15 min and dozens of shots I turned around and hunted on way back to the car and trailer. Back at home I got a few things ready to hunt in morning. Saw another porcupine, lots of them right now.

Tuesday, September 16, 1997—partly cloudy, 33° to 57°. We road hunted in morning. Rested. Worked on truck parts. After supper we hunted west to Mile 120 - no luck. I returned puller to Joe. Talked to a hunter who says caribou are at Alltel Creek!

Wednesday, September 17, 1997—cloudy, rain after dark, 33° to 52°. Road hunted. Took ATV on trail in back of DOT Camp. Saw some tracks of moose. Cal asked me to check out a small are he had seen "brown" movement in. Parked at his place and drove ATV to first swamp. Soon after crossing swamp drainage on foot, two ravens flew over my head making three calls each, then flying 50-60 yards ahead of me and making a different call there. Remembering a similar experience when hunting grizzly bear many years ago, I became very alert. The ravens flew away. I stalked 10 yards closer, stopping when I head the sound of bones crunching. (May also have been bulls pushing each other).

It sounded to me like something was feeding in the trees and brush just ahead. I listened for two or three minutes. Then slow and quietly turned and returned to the Suzuki and went back up the trail about a half mile and walked south to part of old burn. Only saw a small hunting owl. It flew up and perched 15 yards away. No luck there so I went to a lake farther east and tried to call in a moose. I stood on top of a fox den leaning on the down trunk of a very large spruce. The den had been dug down between two of the trees large support roots. No moose came to the call, so I drove to the car and trailer. Told Cal of my experience and went home. Ralph phoned, he'll be here to hunt Thursday evening.

Thursday, September 18, 1997—partly cloudy snow only tree tops, 30° to 52°. Went to Dave's and measured exhaust manifold of Pete's motor. Dave gave me a press. When back at home looked up some pipe fittings and took them to Mendeltna in hopes his dad could use them. Didn't see any moose while driving back and forth. I had my rifle with me just in case. Gather some camping gear in hopes of going sheep hunting on Wood Cr. David and Jacobie came over to borrow some wire but I didn't have the right kind. New snow in mountains to the south of us tonight.

Friday, September 19, 1997—foggy in place in early morning, 26° to 48°. Ralph and I drove the road west hunting very early morning. Then breakfast at home. Then went to Tolsona Ridge to glass for moose – no luck. We then drove Lake Louise Road to 9 mile. Had a short snooze then went home. Sylvia was back from Glennallen and was digging potatoes. We went to gravel pit to check Ralph's rifle sights, and he shot my sig at a target. Went home and hauled the potatoes up the hill and put them in the basement. We took my car, trailer and ATV to trailhead at Mile 133, drove in two miles and walked a mile and a half. Ralph walked farther. He heard a bull moose grunting. We got out to road and home 9:55 PM. Ate supper – tired tonight.

Saturday, September 20, 1997—partly cloudy, nice day, 29° to 52°. Ralph and I went to Tolsona Ridge Communications site and glassed for moose, no luck. Back to Lake Louise Junction and up the road. We went east on 11 mile Seismic Trail to the East Drainage from Old Boot Lake and walked the two lake shores to Old Boot and down its south shore to Odden's cabin. A grizzly bear had torn the clasp loose that held the cabin door shut. It had eaten some food items and generally made a mess, but no real damage. We cleaned up most of the mess and fastened the door shut again. After we got back out to the road we went home.

We parked the car, trailer and ATV. Ralph drove 30 miles east and back home and we didn't see any moose or caribou. Then we drove to mi 133 trailhead and he drove his pickup in about 2 miles. We hunted on foot from there till dark. I tried calling a moose. Ralph thought he heard a moose grunt four times. After supper I called Jim Odden and filled him in on the condition of his cabin.

Sunday, September 21, 1997—cloudy, rain in evening, 27° to 44°. Ralph and I went to gravel pit and salvaged some junk steel that was to be buried. Ralph bolted down the canopy on his pickup and left for Anchorage. I picked up things in preparation for snow. Washed mud off Suzuki. Peter Butaric phoned that he would bring out a motor for the pickup. Ed Farmer unloaded the motor with Allen's backhoe loader. We went to Betty and Jerry's for a cookout Mary Odden had planned.

Monday, September 22, 1997—snow on nearby mountains, 33° to 49°. Worked a little on truck motor. Anchored the large waterline to the hillside. Gather up crane and goose hunting gear and loaded it into Molly the car. Cal and Mary brought some movies back and visited awhile. Sylvia gave them some garden produce.

Tuesday, September 23, 1997—partly cloudy, 35° to 55°. Sylvia fixed a good breakfast for Bob and Karn. After they went home I finished loading the car and headed for Delta Jct. forgetting my wool jacket, clock and extra choke tubes for the 10-gauge. Got waterfowl regulations at Alaska Fish & Game. Cashed a check at bank. Got gasoline. Drove to Delta Junction uneventful but nice trip, got more gas here. Went to shooting range and picked up a lot of .45 ACP and 1 .338 magnum. Drove out to Roy Beaver's. He was away at another farm working. Went to Scott Hollenbeck's. He has been killing geese for three days. Lots of sandhill cranes flying this afternoon. He invited me to hunt in his blind. I parked along the field in short, re-growth trees. Walked out to blind but no birds came close. Ate supper and made coffee for morning at car.

Wednesday, September 24, 1997—40° and windy, warmed up to around 50°, wind died down. I hunted from Scott's "bale" blind. Got three Canadian geese and missed some easy shots. Got a sandhill crane, young of year. Should have had two more. Saw a red fox hunting mice near the blind. It must have been a female as it squatted when it peed. Cleaned the birds. Ate breakfast. Alone in early afternoon Scott started raking this field. I drove him to his house to get the baler. He and E.B. finished the field in the early afternoon. I saw Roy Beaver on road and we visited. I went to his place to hunt birds. It seemed he didn't want me to hunt on his land. Rather park there and walk down a moose trail to the river and hunt.

Almost all the geese had left the river and were sitting in one of Schultz Bros. fields. I could have killed geese as they crossed Roy's line but he wanted me on river. There I would have dropped the geese in the trees and brush and had to search for them under difficult conditions plus possibly lose a wounded one. So I left and went to John Thuringer's place. He said there weren't any birds there but we could hear and see them. He probably has it leased out and didn't want to offer me to hunt so I didn't ask. He did give me a cup of coffee. I came back to Scott's, parked in the same spot. In a few minutes a nice flock of cranes flew over and I shot the last one, again a young bird of the year. As I fixed supper, four geese flew over Scott's decoys. I should have been out there. I did go out after I ate but no birds flew over. Many thousands of cranes flew by in distance on each side. Saw several owls and some hunting hawks. Visited a gun shop near Scott's farm. The beauty of the sun shining on the clouds was outstanding at times.

Thursday, September 25, 1997—partly cloudy, sunny, 34° to 60°. Walked out to the blind as it started to get light. The little fox came back and again "stalked" the decoys, and then hunted mice. I lip-sqeaked and its ears perked up. Then it went on hunting mice. The geese didn't show up. The cranes flew over later. I shot one young one. It fell eight feet from me and hit the ground hard. I cleaned it, ate breakfast and hunted from a clump of trees farther north and east. I shot a mature female there. Tens of thousands of cranes were leaving this morning. I loaded up my things, went up to Scotts, thanked him for his hospitality and left for home. Picked up brass at both shooting ranges on way home. Got belts for truck motor and gas in Glennallen. Got home, unloaded gear, hunting gear. Sylvia washed the birds and put them in ice water. Allen and Roxanne had us down for biscuits and gravy this evening. We got caught up on the news around here.

Friday, September 26, 1997—partly cloudy, 28° to 56°. Shot a spruce hen and cleaned it. Visited Ed a couple min and offered help putting the roof on his new building. Did a few little jobs. Polished the brass I brought home. Rested a while. After supper I hauled 10 buckets of gravel and raked smooth and packed by driving over it. Shot a spruce hen and two snowshoe rabbits.

Saturday, September 27, 1997—partly cloudy, 34° to 48°. Stretched up one waterline. Put longer line into basement and insulated it where it goes through the wall of basement. Cut off the excess. Sealed fertilizer lime sacks. Finished hauling gravel for lane. Went to see Allen about getting his cherry picker.

Sunday, September 28, 1997—mostly sunny, 31° to 47°. Allen phoned early and wanted to take lift the old motor out of the truck and put the new one in. Jim Odden had offered to help also so I called him and he came down. Later after getting the new motor in the truck, Allen went to church pot luck. Jim did most of the work. We got lots of nuts and bolts tightened. Alternator, smog pump and power steering all on the motor. Had quite a few problems with some of the fitting. Actually we accomplished a lot. Jim needed some pipe fittings and a gasoline hose nozzle. Fortunately I had what he needed. David loaded the old motor in the bed of the pickup.

Monday, September 29, 1997—partly cloudy, skim of ice on east end of lake, 19° to 43°. Visited Ed and Sandy. Hooked up tranny oil lines, heater hoses when I installed the radiator and fan shroud. Filled radiator with anti-freeze. Cleaned garage. Ralph phoned – he won't be able to time the truck motor for two weeks.

Tuesday, September 30, 1997—Very nice day, 24° to 45°. Hooked up the gas lines to and from the fuel pump on the truck. Also throttle linkage, 2 grounds, retightening one radiator hose that seeped antifreeze during the night. Moved two brackets from old motor to this one, including the vacuum assist for braking. Walked down to lake, no ducks in range. Hauled garbage to transfer site. Some liquid leaked into rear of car. I washed it out and disinfected the area. Did a little plinking with the .44 magnum, making a pop can jump 5 feet in the air. We have at least two small snowshoe hares, obviously from a late litter.

Wednesday, October 1, 1997—partly cloudy, 30° to 43°. Hooked up a couple small things on truck. Shot a spruce hen. Walked to east end of lake and shot two ducks. Missed some others. Came back home. Took the canoe to retrieve the ducks. Tied a rope to Farmer's gas cylinder and towed it up the lake to our landing and then hauled it up to the house with the Suzuki. After supper we drove to gravel pit on Tazlina Hill and hunted snowshoe hare. Got one, saw two others, and let the Farmers know the location of the cylinder.

Thursday, October 2, 1997—partly cloudy, cloudy evening, 22° to 46°. Epoxy glued a rear sight on the .22, installed a front sight as well. Test firing the rifle. Shot a little to the left. Shot a spruce hen with .223 loaded with one of my cast bullets. Those loads were very accurate. I reloaded 20 more of them for small game hunting. Tried to hunt ducks, no luck though.

Friday, October 3, 1997—mostly sunny, 18° to 41°. Lake ¾ frozen over. Lots of ice melted and a little wave action broke more of it up today. Tried twice to sneak up on some ducks with no luck. Shot a squirrel and two spruce hens. Went rabbit hunting across from DOT this evening and didn't see a rabbit. Slipped and pulled a muscle though in my left leg at hip. We went to Glennallen for lunch and shopping. I drained the last of the gas from the leaking gas tank on the truck. Shot the squirrel with one of my cast bullets. Jim and Elaine Manning visited this evening.

Saturday, October 4, 1997—snow, cloudy, more light snow, 28° to 33°. Shot three spruce hens. Shot four ducks. Dismantled the old top for the well. My hamstring on left side sure is sore. Rest a lot today. Cleaned one rifle. Jim and Elaine Manning here to supper.

Sunday, October 5, 1997—mostly partly cloudy and pretty strong breeze blowing down the lake, 20° to 34°. It kept the lake from freezing over again. I walked down to look for ducks twice but none on our side of lake. Found a couple little jobs to do. We are ready for winter. Allen ate supper with us. I gave him some cartridges and a frame for a homemade hydraulic press.

Monday, October 6, 1997—cloudy and some breeze, windy in the night, 14° to 33°. I brought the canoe up here from the lake. Went spruce hen hunting a couple miles east? Got one and missed two. Piled and burned the slash and brush from around the septic drain field. Cut and threw more on the fire later. Just the coals left now. Did a couple other small jobs.

Tuesday, October 7, 1997—mostly sunny, 21° to 35°. Jim O brought over a blueberry cheese cake. Then he and I went to Glennallen to do a few errands. Had lunch when we got back. Later I put a little protective wire fence around the two tamarack trees. Refastened the large water line anchor to the stump on the hill. Cut a few dowel axels for Elaine. Ice is all around the lake shore. Some ducks still here.

Wednesday, October 8, 1997—sunny, some breeze, 8° to 36°. The lake is frozen over except for a small hole the ducks have kept open. Saw as many as seven ducks at the hole. Shot another spruce hen. Went hunting three miles east and didn't see any game. Went to Harold and Rachel's for supper and home. Movie of their hunting, shooting and spearing a beluga whale, about 2000 lbs.

Thursday, October 9, 1997—partly cloudy, 19° to 36°. On way home snow at the summit and west through the pass. We went to Anchorage to shop. It went pretty good and we got home before dark. Unloaded everything. Allen asked us to go to supper with them at Eureka. Blake Beaudoin came in and visited a long time with Allen, Roxanne, Sylvia and I and Kim H.

Friday, October 10, 1997—mostly cloudy, 16° to 30°. Went to Allen's and dropped off the press frame for him. Allen and I went east four miles and glassed for Denning bears. Later Allen came over for a pistol sighting in session. Patti Billman was here at the time. Sylvia had come home from Glennallen and got to visit with Patti.

Saturday, October 11, 1997—mostly sunny, 4° to 27°. Ralph drove here from Anchorage. Finished hooking up "tubes" on truck, distributor and timed it. Took it for a test ride. Motor runs really good. We'll watch it for a while as there is an ATF leak and antifreeze leak also. Sylvia fixed a moose steak supper. Ralph ate with us and went back to Anchorage.

Sunday, October 12, 1997—sunny, -4° to 25°. Can't figure out why the breather for the front differential is unattached. Glassed Slide Mountain. Saw no animals. Phoned Paul, (Steve's birthday) Steve was out hunting.

Monday, October 13, 1997—sunny, 1° to 21°. Took the old truck motor to Peter at Glennallen. Stopped and picked up a big handful of 6 MM cartridges spilled, lost along the hwy. Drained old water contaminated oil from the front differential on truck. Rinsed it out, replaced the cover and refilled it w/oil. Ck oil in transfer case. Drained the oil from the motor, replaced the old filter and refilled with new oil.

Tuesday, October 14, 1997—mostly cloudy and some snow, 4° to 19°. I went to Anchorage. Very slippery, windy, and snowing and blowing on into Anchorage. Shopped for tarps and blue board at Eagle Hardware. Got groceries at Carr's in Wasilla. Truck stuff at Wal-Mart. Got back home about 4:00 PM. Windy drive home. We put the blue board over the septic drain field and staked tarps over it to keep the blue board in place. Went to Odden's for a chili supper. Lester and Lois Odden are visiting at Jims.

Wednesday, October 15, 1997—1" snow, cloudy, partly cloudy, 19° to 28°. Checked belts on truck for proper tension. Swept garage, burned the limbs and stumps from the trees I cut down last summer. Put the cap on the truck bed. Walked down to the lake. Ordered two tables at the trap swap in Palmer this coming Saturday. Got package back containing gift to Dylan (great grandson).

Thursday, October 16, 1997—snowing all day, 17° to 23°. Spent most of day gathering up and preparing articles to take to Palmer Trap Swap.

Friday, October 17, 1997—sunny, 9° to 22°. A marten hunted around garage and wood shop while Sylvia watched. A little later I saw a coyote walking down our lake. I went outside with a rifle and took a poke at it. I'm sure I over shot the coyote and missed. We rode senior van to Glennallen. I got a gasket for truck thermostat. I had tested in a pan of boiling water and installed it when I got back home. Put oil and gas in car and loaded it for trip to Palmer in the morning.

Saturday, October 18, 1997—cloudy here, sunny in Palmer and very windy, 7° to 12°. We had breakfast and left home about 6:00 AM and went to old Palmer RR depot in Palmer to sell some of our miscellaneous stuff at Trap Swap. Didn't sell much in $ but had fun visiting. Bought some bullets.

Sunday, October 19, 1997—cloudy, some snow in the morning, 9° to 19°. Loaded 20 of new bullets. Fired 3 for group and accuracy. Very good. Did a little reading. Today is sister Virginia's birthday and I phoned her. Phoned Nadia in the morning.

Monday, October 20, 1997—sunny, 8° to 30°. Took ashes and garbage to dumpster. Picked up raven scattered trash. Saw a marten here at home. Fired rifle for velocity. Rotated tires on truck. Cleaned and waxed truck windows.

Tuesday, October 21, 1997—cloudy, partly cloudy. 16° to 32°. Went to Jim Odden's and helped him work on wood - storage shed. We got quite a bit done. Jim's parents Lester and Lois are visiting from Wisconsin.

Wednesday, October 22, 1997—cloudy, 25° to 32°. Helped Jim with his shed again today. We had supper w/Jim, family and his folks.

Thursday, October 23, 1997—cloudy, 3/4" snow, 22° to 27°. Highway is slippery. We finished putting the steel on Jim's woodshed (Mary's Taj Mahal). Pretty stiff and sore.

Friday, October 24, 1997—cloudy, 3/4" snow, 9° to 19°. We went to Glennallen. Pd elect bill, re-mailed package to great grandson Dylan and shopped after lunch. Got our flu and tetanus shots too.

Saturday, October 25, 1997—cloudy, a little snow, 8° to 20°. I couldn't get the snowgo to start. I did start the Suzuki and put a light bulb in the well to thaw the ice. Sylvia fixed a nice meal (bear roast and a meatloaf). Jim, Mary, and Kari Odden, Jim's folks Lester and Lois, Allen Farmer and Ellie and a friend of Jim's, Richard were here to supper.

Sunday, October 26, 1997—sunny, -2° to 12°. I pulled the snowgo into the garage. We visited Cal and Mary, and I got new diaphragms for the fuel pump on the snowgo. Talked to a guy at John Lake Trailhead that had seen 16 caribou (2 bulls) up on top of Slide Mountain.

Monday, October 27, 1997—sunny, -16° to 5°. Rebuilt the fuel pump on snowgo and got it running. Tried to pump water. Had to remove the ice in the lower waterline and repair one fitting. This all took a lot of trips up and down the hill with the snowgo. Had a fire in the garage all day. Attempted repair of a bad break in the snowgo windshield. Allen came over late afternoon and picked up his rifle.

Tuesday, October 28, 1997—partly cloudy, cloudy and snow, 4° to 7°. Tom H. visited several hours. I went with him to Cal' then to Eureka for a hamburger. Back home, Jim, Mary and Jim parents were here. Jim is taking them to Anchorage. They will get to rest over night then catch an early morning flight home. I checked the snowgo windshield repair. It looks as if it might hold, but just in case I might want to wire it together. I melted holes in it to thread the wires through.

Wednesday, October 29, 1997—mostly cloudy, 5° to 15°. Visited Tom and Kim gave them one of Nadia's cook books. Kim made us copies. We gave Steve and Karen a cook book. Then after supper we went to Allen and Roxanne's and gave them a cookbook and visited awhile.

Thursday, October 30, 1997—cloudy and some light snow, 14° to 26°. Allen thought the snow would get to be a storm and waited till noon to decide to go up Slide Mt and hunt caribou. Our waterline was frozen and I worked on it instead of going hunting. Pumped water through the big line and put frozen line in basement. Kyle shot a caribou. Allen brought some of it to us.

Friday, October 31, 1997—cloudy all day, 20° to 24°. Sylvia went to Glennallen I taped a movie. Then pulled the thawed waterline out of basement and down the hill and hooked it up. Then hauled a couple small pickup loads and stacked them in basement. Sylvia cut up and packaged the meat when she got home. Neighborhood kids came trick-or-treating. Nadia phoned.

Saturday, November 1, 1997—low clouds most of day, 17° to 23°. Put two more small loads of wood in basement. We had Harold, Rachel, Rusty and John here to supper. Allen stopped for just a minute.

Sunday, November 2, 1997—low clouds, lots of frost in air and patchy black ice on highway, 12° to 14°. Watched a couple TV shows, read some, went over to Manning and visited a while. Went to Jim and Mary's to a trout supper. Jim and Kari caught a beautiful mess of large trout today.

Monday, November 3, 1997—cloudy, 12° to 13°. Wrote letters. Read a lot. Saw a couple rabbits - no luck hunting them. Sent three inquiries to gunsmiths. Sent application to Juneau.

Tuesday, November 4, 1997—cloudy, fog in area, 5° to 22°. Lots of aches and pains I attribute to this weather. Worked a few min on car. Jim M. visited.

Wednesday, November 5, 1997—cloudy, 4" snow in late afternoon, 13° to 29°. Put snow plow blade on truck. Hooked up the plow lights. Allen visits in evening.

Thursday, November 6, 1997—sunny all day, 7° to 25°. Allen, Roxanne, Samantha were here for breakfast and a nice visit. I then plowed our snow.

Friday, November 7, 1997—mostly cloudy, 3° to 20°. Went to Glennallen on senior van to bank, pay phone bill etc. Went to a potluck at school house harvest party. Games and white elephant bids. Ralph phoned after we got home.

Saturday, November 8, 1997—mostly cloudy, 13° to 35°. Jim was here at 7:30 AM after breakfast we went to Meyer Lake area on Richardson Hwy to hunt caribou. First he drove the snowgo pulling me riding the sled. We explored off to mostly the east and didn't see any caribou and couldn't find those we saw earlier. Lots of people driving snowgos and shooting at caribou when they got a chance. After we ate, some caribou came out on the lake near us. We walked over there. I shot at one and missed!! I was so bummed I didn't shoot again. Somewhat later Jim got a shot at one and winged it. Trailed it a long ways and lost it. Other people were getting some animals. On the way home I spotted 40 or so out on a lake. Jim stopped and we walked back. Kind of spooked them, but they didn't run far. I took a poke at a young bull and missed!! I'm mystified and can't understand why I miss. Jim's didn't get a good clear shot at a large boo in the lead. Soon it was full dark. Once back at home, Sylvia fixed a little supper.

Sunday, November 9, 1997—cloudy, rain in evening, 24° to 37°. Sighted in the .338 and reloaded the brass. Snow slid off the east side of garage and I plowed it away. Jim M. borrowed the air tank. We went over to their place for supper and a nice visit.

Monday, November 10, 1997—cloudy all day, 30° to 35°. I went over to Jim Odden's and helped him get his water room started.

Tuesday, November 11, 1997—cloudy to partly cloudy, 30° to 20°. Helped Jim work on his addition on their house.

Wednesday, November 12, 1997—mostly cloudy, 11° to 30°. Helped Jim put up logs for the water storage addition on his house. Allen visited in evening and ate caribou steak with us.

Thursday, November 13, 1997—mostly sunny, 5° to 14°. Visited Ed and Chuck Farmer when I went after the mail this morning. Didn't do much today. Shot at some targets this afternoon. Don't feel very well.

Friday, November 14, 1997—mostly sunny, 6° to 16°. Went west a ways looking for a couple places to make marten sets, but the snow is so hard there isn't any fresh tracks. Took garbage to dumpster. Stopped by Jim Odden's, knocked on door, no answer. Picked up the meat sacks and brought them home and drying them in basement. Ralph drove down from Fairbanks. Got here just before dark. Good visit. Sylvia fixed a good supper. Almost forgot - Visited Allen in Am and got a tape back from him and loaned the tape to Ron when he brought Sylvia back from Glennallen on senior van. Cal phoned - Jeff phoned.

Saturday, November 15, 1997—partly cloudy, 4° to 16°. Ralph drove and we went up Lake Louise Road. Didn't see any caribou or fresh sign. No fox, coyote etc. Picked up some of his things at Tazlina. Stopped and looked at Jim Oddens new snowgo. Back at our place Ralph loaded his snowgo in his pickup and was on his way to Anchorage and will pick up more things there and then a drive to Fairbanks tomorrow. Jeff is leaving AK for work in Arizona.

Sunday, November 16, 1997—low cloudy and some fog, 10° to 15°. Sylvia made apple pies from some of apples Harold and Rachel brought us last night. She did some laundry. I did a little target shooting. Cal and Mary G visited a while in late morning.

Monday, November 17, 1997—mostly cloudy, some early fog, -5° to 10°. Reloaded some .45 ACP. Pumped water. The water doesn't return through the pump into the well fast enough. Good thing I was there to open the cam locks and let the water back in well.

Tuesday, November 18, 1997—cloudy, quite a bit of fog, 6° to 12°. Reloaded some .223 with home cast bullets for shooting pests. Looked at well fittings in hope of getting a bleeder orifice installed in water line. Jim, Mary, and Kari were here to supper and watched a movie after.

Wednesday, November 19, 1997—cloudy, light snow in afternoon, 9° to 15°. Made a mistake in plumbing in well, so didn't accomplish anything. Visited Allen. Caught and skinned a marten. Phoned Tyler and Beverly.

Thursday, November 20, 1997—cloudy, west snow in afternoon, 5° to 14°. Turned the marten skin on the stretcher. Studied Medicare and insurance. Phoned about changing pharmacies. Read a lot.

Friday, November 21, 1997—sunny, cloudy in afternoon and evening, -3° to +9°. We went to Glennallen on senior van. I got a plastic pipe fitting in town. We put it and some more fittings in the well - above the pump. The box around the well is frost heaved and I made some shims to make the lid fit better, and then tied a tarp over the box.

Saturday, November 22, 1997—snow all night and day, 6+ inches, 8° to 20°. We pumped water and I packed the snowgo trail to the well. Corky and Rusty brought their snow blower over and did some welding on it. I put snow plow on truck and plowed our yard and driveway.

Sunday, November 23, 1997—cloudy, 7° to 14°. Plowed the rest of the snow. Shoveled a lot of snow. Banked with snow some of basement. Took garbage to transfer sight. Shot a varmint today. Saw fresh fox tracks on Tazlina Hill. Did some target shooting, using a pile of snow for a bullet back stop - works good. Mary Gilcrease dropped off a couple plates of left over food from The Mendeltna Chapel Pot Luck Dinner. Thank you Mary!

Monday, November 24, 1997—cloudy all day, 2° to 14°. I shoveled snow of woodshed and brown trailer. Did some more target shooting.

Tuesday, November 25, 1997—mostly cloudy, -6° to +7°. We had a good trip to Anchorage doing shopping. Roads were slippery though. Allen visited in evening.

Wednesday, November 26, 1997—light snow all day, -5° to 10°. Sore back. Reloaded ammo. Allen dropped off a movie.

Thursday, November 27, 1997—sunny, -2° to +2°. We pumped water and I packed trail to well with snowgo. We ate Thanksgiving dinner with Allen and Roxanne and extended family. John Dimmick drove his truck in ditch. Tried to help, was up till 2:00 AM.

Friday, November 28, 1997—low clouds, light snow, -7° to +6°. Rested today.

Saturday, November 29, 1997—cloudy, -2° to +4°. Back is sore. Rested today. Wrote an article for a magazine.

Sunday, November 30, 1997—partly sunny, -6° to +6°. Back is still store. Didn't do anything much today. Allen visited in evening. Forgot to take his jacket along when he left. Note: Sept 15 to Nov 30. 11 days below 0°.

Monday, December 1, 1997—some snow in night, -2° to 15°. Cloudy today. Plowed our snow and around the mailbox's. David F lost control of his dad's pickup and went in the ditch a ½ mile west of Nelchina. After shoveling it out, he drove out on his own power. I went to Cal's and visited a little while. Saw a raven working on something under the snow. Saw two cow moose and one calf. Hoped to see a fox but no luck.

Tuesday, December 2, 1997—skiff snow, mostly cloudy, 4° to 10°. Tried to call a fox at Little Nelchina and at gravel pit, no luck. Did see a moose on Little Nelchina River. Cal came over and welded a part he repaired for a snowgo. He gave us a ptarmigan and bought a Polaris rewind.

Wednesday, December 3, 1997—cloudy, -5° to 10°. I tried to call in a fox at several different locations with no luck. Visited with Allen a few minutes this morning. Saw a couple moose today. Reloaded a few cartridges.

Thursday, December 4, 1997—2° until the afternoon, then warmed up to 27° in the evening. Strong gusty winds in afternoon drifted snow. Blew it off the trees. Checked the oil in both vehicles. Set up shooting bench - ProChrono and Target, testing the load that I put together yesterday.

Friday, December 5, 1997—cloudy, 24° to 29°. We went to Glennallen on senior van, bank, post office, paid phone bill, ate lunch. Back home we pumped water. I plowed snow off our yard and lane. Then Kim phoned and wanted me to do a little plowing at the transfer sight. I also did some off hand rifle practice shooting. Fred Rungee had supper with us. Plowed the transfer sight.

Saturday, December 6, 1997—cloudy and fog around us, 8° to 13°. Did some more off hand rifle shooting and reloaded the brass.

Sunday, December 7, 1997—cloudy and some 2" of snow, 9° to 13°. Wrote Christmas letters. Jim and Kari O. came over and borrowed our water hauling tank.

Monday, December 8, 1997—mostly sunny, -4° to 11°. Plowed our snow. Shoveled some. Moved the table I set the water hauling tank on. Did some pistol target shooting. Cleaned a rifle.

Tuesday, December 9, 1997—cloudy and light snow all day, -12° to +10°. We pumped water again today. Our well gets lower and lower. I shoveled some snow up to the house foundation. Did more pistol target practice. Allen came over to visit after he got off from work. Sylvia had made three apple pies.

Wednesday, December 10, 1997—3" snow in night and cloudy all day. I plowed our snow and shoveled some of it. Went to DOT camp east driveway and checked marten set there.

Thursday, December 11, 1997—cloudy and a couple light snowfalls, 10° to 18°. Shoveled snow up to house the rest of the way around the house.

Friday, December 12, 1997—mostly sunny, 1° to 23°. We went to Glennallen on the senior van. Ate lunch and did a little shopping. Allen visited in later afternoon.

Saturday, December 13, 1997—sunny, cloudy and fog, 0° to -12°. We pumped water and I put a new drain back valve in the water line in well. We went to the Christmas party at the American Legion in Glennallen. Long day!

Sunday, December 14, 1997—rested all day.

Monday, December 15, 1997—sunny, cloudy, -9° to 0°. 1/4" snow in night. Wrote Christmas card letters. Read some. We don't feel up to par.

Tuesday, December 16, 1997—mostly sunny, saw sun dogs this afternoon, -21° to -5°. Visited Cal and Mary in the afternoon. Allen and Sammy visited in evening.

Wednesday, December 17, 1997—cloudy and a little snow, -19° to -7°. I felt sick all day. Read a lot.

Thursday, December 18, 1997—mostly cloudy and 2" snow, -17° to +7°. We went to senior party held at Legion Post. I plowed our snow.

Friday, December 19, 1997—mostly cloudy, -10° to +3°. Helped Tom H. a little with his satellite dish. Dropped off a turkey at Odden's. Didn't feel so good. We went to the school house to see the kids Christmas program and pot luck afterward. Sylvia baked a ham for Kim for the potluck.

Saturday, December 20, 1997—nice day, -8° to +2°. We pumped water. Did target shooting.

Sunday, December 21, 1997—pretty nice day, -20° to -9°. Sylvia has a flu of some kind. I read. The light bulb burned out at the well just after dark and supper. I fired up the snowgo and replaced it.

Monday, December 22, 1997—nice day, -24° to -2°. Lots of aches and pains today. Plus Sylvia is really sick with some kind of crud. Joe Virgin stopped by with some Christmas goodies. Elaine Manning dropped off a home decorative painted can of cookies. Then late in evening Oddens stopped over with tangerines and Norwegian Xmas cookies. Visited a while and I played the "Bush Pilot" video tape.

Tuesday, December 23, 1997—nice day, -8° to -1°. Shoveled snow off roofs. Sylvia is till quite sick.

Wednesday, December 24, 1997—nice day, fog in morning, -6° to 20°. Sylvia is some better. Allen visited in the afternoon. Left goodies and invited us to Christmas dinner. Mary O phoned to see how Sylvia is. Elaine Manning is trying to get a prank set up for her husband Jim's Christmas gift. Jeff Routt visited in early evening.

Thursday, December 25, 1997—snowed a little in night, then started snowing about noon, 5° to 20°. Snowing about noon. We still have the flu. We pumped water this afternoon. I shoveled snow up around the well cover and filled in a low place in the trail with snow. The kids were snowboarding last night and this afternoon. I put the snowplow on the truck before I came in.

Friday, December 26, 1997—cloudy all day, 7° to 21°. I had 6" snow to plow this morning. Cleaned off a couple roofs. Shoveled some snow. Sylvia is better. She did three loads of laundry. Pumped water again today. Tanks are full.

Saturday, December 27, 1997—cloudy, some falling frost and snow, 2° to 9°. Read today. This crud we have is slow to go away. Charlie Trowbridge phoned – they plan to visit us for a few days at New Years.

Sunday, December 28, 1997—near 0° all day. I cleaned snow off several roofs. Plowed about 2" snow. Check my two marten sets. Wrote up a list of questions for Sinclair Inc. Read some. Charlie Trowbridge phoned to give us a time of arrival here (Thursday).

Monday, December 29, 1997—cloudy, low clouds and some breeze just before dark, 0° to 15°. We pumped water again today. Shoveled a little snow. Sylvia did load of laundry and the toilet is slow to flush.

Tuesday, December 30, 1997—cloudy, clearing and some breeze, -8° to +3°. Winds were blowing snow in long streams west to east from off the tops of the mountains to the south of us. Didn't do much, just a little straightening up around the house. Wrote a couple letters. Allen, Roxanne and Samantha brought over rum cake, ice cream later in afternoon. We had a nice visit.

Wednesday, December 31, 1997—partly cloudy, -25° to -7°. We had a phone call from Beverly. I called a couple friends around here.

Norman and Sylvia Wilkins dancing at a local function. Their story continues in book three.

A letter written by Norman Wilkins
to a friend 11-10-96

As I write this a light fog lifts off the lake and a gentle air moves it to the west. From my seat at the kitchen table, I look out on a beautiful, calm and serene part of the world. I set my coffee cup down quietly so as not to break the silence. Suddenly I hear yawns; then shortly, the slap of feet on the way to the bathroom. Then Sylvia says, "Ooh! Look there, spruce hens—four of them!" Another day gets a kick start and we are glad to be part of it.

September 5th a close friend drowned while on a hunting trip. He was trying to get a line across the Maclaren River so they could get hunting equipment across. He and his brother planned to hunt for bull moose. He was 45 years old. Sure wish he was stalking a big bull moose this morning.

Sylvia picked many gallons of currants, blueberries and rose hips. No cranberries this year. We have some cabbage, cauliflower, onions and potatoes in the garden yet. A cold front is supposed to be coming down from the north.

An acquaintance from Minnesota stopped by a couple of weeks ago on his way home. We visited for a couple of hours. He had seen a bull moose cross the highway a few miles west of here. When this fellow continued on his trip, I went down to Allen's with the bull moose story. He, Cal and I drove over there, spread out, still hunting. Allen came on big moose tracks, saw the bull, determined that it had legal brow tines and shot it.

I tweaked my left knee 6 weeks ago. If I have it looked at, it won't be until after hunting season. It doesn't get better or worse, so it will hang in there a while yet.

We have enough meat for ourselves. I would shoot a caribou so the uncle of the friend who drowned could have some meat. He is housebound and can't hunt anymore.

Last Saturday I went on a day trip hunting sheep, mostly to keep my mind occupied. I went to the old "Zigzag" house; it's burned down now. Two trails leave from there. I took the one going over North Pass. My ATV negotiated the mud holes. The dry summer and fall helped in that respect. Once over the pass, an occasional parka squirrel scurried down the trail ahead of me. They were so roly-poly they shook as they ran.

The trail goes down a creek on the other side with quite a bit of ice. Here I watch closely for I had heard that a miner had put a 'Cat' trail in on the mountain side in order to get around the gorge. The miner did a good job. Just at the lower end of the gorge, Willow Creek comes in on the right. It is virtually treeless!

Many years ago when I was here, a couple of brothers I knew were 'glassing' the sheep on the mountains at the end of the valley. They couldn't determine any legal rams from this distance. Since they saw the sheep first, I suggested I wait till they were well up the valley before I started. Either the rams weren't legal or were inaccessible because I didn't hear shots and these two were gone when I got back out of the valley.

I left the ATV and walked slowly, favoring my knee and an old body. At each rise I paused to look over everything ahead, each side and everything to the rear. Safety in grizzly country is being aware. Plus, I was watching for sheep. When I was about a mile and a half from a cabin that I knew was here, it came into view as I crested another rise. Then it was just a matter of holding my course over a few more rises and I was there.

Built of shiplap pine on spruce pole framing, covered with 30 wt. tar paper many, many years ago, it had withstood the ravages of time remarkably well. As I came closer I noticed the door was unlatched and gently swinging on puffs of air movement. It stands on a low mound just at the foot of a steep, rocky entrance to another valley extension. I didn't immediately enter the cabin.

Savoring being there, I took my time and walked around it, looking at the caribou horns, moose horns, some bottles, glass jars, etc. I glassed for sheep once again, but I know I won't shoot one today for I won't be able to pack it out.

Always interested in rock formations, a quartz outcrop caught my eye. Catalog this in my mind as a place to prospect.

Finally, I've completely circled the cabin. It has no window. When I finally do go inside, I mentally measure it to be 8' x 12' with plenty of head room. The shiplap has shrunk until cracks show and is rotted in places at the bottom so squirrels can run in and out. Some tar paper has blown off and it would be wet in a rain.

Someone has brought in an iron cot and a 10" x 12" x 20" sheet metal stove. There is only willow for stove wood; the elevation here is 4300 feet. There was a shelf with a pint bottle half full of apricot brandy and a crude table nailed up against the west wall. I had heard that 20 years ago, the floor was covered with hides. They are gone; bare dirt remains.

A different-looking 30-gallon drum with a lid on it stands at the foot of the cot. Lifting the lid, I see a sleeping bag. I don't dig around in the drum, for it's not mine to dig in.

Going back outside, I look around some more, look for sheep also—no luck. Then I pick another route back to the mouth of Willow Creek. My legs are tired and will be more so. I found a caribou horn on the way out. God, how I like to look and see things when I'm out like that. A motion out of the corner of my eye turned out to be an eagle landing on Sharp Peak, a nearby mountain.

Back at the parked ATV, I dig out the other half of my sandwich, eat it and a cookie. Thus fueled up, I drove the 9 miles back out to trail's head.

—Norman

About the author and his wife

Norman Wilkins and Slovenia-born Ladislava Kolenc (Sylvia to those who know her) met in postwar Gorizia Italy in 1946, marrying there in 1948. They moved to Iowa where Norman grew up, and farmed in several communities until 1957 when they moved to Motley, Minnesota and built the Tamarack Dell dairy farm. There, they raised their family and farmed until the late 1970s.

Norman had long felt the pull of the north, drawn to the mystique of Alaska—"The Last American Frontier" many said, and once the children were on their own, that desire to go north grew stronger. He made more than one hunting trip to Alaska before the 1978 expedition included in this book, and as the trips unfolded, so did Norman's desire to make Alaska his permanent home—to be a part of the expansive wilderness and yes, explore for gold!

Sylvia was not so enthusiastic in the beginning. (Bear in mind, those first few years they lived in a one-room, 12'x16' plywood cabin with no indoor toilet, no electricity and no running water.) Once, after they settled in Nelchina, Sylvia was asked how she liked Alaska, to which she replied, "I really like the people here, but you can take Alaska and give it back to the Eskimos!"

They *did* find gold in Alaska. They found it in the air, the mountains, the wildlife and especially in the people—the people they worked shoulder to shoulder with and shared their table with; each one weaving an independent piece of the tapestry of everyday life in the '70s, '80s, '90s and until 2005 along the Glenn Highway.

From their log cabin overlooking Scoter Lake at Nelchina, radiating outward to Glennallen, Anchorage, Copper Center, Tok, Palmer, Wasilla, Fairbanks, Denali, Matanuska, Susitna, Valdez, Cordova and other arctic communities, Norman Wilkins recorded daily journal entries throughout the entire 25+ years he and Sylvia spent carving out a life on the Alaskan tundra.

Norman and Sylvia currently live in Minnesota, but a big part of Norman's heart remains in Alaska. I'm proud to call them my parents.

—Nadia Giordana, Cloud 9 Publishing

For more information about the author and his wife,
or to learn where to get additional copies of this book,
go to www.10000daysinalaska.com.

10,000 Days In Alaska by Norman Wilkins
is a three-volume, documentary journal.
To contact the publisher,
email Nadia Giordana
at
iinadia@msn.com
or write to:
Cloud 9 Publishing
14051 Oakview Lane North
Daytonn, MN 55327

10,000 Days In Alaska
can also be found as a Facebook page.

Norman Wilkins

10,000 Days In Alaska Book Two 1990-1997

www.ingramcontent.com/pod-product-compliance
Lightning Source LLC
Chambersburg PA
CBHW051411090426
42737CB00014B/2608